THIRD EDITION

Applying Career Development Theory to Counseling

Richard S. Sharf
University of Delaware

BROOKS/COLE

THOMSON LEARNING

Australia • Canada • Mexico • Singapore • Spain • United Kingdom • United States

BROOKS/COLE

THOMSON LEARNING

Sponsoring Editor: *Julie Martinez*
Editorial Assistant: *Cat Broz*
Marketing: *Caroline Concilla/Megan Hansen*
Assistant Editors: *Jennifer Wilkinson/*
  Shelley Gesicki
Project Editor: *Kim Svetich-Will*
Production Service: *ATLIS Graphics & Design*
Manuscript Editor: *Jacqui Brownstein*

Permissions Editor: *Karyn Morrison*
Interior Design: *Roy R. Neuhaus*
Cover Design: *Roy R. Neuhaus*
Proofreader: *Susan Pendleton*
Print Buyer: *Vena Dyer*
Compositor: *ATLIS Graphics & Design*
Printing and Binding: *R. R. Donnelley/*
  Crawfordsville

For more information about this or any other Brooks/Cole product, contact:

BROOKS/COLE
511 Forest Lodge Road
Pacific Grove, CA 93950 USA
www.brookscole.com
1-800-423-0563 (Thomson Learning Academic Resource Center)

Printed in the United States of America

10 9 8 7 6 5 4 3 2 1

Library of Congress Cataloging-in-Publication Data

Sharf, Richard S.
  Applying career development theory to counseling / Richard S. Sharf.— 3rd ed.
    p. cm.
  Includes bibliographical references and index.
  ISBN 0-534-36748-8 (casebound : alk. paper)
  1. Vocational guidance. 2. Career development. I. Title.

HF5381.S515 2002
158.6—dc21   2001035044

Cover Image: *Summer* by Pieter the Younger Brueghel (c. 1564–1638),
Johnny van Haeften Gallery, London, UK/Bridgeman Art Library.

In loving memory of my mother and father,
Edith Sycle Sharf and Nathaniel Sharf

Preface

Students taking a beginning graduate course in career guidance, career theory, or career counseling want to know how to assist clients with career concerns. This book will help them relate career theory and research to the practice of counseling, aiding them in their practicum, their internship, and their jobs as counselors. In the third edition of *Applying Career Development Theory to Counseling*, I show how each career development theory can be used in counseling. Each theory gives special insight into various perspectives on career development as it affects career counseling. Furthermore, the theories organize facts into a comprehensible system for students to understand and use, rather than overwhelm them with unrelated lists of information.

Case examples are a special feature of this book. For each theory and its significant constructs, one or more cases are used to illustrate the conceptual approach of the theory. The examples are given in a dialogue between counselor and client. In the dialogue, the counselor's conceptualization follows most counselor statements and is bracketed. This approach provides a direct application of the theory to counseling practice, making the book useful to both students and practicing counselors. In a few places, narrative descriptions of cases are used to illustrate theories.

THE THIRD EDITION

New to the third edition are several significant additions. Constructivist approaches (Chapter 11) replaces the chapter on Psychodynamic approaches. Two different constructivist methods—personal construct psychology and narrative counseling—illustrate many creative career counseling techniques. Adler's and Bordin's psychodynamic approaches have been dropped. Erikson's psychoanalytical approach has been shortened and placed in Chapter 8, "Adolescent Career Development," replacing Crites's model of vocational maturity. This section focuses on vocational identity reflecting the research of Fred Vondracek and his colleagues. Chapter 12, "Parental Influence Theories," emphasizes new work on attachment theory as it applies to career development. Included also is research by Richard Young and his colleagues on studying the influences of parent–adolescent interactions on career development. Chapter 13 includes a substantial change in presentation of Krumboltz's social learning theory. His emphasis on planned happenstance replaces the section on DECIDES. Chapter 14, "Career Decision-Making Theory," has been significantly changed. A spiritual approach to career decision making, featuring the work of Anna Miller-Tiedeman, is described along with David Tiedeman's emphasis on a developmental approach to decision making (retained from the previous edition). The cognitive information processing theory of Peterson and his colleagues replaces the sequential elimination approach of Gati. Information on the new Standard Occupational Classification System and the O*NET have been added to Chapter 2, "Trait and Factor Theory," and material describing particular issues affecting youth in the labor force has been added to Chapter 15, "The Labor Market: Sociological and Economic Perspectives." Some instructors may choose to assign Chapter 15 to follow Chapter 2, so that students may focus on occupational information in one section of the course. Other instructors may decide to assign Chapter 15 near the end of the course to emphasize the contrast between psychological approaches to career development and sociological or economic approaches. Each chapter in the third edition has been revised to reflect the results of new research and changes in the theory, where there have been changes.

SPECIAL CONSIDERATIONS IN EACH CHAPTER

Each career development theory is discussed in terms of its implication for using occupational information, for using tests, and for special issues that may affect the application of the theory. Some theories use an occupational classification system; others specify how occupational information can be used in counseling. Yet other theories have relatively little to say about the use of occupational information. Since occupational information (and educational information) is such an important part of career counseling, special efforts are made to link theory and career information. Many theories use tests and inventories both as a means of researching career development theory and as tools for the counselor to use in helping clients assess themselves. This book focuses on tests as they relate to theories and does not assume knowledge of testing issues, although some information about reliability and validity is presented. Also, career development theories provide insight into possible conflicts between counselor values and client values, which will present problems to the counselor. Considering problems in applying theory, occupational information, and testing can help students select the career development theories that will help them most in their work as counselors.

In each chapter, a section addresses the application of theories of career development to women and culturally diverse populations. Theories vary greatly in how they address the issues of women. For example, Gottfredson's career development theory deals very specifically with the career issues of women. Other theories deal only tangentially with women's career choice issues. Many career development theories were originally created for white males and were later expanded to include women and diverse cultural groups. The third edition reflects a moderate increase in research that has studied the career development issues of culturally diverse populations. This is a particularly challenging issue to address because of the wide variety of cultural groups and the differences within cultural groups. For example, there are many significant cultural differences among Native American tribal groups. Also, some career development issues may be different for African Americans and for black people in other countries. In the third edition of this text, I refer to culturally diverse populations rather than people of color. This change represents a broader worldview. I have chosen to emphasize cultural diversity rather than skin color, which is only one aspect of cultural diversity.

CONTENTS OF THIS BOOK

This book is divided into an introduction and four parts: "Trait and Type Theories," "Life-Span Theory," "Special Focus Theories," and "Theoretical Integration." Trait and type theories emphasize the assessment of interests, abilities, achievements, personality, and values, along with the acquisition of occupational information. Life-span theory follows a chronological approach, studying people across four broad stages in the life span. Special focus theories include the application to career development issues of research in psychology, such as constructivist theory and learning theory. Part Three also includes contributions from sociology and economics. Part Four deals with how these theories can be combined for effective career counseling. The last chapter, Chapter 16, also discusses the relevance of career development theories to special issues such as noncounseling interventions, group counseling, and job placement among other concerns. Each chapter is briefly described in Chapter 1 on pages 18–20.

COURSE APPLICATION

This book is intended for a beginning graduate course of which career issues are a major component. The book can be used differently, depending on whether the emphasis of the course is on career counseling, career testing, career guidance, or career theory.

Whereas most books that describe career counseling describe one method or many components of methods, this book presents a number of different theoretical and conceptual approaches to career counseling. After studying these various approaches, the student can decide which theories will be most helpful to him or her in counseling work. In general, the chapters are independent of each other, and not all chapters need be assigned. Since trait and factor theory represents a straightforward approach to career choice and adjustment, it is often an appropriate starting place.

The assignment of career tests and inventories, along with their manuals, can be combined with the use of this book. Table 16-1, on pages 458, 459 lists the tests that this book refers to and the theory with which they are associated. Trait and factor theories make the most use of tests and inventories, and life-span theory, decision-making theory, social learning theory, and constructivist approaches make less direct use of them. Many tests and inventories may be assigned along with Part One and before any of the appropriate chapters.

The focus of this book is on career counseling, not on instructional guidance programs for the classroom. One reason is that, when counselors are first employed, they are likely to be assigned counseling functions rather than responsibilities for guidance programs. When they work on guidance programs, they are usually supervised by someone who has established a system for introducing career materials into the classroom. Although classroom activities and school-to-work are described in Part Two, their discussion is limited. However, this book will provide a background for designing guidance activities and programs.

This text combines career development theory with suggestions for using and understanding theory in counseling. Instructors may use the material in the order that suits them. Some may prefer to assign Chapter 11 ("Constructivist Approaches to Career Development") and Chapter 12 ("Parental Influence Theories") before discussing life-span theory, because these chapters describe views that relate to life-span development. The assignment of chapters is likely to depend on the emphasis preferred by the instructor.

SUPPLEMENTS

To provide instructors with materials that they may use in the classroom and to assist in preparation of lectures and examinations, I have expanded the instructor's manual. I have included numerous discussion questions for each chapter as well as suggestions for role playing of counseling in class. For examinations, I have prepared over 538 multiple choice questions (some questions appearing in the previous edition of the manual have been revised for clarity). Also, I have expanded the number of essay questions that instructors may draw from. Included also are about 100 transparency masters that instructors may use in their classroom presentations. I believe that all of these materials will help instructors use *Applying Career Development Theory to Counseling,* Third Edition, in teaching career development and career counseling courses. Some instructors may find that the materials I have provided will suggest other classroom exercises, transparencies, or examination questions that they may wish to develop for their own purposes.

ACKNOWLEDGMENTS

Many people have been extremely helpful in reading one or more chapters of the book. I would like to thank the following people who have read and commented on the third edition of this book: Dr. Kathy Gainor of

Montclair State University, Dr. Deborah Haskins of Loyola College, Dr. John Liptak of Bluefield College, Dr. Susana Lowe of Boston College, Dr. Margaret Pinder of Amber University, Dr. Sarah Toman of Cleveland State University, and Nancy C. Wallace, M.Ed., NCC Assistant Director, University Career Services of George Mason University. I would also like to thank Karen J. Forbes of Lafayette College and Matthew R. Elliott of Holy Cross College who read several early chapters, making suggestions for the ultimate form that the book would take. The following people read, commented on, or supplied materials for chapters in this book: Linda Gott-fredson, James E. Hoffman, Lawrence Hotchkiss, Janice Jordan, Charles Link, Mary C. Miller, and Steven M. Sciscione, of the University of Delaware; Janet Lenz, Gary Peterson, Robert Reardon, and James Sampson of the University of Florida; Deborah P. Bloch of the University of Maryland at Baltimore; David Blustein of Boston College; René V. Dawis of the University of Minnesota; Kimberly Ewing of Loyola University of Baltimore; Gail Hackett of the University of Arizona; John L. Holland; John D. Krumboltz of Stanford University; Robert Lent of the University of Maryland; David Lubinski of Vanderbilt University; Greg Neimeyer of the University of Florida; James Rounds of the University of Chicago; Howard Tinsley of the University of Florida; Mark L. Savickas of Northeastern Ohio Universities College of Medicine; Michael Smith of McGill University; Fred Vondracek of Pennsylvania State University; and Richard Young of the University of British Columbia. I would also like to thank Roseanne Ferri and Lisa Sweder for typing the third edition. Cindy Carroll, Elizabeth Parisan, Nancy Bates, Joy Ferguson, and Dana Shiflett provided additional secretarial support. Finally, I would like to thank my wife, Jane, for her patience and understanding when this book was being prepared.

Richard S. Sharf

Brief Contents

1 Introduction   1

PART ONE   Trait and Type Theories   23
2 Trait and Factor Theory   25
3 Work Adjustment Theory   65
4 Holland's Theory of Types   94
5 Myers-Briggs Type Theory   120

PART TWO   Life-Span Theory   151
6 Introduction to Super's Life-Span Theory   153
7 Career Development in Childhood   162
8 Adolescent Career Development   186
9 Late Adolescent and Adult Career Development   219
10 Adult Career Crises and Transitions   252

PART THREE   Special Focus Theories   277
11 Constructivist Approaches to Career Development   279
12 Parental Influence Theories   307
13 Social Learning and Cognitive Theory   335
14 Career Decision-Making Approaches   374
15 The Labor Market: Sociological and Economic Perspectives   411

PART FOUR   Theoretical Integration   449
16 Theories in Combination   451

Appendix   Tests and Their Publishers   481
Name Index   485
Subject Index   491

Contents

CHAPTER 1 Introduction 1

THE ROLE OF THEORY IN PSYCHOLOGY 4

COUNSELORS' USE OF CAREER DEVELOPMENT THEORY 5

Client Population 6

Theories of Counseling and Theories of Career Development 6

Chunking 7

COUNSELOR SKILLS 8

Helping Skills 8

Testing 13

Providing Occupational Information 15

How Career Development Theory Relates 16

GOALS OF CAREER COUNSELING 16

CAREER DEVELOPMENT OF WOMEN 17

CAREER DEVELOPMENT OF CULTURALLY
DIVERSE POPULATIONS 18

WHAT'S AHEAD 18

REFERENCES 20

PART ONE Trait and Type Theories 23

CHAPTER 2 Trait and Factor Theory 25

STEP 1: GAINING SELF-UNDERSTANDING 27

Aptitudes 28

Achievements 30

Interests 32

Values 34

Personality 35

Example of Step 1 36

STEP 2: OBTAINING KNOWLEDGE ABOUT
THE WORLD OF WORK 38

Types of Occupational Information 38

Classification Systems 39

Trait and Factor Requirements 47

What the Counselor Needs to Know 52

Example of Step 2 52

STEP 3: INTEGRATING INFORMATION ABOUT
ONESELF AND THE WORLD OF WORK 53

How the Counselor Can Help 54

Example of Step 3 55

APPLYING THE THEORY TO WOMEN 56

APPLYING THE THEORY TO CULTURALLY
DIVERSE POPULATIONS 58

COUNSELOR ISSUES 60

SUMMARY 61

REFERENCES 61

CHAPTER 3   **Work Adjustment Theory   65**

ASSESSING ABILITIES, VALUES, PERSONALITY,
AND INTERESTS 67

Abilities 67

Values 68

Personality Styles 71

Interests 71

A Counseling Example 72

MEASURING THE REQUIREMENTS AND CONDITIONS
OF OCCUPATIONS 74

Ability Patterns 75

Value Patterns 75

Combining Ability and Value Patterns 76

MATCHING ABILITIES, VALUES, AND REINFORCERS 77

JOB ADJUSTMENT COUNSELING 82

ADJUSTMENT TO RETIREMENT 84

NEW DEVELOPMENTS 86

THE ROLE OF TESTING 86

THE ROLE OF OCCUPATIONAL INFORMATION 88

APPLYING THE THEORY TO WOMEN AND CULTURALLY
DIVERSE POPULATIONS 88

COUNSELOR ISSUES 90

SUMMARY 90

REFERENCES 91

CHAPTER 4   *Holland's Theory of Types*   94

THE SIX TYPES 95

   Realistic 95

   Investigative 97

   Artistic 98

   Social 99

   Enterprising 99

   Conventional 100

COMBINATIONS OF TYPES 101

EXPLANATORY CONSTRUCTS 102

   Congruence 103

   Differentiation 104

   Consistency 106

   Identity 108

RESEARCH ON HOLLAND'S CONSTRUCTS 108

THE ROLE OF OCCUPATIONAL INFORMATION 110

THE ROLE OF TESTING 111

APPLYING THE THEORY TO WOMEN 112

APPLYING THE THEORY TO CULTURALLY
DIVERSE POPULATIONS 113

COUNSELOR ISSUES 114

SUMMARY 116

REFERENCES 117

CHAPTER 5   Myers-Briggs Type Theory   120

PERCEIVING AND JUDGING 122

The Two Ways of Perceiving 122

The Two Ways of Judging 123

Combinations of Perceiving and Judging 124

Two Counseling Examples 125

The Preference for Perception or Judgment 126

EXTRAVERSION AND INTROVERSION 127

THE SIXTEEN TYPE COMBINATIONS 127

DOMINANT AND AUXILIARY PROCESSES 131

USING THE MYERS-BRIGGS TYPOLOGY IN COUNSELING 132

Example of Career Decision-Making Counseling 134

Example of Career Adjustment Counseling 139

THE ROLE OF OCCUPATIONAL INFORMATION 142

THE ROLE OF TESTING 143

APPLYING THE THEORY TO WOMEN AND
CULTURALLY DIVERSE POPULATIONS 145

COUNSELOR ISSUES 147

SUMMARY 147

REFERENCES 148

PART TWO   LIFE-SPAN THEORY   151

CHAPTER 6   Introduction to Super's Life-Span Theory   153

BASIC ASSUMPTIONS OF SUPER'S THEORY 153

SELF-CONCEPT 154

ROLES 156

DEVELOPMENTAL STAGES   157

THE ROLE OF OCCUPATIONAL INFORMATION AND TESTING   159

APPLYING THE THEORY TO WOMEN AND
CULTURALLY DIVERSE POPULATIONS   159

SUMMARY   160

REFERENCES   160

CHAPTER 7   Career Development in Childhood   162

SUPER'S MODEL OF THE CAREER DEVELOPMENT
OF CHILDREN   163

Curiosity   163

Exploration   165

Information   166

Key Figures   168

Internal versus External Control   169

Development of Interests   169

Time Perspective   170

Self-Concept and Planfulness   170

USING SUPER'S MODEL IN COUNSELING CHILDREN   171

GENDER-ROLE STEREOTYPING AND
GOTTFREDSON'S THEORY   173

Gottfredson's Theory of Career Development   173

Implications of Gottfredson's Theory for Super's Theory   176

Use of Gottfredson's and Super's Concepts in Counseling   176

CAREER DEVELOPMENT OF CHILDREN FROM
CULTURALLY DIVERSE BACKGROUNDS   178

THE ROLE OF OCCUPATIONAL INFORMATION   179

Occupational Information in Counseling   179

School-to-Work Programs Designed for Children   180

THE ROLE OF TESTING   181

COUNSELOR ISSUES   182

SUMMARY   182

REFERENCES   182

CHAPTER 8 *Adolescent Career Development* 186

FACTORS INFLUENCING ADOLESCENT
CAREER DEVELOPMENT 187

GINZBERG'S TENTATIVE STAGES OF ADOLESCENT
CAREER DEVELOPMENT 188

  Development of Interests 189

  Development of Capacities 189

  Development of Values 190

  Transition Period 190

  Comparison of Super's and Ginzberg's Stages 191

  A Counseling Example 192

CAREER MATURITY 193

  Super's Conception of Career Maturity 194

  Using the Concept of Career Maturity in Counseling 198

IDENTITY AND CONTEXT 199

  A Counseling Example 202

THE ROLE OF OCCUPATIONAL INFORMATION 203

THE ROLE OF TESTING 204

GENDER ISSUES IN ADOLESCENCE 205

  Implications of Gender Research for Super's Theory 207

  Implications for Counseling 207

  A Counseling Example 208

CAREER DEVELOPMENT OF ADOLESCENTS
FROM DIVERSE CULTURAL BACKGROUNDS 209

  Case Example 210

COUNSELOR ISSUES 213

SUMMARY 213

REFERENCES 214

CHAPTER 9 *Late Adolescent and Adult Career Development* 219

ROLE SALIENCE 220

  Life Roles 220

Indicators of the Salience of Life Roles   222

ADULT LIFE STAGES   225

Exploration   226

Establishment   230

Maintenance   234

Disengagement   236

Recycling   237

LIFE STAGES OF WOMEN   239

LIFE STAGES OF CULTURALLY DIVERSE ADULTS   242

COUNSELOR ISSUES   246

SUMMARY   247

REFERENCES   248

CHAPTER 10   *Adult Career Crises and Transitions   252*

TYPES OF TRANSITIONS   253

CATEGORIES OF CAREER TRANSITIONS   253

MODELS OF TRANSITIONS AND CRISES   256

HOPSON AND ADAMS'S MODEL OF ADULT TRANSITIONS   258

Immobilization   258

Minimization   259

Self-Doubt   260

Letting Go   261

Testing Out   261

Search for Meaning   262

Internalization   262

CAREER CRISES AFFECTING WOMEN   264

Temporary Reentry into and Leave-Taking from the Labor Force   264

Sexual Harassment   265

CAREER CRISES AFFECTING CULTURALLY DIVERSE POPULATIONS   270

COUNSELOR ISSUES   272

SUMMARY   273

REFERENCES   273

PART THREE   Special Focus Theories   277

CHAPTER 11   Constructivist Approaches to Career Development   279

PERSONAL CONSTRUCT PSYCHOLOGY   280

Values and Interests   282
Developmental Stages of Vocational Construct Systems   283
Assessment and Counseling Strategies   284
The Vocational Reptest   284
Laddering Techniques   287
Vocational Card Sort   289

NARRATIVE COUNSELING   291

Storytelling   292
Goals of Assessment in Narrative Counseling   292
Narrative Career Counseling   293
Cochran's Narrative Career Counseling   294

THE ROLE OF TESTING   301
THE ROLE OF OCCUPATIONAL INFORMATION   302
APPLYING THE THEORIES TO WOMEN AND CULTURALLY DIVERSE POPULATIONS   303
COUNSELOR ISSUES   303
SUMMARY   304
REFERENCES   305

CHAPTER 12   Parental Influence Theories   307

ROE'S PERSONALITY DEVELOPMENT THEORY   308

Roe's Occupational Classification System   308
Maslow's Hierarchy of Needs   315
Propositions of Roe's Personality Development Theory   316
Roe's Model of Parent–Child Interaction   318

ATTACHMENT THEORY   321
PARENT–CHILD CAREER INTERACTIONS   324
FAMILY SYSTEMS THERAPY   325

USING PARENTAL INFLUENCE THEORIES IN COUNSELING   327

APPLYING THE THEORIES TO WOMEN AND
CULTURALLY DIVERSE POPULATIONS   330

SUMMARY   331

REFERENCES   331

CHAPTER 13   Social Learning and Cognitive Theory   335

KRUMBOLTZ'S SOCIAL LEARNING THEORY   336

Genetic Endowment   337

Environmental Conditions and Events   337

Learning Experiences   339

Task-Approach Skills   340

Client Cognitive and Behavioral Skills   341

Counselor Behavioral Strategies   343

Cognitive Strategies for Counseling   346

Social Learning Theory Goals for Career Counseling   349

Applying Planned Happenstance Theory to Career Counseling   350

SOCIAL COGNITIVE CAREER THEORY   356

Self-Efficacy   357

Outcome Expectations   358

Goals   358

The Social Cognitive Model of Career Choice   359

Counseling Example   362

THE ROLE OF OCCUPATIONAL INFORMATION   364

THE ROLE OF TESTING   365

APPLYING SOCIAL LEARNING AND SOCIAL COGNITIVE
CAREER THEORIES TO WOMEN   365

APPLYING SOCIAL LEARNING AND SOCIAL COGNITIVE
CAREER THEORIES TO CULTURALLY DIVERSE POPULATIONS   368

COUNSELOR ISSUES   369

SUMMARY   370

REFERENCES   370

CHAPTER 14   *Career Decision-Making Approaches   374*

TIEDEMAN'S PERSPECTIVE ON THE PROCESS OF
CAREER DECISION MAKING   375

Anticipating a Choice   376

Adjusting to a Choice   380

Research on Tiedeman's Process Perspective   381

A SPIRITUAL PERSPECTIVE ON DECISION MAKING   382

Lifecareer Theory   383

Personal and Common Realities   384

Spirituality   384

A Spiritual Approach to Career Counseling   387

A Case Example of Spiritual Counseling   388

A COGNITIVE INFORMATION PROCESSING APPROACH   391

Assumptions of a Cognitive Information Processing Approach   391

The Pyramid of Information Processing   392

The Executive Processing Domain   401

Career Decision Making   403

The Career Thoughts Inventory   403

Seven-Step Service Delivery Sequence   404

THE ROLE OF OCCUPATIONAL INFORMATION   405

THE ROLE OF TESTING   406

APPLYING THE THEORIES TO WOMEN AND
CULTURALLY DIVERSE POPULATIONS   406

COUNSELOR ISSUES   407

SUMMARY   408

REFERENCES   408

CHAPTER 15   *The Labor Market: Sociological and Economic Perspectives   411*

THE UNITED STATES LABOR MARKET   412

SOCIOLOGICAL AND ECONOMIC APPROACHES   414

YOUTH EMPLOYMENT   417

*THE EFFECT OF THE WORK ENVIRONMENT
ON THE INDIVIDUAL   419*

STATUS ATTAINMENT THEORY   422

HUMAN CAPITAL THEORY   427

DUAL-ECONOMY THEORY   429

WOMEN AND DISCRIMINATION IN THE WORKPLACE   431

*CULTURALLY DIVERSE INDIVIDUALS AND
DISCRIMINATION IN THE WORKPLACE   438*

SUMMARY   441

REFERENCES   442

PART FOUR   Theoretical Integration   449

CHAPTER 16   Theories in Combination   451

COMBINING THEORIES   452

*Combining Life-Span Theory with Trait and Factor
and Career Decision-Making Theories   453*

Combining Trait and Factor Theories   457

Combining Career Decision-Making Theories   457

An Integrative Approach to Life Planning   460

The Counselor's Choice   463

NONCOUNSELING APPLICATIONS OF THEORIES   463

Screening Methods   463

Paper-and-Pencil Materials   463

Computerized Guidance Systems   464

SPECIAL COUNSELING ISSUES   465

Group Career Counseling   467

Career Counseling as a Related Issue   467

Changing Work Settings   467

Placement Counseling   467

TEST USE IN THEORIES   469

OCCUPATIONAL CLASSIFICATION SYSTEMS AND
CAREER DEVELOPMENT THEORIES   470

*HOW THEORIES APPLY TO CAREER DEVELOPMENT
ISSUES OF WOMEN 472*

*HOW THEORIES APPLY TO CULTURAL DIVERSITY
ISSUES IN CAREER DEVELOPMENT 474*

COUNSELOR ISSUES 475

   Trait and Factor Theories 475

   Life-Span Theories 476

   Career Decision-Making Theories 476

   Sociological and Economic Approaches 476

CONCLUSION 477

REFERENCES 477

Appendix: Tests and Their Publishers 481

Name Index 485

Subject Index 491

Introduction

Being satisfied with one's career is one of the most important aspects of an individual's personal happiness. Career concerns occur throughout one's lifetime. As young children are exposed to their parents' occupations, television programs, and the people around them, they become aware of career opportunities and choices. This exposure becomes broader and deeper throughout elementary school, junior high school, and high school. It is difficult for students not to be overwhelmed by the many occupations and choices around them. After high school, temporary and transitional occupations are often chosen, with continued adjustment throughout one's life span to increase career satisfaction. During retirement, questions of career satisfaction continue to be important. Since approximately one-half of a person's waking hours are spent working, dissatisfaction with career demands can spread into other parts of one's life. It is not uncommon for job dissatisfaction to affect relationships with one's family and friends. People who are dissatisfied with their work or find it boring or monotonous must look for satisfaction in other areas of their lives, such as leisure and family. For many people, however, these other satisfactions do not compensate for frustrations at work. The opportunity to help someone adjust to a selected career is an opportunity to affect a person's life positively, in meaningful and significant ways.

The knowledge that several hours spent in counseling can greatly influence the outcome of an individual's life is an exciting challenge to the counselor. Individuals unfamiliar with career counseling have sometimes compartmentalized counseling by saying there is personal counseling, and then there is career counseling. In editing a special section of *The Career Development Quarterly* (Volume 42, No. 2, 1993), Linda Subich asked the question "How personal is career counseling?" She received 32 submissions, of which 10 were published. The clear, virtually unanimous answer was "Very personal."

These respondents recognized that personal issues pervade career counseling, and that career issues are often prominent in personal counseling, thus making the distinction between the two moot. For example, Krumboltz (1993) showed that career and personal concerns are intertwined, in many cases, and that there are strong emotional components within career counseling that counselors should address. Also, Davidson and Gilbert (1993) stated that personal identity is a part of an individual's career development and that personal issues affect career development and vice versa. Croteau and Thiel (1993) also addressed the personal aspects of career counseling by giving examples of how sexual orientation affects career development. Lucas (1993) showed how family and development issues affected her career counseling of three clients. In a study comparing the level of psychological distress of clients who presented career concerns and of clients who presented noncareer concerns, Gold and Scanlon (1993) found that the level of psychological distress was equivalent, but that those who reported career concerns received fewer sessions of counseling. Another way of seeing the relationship between personal and career counseling is to examine Spokane's (1991) three-phase model of career intervention, which is drawn from the literature on psychotherapy. These experienced counselors and therapists pointed out the personal nature of career counseling from many different vantage points. Because career issues do not always have the immediate impact on counselors that negative or stressful events or feelings may have, career issues may be neglected or dismissed if they are not examined thoroughly.

In this text, numerous case examples are used to illustrate the application of career development theory to counseling. Most of the examples have personal as well as career components. Winifred, in Chapter 3, is a 45-year-old farmer who is faced with the difficulty of changing jobs after experiencing chronic back pain. Chester (Chapter 4) is a high school dropout whose boredom and frustration with his life and work are affecting his personal life. George (Chapter 5) is tense and anxious at work and has difficulty dealing with his supervisees. Arthur (Chapter 7), a fourth-grader, is starting to fall behind in school, is withdrawing from his peers, and is frustrated by reading. Personal issues confront Chad (Chapter 8) as he decides between selling drugs and staying in school to prepare for a career. Matthew (Chapter 9) is 64 and confused and afraid as he faces retirement. Having been laid off from a job that he has had for 23 years, John, who is 55, is angry and depressed (Chapter 10). The trauma of sexual harassment and racial discrimination forces Roberta (Chapter 10) to deal with her anger and the perpetrators. Dennis, a 25-year-old grocery store manager, is living at home and coping with his father's negative views of him (Chapter 11). Carlotta (Chapter 12), 26, is facing career crises as she makes decisions about graduate school. Her reactions are affected by her early parental relationships and her sense of responsibility for her family. A senior in high school, Susan is trying to make plans about what to do after graduation as she deals with her mother's terminal cancer (Chapter 14). A spiritual approach to career decision making is illustrated in the case of Bonnie, who is not sure whether or not to attend college and has to contend with her mother's hurt feelings (Chapter 14). This is a sampling of some of the cases that appear in this book, many concerned with both personal and career issues.

Life issues and problems occur at many different times. The developmental nature of career concerns can be seen in the case of Lucy, who is discussed in Chapters 7, 8, and 9. As a fifth-grader, she is upset about her mother's forcing her father out of the house, and her reaction affects her interactions at school and in the family. At 15, the pressures on Lucy from her father and a boyfriend to go to nursing school rather than to medical school are affecting her self-confidence and causing confusion. At 28, Lucy is hurting from the breakup of a three-year relationship and is deciding whether to return to school to become a physician. These personal and career issues are intertwined, as they are for many clients.

The term *career* refers to how individuals see themselves in relationship to what they do. The case studies presented offer snapshots of a person's career or an aspect of a person's working and leisure behavior. The National Career Development Association (Sears, 1982) defines the term *career* as the individual's work and leisure that take place over her or his life span. In this text, *career choice* applies to decisions that individuals make at any point in their career about particular work or leisure activities that they choose to pursue at that time. The focus is on the individual, in contrast to the terms *job* and *occupation*. In this text, jobs refer to positions requiring similar skills within one organization. Occupations refer to similar jobs found in many organizations. Occupations exist regardless of whether individuals are employed in them. Career refers to the lifetime pursuits of the individual.

Career development theory can serve as a guide for career counseling, and for problems similar to those previously described. By tying together research about career choice and adjustment with ideas about these issues, career development theorists have provided a conceptual framework within which to view the types of career problems that emerge during a person's lifetime. To understand these theories, it is first important to understand the role of theory in psychology.

THE ROLE OF THEORY IN PSYCHOLOGY

In reviewing the role of theory in psychology, Heinen (1985) describes theory as "a group of logically organized laws or relationships that constitute explanation in a discipline" (p. 414). Theory has been particularly important in the development of physical and biological science. Within psychology, theory has made a distinct impact in the area of learning. When applied to career development, theory becomes more crude and less precise. Career development theory attempts to explain behavior that occurs over many years and is made up of reactions to thousands of experiences and situations such as school, hobbies, and parents.

Regardless of the type of theory, there are certain general principles for judging the appropriateness of a theory. The following are criteria by which career development theories can be evaluated (Fawcett & Downs, 1986; Hanzel, 1999; Snow, 1973).

1. *Theories should be explicit about their rules and theorems. Terms that are used in describing these rules should be clear.* Theories that attempt to explain how people make career choices often have difficulty in defining terms such as *growth, development,* and *self-concept.* Theorems about career selection are also difficult to make. In general, the broader the theory, the more difficult it is to be specific about the terms that are used.

2. *Theories should be precise about the limitations of their predictions. Theories differ in the breadth of behavior that they attempt to predict.* For example, some theories attempt to explain career development for women, some for both men and women, and some for people of different age groups. Some theories attempt to explain vocational choice, while others try to explain how people adjust to this choice; still others explain both. It is important to understand what the subject of the theory is. It is unfair to criticize a theory for failing to do something that it does not set out to do.

3. *When theories are developed, they need to be tested.* This is accomplished by doing research that can be expressed in terms of quantitative relationships. By doing research studies that use clear and measurable terms, investigators can best determine if data are in agreement with the theory. Within the field of career development, it is sometimes difficult to determine whether or not research supports a theory. The reason may be that an investigator has defined terms in a different way from the theorist or has used an unrepresentative sample to make predictions or generalizations. For example, if a theorist attempts to explain how all people make choices, the research samples should include both men and women, regardless of race, education, and income. Sometimes evidence from a research study is unclear, supporting some propositions of a theory but not others, or supporting the theory for some populations but not others. A helpful method for confirming theoretical constructs is the development of inventories that define constructs and relate them to other constructs within the theory as well as to other theories and instruments. By the accumulation of such information, construct validity is established for the theory and the instrument.

4. *A theory needs to be consistent and clear.* A theory should provide constructs that have a logical relationship to each other. To be clear, the theory should not be too complex. It should provide the simplest way to explain propositions. On

the other hand, there is the danger of oversimplification. Essential components should not be left out of a theory. Because vocational theorists attempt to explain exceedingly complex behavior, it is only natural that they may oversimplify their theories. In doing so, they may provide a useful and understandable guide for the counselor.

In summary, a theory needs to be explicit about its theorems and terms. Further, it needs to be clear about what it is theorizing and the breadth of its propositions. In addition, research should be able to provide positive or negative support for the theory. Sometimes research findings add to and develop a theory, showing that it is open to change. Also, a theory, while being neither too simple nor too complex, must provide a useful way of explaining and understanding career development.

Judgments about the soundness and relative utility of theories are difficult for the counselor to make. Authors such as Osipow and Fitzgerald (1995) and Brown and Brooks (1996) attempt to evaluate how well career development theories meet criteria similar to those described above. While research will receive comment, the primary focus of this book is on the application of the theory by the counselor. Most of the theories that have been included were determined by me to meet, at least minimally, the four criteria just listed. Some theories are quite new and have not yet met these criteria, but they provide new ideas for counselors to consider.

A broad approach to the application of theory to career development and to psychology, in general, has been taken by Dawis (2000a, 2000b). He argues that the Person-Environment Fit model can be used as a way of understanding the important aspects of psychological science. He believes that by studying the interaction between persons and their environment, researchers will have an excellent model for studying many psychological issues including career choice and development. Almost all of the theories in this book can be viewed from this broad perspective as they all focus on how individuals interact with their environment (e.g., school, work, families). Tinsley (2000) has reviewed the adequacy of the Person-Environment Fit model focusing on those theories called trait and factor theories. However, the Person-Environment Fit model is too broad to be applied by counselors, therefore I discuss theories that are more detailed and specific about career development.

COUNSELORS' USE OF CAREER DEVELOPMENT THEORY

To select theories of career development to use, counselors must not only have confidence in the theory as described in the previous section but also make judgments about the advisability of using that theory with their clients. Further, counselors need to consider their own view and style of counseling or psychotherapy. Their theory of counseling is likely to influence their selection of a theory of career development. Still further, the counselor needs to select a theory of career development that is manageable and relatively easy to draw upon in a counseling session. These three concepts are discussed in more detail in the following paragraphs.

Client Population

Counselors work in a wide variety of settings and are likely to encounter a preponderance of one or another type of career problem. For example, elementary and junior high school counselors work with students who are at the beginning of the career information and selection process. High school and college counselors tend to help their clients with vocational choice, development of alternatives, and job placement. Employment counselors, although they deal with some of the same issues as high school and college counselors, may encounter more issues related to satisfaction with and adjustment to a job. Some counselors work in business and industry with a limited number of professions, such as accounting and engineering. These counselors are likely to be involved in issues of work satisfaction, adjustment, and promotion. Vocational rehabilitation counselors and other counselors who work with clients who are physically and mentally challenged deal not only with the issues mentioned previously but must also judge the applicability of the theory to the challenges of their clientele. Moreover, retirement issues have become a greater concern of counselors in recent years. Choosing new, part-time, or volunteer work and scaling down the demands of current work are issues that retirement counselors must consider. Pastoral counselors, physicians, clinical psychologists, and psychiatrists work in settings where their clients may have career choice or adjustment issues that are related to other problems. Although career concerns may not be the presenting problem of the client for these and other mental health workers, they may still be significant issues. Further, the gender of the client can be an important variable in theory selection. Counselors must ask themselves if a theory is as appropriate for younger as older individuals. Since career development theories differ in the age range that they choose to explain, it is for the counselor to decide whether a particular career development theory is appropriate for the population with which he or she works.

Theories of Counseling and Theories of Career Development

Like counseling theories, many theories of career development are derived from theories of personality. Often it is difficult to distinguish theories of counseling and theories of career development clearly from theories of personality. In general, counseling and psychotherapy theories tend to be a subset of personality theory used to bring about a desired change in feeling, thinking, or behavior. Similarly, many theories of career development tend to be a subset of personality theories, which include how people relate to work and career issues. Therefore, since personality, counseling, and career development theory are highly interrelated, it is natural for counselors who prefer a certain personality theory or theory of counseling to be drawn to a similar career development theory.

Because theories of personality and counseling form the core of a counselor's training, they tend to influence the counselor's selection of a theory of career development. Rarely would the selection of a theory of career development determine a counselor's theory of personality or career counseling. For example, counselors attracted to Jungian theory may wish to use the Myers-Briggs theory of types. Those counselors who employ rational emotive behavior therapy, behavioral therapy, or cognitive therapy may find trait and factor theory, Holland's theory of types, social learning, and cognitive information processing approaches to be particularly helpful. Many counselors are eclectic in their practical orientation; that is, they may draw from many theories. Although it is helpful to be open to the value of all theories of career development, it is important to remember the connection between career development theory and counseling theory. The theories presented in this book differ in terms of how similar they are to theories of personality, a few being quite different.

Chunking

The concept of chunking is important for counselors to consider when selecting a theory of career development. Unlike computers, counselors have a limited ability to store information. Psychologists have studied the limited capacity of both short-term and long-term memory. In studying short-term memory, Miller (1956) suggested that people can process five to nine concepts, ideas, numbers, words, or sentences at a time. This processing is done by grouping concepts or ideas and is called *chunking*. In reviewing the literature, Simon (1974) examined a number of different verbal learning areas, basically supporting the findings of Miller. Challenging Miller's findings, Broadbent (1975) suggested that the number *three* was the basic unit of memory. Trying to reconcile the views of Miller and Broadbent, Mac-Gregor (1987) suggested individuals sometimes chunk or group information into three items and other times chunk into seven items.

Recent research has extended knowledge about chunking. Studies of brain wave frequency and the cerebral cortex suggest that working memory handles about seven items at a time (Glassman, 1999; Wickelgren, 1999). Neural network modules are used to understand how individuals "chunk" concepts (Halford, Wilson, & Phillips, 1998). The concept of chunking has been extended to understand the thinking of novice and experienced computer programmers (Ye & Salvendy, 1994) and to training in business (Gordon, 1997).

There is value in applying the concept of chunking to the use of career development theory in career counseling. Theories that have three or four basic constructs are likely to be learned relatively easily. Theories with up to eight or nine concepts may be remembered and used with some difficulty, depending on how often the concepts are reused in counseling.

Theories with more than eight or nine concepts are likely to present a retention problem for the counselor when he or she is starting to put a theory into practice. One solution is to divide the theory into several chunks. It is important to do this, as counselors need to learn information about a number of subjects, such as helping skills, career testing, and occupational information, when assisting clients in career decision making.

COUNSELOR SKILLS

The primary purpose of this book is to describe the usefulness of career development theory in counseling people with problems of career selection and adjustment. Information about theories can be combined with helping skills, which are based primarily on the early work of Carl Rogers (1951). Further, the use of occupational information as found in pamphlets and books and on computers is a necessary component of career counseling. Since the 1940s, career testing has also been an integral part of this type of counseling. These three areas of knowledge—helping skills, testing, and providing occupational information—are described in the following paragraphs in terms of their relationship to career development theory.

Helping Skills

Since the early 1980s, a number of books have described helping skills. The authors of these books appear to agree generally on the helping skills necessary for change in most counseling situations, including career counseling. Their work is based on the precepts of Carl Rogers (1958), which specify four basic conditions necessary for counseling change: unconditional positive regard, genuineness, congruence, and empathy.

Unconditional positive regard can be described as the acceptance of a person as being worthwhile and valuable, regardless of age, gender, race, or what he or she has done. Genuineness refers to sincerity—the need for the counselor to be honest with the client. Congruence requires that the counselor's voice tone, body language, and verbal statements be consistent with one another. Finally, empathy refers to the ability to communicate to the client that the counselor understands the client's concerns and feelings from the point of view of the client. These four basic conditions have become the cornerstone of research involving over 260 studies.

Truax and Carkhuff (1967) and Carkhuff and Berenson (1967) have done considerable research to further define and develop Rogers's work. Recently, authors such as Egan (1998), Ivey and Ivey (1999), Okun (1997), and Patterson and Welfel (2000) have provided methods for learning the basic or core helping skills. In addition, these writers have emphasized (to varying degrees) other important skills such as asking open-ended and nonbiased questions. Besides discussing, paraphrasing, and reflecting feelings (basic empathic listening skills), these writers explain important issues of confrontation and the need for concreteness and specificity. The authors just listed provide texts for courses in basic counseling skills or helping relationships. A detailed explanation of these skills goes beyond the scope of this book. However, I describe the most common interventions and counseling techniques that are likely to be used in career counseling. Many of these interventions are used in the case examples that are found throughout this book.

Attending Skills   A basic counseling skill is the counselor's nonverbal presence in the counseling situation. In an attending position, counselors face their clients squarely, adopting an open posture (legs and arms not crossed) and leaning slightly toward the other person. Maintaining good eye contact, not staring, is natural for people who are having a deep conversation. Counselors also maintain a relaxed, rather than tense or fidgety, presence. These skills are used primarily in North America when addressing clients. In other cultures, people may show attentiveness in other ways (Egan, 1998).

Questions   Questions are used to get specific information or to help clients describe or elaborate on certain subjects, feelings, or events. Closed-ended questions request specific information, and the answers are often of the "yes" or "no" variety. Open-ended questions encourage a broader response, asking the client to explain more fully the what, how, when, or where of a situation, feeling, or event. Both are illustrated in this dialogue:

> *CO:* What grade did you get in English last year? [Closed-ended question]
> *CL:* I got an "A."
> *CO:* Did you like the class? [Closed-ended question]
> *CL:* Yes. It was OK.
> *CO:* What did you learn about in class? [Open-ended question]
> *CL:* We studied modern writers, and I learned how to critique short stories. I was surprised that my ability to develop a good paragraph really changed during the course. My teacher was very helpful and complimented me about my progress.
> *CO:* How does that affect your thoughts about college? [Open-ended question]
> *CL:* It really gets me thinking. I hadn't known that I could write that well. The short reviews we did in class really made me more comfortable with writing and made me think, "Hey, I can do more of this." I could even do it in college.

As shown here, open-ended questions usually elicit a much broader explanation from the client than do closed-ended questions. Questions, in general, and especially closed-ended questions tend to place the burden of the interview on the counselor. In a sense, if questions are used frequently, clients develop an expectation that if they answer the questions the counselor will provide a solution to the problem. In this book, questions are used very sparingly in the case examples. Rather the counselors in the examples are much more apt to use reflections of client statements.

Statements and Reflections   By rephrasing what the client has said, counselors focus on the cognitive or emotional content of a client's statement. When a client makes a statement, restating it directs attention to the situation, the person, or the general idea. The client is thus encouraged to add or to develop his or her statement. Restatements may reflect not only the words of the client, but also the voice tone, gestures, and facial expression. Because information and affect are attached to career issues, it is often helpful to make content and feeling reflections. Feeling reflections contain an emotional word or phrase (or imply it). Content reflections focus on the information that the client provides.

> CL: My work is so boring. All I do is wait on one customer after another. I ring up the sale. Give the customer the receipt. Ring up the sale. Give the customer the receipt. And on and on.
>
> *Content reflection:* Each day you perform the same actions over and over again.
> *Feeling reflection:* Waiting on customers is really boring you and annoying you. You can't wait till the day is over.

In this situation, the content reflection tells only a small part of the story. The feeling reflection provides a fuller expression of the client's experience. In the cases in this book, when feeling or emotional content is provided in the client's response, the counselor response usually reflects the affective component. Content reflections tend to be used mainly when the counselor perceives little affect.

Continuation Responses   Often, in career counseling (and other counseling) it can be helpful to request more information. A nonverbal gesture such as nodding or using a hand movement invites a client to continue. Verbal comments include "Tell me more," "Can you say more about that?" "Go on," "Hmm," "And then?" and "And what happened then?" A brief example will clarify:

> CO: What are your plans for next year? [Open-ended question]
> CL: I think that I'm going to work in the department store's hardware department. I've done it for three years, and it's easy to continue to do so. Besides, I really think I need to get more money before I can continue college.
> CO: Say more about that, if you would. [Continuation]
> CL: It's easy to stay in the hardware department. I know it really well, but I'm not getting very far with it. Sometimes, I think I should go back to school anyway, even though I don't have the money, and just hope things will work out.
> CO: Hmm. Tell me more. [Continuation]
> CL: I don't think that I have the money, but maybe I can get my father to take out a loan. He really doesn't want to, but if I'm really persuasive, maybe he can help me. It sure would be better than having to be back in that old job.

When discussing career issues, continuation techniques bring out more information than the client may volunteer at first. The career development theories in this book focus on the client as an important informational resource about himself or herself. Thus, continuation responses are frequently seen in the examples.

Giving Information, Not Opinion   Often, counselors give clients information about educational or occupational opportunities. It is important that this information be accurate, up-to-date, and clear. Biased information can be destructive and confusing to the client. Opinions that are given by the counselor represent only one person's view. However, because clients are likely to view counselors as experts, the counselors' opinions may be perceived as being information or *the truth*. Counselors who give opinions risk discouraging or encouraging a client inappropriately.

> *CL:*   Now, after I've completed my first year of college, I have a "C" average. I'm not sure whether I should revise my plans to go to medical school.
>
> *Opinion 1:* I think that you should revise your plans. Students with a "C" average have little chance of getting into medical school.
>
> *Opinion 2:* Things are likely to get better. You still have a chance to pull your grades up and probably get into medical school.
>
> *Information:* What do you think about your chances of getting into medical school? [The counselor wants to know what is the basis of the client's information.]
>
> *CL:*   I realize that most students have to have an "A−" average to go to medical school, but I think I can raise my grades.
>
> *Information:* You may find it helpful to go to the premed adviser to get more information about how students have done here in getting into medical school. [The counselor does not have the specific information that the client needs at hand but directs the client to a source.]

Although individuals with a "C" average in their freshman year in college may find it difficult to be admitted to medical school, there are some exceptions. The counselor assumes a powerful role if she or he gives Opinions 1 or 2. The theories that are covered in this book assume that the client, rather than the counselor, is the decision maker, thus providing guidance for career decision making.

Reinforcement   A behavioral technique, verbal reinforcement of the client's behavior is often used in career counseling. This technique is particularly featured in Chapter 13, where social learning theory is described. In verbal reinforcement, it is the client's behavior that is reinforced, rather than the client.

> *CL:*   I've been wanting to tell my boss that he's been giving me too many assignments lately. I've really been afraid to do so, and I've been really anxious. I'm afraid that he will be really mad at me and tell me I'll have to leave my job. This is something I don't want to do. It's a great job otherwise. This has bugged me so much that I've been losing sleep over it and I'm really starting to feel depressed. Finally, I got up the courage and

talked to my boss and told him exactly what it was that was bothering me. He was understanding, and I was really relieved.

CO: That's terrific. You did something that you have wanted to do for quite a while. You explained the problem, explained the difficulties, and you got satisfaction. That's wonderful.

If the client had said, "I told my boss all these things, and he got really angry" the counselor might have replied, "You did what you wanted to do. You explained the problem to him specifically, and told him how it was bothering you. It's great that you were able to do so. It's too bad that he didn't respond the way you wanted him to." In both cases, the counselor is reinforcing the client's behavior. A common behavior that counselors reinforce is information seeking. For example, when a client has read about or talked to people in a particular profession, counselors may say, "That's terrific that you spent so much time in finding out about that. Great!"

Family Background Exploration   Chapter 12 on parental influence theories discusses ways of exploring the role of parenting in career decision making. For example, the genogram is a method of diagramming family relationships and is a tool for discussing the relationship of clients' career plans to those of their families.

Test and Inventory Interpretation   An important career-counseling intervention is test interpretation. Discussed particularly in the theories that are explained in Part One, test interpretation provides information about the client to the client. In interpreting tests or inventories for clients, counselors use many of the skills that have just been described. Throughout the book, examples of test interpretation are given for interest, ability, value, and personality tests and inventories. Some of the specific knowledge that is needed to make accurate test interpretations is discussed briefly in the next section of this chapter. Test interpretation, like many of the techniques described here, is helpful in career counseling. Other techniques, such as confrontation, self-disclosure, and counselor interpretations, can also be helpful and are described in some of the texts mentioned previously.

Career development theories, for the most part, do not specify counseling techniques. Rather, they provide a way of comprehending and organizing the information that is contained in counseling sessions. The tools that produce this information are the content and feeling reflections, open-ended questions, and other techniques mentioned previously. Career development theory, which may indirectly affect the technique used, aids the counselor in understanding the client. It is likely that the counselors using trait and factor theory will ask more questions and will use fewer feeling reflections than those who employ Super's life-span theory. However, this does not have to be the case. The focus of this book is making use of career development theory in conceptualizing career counseling when assisting a client.

Testing

The term *test* refers generally to ability and achievement tests on which there are correct answers, and on which individuals perform as well as possible ("maximum performance"). The term *inventory* refers to instruments that solicit a preference or viewpoint from the counselee and have no "right" or "wrong" answers. Common inventories used in counseling measure interests, values, and personality. Career development theories differ on the weight they give to the importance of tests and inventories in the career development process. Tests and inventories have been in wide use for career counseling since the 1930s and 1940s. Extensive test development took place during World War II because of the need to assign men and women to the military tasks for which they were best suited. Although originally designed for the selection of employees, tests and inventories have been particularly useful in counseling. To be competent in test or inventory selection, counselors need to understand measurement concepts such as validity, reliability, and normative information. Because these concepts are so important in understanding testing, they will be described briefly here. However, this description does not take the place of a course or text on psychological measurement.

Norms   It is useful to compare a client's score on a test or inventory with a normative sample (norms) that is used in developing a standard for scoring. Such a sample should be normal scores, those that are typical of a population. Sometimes, norms are based on a general population and, at other times, on specific groups, such as high school students, accountants, or former drug abusers. In some cases, norms are listed separately for males and females; in other cases, they are combined. Norms are also sometimes separated for people of different races or ages. Good norms are helpful in providing counselors a full understanding of the basis of the comparisons that they will make. For example, a counselor would not want to compare a twelfth-grade client's biology achievement score with the scores of ninth-graders. Although national norms are frequently used, it is sometimes helpful to have local norms, so as to compare students within a school system or a state.

Norms are typically presented in percentile scores, which are easy to understand because counselors can see the percentage of individuals above or below a particular score. Often, standard scores are used because, unlike percentile scores, they provide for a uniform difference between each score. Thus, the difference between 50 and 55 is the same as the difference between 70 and 75, which is not true of percentages.

Reading a test manual to learn about norms and to decide, where appropriate, which norms to use is important for counselors who wish to use the tests or inventories that are described in this book.

Reliability   To be used, a test or inventory must be dependable and consistent. If a student takes a test or inventory one time, the score that he or she receives a second time should be similar. A test that has perfect reliability would be one on which everyone's scores were in the same relative position on every additional administration of the test. There are two major sources of unreliability: variation in human performance and variation in the technical aspects of measurement. For example, a measurement of math ability should be more stable than a measure of depression, which varies according to mood. Error may be due to the testing conditions, such as lighting, heat or cold, and poor instructions. On many tests, the reliability coefficients usually exceed .80, but there are some situations in which an acceptable reliability may be less. Reliability may be measured by administering the same test on two different occasions or two different forms of the same test on different occasions. Split-half reliability is obtained by dividing a single test into two comparable halves and comparing the results from the two halves. Yet another measure is interitem consistency, which is arrived at by examining the average intercorrelations among the items on a test. Knowledge of the reliability of an instrument is important in deciding whether to use it with clients.

Validity   Does a test or inventory measure what it is supposed to measure? Does a measure of English skills really measure skills in English? How well a test or inventory measures what is requested of it is referred to as *validity*. For a test or inventory to be valid, it must first be reliable; that is, it must be a consistent measure of a trait or other variable. Different types of scales require different types of validity. *Content validity* refers to the actual content of the items. Do the items reflect the area, such as knowledge of algebra, that the test is attempting to measure. *Concurrent validity* is a measure against a specific criterion. For example, scores on a test of clerical ability can be compared to the performance of secretaries who have established clerical abilities. *Predictive validity* also refers to a criterion, but in the future. For example, does a test of clerical aptitude predict how well applicants for secretarial positions will perform on clerical aspects of their positions in a year? *Construct validity* is more complex, referring to whether or not the scales make psychological sense and are related to the variables that they should be related to. A depression inventory should be related to other tests of depression or psychiatric ratings of depressed people on specific symptoms of depression. Test and inventory manuals provide the counselor with information on these types of validity. A test that is not valid has little value for the counselor. In this book, many tests and inventories are mentioned, and all have at least moderate validity in some, but not all, of the four types of validity described here.

Testing plays two major roles in career development theory. First, tests and inventories can be used to develop and verify a theory. Second, tests and inventories can provide the counselor with information that can then be used as a means of understanding the client from the point of view of career development theory. For example, John Holland developed and used the Self-Directed Search and the Vocational Preference Inventory as a way to test the constructs of his theory. Another example is Super's career development theory. Donald Super developed the Values Scale and the Career Development

Inventory, among many other inventories; other investigators have developed career maturity scales, all of which can be used to test various aspects of Super's theory. Counselors can use these instruments to develop knowledge about the client that they can then relate directly to a theoretical context.

For the counselor, tests and inventories have three major features: selection, administration, and interpretation. Norms, reliability, and validity are important considerations in deciding which tests or inventories to select. Test and inventory selection may also be based on theoretical concepts that are relevant to the counselees, which will be discussed further in this text. Administration is described in detail in each test manual, and different considerations apply to individual and group test-taking procedures. Interpreting a test requires a knowledge of both the client and the test or inventory. In this text, examples of test and inventory interpretation are given to show how a counselor might discuss portions of results with a client.

Providing Occupational Information

Career counseling differs from other types of counseling in its reliance on occupational and educational information. Hoppock (1976) describes in detail the information that counselors should know about occupations and the importance of occupational information in counseling. Hoppock believes that counselors should:

- Know where their clients get their first jobs or where their clients go to work after they've completed counseling.
- Determine the principal employment opportunities in their local area. The geographic area within which college students search for jobs is likely to be much larger than for high school students, who are more likely to look for work close to home.
- Learn about occupations that are being considered by their clients, so they can provide information appropriate for their clients.
- Learn about at least one occupation that is central to each of three of the most important and largest local employers. This will entail visiting and developing contacts with these employers.
- Know how to obtain information and to evaluate it for accuracy and usefulness.

Essentially, counselors need to know certain types of information and specific sources of career information. The types of information that are perhaps most important (Sharf, 1984) include descriptions of the occupation, working conditions, qualifications required by the job duties, beginning and average salaries, the employment outlook, the education (courses, majors, or degrees) required by the job, and where one can get more information about the occupation. Answers to these questions are provided in publications such as the *Occupational Outlook Handbook* (2000) and the *Encyclopedia of Careers and Vocational Guidance* (Hopke, 2000). These publications offer occupational information about a broad and representative sample of occupations. In addition, pamphlets produced by publishers specializing in occupational information and by trade organizations describe hundreds of occupations that are available. Textbooks and courses on occupational information deal fully with these topics and are helpful for effective career counseling. Furthermore, a number of computerized guidance products such as DISCOVER and SIGI PLUS provide occupational information along with career assessment.

Career development theories vary widely in the attention that they pay to occupational information. For example, Holland's theory provides a system for classifying all occupational information through the use of six categories. Holland provides an identifiable code for each occupation that has clear meaning according to his theory. On the other hand, the Myers-Briggs theoretical formulation focuses almost entirely on the person's type and not on occupational information. Super and his colleagues (Starishevsky & Matlin, 1963) used the term *occtalk* to describe occupational information that clients learn; they used the term *psychtalk* to delineate the views that clients have of themselves. For instance, "It is helpful for musicians to know a number of instruments" is an example of occtalk; "I enjoy learning music theory" is an example of psychtalk. This example illustrates how theorists built a bridge between occupational information and information about the client from a counseling interview. Although occupational information is described in this chapter, it is explained in detail in Chapter 2 as a means of classifying careers, and in Chapter 15 as a way of viewing the labor market. Classifying occupations and learning about the labor market are two important aspects of occupational information.

How Career Development Theory Relates

Just as counseling theories provide a framework for the conceptualization of client problems, career development theory provides a framework for helping with a client's career problems. Career development theory can be considered the part of the process of career counseling that offers a means of conceptualizing career concerns. Basic helping skills are the essential ingredient in bringing about change and progress in career issues. Tests and inventories, as well as occupational information, can be seen as additional information that aids in the conceptualization process. Counseling skills are used to provide feedback about tests and inventories or to give information about occupations. Overall, it is career development theory that can give counselors an idea of how they are going to help their clients and what the eventual outcome of counseling may be. The goal-directedness that career development theory can provide gives counselors, particularly beginning counselors, a sense of confidence.

GOALS OF CAREER COUNSELING

The two most common goals of career counseling are the selection of an occupation and the adjustment to an occupation. As shown in Chapters 7 and 8, career selection usually takes place anytime after the age of 14, but most commonly during high school and/or college. When helping a client in the process of choosing occupations, counselors often use information about the client's satisfaction with any previous work. When adults are trying to find more satisfaction in an occupation, they often question their current career choice and review their reasons for seeking that occupation. This may happen at any time during a person's working life. Some theorists, such as Dawis and Lofquist (1984), focus on vocational adjustment as well as vocational selection. Implicit in all career development theories is the notion that the client, rather than the counselor, makes the final choice.

Goals, whether explicit or implicit, are essential to counseling. Goals serve as a guide for the work that is done in the counseling session. An example of making goals explicit is when the counselor and the client agree that the purpose of counseling is to select from appropriate career alternatives. An example of making goals implicit is when the counselor assumes that the client wishes to select appropriate career alternatives. Whether the goals are explicit or implicit, the use of career development theories can make goals clear and specific for the counselor.

For each theory in this book, methods of conceptualizing theoretical constructs in terms of counseling goals will be described to the extent that the theory permits. A counselor using theoretical constructs in conceptualizing client goals should have a sense of how well the counseling is progressing, what (in general) should happen next in the counseling, and what needs to take place for the counseling to be completed. These goals and their implementation may not be identical for all people. Research on the career development of women and culturally diverse populations has provided information that has changed the way many of the theories can be conceptualized for these groups.

CAREER DEVELOPMENT OF WOMEN

Some career development theories were created before 1960 and were based solely on research on white males from middle-class or upper-middle-class families. Although most of these theories have since incorporated women into their sampling and theoretical statements, career development theorists have been criticized for their neglect of women's career development issues. The role of women in the workplace has changed greatly since the early 1960s. Because women represent over half the population of the United States and of the world, it is particularly important to illustrate the application of career development theories to women.

In this book, each chapter has a section dealing with applications of theory to career counseling issues for women. In some cases, this section is quite brief, as the theory may not be sufficiently detailed and researched to include information about women. In other cases, especially life-span and social cognitive career theory, much space is devoted to career development issues for women, as well as to examples of counselor conceptualizations of client concerns. Theories of women's life-span career development are incorporated into Part Two. There is approximately equal representation of men and women in the case examples illustrating career development theory.

CAREER DEVELOPMENT OF CULTURALLY DIVERSE POPULATIONS

While there are only two genders, there are many cultures. No theories of career development have been formulated to apply specifically to one culture or another. However, research has been done on the applicability of particular career development theories to specific cultural groups. When this research will help in understanding the context of the theory for a particular group, it is presented.

Within the field of career development, more research has been done on African Americans than on other people of color. Some research has also studied the career development of Latinos, Asians, and Native Americans, but even these groups do not represent uniform cultural backgrounds. For example, Asians include Japanese, Chinese, Vietnamese, Cambodians, and East Indians, as well as many other nationalities. Within each of these nationalities, there are groups that may have little in common with each other. For example, there are many regions in India that do not share a common language, religion, or social customs. Immigrants to the United States may come as refugees from wars. Many Vietnamese people have come to the United States seeking employment after being forced to flee their country after the Vietnam War. Discussion of these different cultures is beyond the scope of this book and can be found in other sources (for example, Atkinson, Morten, & Sue, 1998; Axelson, 1999), although their emphasis is not on career or employment issues. This book gives some examples of the conceptualization of career development issues when counseling people from some of these cultures, but it is not possible to include examples from all cultures.

In this book, the term *cultural diverse populations* is used to designate African Americans and other blacks, Latinos, Native American, and Asian/Pacific Islander people. The term *minority* is reserved for people who represent a minority of a given population. Worldwide, people of color are a majority, and Caucasians are a minority.

WHAT'S AHEAD

The theories described in this book are grouped into four parts: type and trait theories, life-span theories, special focus theories, and theoretical integration. Part One deals with characteristics or types of people, focusing on the behavior and concerns of a person at the present moment. Chapter 2 discusses the earliest formal theory of career development: trait and factor theory. This theory deals with the study of interests, values, aptitudes, and other traits that are used in assisting clients with career decisions. In

Chapter 3, Lofquist and Dawis's theory focusing on adult adjustment to work is detailed. The fourth chapter describes John Holland's typology of people and environments, including an explanation of the six Holland types and their application to career counseling. Another typology, based on Carl Jung's approach to personality theory, is the focus of Chapter 5, featuring the Myers-Briggs view of personality types as it affects career development.

Part Two includes life-span theories, introduced in Chapter 6. Unlike Parts One and Three, in which each chapter describes a specific theory, Part Two focuses on four aspects of life-span development: childhood (Chapter 7), early adolescence (Chapter 8), late adolescence and adulthood (Chapter 9), and adult career crises and career transitions (Chapter 10). This format is followed for several reasons. Super's life-span theory is more developed than other life-span theories, having produced much more research and instrumentation. Most other life-span theories do not cover the entire life span. Further, the conceptualization of career counseling is similar among all life-span theories. In Chapters 7, 8, and 9, Super's theory is used as the basis for explaining career development concepts. Other theories are used to add to Super's work, particularly as it relates to the career development of women and culturally diverse populations. In Chapter 10, Hopson and Adams's theory of adult transitions is used to discuss career crises. It is placed within the context of Super's life-span theory.

In Part Three, additional theories emphasize various aspects of career development. Chapter 11 explains two different constructivist approaches— ways of viewing individuals as creating their own views of events and relationships in their lives. Parental influence on career choice, along with Roe's classification of occupations, is explained in Chapter 12. Krumboltz's behavioral approach to career decision making, along with social cognitive career theory, both based on social learning theory, is described in Chapter 13. How one makes career decisions is examined by comparing a developmental approach, a spiritual approach, and a cognitive information processing perspective on career decision making in Chapter 14. As described in Chapter 15, sociologists and economists have developed broad views of career development. These views focus on the effect of societal expectations of individuals, as well as stereotypes of women and minorities and their impact on employment. This research examines the importance of family, school, and the work setting in the career decision-making process.

The final part (Chapter 16) shows counselors how to integrate several theories in their counseling conceptualization. Examples of how this integration can take place, depending on the work setting and the counselor's theoretical preferences, are given. Also, special issues, such as the use of computer guidance programs, career group counseling, and job placement counseling, are discussed.

Each chapter follows the same format. The first part of the chapter describes a specific theory and its important constructs. Integrated into the description of the theories is information about counseling strategies, with examples of how to conceptualize client concerns by using theoretical constructs. Brief dialogues between counselor and client, which include counselor conceptualizations, illustrate the application of each career development theory. The use of dialogue enables readers to learn about the thought process a counselor goes through to conceptualize a client problem. Occasionally, narrative case studies are also used. Included in each chapter is a discussion of how the theory incorporates testing and occupational information. Applicability to women and culturally diverse populations is also described, with reference to reviews of the literature and to general research findings. Another section of each chapter deals with counselor problems in applying the theory, including feelings and thoughts that counselors may have that interfere in applying a particular theoretical approach. After reading each chapter, readers should have a clear idea of how to think about client problems by using a particular theory.

There are several ways readers can apply the information in this book to make it more meaningful for them. Readers who counsel clients can try to picture a client and think about his or her presenting concerns in terms of a particular theory. Another approach is to think of one's own life or that of friends or family in terms of the theory. For students, an effective way of integrating career development theory into counseling is to role-play counseling situations with other students, using a particular theoretical orientation. All of these approaches are likely to make the material seem more helpful and applicable.

References

Atkinson, D. R., Morten, G., & Sue, D. W. (1998). *Counseling American minorities: A cross-cultural perspective* (5th ed.). Boston: McGraw-Hill.

Axelson, J. A. (1999). *Counseling and development in a multicultural society* (3rd ed.). Pacific Grove, CA: Brooks/Cole.

Broadbent, D. E. (1975). The magic number seven after fifteen years. In A. Kennedy & A. Wilkes (Eds.), *Studies in long term memory* (pp. 3–18). London: Wiley.

Brown, D., & Brooks, L. (Eds.). (1996). *Career choice and development* (3rd ed.). San Francisco: Jossey-Bass.

Carkhuff, R., & Berenson, B. (1967). *Beyond counseling and therapy*. New York: Holt, Rinehart & Winston.

Croteau, J. M., & Thiel, M. J. (1993). Integrating sexual orientation in career counseling: Acting to end a form of the personal-career dichotomy. *The Career Development Quarterly, 42,* 174–179.

Davidson, S. L., & Gilbert, L. A. (1993). Career counseling is a personal matter. *The Career Development Quarterly, 42,* 149–153.

Dawis, R. V. (2000a). The person-environment tradition in counseling psychology. In W. E. Martin, Jr., & J. L. Swartz (Eds.), *Person-environment psychology: Clinical and counseling applications for adolescents and adults* (pp. 91–111). Mahwah, NJ: Erlbaum.

Dawis, R. V. (2000b). Response: P-E fit as paradigm: Comment on Tinsley (2000). *Journal of Vocational Behavior, 56,* 180–183.

Dawis, R. V., & Lofquist, L. H. (1984). *A psychological theory of work adjustment.* Minneapolis: University of Minnesota Press.

Egan, G. (1998). *The skilled helper* (6th ed.). Pacific Grove, CA: Brooks/Cole.

Fawcett, J., & Downs, F. S. (1986). *The relationship of theory and research*. Norwalk, CT: Appleton-Century-Crofts.

Glassman, R. B. (1999). Hypothesized neural dynamics of working memory: Several chunks might be marked simultaneously by harmonic frequencies within an octave of brain waves. *Brain Research Bulletin, 50*, 77–93.

Gold, J. M., & Scanlon, C. R. (1993). Psychological distress and counseling duration of career and noncareer clients. *The Career Development Quarterly, 42*, 186–191.

Gordon, J. (1997). Infonuggets: The bite-sized future of corporate training? *Training, 34*, 26–33.

Halford, G. S., Wilson, W. H., & Phillips, S. (1998). Processing capacity defined by relational complexity: Implications for comparative, developmental, and cognitive psychology. *Behavioral and Brain Sciences, 21*, 803–864.

Hanzel, J. (1999). *The concept of scientific law in the philosophy of science and epistemology: A study of theoretical reason*. Boston: Kluwer.

Heinen, J. R. (1985). A primer on psychological theory. *Journal of Psychology, 119*, 413–421.

Hopke, W. E. (Ed.). (2000). *Encyclopedia of careers and vocational guidance* (11th ed.). Chicago: L. G. Ferguson.

Hoppock, R. (1976). *Occupational information*. New York: McGraw-Hill.

Ivey, A. E., & Ivey, M. B. (1999). *Intentional interviewing and counseling: Facilitating client development in a multicultural society* (4th ed.). Pacific Grove, CA: Brooks/Cole.

Krumboltz, J. D. (1993). Integrating career and personal counseling. *The Career Development Quarterly, 42*, 143–148.

Lucas, M. S. (1993). Personal aspects of career counseling: Three examples. *The Career Development Quarterly, 42*, 161–166.

MacGregor, J. N. (1987). Short-term memory capacity: Limitation or optimization? *Psychological Review, 94*, 107–108.

Miller, G. A. (1956). The magical number seven, plus or minus two: Some limits on our capacity to process information. *Psychological Review, 63*, 81–97.

Occupational outlook handbook. (2000). Washington, DC: U.S. Department of Labor.

Okun, B. F. (1997). *Effective helping: Interviewing and counseling techniques* (5th ed.). Pacific Grove, CA: Brooks/Cole.

Osipow, S. H., & Fitzgerald, L. F. (1995). *Theories of career development* (4th. ed.). Boston: Allyn & Bacon.

Patterson, L. E., & Welfel, R. E. (2000). *The counseling process* (5th ed.). Pacific Grove, CA: Brooks/Cole.

Rogers, C. (1951). *Client-centered therapy*. Boston: Houghton Mifflin.

Rogers, C. (1958). The characteristics of a helping relationship. *Personnel and Guidance Journal, 37*, 6–16.

Sears, S. (1982). A definition of career guidance terms: A National Vocational Guidance Association perspective. *Vocational Guidance Quarterly, 31*, 137–143.

Sharf, R. S. (1984). Vocational information-seeking behavior: Another view. *Vocational Guidance Quarterly, 33*, 120–129.

Simon, H. A. (1974). How big is a chunk? *Science, 183*, 482–488.

Snow, R. E. (1973). Theory construction for research and testing. In R. W. Travers

(Ed.), *Second handbook of research on teaching* (pp. 77–112). Chicago: Rand McNally.

Spokane, A. R. (1991). *Career interventions*. Englewood Cliffs, NJ: Prentice Hall.

Starishevsky, R., & Matlin, N. A. (1963). A model for the translation of self-concept into vocational terms. In D. E. Super, R. Starishevsky, N. A. Matlin, & J. P. Jordaan (Eds.), *Career development: Self-concept theory* (Research Monograph No. 4, pp. 33–41). New York: College Entrance Examination Board.

Subich, L. M. (1993). How personal is career counseling? *The Career Development Quarterly, 42*, 129–131.

Tinsley, H. E. A. (2000). The congruence myth: An analysis of the efficacy of the person-environment fit model. *Journal of Vocational Behavior, 56*, 147–179.

Truax, C. B., & Carkhuff, R. R. (1967). *Toward effective counseling and psychotherapy. Training and practice.* Chicago: Aldine.

Wickelgren, W. A. (1999). Webs, cell assemblies, and chunking in neural nets: Introduction. *Canadian Journal of Experimental Psychology, 53*, 118–131.

Ye, N., & Salvendy, G. (1994). Quantitative and qualitative differences between experts and novices in chunking computer software knowledge. *International Journal of Human Computer Interaction, 6*, 105–118.

PART ONE
Trait and
Type Theories

Trait and type theories were the first career development theories to be described. In general, they were developed to analyze traits or characteristics of individuals so these traits could be matched with qualifications required by jobs. Groups of traits or characteristics could be combined so that types of individuals could be identified. Likewise, qualifications of jobs and work requirements could be combined to describe types of work.

In this part, four trait or type theories are presented. Trait and factor theory, described in Chapter 2, assesses characteristics of people and characteristics of jobs, which are then matched to help an individual select an occupation. As described in Chapter 3, work adjustment theory provides a framework for assessing an individual's needs and skills so that they can be matched with similar needs and skills required by a small group of different occupations. Holland's typological theory, the focus of Chapter 4, describes six types of people and six types of environments. The counselor assists in career selection by matching the person with the environment. The Myers-Briggs type theory, introduced in Chapter 5, describes ways of perceiving and judging the world. Matching an individual's style of judging and perceiving with the styles of judging and perceiving used by people employed in certain careers can assist an individual in finding an appropriate work environment. Each of these theories shares the goal of attempting to measure characteristics or types of individuals so that they can be matched with characteristics or types of work to provide assistance in career selection.

2

Trait and
Factor Theory

In 1909, Frank Parsons described his concept of vocational guidance in his book *Choosing a Vocation*. These views and his contribution to career development have been described in a special issue (Volume 20, Number 4, 1994) of the *Journal of Career Development*. His views became the foundation for what later evolved into trait and factor theory. The term *trait* refers to a characteristic of an individual that can be measured through testing. *Factor* refers to a characteristic required for successful job performance. It also refers to a statistical approach used to differentiate important characteristics of a group of people. Thus, the terms *trait* and *factor* refer to the assessment of characteristics of the person and the job.

Assessment of traits is referred to in the first and most crucial of the steps Parsons identified that describe his approach to occupational selection. Parsons (1909, p. 5) proposed that, to select an occupation, an individual should ideally have

1. A clear understanding of yourself, your attitudes, abilities, interests, ambitions, resource limitations, and their causes;
2. A knowledge of the requirements and conditions of success, advantages and

25

disadvantages, compensation, opportunities, and prospects in different lines of work;

3. True reasoning on the relations of these two groups of facts.

Frank Parsons's book, derived from his work in career counseling with adolescents in the Boston area, was not the only contribution to trait and factor theory. At about the same time, Elton Mayo at Harvard and Frederick Taylor working in business were doing early industrial psychological work that involved the study of working conditions such as fatigue and boredom. They developed various ways to study how an individual reacts to his or her work environment. It was natural that their objective measurements would fit into the discipline of trait and factor psychology. In the 1930s and 1940s, particularly during World War II, much work was done on assessing abilities of personnel. It was necessary for the U.S. Employment Service and the War Manpower Commission to develop a research testing and placement program so that Americans would be better able to serve the war effort. One of the most important tests that grew out of that program was the Army General Classification Test. It set new standards for test development and was used to select recruits for a wide variety of tasks. Many other tests were also developed through federal funding. This gave a boost to the assessment techniques that were needed for the development of trait and factor theory. After World War II, research continued in the area of assessment, much of it taking place at the University of Minnesota. In fact, trait and factor theory has also been called the *Minnesota point of view* and *actuarial counseling*.

The most well-known contributor to "the Minnesota point of view" was Edmund G. Williamson, dean of students at the University of Minnesota between 1941 and 1969. His writings epitomize the trait and factor approach (Williamson, 1939, 1965). Although Williamson, like Carl Rogers, was concerned with the whole person, his approach was entirely different from Rogers's and was labeled *directive* in contrast to the nondirective approach of Carl Rogers. Among Williamson's methods were information giving and direct suggestion. It was his view that the counselor should share his or her wisdom with the client in guiding the client to a correct decision. In contrast, Rogers emphasized reflection of the client's feelings rather than imparting information. Williamson's approach has been criticized by a number of writers; its criticism is documented by Aubrey (1977).

There is little research supporting or refuting trait and factor theory itself as a viable theory of career development. Rather, the research that has been done, of which there is a large amount, has related traits and factors to one another or has established the validity and reliability of measurements of traits and factors. Aptitudes, achievements, interests, values, and personality have been correlated with each other by developers of tests and inventories. When validating and developing tests, it is necessary to relate the scales of one test to the scales of very similar tests. For example, Schmidt (1988) and Gottfredson (1988) reviewed studies that use, with moderate success, general ability to predict job performance.

In this chapter, a broad view of trait and factor theory will be taken to show how it can be used to conceptualize career development. Parsons's (1909) concepts of almost a century ago have been embellished by integrating tests and occupational information with his precepts. Parsons characterized the first step of career choice as gaining "a clear understanding of yourself, your attitudes, abilities, interests, ambitions, resource limitations, and causes." We will look at this step in terms of aptitudes, achievements, interests, values, and personality to reflect five types of assessment that have emerged as important to career counseling. Parsons's second step is obtaining "a knowledge of the requirements and conditions of success, advantages and disadvantages, compensation, opportunities, and prospects in different lines of work." We will discuss how the counselor can assist the client in gaining a knowledge of occupations. Third, Parsons said that a wise choice is made by "true reasoning on the relations on these two groups of facts." We will consider integration of information about oneself and the world of work, giving a focus that is not limited to the use of cognitive skills but that also includes reflecting and questioning skills. Information regarding various traits and factors in women and culturally diverse populations will also be given. This will be followed by a discussion of potential counseling difficulties in using trait and factor theory.

STEP 1: GAINING SELF-UNDERSTANDING

When Parsons and early career counselors started to help young people choose a career, they had few resources available to them (such as tests, inventories, and occupational information). They relied primarily on interviews and discussions with clients. Asking a client what she enjoyed doing (interests) and how well she did it (aptitude and achievement) was an important method of helping the client gain self-understanding. As a client talked about aspects of her life that were important to her (her values), the counselor was able to make a further assessment. As the counselor observed the client and listened to her comments about herself and others, the counselor could make observations about the client's personality. The counseling interview continues to be an important part of the trait and factor assessment process. However, the development of tests and inventories has given counselors additional useful tools.

Since the beginning of the twentieth century, psychologists have been very productive in the development of psychometric measures. These are reviewed in the *Fourteenth Mental Measurements Yearbook* (Buros Institute of Mental Measurement, 1999) and in *Tests in Print V* (Murphy, Impara, & Plake, 1999), which lists 2,939 tests, of which 88 are achievement batteries, 223 are intelligence and academic aptitude tests, 560 are vocational tests, and 676 are personality inventories. For the counselor to become familiar with each of these is, of course, practically impossible. Here we will describe only a few well-accepted tests that counselors are likely to use in the trait and factor approach and that are frequently used by counseling psychologists (Watkins, Campbell, & Nieberding, 1994). This does not necessarily mean that these are the best tests, but they are ones in wide usage that are different enough from each other so that their main features can be contrasted. *A Counselor's Guide to Career Assessment Instruments* (Kapes, Mastie, & Whitfield, 1994) presents test reviews of most of the instruments described in this text. Additionally, many of these tests and inventories are available online. When a counselor chooses a test to use with clients, the counselor may incorporate the concepts of the tests into his or her thinking about the client. For example, a counselor wishing to conceptualize a client's sociability may use the definition of *sociability* on the Sociability scale of the California Psychological Inventory rather than invent a new definition of sociability. It is the purpose of this chapter not to evaluate these tests and inventories, but to show how tests can be used in conceptualizing clients' career concerns.

The five basic traits and factors that can be assessed by testing and interviewing are aptitudes, achievements, interests, values, and personality. We will consider each of these areas in turn.

Aptitudes

The terms *aptitude, ability,* and *achievement* are easily confused, as are the tests that measure these traits. It is helpful to make these distinctions: An achievement test is designed to reveal how much an individual has learned; an ability test measures maximum performance and reveals the level of a person's present ability to perform a task; and an aptitude test reveals a person's probable future level of ability to perform a task (Goldenson, 1984). In other words, these tests measure past achievement, present ability, and future aptitude. Often the line between them is not very clear. For example, the assessment of past achievement may provide a measure of possible aptitude. Aptitude tests have been particularly attractive to clients who believe that, if they can find the occupations in which they have aptitude, they can predict their future success in a specific occupation. Unfortunately, aptitude tests measure a number of general aptitudes, and there are no aptitude tests precise enough to predict with certainty the eventual success of an individual.

Aptitude tests have been used to predict future success in either further educational endeavors or occupational training. Table 2-1 lists a sample of well-known aptitude tests, along with their subtests. The first two tests listed—the College Board Scholastic Assessment Test (SAT) and the American College Testing Assessment Program: Academic Test (ACT)—are used for predicting college success. The Differential Aptitude Tests (DAT) are used to assist people in selecting a career. The U.S. Employment Service General Aptitude Test Battery (GATB) and the Armed Services Vocational Aptitude Battery (ASVAB) are used by the U.S. Employment Service and Armed Services, respectively, for counseling and selection by these two agencies and by educational and other institutions. Note that all five of the tests measure verbal and quantitative (mathematical or numerical) aptitudes.

Table 2-1 *Five Aptitude Tests and Their Subtests*

College Board Scholastic Assessment Test (SAT)	ACT Assessment Program: Academic Tests (ACT)	Differential Aptitude Tests (DAT)	U.S. Employment Service General Aptitude Test Battery (GATB)	Armed Services Vocational Aptitude Battery (ASVAB)
Verbal	English usage	General learning	General learning	Coding speed
Mathematical	Mathematics usage	Verbal reasoning	Verbal	Word knowledge
Standard written English	Social studies reading	Numerical ability	Numerical	Arithmetic reasoning
	Natural sciences reading	Abstract reasoning	Spatial	Tool knowledge
		Clerical speed and accuracy	Form perception	Space perception
		Mechanical reasoning	Clerical perception	Mechanical comprehension
		Space relations	Eye/hand coordination	Shop information
		Spelling	Finger dexterity	Automotive information
		Language usage	Manual dexterity	Electronics information

These two, verbal and mathematical aptitude, are common to almost all academic aptitude tests. Note also that fewer subtests are used for measuring college aptitude than are used for predicting aptitude for occupations not requiring college skills, such as secretary, mechanic, and electronics technician. Further, the DAT, GATB, and ASVAB give occupational profiles that match high scores on various aptitudes. Thus, one can look up an occupation in one of the test manuals and find the scores that are needed on various subtests for suggested entry into that specific occupation. These scores should be considered guidelines rather than requirements. Research on the validity of these instruments continues to be important. For example, the U.S. Department of Labor has critically reviewed the GATB because of questions about validity and fairness to minority and majority test takers (Adler, 1991).

More than most other types of tests, the aptitude test that a counselor uses depends upon his or her setting. For example, high school and college counselors in the eastern and western parts of the United States tend to use the SAT, whereas their colleagues in the Midwest tend to use the ACT. Counselors working at a federal employment service are likely to use the GATB, whereas those working with the military or prospective applicants to the military will use the ASVAB. The selection of appropriate norms is necessary, so that clients' aptitudes are compared to an appropriate comparison group. Clients' self-estimates of their own aptitudes can be useful, so that comparisons can be made with measured aptitudes, allowing the client to develop a fuller understanding of his or her aptitudes.

Although discussion with a client may produce information to make an objective judgment about aptitude and abilities, counselors should be wary of making *predictions* about a client's success based on aptitude test scores. It is one thing for employers to make selections based on aptitude; it is another for a counselor to say to a client, "You could not become a physician because your scores are not high enough." There are examples in our society of how the client proved the counselor wrong by doing much better than was predicted. Clients are in a better position than the counselor to determine the risk they are willing to take in trying to enter an occupation in which they would appear to have little chance for success. Clients must live with the effects of their decisions. For example, a client with mediocre grades who has always wanted to be a doctor but who does not apply to medical school may regret that decision for many years.

Achievements

Achievement refers to a broad range of events that individuals participate in and accomplish during their lifetime. These can be separated into three types of achievements. The first is academic accomplishment, measured most often by grades, but also by honors and specific test scores. The second is accomplishments in work, such as tasks completed and supervisor ratings. The third, and the one that most easily fits with the trait and factor approach, pertains to tests of achievement for certification or entry into an occupation.

Over the years, research studies have shown that the best single predictor of academic performance is previous academic performance. In other words, one can predict performance in college better from high school grades than from aptitude test scores, with aptitude tests accounting for about 15% of the variance in predicting college grades (Leman, 1999). In fact, high school grades can be given twice the weight of scholastic aptitude tests when predicting college grades (Astin, 1993). Although not strictly traits or factors, accomplishments that can be attained at work, through hobbies, or through extracurricular activity can be very useful in determining the nature of an individual's abilities and achievements. These accomplishments can be very diverse and include such activities as athletic honors, ability to help a sick person, ability to type a paper quickly, ability to tally numbers with speed and accuracy, and ability to give a speech in front of an audience. Although such activities are important, many may be very difficult to measure quantitatively.

Achievement *can* be measured quantitatively through tests that are used for licensure, certification, or entry into a particular field or profession. For example, psychologists, doctors, nurses, and lawyers must pass board examinations of a particular state prior to becoming licensed to do their specific work. Similarly, plumbers, police officers, and many other professionals must take tests before advancing from one level to another. The wide range of achievement tests available at present includes tests pertaining to the following kinds of work:

Accountant	Nurse
Actuary	Physician
Artist	Plumber
Cosmetologist	Police officer
Electrician	Psychologist
Funeral director	Real estate agent
Life insurance agent	Teacher
Mechanic	Typist
Musician	X-ray technician

What characterizes all of these tests is that they are very specific to a given task or profession. For example, the best test of typing ability is to obtain a typing sample from an individual. A written or multiple-choice test about typing would not be adequate. Likewise, the best test of artistic or musical ability is to look at a portfolio of artwork or listen to a musical audition.

One of the problems in using client self-report of accomplishments, such as helping someone in distress, is that in the United States and Japan people are often taught to be modest about their achievements. Encouragement is often needed for people to accurately present their successes. Emphasizing these accomplishments can be useful as they may serve as building blocks for further accomplishments. For example, if a student has successfully presented a project at a science fair, that becomes a starting place to discuss other types of projects and science interests that the person may have.

Interests

Over the years, interests have become the most important trait used in occupational selection. The reason is that occupational entry can be predicted better from interests than from aptitude for individuals with many abilities who are able to choose from a wide range of occupations. Reviews of the relationship between interests and abilities have shown a small but significant correlation between the two ($r = .20$) (Ackerman & Heggestad, 1997; Lent, Brown, & Hackett, 1994). For example, studying the relationship between the Self-Directed Search (interests) and the Ball Aptitude Battery Carson (1998) and Harmon, Barton, & Carson (1999) find minimal overlap between interests and abilities. Thus, some individuals may like some things that they don't do well, and some may be good at activities they don't like. Unlike aptitude tests, interest inventories have scales for specific occupations. Two particularly well-known interest inventories that use occupational scales are the Kuder DD and the Strong Interest Inventory. By measuring the interests of successful and satisfied people in an occupation, the authors of these instruments were able to develop a scale that compares the interests of these individuals to the interests of those who are unsure of their career choice. Such scales tend to predict occupational success and satisfaction decades after the test was taken.

Besides occupational interests, general areas of interest have been measured. Whereas occupational interest scales describe interests of people in a specific occupation, such as secretary, basic interest scales measure interests in activities, such as office practices. An office practice interest scale may include tasks such as typing, taking dictation, and answering the phone. To use another example, a mathematics scale may measure interests in abstract math and computation, whereas a mathematician scale measures the similarity of the interests of the test taker to the interests of those who are employed as mathematicians. Several inventories measure a broad spectrum of general interests. Three of them are listed in Table 2-2: the Kuder Career Search™ (KCS); the Basic Interest Scales of the Strong Interest Inventory (SII); and the California Occupational Preference Survey (COPS). Note that the California Occupational Preference Survey has separate professional and skilled interest scales for five different interest areas. In general, the basic interest scales are quite similar for all three of the inventories. Any one of these inventories can provide a framework for categorizing interests in counseling.

By using a particular structure to evaluate a client's interests, the counselor can more easily understand the client's experience. For example, if a counselor uses the ten interest scales of the KCS as a framework, he or she can categorize the client's discussion of preferences during an interview. If a client talks of enjoying painting and drawing throughout his school experience as well as writing for high school and college publications, the counselor can conceptualize and categorize these interests as art and communications. Later, when the client talks about enjoying going to art museums and discussing art with friends, this same conceptualization of artis-

Table 2-2   *Three Interest Inventories and Their Scales*

Kuder Career Search (KCS)	Strong Interest Inventory (SII) Basic Interest Scales	California Occupational Preference Survey (COPS)
Nature	Agriculture	Consumer economics
Mechanical	Applied arts	Outdoor
Computations	Art	Clerical
Science/Technical	Athletics	Communication
Sales/Management	Computer activities	Science—professional
Art	Law/Politics	Science—skilled
Communications	Mathematics	Technology—professional
Music	Mechanical activities	Technology—skilled
Human services	Medical science	Business—professional
Office detail	Medical service	Business—skilled
	Merchandising	Arts—professional
	Military activities	Arts—skilled
	Music/Dramatics	Service—professional
	Nature	Service—skilled
	Office services	
	Organizational management	
	Public speaking	
	Religious activities	
	Sales	
	Science	
	Social service	
	Teaching	
	Writing	

tic interests can be made. Having this frame of reference allows the counselor to group concepts and ideas that come from the counseling interview. If the counselor then administers the KCS to the student, the counselor can get further validation of the client's interest in art if the score is high. If the score is low, the counselor can discuss the discrepancy between the client's expressed interest in art and low inventoried interest in art. When selecting inventories to use with clients, it is helpful to use those that make conceptual sense to the counselor. For example, it is possible but more difficult to use the Strong Interest Inventory Basic Interest Scales as a conceptual base when using the KCS. Trying to conceptualize or chunk 10 scales (KCS), 14 scales (COPS), or 23 scales (SII) can be very difficult. Holland's theory, which is described in Chapter 4, uses only 6 scales or constructs. When discussing the interests of clients in one trait, it is often helpful to discuss abilities and achievements in that trait at the same time. This helps the counselor to better organize the client's previous experiences and to use fewer chunks of material.

Table 2-3   *Two Values Inventories and Their Scales*

Study of Values (SV)	Values Scale (VS)
Theoretical	Ability utilization
Economic	Achievement
Aesthetic	Advancement
Social	Aesthetics
Political	Altruism
Religious	Authority
	Autonomy
	Creativity
	Economic rewards
	Lifestyle
	Personal development
	Physical activity
	Prestige
	Risk
	Social interaction
	Social relations
	Variety
	Working conditions
	Cultural identity
	Physical prowess
	Economic security

Values

Neglected by many trait and factor counselors, values represent an important but difficult concept to measure. For career counseling, two types of values are considered important: general values and work-related values. Table 2-3 lists the 6 general values that are found in the Study of Values (SV) and the 21 work values listed in the Values Scale (VS). Inspection of Table 2-3 shows the contrast between the general values of the SV and the more specific work-related values of the VS. However, counselors may not make use of any value inventories, preferring to conceptualize work values or general values rather than to measure them. One reason is that it is very difficult to develop a reliable and valid value inventory, as these concepts are often elusive and not ones that can be predicted easily.

Values, as difficult to assess as they may be, are often helpful to clients who are deciding on a career direction. For example, the client who wishes to help others may feel that this desire is more important than any of his or her other traits or factors, such as interests or abilities. In such a case, the counselor helps the client find an interesting way to satisfy his or her values. For example, a client who wishes to help the homeless may pursue social work or business management, depending on the direction of the

Table 2-4   Two Personality Inventories and Their Scales

California Psychological Inventory (CPI)	Sixteen Personality Factor Questionnaire (16 PF)
Dominance	Cool vs. warm
Capacity for status	Concrete thinking vs. abstract thinking
Sociability	Affected by feelings vs. emotionally stable
Social presence	Submissive vs. dominant
Self-acceptance	Sober vs. enthusiastic
Independence	Expedient vs. conscientious
Empathy	Shy vs. bold
Sense of well-being	Tough-minded vs. tender-minded
Responsibility	Trusting vs. suspicious
Socialization	Practical vs. imaginative
Self-control	Forthright vs. shrewd
Tolerance	Self-assured vs. apprehensive
Good impression	Conservative vs. experimenting
Communality	Group-oriented vs. self-sufficient
Achievement via independence	Undisciplined self-conflict vs. following self-image
Achievement via conformance	
Intellectual efficiency	Relaxed vs. tense
Psychological-mindedness	
Flexibility	
Femininity/Masculinity	

client's interests. The value of helping others is called altruism on the VS. Being able to label a value and compare it to other values can be very useful for the counselor. Although the list of 21 work values in the VS is long, it does give the counselor a framework to assess the values important to a client. Some counselors may wish to use a shortened version of such a list of values, while others may be satisfied using the 6 values of the SV.

Personality

The measurement of personality has been an important area of study for the last 80 years. Although much of the work has centered on abnormal personality, with the development of the Minnesota Multiphasic Personality Inventory-2 (MMPI), the Rorschach, and the Thematic Apperception Test (TAT), work has also been done in the area of normal personality. For purposes of illustration, two different measures of personality are listed in Table 2-4 that give insight into the conceptualization of personality for vocational selection. The two tests that will be described here are the California Psychological Inventory (CPI) and the Sixteen Personality Factor Questionnaire (16 PF). The CPI represents a commonsense or folk approach to personality, and the 16 PF represents a statistical approach.

The CPI, developed by Harrison Gough (Gough & Bradley, 1996), uses 20 scales to measure different aspects of personality. The terms are inoffensive ones to which clients might not object and are called "folk scales" (Table 2-4). Gough used many items from the MMPI to develop this inventory; however, the two inventories are very different in that the MMPI uses pathological terminology and the CPI does not. For example, the MMPI uses scale names such as "schizophrenia" and "hypochondriasis," whereas the CPI uses names such as "self-control" and "flexibility." People who score high on flexibility are likely to be rated by others as flexible. Such comparisons between scores on a scale and ratings by experts or peers were widely used in developing the CPI. The scale names represent terms that counselors can use when trying to assess the characteristics of individual clients.

The 16 PF lists 16 primary personality factors. These are presented using a bipolar method, indicating the two extremes of each trait. Examples are cool versus warm, submissive versus dominant, and shy versus bold. These factors are similar in many ways to the 20 scales of the CPI; the difference is in their development. A statistical technique, factor analysis, was used to try to make the scales as different from each other as possible. These factors can be useful in conceptualizing a client who is trying to make occupational selection decisions.

Personality profiles have been developed using the CPI and the 16 PF for individuals in a variety of occupations. Therefore, a counselor is able to match the profile of a client with an appropriate occupational pattern. Personality inventories are more difficult to learn to use than are ability, achievement, interest, or values tests because of the complexity of the variables involved and their abstraction. Additionally, personality inventories may present a cultural bias reflecting the culture of the developers or the sample used for measuring participants' personality. In fact, many counselors who use the trait and factor approach may not use personality tests at all. Both personality and interests are moderately related to occupational abilities (Ackerman & Heggestad, 1997). For example, an accountant may have needs for order and deference, which may influence occupational selection, as does interest in business, accounting principles, and math. Further, intelligence and mathematical ability are likely to be important factors in the choice of accounting. Being able to integrate the concepts of order and deference with interests, abilities, achievements, and values is very helpful.

Example of Step 1

Jack, a white freshman at a large university, is undecided about his career choice. He has already met with the counselor for one session and has gone over his results on the KCS, the VS, and the CPI (Table 2-5). The counselor now has the results of his SAT. This dialogue might occur in the second session as the counselor attempts to integrate the test results. Test results are usually discussed interactively rather than just reported or delivered to

Table 2-5 *Jack's High and Low Scores on Selected Tests and Inventories*

	SAT	KCS	VS	CPI
High	Verbal	Art Sales/Management	Creativity Ability utilization	Social presence Socialization
Low	Math	Nature Computations Office detail	Economic security Altruism	Independence

the client, as the results usually have a deeper impact with an interactive approach and the counselor may be seen as more expert and trustworthy than when results are just reported (Hanson, Claiborn, & Kerr, 1997). Zunker and Norris (1998) go into detail about test interpretation, whereas this dialogue focuses on conceptualizing the client's use of information about his traits and factors taken from assessment instruments:

CL: Some of my courses this semester are really boring. I wish I didn't have so many course requirements.

CO: I'd like to hear more about them. [Detail is needed to evaluate the client's experience in terms of his various traits and factors.]

CL: Calculus is a nuisance. It takes a lot of time, there doesn't seem to be any use for it, and I just feel so bored after the class. My history course isn't much better—medieval civilization is not exactly earthshaking to me. I knew I had to take a history course, but maybe I should have taken something else.

CO: Having to fulfill requirements is really quite difficult for you. [It is not surprising that Jack is having difficulty with math and does not like it— low SAT and KCS scores. The counselor lets Jack determine what he wants to talk about next by using a feeling reflection.]

CL: Fortunately, not all my courses are so bad. My speech course is easy and kind of fun. I've enjoyed standing up in front of class and trying to capture the attention of the other students, which really is a challenge, as many of them like the class as much as I like math. That class reminds me a bit of when I worked at carnival concessions two summers ago and I had to give a spiel to people about why they should play a game.

CO: It sounds like fun, trying to present yourself in an impressive way to others. It reminds me of what we were talking about last time when we were going over the California Psychological Inventory. [The counselor makes a direct connection between the client's high score on the Social Presence scale of the CPI and his desire to present his work in the speech class and be involved in the carnival situation.]

CL: Yes, I sure enjoy the attention I get. It's kind of fun. I remember when I first came to visit this campus, I was impressed with the guy who showed us around. In fact, even though I'm just a freshman, I think I want to try to see if I can give campus tours, too.

CO: You really are enjoying doing a lot of things that get you out in front of others. [Jack seems quite aware and accepting of his own enjoyment of getting the attention of others.]

CL: I guess so. I'm all over the place. I've got our whole dorm working on this massive homecoming float. It really looks good. I think we're going to win first prize.

CO: You really seem to enjoy designing and developing new things. [The counselor is aware of the client's high score on Creativity on the Values Scale and chooses to comment on this trait of the client without mentioning the test score itself.]

CL: Yes, I don't know how to find time to study sometimes, but I also seem to manage. There's so much to learn here and so much to do. I need some 48-hour days.

CO: It really is hard to decide what to do sometimes. [The counselor is aware of Jack's interest in socializing and communicating with others from the CPI, as well as his desire to use his skills, indicated by his ability utilization score on the VS. The counselor is also aware that this may create some problems for Jack in deciding what to do. Note that the counselor combines traditional nondirective responses with trait and factor conceptualization.]

STEP 2: OBTAINING KNOWLEDGE ABOUT THE WORLD OF WORK

Occupational information is the second ingredient of trait and factor theory. It is the counselor's role to help the client gather occupational information. To do this, it is not necessary to rely solely on the counselor's knowledge of occupations, but to use many resources to supplement this knowledge. There are three aspects of occupational information to consider. The first is the type of information; for example, a description of the occupation, the working conditions, or the salary. The second important aspect is classification. There are several classification systems that enable the client and the counselor to see thousands of occupations organized in meaningful ways. Third, it is helpful to know the trait and factor requirements for each occupation that one is seriously considering. For example, if a client is thinking about becoming a veterinarian, it is helpful to know which aptitudes, achievements, interests, values, and personality traits predict success and satisfaction in veterinary medicine.

Types of Occupational Information

Occupational information is available from a variety of different sources. These include booklets made available by professional trade associations, pamphlets available through publishers that specialize in producing occupational information, and lengthier books or encyclopedias. Furthermore, occupational information is available on audio- and videocassettes, as well as on microfiche, in computer-based information systems, and many websites. At its most basic, almost all occupational information includes a description of the occupation, the qualifications required for entry, the necessary education, the working conditions, the salary, and the employment outlook. Many publications go beyond this by giving information about career ladders, similar occupations, examples of people working in the profession, and special information for women and culturally diverse populations. A more detailed explanation of types of occupational information is given in the next section.

It is impossible for counselors to remember all of this information about many occupations. Perhaps the most important type of information for counselors to know is the description of an occupation. Beyond that, it is helpful to have books such as the *Occupational Outlook Handbook* (OOH) (2000), which is issued every two years and is available to answer questions about occupations. The OOH is also available online and is linked to several inventories such as the KCS. To make matters more complex, occupational information changes from year to year. Specifically, the salary and employment outlook is apt to vary. Further, these two variables are apt to differ depending on what section of the country one lives in. For example, plumbers make a higher salary in New York City than they do in Des Moines, Iowa, or Augusta, Maine. When evaluating occupational information, it is useful to examine language, content, and pictures for race or gender bias. *The Career Development Quarterly* evaluates occupational material according to guidelines established by the National Vocational Guidance Association (1980).

The National Vocational Guidance Association (1980), now the National Career Development Association, has published guidelines that address the quality and content of occupational information. Regarding quality, questions such as the following are asked: Are the written information and pictures accurate and nonbiased with regard to gender and race? Is the information clear and interesting, and is it appropriate for the intended audience? Is the material updated frequently? Regarding content, the following areas are covered: the duties and nature of the work, the physical activities required, social and psychological satisfactions and dissatisfactions, the type of preparation required, earnings and benefits, advancement possibilities, the employment outlook, part-time and volunteer opportunities for exploring the occupation, related occupations, sources of training, and sources of additional information. By examining a description of one occupation in the *Occupational Outlook Handbook* (2000), readers can see how these topics are covered.

Classification Systems

Because it is easy to be overwhelmed by the volume of information available to counselors and clients, it is essential to have a way to organize occupational information. Classification systems have been developed to fill this need. Three different government classification systems that have evolved over the years are particularly important. In addition, Holland's classification of occupations (see Chapter 4) has been found helpful by a number of counselors. The most comprehensive listing of occupations is the *Dictionary of Occupational Titles* (DOT), which was last published in 1991. It classifies about 20,000 occupations that exist in the United States. To organize these occupations, it uses a nine-digit code. The first three numbers designate an occupational group. The first digit identifies one of nine broad categories. The second digit breaks up the occupations into 82 divisions (Table 2-6) and the third digit divides the occupations into 559 groups. For example, the occupation of counselor has the first three digits 045. The 0 refers to professional, technical, and managerial occupations. The 04 makes reference to occupations in the life sciences. Within that division, 045 designates occupations in psychology. The next three digits relate to three ways of doing tasks. The fourth digit describes how the individual deals with data; the fifth, how a person deals with people; and the sixth, how a person uses things. The assignment to categories of data, people, and things is based on an analysis of the tasks done by people in the occupation. The last three digits indicate the alphabetical order of the occupational titles that have the same six-digit code. Many other sources give further details of this system, for example, *Improved Career Decision Making Through the Use of Labor Market Information* (1991), a U.S. Department of Labor publication. The DOT classification system continues to be used by counselors and by test publishers to classify occupations. However, in 1998 it was replaced by the U.S. government with the O*NET classification system.

Working from the *Dictionary of Occupational Titles*, hundreds of people worked together to develop the O*NET, the *Occupational Information Network*, which will replace the DOT. Unlike other classification systems, the O*NET was designed to be presented on the computer so that it could be updated frequently. Table 2-7 lists the 9 sections and the 103 major groupings of the O*NET.

Whereas the DOT contains 12,741 occupational titles, the O*NET has information on 1,172 occupations. Over the years, new occupations will be added to this database. What makes this classification system so different from others is that each occupation has about 445 data descriptors. Contrast this with the 8 descriptors that are used in the *Occupational Outlook Handbook* (nature of the work, working conditions, employment, training, job outlook, earnings, related occupations, and sources of additional information).

Having 445 descriptors available does not mean that all are used for each occupation. Most individuals will not use the O*NET itself, but will look at a version that has been abstracted from the O*NET onto the computer or into a book such as *The O*NET Dictionary of Occupational Titles* (Farr, Ludden, & Mangin, 1998). The information that is provided in this book includes 14 relevant descriptions, not 445. The six categories of O*NET descriptors are described here. Because the six categories of 445 descriptors include so many characteristics, only the more common ones will be listed.

1. *Worker characteristics* include abilities, interest, and work styles. Among the *abilities* are cognitive (verbal, numerical, perceptual, and spatial), psychomotor abilities (manual and finger dexterity), physical abilities (strength, endurance, balance, and coordination), and sensory abilities (visual, auditory, and speech). *Interests* are represented by the six Holland types (Chapter 4). Included under interests are occupational values such as ability utilization, achievement, variety, compensation, and advancement. *Work styles* include achievement in interpersonal orientations, social influence, adjustment, independence, and practical intelligence.

2. *Worker requirements* include skills that are basic as well as specific knowledge requirements. Educational requirements are also a part of this category. *Basic skills* refer to reading comprehension, active listening, writing, speaking, math, and science, whereas *process skills* include critical thinking, active learning, learning strategies, and monitoring. *Cross-functional skills* are social (persuading negotiating, and instructing), problem solving, technical (testing, maintaining, repairing), judging and decision making, and managing time and finances. *Knowledge requirements* refer to principles and facts about a variety of subjects such as business, engineering, math, and communication. *Education requirements* refer to the level of education required for a specific subject.

3. *Experience requirements* describe specific preparation or past work experience. Licenses or certificates are also used to identify levels of skill or performance needed to enter an occupation.

4. *Occupation requirements* are presented as general types of work activities, the context of the organization, and the context of the work. *General types of work activities* are those that occur in many types of jobs. They include getting information needed to do the job, processing and evaluating information, making decisions, solving problems, performing physical and technical work, and communicating with others. *Organizational contexts* refer to the way that people do their work. Some of the organizational context factors include the amount of control the workers have in making decisions, the variety of skills used in the work, autonomy, feedback, recruitment and selection of employees, training and development, and pay and benefits. *Work contexts* are the social and physical factors that affect how individuals do their work. These include methods of communication, job interactions, the work setting, job hazards, physical demands, challenging nature of the work, and the pace and schedule of the work.

5. *Occupation-specific requirements* describe characteristics of each occupation in terms of skills, knowledge, tasks, duties, machines, tools, and equipment.

6. *Occupational characteristics* include information about the occupation, such as *job* opportunities and pay.   .

The vast information available in the O*NET can be overwhelming. The information abstracted above has been taken from Lock (2000). Because this information is so comprehensive, *The O*NET Dictionary of Occupational Titles* (Farr, Ludden, & Mangin, 1998) provides one of the best resources for understanding and using the O*NET. Included in this book are crosswalks (a bridge or cross-reference) to the *Dictionary of Occupational Titles*, the *Guide for Occupational Exploration*, and descriptions of 218 of the O*NET data elements. There is also information on the O*NET database's structure and development as well as an alphabetical index of O*NET job titles.

Table 2-6 *Dictionary of Occupational Titles: Two-Digit Occupational Divisions*

Code	Occupation
0/1	*Professional, Technical, and Managerial Occupations*
00/01	Occupations in architecture, engineering, and surveying
02	Occupations in mathematics and physical sciences
03	Computer-related occupations
04	Occupations in life sciences
05	Occupations in social sciences
07	Occupations in medicine and health
09	Occupations in education
10	Occupations in museum, library, and archival sciences
11	Occupations in law and jurisprudence
12	Occupations in religion and theology
13	Occupations in writing
14	Occupations in art
15	Occupations in entertainment and recreation
16	Occupations in administrative specializations
18	Managers and officials, n.e.c.*
19	Miscellaneous professional, technical, and managerial occupations
2	*Clerical and Sales Occupations*
20	Stenography, typing, filing, and related occupations
21	Computing and account-recording occupations
22	Production and stock clerks and related occupations
23	Information and message distribution occupations
24	Miscellaneous clerical occupations
25	Sales occupations, services
26	Sales occupations, consumable commodities
27	Sales occupations, commodities, n.e.c.*
29	Miscellaneous sales occupations
56	Occupations in processing of wood and wood products
57	Occupations in processing of stone, clay, glass, and related products
58	Occupations in processing of leather, textiles, and related products
59	Processing occupations, n.e.c.*
6	*Machine Trades Occupations*
60	Metal machining occupations
61	Metalworking occupations, n.e.c.*
62/63	Mechanics and machinery repairers
64	Paperworking occupations
65	Printing occupations
66	Wood machining occupations
67	Occupations in machining stone, clay, glass, and related materials
68	Textile occupations
69	Machine trades occupations, n.e.c.*
7	*Benchwork Occupations*
70	Occupations in fabrication, assembly, and repair of metal products, n.e.c.*
71	Occupations in fabrication and repair of scientific, medical, photographic, optical, horological, and related products
72	Occupations in assembly and repair of electrical equipment
73	Occupations in fabrication and repair of products made from assorted materials
74	Painting, decorating, and related occupations

42

3	*Service Occupations*
30	Domestic service occupations
31	Food and beverage preparation and service occupations
32	Lodging and related service occupations
33	Barbering, cosmetology, and related service occupations
34	Amusement and recreation service occupations
35	Miscellaneous personal service occupations
36	Apparel and furnishing service occupations
37	Protective service occupations
38	Building and related service occupations
4	*Agricultural, Fishery, Forestry, and Related Occupations*
40	Plant farming occupations
41	Animal farming occupations
42	Miscellaneous agricultural and related occupations
44	Fishery and related occupations
45	Forestry occupations
46	Hunting, trapping, and related occupations
5	*Processing Occupations*
50	Occupations in processing of metal
51	Ore refining and foundry occupations
52	Occupations in processing of food, tobacco, and related products
53	Occupations in processing of paper and related materials
54	Occupations in processing of petroleum, coal, natural and manufactured gas, and related products
55	Occupations in processing of chemicals, plastics, synthetics, rubber, paint, and related products
75	Occupations in fabrication and repair of plastics, synthetics, rubber, and related products
76	Occupations in fabrication and repair of wood products
77	Occupations in fabrication and repair of sand, stone, clay, and glass products
78	Occupations in fabrication and repair of textile, leather, and related products
79	Benchwork occupations, n.e.c.*
8	*Structural Work Occupations*
80	Occupations in metal fabricating, n.e.c.*
81	Welders, cutters, and related occupations
82	Electrical assembling, installing, and repairing occupations
84	Painting, plastering, waterproofing, cementing, and related occupations
85	Excavating, grading, paving, and related occupations
86	Construction occupations, n.e.c.*
89	Structural work occupations, n.e.c.*
9	*Miscellaneous Occupations*
90	Motor freight occupations
91	Transportation occupations, n.e.c.*
92	Packaging and materials handling occupations
93	Occupations in extraction of minerals
95	Occupations in production and distribution of utilities
96	Amusement, recreation, motion picture, radio, and television occupations, n.e.c.*
97	Occupations in graphic art work

*n.e.c. is an abbreviation for "not elsewhere classified."

Source: based on *Dictionary of Occupational Titles* (Vol. 1, 4th ed., rev.). Washington, DC: U.S. Department of Labor, Employment and Training Administration, 1991.

Table 2-7　*O*NET Occupations Within Groupings of Related Jobs*

Section 1　Executives, managers, and administrators
13– – –　General managers
15– – –　Specialty managers
190– –　Executives
199– –　Services managers

Section 2　Professional and support specialists, financial specialists, engineers, scientists, mathematicians, social scientists, social services workers, religious workers, and legal workers
211– –　Financial specialists
213– –　Purchasers and buyers
215– –　Human resource workers
219– –　Inspectors and compliance officers
219– –　Management support workers
221– –　Engineers
223– –　Architects and surveyors
225– –　Engineering technologists and technicians
241– –　Physical scientists
243– –　Life scientists
245– –　Life and physical sciences technologists and technicians
251– –　Computer scientists
253– –　Mathematical scientists and technicians
271– –　Social scientists
273– –　Social service workers
275– –　Religious workers
281– –　Lawyers and judges
283– –　Legal assistants

Section 3　Professional and support specialists, educators, librarians, counselors, health care workers, artists, writers, performers, and other professional workers
311– –　College and university faculty
313– –　Preschool, kindergarten, elementary, secondary, and special education
　　　　teachers and instructors
315– –　Librarians, curators, and counselors
321– –　Diagnosing and treating practitioners (health)
323– –　Medical therapists
325– –　Health care providers
329– –　Medical technologists and technicians
340– –　Artistic, creative, and entertainment providers
39– – –　Other professional, paraprofessional, and technical workers

Section 4　Sales workers
410– –　Sales supervisors and managers
430– –　Sales agents
490– –　Technical, wholesale, and retail sales workers
499– –　Sales consultants and estimators

Table 2-7 *(continued)*

Section 5 Administrative support workers
510– – Administrative supervisors
531– – Financial transaction workers
533– – Insurance specialists
535– – Investigators and collectors
537– – Government clerks
538– – Travel and hotel clerks
539– – Other clerical workers
551– – Secretaries
553– – General office support workers
560– – Office machine operators
571– – Communications equipment operators
573– – Mail clerks, carriers, and messengers
580– – Material recording, scheduling, and distributing workers

Section 6 Service workers
610– – Service supervisors and managers
620– – Private household workers
630– – Protective services workers
650– – Food service workers
660– – Medical assistants and aides
670– – Cleaning and building service workers
680– – Personal service workers

Section 7 Agricultural, forestry, and fishing workers
720– – Agriculture, forestry, and fishing supervisors
730– – Timber cutting and related logging workers
790– – Plant and animal workers
798– – Farm workers
799– – Other agricultural workers

Section 8 Mechanics, installers, repairers, construction trades, extractive trades, metal and plastic working, woodworking, apparel, precision printing, and food processing workers
810– – Blue-collar worker supervisors
830– – Inspectors, testers, and graders
851– – Industrial equipment mechanics
853– – Motor vehicle mechanics
855– – Communications equipment mechanics
857– – Line installation and electronic equipment repairers
859– – Other mechanics, installers, and repairers
871– – Carpenters, drywall workers, and lathers
872– – Electricians
873– – Masons, concrete workers, tile setters, and reinforcing metal workers
874– – Painters and paper hangers
875– – Plumbing workers

(continued)

Table 2-7   *(continued)*

876– –   Flooring installers
877– –   Highway and rail workers
878– –   Other construction workers
879– –   Extractive trade workers
891– –   Metal working and plastics working occupations
893– –   Woodworking occupations
895– –   Apparel occupations

Section 9   Machine setters, operations, and tenders, production workers, hand
workers, plant and systems workers, transportation workers, and helpers
911– –   Machine cutting, trimming, drilling, grinding, and polishing setters,
             operators, and tenders
913– –   Punching, pressing, extracting, rolling, and forming machine setters and
             operators
917– –   Metal fabricating machine setters, operators, and related workers
919– –   Molding, casting, plating, and heating machine setters, and operators
921– –   Other metal and plastic machine setters and operators
923– –   Woodworking machine setters and operators
925– –   Printing, binding, and related machine setters and operators
927– –   Textile and related machine setters, operators, and related workers
929– –   Other machine setters, operators, and tenders
931– –   Precision production occupations
939– –   Hand workers, including assemblers and fabricators
950– –   Plant and systems occupations
971– –   Motor vehicle operators
973– –   Rail transportation workers
975– –   Water transportation and related workers
977– –   Air transportation workers
978– –   Other transportation-related workers
979– –   Material moving equipment operators
981– –   Helpers—mechanics and repairers
983– –   Helpers—construction
985– –   Helpers—feeders and offbearers
987– –   Helpers—material movers
989– –   Helpers—production, washing, and packing
990– –   Military

Source: O*NET Database, U.S. Department of Labor, Washington, DC, 1998.

The 14 descriptors that are provided in *The O*NET Dictionary of Oc-cupational Titles* are listed briefly here. This information is somewhat sim-ilar to that provided by the *Dictionary of Occupational Titles.*

- *O*NET Number*—Each O*NET occupation has its own number that relates to occupational groups and subgroups within the O*NET.
- *O*NET Occupational Title*
- *Occupational Handbook Titles*

- *O*NET Occupational Description*—This contains a brief description of the job followed by a list of occupational tasks performed by individuals in that occupation.
- *Yearly earnings*—The average pay received by those in the occupation.
- *Education*—This includes education, training, and work experience required for entry into the occupation.
- *Knowledge*—This includes knowledge that is required for the job that may come from sources such as high school, college, training programs, self-employment, or other life experience.
- *Abilities*—These are enduring attributes which are required for the job and do not change over periods of time.
- *Skills*—These are the many small skills that may be needed for each job.
- *General work activities*—These include both basic and complex work activities.
- *Job characteristics*—This includes such information as interacting with others, mental processes, role relationships, communication methods, and more.
- *The Guide for Occupational Exploration* groupings (GOE)
- *The classification of instructional programs*—This is a system of categorizing training and educational programs and courses.
- *Related Dictionary of Occupational Titles jobs*—This includes the nine-digit DOT code and the title for related DOT jobs.

Another government classification system, the *Enhanced Guide for Occupational Exploration* (GOE; 1991), uses a three-digit code somewhat similar to the first three digits of the DOT code. The difference is that the codes are more related to the interest requirements of occupations than are the DOT codes. The 12 basic interest areas are listed in Table 2-8. The GOE lists occupations in 348 subgroups, with the DOT code given for each code or occupation in the subgroup. Because the GOE makes more intuitive sense to the client, using the GOE, requires less help from the counselor than using the DOT.

A more complex system is the *Standard Occupational Classification Manual* (SOC; 1998). It has three levels: major groups, minor groups, and broad occupations. The SOC code clusters jobs by similar work function, rather than by interests as in the GOE. The 23 major groups that make up this classification system are listed in Table 2-9 along with the 98 minor groups. The SOC was developed to bridge the DOT and a classification system used by the U.S. Census Bureau. Because the National Occupational Information Coordinating Committee (NOICC) has adopted this system for its work, many career centers have also used it. Since these four classification systems (DOT, O*NET, GOE, and SOC) all attempt to classify about several thousand occupations, they are a helpful tool for the counselor in organizing a large amount of material.

Trait and Factor Requirements

Occupational information can be related directly to the client's traits and factors. Information about required aptitudes, achievements, interests, values, and personality is contained in occupational pamphlets and books. For

Table 2-8 *Guide for Occupational Exploration System: Interest Areas, Work Groups, and Subgroups*

01	*Artistic*		06.03	Quality control
01.01	Literary arts		06.04	Elemental work: Industrial
01.02	Visual arts		07	*Business Detail*
01.03	Performing arts: Drama		07.01	Administrative detail
01.04	Performing arts: Music		07.02	Mathematical detail
01.05	Performing arts: Dance		07.03	Financial detail
01.06	Craft arts		07.04	Oral communications
01.07	Elemental arts		07.05	Records processing
01.08	Modeling		07.06	Clerical machine operation
02	*Scientific*		07.07	Clerical handling
02.01	Physical sciences		08	*Selling*
02.02	Life sciences		08.01	Sales technology
02.03	Medical sciences		08.02	General sales
02.04	Laboratory technology		08.03	Vending
03	*Plants and Animals*		09	*Accommodating*
03.01	Managerial work: Plants and animals		09.01	Hospitality services
			09.02	Barber and beauty services
03.02	General supervision: Plants and animals		09.03	Passenger services
			09.04	Customer services
03.03	Animal training and service		09.05	Attendant services
03.04	Elemental work: Plants and animals		10	*Humanitarian*
			10.01	Social services
04	*Protective*		10.02	Nursing, therapy, and specialized teaching services
04.01	Safety and law enforcement			
04.02	Security services		10.03	Child and adult care
05	*Mechanical*		11	*Leading-Influencing*
05.01	Engineering		11.01	Mathematics and statistics
05.02	Managerial work: Mechanical		11.02	Educational and library services
05.03	Engineering technology			
05.04	Air and water vehicle operation		11.03	Social research
			11.04	Law
05.05	Craft technology		11.05	Business administration
05.06	Systems operation		11.06	Finance
05.07	Quality control		11.07	Services administration
05.08	Land and water vehicle operation		11.08	Communications
			11.09	Promotion
05.09	Materials control		11.10	Regulations enforcement
05.10	Crafts		11.11	Business management
05.11	Equipment operation		11.12	Contracts and claims
05.12	Elemental work: Mechanical		12	*Physical Performing*
06	*Industrial*		12.01	Sports
06.01	Production technology		12.02	Physical feats
06.02	Production work			

Source: Based on *Guide for Occupational Exploration.* Washington, DC: U.S. Department of Labor, 1979.

Table 2-9 *Standard Occupational Classification System:*
23 Major Groups and 98 Minor Groups

11–0000	*Management Occupations*
11–1000	Top executives
11–2000	Advertising, marketing, promotions, public relations, and sales managers
11–3000	Operations specialties managers
11–9000	Other management occupations
13–0000	*Business and Financial Operations Occupations*
13–1000	Business operations specialists
13–2000	Financial specialists
15–0000	*Computer and Mathematical Occupations*
15–1000	Computer specialists
15–2000	Mathematical scientists
15–3000	Mathematical technicians
17–0000	*Architecture and Engineering Occupations*
17–1000	Architects, surveyors, and cartographers
17–2000	Engineers
17–3000	Drafters, engineering, and mapping technicians
19–0000	*Life, Physical, and Social Science Occupations*
19–1000	Life scientists
19–2000	Physical scientists
19–3000	Social scientists and related workers
19–4000	Life, physical, and social science technicians
21–0000	*Community and Social Services Occupations*
21–1000	Counselors, social workers, and other community and social service specialists
21–2000	Religious workers
23–0000	*Legal Occupations*
23–1000	Lawyers, judges, and related workers
23–2000	Legal support workers
25–0000	*Education, Training, and Library Occupations*
25–1000	Postsecondary teachers
25–2000	Primary, secondary, and special education school teachers
25–3000	Other teachers and instructors
25–4000	Librarians, curators, and archivists
25–9000	Other education, training, and library occupations
27–0000	*Arts, Design, Entertainment, Sports, and Media Occupations*
27–1000	Art and design workers
27–2000	Entertainers and performers, sports and related workers
27–3000	Media and communications workers
27–4000	Media and communications equipment workers
29–0000	*Health Care Practitioners and Technical Occupations*
29–1000	Health diagnosing and treating practitioners
29–2000	Health technologists and technicians
29–9000	Other health care practitioners and technical occupations

(continued)

Table 2-9 *(continued)*

31–0000	*Health Care Support Occupations*
31–1000	Nursing, psychiatric, and home health aides
31–2000	Occupational and physical therapist assistants and aides
31–9000	Other health care support occupations
33–0000	*Protective Service Occupations*
33–1000	First-line supervisors/managers, protective service workers
33–2000	Fire fighting and prevention workers
33–3000	Law enforcement workers
33–9000	Other protective service workers
35–0000	*Food Preparation and Serving-Related Occupations*
35–1000	Supervisors, food preparation and serving workers
35–2000	Cooks and food preparation workers
35–3000	Food and beverage serving workers
35–9000	Other food preparation and serving-related workers
37–0000	*Building and Grounds Cleaning and Maintenance Occupations*
37–1000	Supervisors, building and grounds cleaning and maintenance workers
37–2000	Building cleaning and pest control workers
37–3000	Grounds maintenance workers
39–0000	*Personal Care and Service Occupations*
39–1000	Supervisors, personal care and service workers
39–2000	Animal care and service workers
39–3000	Entertainment attendants and related workers
39–4000	Funeral service workers
39–5000	Personal appearance workers
39–6000	Transportation, tourism, and lodging attendants
39–9000	Other personal care and service workers
41–0000	*Sales and Related Occupations*
41–1000	Supervisors, sales workers
41–2000	Retail sales workers
41–3000	Sales representatives, services
41–4000	Sales representatives, wholesale and manufacturing
41–9000	Other sales and related workers
43–0000	*Office and Administrative Support Occupations*
43–1000	Supervisors, office and administrative support workers
43–2000	Communications equipment operators
43–3000	Financial clerks
43–4000	Information and record clerks
43–5000	Material recording, scheduling, dispatching, and distributing workers
43–6000	Secretaries and administrative assistants
43–9000	Other office and administrative support workers
45–0000	*Farming, Fishing, and Forestry Occupations*
45–1000	Supervisors, farming, fishing, and forestry workers
45–2000	Agricultural workers
45–3000	Fishing and hunting workers

Table 2-9   *(continued)*

45–4000	Forest, conservation, and logging workers
45–9000	Other farming, fishing, and forestry workers
47–0000	*Construction and Extraction Occupations*
47–1000	Supervisors, construction and extraction workers
47–2000	Construction trades workers
47–3000	Helpers, construction trades
47–4000	Other construction and related workers
47–5000	Extraction workers
49–0000	*Installation, Maintenance, and Repair Occupations*
49–1000	Supervisors of installation, maintenance, and repair workers
49–2000	Electrical and electronic equipment mechanics, installers, and repairers
49–3000	Vehicle and mobile equipment mechanics, installers, and repairers
49–9000	Other installation, maintenance, and repair occupations
51–0000	*Production Occupations*
51–1000	Supervisors, production workers
51–2000	Assemblers and fabricators
51–3000	Food processing workers
51–4000	Metal workers and plastic workers
51–5000	Printing workers
51–6000	Textile, apparel, and furnishings workers
51–7000	Woodworkers
51–8000	Plant and systems operators
51–9000	Other production occupations
53–0000	*Transportation and Material Moving Occupations*
53–1000	Supervisors, transportation and material moving workers
53–2000	Air transportation workers
53–3000	Motor vehicle operators
53–4000	Rail transportation workers
53–5000	Water transportation workers
53–6000	Other transportation workers
53–7000	Material moving workers

Source: Based on *Standard Occupational Classification Manual.* Washington, DC: U.S. Department of Commerce, 1998.

example, when reading that a lawyer must learn the law, must write arguments, and so forth, a client can ask himself or herself if he or she has interest in doing those activities. When the qualifications and the educational requirements of an occupation are explained in occupational resources, clients can determine whether they have the necessary ability to proceed into that occupation. With regard to working conditions, a client can decide whether or not he or she has the appropriate personality and abilities to find the working conditions satisfying. For example, a person with a need for organization and cleanliness may find work in factories with dirt and scrap parts objectionable. A client's values are tested when the client must consider if the salary is sufficient or if the employment outlook is too risky. Occupational literature contains information that allows a client to assess the fit between his or her aptitudes, achievements, interests, values, and personality and the occupation being described.

What the Counselor Needs to Know

Since there are thousands of occupations open to clients, it is helpful for the counselor to be able to decide what he or she must know about occupations. For example, if a counselor uses the Strong Interest Inventory (SII), it is helpful to know the description of all occupations listed, as clients are likely to ask about them. If a counselor uses a personality inventory or an aptitude test such as the GATB, or ASVAB, it is beneficial to have at hand a list of occupations that match scores on those inventories or tests. Often the classification system that the counselor uses is determined by the classification system used by the occupational library in his or her setting. By making use of an organized library, the counselor can direct the client to appropriate occupational information. Then the client can read information not only about a specific occupation, but also about occupations with similar codes. For example, by looking under the DOT code with the first three digits of 045, the client will find information about several different kinds of counseling and psychology occupations.

Example of Step 2

As Jack and the counselor discuss Jack's experience and test scores (Table 2-5), they arrive at several occupations that Jack may want to examine. They've chosen these occupational titles because these are occupations that seem to fit some of Jack's interests, aptitudes, values, and personality.

> CL: Although I had thought of sales before, I had never given it much thought because my knowledge of sales was limited to door-to-door or telephone sales, and I never really liked that.
>
> CO: There is a wide variety of sales occupations, and I can help you learn about them by showing you information about some of the job descriptions that we have in our career library. [The counselor is aware that books such as the *Occupational Outlook Handbook* and other pamphlets on occupations may be a good start in broadening Jack's knowledge about sales. The counselor does not need to know all of the sales occupations that exist. If he or she wishes to find as large a number of sales occupations as possible, then the O*NET titles will provide that information.]
>
> CL: Although sales seems OK, I'm still interested in doing artwork. But on the other hand, I don't want to be a starving artist. There must be some ways to use art and still make a living.
>
> CO: There are. Although some artistic occupations are extremely competitive, there are some that are not as competitive. It is really worth looking into some of these, such as graphic arts. [Even though painting for a

living is very competitive, it is not appropriate to discourage the client from learning more about this occupation or others like it. The counselor wishes to encourage the client to read about a wide variety of artistic occupations that may include the use of drawing, painting, or sculpting.]

CL: I haven't taken any art courses in college, but in high school last year, I worked closely with my art teacher. Perhaps that's something that I should look into.

CO: Maybe you will be able to talk to your teacher during your vacation. [Jack is being encouraged to get occupational information. Even though the test and inventory scores may not fit with art teaching as much as they may with other occupations, it is helpful to encourage Jack to make this decision himself. This decision is best made after getting more information about being an art teacher.]

CL: When I think of it, there are a lot of people I know in careers that I'm considering. And some in careers I'm really not considering. My uncle sells Cadillacs in Philadelphia.

CO: Even though you're not considering selling cars, you're interested in sales. Perhaps you could talk to him about sales. [Getting information from all sources, both direct and indirect, is helpful.]

CL: Yes, but my uncle's like me. He'll probably try to sell me on selling.

CO: But you're able to separate the good information from opinion. Further, you can compare what he says to information that you learn when you read about sales occupations. [Being aware of the subjectivity of one person's impressions of an occupation, the counselor encourages Jack to consult other sources of more objective information, such as books or pamphlets.]

STEP 3: INTEGRATING INFORMATION ABOUT ONESELF AND THE WORLD OF WORK

According to trait and factor theory, this third step, integrating information about oneself and about occupations, is the major goal of career counseling. As mentioned previously, the manuals that accompany many tests and inventories indicate which occupations match specific patterns of scores. Further, occupational information has within it material indicating the aptitudes, achievements, interests, values, and personality characteristics required for each occupation. In a sense, the matching is built into the first two steps of trait and factor theory. However, this all sounds neater in theory than it is in practice. It is possible for a person's abilities as measured on the GATB to suggest one set of occupations, interests as measured on the SII to suggest another group of occupations, and personality as measured on the 16 PF to suggest yet a third group of occupations. There may also be disagreement among tests that measure the same trait, emphasizing the fallibility of testing and the need for care in test interpretation. In addition to the fallibility of tests is the notion that much information that is useful in making career decisions may not come necessarily from tests, but from the counseling interview.

Tests are not the only methods for measuring and assessing traits and factors. Computer guidance systems tend to fit neatly into trait and factor theory. They often combine tests and occupational information in such a way that clients can meet their own individual needs for self-assessment and occupational information. Two of the more comprehensive systems are SIGI PLUS (1985) and DISCOVER (1984). Both systems allow an opportunity to measure interests, values, and self-reported competencies. These systems do not measure personality, but they do provide assessment of work values. Occupational information is then matched with the student's competencies, values, and interests so that the student can examine information about occupations that match his or her self-assessment. Both instruments provide an opportunity to help with the decision-making process by reducing a list of occupational alternatives. In fact, DISCOVER allows the opportunity to put into the system test scores from a number of instruments such as those that have been discussed previously.

One advantage that both SIGI PLUS and DISCOVER have over the tests and inventories previously described is that the computer programs are interactive. In other words, as a student answers some questions and receives information, he or she can choose to move to any one of several sections. There is an interplay of information between the client and the computer, resulting in immediate feedback to the client. Computers can be used instead of or with other tests or inventories. However, neither tests nor computers can help clients in working out difficult and unusual concerns such as parental pressure to enter an unwanted occupation.

How the Counselor Can Help

The process of counseling by using trait and factor theory requires moving between the assessment of oneself and occupational information. Since much occupational information can be obtained outside the counseling session, most of the focus within the session is on self-assessment.

Counselors have available to them a full range of helping skills as described in Chapter 1. In using trait and factor theory, a counselor need not be limited to making suggestions and giving information. Both reasoning and feelings are important in making a career decision. When a client expresses a feeling, it is often helpful to find the reason behind it. For example, if a client says, "I wouldn't like to be a nurse," the counselor can respond in a number of ways: "What is it about nursing that you don't like?" or "Nursing doesn't feel right to you." By doing this, the counselor is likely to find out what lies behind the feelings. If the client replies, "I don't have what it takes to get into a nursing school," the counselor can reply, "You believe a nursing school wouldn't accept you" (content reflection) or "You feel anxious about entering a nursing school" (feeling reflection) or "What makes you think you couldn't enter a nursing school?" (open question). These are examples of helping skills that would assist the student in exploring his or her interest or abilities in nursing. Counseling can proceed by going repeatedly over a client's aptitudes, achievements, interests, abilities, and values so that understanding is reached.

As counseling progresses, it may be important to get more specific occupational information as well as more specific information about interests, aptitudes, achievements, values, and personality. An excellent way to do this is for the client to talk with people in a specific job. He or she can obtain even more detailed information by trying out an activity as a volunteer or part-time worker. For example, if a student is trying to choose between becoming an occupational therapist and a salesperson, it may be helpful to get a summer job as a salesperson in a retail store and volunteer to work in a hospital doing occupational therapy. A potential problem is that occasionally one may work in a setting that is unrepresentative because of low morale, inadequate administrative structure, or unhelpful colleagues. Counselors can help the client separate the setting from the idiosyncrasies of the people in the work setting. As occupational experience and exploration in the counseling session help the client define his or her interests and ability more clearly, the client moves toward a career decision. Although a career decision has been reached, it may be only temporary. Career counseling can be repeated at various times in the client's lifetime. Traits and factors can be reassessed as clients have new experiences that affect their assessment of their aptitudes, achievements, interests, values, and personality.

Example of Step 3

The following illustration is from a session that occurs after Jack has talked to others and read about occupations of interest to him:

> *CL:* Some of the information that I read was really helpful. I hadn't realized that there were so many different types of sales occupations and so many different places where you could work.
>
> *CO:* That's great. It sounds as if you've done a lot of work. [The counselor chooses to reinforce the client's information seeking. Without occupational information, career counseling will be unsuccessful.]
>
> *CL:* I think I would really like to take more art courses, perhaps in graphic arts. I know that graphic arts is a competitive field; at least that's what the material said. But I still think it would be good for me.
>
> *CO:* Tell me a little more about what you like about it. [The counselor is aware of Jack's low score on economic security on the VS. His lack of concern about the competitiveness of graphic arts seems consistent with this.]
>
> *CL:* Well, there is really an opportunity to draw, to be precise, to create new things. I could see myself doing advertising work.
>
> *CO:* The artistic work really seems to fit for you. [Jack's high score on art on the KCS and creativity on the VS are consistent with this statement.]
>
> *CL:* When I was looking in the career library, I found information about public relations. That got me thinking, too, because you can use all kinds of methods to try to persuade people to a certain point of view. I guess I hadn't realized that there are a lot of ways of doing this. I suppose you can do this artistically as well as by talking to people.
>
> *CO:* That's a clever way of looking at that. You can combine several interests of yours, perhaps. [Reinforcing the client's insight into how to combine

art and sales/management interests, as indicated on the KCS, furthers the client in his decision making.]

CL: I wonder if you can really do this in public relations or maybe advertising.

CO: Perhaps we can find some people for you to talk to about this idea. [The counselor realizes that written occupational information may not suffice to answer the client's question. The counselor is prepared to provide other resources to help Jack clarify his career decision making. Note how the counselor moves back and forth between self-assessment and occupational information, gradually moving the client closer to a career decision.]

APPLYING THE THEORY TO WOMEN

Differences in the abilities, achievements, values, personality, and interests of men and women have been a frequent source of study. Much research has focused on the differences between men and women in their real and perceived mathematical and verbal ability, resulting in differential educational and occupational achievements by men and women. Although the values and interests of men and women are becoming more similar, there are some significant variations. These issues are the focus of this section.

Perhaps more important than the minor differences that exist between males and females in terms of verbal and mathematical ability are the factors that bring about or affect these differences. As Betz and Fitzgerald (1987) point out, the differences may be cultural. Asian women and Finnish women tend to do as well as, if not better than, men on measures of math ability. In the United States, Fennema and Sherman (1977) have reported that there are no sex differences in mathematical ability of high school girls when the number of high school courses that emphasize spatial ability, such as drafting courses, are the same for both men and women. The relationship between math ability and later career achievement has been the focus of several informative investigations.

As Betz and Fitzgerald (1987) and Fitzgerald and Betz (1994) observe, women's own achievements have not always been considered important. In earlier times, women were recognized for being wives, mistresses, or mothers of famous men, rather than for their own accomplishments. Research focuses on the comparative achievement of men and women. In a study of 440,000 high school students, Card, Steel, and Abeles (1980) found that, although women had higher high school grades than men, 5 and 11 years later men had obtained more education and were being paid more for their work than women. Betz and Fitzgerald (1987) point out that those women who continue to study math have a much broader range of career options than those who do not. Examing the persistence of undergraduate students in engineering, Schaefers, Epperson, and Nauta (1997) found that men and women were similar in their attitudes. They suggest that ability, confidence in one's ability, external support, and interest are important in persistence in engineering for women and men. However, Kerr and Maresh (1994) find that gifted women do not use their intellectual abilities as fully as possible in achieving occupational success. Related to the differing achievements of women in school and in careers is their attitude toward their ability to be successful.

Personality factors such as confidence and self-esteem have been a focus of research that attempts to explain the different levels of accomplishment and ability of women when compared to men. Chipman, Krantz, and Silver (1992) reported that math anxiety negatively affected interest in science careers. Well-adapted women or vocationally secure women shared strong interest and ability in the sciences (Meldahl & Muchinsky, 1997). Related to this is the concept of self-efficacy, which is discussed in more detail in Chapter 13, "Social Learning Theory." The research on math self-efficacy, as reviewed by Lent and Hackett (1987), shows that women are often less confident and more anxious about their math ability than are men. Girls aged 7–10 are also less confident about math than boys (Eccles, Wigfield, Harold, & Blumenfeld, 1993) but are more confident about reading and music activities.

Lack of self-confidence about career-related activities is not confined to math. For example, Swanson and Lease (1990) found that women rated the general abilities of peers higher than their own abilities, while men rated the abilities of peers lower than their own abilities. Read (1994) found that women in nontraditional training programs had greater confidence in being able to succeed in school and on the job than did women in traditional and gender-balanced programs. In a study of 198 working women aged 18 to 55, Betsworth (1999) reported that the women significantly underestimated their abilities on general learning ability, verbal ability, spatial ability, form perception, clerical perception, and motor coordination. Betz and Fitzgerald (1987) stated that women, in general, are more likely to underestimate their own abilities and probable levels of future performance than are men. Clearly, the lack of self-esteem and confidence of many women has kept them from greater educational and occupational accomplishments.

In a very broad sense, the interests of men and women have been shown to be different (Hansen, Collins, Swanson, & Fouad, 1993). Interest inventories have revealed that, in general, women have more interest in artistic, clerical, and social occupations than men. Conversely, they have less interest in scientific and technical occupations (Betz & Fitzgerald, 1987). One of the problems in measuring interests has been that early forms of interest inventories were often sex-biased. For example, separate forms were used for men and women, and occupational titles were often male-oriented, such as mailman, rather than mail carrier (Diamond, 1975). Although interest inventories have been improved to measure interests more accurately, without sex bias contaminating the assessment, interest inventories still reflect social values about occupations. Social values that women should enter occupations such as teaching, nursing, and social work continue. For counselors, the challenge is to help women develop occupational interests in areas such as science and math.

Some research has focused on the different values that men and women have regarding work. Studying medical students, Kutner and Brogan (1980) found that the men's and women's work values were somewhat similar, but the men rated income and prestige as more important than the women did. In terms of commitment to work, Luzzo (1994) found that college women had a stronger commitment to work than did college men. Lips (1992) found that college women rated people-related values and intrinsic values higher than did college men. Although there are differences in the values of men and women within various professions and occupations, the differences in the career values of men and women appear to be decreasing, with both males and females valuing accomplishment, salary, security, and so on.

Although differences in abilities, achievements, personality, interests, and values between men and women do exist, they are often rather small. The differences between workers within occupational groups are often much greater than those between men and women in general. Being aware of how men and women differ on various traits and factors may help counselors attend to societal pressures on their female clients, while attempting to maximize their educational and occupational opportunities.

APPLYING THE THEORY TO CULTURALLY DIVERSE POPULATIONS

Regarding the traits of culturally diverse individuals, perhaps the most research has focused on the interests and work values of different cultural groups. For the purposes of this section, the interests and work values of Asian Americans, African Americans, Hispanics, and Native Americans will be discussed. Related to the formation of work values is the availability of occupational information. It is not valid to assume that occupational information is equally available to all Americans.

Research on the interests of culturally diverse people has focused mainly on measures of interests. For example, Sewell and Martin (1976) found, in general, that African American high school students tended to have fewer interests than white students and scored higher than white students in artistic interests and lower in scientific, technical, mechanical, and outdoor interests. However, Helms and Piper (1994) cite studies to show that the interests of black and white Americans are more similar to each other than prior research would suggest. Much of the research has used Holland's inventories, discussed in Chapter 4. There is not sufficient information to reveal how accurately interest inventories measure the likes and dislikes of culturally diverse people. Tracey, Watanabe, and Schneider (1997) caution that some models of career interests that fit American students do not fit Japanese students. Leung, Ivey, and Suzuki (1994) found that Asian American college students had interests in social as well as scientific and technical occupations, in contrast to the traditional view that Asian American interests are primarily scientific. Using a sample of over 55,000 employed adults, Lattimore and Borgen (1999) reported that the Strong Interest Inventory generally predicted the interests of African Americans, Hispanic Americans, Asian Americans, and Native Americans as well as it did the interests of Caucasian Americans.

In his discussion of the work values of different cultural groups, Axelson (1999) described studies that emphasize the various characteristics of cultural groups but cautioned against generalizing about the behavior of individuals in a particular cultural group. Observing that Asian Americans are often willing to adopt the work values of a new culture and to assimilate into it, Sue (1975) states that this is due in part to the development of independent work behavior in their native country. Leong (1991) found that Asian Americans placed a greater emphasis on making money and on security than did white Americans. Studying the values of adolescents in Hong Kong, Lau and Wong (1992) found that they valued personal and competency factors, enjoyment, and security in contrast to independence and obedience. This finding contradicts traditional views of the values of Chinese adolescents. Weathers, Thompson, Robert, and Rodriguez (1994) found that, when making career decisions, African American college women valued flexibility in pursuing career and family concerns as most important.

Studying Mexican Americans, Gowan and Trevino (1998) found that men were more likely to hold traditional views of the roles of women in the workplace than were women. Developing a model to explain the educational plans and career expectations of Mexican American high school girls, McWhirter, Hackett, and Bandalos (1998) found evidence to show that cultural influences were more important than gender in predicting career expectations of Mexican American girls. In a study of Latina undergraduates, Gomez and Fassinger (1994) found that women who were more bicultural in their value system tended to show a wider array of achievement behaviors than those who were less acculturated.

Regarding Native Americans, Richardson (1981) pointed out that the values of Native Americans are very different from those of white Americans. Native Americans tend to work for a specific purpose and stop when they have enough money to enjoy life. They may value working with their hands rather than doing mental work or paperwork. Native American students who valued working with their hands were more likely to drop out of high school than those who had other values (Gade, Hurlburt, & Fuqua, 1992). These studies are examples of the findings on different cultural values among culturally diverse people. Such generalizations help us to recognize the variety of work values that exist in society.

To choose an occupation, one must have, according to trait and factor theory, information not only about oneself, but also about occupations. Limited occupational information has been a problem for Native American youth (Spencer, Windham, & Peterson, 1975) and for Mexican American adolescents (Kuvlesky & Juarez, 1975). Furthermore, Davidson (1980) and Gottfredson (1978) note that African American teenagers have less occupational information than white teenagers and are thus hampered in career decision making. A possible solution to the problem of inadequate occupational information for culturally diverse populations is to make available biographical information about specific workers, including discussions of how they overcame discrimination or financial hardship (Rodriguez, 1994). A question-and-answer format in printed materials, as well as pictures of people of different ethnic groups working in the profession, can also help to make occupational literature more attractive.

Differences in work values and interests combined with limited access to occupational information make the career choice process difficult for nonwhite Americans. Being aware of such information can help counselors avoid making assumptions about the occupational knowledge and values of their clients.

COUNSELOR ISSUES

One concern about trait and factor theory is its emphasis on testing. One hopes that a client will not leave the final counseling session saying, "The test told me I should be a . . ." Although tests and inventories are used in trait and factor counseling, they are not necessarily the determinant of a final career choice. Since many clients are often looking for a quick solution, it is easy to allow the client to avoid the responsibility of making a career decision. Beginning counselors may find themselves giving test information rather than using more difficult counseling skills such as content and feeling reflections.

Trait and factor theory is deceptively simple. It is easy for the beginning counselor to develop a style in which he or she asks questions and the client gives the answers. Because tests seem so authoritative to the client, they can prevent an easy interaction and rapport between the client and the counselor. However, by taking ample time to leave the test information and discuss relevant client personal experience, the counselor can help the client accept responsibility for career decision making.

Another reason that trait and factor theory is so deceptively simple is that the three basic tenets of trait and factor theory provide an overview but do not provide much detail. Trait and factor theory does not provide a guide to which tests or inventories the counselor will include in his or her repertoire. It is up to the counselor to choose from hundreds of tests and inventories and to choose which traits and factors are most important. Conceptually, the theory provides less guidance for the counselor than do most of the other theories discussed in this book.

Trait and factor theory is a static rather than a developmental theory. It does not focus on how achievements, aptitudes, interests, values, and personalities grow and change; rather, it focuses on identifying traits and factors. This does not mean that this information cannot be useful in counseling. The counselor needs to help the client assess his or her interests and abilities. One way to do this is to discuss how these interests or aptitudes have changed over a period of years. This is certainly permissible within the guidelines of trait and factor theory; however, it is not emphasized. Often, the discussion of previous choices will be helpful in making a present choice. Thus, past traits and factors and their evolution may be useful in assessing current traits and factors.

Another problem that counselors may encounter is the difference between their own aptitudes, achievements, interests, values, and personality and those of the client. In particular, if the counselor has work values that are very different from those of the client, the counselor should recognize this and be tolerant. Counselors often value altruism and good working relationships with their associates. They need to be careful to understand those who do not value these factors and prefer prestige or management, which counselors might not value. This and the other problems mentioned make trait and factor theory one of the more difficult theories for a counselor to implement.

SUMMARY

Being the oldest and arguably the most widely used of all career development theories, trait and factor theory focuses on the match between an individual's aptitudes, achievements, interests, values, and personality and the requirements and conditions of occupations. Having obtained relevant information, the counselor and client work to bring about a match between the individual and the world of work. This approach relies heavily on the use of tests and inventories to measure aptitudes, achievements, interests, values, and personality. In test selection, the theory is vague, allowing the counselor to select those instruments that seem most appropriate to the counselor and the client. Selection of tests and inventories may determine the occupational classification system that the counselor will use. Such a system is helpful to the client in organizing information about occupations. The research focus in trait and factor theory has been on the traits and factors themselves rather than on the applicability of trait and factor theory as a career counseling approach. Additional research has been done delineating the aptitudes, achievements, interests, values, and personality of women and culturally diverse people. However, there is a vast need for more research, particularly on the latter group. The general trait and factor theory described in this chapter can be seen as a precursor to the more highly defined trait and factor theories of Holland (Chapter 4) and Lofquist and Dawis (Chapter 3).

References

Ackerman, P. L., & Heggestad, E. D. (1997). Intelligence, personality, and interests: Evidence for overlapping traits. *Psychological Bulletin, 121,* 219–245.

Adler, T. (1991). Tug of war develops over use of GATB. *American Psychological Association Monitor, 22*(5), 14.

Astin, A. W. (1993). *What matters in college? Four critical years revisited.* San Francisco: Jossey-Bass.

Aubrey, R. F. (1977). Historical development of guidance and counseling and implications for the future. *Personnel and Guidance Journal, 55,* 288–295.

Axelson, J. A. (1999). *Counseling and development in a multicultural society* (3rd ed.). Pacific Grove, CA: Brooks/Cole.

Betsworth, D. G. (1999). Accuracy of self-estimated abilities and the relationship between self-estimated abilities and realism for women. *Journal of Career Assessment, 7,* 35–43.

Betz, N. E., & Fitzgerald, L. F. (1987). *The career psychology of women.* Orlando, FL: Academic Press.

Buros Institute of Mental Measurement. (1999). *The fourteenth mental measurements yearbook.* Silver Platter Database, Lincoln: University of Nebraska Press.

Card, J. J., Steel, L., & Abeles, R. P. (1980). Sex differences in realization of individual potential for achievement. *Journal of Vocational Behavior, 17,* 1–21.

Carson, A. D. (1998). The relation of self-reported abilities to aptitude test scores: A replication and extension. *Journal of Vocational Behavior, 53,* 353–371.

Chipman, S. F., Krantz, D. H., & Silver, A. (1992). Mathematics anxiety and science careers among able college women. *Psychological Science, 3,* 292–295.

Davidson, J. P. (1980). Urban black youth and career development. *Journal of Non-White Concerns in Personnel and Guidance, 8,* 119–142.

Diamond, E. E. (1975). Guidelines for the assessment of sex bias and sex fairness in career interest inventories. *Measurement and Evaluation in Guidance, 8,* 7–11.

Dictionary of occupational titles (4th ed.). (1991). Washington, DC: U.S. Department of Labor, Employment and Training Administration.

DISCOVER: A computer-based career development and counselor support system. (1984). Iowa City, IA: American College Testing Foundation.

Eccles, J., Wigfield, A., Harold, R. D., & Blumenfeld, P. (1993). Age and gender differences in children's self and task perceptions during elementary school. *Child Development, 64,* 830–847.

Enhanced guide for occupational exploration. (1991). Indianapolis, IN: JIST Works.

Farr, J. M., Ludden, L., & Mangin, P. (1998). *The O*NET Dictionary of Occupational Titles.* Indianapolis, IN: JIST Works.

Fennema, E., & Sherman, J. A. (1977). Sex-related differences in mathematics achievement, spatial visualization, and affective factors. *American Educational Research Association Journal, 14,* 51–71.

Fitzgerald, L. F., & Betz, N. E. (1994). Career development in cultural context: The role of gender, race, class, and sexual orientation. In M. L. Savickas & R. W. Lent (Eds.), *Convergence in career development theories* (pp. 103–118). Palo Alto, CA: CPP Books.

Gade, E. M., Hurlburt, G., & Fuqua, D. (1992). The use of the self-directed search to identify American Indian high school dropouts. *School Counselor, 39,* 311–315.

Goldenson, R. M. (Ed.). (1984). *Longman dictionary of psychology and psychiatry.* New York: Longman.

Gomez, M. J., & Fassinger, R. E. (1994). An initial model of Latina achievement: Acculturation, biculturalism, and achieving styles. *Journal of Counseling Psychology, 41,* 205–215.

Gottfredson, L. S. (1978). *Race and sex differences in occupational aspirations: Their development and consequences for occupational segregation.* (Grant No. NIE-G-78-0210). Washington, DC: National Institute of Education.

Gottfredson, L. S. (1988). Reconsidering fairness: A matter of social and ethical priorities. *Journal of Vocational Behavior, 33,* 293–319.

Gough, H. G., & Bradley, P. (1996). *California Psychological Inventory: Administrator's guide* (3rd ed.). Palo Alto, CA: Consulting Psychologists Press.

Gowan, M., & Trevino, M. (1998). An examination of gender differences in Mexican-American attitudes toward family and career roles. *Sex Roles, 38,* 1079–1093.

Hansen, J. C., Collins, R. C., Swanson, J. L., & Fouad, N. A. (1993). Gender differences in the structure of interests. *Journal of Vocational Behavior, 42,* 200–211.

Hanson, W. E., Claiborn, C. D., & Kerr, B. (1997). Differential effects of two test-interpretation styles in counseling: A field study. *Journal of Counseling Psychology, 44,* 400–405.

Harmon, V., Barton, M., & Carson, A. (1999, August). Further examination of relations between abilities and interest codes [Poster]. American Psychological Association Convention, Boston, MA.

Helms, J. E., & Piper, R. E. (1994). Implications of racial identity theory for vocational psychology. *Journal of Vocational Behavior, 44,* 124–138.

Improved career decision making through the use of labor market information. (1991). Garrett Park, MD: Garrett Park Press.

Kapes, J. T., Mastie, M. M., & Whitfield, E. A. (Eds.). (1994). *A counselor's guide to career assessment instruments* (3rd ed.). Alexandria, VA: National Career Development Association.

Kerr, B., & Maresh, S. (1994). Career counseling for gifted women. In W. B. Walsh & S. H. Osipew (Eds.), *Career counseling for women* (pp. 197–235). Hillsdale, NJ: Erlbaum.

Kutner, N. G., & Brogan, D. R. (1980). The decision to enter medicine: Motivation, social support, and encouragements for women. *Psychology of Women Quarterly, 5,* 321–340.

Kuvlesky, W. P., & Juarez, R. (1975). Mexican American youth and the American dream. In J. S. Picou & R. E. Campbell (Eds.), *Career behavior of special groups: Theory, research, and practice* (pp. 241–296). Columbus, OH: Merrill.

Lattimore, R. R., & Borgen, F. H. (1999). Validity of the 1994 Strong Interest Inventory with social and ethnic groups in the United States. *Journal of Counseling Psychology, 46,* 185–195.

Lau, S., & Wong, A. K. (1992). Value and sex-role orientation of Chinese adolescents. *International Journal of Psychology, 27,* 3–17.

Leman, N. (1999). *The big test: The secret history of the American meritocracy.* New York: Farrar, Straus & Giroux.

Lent, R. W., Brown, S. D., & Hackett, G. (1994). Toward a unifying social cognitive theory of career and academic interest, choice and performance. *Journal of Vocational Behavior, 45,* 79–122.

Lent, R. W., & Hackett, G. (1987). Career self-efficacy: Empirical status and future directions. *Journal of Vocational Behavior, 30,* 347–382.

Leong, F. T. L. (1991). Career development attributes and occupational values of Asian American and white American college students. *The Career Development Quarterly, 39,* 221–230.

Leung, S. A., Ivey, D., & Suzuki, L. (1994). Factors affecting the career aspirations of Asian Americans. *Journal of Counseling & Development, 72,* 404–410.

Lips, H. M. (1992). Gender and science-related attitudes as predictors of college students' academic choices. *Journal of Vocational Behavior, 40,* 62–81.

Lock, R. D. (2000). *Taking charge of your career direction.* Pacific Grove, CA: Brooks/Cole.

Luzzo, D. A. (1994). An analysis of gender and ethnic differences in college students' commitment to work. *Journal of Employment Counseling, 31,* 38–45.

McWhirter, E. H., Hackett, G., & Bandalos, D. L. (1998). A casual model of the educational plans and career expectations of Mexican American high school girls. *Journal of Counseling Psychology, 45,* 166–181.

Meldahl, J. M., & Muchinsky, P. M. (1997). The neurotic dimension of vocational indecision: Gender comparability? *Journal of Career Assessment, 5,* 317–331.

Murphy, L. L., Impara, J. C., & Plake, B. S. (1999). *Tests in print V.* Lincoln: University of Nebraska Press.

National Vocational Guidance Association. (1980). Guidelines for the preparation and evaluation of career information literature. *The Vocational Guidance Quarterly, 28,* 291–296.

Occupational outlook handbook (2000). Washington, DC: U.S. Department of Labor.

Parsons, F. (1909). *Choosing a vocation.* Boston: Houghton Mifflin.

Read, B. K. (1994). Motivational factors in technical college women's selection of nontraditional careers. *Journal of Career Development, 20,* 239–258.

Richardson, E. H. (1981). Cultural and historical perspectives in counseling American Indians. In D. W. Sue (Ed.), *Counseling the culturally different* (pp. 216–255). New York: Wiley.

Rodriguez, M. A. (1994). Preparing an effective occupational information brochure for ethnic minorities. *The Career Development Quarterly, 43,* 178–184.

Schaefers, K. G., Epperson, D. L., & Nauta, M. M. (1997). Women's career development: Can theoretically derived variables predict persistence in engineering majors? *Journal of Counseling Psychology, 44,* 173–183.

Schmidt, F. L. (1988). The problem of group differences in ability test scores in employment selection. *Journal of Vocational Behavior, 33,* 272–292.

Sewell, T. E., & Martin, R. P. (1976). Racial differences in patterns of occupational choice in adolescents. *Psychology in the Schools, 13,* 326–333.

SIGI PLUS: Counselor's manual. (1985). Princeton, NJ: Educational Testing Service.

Spencer, B. F., Windham, G. O., & Peterson, J. H., Jr. (1975). Occupational orientations of an American group. In J. S. Picou & R. E. Campbell (Eds.), *Career behavior of special groups: Theory, research, and practice* (pp. 199–223). Columbus, OH: Merrill.

Standard occupational classification manual. (1998). Washington, DC: U.S. Department of Commerce.

Sue, D. W. (1975). Asian-Americans: Social-psychological forces affecting their life styles. In J. S. Picou & R. E. Campbell (Eds.), *Career behavior of special groups: Theory, research, and practice* (pp. 97–121). Columbus, OH: Merrill.

Swanson, J. L., & Lease, S. H. (1990). Gender differences in self-ratings of abilities and skills. *Career Development Quarterly, 38,* 347–359.

Tracey, T. J. G., Watanabe, N., & Schneider, P. L. (1997). Structural invariance of vocational interests across Japanese and American cultures. *Journal of Counseling Psychology, 44,* 346–354.

Watkins, C. E., Jr., Campbell, V. L., & Nieberding, R. (1994). The practice of vocational assessment by counseling psychologists. *The Counseling Psychologist, 22,* 115–128.

Weathers, P. L., Thompson, C. E., Robert, S., & Rodriguez, J., Jr. (1994). Black college women's career values: A preliminary investigation. *Journal of Multicultural Counseling and Development, 22,* 96–105.

Williamson, E. G. (1939). *How to counsel students.* New York: McGraw-Hill.

Williamson, E. G. (1965). *Vocational counseling.* New York: McGraw-Hill.

Zunker, V. G., & Norris, D. S. (1998). *Using assessment results for career development* (5th ed.). Pacific Grove, CA: Brooks/Cole.

3

Work Adjustment Theory

Work adjustment theory is the outgrowth of more than 35 years of research by René Dawis and Lloyd Lofquist and their colleagues. Their work, which reflects the trait and factor tradition of the University of Minnesota, evolved into a growing body of research that led to several revisions and refinements of their theory. In the process of this development, the Work Adjustment Project was designed to provide improved rehabilitation services for vocationally challenged clients. At the University of Minnesota, an adult Vocational Assessment Clinic treated clients and a Vocational Psychology Research unit was designed to develop and score the tests that are part of work adjustment theory. Originally designed to meet the needs of vocational rehabilitation clients, the theory is now applicable to adults who wish to make career choices or are experiencing work adjustment problems.

Work adjustment theory (Dawis & Lofquist, 1984) consists of 18 propositions and corollaries. The current theory (Dawis 2000a, 2000b) is based on research that has modified earlier work (Dawis, England, & Lofquist, 1964; Dawis, Lofquist, & Weiss, 1968; Lofquist & Dawis, 1969). Each of these statements of theory has had as a goal the prediction of work adjustment. Dawis and Lofquist (1984) define work adjustment as a "continuous and dynamic process by which a worker seeks to achieve and maintain correspondence with a work environment" (p. 237). Put another way, work adjustment is indicated by the length of time, or tenure, on the job. This concern with job tenure and a similar concept, job performance, distinguishes work adjustment theory from most other theories described in this book, which are concerned with career selection or work adjustment but not actual performance on the job.

There are two major components to the prediction of work adjustment (and therefore tenure): satisfaction and satisfactoriness. *Satisfaction* refers to being satisfied with the work that one does. In contrast, *satisfactoriness* refers to the employer's satisfaction with the individual's performance. Or to rephrase, satisfaction refers to the extent to which an individual's needs and requirements are fulfilled by the work that he or she does. Satisfactoriness concerns the appraisal of others, usually supervisors, of the extent to which an individual adequately completes the work that is assigned to him or her, and it is of interest to industrial and organizational psychologists.

"Satisfaction is a key indicator of work adjustment," state Lofquist and Dawis (1984, p. 217). Satisfaction is important because the individual must be satisfied with many aspects of the work, such as salary and type of work task. This chapter will focus primarily on the individual's satisfaction with work. However, work adjustment theory is also concerned with other indicators of satisfaction and satisfactoriness, including the amount of turnover, absenteeism, and tardiness on the job; devotion to a job; job morale; and productivity on a job. These aspects of job performance are all indicators of work adjustment. The work environment must satisfy the individual's needs, and he or she must have the requisite skills to meet the job's needs.

Skills and needs are observable entities that are the essence of work personality. However, hundreds of skills may be required in different types of jobs, as well as many needs, so that measurement of them is awkward and difficult. Dawis and Lofquist (1984) propose the concept of abilities, which combines the common elements of skills required in many jobs. In a similar vein, values serve to group needs together in a meaningful way. Much of these researchers' theoretical work concerns the discussion and measurement of abilities and values. They also discuss personality style and interests. Their experimental work on personality styles and adjustment styles is not as highly developed as is their work on needs and values. They view interests as a derived construct, being a reflection of ability-value relationships.

In describing work adjustment theory, a specific application of trait and factor theory, an approach similar to that employed in Chapter 2, "Trait and Factor Theory," will be used. Work adjustment theory differs from general trait and factor theory in that it makes use of clearly defined concepts and follows an articulated theoretical model. The first section of this chapter will be concerned with assessing abilities, values, personality, and interests (similar to Parsons's first step). Since abilities and values are the major emphasis of Lofquist and Dawis's (1984) work, they will receive the most attention. The second section, also similar to Parsons's second step, will be concerned with knowledge of the requirements and conditions of occupations. In this section, abilities required by work and reinforcement of individual needs will be discussed. The third section, similar to Parsons's third step, will outline the matching of the abilities and values of an individual with the abilities required by the job and the reinforcers provided by the job.

Work adjustment theory also has implications for helping clients with adjustment problems, such as problems with coworkers and superiors, boredom, inability to meet job demands, and retirement, as well as many other issues. In addition, work adjustment theory provides some psychometric data on the ability and values differences of women and culturally diverse populations. This is not a major focus of the theory, as it is concerned with differences among individuals, not group differences.

ASSESSING ABILITIES, VALUES, PERSONALITY, AND INTERESTS

Consistent with trait and factor theory, measurement of values and abilities is crucial to the understanding of work adjustment theory. To assess abilities, Dawis and Lofquist (1984) make use of the General Aptitude Test Battery (GATB) developed by the U.S. Department of Labor (1982). As a measure of values and needs, they have developed the Minnesota Importance Questionnaire (MIQ) (Rounds, Henly, Dawis, Lofquist, & Weiss, 1981), which is critical to the use and understanding of work adjustment theory. They are also in the process of developing measures of personality style and adjustment style as they relate to work adjustment (Lawson, 1993). Because Dawis and Lofquist (1984) see interests as an expression of abilities and values, their focus is on ability and value assessment. Each of these components of work adjustment theory will be discussed and illustrated.

Abilities

Dawis and Lofquist (1984) define abilities as "reference dimensions for skills" (p. 233). Abilities are viewed as encompassing aptitudes, which are predicted skills as contrasted to acquired skills. For Lofquist and Dawis, the notion of abilities is needed in order to conceptualize a vast array of work skills. The latter can include typing, waiting on tables, fixing teeth or engines, planing wood, plastering walls, selling insurance policies, and so forth. There are hundreds, perhaps thousands, of such skills. Ability tests measure factors common to many skills. Many ability tests measure between 8 and 15 ability dimensions. Dawis and Lofquist (1984) describe the General Aptitude Test Battery (U.S. Department of Labor, 1982) as an example of a measure of ability. The GATB is used widely by employment counseling agencies and measures nine specific abilities:

G —General learning ability: Overall ability to learn as well as general knowledge

V —Verbal ability: Understanding of words and paragraphs

N—Numerical ability: Ability to perform arithmetic quickly

S —Spatial ability: Ability to see objects in space and understand relationships between two-dimensional and three-dimensional objects

P —Form perception: Ability to see details in two- or three-dimensional drawings and to make discriminations in shapes and shadings

Q—Clerical ability: Ability to see differences in tables and lists that include both words and numbers

K —Eye/hand coordination: Ability to coordinate hand movements with visual perception

F —Finger dexterity: Ability to move small objects quickly and with precision

M—Manual dexterity: Ability to use hands and arms in manipulating objects quickly and skillfully

Although other abilities could be used in addition to those listed, these nine abilities are used by Dawis and Lofquist in their application of work adjustment theory. Other ability tests could be used that would be consistent with work adjustment theory, but the GATB is most practical because of the information it provides for counselors to use in matching jobs with individuals' abilities and values. In general, the GATB incorporates abilities required for many jobs and measures a broader base of abilities than many academic aptitude tests. For example, one would expect an electrician to have, among other abilities, numerical ability, form perception, and eye/hand coordination. The GATB manual (U.S. Department of Labor, 1982) provides a list of abilities that are needed in a vast variety of jobs. A new version of the GATB, the *Ability Profile* is in the planning stages.

Values

Just as abilities represent a distillation of many work skills, values represent a grouping of needs. Unlike the hundreds of work skills that may exist, the number of needs is fewer. The Minnesota Importance Questionnaire (Rounds, Henly, Dawis, Lofquist, & Weiss, 1981) is a measure of needs. Although not encompassing all needs, the 20 need scales of the Minnesota Importance Questionnaire characterize important work-related concepts. The 20 need scales are listed in Table 3-1 along with the statement that represents each scale. In the questionnaire each statement is paired in a comparison with every other statement, to constitute 190 items. For example, an individual is asked whether he or she would rather "be busy all the time" (activity) or "do things for other people" (social service). By comparing the relative importance of each need, scores on each scale are determined. The disadvantage of this method is that it represents a narrower

Table 3-1   *Values, Need Scales, and Statements from the Minnesota Importance Questionnaire*

Value	Need Scale	Statement
Achievement	Ability utilization	I could do something that makes use of my abilities.
	Achievement	The job could give me a feeling of accomplishment.
Comfort	Activity	I could be busy all the time.
	Independence	I could work alone on the job.
	Variety	I could do something different every day.
	Compensation	My pay would compare well with that of other workers.
	Security	The job would provide for steady employment.
	Working conditions	The job would have good working conditions.
Status	Advancement	The job would provide an opportunity for advancement.
	Recognition	I could get recognition for the work I do.
	Authority	I could tell people what to do.
	Social status	I could be "somebody" in the community.
Altruism	Coworkers	My coworkers would be easy to make friends with.
	Moral values	I could do the work without feeling it is morally wrong.
	Social service	I could do things for other people.
Safety	Company policies and practices	The company would administer its policies fairly.
	Supervision—Human relations	My boss would back up the workers (with top management).
	Supervision—Technical	My boss would train the workers well.
Autonomy	Creativity	I could try out some of my ideas.
	Responsibility	I could make decisions on my own.

Source: A Psychological Theory of Work Adjustment, by R. V Dawis and L. H. Lofquist. Copyright © 1984, University of Minnesota Press, p. 29. Reprinted by permission.

definition of the need than if several items were used for a particular scale. Choosing this method to define needs reflects Dawis and Lofquist's emphasis on the importance of rigorous measurement in their theory.

Using the statistical technique of factor analysis, Dawis and Lofquist (1984) have derived six values from the 20 needs, also listed in Table 3-1. Values are clustered with their opposites: achievement is negatively related to comfort, status is very different from altruism, and safety is negatively related to autonomy. The relationship of the needs to the values and the values to each other provides a way for a counselor to chunk and derive meaning from the need scales of the MIQ. The values are described as follows:

Achievement   This value is reflected in the need to make use of one's abilities and to do things that give one a sense of accomplishment. For example, a carpenter who is proud of his or her abilities and the products he or she makes is likely to value achievement.

Comfort   Included in this value are a variety of needs dealing with specific aspects of work that make the job less stressful for the worker. These are quite diverse, including being busy all the time (activity), working alone (independence), doing different things (variety), and being paid well (compensation). Other aspects of comfort can be long range; for example, a desire for steady employment (security). Also, specific working conditions can be important. These might include lighting, heating, and amount of space. All of these have in common an emphasis on a nonstressful work environment, one that will yield benefits to the employee, such as security and compensation.

Status   How one is perceived by others and the recognition one gets are the emphasis of this value. Status can be attained by an opportunity for advancement, recognition for the work that one does, or, more generally, prestige (social status) that comes from being important in the community. In addition, telling people what to do (authority) is another way of achieving status. Recognizing that status needs are important to some individuals can be particularly helpful both in career choice and in recognizing a problem with work dissatisfaction. For example, some people who have initially enjoyed a particular job may lose interest in it when they find that they are not advancing and are not being recognized for what they do.

Altruism   Altruism is quite the opposite of status because it is concerned not with how one is perceived by others but with how one can help or work with others. Doing things for other people (social service) and, more specifically, getting along with colleagues at work (coworkers) can be a very important aspect of work. In particular, being able to do work that feels morally correct (moral values) can be a need that is directly tied to work satisfaction. For example, persons who are required to sell products that they feel are harmful or worthless may find that they must terminate their jobs because their moral values are being violated.

Safety   Rather than being seen in the narrow sense of avoiding hazardous conditions, this value is broader in that it reflects the importance of orderliness and predictability. It includes the enforcement of policies in a fair manner (company policies and practices) as well as support from supervisors (supervision—human relations). Also, safety includes how coworkers are trained (supervision—technical), as it can affect how a person does his or her job. For example, an automobile assembly worker who could not count on coworkers to do their jobs well and who felt that management was lax in providing workers with training and materials would not have his or her safety needs met.

Autonomy   Some people are not concerned with how they are treated by their bosses (safety) but want the opportunity to work on their own. This might include trying out some of their own ideas (creativity) or making decisions on their own (responsibility). For example, an auto assembly worker who wants to try out new ideas to make her work easier or more efficient is concerned with autonomy rather than safety.

These values and needs provide a way for the counselor to understand a person's work experience. Without such a guideline, work experience can appear to be a series of unrelated events. The MIQ is a method of measuring the importance of needs that emerge from experience. For example, individuals who want to accomplish a lot in their work, help others, and make decisions on their own (achievement, altruism, and autonomy) will find satisfaction in very different occupations from persons who are concerned with pay and steady employment, getting recognition for the work they do, and being in a company with fair policies (comfort, status, and safety).

Personality Styles

According to Dawis and Lofquist (1984), personality style is concerned with how an individual with particular abilities and values interacts with his or her work situation. They have identified four characteristics of personality style: celerity, pace, rhythm, and endurance. These describe ways in which people respond to their environment: how quickly, with how much intensity, in what particular pattern, and for how long. Celerity is concerned with the speed with which one approaches tasks; pace is concerned with the effort one spends in working; rhythm is the pattern of one's effort or pace; and endurance concerns how long one is likely to continue working at a task. Thus, someone who is high on celerity, pace, rhythm, and endurance works quickly, is involved in a large number of activities, is consistent in his or her work, and can be relied on to complete projects. These work personality styles are an interesting addition to the ability and values concepts of Lofquist and Dawis. However, scales for the assessment of celerity, pace, rhythm, and endurance are still in the developmental stage (Lawson, 1993). Questions such as "Do individuals maintain the same work personality style (celerity, pace, rhythm, and endurance) in one work environment that they do in another?" remain to be answered.

Interests

As stated earlier, interests are seen by Dawis and Lofquist (1984) as derived from values and abilities in that they are an expression of ability-value relationships. For these researchers, an interest in being an engineer or a bricklayer is derived from the abilities and values that one has. They believe that interest inventories can be helpful in counseling but do not feature them in their approach to work adjustment counseling. Rounds (1990) analyzed data that assessed the relative contribution of work values and vocational interests. His conclusion was that both are important, but that work values appear to be a slightly better predictor of job satisfaction than interests. Differences were also found for females and males. This study lends support to the weight that Dawis and Lofquist put on values as an important aspect of prediction of job satisfaction.

A Counseling Example

In the following example, the GATB and MIQ are used to assist a client with self-assessment. Later in this chapter, after a description of the work adjustment theory approach to occupational information, a continuing discussion with the client will show how work adjustment theory matches information about values and abilities with occupational information.

Winifred is a 45-year-old white farmer living with her husband in rural Missouri. Her husband is an auto mechanic in the local village, and Winifred runs the family farm. They have no children but cared for foster children until about 10 years ago. Winifred has been the principal farm manager and farm laborer for 20 years, raising feed corn and hogs. Winifred has been primarily responsible for planting, fertilizing, and harvesting the corn. She also takes the major responsibility for the constant activity of feeding the hogs. Winifred had no formal training in farming and learned most of it from her parents and from attending special agricultural extension programs. Recently, she sprained her back badly while harvesting. This came as an addition to chronic back pain that she had experienced over the last 3 years. After consulting with her physician, who has taken several X-rays of her spine, Winifred has come to the realization that she can no longer handle the heavy task of farming. Furthermore, she has become dissatisfied and bored with the work. Because Winifred is self-employed, she is both employee and employer. One measure of her satisfactoriness as a farmer is the productivity of the farm. Winifred has made the farm financially productive in good weather conditions and has been able to maintain the farm's solvency in times of drought.

When discussing her concerns with her physician, Winifred was referred to a local career counselor. He asked her to complete the GATB and the MIQ after talking with her briefly. Winifred's scores are summarized in Table 3-2. Her scores are highest in numerical ability, spatial ability, form perception, eye/hand coordination, and finger dexterity. Her highest needs as registered on the MIQ are for ability utilization and achievement.

> CL: It was strange taking those tests. When I was in high school, I remember tests like that aptitude test I took [The GATB]. It's been 25 years. I never thought I'd see one of those again. But I was surprised to be playing with blocks and washers and things. [Winifred is referring to the finger and manual dexterity tests.]

Table 3-2 *Test Scores for Winifred*

	High	Moderate	Low
GATB	Numerical ability Spatial ability Form perception Eye/hand coordination Finger dexterity		Verbal ability Clerical ability
MIQ	Ability utilization Achievement	Creativity Responsibility Activity Independence Compensation	

CO: Well, you seemed to do fine. There's a lot of information for us to look at. [The counselor wants to explore Winifred's abilities, and the GATB seems to be a good place to start.]

CL: My husband always says that I can fix the tractor faster than he can. He says that my hands really whiz around when I get going.

CO: Well, you also have the abilities to visualize objects and to understand relationships of objects on paper. [The counselor wants to talk to Winifred about her spatial ability and her form perception.]

CL: When I was a girl in school 25 years ago, I couldn't take courses that I wanted to. Shop courses were for boys; home economics and business education were for girls. I know my mom wanted me to be a secretary. What a mess I would have been! I know that I don't have those kinds of skills. It drives me nuts even when I have to do some of that at the farm. I can't type lists, and I don't like it.

CO: Tell me more about what you're good at and not so good at on the farm. [So far, it seems as if Winifred's perception of her own abilities matches that of the GATB. The counselor wants to check further.]

CL: Well, I'm good at fixing things. My husband has taught me a lot of mechanical stuff that he learned when he took courses in high school. I seem to pick it up real well. Later, I learned about electrical things. That's probably the most fun for me. My husband keeps telling me how good I am at it. I guess I am. That's the good part. The bad part is moving around and lifting. It really hurts. I used to do a lot more heavy work. Now I look for ways I can get other people to do it or get some machine to do it. You should see the way I use a tractor. I practically try to wash dishes with it. We've got all kinds of additions for the tractor, but sometimes it's real hard to hook them up.

CO: Seems like working on the farm has really given you a chance to see what you can do and what you can't do. [Winifred's own perception of her abilities seems to check out with her scores on the GATB.]

Winifred and the counselor continue to discuss the GATB and then move to a discussion of her work values, needs, and the MIQ. Even from the discussion so far, the counselor senses that achievement is important to Winifred. She seems proud of her abilities and of what she has done.

CL: I like what I've done on the farm. A lot of my friends sit around and make pies. That's not me. At first, that bothered my husband. Now, he's OK with it. We figure it's OK to buy frozen foods, desserts, and such. He doesn't seem to mind that I don't cook. He doesn't want to, either.

CO: You've done a lot with the farm. What else have you done? [The counselor hears the achievement value and wants to inquire further.]

CL: I've done a lot of different things. I do so much on my own, particularly in the last few years. My husband seems to have lost some interest in the farm, too. I wish he hadn't. I kind of like it, but it gets to be a burden sometimes. I don't mind deciding what to do, but I guess I get tired of having to be there all the time. We can never leave the farm, it seems. A few times we have; my folks come in. It's hard. You know pigs. You can't leave them for long.

CO: I would like to talk to you about the Minnesota Importance Questionnaire. Some of the scores fit in with what you're saying about what's important to you. You really do seem to like to be active and to work on your own. [Finding that Winifred's expressed values seem to fit with the MIQ makes things go smoothly.]

CL: I wondered how I did with the MIQ. That was easy. Not like the GATB.

CO: Well, your high scores show that you like to use your abilities and want to be able to get a sense of accomplishment in what you do.

CL: That's for sure. I can't imagine doing something that didn't matter. To do the same thing time after time that didn't matter would be awful. I want to feel like I'm getting somewhere, making progress.

CO: Well, we will consider that when we start to look at things that you might want to do. [The counselor makes a mental note that achievement is, again, important to Winifred. Its opposite, comfort, is not. Work conditions do not seem to be important to her.]

The counselor and Winifred continue to talk about Winifred's abilities, values, and interests. Later they will discuss possible occupations and matching occupations that fit the GATB.

MEASURING THE REQUIREMENTS AND CONDITIONS OF OCCUPATIONS

Just as there are methods to measure individuals' values and abilities, there are methods to measure the abilities and values needed for many occupations. In brief, this is done by averaging scores for people in various occupations on the GATB and the MIQ. Such information is not available for the work personality styles of celerity, pace, rhythm, and endurance. Also, information about interest patterns of people in various occupations has not been used by Dawis and Lofquist in their psychometric application of work adjustment theory. This is because Lofquist and Dawis believe that interest is a secondary concept, as mentioned earlier, and that the information provided by the occupational patterns of abilities and values is sufficient. These two will be discussed in more detail here.

Ability Patterns

Occupational Ability Patterns have been developed by the U.S. Department of Labor to describe the important abilities that are required for a great variety of jobs. To do this, job analysts assessed an occupation at various sites. Furthermore, individuals employed in occupations were administered the GATB. From these two methods, a set of GATB ability requirements (three or four) was developed for each occupation. Furthermore, cutoff scores were selected. Those scoring above the cutoff point were people who had done their jobs successfully as determined by supervisor ratings or other means. This information enables an individual to assess whether he or she has abilities similar to those of successful people in a given occupation. However, in determining cutoff scores for occupations, it is important not to set the scores too high and possibly exclude adequate potential candidates.

Value Patterns

Work environments differ in the degree to which they meet the needs and values of an individual. Lofquist and Dawis have developed a list of Occupational Reinforcer Patterns to assess how much an occupation reinforces the values of individuals. To do that, they developed the Minnesota Job Description Questionnaire (MJDQ; Borgen, Weiss, Tinsley, Dawis, & Lofquist, 1968a), which assesses how well an occupation reinforces or meets each of 20 needs. The MJDQ uses the same needs as the Minnesota Importance Questionnaire. Table 3-3 shows the wording of the items on the MJDQ. Comparing the items in Table 3-1 with those in Table 3-3 will illustrate the similarity. For example, on the MIQ the need for activity is assessed by the item "I would be busy all the time." Activity as a reinforcer is assessed through this MJDQ item: "Workers on this job are busy all the time." Thus, the needs of an individual are matched with the reinforcers, provided by the job. Many occupations were assessed with the MJDQ so that reinforcer patterns could be established (Borgen et al., 1968b). Recently, Dawis, Dohm, and Jackson (1993) have described occupations as reinforcer systems, which can offer predictable versus unpredictable reinforcements, self-reinforcements versus non-self-reinforcements, and social versus nonsocial reinforcement. These ratings of reinforcement schedules are related to, but different from, occupational reinforcement patterns. Using information about value patterns helps counselors to see how the values of their clients match the values that are met or reinforced by a large number of occupations.

Table 3-3 *Need Scales and Statements from the Minnesota Job Description Questionnaire*

Need Scale	Statement (Workers on this job . . .)
Ability utilization	Make use of their individual abilities
Achievement	Get a feeling of accomplishment
Activity	Are busy all the time
Advancement	Have opportunities for advancement
Authority	Tell other workers what to do
Company policies and practices	Have a company that administers its policies fairly
Compensation	Are paid well in comparison with other workers
Coworkers	Have coworkers who are easy to make friends with
Creativity	Try out their own ideas
Independence	Do their work alone
Moral values	Do work without feeling that it is morally wrong
Recognition	Receive recognition for the work they do
Responsibility	Make decisions on their own
Security	Have steady employment
Social service	Have work where they do things for other people
Social status	Have a position of "somebody" in the community
Supervision— Human relations	Have bosses who back up their workers (with top management)
Supervision— Technical	Have bosses who train the workers well
Variety	Have something different to do every day
Working conditions	Have good working conditions

Source: Minnesota Job Description Questionnaire, by Borgen, Weiss, Tinsley, Dawis, and Lofquist. Copyright © 1968, Vocational Psychology Research, Department of Psychology, University of Minnesota. Reprinted by permission.

Combining Ability and Value Patterns

Important information about occupations can be provided by combining information about Occupational Ability Patterns and Occupational Reinforcer Patterns. The combined data were used to create the Minnesota Occupational Classification System (MOCS). The original MOCS had 337 occupations. The third revision of the MOCS has 1769 occupations. The relationship of instruments used to assess individual abilities and values and those found in occupations is shown in Table 3-4. The individual and occupational patterns are matched by using the MOCS, which is described in the next section.

Table 3-4   *Instruments Used in Work Adjustment Theory*

Assessment of Individuals	Assessment of Occupations
Abilities	Ability Patterns
General Aptitude Test Battery (GATB)	Occupational Ability Patterns
Values	Value Patterns
Minnesota Importance Questionnaire	Minnesota Job Description
(MIQ)	Questionnaire (MJDQ)
Personality Styles	Personality Styles
Instruments are being developed	Instruments are being developed

Matching Assessment of Individual and Occupation
Minnesota Occupational Classification System (MOCS)
Adjustment Styles (Instruments are being developed)

MATCHING ABILITIES, VALUES, AND REINFORCERS

When matching values and abilities with the Occupational Ability Patterns and Occupational Reinforcer Patterns, the counselor has three tools available: the Minnesota Importance Questionnaire report form, the GATB manual (U.S. Department of Labor, 1982), and the Minnesota Occupational Classification System (MOCS). All can be helpful in identifying occupations for clients to explore further. In addition, a relatively new but useful concept is adjustment style. This concept concerns the degree of fit between the person and the environment. Four qualities describe this fit: flexibility, activeness, reactiveness, and perseverance. All of these tools can help the client and the counselor make use of a wealth of information and narrow the number of occupational alternatives so that the client has a manageable number of choices.

When clients take the Minnesota Importance Questionnaire, they receive scores on the 6 values and 20 needs described earlier and on 90 occupations. Table 3-5 shows an example of a report. It lists occupations whose reinforcer patterns match the client's identified needs. The strength of the correspondence (or relationship) between the individual's rating of the importance of a need on the MIQ and the importance attached to that need by a sample of people in an occupation is indicated by the C Index. By using this, a counselor can help the client locate occupations for future consideration. If the sample of 90 occupations is not sufficient, the counselor can request an extended report, which lists the scores of more than 183 occupations.

The client and counselor can also match the client's ability scores and need patterns to occupations by using the Minnesota Occupational Classification System. Since the MOCS lists both Occupational Ability Patterns and Occupational Reinforcer Patterns for more than 1,700 occupations, it

Table 3-5 *Minnesota Importance Questionnaire Sample Report Form (Winifred's Scores)*

MIQ profile is compared with Occupational Reinforcer Patterns for 90 representative occupations. Correspondence is indicated by the C Index. A prediction of Satisfied (S) results from C values greater than .50, Likely Satisfied (L) for C values between .10 and .49, and Not Satisfied (N) for C values less than .10. Occupations are clustered by similarity of Occupational Reinforcer Pattern. Abbreviations after each cluster refer to the primary values (all capitals) and secondary values: For example, Achievement (ACH) is a primary value, and Comfort (Com) is a secondary value.

	C Index	Prediction Satisfied		C Index	Prediction Satisfied
Cluster A (ACH-AUT-Alt)	.30	L	Cluster B (ACH-Com)	.15	L
Architect	.25	L	Bricklayer	−.07	N
Dentist	.21	L	Carpenter	.24	L
Family practitioner	.21	L	Cement mason	−.16	N
Interior designer/decorator	.43	L	Elevator repairer	.48	L
Lawyer	.35	L	Heavy equipment operator	.30	L
Minister	.13	L	Landscape gardener	−.11	N
Nurse, occupational health	.12	L	Lather	−.05	N
Occupational therapist	.33	L	Millwright	.10	L
Optometrist	.39	L	Painter–paperhanger	.11	L
Psychologist, counseling	.21	L	Patternmaker, metal	.28	L
Recreation leader	.15	L	Pipefitter	.34	L
Speech pathologist	.28	L	Plasterer	−.13	N
Teacher, elementary school	.23	L	Plumber	.37	L
Teacher, secondary school	.28	L	Roofer	−.04	N
Vocational evaluator	.36	L	Salesperson, automobile	.43	L
Cluster C (ACH-Aut-Com)	.44	L	Cluster D (ACH-STA-Com)	.57	S
Alteration tailor	.27	L	Accountant, certified public	.43	L
Automobile mechanic	.25	L	Airplane copilot, commercial	.25	L
Barber	.46	L	Cook (hotel–restaurant)	.48	L
Beauty operator	.44	L	Department head, supermarket	.39	L

	C Index	Prediction Satisfied
Caseworker	.28	L
Claim adjuster	.51	S
Commercial artist, illustrator	.56	S
Electronics mechanic	.39	L
Locksmith	.28	L
Maintenance repairer, factory	.41	L
Mechanical engineering tech	.40	L
Office-machine servicer	.53	S
Photoengraver (stripper)	.54	S
Sales agent, real estate	.32	L
Salesperson, general hardware	.15	L
Cluster E (COM)	.19	L
Assembler, production	.05	N
Baker	.16	L
Bookbinder	.28	L
Bookkeeper I	.31	L
Bus driver	.17	L
Keypunch operator	.10	L
Meat cutter	.16	L
Post office clerk	.13	L
Production helper (food)	.24	L
Sales, general (department store)	.20	L
Sewing machine operator, auto	.03	N
Solderer (production line)	.16	L
Telephone operator	.17	L
Teller (banking)	.18	L

	C Index	Prediction Satisfied
Drafter, architectural	.41	L
Electrician	.44	L
Engineer, civil	.45	L
Engineer, time study	.59	S
Farm equipment mechanic I	.52	S
Line-installer-repairer (tel)	.13	L
Machinist	.54	S
Programmer (bus., eng., sci.)	.65	S
Sheet metal worker	.50	S
Statistical machine servicer	.56	S
Writer, technical publications	.61	S
Cluster F (Alt-Com)	.21	L
Airplane flight attendant	.02	N
Clerk (gen. ofc., civil svc.)	.03	N
Dietitian	.56	S
Firefighter	.16	L
Librarian	.28	L
Medical technologist	.21	L
Nurse, professional	.15	L
Orderly	−.08	N
Physical therapist	.34	L
Police officer	.13	L
Receptionist, civil service	.29	L
Secretary (general office)	.26	L
Taxi driver	.12	L
Telephone installer	.42	L
Waiter/waitress	.18	L

Source: *A Psychological Theory of Work Adjustment*, by R. V. Dawis and L. H. Lofquist. Copyright © 1984, University of Minnesota Press. Reprinted by permission.

can be a particularly helpful resource. The counselor and client can examine occupations, perhaps taken from the Minnesota Importance Questionnaire report (Table 3-5), and ascertain the match between the client and the occupational group, a very thorough matching process. However, this is not the only way of looking at the correspondence between the individual and the working environment.

Although still in an experimental stage, the notion of adjustment style can be useful to the counselor. *Adjustment style* refers to how an individual relates to the occupational environment (Dawis & Lofquist, 1984). The concepts of flexibility, activeness, reactiveness, and perseverance all concern the relationship of the individual to the occupation. *Flexibility* refers to the ability of an individual to tolerate unpleasant or difficult aspects of the job. For example, individuals differ in terms of their flexibility in working in a cramped working environment or with an unpleasant superior. When individuals are faced with unpleasant or difficult work situations, they may try to change the environment—*activeness;* or make a change in themselves—*reactiveness.* For example, a person who must deal with an unpleasant superior may choose to confront the superior and try to resolve the discomfort (activeness). On the other hand, an individual may demonstrate reactiveness by trying to ignore the superior and by paying attention to other colleagues or the job itself. *Perseverance* refers to how long an individual can tolerate adverse conditions before changing jobs. For example, some people can persevere longer than others in cramped quarters or with an unpleasant superior. These concepts show how individuals deal with a conflict between themselves and their job.

These dimensions may be helpful in conceptualizing different solutions to irritating job circumstances. Lawson (1993) has had success in measuring three of these dimensions. She has developed an Inflexibility Scale, which measures the low end of the flexibility dimension, an Achievement Scale, which measures the high end of the activeness continuum, and a Reactiveness Scale, which measures some components of poor mental health. Studying activeness and reactiveness, Maximovitch (1998) found that mid-career adults were confident in changing themselves (reactive) when they decided to make changes in the environment. When the environment required change, they were active rather than reactive. Maximovitch suggests it was not where change occurred in a work situation that was most important, but where the request for change came from. In a study of developers of innovative software, Gallivan (1998) suggests that tolerance of ambiguity, resilience to stress, and innovative creative style add to work adjustment theory in predicting job satisfaction but not satisfactoriness. These studies help to explore the ways that individuals adjust to their environment and to expand work adjustment theory.

By matching the individual's abilities and values with Occupational Ability Patterns and Occupational Reinforcer Patterns, the counselor attempts to increase the likelihood of the client's future job satisfaction and satisfactoriness. This is a major focus of work adjustment theory. Thus, the counselor is trying to find not just an occupation that will be appealing to the client at the moment, but one that will lead to long-term satisfaction or job tenure.

By returning to our example of Winifred, we can illustrate this concept further:

CL: I'm wondering what other careers I can consider now that farming looks like it's going to be difficult for me.

CO: Let's look at your Minnesota Importance Questionnaire. [Winifred's scores are those reported in Table 3-5.] Note that it lists some occupations that it predicts would satisfy you (S) or are likely to satisfy you (L). Let's take a look at some of the S occupations. [The counselor wants to work with matches between the client's values as measured by the Minnesota Importance Questionnaire and the Occupational Reinforcer Patterns.]

CL: Oh, this is interesting. I don't think that I would want to be a claim adjuster. There isn't much call for that around here. Commercial artist—that's interesting. I guess that's a dream occupation. I don't think I have the ability to do that, however. Oh, look, farm equipment mechanic. I am doing that now, sort of. I know there is a demand for that around here. If I could do some light work, maybe that would work out for me.

CO: Well, that is one that we can look into. We may need to find out about some specific employers and the kind of work they do. [The counselor's concern is that the client's physical condition will preclude being a farm equipment mechanic. However, some employers may have opportunities for work that requires little lifting or standing.]

CL: I see time study engineer on there, too. I don't know what that is.

CO: We can find out more about it. We can use the *Dictionary of Occupational Titles* to tell us more about it.

CL: Wow! Programmer—I think that I would like that. I just don't think that I could go back to school. Also, I'm not sure whether I have the mathematical ability that would be necessary.

CO: Well, let's look into that. Let us see how your GATB scores compare to those of programmers. [The counselor then consults the Minnesota Occupational Classification System.]

CL: But what kind of schooling would I need?

CO: Let's look in the *Occupational Outlook Handbook*. [The client and the counselor look at it together. They see that there are several ways of entering the occupation of programmer.]

The client and counselor continue in this manner to investigate possible occupations that the client may consider. The counselor will ask the client to do more reading to find out more about occupations that seem initially attractive. While using a method of matching the client with potential occupations, the counselor has narrowed the number of potential occupations to be considered to about 15. The client and counselor not only will explore occupational information but will also examine educational opportunities, physical limitations, salary, and other issues that will affect the client's eventual choice.

Work adjustment theory has produced over 250 studies that lend support to its validity as an effective method of helping individuals with career choice and work adjustment problems. Research such as that done by Breeden (1993), which followed up 436 adults who had received career counseling, found that, after two years, those who had changed jobs and occupations were more satisfied after counseling than before counseling. Following up high school seniors eight years after graduation, Bizot and Goldman (1993) found that the match between the aptitude of the individual and the aptitude required by the job were good predictors of satisfactoriness and, to a somewhat smaller extent, job satisfaction. Bretz and Judge (1994) support work adjustment theory as useful in describing the fit between individuals and organizations, as well as between individuals and jobs. Work adjustment theory has also been found to predict satisfaction of 17 vocational needs for workers who are mentally challenged (Melchiori & Church, 1997). Such studies are examples of those that support the value of work adjustment theory in career counseling.

JOB ADJUSTMENT COUNSELING

Work adjustment theory can also be used to conceptualize the types of problems that an individual may have in adjusting to the job. An individual's skills may not yet have been developed sufficiently to meet the skill requirements of the job. Furthermore, the job may require skills that the individual is unable to develop because of lack of education or ability. A frequent problem is that an individual's values and needs are not met by the work environment. Another concern could be that the individual does not understand the reinforcer patterns of the work involved. Sometimes, dissatisfaction with the job is due not to the job itself but to problems outside work. For example, a person who is having difficulty at home may carry these problems into the workplace and become dissatisfied with the job as well.

When a client complains of problems at work, the basic approach is to make an assessment of the client's work personality and the working environment. Assessing the work values and needs of a client can be done by using the MIQ or, if this is not possible, by using the conceptual schema of the MIQ. Thus, a counselor can determine the significance of each of the 6 values (achievement, comfort, status, altruism, safety, and autonomy) during the counseling session. Furthermore, the counselor can determine which of the 20 needs that make up the 6 values are most relevant for the client, discussing the work environment in terms of the reinforcers offered. The counselor need not ask about each reinforcer specifically, but using the 20 reinforcers as a conceptual system can determine the correspondence between the individual's most important needs and the reinforcers offered by the job.

Similarly, using the nine abilities described by the GATB as a guide, the counselor can assess, in a general sense, the abilities that the client has and the occupational ability patterns of the job itself. Correspondence between the abilities of the client and the abilities required by the job can then be assessed. Although it is possible to use tests such as the GATB, the counselor may not choose to do so, as they take several hours to complete.

Possible solutions for problems can come by assessing the discrepancies between the individual's values and abilities and the ability patterns and reinforcer patterns of the job. By further understanding the reinforcer patterns of work, the client may be able to improve his or her satisfaction level. Another possibility is to make changes in the work itself so that the reinforcer patterns are altered. For example, a person who values independence may discuss with her supervisor ways in which she can work alone on the job. When these solutions fail, individuals can look for reinforcers outside the work environment. These might include hobbies and part-time or volunteer work. If none of these suggestions are appropriate, then an individual may consider changing jobs.

The next example shows how a counselor can use work adjustment theory to assist a client with job adjustment counseling. Nick is a 37-year-old Russian American construction worker who is experiencing increasing job dissatisfaction. He works for a construction firm that builds new houses. Doing a variety of construction tasks, especially carpentry, he has worked with the same crew of construction workers for the last five years. However, there have been some changes as the crew has grown or shrunk in size and workers have left for other jobs. Recently, a new supervisor has been assigned to the crew. Nick is finding that he dislikes the new supervisor and is considering quitting his job. He returns to talk to a Veterans Administration counselor whom he had talked to four years ago when he was having problems in his marriage. The following is an excerpt from their first session.

CL: My new supervisor, Wally, drives me nuts. I can't stand working with him. I never know where I stand. He never says anything. Other supervisors would give me direction. This guy just stands around like a two-by-four. I always knew where I stood with the other supervisors. With Wally I have no idea. I even ask him questions, and he doesn't give me much of an answer.

CO: Nick, tell me more about what you're doing at work. [The counselor hears that Nick values safety. He seems to feel that supervision, both human relations and technical, is lacking. The counselor wants to hear more before jumping to conclusions.]

CL: Well, we're building some real fancy homes now. We have to follow blueprints and make sure that everybody's doing what they're supposed to— that people aren't knocking into each other, getting in the way. It seems to be the same whether we're framing the house, putting up drywall, or whatever. All Wally does is stand around. Since I've been there a long time, some of the guys look to me for help. That is not my job.

CO: You don't want to be a supervisor? [Nick doesn't seem to want responsibility; he seems to place little value on autonomy, the opposite of safety. On the other hand, his supervisor seems to be reinforcing responsibility and not providing much supervision.]

    CL: No, I just want to do my job. I want to get paid. I don't want to do the same thing all the time. I don't mind keeping busy, but I'd just as soon do what I'm told.

    CO: Sounds as if before, you knew what to expect. You knew what to do and what you were going to do. Now you don't, and it's real frustrating. [Nick needs to be active, to do a variety of work, and to receive compensation. These indicate that Nick values comfort as opposed to achievement. A sense of achievement does not seem to be important to him.]

    CL: I want to figure out some way to be more comfortable. It's terrible not knowing what to do.

Nick and the counselor will explore how Nick's values of safety and comfort can be met on the job. One solution that may emerge from counseling is discussing strategies of receiving more direction from Wally. Another possibility would be to determine if Nick can transfer to a different construction crew. The counselor may also wish to consider Nick's adjustment style. Nick does not appear to be flexible. He does not seem to be able to tolerate much discomfort in the work environment. The counselor, along with Nick, may try to decide whether Nick is likely to be able to actively change his environment by talking to his supervisor or to react to the problem by focusing on out-of-job activities and his relationship with his coworkers. In this way, work adjustment theory provides a conceptualization system for the counselor to use to help Nick improve his current work adjustment.

ADJUSTMENT TO RETIREMENT

When individuals face retirement, they may encounter some problems that have components of both job adjustment and career selection. Often, individuals have maintained a satisfactory correspondence with the work environment. In other words, their work satisfaction is usually good, and their abilities and values match the abilities and reinforcers required and offered by the job. Now, the task is to find work in a "nonwork environment." If the individual has found the reinforcers offered by his or her current work to be satisfactory, then the counselor should help the individual find similar reinforcers in a nonwork environment.

To help the client, the counselor will need to make some assessment of skills and ability, as well as needs and values. This can be done by discussing in some detail the aspects of the current work that the individual finds particularly valuable. Then, the counselor and client will try to identify environments that will match the individual's needs and abilities. One difficulty for the counselor is that there is relatively little organized information about retirement activities. There are many books and pamphlets on career options and there are several occupational classification systems. However, no comparable system exists for retirement activities. Ideally, a counselor could assess the abilities and needs of a client who was about to retire and match them by using a system similar to the Minnesota Occupational Classification System. However, there is no system for classifying volunteer or retirement activities.

In addition to this concern is the changing nature of the retiree in his or her situation. As people age, their physical abilities change. Assessing these changes is an important aspect of helping the retiring worker. In addition, the financial needs of an individual must be assessed, as the need for earning income may continue. Furthermore, retirees may not be able to move from their current location to take advantage of a variety of community activities, hobbies, and part-time or volunteer work. Thus, there are more constraining factors in retirement counseling than in career decision making or job adjustment counseling. A case study will help to illustrate some of the factors involved in using work adjustment theory to counsel people on retirement issues.

Henrietta is a 64-year-old African American first-grade teacher living in New Orleans. She is widowed and living alone. Her two children are married and living out of state. Henrietta has been depressed for several months and has sought counseling because of the depression. As the counselor and Henrietta have talked, it has become clear that her impending retirement is disturbing her very much.

Henrietta has always enjoyed working with small children. Helping others is very important to her. One reason that she has enjoyed teaching so much is that most of her colleagues share her views. When her husband died 12 years ago, she became very active in her church. This activity helped her deal with her husband's death. Henrietta's religious values are strong. She not only is involved in attending services weekly but also participates in social service projects that her church undertakes. Henrietta wants to be busy. She has enjoyed teaching so much because it has given her an extraordinary sense of accomplishment. She has never felt that her aging has distanced her from her young students. Each year, she has looked forward to a new class.

The counselor recognizes how much Henrietta values altruism. She sees that the reinforcers offered by teaching first-grade children clearly match Henrietta's moral values and social service needs. Further, the counselor assesses how important achievement is to Henrietta. Their task is to discuss alternatives to teaching that will provide similar reinforcers. Because of the retirement plan of her school district, it is economically appropriate for Henrietta to retire at the age of 65. However, she feels a need to continue some work to supplement her income. Furthermore, she has many friends in her neighborhood and has strong ties with her church. She has no desire to move.

Many of the options that Henrietta and the counselor discuss have to do with part-time and volunteer activities that would satisfy her values of altruism and achievement. Some of these are working at, or possibly supervising, day care activities at a nearby church that is larger than her own. Other alternatives are to assist at a senior center in the neighborhood. Henrietta also considers work with the homeless but is concerned about transportation and safety. After talking with Henrietta for a little while, it is evident to the counselor why Henrietta has been rewarded by the school district for her teaching skills and her human relationship abilities. By concentrating on activities that would reinforce Henrietta's values of altruism and achievement, the counselor gets a sense of which activities would be appropriate to consider and which are likely to be unattractive. Henrietta feels helped by the counselor, because the suggested alternatives appear to meet her social service and achievement needs.

NEW DEVELOPMENTS

Recently, work adjustment theory has been applied to young gifted adolescents. Benbow and Lubinski have studied 13-year-old adolescents who have scored above 370 on the SAT verbal and 390 on the SAT math for some studies and above 430 on the SAT verbal and 500 on the SAT math for others (Achter, Lubinski, & Benbow, 1996; Achter, Lubinski, Benbow, & Eftekhari-Sanjoni, 1999; Benbow & Lubinski, 1997; Schmidt, Lubinski, & Benbow, 1998). Their research supports the view of Lubinski (2000) and Benbow and Lubinski (1997) that the concepts of satisfaction and satisfactoriness, crucial to work adjustment theory, can be applied to the educational adjustment and achievement of 13-year-old gifted students. They examine educational reinforcer patterns of gifted adolescents and describe how these young people are able to make educational and vocational decisions at an earlier age than their contemporaries by referring to concepts basic to work adjustment theory. Studying 13-year-old gifted adolescents over a 20-year period, Benbow, Lubinski, and their colleagues find the theory of work adjustment helpful in understanding the educational and vocational choices of these talented students. They believe this is because work adjustment theory considers abilities (satisfactoriness as measured by educational achievement measure) and preferences (satisfaction as measured by interest and values inventories). Lubinski and Benbow (2000) suggest counselors reinforce the effective behaviors of young adolescents rather than reinforce the feelings of these clients, which may be more vague and diffuse.

THE ROLE OF TESTING

Although the preceding examples show that work adjustment theory can be used in counseling without testing, tests are an extremely important component of work adjustment theory. Particularly with regard to career selection, testing is essential. Furthermore, the development of psychometric instruments has gone hand in hand with the development of work adjustment theory. Of all the instruments developed by the Work Adjustment Project, the Minnesota Importance Questionnaire is the one most likely to be used by counselors. Other instruments have been developed to test the theory: the Minnesota Job Description Questionnaire, the Min-

Satisfaction

	Low	Moderate	High
Low			
Moderate		Creativity Responsibility Independence Compensation	Activity
High	Ability utilization Achievement		

Importance (vertical axis label)

Figure 3-1   The importance × satisfaction grid, including Winifred's data for seven vocational needs. (Adapted from Thompson and Blain, 1992.)

nesota Satisfaction Questionnaire, the Minnesota Satisfactoriness Scales, and a biographical information form. Described briefly by Dawis and Lofquist (1984), these instruments, as well as other research, are the subject of 30 monographs published by the University of Minnesota over a period of more than 35 years. Research on psychometric qualities of these instruments continue to be done (Eggerth, 1998), as do psychometric analysis of concepts such as tenure (Myors, 1996). This emphasis on the importance of testing in theory development carries over to Dawis and Lofquist's (1984) approach to counseling. More than other theorists, even other trait and factor theorists, Dawis and Lofquist emphasize the importance of measuring an individual's traits and matching them with information about occupations. Unlike most tests and inventories, their materials are not published commercially, but they can be purchased from Vocational Psychology Research, Department of Psychology, University of Minnesota.

These instruments can be used in combination with each other. For example, Thompson and Blain (1992) describe how a grid can be used to present information from the Minnesota Importance Questionnaire (MIQ). They suggest using a 3 × 3 grid that combines MIQ and MSQ data in low, moderate, and high categories (Figure 3-1). In this way, counselors can group the importance of the 20 client needs and the degree to which they are being satisfied into 9 areas.

The use of this grid can be illustrated by applying it to Winifred, discussed earlier. Winifred has studied computer programming and has worked at a grain company as a programmer for five months. She tells the counselor that she has enjoyed learning programming but does not find her current job fulfilling. The counselor asks her to take the MSQ, and then writes in seven of her highest MIQ needs (see Table 3-2, p. 73) in a 3 × 3 grid, placing them in boxes depending on Winifred's MSQ scores (Figure 3-1). Winifred discusses these scores with her counselor. Her frustration with the lack of challenge in her current job becomes clearer. Although she enjoys keeping busy (activity), she feels she is basically rewriting programs used in the first few months of her job. She does not feel that she is accomplishing very much (achievement) or using her new skills (ability utilization), needs that are very important to her. Going over the grid helps Winifred decide that it is important that she get her supervisor to assign her more varied and challenging tasks.

THE ROLE OF OCCUPATIONAL INFORMATION

Occupational information presents a particular challenge for the counselor using work adjustment theory. Normally, a counselor using this theory would make use of the MIQ and the GATB. As shown earlier, each of these instruments provides a list of occupations that fit occupational patterns. In addition, the Minnesota Occupational Classification System lists Occupational Ability Patterns and Occupational Reinforcer Patterns for more than 1700 occupations. Therefore, if the counselor is to use this system, it is important to have information available that explains these occupations. Perhaps the most essential reference is the *Dictionary of Occupational Titles,* which lists definitions of 12,000 occupations. Furthermore, pamphlets and books that more fully explain occupations are necessary so that the client can learn more about any occupation that is suggested by the results of the MIQ and the GATB. Although it is not necessary for counselors to memorize the descriptions of each of the 1769 occupations in the Minnesota Occupational Classification System, the system is so specific in its recommendations of occupations for individual clients that a wide knowledge of occupational information is extremely helpful to the counselor.

APPLYING THE THEORY TO WOMEN AND CULTURALLY DIVERSE POPULATIONS

Group differences have not been a focus of work adjustment theory. Dawis and Lofquist (1984) have focused on the large differences within groups, rather than the small differences that may exist between groups. For example, there is a very wide range of scores on the achievement scale for men and for women (within groups), but there are very small differences between men and women on the achievement scale. Although Rounds, Dawis, and Lofquist (1979) found some differences between males and females on various MIQ needs, Flint (1980) and Borgen et al. (1968b) found few differences. Gay, Weiss, Hendel, Dawis, and Lofquist (1971) found that women scored higher than males on the following needs: achievement, activity, company policies and practices, coworkers, independence, and working conditions. Men scored higher than women on advancement, authority, creativity, responsibility, security, social status, and supervision. Fitzgerald and Rounds (1993) conclude that few gender differences are found in variables related to work adjustment theory.

The GATB manual (U.S. Department of Labor, 1982) shows that boys score higher than girls on spatial ability, but lower than girls on form perception, clerical ability, eye/hand coordination, and finger dexterity. A review of other research shows very minor differences in the cognitive abilities of men and of women (Fitzgerald & Rounds, 1993). Gustafson (1997) suggests that cognitive factors can be helpful in predicting intrinsic job satisfaction. Although there are some differences between men and women in their abilities and preferences for needs, the implications for counseling are negligible. The information available for women and men from the Minnesota Occupational Classification System is identical.

Fitzgerald and Rounds (1993) suggest how work adjustment theory can be expanded to encompass two issues related to women: integrating work and family and sexual harassment. For example, they suggest that "variables such as convenient and flexible hours of work, or benefits" (e.g., leave for a sick child) (p. 343) could be added to the theory's list of needs. Further needs such as "compensation" could be broadened to include benefits such as parental leave for a sick child or child care at the workplace. Regarding sexual harassment, they suggest that the need for "company policies and practices" could include how clear organizations make guidelines on sexual harassment and how well they are implemented. Furthermore, measures of satisfaction that include questions about sexual harassment or measures of sexual harassment could be included to broaden the theory. Another suggestion, focusing on the environment rather than the person, is to study how sexual harassment affects the workplace.

Dawis (1992) is clear in stating that work adjustment focuses on individual differences in needs, values, abilities, and skills. More specifically, Dawis (1994) says that "gender, ethnicity, national origin, religion, age, sexual orientation, and disability status are seen as inaccurate and unreliable bases for estimating the skills, abilities, needs, values, personality styles, and adjustment style of a particular person" (p. 41). Adding to this view, Rounds and Hesketh (1994) suggest ways in which work adjustment theory could address discrimination based on race or sex. They say that work needs and values could be broadened to include statements that address fairness issues, such as "supervisors create an environment of mutual respect," "my supervisors and coworkers treat me fairly," "promotions are based on merit," and "company policies concerning discriminatory practices are enforced" (p. 184). Such statements give counselors ideas on how work adjustment issues can be conceptualized when clients discuss problems at work related to discrimination by coworkers, supervisors, or customers. Bowman (1998) gives a case example of how work adjustment theory can be useful in helping a woman who experienced racism at work. These writings provide suggestions on how work adjustment theory can be used with culturally diverse populations.

COUNSELOR ISSUES

Lofquist and Dawis have applied work adjustment theory to nonwork areas of life—called person-environment-correspondence theory—in their book *Essentials of Person-Environment-Correspondence Counseling* (1991). Dawis and Lofquist (1993) and Lofquist and Dawis (1991) show the value of expanding work adjustment theory in a broader approach to counseling. Lofquist and Dawis (undated) suggest that it is helpful for counselors to see themselves, as well as their clients, as environments. Both the client and the counselor can serve as reinforcers for each other, just as a job environment can serve as a reinforcer for a worker. Dawis (2000a) suggests that it is helpful to attend to the counselor's satisfaction and the reinforcement that the counselor gets from working with the client. Lofquist and Dawis suggest that, in the course of training, counselors should identify their own needs and values. Awareness of their needs and values can help counselors understand the effect that they can have on a client. In a counseling session, a counselor should be able to identify the needs of a client. For example, if a counselor has a high need for social service (doing things for others) and the client has a high need for responsibility (deciding on one's own), the altruistic counselor may be frustrated. Realization that there are differences between the values of the counselor (altruism) and the reinforcement pattern of the client (responsibility) will help the counselor be less frustrated and more effective. Examining another example, a client who has a strong safety value may be frustrated by a counselor who uses an unstructured style. Lofquist and Dawis (undated) believe that it is necessary for the counselor to identify basic abilities and reinforcers within himself or herself and the client so that effective counseling can take place. A key characteristic for a counselor is flexibility. It is important for the counselor to be able to adapt to the environment of the client so that the client's needs can be met. This can be done best when a counselor has knowledge about his or her needs and response requirements so that the counselor can suspend, when necessary, his or her own needs, to meet those of the client.

SUMMARY

The work adjustment theory of Lofquist and Dawis is notable because of its emphasis on specifying the traits and factors of an individual and matching them with job requirements and reinforcers. Work adjustment theory is made up of 18 theoretical propositions that have been supported by research (Dawis & Lofquist, 1984; Lofquist & Dawis, 1991). The focus of the theory is the prediction of adjustment to work. For Dawis and Lofquist, an individual's abilities and values can be predictive of work adjustment and length of time on a particular job, if the ability requirements and reinforcer pattern of the job are known. A major contribution of work adjustment theory is the development of the Minnesota Importance Questionnaire, which measures an individual's work needs. Combined with information about abilities, scores on the MIQ can be matched with Occupational Ability Patterns and Occupational Reinforcer Patterns. This matching yields specific occupations for an individual to consider in making a job choice. Broader than many career development theories, work adjustment theory has implications not only for career selection but also for a great variety of other counseling situations. Two that were discussed in this chapter were job adjustment counseling and retirement counseling. More than any other theory, work adjustment theory represents a clear application of trait and factor theory.

References

Achter, J. A., Lubinski, D., & Benbow, C. P. (1996). Multipotentiality among intellectually gifted: "It was never there and already it's vanishing." *Journal of Counseling Psychology, 43,* 65–76.

Achter, J. A., Lubinski, D., Benbow, C. P., & Eftekhari-Sanjoni, E. (1999). Assessing vocational preferences among gifted adolescents adds incremental validity to abilities. *Journal of Educational Psychology, 91,* 777–789.

Benbow, C. P., & Lubinski, D. (1997). Intellectually talented children: How can we best meet their needs? In N. Colangelo & G. A. Davis (Eds.), *Handbook of gifted education* (2nd ed., pp. 155–169). Boston: Allyn & Bacon.

Bizot, E. B., & Goldman, S. H. (1993). Prediction of satisfactoriness and satisfaction: An 8-year follow-up. *Journal of Vocational Behavior, 43,* 19–29.

Borgen, F. H., Weiss, D. J., Tinsley, H. E. A., Dawis, R. V., & Lofquist, L. H. (1968a). *Minnesota Job Description Questionnaire.* Minneapolis: University of Minnesota, Psychology Department, Vocational Psychology Research.

Borgen, F. H., Weiss, D. J., Tinsley, H. E. A., Dawis, R. V., & Lofquist, L. H. (1968b). Occupational reinforcer patterns. *Minnesota Studies in Vocational Rehabilitation, 24.*

Bowman, S. L. (1998). Minority women and career adjustment. *Journal of Career Adjustment, 6,* 417–431.

Breeden, S. A. (1993). Job and occupational change as a function of occupational correspondence and job satisfaction. *Journal of Vocational Behavior, 43,* 30–45.

Bretz, R. D., Jr., & Judge, T. A. (1994). Person-organizations fit and the theory of work adjustment. Implications for satisfaction, tenure, and career success. *Journal of Vocational Behavior, 44,* 32–54.

Dawis, R. V. (1992). Individual differences tradition in counseling psychology. *Journal of Counseling Psychology, 39,* 7–19.

Dawis, R. V. (1994). The theory of work adjustment as convergent theory. In M. L. Savickas & R. W. Lent (Eds.), *Convergence in career development theories* (pp. 33–44). Palo Alto, CA: Consulting Psychologists Press.

Dawis, R. V. (2000a). The person environment tradition in counseling psychology. In W. E. Martin & J. L. Swartz (Eds.), *Person-environment psychology: Clinical and counseling applications for adolescents and adults* (pp. 91–111). Mahwah, NJ: Erlbaum.

Dawis, R. V. (2000b). Work adjustment theory. In A. E. Kazdin (Ed.), *Encyclopedia of psychology*. New York: Oxford University Press.

Dawis, R. V., Dohm, T. E., & Jackson, C. R. S. (1993). Describing work environments as reinforcer systems: Reinforcement schedules versus reinforcer classes. *Journal of Vocational Behavior, 43,* 5–18.

Dawis, R. V., England, G. W., & Lofquist, L. H. (1964). A theory of work adjustment. *Minnesota Studies in Vocational Rehabilitation, 15.*

Dawis, R. V., & Lofquist, L. H. (1984). *A psychological theory of work adjustment.* Minneapolis: University of Minnesota Press.

Dawis, R. V., & Lofquist, L. H. (1993). From TWA to PEC. *Journal of Vocational Behavior, 43,* 113–121.

Dawis, R. V., Lofquist, L. H., & Weiss, D. J. (1968). A theory of work adjustment (a revision). *Minnesota Studies in Vocational Rehabilitation, 23.*

Eggerth, D. E. (1998, March). A rescaling of the instrumentation of the Minnesota Theory of Work Adjustment: An application of the Bradly-Terry-Luce method for paired companion data. *Dissertation Abstracts International: Section B: The Sciences and Engineering.* Vol. 58 (9-B): 5184.

Fitzgerald, L., & Rounds, J. (1993). Women and work: Theory encounters reality. In W. Walsh & S. Osipow (Eds.), *Career counseling for women* (pp. 327–354). Hillsdale, NJ: Erlbaum.

Flint, P. L. (1980). *Sex differences in perceptions of occupational reinforcers.* Unpublished doctoral dissertation, University of Minnesota.

Gallivan, M. J. (1998, May). Reskilling IS professionals: Individual and organizational adaptation to software process innovations. *Dissertation Abstracts International: Section A: Humanities and Social Sciences.* Vol. 58 (11-A): 4343.

Gay, E. G., Weiss, D. J., Hendel, D. D., Dawis, R. V., & Lofquist, L. H. (1971). Manual for the Minnesota Importance Questionnaire. *Minnesota Studies in Vocational Rehabilitation, 28.*

Gustafson, S. A. (1997). Cognitive processes as dispositional factor in job satisfaction. *Dissertation Abstracts International: Section B: The Sciences and Engineering.* Vol. 57 (7-B): 4760.

Lawson, L. (1993). Theory of work adjustment personality constructs. *Journal of Vocational Behavior, 43,* 46–57.

Lofquist, L. H., & Dawis, R. V. (undated). *Client and counselor as environments: Implications for counseling.* Unpublished manuscript, University of Minnesota, Psychology Department.

Lofquist, L. H., & Dawis, R. V. (1969). *Adjustment to work.* New York: Appleton-Century-Crofts.

Lofquist, L. H., & Dawis, R. V. (1984). Research on work adjustment and satisfaction: Implications for career counseling. In S. Brown & R. Lent (Eds.), *Handbook of counseling psychology* (pp. 216–237). New York: Wiley.

Lofquist, L. H., & Dawis, R. V. (1991). *Essentials of person-environment-correspondence counseling.* Minneapolis: University of Minnesota.

Lubinski, D. (2000). Assessing individual differences in human behavior: "Sinking shafts at a few critical points." *Annual Review of Psychology, 41,* 405–444.

Lubinski, D., & Benbow, C. P. (2000). States of excellence. *American Psychologist, 53,* 1–14.

Maximovich, T. M. (1998, March). The dynamics of person-environment fit: Active and reactive responses within the theory of work adjustment. *Dissertation Abstracts International: Section B: The Sciences and Engineering.* Vol. 58 (9-B): 5716.

Melchiori, L. G., & Church, A. T. (1997). Vocational needs and satisfaction of supported employees: The applicability of the theory of work adjustment. *Journal of Vocational Behavior, 50,* 401–417.

Myors, B. (1996, December). Utility analysis based on tenure. *Dissertation Abstracts International: Section B: The Sciences and Engineering.* Vol. 57 (6-B): 4071.

Rounds, J. B. (1990). The comparative and combined utility of work value and interest data in career counseling with adults. *Journal of Vocational Behavior, 37,* 32–45.

Rounds, J. B., Dawis, R. V., & Lofquist, L. H. (1979). Life history correlates of vocational needs for a female adult sample. *Journal of Counseling Psychology, 26,* 487–496.

Rounds, J. B., Henly, G. A., Dawis, R. V., Lofquist, L. H., & Weiss, D. J. (1981). *Manual for the Minnesota Importance Questionnaire.* Minneapolis: University of Minnesota, Psychology Department, Work Adjustment Project.

Rounds, J. B., & Hesketh, B. (1994). Emerging directions of person-environment fit. In M. L. Savickas & R. W. Lent (Eds.), *Convergence in career development theories* (pp. 177–186). Palo Alto, CA: Consulting Psychologists Press.

Schmidt, D. B., Lubinski, D., & Benbow, C. P. (1998). Validity of assessing educational-vocational preference dimensions among intellectually talented 13-year-olds. *Journal of Counseling Psychology, 45,* 436–453.

Thompson, J. M., & Blain, M. D. (1992). Presenting feedback on the Minnesota Importance Questionnaire and the Minnesota Satisfaction Questionnaire. *The Career Development Quarterly, 41,* 62–66.

U.S. Department of Labor. (1982). *Manual for the USES General Aptitude Test Battery: Section II. Occupational aptitude pattern structure.* Washington, DC: U.S. Government Printing Office.

Holland's Theory
of Types

It is John Holland's view that career choice and career adjustment represent an extension of a person's personality. People express themselves, their interests and values, through their work choices and experience. In his theory, Holland assumes that people's impressions and generalizations about work, which he refers to as *stereotypes*, are generally accurate. By studying and refining these stereotypes, Holland assigns both people and work environments to specific categories.

Holland (1966, 1973, 1985a, 1992, 1997) has published five books that explain his typological theory. Each book represents an update and a further-refined version of earlier work in the development of his theory. The August 1999 issue of *The Journal of Vocational Behavior* contains 12 articles which describe John Holland's 40-year contribution to career development theory. Two psychological inventories were important in the development of his theory: the Vocational Preference Inventory (Holland, 1985b) and the Self-Directed Search (Holland, 1994). These instruments, in different ways, measure self-perceived competencies and interests, which are an assessment of an individual's personality. Holland (Holland, 1997) recognizes that his theory can account for only a portion of the variables that underlie career selection. He is clear in stating that his theoretical model can be affected by age, gender, social class, intelligence, and education. With that understood, he goes on to specify how the individual and the environment interact with each other through the development of six types: Realistic, Investigative, Artistic, Social, Enterprising, and Conventional. Both individuals and environments consist of a combination of types.

THE SIX TYPES

In the following pages, each of the six work environments (Gottfredson & Richards, 1999) is described, followed by a description of the personality type of the person who matches that environment. Next, behavior that can be expected from each type in the context of counseling is discussed. Other important concepts, such as congruence and differentiation, to be discussed later, describe the interaction between the person and the environment. When describing real people and work environments, which are never purely of one type, Holland uses a combination of three types, also discussed later. The relationships among the six types are illustrated in Figure 4-1. The placement of the types on the hexagon is purposeful; the arrangement is explained later when the concept of consistency is described.

Realistic

The Realistic Environment   The Realistic (R) environment makes physical demands on the person. Such work settings have tools, machines, or animals that the individual manipulates. In such a setting, individuals are required to have technical competencies that will allow them to do such things as fix machines, repair electronic equipment, drive cars or trucks, herd animals, or deal with other physical aspects of their environment. The ability to work with things is more important than the ability to interact with other people. Construction sites, factories, and auto garages are examples of environments that provide machinery or other things for Realistic people to master. Some Realistic environments require a great deal of physical agility or strength, such as roofing, outdoor painting, and pipe fitting. These environments may be hazardous and may produce more physical illness or accidents than other work environments.

The Realistic Personality Type   Realistic people are likely to enjoy using tools or machines in their hobbies or work. They tend to seek to develop competencies in such areas as plumbing, roofing, electrical and automotive repair, farming, and other technical disciplines. They are apt to like courses that are very practical and teach the use of mechanical or physical skills. Realistic people are likely to have little tolerance of abstract and theoretical descriptions. Often, they approach problems, whether mechanical or personal, in a practical or problem-solving manner. They are likely to value

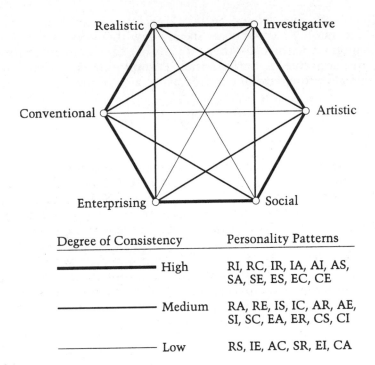

Degree of Consistency	Personality Patterns
━━━━━━━━━━ High	RI, RC, IR, IA, AI, AS, SA, SE, ES, EC, CE
──────────── Medium	RA, RE, IS, IC, AR, AE, SI, SC, EA, ER, CS, CI
───── Low	RS, IE, AC, SR, EI, CA

Figure 4-1   The relationships among Holland types. (Adapted from *Holland's Hexagon, ACT Research Report No. 29*, by J. L. Holland, D. R. Whitney, N. S. Cole, and J. M. Richards, Jr. Copyright © 1969 The American College Testing Program. Reprinted by permission.)

money, power, and status, while placing a lesser value on human relationships.

Behavior of Realistic Clients   In the counseling situation, Realistic clients are likely to expect specific suggestions and advice to solve their career problems—a practical solution. Such clients may be somewhat resistant to expressing their feelings about their career choice and prefer to move directly to an answer to the problem of choosing a career. When discussing their activities, they are likely to enjoy talking about such activities as hunting, fishing, and fixing cars. They are apt to discuss things they have done that show an expertise in using tools. They may also talk about specific possessions, such as cars, radios, or other machinery, with which they like to tinker.

Women may encounter more resistance and harassment from males in a Realistic environment than in any other of the six types. Since many of the activities and participants in the Realistic environment tend to be traditionally masculine, Realistic women may encounter a considerable amount of sexism in trying to enter a Realistic occupation such as auto mechanics, coal mining, or roofing. Women who have received encouragement from their fathers and brothers in the development of Realistic competencies may become hurt and angry when they encounter resistance from men in a Realistic working environment. Dealing with such issues requires that the counselor be sensitive to and support women who have Realistic interests and competencies. Still, not all Realistic occupations present such problems. Many occupations have significant Realistic components, yet are not traditionally masculine. Examples include silversmith, dressmaker, floral designer, and inventory clerk.

Investigative

The Investigative Environment   The Investigative (I) environment is one in which people search for solutions to problems through mathematical and scientific interests and competencies. In such a situation, people are encouraged to use complex and abstract thinking to solve problems creatively. Examples of occupations that offer the opportunity to use analytical thinking skills are computer programmer, physician, mathematician, biologist, science teacher, veterinarian, and research and development manager. In each of these environments, cautious and critical thinking is valued. Individuals are likely to need to use logic and precise methodical thinking in order to find solutions to problems in these fields. These jobs require that people use their intellect to work independently to solve problems. They are not required or encouraged to use human relations skills to solve problems, nor are they likely to need to use machines. For example, a computer programmer uses logic to figure out solutions to problems (an Investigative environment), whereas the computer technician works with machinery and may assemble it or fix it (a Realistic environment).

The Investigative Personality Type   The Investigative person is likely to enjoy puzzles and challenges that require the use of intellect. Such a person is apt to enjoy learning and to feel confident about his or her ability to solve mathematical and scientific problems. Such people often enjoy reading about science and discussing scientific issues. They seek to work independently to solve problems such as mathematical or scientific questions. They are likely to enjoy courses in math, physics, chemistry, biology, geology, and other physical or biological sciences. They are not likely to enjoy supervising other people or dealing directly with personal problems, but they may enjoy analyzing or searching for solutions to psychological problems.

Behavior of Investigative Clients   Clients who are primarily Investigative in their personality tend to enjoy the challenge of an unanswered question. They are often excited by a problem and want to work hard to find a solution even though there may be relatively little financial or other reward. When it comes to solving a career problem, they may wish to solve it themselves and to approach it from a rational rather than emotional point of view. When the career problem itself is seen as a challenge, they may feel better if they view the counselor as a fellow investigator rather than as an expert who is telling them what to do.

Artistic

The Artistic Environment   The Artistic (A) environment is one that is free and open, encouraging creativity and personal expression. Such an environment offers much freedom in developing products and answers. Examples of occupations in which people can use creative and unconventional ways to express themselves are musician, fine artist, and freelance writer. Such settings allow people to dress the way they wish, keep few appointments, and structure their own time. These work environments encourage personal and emotional expression rather than logical expression. If tools are used, they are used to express oneself (for example, a clarinet or a paintbrush) rather than as a means to complete a task (for example, an electric drill or a wrench).

The Artistic Personality Type   The Artistic person likes the opportunity to express himself or herself in a free and unsystematic way, creating music, art, or writing. Such people may use instruments to do this, such as a violin, the voice, sculpting tools, or a word processor. They are likely to want to improve their ability in language, art, music, or writing. Originality and creativity are particularly important in expression. To use a paint-by-numbers kit would be deeply offensive to an Artistic type, who needs and desires the opportunity to express herself or himself in a free and open manner. A pure Artistic type would dislike technical writing and would prefer writing fiction or poetry.

Behavior of Artistic Clients   In a counseling session, Artistic clients often make clear how important art, music, or writing is in their lives. They may prefer a nonstructured counseling approach to one that uses worksheets and written materials. They may enjoy discussing the expression and development of an Artistic product. They may also like to comment on or criticize the products of others. When talking to Artistic people, it becomes clear that their excitement centers on their creative activity. They may enjoy using humor or other methods of expression to show that they are unique and not like other clients. Their expression may be unclear or may appear disordered. Often, they discuss their own thinking and creative process. More than any other type, Artistic people are likely to rely on emotions in their discussion of career issues and to see the choice process as an affective rather than a logical one.

Social

The Social Environment The Social (S) environment is one that encourages people to be flexible and understanding of each other, where people can work with others through helping with personal or career problems, teaching others, affecting others spiritually, and being socially responsible. The Social environment emphasizes human values such as being idealistic, kind, friendly, and generous. These ideals most commonly exist in the education, social service, and mental health professions. Examples of these occupations are elementary school teacher, special education teacher, high school teacher, marriage counselor, counseling psychologist, speech therapist, school superintendent, and psychiatrist.

The Social Personality Type The Social person is interested in helping people through teaching, helping with personal or vocational problems, or providing personal services. Social people enjoy solving problems through discussion and teamwork rather than through delegation. Preferring to talk and resolve complex problems that may be ethical or idealistic in nature, they often choose to avoid working with machines. They seek out environments where they can use verbal and social skills, such as in education, welfare, and mental health.

Behavior of Social Clients In a counseling situation, Social people express their idealism, wanting to help others through religion, politics, or social service. Often altruistic, they are more concerned with contributing to a better world than with economic achievement for themselves. They are likely to value informal activities that they have done such as teaching young children and helping friends with personal problems. When talking with a counselor, they may be interested in the counselor's profession (a Social environment) and may be appreciative of the counselor's help. Because it is in their nature to be helpful, they may wish to cooperate with their counselor's plans to assist them. Also, their Social nature may make them good candidates for career group counseling, where they may enjoy the opportunity to help others. On the other hand, they may be too verbal, since they value talking, making it difficult for the counselor to assist them and other career group members in dealing with questions of career planning.

Enterprising

The Enterprising Environment The Enterprising (E) environment is one where people manage and persuade others in order to attain organizational or personal goals. These are situations where finance and economic issues are of prime importance and risks may be taken to achieve rewards. In such an environment, people tend to be self-confident, sociable, and assertive.

It's an environment where promotion and power are important, and persuasion and selling take place. Examples of Enterprising environments are sales work, buying, business management, restaurant management, politics, real estate, the stock market, insurance, and lobbying. All of these environments provide the opportunity for power, status, and wealth.

The Enterprising Personality Type   The acquisition of wealth is particularly important for Enterprising people. They enjoy being with others and like to use verbal skills in order to sell, persuade, or lead. They tend to be assertive and popular, trying to take on leadership positions. They enjoy working with people but prefer to persuade and manage rather than to help.

Behavior of Enterprising Clients   Enterprising people may present themselves in a self-assured manner. They may appear to be more self-confident than they feel. Some Enterprising people may be quite open about their goal to accomplish wealth, whereas others may be very reluctant to admit to a goal that they see as socially inappropriate. Like Social types, they may be very verbal with a counselor and willing to talk about past accomplishments. Unlike Social types, they will value convincing and persuading others rather than helping others. In part, because of their self-confidence, Enterprising types may have difficulty seeing their competencies accurately and may overestimate their abilities. Enterprising types may be impatient with entry-level positions or occupations that don't lead quickly to the accumulation of wealth or power. They are also likely to experience conflict with other Enterprising types who are competing for both power and money.

Conventional

The Conventional Environment   Organization and planning best describe the Conventional (C) environment. Much of the Conventional environment is an office environment, where one needs to keep records, file papers, copy materials, and organize reports. In addition to written material, the Conventional environment includes mathematical materials, such as bookkeeping and accounting records. Word processing, calculating, and copy machines are the type of equipment that is found in a Conventional environment. Competencies that are needed to work well in a Conventional environment are clerical skills, an ability to organize, dependability, and an ability to follow directions.

The Conventional Personality Type   The Conventional person is one who values money, being dependable, and the ability to follow rules and orders. These people prefer being in control of situations and not dealing with ambiguous requests. They enjoy an office environment where their values of earning money and following rules, regulations, and guidelines can be met. Their strengths are their clerical and numerical ability, which they use to solve straightforward problems in their environment. Their relationships with people tend to be directed toward accomplishing tasks and establishing an organized approach to problems.

Behavior of Conventional Clients   In a counseling situation, Conventional people are likely to present themselves as organized, yet dependent on others for direction. They may have difficulty being open to examining new occupations or career paths on their own initiative. However, they are often proud of their organizational ability in high school extracurricular activities and in business activities. If they have had work experience, they are likely to have had the opportunity to work in an office and to have enjoyed that. If they have worked in environments that are not Conventional, they are likely to have been frustrated by the lack of organization in these environments and will have tried to bring some type of order into their working world. When they explore occupational possibilities, they are most likely to be excited and interested in jobs in financial institutions, such as banks, or in occupations where they can use counting skills, such as tax expert, inventory controller, and data processor. They are also likely to be interested in financial and accounting analysis. Other personality types are likely to see these jobs as routine or boring. Conventional types appreciate the opportunity to organize and regulate.

COMBINATIONS OF TYPES

Clearly, no real work environment is purely of one type. Rather, most working situations involve a combination of types. When describing occupational environments in *The Occupations Finder* (Holland, 1994) and training environments in *The Educational Opportunities Finder* (Rosen, Holmberg, & Holland, 1994), which accompanies his *Self-Directed Search Professional User's Guide* (Holland, Powell, & Fritzsche, 1994), Holland uses a three-letter code to describe each of these environments. Holland's *The Occupations Finder* lists three-letter codes for 1156 occupations, and *The Educational Opportunities Finder* lists over 750 programs of study. For example, a bookkeeping environment is not one that is strictly Conventional. It is primarily Conventional, secondly Investigative, and thirdly Social, summarized as CIS. Environments differ in terms of how much they are dominated by one or two types. For example, the bookkeeper may work in a primarily Conventional environment, but a detective may work in an environment that is Social, Realistic, and Enterprising. It would be Social because of the need to help other people; Realistic because of the importance of driving cars, using guns and fingerprint material, and so forth; and Enterprising because of the persuasiveness and assertiveness that are required. Another book, the *Dictionary of Holland Occupational Codes* (Gottfredson & Holland, 1996a), lists more than 12,000 occupations that have been coded by translating the U.S. Department of Labor system of DOT codes into Holland codes. Thus, it is possible to look up any occupation and determine its three-letter code.

Just as no single environment can be described by one code, it is rare for a person to fit only one Holland psychological type. Through their experiences in school, with hobbies, and with parents, people are exposed to a large number of situations that help them become familiar with certain types of environments. For example, repairing a car exposes one to a Realistic environment, being involved in clubs at school is likely to involve one in a Social environment, and drawing and painting are examples of an Artistic environment. As people are exposed to these activities, they become more interested in certain environments and develop many specific abilities. They become better able to be successful in some environments than in others. As they do this, certain of the Holland types become stronger than others, and their personality type becomes more definite.

These types can be measured by instruments Holland has developed such as the Vocational Preference Inventory (VPI) or the Self-Directed Search (SDS). In addition, other inventories, such as the Strong Interest Inventory (SII), use Holland's types and can be used to code the interests of individuals according to a three-letter Holland code.

When listening to a client describe his or her career history, it is helpful to think in terms of Holland's six types of people and environments. As a client describes a particular experience, a fit between personality type and interest and experience is likely to become apparent. As the client moves on to another topic, another type is likely to emerge. In this way, the counselor can keep a rough count or impression of the dominant personality types. For example, as a client describes her interest in military activities and parachuting, the counselor conceptualizes these activities in terms of Holland's Realistic type. When she talks about her interest in biology class in high school and her desire to take an advanced course in biology, the notion of interests and abilities in Investigative activities arises. As counselors become more familiar with Holland's theory, it is possible that the mention of activities will "ring a bell" and they will recall the appropriate type that the person is fitting at the moment. For the beginning counselor, it is often necessary to consciously memorize the Holland types and bring them into active memory to compare the type with the activity being discussed by the client. Sometimes, it is helpful to explain Holland's system to clients, providing them with an opportunity to organize their thoughts about themselves and the world of work.

EXPLANATORY CONSTRUCTS

Four important constructs for conceptualizing and using Holland's types in counseling are congruence, differentiation, consistency, and identity. These refer to the relationship between the personality and the environment (congruence), the relationship between and the relative importance of types (differentiation), and the relationship of the types to each other (consistency). In addition, the concept of identity, which is less directly tied to types, is important for counselors to be familiar with.

Congruence

The term *congruence* refers to the relationship of the personality to the environment. The more similar the personality is to the environment, the more congruent the relationship. Social types tend to enjoy working in a Social environment; Investigative types prefer the Investigative environment. Thus, a Social type working in a sales environment (Enterprising) might find the environment incongruent. An Investigative type working in an Artistic environment might also find that incongruent and would be frustrated by the ambiguity and flexibility that are required in the production of artistic or musical products. Using Holland's three-letter code, an SRA personality would be most congruent with an SRA environment and slightly less congruent with an SRC environment. Likewise, an SIC environment would be more incongruent, and an ICR environment would be quite incongruent with an SRA type of person. Thus, congruence decreases as the similarity of the three-letter code of the person and of the environment decreases.

Counseling Implications   The concept of congruence is essential in counseling, where it can provide an important goal. A client wishing to make a career choice will want to find an environment that is congruent with his or her personality. It is the counselor's job to assess the client's personality and assist in finding environments that will fit the counselee according to the Holland type. Working toward the discovery of congruent occupations becomes the major purpose of career-counseling sessions. The counselor thinks about the client and possible career choices in terms of the six Holland types and the degree to which they match.

Example of Congruence   Jane, a white high school sophomore, has a counseling session with her guidance counselor that includes this dialogue:

CL: Recently, I was working with a friend who was making a project for her high school science fair. It got kind of messy—we spent a lot of time sorting ants into different piles and developing different terrains—but it was a lot of fun. I was surprised how the time just went by so quickly. In fact, I got in trouble for getting home late. We worked on it Thursday night and then most of last Saturday.

CO: Sounds like you really got intrigued with all of the different things that you could do. [The counselor encourages the client to keep talking about her interest in the science project to see if her interest in Investigative activities will sustain itself.]

CL: It was a lot of fun. I never knew that observing ants could be so interesting. It really got me thinking about what I might do. I wish that I had thought about doing a science project. But it's too late now.

CO: If you were to do a science project now, what do you think it might be? [The exploration of Investigative activities continues.]

CL: I'm not sure, really. But I think it might have something to do with mice and how they act. I'm taking biology now, and I really like it. I wish that I had room in my schedule next year for another biology course.

CO: You seem surprised that you have so much interest in biology. [The counselor tries to understand how important Investigative activities are to the client and if this is a recent awareness for the client.]

CL: I *am* surprised. I never thought I would like science so much. I've known all along that I enjoy art. My art teachers really like my work, and I enjoy painting. Last summer, I won first place in a contest with my paintings.

CO: That sounds exciting. It's great to have things that seem different from each other but are so enjoyable. [While reinforcing the client's enjoyment, the counselor acknowledges the existence of both Investigative and Artistic interests.]

CL: I've thought that it would be neat to do something with these after college. I've thought of doing something with biology, becoming a biologist or geneticist or something like that. But I'm not sure what I'd do with art. Sometimes, I think that I might like to be an artist or an architect.

CO: These are occupations worth looking into. They certainly fit with the things that you've been telling me so far about yourself. [Without knowing the exact Holland codes for the occupations that the student mentions, the counselor can still tell that the occupations that have been described are congruent with the client's emerging personality type. The counselor is then in a position to find other occupations that may be congruent with the AI type. Further, the counselor will have the opportunity to see if there are other Holland types that reflect the individual's personality. If so, this may help the counselor in finding other occupations to suggest that will be congruent with her type.]

Differentiation

Both people and environments may differ in terms of how clearly they belong to one or two types. Some people may predominantly resemble one Holland type, whereas others may be quite undifferentiated and have interests and competencies across all six types. Most people are likely to have one, two, or three dominant types. For example, some people enjoy painting, writing, helping others, leading youth groups, and doing volunteer work in a hospital. They may dislike working with machinery, office work, science, and business. Such people would be readily identified as differentiated, as their interests (Social and Artistic) are clearly different from their dislikes (Investigative, Realistic, Conventional, and Enterprising). On the other hand, some people enjoy doing all kinds of activities and they do them well. These people are undifferentiated according to Holland's system. Holland determines *differentiation* by subtracting the lowest score of any type from the highest score of any type on the SDS or VPI. Any inventory that measures his six types can be used. A high result indicates a differentiated profile and a low result an undifferentiated profile.

Just as people vary in terms of differentiation, so do environments. Some environments allow for more freedom of movement to various Holland environments than do others. For example, assembly line work usually allows an individual only the opportunity to do Realistic work—a differentiated environment. On the other hand, a teacher working in a university may have the opportunity to do research in his or her field (Investigative), teach students and help them select courses (Social), and possibly consult with industry (Enterprising)—an undifferentiated environment. Sometimes, environments are varied enough so that people who at first find that their personality and environment are not congruent can find a way to work within the environment that provides eventual congruence.

For example, a physician who is predominantly Enterprising rather than Investigative (the predominant type of physician) may find enough diversity in a hospital environment to work as a hospital administrator or fund-raiser, thus meeting his or her Enterprising needs. To use another example, a secretary working in an office that requires typing, filing, and reception work will find an opportunity to meet both Conventional and Social needs, whereas a secretary in a typing pool will be able to meet only Conventional needs. Thus, environments differ in the degree to which they are differentiated.

Counseling Implications   Undifferentiated people are likely to have difficulty in making career decisions and may seek career counseling. One goal of counseling is to help clients to differentiate and broaden their knowledge of their interests, abilities, and values within each of the six types. Some clients who are trying to find a new career goal will find that they have interests and abilities in many different areas (undifferentiated). It is then the counselor's role to discuss more deeply their interests, values, and experiences, and to make explicit the differing values of each of the six types for the client. Other clients may find that they have few interests and low self-estimates of their abilities across all types. Such clients may need to address issues of depression or low self-esteem. The typology serves as a frame of reference for exploring areas of interest of which the client may not be aware. A discussion of a client's experiences with hobbies, part-time work, volunteer work, full-time work, extracurricular activities, and leisure time is apt to give the counselor an opportunity to conceptualize the client according to all six of Holland's personality types. Sometimes, it is not possible to provide further differentiation for a client without more work experience—whether part time, volunteer, or full time. The pursuit of differentiation can be a means of finding a congruent occupation for a client.

Example of Differentiation   The client, Chester, is a young Chinese American man who dropped out of high school at the end of the 11th grade. For the past three years, he has been employed on an automobile assembly line. He has taken the Self-Directed Search (SDS) at a guidance program offered in the evening at his local high school. His highest score on the SDS was E, considerably higher than R and I, the next highest scores. His counselor uses this information along with Chester's description of career-related experiences to help Chester in career selection:

> CL: When I was in school, there just wasn't very much that interested me. Now I have a job that gets more and more boring. When I first worked in auto-body assembly, I didn't mind it. Things were kind of fun then. Now

I've done most of the jobs on the line, and there's never a challenge. It's the same thing all over again.

CO: The assembly work really sounds as if it is bothering you and making you rethink what you want to do. [Perhaps Realistic activities are not for this client. Do the client's R interests match his SDS scores?]

CL: Yes. There are a lot of things that I enjoy doing much more.

CO: Can you tell me about them? [More information about the client's personality, according to the six Holland personality types, is needed to compare with his scores on the SDS.]

CL: Well, on weekends my friend and I work on cars to resell. It's fun and interesting, and I'm making a lot of extra cash.

CO: Sounds good; I'd like to hear more.

CL: Well, we get old cars from people who are about ready to junk them. We fix the mechanical problems, touch them up with paint, and list them in the newspaper.

CO: Which aspect of this work do you do most? [Realistic interests, in terms of working on cars, and Enterprising interests, selling the cars, sound like possibilities. The counselor revises the original view that Realistic activities are not of interest to this client.]

CL: My friend really knows cars. I help him in some of the simple work. As I've worked with him, I've been able to help him when he takes an engine apart. But I couldn't do that myself. When it comes to people buying the car, I'm the one who sells it. It really is a challenge for me to take something that we've worked on and get someone to buy it. I feel as if we've got a good product, and I want them to know about it.

CO: Is selling something new for you? [The counselor is differentiating between the Realistic and Enterprising interests of the client, choosing to follow up and get more detail on the Enterprising aspect, Chester's highest score on the SDS.]

CL: No, I've sold before. When I was in high school I used to work in a tire store. I sold truck tires and auto tires, then put them on. Although I didn't mind putting on new tires, it was more interesting to me to help the customer select tires and buy a real good set. I'd get a commission on what I sold, not a big one, but I liked it.

CO: That sounds as if there were a lot of things that you could take advantage of on that job. [The counselor continues to differentiate the interests in Realistic and Enterprising activities from each other, exploring the differentiation suggested by the difference between the E and R scores on the SDS. This content reflection asks for further differentiation.]

Consistency

Consistency refers to the similarity or dissimilarity of types. Certain types, whether environment or personality, have more in common with some types than with others. For example, as shown in Figure 4-1 (page 96), Social and Artistic types are similar (close together). On the other hand, Social types and Realistic types are quite different from each other, as are Enterprising types and Investigative types. The closer the types are to each other on the chart, the more consistent they are. For example, Social people tend to like to help others, work as a team, and value their interactions with people; Realistic types prefer not to work with people, but to work with machines and technical challenges. Social people may often have an aversion to machines, or put another way, Social people tend to have more in common with Artistic and Enterprising types than they do with Realistic individuals. Likewise, Realistic people are apt to have more in common with Investigative and Conventional individuals than with Social people.

Consistency also applies to environments. Some environments require skills and interests that are generally inconsistent. One example is athletic trainer (SRE). The Social and Realistic environments are inconsistent, yet athletic trainers must help injured athletes who may be under emotional and physical stress. Further, they use a variety of sophisticated medical equipment to remedy injuries. In general, there are very few occupations that have codes that are inconsistent. For example, there are no occupations that could be labeled CA. When applied to a working environment, the term *inconsistent* means that the environment requires types of interests and abilities that rarely are required in the same job. Creative and artistic production (A) is seldom seen in conjunction with demands for numerical skill (C) in any occupation. On the other hand, individuals with inconsistent types may be able to identify a special niche for themselves. For example, an individual with a CA personality may enjoy organizing a music library for a symphony orchestra.

Consistency is not a goal of counseling, whereas differentiation and congruence can both be goals. Consistency is a more subtle concept than the others. Lack of consistency does not mean that a choice is poor. For example, a person who has an inconsistent type (SIC) has not made a poorer career choice than a person who has a more consistent type (SAI). Perhaps the notion of consistency can best be used in counseling by making the counselor aware that it may be difficult to find an environment that will fit two or three inconsistent Holland codes. Often, the client may have to choose an occupation that fits one of the two inconsistent types, but not both. For example, a client with strong Artistic and Conventional interests and skills may choose to do accounting during the day and then moonlight as a musician. It would not be possible to find occupations that would easily incorporate both of these personality types.

Recently, Holland (1997) described a new form of consistency, *consistency of aspirations*. Some clients may have a variety of aspirations or future dreams that vary in their degree of consistency. Some codes may be within one type or two adjoining types. Other codes may be found in types inconsistent with each other. A measure of consistency of aspirations can be obtained by examining the Daydreams section of the SDS. Aspirations or daydreams have always been an important concept to Holland (Reardon & Lenz, 1998). Knowing what clients daydream about, desire, or aspire to provides useful information to the career counselor in both assessing Holland type and the counseling process itself.

Identity

Identity refers to the clarity and stability of a person's current and future goals. It also refers to the stability of the working environment. If an organization has identity, the tasks and goals of an occupation or employer do not vary widely. Identity is different from any of the other concepts relevant to Holland's system because it does not relate directly to his typology. It is measured not by the VPI or the SDS, but through a third instrument titled My Vocational Situation (MVS) (Holland, Daiger, & Power, 1980).

Although the inventory, My Vocational Situation, will measure the concept of identity, the counselor's assessment of identity in a counseling interview can also prove to be helpful. A question for the counselor to consider is: Now that we are completing career counseling, does this client have a clear idea of career plans and contingency plans, as well as knowledge of how to implement the plans? For example, a man who decides to pursue acting should not only be aware of his interest in this profession but also be able to assess feedback he has received from directors and acting teachers. This man should be aware of the risks in obtaining work, alternative careers when unemployed, contacts for employment, and so on. To start looking for work without planning would be to have a diffuse sense of identity. To use another example, a young woman who wants to be a lawyer because lawyers make good salaries and work on exciting cases has not yet formed a sense of identity. When she has information about how to become a lawyer and whether she would like the duties of a lawyer, then her sense of identity will become clearer.

Identity can be an important goal of career counseling. Achievement of identity may occur when the goal of congruence has been accomplished. If a woman decides on the occupation of roofer, feeling that laying new roofs would be something that she is able to do and would enjoy (congruence between person and environment), a sense of identity will develop. As she moves from one job site to another, her goals may stabilize, and she may grow more certain of her interests and abilities.

RESEARCH ON HOLLAND'S CONSTRUCTS

Holland's theory has produced over 500 studies, more research than any other career development theory. Holland himself has been very influential in the production of research and the compilation of it. His five books (1966, 1973, 1985a, 1992, 1997) are indications of his continuing work to refine existing and develop additional theoretical constructs. Research on career development is reviewed periodically in the *Journal of Vocational Behavior*, the *Career Development Quarterly*, and the *Journal of Career Assessment*. These reviews devote a section to discussions of current research on Holland's theory.

Congruence is the most important of Holland's concepts and the one that is most widely researched. What seems like a straightforward concept is actually quite complex. For example, Brown and Gore (1994) evaluated 10 different methods of measuring congruence between personality type and employment, and Camp and Chartrand (1992) examined 13 methods. Many studies have related congruence to other important variables such as stress, job satisfaction, and personality variables. Using nine female and seven male samples to assess measures of complexity, Hoeglund and Hansen (1999) found very small relationships between congruence and satisfaction across Holland types. In reviewing recent studies, the relationship between congruence measures and job satisfaction appears to be quite small (Tokar, Fischer, & Subich, 1998). Chartrand and Walsh (1999) also examined the validity of the concept of congruence and the difficulties in measuring it, providing an overview of research in this area. Because of the different ways that congruence can be measured and the different variables, such as personality and achievement, that it can be related to, congruence is likely to be an important focus of research for some time, although current research suggests a small relationship between job satisfaction and congruence.

Another area of research involves studying the relationship of Holland's personality types to various personality characteristics. For example, Tokar and Swanson (1995) found that Holland's six personality types fit with those of the NEO Five-Factor Model (FFM). This inventory measures five broad factors known as the big five: Extraversion, Neuroticism, Agreeableness, Conscientiousness, and Openness to Experience. The big five supported Holland's characterization of six personality types, and the Openness and Extraversion factors were particularly relevant to Holland's typology. This finding was also supported by Tokar and Fischer (1998). Tokar, Fischer, and Subich (1998) found neuroticism, extroversion, and conscientiousness to be most frequently associated with a variety of vocational behaviors. In comparing the Five-Factor Model of personality with Holland's typology, Hogan and Blake (1999) concluded that Holland's inventories measure identity, whereas the FFM personality inventory measures reputation, an observer's view of an individual's personality. In a study contrasting the Self-Directed Search with the FFM, DeFruyt and Mervielde (1999) conclude that Holland's typology was better at predicting the nature of employment, whereas the FFM was better in predicting the employability and employment status of applicants. The FFM was more employer-oriented, in keeping with the conclusions of Hogan and Blake, who believe that personality inventories are more likely to be consistent with observers' (employers') ratings than vocational measures. Comparisons between Holland's typology and the FFM appear to be a significant area of current research.

Although some studies have focused on redefining and developing consistency (Latona, 1989; Pazy & Zin, 1987) and differentiation (Asama, 1997), vocational identity has received the most recent attention. Osipow (1999) has reviewed Holland's concept of vocational identity and supporting evidence or lack of it. Leung, Conoley, Scheel, and Sonnenberg (1992) reported no relationship between scores on the Vocational Identity scale of My

Vocational Situation and consistency and differentiations. Conneran and Hartman (1993) found that chronically career-undecided high school students showed lower levels of congruence and vocational identity than those students who were not chronically undecided. Adults seeking career services with low differentiations scores and low overall scores on the SDS were found to have less education and score lower on vocational identity than more highly differentiated adults and those with higher scores on the SDS (Pusateri, 1997). For male substance abusers, success in treatment was associated with a higher degree of identity as measured by the My Vocational Situation (MVS) (Hankinson, 1998). Regarding Holland's concept of congruence, identity was related to college major choice congruence, but not career choice congruence for gifted high school juniors (Leung, 1998). Studying high-risk inner-city high school students, Ladany, Melincoff, Constantine, and Love (1997) showed that students' level of commitment to their career choices was related to their vocational identity, their need for occupational information, and the barriers that they felt hindered them in pursuing career goals. On a theoretical level, Vondracek (1991, 1992) has criticized Holland's definition of identity as being oversimplified and less complex than "identity" as originally described by Erik Erikson.

Holland's theory has attracted researchers for several reasons. Holland defines his terms clearly and simply. His theory is directly related to the practice of vocational counseling. Most studies on Holland's concepts do not require longitudinal research or extensive follow-up studies. Also, John Holland has been very involved in research on his theory and helpful to those who wish to engage in research related to his work. In general, the research on Holland's theory offers counselors confidence that Holland's concepts have merit and can be used for counseling conceptualization.

THE ROLE OF OCCUPATIONAL INFORMATION

Holland's typological system is particularly useful to clients because it helps to integrate occupational information into the counseling process. By dividing all occupations (or environments) into six types, Holland gives the client an easy framework to use for conceptualizing all occupations. With this system, clients are less likely to ask, "Are there some occupations that I have never considered?" Using this system, counselors have a clear approach to explaining the world of work. Both client and counselor can use *The Occupations Finder* (Holland, 1994) to identify a thousand of the more common occupations and *The Educational Opportunities Finder* (Rosen et al., 1994) to identify over 750 programs of study. If more detail is wanted, Holland's *Dictionary of Holland Occupational Codes* (Gottfredson & Holland, 1996a) lists 12,099 occupations sorted by Holland code.

For the counselor, Holland's typological system is a helpful way to group occupational information. Not only can Holland's system be used to classify items in an occupational library, but it can also be used by a counselor to classify the client's experiences with environments. For example, as a counselor talks to employers about their needs for employees, the environment that the employers describe can be classified mentally by the counselor. In a similar way, as a client describes work experience that he or she has enjoyed or disliked, the environment can also be classified according to Holland type. The knowledge gained from experiences such as visiting plants, reading occupational information, and talking to other counselors about work can be used to help in coding occupations according to Holland type. By practicing with the Holland system, whether formally or informally, the counselor becomes increasingly familiar with it.

THE ROLE OF TESTING

Testing has had two purposes in Holland's system. The first is in the development of the theory. For example, the Vocational Preference Inventory was initiated prior to Holland's theory and was partly responsible for the definition of his six types of people and environments. The VPI and the SDS then became research instruments to verify and validate Holland's theory. The second use of tests is for individuals in need of career assistance. By using the SDS, the VPI, or another inventory that yields Holland types, the counselor can get an objectively determined personality type for the client. By comparing the counselor's assessment of the client's Holland type with that of an objective inventory, the counselor can get confirmation or try to determine why there is a discrepancy, if one exists. By doing so, the counselor is likely to gain further insight into the client's interests, abilities, and values. Testing is an important part of the development of Holland's theory. Making use of validated and reliable information can be a great help to counselors in working with clients.

Inventories related to Holland's typology have been very popular. The publishers of Holland's instruments, Psychological Assessment Resources, estimates that over 21 million people have used one or more of them, worldwide (Reardon & Lenz, 1998). Since the original version of the Self-Directed Search-R (regular), several other versions have been developed. There are Canadian and Spanish forms of the SDS, and a Chinese version has been tested (Yu & Alvi, 1996). Also, an easier form of the SDS-Form E has been designed for adolescents and adults with limited reading skills (sixth grade). The SDS-Career Planning has been developed for adults who aspire to greater levels of professional responsibility. It does not include Daydream or Self-Estimate sections. The SDS-Career Explorer focuses on helping middle school students with educational and vocational planning. Although the SDS was designed to be self-scoring, scan sheets are available as are computer-based interpretive reports.

In addition to the SDS, Holland and his colleagues have developed several other useful inventories. The Career Attitudes and Strategies Inventory (CASI) was designed to assess the views of adults toward work. Scales include Job Satisfaction, Work Involvement, Skill Development, Dominant

Style, Career Worries, Interpersonal Abuse, Family Commitment, Risk-Taking Style, and Geographical Barriers (Holland & Gottfredson, 1994). The Position Classification Inventory (Gottfredson & Holland, 1991) was developed to classify positions according to Holland type. Taking only 10 minutes, this 84-item inventory can be given to large numbers of people who do the same type of work in order to determine the Holland code for a specific job. The Environmental Identity Scale (EIS) (Gottfredson & Holland, 1996b) assesses workers' views about the explicitness and consistency of employers' goals, work rules, and rewards. These instruments show that Holland and his colleagues are active in the development of measures to assess individuals as well as their environments.

APPLYING THE THEORY TO WOMEN

Because Holland's system has six clearly defined types supplemented by explanatory constructs such as congruence, consistency, and differentiation, it has been the subject of a great deal of research. Much of the research has used both males and females, thus providing data on the appropriateness of Holland's theory for women. Holland (1997) has shown that men are more likely to score high on the Realistic, Investigative, or Enterprising scales, whereas women may score higher on the Social, Artistic, and Conventional scales. Holland's conclusion about summary codes is somewhat similar to that of Arbona (1989), who used an analysis of 1980 census data that reflected the occupational choices of 97 million Americans. Men predominated in the Realistic and Enterprising categories, whereas women were found more often in Social and Conventional careers. Investigative and Artistic occupations made up a small proportion of workers. Some critics of Holland's theory have taken these differential preferences to mean that Holland's theory is biased against women. Holland points out that his system is a reflection of society and cultural expectations; it does not determine them.

Regarding Holland's concept of congruence, his review (1997) shows that the SDS or the VPI can predict occupational choice or entry about equally well for men and women. In general, Holland, Powell, and Fritzsche (1994) conclude that the predicted validities of aspirations and assessment tend to be higher for women than for men. Although there is less research on consistency and differentiation, there seems to be little difference in these two concepts when the gender variable is examined. In concluding their discussion of sex differences, Holland, Powell, and Fritzsche (1994) state that "women are most likely to have low scores on R and high scores on S" (p. 37). Thus, Holland points out those types that have been most influenced by cultural stereotyping.

Research on Holland's typology and theoretical constructs usually contains information that addresses the issue of male–female differences on relevant variables. Hansen, Collins, Swanson, and Fouad (1993) found that Holland's hexagon generally represented the interests of men quite accurately, but that there was little discrimination between women's Realistic and Investigative interests. Social interests stood out as being particularly important in the structure of women's interests. Relating Millon's personality styles to Holland's typology, Rees (1999) found that women's orientation to relationships was related to high scores on Social and to a lesser extent on Artistic. Women's orientation toward independence, separation, and autonomy was related to higher scores on Enterprising and Conventional scales. When studying self-efficacy, there were minimal differences between genders on the six Holland types (Betz, Borgen, Kaplan, & Harmon, 1998; Betz, Harmon, & Borgen, 1996). Examining gender differences on the Big Five Personality factors, Ozone (1998) reports that Experience and Agreeableness were factors that discriminated among Holland types for women, and Experience discriminated among Holland types for men. Studies such as these help to show how Holland's theory applies differently to men and women.

APPLYING THE THEORY TO CULTURALLY DIVERSE POPULATIONS

Holland's theory and instruments have been used internationally as well as with culturally diverse populations in the United States. Research (Holland, 1997; Holland, Powell, & Fritzsche, 1994) in China, Israel, France, Nigeria, New Zealand, and Australia gives some support to the use of Holland's six categories and the constructs of congruence, consistency, and differentiation (although there has been less work on the latter two concepts).

Recent studies have examined how well Holland's hexagon fits people from a variety of backgrounds and cultures. Comparing the interests of African Americans, Mexican Americans, Asian Americans, Native Americans, and Caucasians, Day, Rounds, and Swaney (1998) found that Holland's circular structure of interests adequately represented the interest structure of these groups. Swanson (1992) found that, in general, Holland's typology fit African American female college students somewhat better than African American males. Kaufman, Ford-Richards, and McLean (1998) reported that African Americans scored higher on Social, Enterprising, and Conventional scales on the Strong Interest Inventory, and whites scored higher on Realistic and Investigative themes in their sample. Contrasting white American college students with Asian Americans, Havercamp, Collins, and Hansen (1994) supported the similarity of interest for these two groups. Also, comparing Asian American and white American college students, Leung, Ivey, and Suzuki (1994) found that Asian Americans were more likely to have considered Investigative occupations and less likely to have considered Enterprising and Conventional occupations than white college students. However, Asian Americans showed interests in both Investigative and Social occupations. In examining factors influencing career choices of Asian Americans, Tang, Fouad, and Smith (1999) reported that lower acculturated Asian Americans scored higher on Realistic and

Investigative occupations than did more acculturated college students. Other studies, such as Day and Bedeian's (1995) research on the fit of person-environment models (including Holland's) with African American nursing-service employees, extend the information available about the applicability of Holland's model to individuals from diverse cultures and employment settings. However, information about the appropriateness of Holland's typological system for specific cultural groups is neither sufficient nor consistent enough to allow generalizations about its usefulness for specific groups.

Holland's typological system has also been studied in cultures outside of North America. First-year university students in Hong Kong (Farh, Leong, & Law, 1998) had interests that fit within Holland's hexagonal model. However, students who had more traditional Chinese beliefs responded less consistently than those with weaker beliefs. In India, a sample of adults showed interests that were internally consistent, but the researchers did not find a relationship between Holland's concepts of congruence and job satisfaction (Leong, Austin, Sekaran, & Komarraju, 1998). In South Africa, Watson, Stead, and Schonegevel (1998) found that Holland's typology did not provide a good fit with the interests of disadvantaged black South African adolescents. These studies are typical of some of the more recent cross-cultural research that has tested Holland's theory.

Information about the distribution of the Holland types of different cultural groups working in the United States provides a useful perspective on the employment of culturally diverse populations. In her study of the distribution of workers by ethnic group, Arbona (1989) reported that more Hispanic men (71%) and African American men (68%) than white men (54%) were in Realistic types of work. Furthermore, fewer African American men (10%) and Hispanic men (6%) than white men (23%) were in Enterprising occupations. With regard to women, more African American women (37%) and Hispanic women (41%) than white women (24%) were in Realistic jobs. More white women (15%) than African American women (7%) and Hispanic women (10%) were in Enterprising occupations. In a further analysis of these data, Arbona found that African American and Hispanic men were found more often in low-level Realistic jobs. Arbona (1989) suggests that African American and Hispanic students may be exposed to role models working in relatively low-level jobs. Such data are not a critique of Holland's theory but show its utility in identifying social inequities.

COUNSELOR ISSUES

Research on providing appropriate counseling techniques and approaches for different Holland types yields insights into how best to meet the career counseling needs of individuals who are predominantly of one Holland type. Boyd and Cramer (1995) found that Social and Enterprising college students preferred counseling with unlimited sessions, with little structure in the sessions, with a focus on self-awareness, and with the opportunity for follow-up counseling. They preferred a less concrete focus than did Realistic or Conventional college students. Using a description of six counseling approaches that corresponded to each of Holland's six environments, Niles (1993) found that students identified as a specific Holland type tended (but not strongly) to select a counseling approach similar to their type. This was particularly true of Realistic and Enterprising males and was less true of Investigative, Artistic, and Conventional males, and of females, in general. Speculating from their research on Holland's types and personality variables, Holland, Johnston, Hughey, and Asama (1991) concluded that Realistic and Conventional individuals would be poor candidates for traditional psychotherapy because they are not very open to feelings or new ideas. Reardon and Lenz (1998) provide suggestions for counseling individuals who score high on one Holland type. They describe strategies that clients of different types may use that may interfere with their career exploration process. Issues that face counselors in using Holland's theory with clients of different Holland types are discussed next.

Although there are a number of counselor aids built into the Holland system, such as methods for conceptualizing client problems, classifying occupational information, and incorporating inventories, there are some problems that counselors are likely to encounter. By using the concepts of congruence and differentiation, a few potential problem issues can be described.

In this chapter, discussion has focused on the congruence between the client's personality and his or her working environment. Often, the client's personality type and the counselor's personality type are incongruent. For counselors, the most common types are SE, SI, or SA. Most counselors are predominantly Social; many are secondarily Enterprising, Investigative, or Artistic. When counselors with these Holland codes encounter clients who are primarily Realistic and/or Conventional, they are dealing with a type quite opposite to and incongruent with their own. The danger is that the values of the counselor, in terms of valuing personal interaction and helping, are likely to be very different from those of the client. Being aware of this divergence of values can help counselors be more open toward and understanding of interests, abilities, and values that are very different from theirs. Many counselors may not respect hunting, fishing, being outdoors, fixing cars, and such, but their Realistic clients will. Appreciating the differences among incongruent types can be very helpful in counseling.

Another problem concerns Holland's concept of differentiation. Counselors are likely to be differentiated according to their preference for types of environments. Because they have made a career choice, they are likely to have preferences for two or three types and lack interest in three or four types. For clients of any age who are having difficulty with career selection, there may be little differentiation among four, five, or all six types. For example, a client may enjoy and have abilities in Social, Realistic, Enterprising, Conventional, and Artistic activities. It then becomes the counselor's role to help further differentiate the client's experiences and de-sires, perhaps ascertaining that Realistic and Conventional activities are most satisfying. Counselors may become frustrated with the client's diffi-culty in differentiating, when the counselor is not having that difficulty. Being aware of this divergence often helps the counselor become more pa-tient.

There are times when Holland's personality theory will not suffice. For example, there are 53 RIE, 30 REI, and 17 SEA occupations listed in *The Occupations Finder* (Holland, 1994). Holland's theory does not provide enough information for the client to choose within a specific three-letter category, such as RIE. Other factors such as location or non-Holland per-sonality factors may also need to be considered. Arriving at a code for a client is a help in counseling, not the end of the counseling process. For some clients, Holland's theory will provide a start for differentiating inter-ests and talents or for developing a sense of identity. Other factors such as education, ability, location, and/or personal responsibilities to family may be equally important, if not more so, than personality types. In their book, *The Self-Directed Search and Related Holland Career Materials: A Practi-tioner's Guide,* Reardon and Lenz (1998) provide many useful ideas for counselors using Holland's system. Holland's theory is a useful way of con-ceptualizing client concerns, but it does not provide a conceptualization system that will work with all clients, all problems, all of the time.

SUMMARY

John Holland's typological theory has been accepted widely by counselors and psychologists for several reasons. Conceptually, it is easy to use be-cause the six personality types (Realistic, Investigative, Artistic, Social, En-terprising, and Conventional) can be matched with a corresponding envi-ronment. Usually, an individual and an environment are described by the most important, second in importance, and third in importance of the six categories. When the three letters of the code describing the person and the environment match or approximate a match, then congruence results. Con-gruence, the most important of Holland's constructs, is sought by assess-ing the type of the client and trying to match it with appropriate occupa-tions. Other constructs, such as consistency, consistency of aspirations, differentiation, and identity are also valuable in using Holland's theory conceptually. Because Holland's theoretical constructs are clearly defined, they have generated much research relevant to the applicability of his the-ory to all individuals, including women and culturally diverse populations. The occupational classification system that has been developed using the three-letter code is another practical aid for counselors. Several inventories besides Holland's Self-Directed Search and Vocational Preference Inventory are useful in identifying the client's type. Because of its wide acceptance by counselors and the abundance of supportive research, Holland's theory is likely to be used widely in the future.

References

Arbona, C. (1989). Hispanic employment and the Holland typology of work. *Career Development Quarterly, 37,* 257–268.

Asama, N. (1997, March). Creating new differentiation indices for Holland's theory of vocational personalities and work environments. *Dissertation Abstracts International: Section B: The Sciences and Engineering.* Vol. 57 (9-B): 5961.

Betz, E., Borgen, H., Kaplan, A., & Harmon, L. W. (1998). Gender and Holland type as moderators of the validity and interpretive utility of the Skills Confidence Inventory. *Journal of Vocational Behavior, 53,* 281–299.

Betz, N., Harmon, L., & Borgen, F. H. (1996). The relationships of self-efficacy for the Holland themes to gender, occupational group membership, and vocational interests. *Journal of Counseling Psychology, 43,* 90–98.

Boyd, C. U., & Cramer, S. H. (1995). Relationship between Holland high-point code and client preference for selected vocational counseling strategies. *Journal of Career Development, 21,* 213–221.

Brown, S. D., & Gore, R. A., Jr. (1994). An evaluation of interest congruence indices: Distribution, characteristics, and measurement properties. *Journal of Vocational Behavior, 45,* 310–327.

Camp, C. C., & Chartrand, J. M. (1992). A comparison and evaluation of interest congruence indices. *Journal of Vocational Behavior, 41,* 162–182.

Chartrand, J., & Walsh, W. B. (1999). What should we expect from congruence? *Journal of Vocational Behavior, 55,* 136–146.

Conneran, J. M., & Hartman, B. W. (1993). The concurrent validity of the Self-Directed Search in identifying chronic career indecision among vocational education students. *Journal of Career Development, 19,* 197–208.

Day, D. V., & Bedeian, A. G. (1995). Personality similarity and work-related outcomes among African-American nursing personnel: A test of the supplementary model of person-environment congruence. *Journal of Vocational Behavior, 46,* 55–70.

Day, S. X., Rounds, J., & Swaney, K. (1998). The structure of vocational interests for diverse racial-ethnic groups. *Psychological Science, 9,* 40–44.

DeFruyt, F., & Mervielde, I. (1999). RIASEC types and big five traits as predictors of employment status and nature of employment. *Personnel Psychology, 52,* 701–727.

Farh, J., Leong, F. T. L., & Law, K. (1998). Cross-cultural validity of Holland's model in Hong Kong. *Journal of Vocational Behavior, 52,* 425–440.

Gottfredson, G. D., & Holland, J. L. (1991). *Position Classification Inventory professional manual.* Odessa, FL: Psychological Assessment Resources.

Gottfredson, G. D., & Holland, J. L. (1996a). *Dictionary of Holland Occupational Codes* (3rd ed.). Odessa, FL: Psychological Assessment Resources.

Gottfredson, G. D., & Holland, J. L. (1996b). *Environmental Identity Scale.* Unpublished instrument.

Gottfredson, L. S., & Richards, J. M., Jr. (1999). The meaning and measurement of environments in Holland's theory. *Journal of Vocational Behavior, 55,* 57–73.

Hankinson, G. L. (1998, July). The relationship of vocational identity and other mitigating variables to progress in substance dependence treatment in a therapeutic community. *Dissertation Abstracts International: Section-A: Humanities and Social Sciences.* Vol. 59(1-A): 0092.

Hansen, J. C., Collins, R. C., Swanson, J. L., & Fouad, N. A. (1993). Gender differences in the structure of interests. *Journal of Vocational Behavior, 42,* 200–211.

Haverkamp, B. E., Collins, R. C., & Hansen, J.-I. C. (1994). Structure of interests of Asian-American college students. *Journal of Counseling Psychology, 41,* 256–264.

Hoeglund, T. J., Hansen, J.-I. C. (1999). Holland-style measures of congruence: Are complex indices more effective predictors of satisfaction? *Journal of Vocational Behavior, 54,* 471–482.

Hogan, R., & Blake, R. (1999). John Holland's vocational typology and personality theory. *Journal of Vocational Behavior, 55,* 41–56.

Holland, J. L. (1966). *The psychology of vocational choice.* Waltham, MA: Blaisdell.

Holland, J. L. (1973). *Making vocational choices: A theory of careers.* Englewood Cliffs, NJ: Prentice Hall.

Holland, J. L. (1985a). *Making vocational choices: A theory of personalities and work environments* (2nd ed.). Englewood Cliffs, NJ: Prentice Hall.

Holland, J. L. (1985b). *Manual for the Vocational Preference Inventory.* Odessa, FL: Psychological Assessment Resources.

Holland, J. L. (1992). *Making vocational choices: A theory of vocational personalities and work environments.* Odessa, FL: Psychological Assessment Resources.

Holland, J. L. (1994). *The Occupations Finder.* Odessa, FL: Psychological Assessment Resources.

Holland, J. L. (1997). *Making vocational choices: A theory of vocational personalities and work environments* (3rd ed.). Odessa, FL: Psychological Assessment Resources.

Holland, J. L., Daiger, D. C., & Power, P. G. (1980). *My Vocational Situation: Description of an experimental diagnostic form for the selection of vocational assistance.* Palo Alto, CA: Consulting Psychologists Press.

Holland, J. L., & Gottfredson, G. D. (1994). *Career Attitudes and Strategies Inventory: An inventory for understanding adult careers.* Odessa, FL: Psychological Assessment Resources.

Holland, J. L., Johnston, J. A., Hughey, K. F., & Asama, N. E. (1991). Some explorations of a theory of careers: VII. A replication and some possible exceptions. *Journal of Career Development, 18,* 91–100.

Holland, J. L., Powell, A. B., & Fritzsche, B. A. (1994). *The Self-Directed Search professional user's guide.* Odessa, FL: Psychological Assessment Resources.

Kaufman, A. S., Ford-Richards, J. M., & McLean, J. E. (1998). Black-White differences on the Strong Interest Inventory General Occupational Themes and Basic Interest Scales at ages 16 to 65. *Journal of Clinical Psychology, 54,* 19–33.

Ladany, N., Melincoff, D. S., Constantine, M. G., & Love, R. (1997). At-risk urban high school students' commitment to career choices. *Journal of Counseling and Development, 76,* 45–52.

Latona, J. R. (1989). Consistency of Holland code and its relation to persistence in a college major. *Journal of Vocational Behavior, 34,* 253–265.

Leong, F. T. L., Austin, J. T., Sekaran, U., & Komarraju, M. (1998). An evaluation of the cross-cultural validity of Holland's theory: Career choices by workers in India. *Journal of Vocational Behavior, 52,* 441–455.

Leung, S. A. (1998). Vocational identity and career choice congruence of gifted and talented high school students. *Counseling Psychology Quarterly, 11,* 325–335.

Leung, S. A., Conoley, C. W., Scheel, M. J., & Sonnenberg, R. T. (1992). An examination of the relation between vocational identity, consistency, and differentiation. *Journal of Vocational Behavior, 40,* 95–107.

Leung, S. A., Ivey, D., & Suzuki, L. (1994). Factors affecting the career aspirations of Asian Americans. *Journal of Counseling and Development, 72,* 404–410.

Niles, S. G. (1993). The relationship between Holland types preferences for career counseling. *Journal of Career Development, 19,* 209–220.

Osipow, S. H. (1999). Assessing career indecision. *Journal of Vocational Behavior, 55,* 147–154.

Ozone, S. J. (1998, January). The relationship between Holland's theory of vocational interest and the Five Factor Model of Personality. *Dissertation Abstracts International: Section B: The Sciences and Engineering.* Vol. 58(7-B): 3962.

Pazy, A., & Zin, R. (1987). A contingency approach to consistency: A challenge to prevalent views. *Journal of Vocational Behavior, 30,* 84–101.

Pusateri, M. L. R. (1997, March). The meaning of low flat Holland code profiles. *Dissertation Abstracts International: Section B: The Sciences and Engineering.* Vol. 57(9-B): 5929.

Reardon, R. C., & Lenz, J. G. (1998). *The Self-Directed Search and related Holland career materials: A practitioner's guide.* Odessa, FL: Psychological Assessment Resources.

Rees, A. M. (1999, April). Can relational personality theory provide a framework for differences on Holland typology for women? *Dissertation Abstracts International: Section B: The Sciences and Engineering.* Vol. 59(10-B): 5610.

Rosen, D., Holmberg, K., & Holland, J. L. (1994). *The Educational Opportunities Finder.* Odessa, FL: Psychological Assessment Resources.

Savickas, M. L., & Gottfredson, G. D. (1999). Holland's theory (1959–1999): 40 years of research and application. *Journal of Vocational Behavior, 55,* 1–4.

Swanson, J. L. (1992). The structure of vocational interests for African-American college students. *Journal of Vocational Behavior, 40,* 144–157.

Tang, M., Fouad, N. A., & Smith, P. L. (1999). Asian Americans' career choices: A path model to examine factors influencing their career choices. *Journal of Vocational Behavior, 54,* 142–157.

Tokar, D. M., & Fischer, A. R. (1998). More on RIASEC and the Five-Factor Model of Personality: Direct assessment of Prediger's (1982) and Hogan's (1983) dimensions. *Journal of Vocational Behavior, 52,* 246–259.

Tokar, D. M., Fischer, A. R., & Subich, L. M. (1998). Personality and vocational behavior: A selective review of the literature, 1993–1997. *Journal of Vocational Behavior, 53,* 115–153.

Tokar, D. M., & Swanson, J. L. (1995). Evaluation of the correspondence between Holland's vocational personality typology and the Five-Factor Model of Personality. *Journal of Vocational Behavior, 46,* 89–108.

Vondracek, F. W. (1991). Current status of the concept of vocational identity. *Man and Work, 3,* 291–301.

Vondracek, F. W. (1992). The construct of vocational identity and its use in career theory and research. *Career Development Quarterly, 41,* 130–144.

Watson, J., Stead, G. B., & Schonegevel, C. (1998). Does Holland's hexagon travel well? *Australian Journal of Career Development, 7* (2), 22–26.

Young, G., Tokar, D. M., & Subich, L. M. (1998). Congruence revisited: Do 11 indices differentially predict job satisfaction and is the relation moderated by person and situation variables? *Journal of Vocational Behavior, 52,* 208–233.

Yu, J., & Alvi, S. A. (1996). A study of Holland's typology in China. *Journal of Career Assessment, 4,* 245–252.

Myers-Briggs
Type Theory

5

Unlike most other theories in this book, the Myers-Briggs type theory was not designed to be a theory of career development. Why then is it included? The Myers-Briggs type theory has become very popular with career counselors as many find that it is applicable to their work with clients. The Myers-Briggs type theory is a psychological theory based on the work of Carl Gustav Jung and adapted by Katharine Briggs in the 1920s.

Because the development of the Myers-Briggs typology is unusual, it would be helpful to describe its origins briefly. Katharine Briggs was not a psychologist but was an acute observer of people. Prior to reading Jung's (1921/1971) book *Psychological Types*, she had developed her own categories of people's behavior. Becoming intrigued with Jung's work, she studied it extensively. During the next 20 years, she continued to observe people and to try to classify them into Jungian types. In the 1940s, she was joined by her only child, Isabel Myers, in the development of the Myers-Briggs Type Indicator (MBTI). They worked together sorting and analyzing responses to the MBTI. In 1956, she was able to persuade the Educational Testing Service to publish the MBTI. In 1962, a manual for the MBTI was published, and Isabel Myers spoke at the American Psychological Association meeting. Gradually, the MBTI attracted the attention of psychologists.

In 1969, Isabel started to work with Mary McCaulley and began a typology laboratory at the University of Florida in Gainesville. In 1972, this laboratory became the Center for the Application of Psychological Type, sponsoring research on the MBTI and coordinating research efforts in the development of the Myers-Briggs typology. Sponsored by the Association for Psychological Type are a research journal, *Journal of Psychological Type*, and a newsletter, *Bulletin of Psychological Type*. Although the Myers-Briggs typology has increased in popularity among psychologists and counselors over the years, it is not without its critics. Some psychologists have questioned both the theory and the methodology of the MBTI. This criticism is discussed in more detail in a later section of this chapter.

In his book *Psychological Types* (1921/1971), Jung wrote about different ways that individuals use perception and judgment. He was concerned both with what people pay attention to and how they make decisions about what they see. Further, he viewed some people as being more concerned about what is happening in the world outside themselves and others as being more concerned with their own views and ideas. This is a very brief synopsis of the groundwork on which the Myers-Briggs typology is based. To put Jung's typology into perspective, it is only one of the many aspects of his theory of personality. Many Jungian psychotherapists are concerned with analysis of dreams and other concepts besides those of personality type. However, many psychologists and counselors who use Jungian theory do so only within the limited confines of the Myers-Briggs typological system.

To put the Myers-Briggs type system within the context of career development, it is helpful to think of it as a trait and factor theory. In Chapter 2, the first step in selecting a career, according to trait and factor theory, was listed as gaining a clear understanding of your aptitudes, achievements, interests, values, and personality. Within that context, the Myers-Briggs typology can be seen as a theory of personality. Those counselors who use Myers-Briggs theory in helping clients with career choices use the Myers-Briggs theory as a personality theory. Rarely, if ever, would the Myers-Briggs theory be used without an assessment of aptitudes, achievements, or interests as well. Certainly, the Myers-Briggs theory can be used with other theories besides trait and factor theory. However, it fits rather neatly into that model. Available in the MBTI manual (Myers, McCaulley, Quenk, & Hammer, 1998) are listings of environments (or occupations) in which various types of people work. This information, along with knowledge of a person's type, enables a counselor to help a client with the third step of trait and factor career selection: integrating information about self and the world of work. In addition, the Myers-Briggs typology can be used in assisting a client with career adjustment, applying type concepts to both individuals and their current working conditions.

In this chapter, the four bipolar dimensions basic to Myers-Briggs theory will be explained: extraversion–introversion, sensing–intuition, thinking–feeling, and judgment–perception. Although the number of concepts in the Myers-Briggs typology is not great, the interrelationships among the types make for a complex and sometimes difficult theory to "chunk," or learn. Thus, to understand the theory, it is necessary to understand the four bipolar categories and how they work in conjunction with each other. Examples of counseling for career decision making and for work adjustment will illustrate the interrelationships among the constructs. Because the MBTI is such an important part of the use of the Myers-Briggs type theory, it will receive considerable attention. The interaction between the counselor's MBTI type and the client's MBTI type also has interesting ramifications. Because of its complexity, readers will find that the information in this chapter is insufficient to enable them to use the Myers-Briggs type theory in counseling without formal course work or attendance at workshops, as well as further reading.

Within the Myers-Briggs typology, the two most basic concepts are perception–judgment and extraversion–introversion. The next section deals with how individuals perceive their surroundings and then make judgments or decisions about their observations. This then can be related to an individual's view of the world, that is, focus on the outer world (extraversion) or on the inner world (introversion). These can be seen as "preference patterns," or different ways that individuals prefer to make decisions and choices.

PERCEIVING AND JUDGING

Myers-Briggs theory pertains to the way that individuals observe their world and make decisions based on their perceptions (Myers, 1993). In dealing with the world, the first step is perception. Becoming aware of events, people, objects, or ideas, the individual perceives this information. Then, the individual must decide or make conclusions about the observed events, people, objects, or ideas. In doing so, the individual is judging the events and ideas that have been perceived. According to Myers, much of an individual's mental activity is devoted to *perceiving* and/or *judging*. For example, when an adolescent watches a movie, he or she takes in information (perceives) and then makes decisions about the movie: whether it was liked, appreciated, informative, and so on (judges). Throughout school and work activities, individuals are constantly perceiving and judging. There are two modes of perceiving and two modes of judging.

The Two Ways of Perceiving

The two contrasting ways of perceiving are *sensing* and *intuition*. Sensing is taking in information by using visual and auditory processes along with smell, taste, and touch. In contrast, intuition concerns the use of the unconscious, a concept of great importance in Jungian theory. Rather than direct perception, as in sensing, intuition is indirect and adds ideas to external perceptions. It was the belief of Jung, incorporated into the Myers-Briggs theory, that a preference for perception (and other Myers-Briggs concepts) was innate and not learned through interaction with the environment.

People who prefer sensing prefer to observe, primarily through hearing, vision, and touch. Their focus is on events that happen immediately around them. People who prefer sensing often have a good memory for details and are able to make clear observations. An adolescent who visits the dentist and makes use of the sensing perception may well be aware of the tools the dentist uses, the mannerisms of the dentist, and the location of the dental tools in the mouth. This common experience may eventually have some effect on occupational choice at a later time. At this point, the detailed information about the dental experience is stored in memory. This is in marked contrast to the opposite mode of perceiving: intuition.

By use of insight, an individual may perceive meanings and relationships in events. This insight into observations and ideas can be called *intuition*. Intuition takes visible and auditory (and other) information as a base and goes beyond it. Often the individual using intuition is focused not on the current event, but on a future event. Rather than being concrete, intuition is abstract, imaginative, and often creative. An adolescent who uses intuition while at the dentist's office is likely to imagine what the next dental appointment may be like (that it may be much worse than the current one) or may imagine himself or herself as a dentist (filling cavities and doing other dental work). This response to the dentist is in marked contrast to the practical, present-oriented sensing response described in the previous paragraph. After an idea is perceived, whether sensed or intuited, a judgment is often made about it.

The Two Ways of Judging

Just as there are two kinds of perception (sensing and intuition), there are two types of judgment: *thinking* and *feeling*. After perceiving an event, an individual is likely to act primarily in one way, thinking or feeling. Thinking refers to analyzing and being objective about an observed idea or event. Feeling is a subjective reaction, often related to one's own values.

When using thinking judgment, an individual may be concerned with logic or analysis. The person tries to be objective in making a judgment about a perceived event. He or she may be concerned with judging the event or idea fairly and in the process may use objective criticism to analyze his or her perception. Returning to the adolescent in the dentist's chair, the individual may judge whether the experience will be similar next time, whether he or she would like to be a dentist and could perform dental functions, or what the dentist will do next.

A feeling judgment is deciding based on the values applied to observations or ideas. In making a feeling judgment, an individual is concerned with the impact of the judgment. Such individuals are more likely to be interested in human as opposed to technical problems. Again returning to the dentist's chair as an example, a feeling judgment may be concerned with wondering what it would be like to be a dentist who helps someone but creates physical pain in the process. This concern for others is in marked contrast to the previous example, which uses thinking judgment.

Combinations of Perceiving and Judging

Since perceiving precedes judging, these two functions are combined in individuals. Myers et al. (1998) describes the four combinations of perceiving and judging that can occur:

Sensing and Thinking
Sensing and Feeling
Intuition and Feeling
Intuition and Thinking

According to Myers (1993), individuals prefer one of these four categories. How people perceive and judge has an impact not only on their own way of life, but also on how they interact with others. People who use sensing and thinking abilities to perceive events and make judgments about events are very different from those who use primarily intuition and feeling. Some examples will help to illustrate.

Sensing and Thinking   People who rely on sensing for perceiving and on thinking for judging are likely to focus on collecting facts that can be verified by their observations. They may want to see or hear what has happened. They may want to count the profits or assess the output of a machine. Such people are quite practical and pragmatic. They are likely to choose occupations that demand analysis of facts. Examples of such occupations are law, business management, accounting and auditing, and production and purchasing. When making a career decision for themselves, they are likely to use a rational decision-making process based on information they have acquired through occupational literature and talking with others.

Sensing and Feeling   Although relying on vision, hearing, and other senses, these people make decisions based on feeling. They are aware of the importance of feelings to themselves and others when making a decision. Because of their emphasis on others, they are more likely to be interested in observations about people than objects. Examples of occupations that they are likely to seek out are the medical profession, social work, teaching children, and providing customer services. In making a career decision, they will focus on information about people and occupations, being aware of how they will feel doing a certain kind of work on a day-to-day basis.

Intuition and Feeling   Rather than focus on current observations or happenings, people who intuit are likely to be concerned about future possibilities. Their feeling involvement is likely to be personal, warm, and inspired. They are apt to take a creative approach to meeting human needs and to be less concerned about objects. Examples of occupations would include clergy, teaching at the college or high school level, advertising, and social service occupations. When making a career decision, they are likely to use hunches based on what is best for them. Their emphasis is on feelings about observations rather than weighing the observations themselves.

Intuition and Thinking   Those who use intuition and thinking are likely to make decisions based on analysis that uses hunches and projections about the future. They tend to enjoy solving problems, particularly those of a theoretical nature. Occupations that they tend to seek out include scientific research, computing, business (particularly financial) decision making, and development of new projects. In making their own career decisions, people using intuition and thinking are likely to project themselves into the future, thinking about what types of work would offer particular opportunities. Although based on projections about the future, their decision making would be logical and clear to them.

Two Counseling Examples

Two brief counseling dialogues will illustrate two different combinations of perception and judgment. The first will illustrate a counselor's assessment of sensing and thinking, and the second will illustrate intuition and feeling.

Sharon is a college sophomore who has sought career counseling because she is thinking of entering a business occupation but is not sure which one.

CL: Since we talked last week, I've been looking into a number of occupations. I went to the career library and started to read about careers such as stockbroker and banker. I only had time to read about six, but I intend to go back.

CO: It's good to hear that you got off to a quick start. [The concrete approach of the client sounds as if she is perceiving by using her sensing abilities.]

CL: There are several brochures on stockbroker and banker, not to mention other careers. I want to make sure that I have time to read them and weigh the information. Do you think it would be helpful for me to take notes?

CO: You seem to have a systematic way of doing things; notes seem to fit for you. [The counselor wants to reinforce the logical method that the client uses, which fits with people who use sensing and thinking.]

CL: I know that the occupational scales that I scored high on on that interest inventory fit with these careers. But I do want to find out more about them. Maybe I'll talk with my father about it.

CO: That sounds like a good idea. You're really getting a lot of information to make a decision. [Getting and collecting information about occupations and then analyzing it seems to be the style of this client, which fits in well with the sensing and thinking modes of perceiving and judging.]

Harvey uses a very different approach to career decision making. Also a sophomore in college, Harvey is exploring occupations in the social sciences and uses an approach that combines intuition with feeling.

> CL: I'm so bored with school. I want to get out and do something, something that is going to mean something. I feel as if I'm just marking time. I'm not doing anything that's meaningful.
>
> CO: You'd feel happier if you were doing something now that would make you feel worthwhile. [The client's feeling of frustration is strong and there is an absence of observations about events in his statements.]
>
> CL: Yes, I feel that I'd like to make a difference. I am working on an adult literacy project at the Literacy Center at school. That's probably the thing I get the most out of, even more than my courses. Helping an adult, like this man I'm working with, to learn to read really makes me feel good. I just wish that I could do more of it.
>
> CO: You really want to have an impact on others. [Harvey's perceptions of what goes on at the Literacy Center are intuitive. The counselor hears how important feeling is to Harvey in making judgments about his work with the literacy project.]
>
> CL: I know that I want to help people; that's why I've tried to keep my grades up. I figure I have to in order to get into clinical psychology or psychiatry.
>
> CO: It sounds as if it's difficult, but you really seem to be putting a lot of effort into what you eventually might do, even though you're not sure. [Being aware of Harvey's commitment, the counselor wants to reinforce it, even though Harvey's exact choice about the future is not yet determined.]

Note the contrast between Harvey and Sharon. Sharon's approach is very practical and systematic. On the other hand, Harvey has a mission, which he is enthusiastic about. He just hasn't defined it very clearly at this point. This contrast between a sensing–thinking and an intuitive–feeling approach is an illustration of how Myers-Briggs theory can aid in understanding career decision making.

The Preference for Perception or Judgment

When using the Myers-Briggs typology, it is important not only to understand how a client perceives and judges, but also to know which process is more important. People differ as to how important they consider perceiving objects and people around them in contrast to making judgments or decisions. Some people prefer to make decisions based on relatively few facts *(judgment)*, while others prefer to weigh many facts before reaching a judgment *(perception)*. In order to make a decision, people must stop perceiving and then judge. People who have a perceiving attitude continue to take information in and do not decide. Those who have a judging attitude are apt to stop perceiving and make a judgment without including anymore evidence. People who use judgment are apt to have a sense of order in their lives, whereas people who use perception just live their lives.

EXTRAVERSION AND INTROVERSION

Another factor that adds to the understanding of how individuals use perception and judgment is introversion versus extraversion. The common meanings of introvert and extravert are different from those used by Jung and Myers. In common terminology, *introversion* is generally associated with being shy and quiet, whereas *extraversion* refers to being louder and more outgoing. For Jung and Myers, the terms introversion and extraversion refer to how one sees the world. *Introversion* refers to making perceptions and judgments based on one's interests in his or her inner world. In contrast, *extraversion* refers to using perceptions and judgments in the outer world. For the introvert, the inner world, consisting of concepts and ideas, is important. For the extravert, the outer world, concern with other people and objects, is important. Obviously, both introverts and extraverts live in the inner and outer world. The difference is that introverts prefer the inner world, whereas extraverts prefer the outer world.

Extraverts often like to take action. They want to work with people or things by talking and interacting. They prefer to speak directly to an individual rather than to write a memo. Being verbally and physically active is important to them.

In contrast, introverts enjoy thinking. They may like to work out problems or think for a long time before acting on an experience. They may be more quiet than extroverts, not necessarily due to shyness, but due to the need for time to think.

Introversion and extraversion are used in combination with judgment and perception in the Myers-Briggs system. Some people prefer to use judgment and perception in the outer world, others in the inner world. Each of the four perceiving and judging types described earlier will have a preference for either the inner world (introvert) or the outer world (extravert).

Regarding preference for work, extraverts tend to like activity that provides contact with people, whereas introverts are likely to prefer activity where there is time for concentration. Thus, extraverts may prefer sales and business management occupations as well as social service occupations. On the other hand, introverts may prefer occupations such as science and accounting, where they spend time solving problems on their own. When they do this, they are likely to be more careful in dealing with details than extraverts, being more patient in that they can work on one project for a long time. Introverts do not need to work as part of a team; rather, they prefer to work alone without interruptions.

THE SIXTEEN TYPE COMBINATIONS

In the Myers-Briggs typology, the different ways of judging and perceiving, the preference for judgment or perception, and the preference for introversion or extraversion act in concert with each other to yield 16 different types. Type tables, such as Table 5-1 (pp. 128–129), are often used to

Table 5-1 *Characteristics Frequently Associated with Each Type*

	Sensing Types		Intuitive Types	
	ISTJ	*ISFJ*	*INFJ*	*INTJ*
	Quiet, serious, earn success by thoroughness and dependability. Practical, matter-of-fact, realistic, and responsible. Decide logically what should be done and work toward it steadily, regardless of distractions. Take pleasure in making everything orderly and organized—their work, their home, their life. Value traditions and loyalty.	Quiet, friendly, responsible, and conscientious. Committed and steady in meeting their obligations. Thorough, painstaking, and accurate. Loyal, considerate, notice and remember specifics about people who are important to them, concerned with how others feel. Strive to create an orderly and harmonious environment at work and at home.	Seek meaning and connection in ideas, relationships, and material possessions. Want to understand what motivates people and are insightful about others. Conscientious and committed to their firm values. Develop a clear vision about how best to serve the common good. Organized and decisive in implementing their vision.	Have original minds and great drive for implementing their ideas and achieving their goals. Quickly see patterns in external events and develop long-range explanatory perspectives. When committed, organize a job and carry it through. Skeptical and independent, have high standards of competence and performance—for themselves and others.
	ISTP	*ISFP*	*INFP*	*INTP*
	Tolerant and flexible, quiet observers until a problem appears, then act quickly to find workable solutions. Analyze what makes things work and readily get through large amounts of data to isolate the core of practical problems. Interested in cause and effect, organize facts using logical principles, value efficiency.	Quiet, friendly, sensitive, and kind. Enjoy the present moment, what's going on around them. Like to have their own space and to work within their own time frame. Loyal and committed to their values and to people who are important to them. Dislike disagreements and conflicts, do not force their opinions or values on others.	Idealistic, loyal to their values and to people who are important to them. Want an external life that is congruent with their values. Curious, quick to see possibilities, can be catalysts for implementing ideas. Seek to understand people and to help them fulfill their potential. Adaptable, flexible, and accepting unless a value is threatened.	Seek to develop logical explanations for everything that interests them. Theoretical and abstract, interested more in ideas than in social interaction. Quiet, contained, flexible, and adaptable. Have unusual ability to focus in depth to solve problems in their area of interest. Skeptical, sometimes critical, always analytical.

Introverts

ESTP	ESFP	ENFP	ENTP
Flexible and tolerant, they take a pragmatic approach focused on immediate results. Theories and conceptual explanations bore them—they want to act energetically to solve the problem. Focus on the here-and-now, spontaneous, enjoy each moment that they can be active with others. Enjoy material comforts and style. Learn best through doing.	Outgoing, friendly, and accepting. Exuberant lovers of life, people, and material comforts. Enjoy working with others to make things happen. Bring common sense and a realistic approach to their work, and make work fun. Flexible and spontaneous, adapt readily to new people and environments. Learn best by trying a new skill with other people.	Warmly enthusiastic and imaginative. See life as full of possibilities. Make connections between events and information very quickly, and confidently proceed based on the patterns they see. Want a lot of affirmation from others, and readily give appreciation and support. Spontaneous and flexible, often rely on their ability to improvise and their verbal fluency.	Quick, ingenious, stimulating, alert, and outspoken. Resourceful in solving new and challenging problems. Adept at generating conceptual possibilities and then analyzing them strategically. Good at reading other people. Bored by routine, will seldom do the same thing the same way, apt to turn to one new interest after another.
ESTJ	**ESFJ**	**ENFJ**	**ENTJ**
Practical, realistic, matter-of-fact. Decisive, quickly move to implement decisions. Organize projects and people to get things done, focus on getting results in most efficient way possible. Take care of routine details. Have a clear set of logical standards, systematically follow them and want others to also. Forceful in implementing their plans.	Warmhearted, conscientious, and cooperative. Want harmony in their environment, work with determination to establish it. Like to work with others to complete tasks accurately and on time. Loyal, follow through even in small matters. Notice what others need in their day-by-day lives and try to provide it. Want to be appreciated for who they are and for what they contribute.	Warm, empathetic, responsive, and responsible. Highly attuned to the emotions, needs, and motivations of others. Find potential in everyone, want to help others fulfill their potential. May act as catalysts for individual and group growth. Loyal, responsive to praise and criticism. Sociable, facilitate others in a group, and provide inspiring leadership.	Frank, decisive, assume leadership readily. Quickly see illogical and inefficient procedures and policies, develop and implement comprehensive systems to solve organizational problems. Enjoy long-term planning and goal setting. Usually well informed, well read, enjoy expanding their knowledge and passing it on to others. Forceful in presenting their ideas.

Extraverts

Source: Modified and reproduced by special permission of the Publisher, Consulting Psychologists Press, Inc., Palo Alto CA 94303 from *Introduction to Type,* 6th Edition by Isabel Briggs Myers. Copyright 1998 by Consulting Psychologists Press, Inc. All rights reserved. Further reproduction is prohibited without the Publisher's written consent.

ISTJ	ISFJ	INFJ	INTJ
ISTP	ISFP	INFP	INTP
ESTP	ESFP	ENFP	ENTP
ESTJ	ESFJ	ENFJ	ENTJ

Extraversion–
Introversion

Sensing–Intuition

I
E

S	N

Thinking–Feeling

Judgment–Perception

T	F	F	T

J
P
P
J

Figure 5-1 Format of the type tables. (Modified and reproduced by special permission of the publisher, Consulting Psychologists Press, Inc., Palo Alto, CA 94303, from *MBTI Manual: A Guide to the Development and Use of the Myers-Briggs Type Indicator* by Isabel Briggs Myers, Mary H. McCaulley, Naomi L. Quenk, and Allen L. Hammer [3rd ed., p. 36.] Copyright by Consulting Psychologists Press, Inc.)

describe the relationships among types. In order to examine the interrelationships of the four basic bipolar dimensions, it is helpful to use abbreviations. The following abbreviations will be used throughout the rest of the chapter:

extravert	=	E	introvert	=	I
sensing	=	S	intuition	=	N
thinking	=	T	feeling	=	F
judgment	=	J	perception	=	P

Figure 5-1 illustrates the format of the type tables in terms of the four bipolar dimensions. At the top of the figure are the 16 combinations of four dimensions. By examining the diagrams directly below the 16 combinations, you can see the relationships of the dimensions more clearly. Note that introversion appears in the top half and extraversion in the bottom half of the 16 combinations. Sensing functions appear on the left side of the table and intuition on the right side. Likewise, thinking and feeling dimensions as well as judgment and perception dimensions are distributed in a systematic manner. Figure 5-1 serves as an outline for the descriptions found in Table 5-1. These descriptions give a brief overview of the characteristics of people who fall into each of the 16 categories. In their extensive manual, Myers et al. (1998) caution that type definitions are not to be taken literally; they describe general characteristics of individuals falling into 16 types. They see these types as gifts or attributes that people make use of. They discourage the notion that there are only 16 types of people in the world and that all people within a category are similar to each other. These types are described in far greater detail in the manual, along with the various letter combinations. The Myers-Briggs Type Indicator yields scores on each of the four dimensions that point in the direction of sensing or intuiting, thinking or feeling, judging or perceiving, and extraversion or introversion. The MBTI, an important component when using the Myers-Briggs theory, will be discussed in more detail in a later section. When using the Myers-Briggs typology, it is helpful to be aware that either the judging or the perceiving process may be more significant, an important consideration in how the categorization by type is to be interpreted.

DOMINANT AND AUXILIARY PROCESSES

Probably the most complex and confusing concept to those who are beginning to learn the Myers-Briggs type theory is dominant and auxiliary processes. Perhaps the easiest way to understand this concept is to think of the last letter of the type code as determining the dominant or auxiliary process. If the last letter is P, then the style of perceiving (either intuitive or sensing) is the key process. If the last letter is J, then the way of judging (either thinking or feeling) is the key process.

The dominant process is the guiding one. It is the general, and the auxiliary process is the lieutenant. What makes this particularly complex is that for extraverts, the last letter of the code (J or P) indicates the dominant process; for introverts, the last letter indicates the auxiliary function. The reason is that since introverts function in the inner world, the dominant function is an inner-world function rather than an outer-world function. For extraverts, the dominant process is in the outer world of people and things. For introverts, the dominant process is in ideas and thoughts.

Another way of describing why the introvert's dominant process is the opposite of that indicated by the last letter of the Myers-Briggs code (J or P, judging or perceiving) is that introverts use their dominant process for the inner world and their auxiliary process for the outer world, whereas extraverts use their auxiliary process for the inner world and their dominant process for the outer world. The last letter of the code (J or P) thus refers to a preference for perceiving or judging in the outer world. Introverts whose dominant process is a judging process (thinking or feeling) show perceptiveness of their auxiliary process in dealing with the outer world and live their outer lives in this perceptive framework. The inner judgingness is not apparent to others. Also, introverts whose dominant process is perceptive (sensing or intuition) do not outwardly behave as if they were perceptive people. Rather, they show the judgingness of the auxiliary process. Others would see them as leading their outer lives in the judging attitude.

The preceding discussion is complex. Describing the auxiliary and dominant processes requires thorough familiarity with the Myers-Briggs typology. Critics of the Myers-Briggs theory may point to the dominant and auxiliary processes as having little research support (Healy, 1989). On the other hand, some who find the Myers-Briggs theory to be useful in their counseling claim that the concept of dominant and auxiliary processes is essential. Because not all counselors apply the concepts of dominant and auxiliary, the examples that will be used to illustrate Myers-Briggs conceptualization in counseling will focus on the types themselves rather than on the dominant and auxiliary processes.

USING THE MYERS-BRIGGS TYPOLOGY IN COUNSELING

This section will focus on examples that illustrate two major career issues: career decision making and career adjustment. Over a period of many years, researchers have accumulated a considerable amount of data that relate Myers-Briggs type to occupational choice. In their manual, Myers et al. (1998) describe the types of people in many different occupations. These are listed primarily by four-letter codes. More data are available in the *Atlas of Type Tables* (1987), which includes more information about occupational groups and their codes. To summarize this information, Table 5-2 lists examples of frequent occupational choices that are made by people of each type. Some occupations occur in more than one category. Still, this table gives an idea of those occupations that are most commonly associated with certain Myers-Briggs types. This information that categorizes occupations by type can be useful in both career decision making and work adjustment counseling.

Tables 5-3, 5-4, 5-5, and 5-6 can also be useful in that they list the effects of each of the eight poles (extravert–introvert, Table 5-3; sensing–intuition, Table 5-4; thinking–feeling, Table 5-5; and judgment–perception, Table 5-6) on individuals' preferences for work situations. For example, extraverts tend to prefer variety and action, whereas introverts prefer quiet and working alone. Sensing types like established ways of doing things, whereas intuitive types dislike doing the same thing repeatedly. Thinking types tend to respond to people's ideas rather than their feelings, whereas feeling types respond more to people's values than their thoughts. Judging types work best when they can follow a plan, while perceptive types do not

Table 5-2   *Examples of Frequent Occupational Choices Made by Each Type*

ISTJ	ISFJ	INFJ	INTJ
Accountants	Health workers	Artists	Computer analysts
Auditors	Librarians	Clergy	Engineers
Engineers	Service workers	Musicians	Judges
Financial managers	Teachers	Psychiatrists	Lawyers
Police officers		Social workers	Operations
Steelworkers		Teachers	researchers
Technicians		Writers	Scientists
			Social scientists

ISTP	ISFP	INFP	INTP
Crafts workers	Clerical workers	Artists and	Artists
Construction	Construction	entertainers	Computer analysts
workers	workers	Editors	Engineers
Mechanics	Musicians	Psychiatrists	Scientists
Protective service	Outdoor workers	Psychologists	Writers
workers	Painters	Social workers	
Statisticians	Stock clerks	Writers	

ESTP	ESFP	ENFP	ENTP
Auditors	Child care	Actors	Actors
Carpenters	workers	Clergy	Journalists
Marketing	Mining engineers	Counselors	Marketing
personnel	Secretaries	Journalists	personnel
Police officers	Supervisors	Musicians	Photographers
Sales clerks		Public relations	Sales agents
Service workers		workers	

ESTJ	ESFJ	ENFJ	ENTJ
Administrators	Beauticians	Actors	Administrators
Financial	Health workers	Clergy	Credit managers
managers	Office managers	Consultants	Lawyers
Managers	Secretaries	Counselors	Managers
Salespeople	Teachers	Home economists	Marketing
Supervisors		Musicians	personnel
		Teachers	Operations
			researcher

Table 5-3 *Effects of Extraversion–Introversion in Work Situations*

Extraverts	Introverts
Like variety and action	Like quiet for concentration
Tend to be faster, dislike complicated procedures (especially ES types)	Tend to be careful with details, dislike sweeping statements (especially IS types)
Are often good at greeting people (especially EF types)	Have trouble remembering names and faces (especially IT types)
Are often impatient with long, slow jobs done alone	Tend not to mind working on one project for a long time alone and uninterrupted
Are interested in the activities of their job, in getting it done, and in how other people do it	Are interested in the details and/or ideas behind their job
Often do not mind the interruption of answering the telephone (especially EF types)	Dislike telephone intrusions and interruptions (especially IT types)
Often act quickly, sometimes without thinking it through	Like to think a lot before they act, sometimes without acting
Like to have people around (especially EF types)	Work contentedly alone (especially IT types)
Usually communicate freely (especially EF types)	Have some problems communicating to others since it's all in their heads (especially IT types)

Source: Modified and reproduced by special permission of the Publisher, Consulting Psychologists Press, Inc., Palo Alto, CA 94303, from *MBTI Manual: A Guide to the Development and Use of the Myers-Briggs Type Indicator* 3rd Edition by Isabel Briggs Myers, Mary H. McCaulley, Naomi L. Quenk, Allen L. Hammer. Copyright 1998 by Consulting Psychologists Press, Inc. All rights reserved. Further reproduction is prohibited without the Publisher's written consent.

mind last-minute changes. In the examples that follow, some reference will be made to these tables.

Example of Career Decision-Making Counseling

Edna is a 25-year-old African American female who has just been discharged from the U.S. Army after spending three years of active duty on a large military base. Much of her work entailed keeping records of supplies and office management. Although she liked her military experience, enjoying the colleagues whom she worked with, she did not want to reenlist. Rather, she decided to take advantage of the GI Bill, which would finance much of her future education. Prior to entering the military, she had been a waitress. This is not an occupation that she wishes to return to. She is living in a small apartment with her sister and her sister's husband in Pittsburgh. Now she has decided to seek counseling to help her decide on future plans.

The following segment is part of the second interview. During the first appointment with the counselor, Edna went over her work experience, discussing activities that she had enjoyed. Immediately after finishing the ses-

Table 5-4   *Effects of Sensing–Intuition in Work Situations*

Sensing Types	Intuitive Types
Like focusing on the here and now and reality	Like focusing on the future and what might be
Rely on standard ways to solve problems and dislike problems in which this approach doesn't work	Like solving new problems in unusual ways and dislike solving routine problems
Like an established order of doing things (especially SJ types)	Dislike doing the same thing repeatedly (especially NP types)
Enjoy using and perfecting skills already learned more than learning new ones	Enjoy learning a new skill more than using it
Work more steadily, with realistic idea of how long it will take (especially ISJ types)	Work in bursts of energy, powered by enthusiasm, with slack periods in between (especially ENP types)
Reach a conclusion step by step (especially ISJ types)	Reach an understanding quickly (especially ENP types)
Are patient with routine details (especially ISJ types)	Are impatient with routine details (especially ENP types)
Are impatient when the situation gets complicated (especially ES types)	Are patient with complex situations (especially IN types)
Are not often inspired and rarely trust the inspiration when they are	Follow their inspirations, good or bad, regardless of the data (especially with inadequate type development)
Seldom make factual errors	Frequently make errors of fact, preferring instead the big picture
Tend to be good at precise work (especially IS types)	Dislike taking time for precision (especially EN types)
Create something new by adapting something that exists	Create something new through a personal insight

sion, she completed the Myers-Briggs Type Indicator as well as the Strong Interest Inventory. On the Myers-Briggs Type Indicator, she scored ESFJ, or extraverted feeling with sensing. The last letter, J, means that her dominant process is feeling, which is a judging process; therefore, her auxiliary process is one of perception, which is sensing. Thus, she uses her favorite process, feeling, in dealing with others, and the auxiliary function, sensing, in her inner world. The counselor has just gone over this information with Edna and has reviewed the results of her Strong Interest Inventory. Her high scores were on the occupational theme S, Social, and on the basic interest scales for teaching and social service; she received many high scores

Table 5-5   *Effects of Thinking–Feeling in Work Situations*

Thinking Types	Feeling Types
Like analysis and putting things into logical order	Like harmony
Can get along without harmony	Efficiency may be badly disrupted by office feud
Tend to be firm minded	Tend to be sympathetic
Do not show emotion readily and are often uncomfortable dealing with people's feelings (especially IT types)	Tend to be very aware of other people and their feelings (especially EF types)
May hurt people's feelings without knowing it	Enjoy pleasing people, even in unimportant things
Tend to decide impersonally, sometimes paying insufficient attention to people's wishes	Often let decisions be influenced by their own or other people's personal likes and dislikes
Need to be treated fairly in accordance with the prevailing standards	Need praise and personal attention
Are able to reprimand people impersonally, although they may not like doing so	Dislike, even avoid, telling people unpleasant things
Are more analytically oriented—respond more easily to people's thoughts (especially IT types)	Are more people oriented—respond more easily to people's values

on S and E (Enterprising) occupational scales. Examples of these include human resources director, public administrator, social worker, and elementary school teacher.

Edna is a soft-spoken young woman with a pleasant smile and a very friendly presentation. This portion of the dialogue will focus on the counselor's use of the Myers-Briggs typology in conceptualizing Edna's career decision-making concerns.

> *CL:*   It's helpful to look at these tests. I knew that I didn't like the work in the army. It really was boring for me to monitor inventory records and to keep track of purchase requisitions and things like that. It was funny: People thought I liked my work, I guess because I got along so well with the others. The other women that I worked with were real nice. Sure, there was turnover, but I seemed to be able to get along with everyone.

Table 5-6 *Effects of Judging–Perceiving in Work Situations*

Judging Types	Perceiving Types
Work best when they can plan their work and follow the plan	Adapt well to changing situations
Like to get things settled and finished	Prefer leaving things open for alterations
May decide things too quickly (especially EJ types)	May unduly postpone decisions (especially IP types)
May dislike to interrupt the project they are on for a more urgent one (especially ISJ types)	May start too many projects and have difficulty finishing them (especially ENP types)
May not notice new things that need to be done in their desire to complete what they are doing	May postpone unpleasant jobs while finding other things more interesting in the moment
Want only the essentials needed to begin their work (especially ESJ types)	Want to know all about a new job (especially INP types)
Tend to be satisfied once they reach a judgment on a thing, situation, or person	Tend to be curious and welcome a new light on a thing, situation, or person

CO: Sounds as if getting along with others is very important to you in your work. [Feeling is an important process for Edna. It is not surprising that she emphasizes her feelings about others and wants to get along well with others.]

CL: Oh, yes, it is. I know some friends who worked in offices that were unfriendly, and I would have hated that. It seemed to me that the more my work had to do with people, the more I liked it. When I would have to fill in for the receptionist sometimes, I liked that more than my usual work, even though my usual work required more training. Often, when people would come into my office, they were looking for help, trying to find the right person, or trying to find a requisition. When I could help them, I really felt good, but I sometimes think I want to help in a different way.

CO: What kind of helping gives you a really good feeling? [The counselor speaks to Edna's emphasis on feeling. He wants to know what things are important to her. He suspects that it will be more difficult to get at her auxiliary process, sensing, which deals with her inner world, than to talk with her about her outer world, the dominant process of feeling.]

CL: I think I feel best when I'm helping children. It seems when I'm at home, not when I'm with my sister, I am always helping kids. I help them read;

CL: I help them when they're crying. All my mother's friends know I'm a soft touch. They can rely on me to help out.

CO: Yet you don't mind being a soft touch. [Again, the focus is on Edna's feeling type.]

CL: No, I don't. When we looked at the Strong Interest Inventory, I was glad to see teaching show up. I was afraid that maybe it would, and maybe it wouldn't.

CO: Can you tell me what you mean by would and wouldn't? [Because this is confusing, the counselor wants to hear what Edna seems to have mixed feelings about.]

CL: Well, sometimes I think deep down I've wanted to be a teacher.

CO: Tell me your thoughts about teaching. [Teaching is an occupation that ESFJ people often enter; see Table 5-2.]

CL: My father wanted me to work right away. We really didn't have any money. There were four children, all girls. I was the second youngest, and my oldest sister had gone to college. My father was pretty strict with me, and he didn't really let me do what I wanted. But I really admired him. He worked very hard, and I wanted to please him very much.

CO: But it seems as if now you want to please yourself. [Being compliant and wanting to be loyal to people they respect can be characteristic of ESFJ people.]

CL: My father died two years ago, and I hate to say this, but somehow I feel relieved a little bit. Like now there are no blockades in my way.

CO: It's hard to be critical of your father now. [The counselor wants to be gentle with Edna, because her father is an important part of her.]

CL: I want to do something that I will enjoy. Now with money available, I think that I could go to school. It really seems like that would be a wonderful thing to do. Even my father wouldn't have objected if I had support from the government like I do.

CO: It really is nice to be able to be concerned about a decision that can be helpful for you. [The counselor is aware that Edna is starting to appreciate his confidence in her. Knowing that people who are ESFJ often appreciate support, he starts to offer more. He knows that Edna was disappointed by her father's lack of support.]

CL: I guess sometimes down inside I feel that teaching small children would be marvelous for me. I guess it scares me sometimes to think that. I used to hear that there weren't many jobs in teaching and things like that. I don't hear that much anymore. But I guess I never really had much confidence that I could do it.

CO: You seem to be excited when you think of it now, though. [Again, the counselor wants to reinforce feelings that Edna has inside that this is right. Her judgment about career choice is based on feeling. The fact that her Myers-Briggs type code and her Strong Interest Inventory results are in agreement with her preference relates to the thinking aspect of judging, which Edna does not use much.]

In this example, the Myers-Briggs Type Indicator serves as a source for guiding the counselor in conceptualizing Edna's issues about her future career choices. He chooses not to introduce the terminology to her, but to use the conceptual framework of the Myers-Briggs theory as a basis for his own work. If it seems helpful to him to explain the concepts to Edna again, or to use them with her, then he will.

Example of Career Adjustment Counseling

Often, in counseling, a counselor finds it helpful to develop weaker components of an individual's perception and judgment. For example, a person whose Myers-Briggs type is INTP uses sensing and feeling less frequently than intuition and thinking. Myers and McCaulley (1985, p. 65) suggest that a counselor should work on one process at a time, for example, should work on judgment but not perception and judgment at the same time. Further, the work should be conscious and purposeful, and the counselor should not let other processes interfere. When working with people who are having difficulty on their job, counselors often find it helpful to make use of functions that are not a strong part of the individual's personality. These weaker functions are called *tertiary* and *inferior functions*. They are described in more detail in other publications, such as Myers et al. (1998) and Quenk (1996). An example of making use of weaker functions follows.

George is a 45-year-old Native American raised in New Mexico. He is married, with two teenage children. He has a doctorate in biology and has been employed at a large cancer research hospital to do basic research for the past 12 years. Two years ago, he was put in charge of a research team. Research progress has been frustrating. As a result, his team of five people have become upset with each other. Two of the team members don't talk to each other any longer. George's supervisor has been concerned about this lack of progress. Members of George's team have talked to the supervisor about the fact that there is much tension among members of the group.

George recently complained of chest pain. After being checked thoroughly by a physician, George was referred to a counselor for help with work-related issues. The physician felt, after talking with George, that tension experienced at work might be the cause of the pain. Although somewhat reluctant to seek counseling, feeling that he should be able to handle the problems himself, George has come back for his second meeting with the counselor. After their first meeting, he completed the Myers-Briggs Type Indicator. His scores are summarized as INTP.

CL: I've been having a lot of trouble at work. I find myself distracted constantly. We're involved in much important research, and the people who work with me seem to spend more time bickering with each other and less time researching. I can't concentrate, and I don't like it. I find that I'm upset at the end of the day. I keep hoping things will work out, but they do not.

CO: This sounds very disturbing for you. You can't get your work done, and other people aren't getting their work done. [The counselor is aware that George's dominant process is thinking. He is thinking a lot about his research and the problems at work without the input of others. This process is an introverted one; thus it stays in his mind.]

CL: Yes. I am working often in my own head. I'm thinking constantly. I think at work; I can't stop thinking at home. I find that I'm distracted. My children notice this, too.

CO: What seems to be bothering you the most? [The counselor wishes to focus on a problem that she may be able to help with.]

CL: Part of it is we have some new doctoral-level people who have done good work before but haven't worked under my supervision. They don't say much to me, and I don't say much to them. I know I need to do something about it. Sometimes I can feel the tension; sometimes I can feel it in my chest.

CO: Tell me more about that feeling in the chest. [The counselor seizes the opportunity to talk about the least well-developed function, the inferior function, feeling, which is the opposite of George's dominant function, thinking.]

CL: I guess I feel tight. I usually feel upset, and I don't want to say anything.

CO: That's important information. [The counselor wants to deal with the feeling process, the least well developed of George's perception and judgment functions.]

CL: I guess it is important. It's hard for me sometimes to focus on things other than my research. These personal matters seem so trivial to me. But I'm starting to find that they are not. I remember what you said earlier when we were talking about the Myers-Briggs Type Indicator. You spoke of how important thinking is to me. It really is.

CO: I know, George. One of the things that we can work on is developing that other side of thinking, feeling. [The counselor avoids a long technical discussion of the Myers-Briggs Type Indicator and is eager to follow the lead-in that George has provided.]

CL: I know what happens at work is important. Sometimes I will tell myself it's not.

CO: It's good that you recognize that, George. Perhaps we can work more on that—recognizing not only your own feelings, but the feelings of others also.

CL: It is just uncomfortable for me. Sometimes I find myself almost rushing to get through the laboratory into my own little office, where I can work alone. I need to do more.

CO: What is it that you need to do more of, George?

CL: I need to talk to the people working at their desks and tables in the lab.

CO: That sounds good, George. How might you do it? [The counselor is pleased that George recognizes the need to develop his feeling side. She wants to see what he can do to develop his feeling function.]

CL: I think I need to stop and talk with them, see how things are going, maybe relax. I have some idea that my tension may be communicated to them.

CO: That sounds good, George. That could be happening. [George may be taking advantage of his intuitive process at this point. The counselor is pleased to hear that and yet can return to working on the feelings that are being discussed.]

CL: I know I need to slow down; I need to relax when I'm talking with someone in the lab and not pull away as quickly as I do. How can I do that?

CO: Being in a comfortable position, slowing your breathing, relaxing your hands. Anything to slow yourself down might help. [The counselor responds to this specific request for information, knowing that problem solving is something that is likely to appeal to George because of his emphasis on thinking.]

CL: It sounds simple.

CO: It's not so simple. Maybe we can work on some relaxation techniques later today. There are different ways of slowing down. [The counselor does not want to let relaxation be the only answer to dealing with the feeling function. She wants to return to ways that George can feel more and understand the feelings of others at his work site.]

In this example, the counselor tries to strengthen and develop George's weakest function, the judging function of feeling. For her, the Myers-Briggs Type Indicator provides a way of conceptualizing George's work adjustment problem. Being well versed in the Myers-Briggs theory, she can think about George in terms of the concepts themselves. She can then relate George's type to her knowledge of the concepts, integrating this relationship into her counseling conceptualization. The counselor recognizes that the problem is a difficult one. Developing one's inferior function is not easy. In her continuing work with George, she may look at ways in which he can change his work environment to alleviate the situation, believing that it is easier for George to change his work environment to match his type than to change his type to match his work environment (Myers et al., 1998). Some examples of such changes would be getting others to assist him in supervision or changing his assignment to return to more research and less supervision. Certainly, George's choice of work, science, is a frequent choice of INTP individuals (Table 5-2). His difficulty with supervision is consistent with the description of thinking in Table 5-5. It is for the counselor and George to decide how much George can change and how much the environment can change.

The counseling dialogues used in this chapter give a small sample of the use of Myers-Briggs typological theory in counseling on career issues. Several books have been written that describe the 16 types in detail and include case studies that emphasize the conceptualization of the Myers-Briggs Indicator. Keirsey and Bates (1978) describe both temperaments and types in detail. A good overview of MBTI theory and its relationship to careers is *Introduction to Type and Careers* (Hammer, 1993). Particularly helpful for work adjustment counseling is *Introduction to Type in Organizations* (Hirsh & Kummerow, 1998). Specifically focusing on career counseling is *Do What You Are: Discover the Perfect Career for You through the Secrets of Personality Type* (Tieger & Barron-Tieger, 1992). How different types handle work tasks differently and how to adapt tasks to type is described in *WORK-Types* (Kummerow, Barger, & Kirby, 1997). A casebook approach, such as the one by Provost (1993), which has case illustrations for a variety of the 16 types, can be particularly helpful to counselors learning the Myers-Briggs typology. Possibly, the single best overview of the Myers-Briggs topological theory is *Gifts Differing* (1993) by Isabel Myers with

Peter Myers. These books use numerous examples and cases to explore and explain the intricacies of the Myers-Briggs system of types.

THE ROLE OF OCCUPATIONAL INFORMATION

From a career development point of view, Myers-Briggs type theory can be conceived of as a matching kind of trait and factor theory. Using the Myers-Briggs Type Indicator (or its conceptual system), the counselor can match the client's Myers-Briggs type with the Myers-Briggs types of occupations. By using information such as that in Tables 5-3 to 5-6 and in *Introduction to Type and Careers* (Hammer, 1993), the counselor can gain an idea of the preferred work setting of different Myers-Briggs types. Knowledge of an individual's type can be matched with knowledge of which types select which work settings most frequently (Table 5-2). In their manual, Myers and McCaulley (1985) give an example of a counselor giving occupational information to a client based on information known about various types. An excerpt from their example will help illustrate this:*

> Q. I am an ISTJ and want to enter psychology. Where would I fit?
> A. You are more likely to like the work of an experimental psychologist. In one study, more than twice the expected number of ISTJs chose experimental (I ratio 2.4, $p < .01$). In fact, all the ISTJs in that study chose one of the experimental fields. Remember that most of your colleagues are likely to prefer intuition, but you will probably find more people who share your interest in the experimental fields.
> Q. I know I want psychology, but I'm not sure which field to choose. What is the difference between clinical and experimental psychology?
> A. Clinical psychology attracts more psychologists who are concerned with possibilities (N-intuition) for people (F-feeling) (NF 72%; ratio 1.6, $p < .01$). Experimental psychology attracts more people interested in theory (N) and logical analysis (T-thinking), but there is also a sizable number of more practical people in experimental psychology (S ratio 1.8, $p < .001$). You will find all types in each area, but these facts may help you think about how your interests relate to the psychological specialties. (pp. 83, 84).

This example shows how a counselor who is extremely knowledgeable about Myers-Briggs type theory can extrapolate knowledge from the *Atlas of Type Tables* (1987) and the *MBTI Manual* (Myers et al., 1998) to give information to clients. There is no single source of occupational information that describes occupations solely in terms of Myers-Briggs types. Because

---

*Modified and reproduced by special permission of the Publisher, Consulting Psychologists Press, Inc., Palo Alto, CA 94303 from *MBTI Manual: A Guide to the Development and Use of the Myers-Briggs Type Indicator* 3rd Edition by Isabel Briggs Myers, Mary H. McCaulley, Naomi L. Quenk, Allen L. Hammer. Copyright 1998 by Consulting Psychologists Press, Inc. All rights reserved. Further reproduction is prohibited without the Publisher's written consent.

many Myers-Briggs types can exist within a given occupation, counselors need to be careful not to give the impression that only certain Myers-Briggs types can work in specified occupations. People with different Myers-Briggs types who enjoy the same occupations are likely to approach their work in a way that allows them to express their type. In their manual, Myers et al. are careful to describe the advantages of different points of view of various Myers-Briggs types within any given occupation.

However, there are some general suggestions that can be gathered from research into the ways that people of different types process information (Myers et al., 1998). In discussing occupational information with Sensing types, counselors may want to be concrete and specific, whereas with Intuitive types, they can be more abstract. For individuals whose thinking score is high, data about occupations should be objective; with those for whom feeling is strong, relating occupational information to the client's experiences may be most helpful. An introverted approach to learning career information is likely to focus on reading information and thinking about it. An extraverted approach may be to talk to others about occupations. Recently, Linnehan and Blau (1998) investigated job search behavior and found extraverted individuals preferred interactive job search behaviors, whereas introverted individuals preferred detached or less personal job search approaches. Counselors may want to help clients use both introverted and extraverted approaches.

THE ROLE OF TESTING

The Myers-Briggs Type Indicator and the Myers-Briggs typological theory are very closely wedded. Even counselors who are very familiar with the Myers-Briggs theory rarely use the theory with a client without administering the Myers-Briggs Type Indicator. More than for any other theory discussed in this book, the inventory is closely tied to the conceptualization process that a counselor uses with a client. The 420-page manual is extensive in its description of research that supports the use of the four Myers-Briggs dimensions. Furthermore, Thorne and Gough (1991) have summarized 30 years of research on types done at the Institute of Personality and Social Research at the University of California at Berkeley and Hammer (1996) summarizes a decade of research on the MBTI.

The manual describes the construction of the Myers-Briggs Type Indicator, Form M, as well as the construction of the earlier forms of the MBTI. Hundreds of studies that provide information about the reliability and validity of the MBTI are referred to in the manual (Myers et al., 1998). A few recent studies are mentioned here. For example, Bents and Wierschke (1996) found the German translation of the MBTI to be highly reliable. Marlow (1997) investigated the validity of adjectives used to describe the 16 MBTI types. The adjectives described the bipolar scales in a way that was usually theoretically consistent. Tischler (1994) and Karesh, Pieper, and Holland (1994) found support for the bipolar scales of the MBTI. In a study of 348 successful chief executive officers, Rytting, Ware, and Prince (1994) found a bimodal distribution of scores supporting the polarity of the four scales of the MBTI. Some attempts have been made to develop short forms of the MBTI. Harvey, Murray, and Markham (1994) tested three different short forms and found that they provided less information than the long form and that there were unacceptably high disagreement rates between the short forms and the long form.

The MBTI has been compared to other measures of personality. These studies provide construct validity for the MBTI and help counselors understand the eight constructs more clearly. For example, Tuel and Betz (1998) report predicted relationships between the MBTI and the six Holland themes and the personal styles score of the Strong Interest Inventory. The NEO Personality Inventory Form (Big Five) Extraversion score was found to be related to extraversion on the MBTI. Neuroticism was not correlated with any of the MBTI scales (Furnham, 1996). Other comparisons between the MBTI and the NEO can be found in the MBTI manual and in Mac-Donald, Anderson, Tsagarakis, and Holland (1994). The MBTI manual also reports relationships to other personality constructs and inventories.

Some writers have specifically addressed the relevance of the MBTI to career counseling. McCaulley (2000) describes some ways that the MBTI can be used with career services. Studying software technical professionals, Garden (1997) found that different psychological types had different views of their future career paths, especially when it concerned starting their own company. In career counseling with community college students, the MBTI was rated as being as useful as the Strong Interest Inventory (Katz, Joyner, & Seaman, 1999). When used to help understand how clients deal with career obstacles, such as reluctance to change, or problems due to anxiety or depression, the thinking and feeling scores were related to obstacles for males and the judgment–perception scores were related to obstacles for all clients (Healy & Woodward, 1998). Regarding resumé writing, the MBTI can help clients focus on strengths related to their psychological type in dealing with confidence in writing résumés (Peterson, 1998). Career counseling continues to be a significant research focus of the MBTI.

However, the Myers-Briggs Type Indicator is not above question, and several writers have challenged the findings presented previously. Pittenger (1993) provides evidence that the MBTI has limited counseling utility, reliability, and validity. Using a sample of men, Lorr (1991) was critical of the factor structure of the MBTI. Also, Healy (1989) argues against using the MBTI in counseling. He believes that there is limited evidence that classifying people into 16 types will enhance counseling, a view challenged by Murray (1990) and Tischler (1994). Further, Healy questions whether the Myers-Briggs Type Indicator measures the constructs defined by Jung. He also finds that there is no evidence that using the MBTI in counseling will help clients with their concerns. However, Healy and Woodward (1998) show the value of the MBTI in dealing with obstacles to clients' career development. In general, the research on the MBTI tends to focus on the four dimensions and not on the complex concepts that are used in counseling, such as the dominant and auxiliary processes. Despite these criticisms, researchers continue to develop and study the Myers-Briggs Type Indicator.

Several report forms and scoring systems are available for the MBTI. For the regular form of the MBTI, a special report is available called the *MBTI Career Report* (Hammer & MacDaid, 1994), which lists work behaviors and preferences that match the clients' type. Two instruments are available that provide more information, through more scales, for the four basic Myers-Briggs dimensions. The *MBTI Expanded Analysis* (Saunders, Myers, & Briggs, 1989a) offers 5 subscales for each of the four dimensions. Also, the *Type Differentiation Indicator* (Saunders, Myers, & Briggs, 1989b) includes the same 20 subscales for the four dimensions as the *MBTI Expanded Analysis*, as well as 7 other subscales. These instruments are relatively recent and have not been available long enough to generate validating research. However, they would appear to be useful to counselors as they help individuals explore MBTI concepts in depth and make a bridge to occupational choices that could be considered.

APPLYING THE THEORY TO WOMEN AND CULTURALLY DIVERSE POPULATIONS

In general, cultural and gender differences have recently become a greater focus of research in the study of the Myers-Briggs typology. The MBTI manual (Myers et al., 1998) does report the percentage of males and females at four levels of preference (slight, moderate, clear, or very clear) for each of the eight types. The sample sizes ranged between 15,000 and 25,000 for two different forms of the Myers-Briggs Type Indicator. By way of summary, the MBTI manual estimated that about 75% of women in the United States prefer feeling to thinking, and about 56% of men in the United States prefer thinking to feeling. Another view into this difference is provided by Laribee (1994), who studied accounting students, who would be expected to have a preference for thinking over feeling. The male preference for thinking was 83 to 85%, and the female preference ranged from 44 to 63%. With regard to the gender distribution of type for the other scales, it appears that slightly more men (54%) prefer introversion to extraversion, and slightly more women (52%) prefer extraversion to introversion. Regarding sensing and intuition, both men (72%) and women (75%) prefer sensing to intuition. These gender differences represent United States national samples (Myers et al., 1998).

A new emphasis in the MBTI manual is that of using type in multicultural settings (see Chapter 14, Kirby & Barger, 1998). The MBTI (Form G) has been translated into many languages: Anglicized English, Australian English, Bahasa Malay, Chinese, Danish, Dutch, European French, French Canadian, German, Italian, Korean, Norwegian, Portuguese, Spanish, Spanish/Castellano, and Swedish. All of these translations are available commercially and were deemed valid and reliable. Other translations are currently being tested as to their validity and reliability. The MBTI manual presents samples of the distribution of the 16 types combinations for high school, college, management, and other groups from many countries, such as Canada, Australia, New Zealand, Singapore, France, South Africa, Korea, Japan, Mexico, and several Latin American countries. Within the United States, samples of type distributions are also reported for African Americans and Hispanics. Kirby and Barger (1998) suggest that the MBTI can be used with clients of many cultures. They do suggest caution in using the MBTI with people from cultures that are group or collectivist in orientation such as black South Africans, the Maori of New Zealand, and certain Native American cultures.

Some recent studies of differences in type for individuals from different cultures will provide examples of the worldwide interest in Myers-Briggs theory. Comparisons were made between MBTI scores and college student preference for descriptions of specific types. African American females tended to be over represented on the ISTJ categories on the MBTI (Posey, Thorne, & Carskadon, 1999). Comparing the types of female middle school students and female counselors in Puerto Rico, Alvarado (1997) reported that both groups scored high in sensing and thinking, but the students scored higher on intuition. Comparing Canadian college students from a French-speaking background with those of an English-speaking background, Stalikas, Casas, and Carson (1996) reported that more of the English students scored high on feeling, intuition, and perception than the French. More of the French students scored high on introversion, sensation, thinking, and judging. Comparing managers from Mexico and the United States, Osborn, Osborn, and Twillman (1996) found Mexican managers to more frequently fit the STJ profile than did the managers from the United States. Mexican American ninth-graders also preferred sensing and thinking, whereas their Anglo-American counterparts preferred intuition and feeling (Lundberg, Osborne, & Miner, 1997). Comparing African American and Native American high school students, Nuby and Oxford (1998) found that African Americans preferred judging much more than Native Americans.

In characterizing the values of Native Americans, Little Soldier (1989) stressed the importance of cooperation, sharing, and the extended family. In a study of 210 non reservation Native American college freshmen, Simmons and Barrineau (1994) found that sensing for males and sensing and feeling for females were overrepresented among Native Americans compared to other freshmen, preferences that fit with the values described by Little Soldier. It is likely that in the future more studies such as these will be reported.

An interesting concept of the Myers-Briggs typology that may be particularly appropriate to understanding populations that may be oppressed, such as women and people from different cultural backgrounds, is *falsification* of type. Since the development of type is assumed to be inborn, environmental influences can distort or falsify it. Individuals who are taught to respond in a certain way may learn and outwardly behave as one type, while inwardly their true type is being frustrated. This interesting clinical concept presents a difficult research problem: How can one separate the real type from the falsified type? Those who counsel using Myers-Briggs typology may find that they are able to do this. Whether some women and some individuals from minority cultures have been trained or expected by society to behave in a certain way that does not fit their true type remains to be proved.

COUNSELOR ISSUES

Meyers et al. (1998) make several suggestions for dealing with clients of different types that are based on some of the research on how counselors communicate with their clients. These findings suggest that counselors need to adjust their style of communication for different Myers-Briggs types. In exploratory research, Yeakley (1982, 1983) suggested that it may be helpful for two people to be using the same communication style at the same time, whether it is in a business, a marriage, or a counseling relationship. For Yeakley, listening to sensing types means listening at a pragmatic and literal level. On the other hand, listening to an intuitive type requires listening to the underlying meaning. What does the speaker really mean, and what are the implications? When listening to a thinking type of person, the counselor should focus on the organization of the individual's comments, as in reading an essay: What are the main points, the less important points, and the overall concept? In contrast, listening to a feeling type would mean being aware of feelings about the client and the values or feelings projected by the client in the message. The implication is that counselors whose types are very different from those of their clients will have to expend considerable effort to alter their style of interaction to fit with that of their clients. For example, a counselor whose perceiving style is sensing and whose judging style is feeling may have to adjust to a client whose perceiving style is intuitive and whose judging style is thinking. Erickson (1993) found that, among 23 counselors, thinking types tended to choose to use behavioral, cognitive, rational-emotive, and reality therapies, whereas feeling types preferred Gestalt and person-centered approaches. Thus, counselors may perceive treatment methods for similar problems differently, depending on their type.

SUMMARY

Although not generally considered a theory of career development, the Myers-Briggs type theory has been used as such by many counselors. Its broad focus is on how people perceive and judge the world. There are two different ways of perceiving (sensing and intuition), as well as two different ways of judging (thinking and feeling). Individuals must use the perceiving and judging functions many times during the course of a day. In addition, they deal with their inner world of ideas (introversion) and with the outer world of people and objects (extraversion). In this chapter, the focus has been on relating these styles to career decision making and work adjustment. The complex interactions between the eight Myers-Briggs types, which represent four bipolar dimensions, have been illustrated in several counseling situations. Because the Myers-Briggs Type Indicator is an essential part of the Myers-Briggs theory of types, a discussion of research on the Myers-Briggs Type Indicator, as well as criticism of it, was presented. Readers will find that the presentation in this chapter is insufficient to enable them to use the Myers-Briggs Type Indicator in career counseling. Attendance at workshops that teach the use of the Myers-Briggs Type Indicator, as well as a thorough study of the MBTI manual (Myers et al., 1998), is strongly recommended.

References

Alvarado, I. Y. (1997, March). Psychological preference types of Puerto Rican school counselors and students using the Myers-Briggs Type Indicator. *Dissertation Abstracts International: Section A: Humanities and Social Services*, Vol. 57 (9-A): 3822.

Atlas of type tables. (1987). Gainesville, FL: Center for the Application of Psychological Type.

Bents, R., & Wierschke, A. (1996). Test-retest reliability of the Myers-Briggs Type Indicator. *Journal of Psychological Type, 36,* 42–46.

Erickson, D. B. (1993). The relationship between personality type and preferred counseling model. *Journal of Psychological Type, 27,* 39–41.

Furnham, A. (1996). The big five versus the big four: The relationship between the MBTI and NEO-PI Five Factor Model of Personality. *Personality and Individual Differences, 21,* 303–307.

Garden, A. (1997). Relationships between MBTI profiles, motivation profiles, and career paths. *Journal of Psychological Type, 41,* 3–16.

Hammer, A. L. (1993). *Introduction to type and careers.* Palo Alto, CA: Consulting Psychologists Press.

Hammer, A. L. (Ed.) (1996). *MBTI applications: A decade of research on the MBTI.* Palo Alto, CA: Consulting Psychologists Press.

Hammer, A. L., & MacDaid, G. P. (1994). *MBTI Career Report.* Palo Alto, CA: Consulting Psychologists Press.

Harvey, R. J., Murray, W. D., & Markham, S. E. (1994). Evaluation of three short-form versions of the Myers-Briggs Type Indicator. *Journal of Personality Assessment, 63,* 181–184.

Healy, C. C. (1989). Negative: The MBTI: Not ready for routine use in counseling. *Journal of Counseling and Development, 67,* 487–488.

Healy, C. C., & Woodward, G. A. (1998). The Myers-Briggs Type Indicator and Career Obstacles. *Measurement and Evaluation in Counseling and Development, 31,* 74–86.

Hirsh, S. K., & Kummerow, J. M. (1998). *Introduction to type in organizations* (3rd ed.). Palo Alto: Consulting Psychologists Press.

Jung, C. G. (1971). *Psychological types* (H. B. Baynes, Trans., rev. by R. F. C. Hull), *The collected works of C. G. Jung* (Vol. 6). Princeton, NJ: Princeton University Press. (Original work published 1921.)

Karesh, D., Pieper, W. A., & Holland, C. L. (1994). Comparing the MBTI, the Jungian Type Survey, and the Singer-Loomis Inventory of Personality. *Journal of Psychological Type, 30,* 30–38.

Katz, L., Joyner, J. W., & Seaman, N. (1999). Effects of joint interpretation of the Strong Interest Inventory and the Myers-Briggs Type Indicator in career choice. *Journal of Career Assessment, 7,* 281–297.

Keirsey, D., & Bates, M. (1978). *Please, understand me* (3rd ed.). Del Mar, CA: Prometheus Nemesis Books.

Kirby, L. K., & Barger, N. J. (1998). Uses of type in multicultural settings. In I. B. Myers, M. H. McCaulley, N. L. Quenk, & A. L. Hammer, *MBTI Manual* (3rd ed.). Palo Alto, CA: Consulting Psychologists Press.

Kummerow, J. M., Barger, N. J., & Kirby, L. K. (1997). *WORK-Types.* New York: Warner Books.

Laribee, S. F. (1994). The psychological types of college accounting students. *Journal of Psychological Type, 28,* 37–38.

Linnehan, F., & Blau, G. (1998). Exploring the emotional side of job search behavior for younger workforce entrants. *Journal of Employment Counseling, 35,* 98–113.

Little Soldier, L. (1989). Cooperative learning and the Native American student. *Phi Delta Kappa, 71,* 161–163.

Lorr, M. (1991). An empirical evaluation of the MBTI typology. *Personality and Individual Differences, 12,* 1141–1145.

Lundberg, D. J., Osborne, W. L., & Miner, C. U. (1997). Career maturity and personal preferences of Mexican-American and Anglo-American adolescents. *Journal of Career Development, 23,* 203–213.

MacDonald, D. A., Anderson, P. E., Tsagarakis, C. I., & Holland, C. J. (1994). Examination of the relationship between the Myers-Briggs Type Indicator and the NEO Personality Inventory. *Psychological Reports, 74,* 339–344.

Marlow, D. B. (1997). Defining the 16 MBTI inventory personality types through self-descriptive adjectives: Correlations and analysis of variance. *Dissertation Abstracts International: Section B: The Sciences and Engineering,* Vol. 57 (7-B): 4766.

McCaulley, M. H. (2000). The Myers-Briggs Type Indicator in counseling. In C. E. Watkins, Jr., & V. L. Campbell (Eds.), *Testing and assessment in counseling practice; Contemporary topics in vocational psychology.* (2nd ed, pp. 111–173). Mahwah, NJ: Erlbaum.

Murray, J. B. (1990). Review of research on the Myers-Briggs Type Indicator. *Perceptual and Motor Skills, 70,* 1187–1202.

Myers, I. B. (1962). *Manual: The Myers-Briggs Type Indicator.* Princeton, NJ: Educational Testing Service.

Myers, I. B. (1993). *Gifts differing.* Palo Alto, CA: Consulting Psychologists Press.

Myers, I. B. (1998). *Introduction to type.* Palo Alto, CA: Consulting Psychologists Press.

Myers, I. B., & McCaulley, M. H. (1985). *Manual: A guide to the development and use of the Myers-Briggs Type Indicator*. Palo Alto, CA: Consulting Psychologists Press.

Myers, I. B., McCaulley, M. H., Quenk, N. L., & Hammer, A. L. (1998). *MBTI Manual: A guide to the development and use of the Myers-Briggs Type Indicator* (3rd ed.). Palo Alto, CA: Consulting Psychologists Press.

Nuby, J. F., & Oxford, R. L. (1998). Learning style preferences of Native American and African-American secondary students. *Journal of Psychological Type, 44,* 5–19.

Osborn, T. N., Osborn, D. B., & Twillman, B. (1996). MBTI, FIRO-B, and NAFTA: Psychological profiles of not-so-distant business neighbors. *Journal of Psychological Type, 36,* 3–15.

Peterson, A. C. (1998). Using psychological type to assist career clients with resume writing. *Journal of Psychological Type, 44,* 32–38.

Pittenger, D. J. (1993). The utility of the Myers-Briggs Type Indicator. *Review of Educational Research, 63,* 467–488.

Posey, A. M., Thorne, B. M., & Carskadon, T. G. (1999). Differential validity and comparative type distributions of Blacks and Whites in the Myers-Briggs Type Indicator. *Journal of Psychological Type, 48,* 6–21.

Provost, J. A. (1993). *Applications of the Myers-Briggs Type Indicator in counseling: A casebook*. Gainesville, FL: Center for the Application of the Psychological Type.

Quenk, N. L. (1996). *In the grip: Our hidden personality*. Palo Alto, CA: Consulting Psychologists Press.

Rytting, M., Ware, R., & Prince, R. A. (1994). Bimodal distributions in a sample of CEOs: Validating evidence for the MBTI. *Journal of Psychological Type, 31,* 16–23.

Saunders, D., Myers, I. B., & Briggs, K. C. (1989a). *MBTI expanded analysis*. Palo Alto, CA: Consulting Psychologists Press.

Saunders, D., Myers, I. B., & Briggs, K. C. (1989b). *Type differentiation indicator*. Palo Alto, CA: Consulting Psychologists Press.

Simmons, G., & Barrineau, P. (1994). Learning style and the Native American. *Journal of Psychological Type, 28,* 3–10.

Stalikas, A., Casas, E., & Carson, A. D. (1996). In the shadow of the English: English and French Canadians differ by psychological type. *Journal of Psychological Type, 38,* 4–12.

Thorne, A., & Gough, H. (1991). *Portraits of type: An MBTI research compendium*. Palo Alto, CA: Consulting Psychologists Press.

Tieger, P. D., & Barron-Tieger, B. (1992). *Do what you are: Discover the perfect career for you through the secrets of personality type*. Boston: Little, Brown.

Tischler, L. (1994). The MBTI factor structure. *Journal of Psychological Type, 31,* 24–31.

Tuel, B. D., & Betz, N. E. (1998). Relationships of career self-efficacy expectations to the Myers-Briggs Type Indicator and the Personal Styles Scales. *Measurement and Evaluation in Counseling and Development, 31,* 150–163.

Yeakley, F. R. (1982). Communication style preferences and adjustments as an approach to studying effects of similarity in psychological type. *Research in Psychological Type, 5,* 30–48.

Yeakley, F. R. (1983). Implications of communication style research for psychological type theory. *Research in Psychological Type, 6,* 5–23.

PART TWO
Life-Span Theory

Life-span theory, as it applies to career development, concerns the growing and changing ways that an individual deals with career issues over the entire life span. This approach is in marked contrast to that of the theories in Part One, which dealt with career issues at one point in time. Because life-span theory covers a long period of time, it tends to be more complex, in terms of the number of constructs that are used, than typological or trait and factor theories. Therefore, four chapters are needed to cover the entire life span. Chapter 7 discusses the development of career decision making in childhood. Included is the development of curiosity and exploration, which leads to obtaining information from role models and observed events. This approach leads to the development of interests and a self-concept, resulting in the ability to plan and problem solve. Chapter 8 covers the development of interests, capacities, and values in adolescence. Related is the development of career maturity, which includes knowledge about decision making and occupational information. Chapter 9 is a discussion of career issues in late adolescence and adulthood. It focuses on life roles as well as developmental stages. In Chapter 10, the emphasis is on the career transitions and crises that often occur in adulthood. Each chapter treats special problems related to women and culturally diverse populations that occur during each aspect of the life span. Theoretical concepts are used to provide a conceptual framework for dealing with counseling issues that occur in childhood, adolescence, and adulthood.

The theoretical approach used in Part Two is based on the work of Donald Super and his colleagues, although other theories are used to augment their life-span concepts. The theory, which is introduced in Chapter 6, will be referred to as *Super's theory*, even though it represents the work of many researchers throughout the world who have collaborated with Super in developing his theory. There are several reasons for selecting Super's theory as the basis for the chapters on life-span theory. First, Super's developmental theory is one of the few to cover the entire life span. Second, more than any other life-span theorist, Super developed inventories to validate the constructs of his theory and thus provided instruments to be used in counseling. Third, much more research has been done in conjunction with the concepts of Super's developmental theory than with others. Fourth, unlike trait and factor and other career development theories, life-span theories are rather similar to each other. Discussing each life-span theory separately in terms of its implication for counseling would tend to produce similar suggestions for each theory. Therefore, other developmental theories are integrated into Part Two to supplement Super's life-span theory.

Several theorists have contributed to an understanding of career issues at various points during the life span. Gottfredson's developmental theory of occupational aspirations has much to say about the development of gender-role stereotyping in childhood. Her theory, discussed in Chapter 7, provides an understanding of the development of women's career choices. A theory that had a significant and early impact on career development theory is that of Ginzberg, Ginsburg, Axelrad, and Herma. Their focus is the stages of development that young people go through in choosing an occupation. These stages are quite similar to those formulated by Super and are presented in Chapter 8, along with a discussion of the differences between the two theories. The work of Vondracek and his colleagues shows the relevance of vocational identity in the study of adolescent development in Chapter 8. This recent approach is likely to have a great impact on life-span theory as it emphasizes the social context in which adolescents make career choices. The model of minority identity development proposed by Atkinson, Morton, and Sue, although not a career development theory, helps in conceptualizing life-span issues that affect the career development of minorities. Discussed in Chapter 9, the theory focuses on the development of adults but is applicable to adolescents as well. Another theory that is not a career development theory is used as the basis for a discussion of adult career crises and transitions in Chapter 10. Hopson and Adams's theory for understanding adult transitions is integrated into the developmental stages of Super's theory. By combining these theories with work done by Super and his colleagues, we can arrive at a conceptual framework for counseling clients of all ages.

Introduction to Super's Life-Span Theory

An overview of Super's theory will be given in this brief chapter. The details of Super's theory are provided in the next three chapters. Underlying Super's theory of career development are assumptions about individuals and the world they live in. Super (1990) considers individual roles that include study, community service, leisure, work, and family to be important when studying career development across the life span. Developmental tasks and stages are an important aspect of Super's (1990) theory. Life roles within developmental tasks may vary for individuals at different points during their life. The assumptions of Super's theory, roles, and developmental stages are discussed further in the following pages.

BASIC ASSUMPTIONS OF SUPER'S THEORY

Super (1990, p. 205) described his theory as a segmental theory, one that includes the work of many other theorists: Thorndike, Hull, Bandura, Freud, Jung, Adler, Rank, Murray, Maslow, Allport, Rogers, and others. From the work of these theorists, he derived basic assumptions that allowed him to develop his own theory. Perhaps most basic is the assumption that physiological aspects, such as genetic predisposition, along with geographic aspects (country of origin) have an impact on other aspects of career development. These aspects include the development of psychological characteristics and the social-economic structure of the environment, which are all incorporated into the self-concept. Psychological characteristics include the development of needs, values, interests, intelligence, ability, and special aptitudes. These lead to the development of the personality of an individual and to his or her accomplishments. The social-economic factors include one's community, school, family, and peer groups, along with the state of the economy and the labor market. These influence the job structure and employment practices—the conditions outside the individual with which he or she must interact. Psychological and social-economic factors combine in the development of the self. As individuals learn about themselves and their environment, they go through developmental stages in which they evolve a concept of themselves.

This model is discussed more fully in Super (1990) and is illustrated by the diagram of an archway. It is presented here (Figure 6-1) because it is the basis of the research and writing by Super and his colleagues on life roles and developmental stages. Since Super's death in 1994, other researchers have sought to continue and further develop his theory. Herr (1997) and Savickas (1997) suggest that *adaptability* would be a more productive concept to use than career maturity. Blustein (1997) suggests the importance of context or social factors in studying client exploration. These ideas serve to relate Super's work to individual career development.

SELF-CONCEPT

Self-concept has been at the core of Super's developmental theory. Super (1953) described vocational development as the process of developing and implementing a self-concept. He saw self-concept as a combination of biological characteristics, the social roles individuals play, and evaluations of the reactions other individuals have to the person. *Self-concept* refers to how individuals view themselves and their situation. Figure 6-1 shows Super's arch, which illustrates his segmental theory, and the subject of the next three chapters. Note that the self is at the top of the arch. How individuals perceive themselves and interact is a reflection of personality, needs, values, and interests (the left-hand column). These perceptions change over the life span. Discussed in *Career Development: Self-Concept Theory* (Super, Starishevsky, Matlin, & Jordaan, 1963), the developing nature of the self-concept is of particular importance. Super et al. described processes such as self-differentiation, role playing, exploration, and reality testing, which led to the development of the self-concept. Interaction with society (the right-hand column) brings about the development of the self-concept as the individual interacts with family, school, peers, and coworkers. The self-concept refers to individuals' views of themselves and society

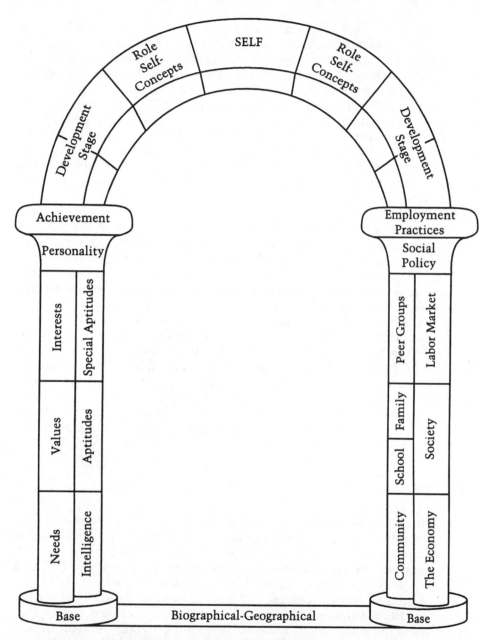

Figure 6-1   The archway of career determinants.
Source: "A Life-Span, Life-Space Approach to Career Development" by Donald E. Super (1990). In D. Brown, L. Brooks, and Associates, *Career Choice and Development: Applying Contemporary Theories to Practice* (2nd ed., p. 200). Copyright © 1990 by Jossey-Bass. Reprinted by permission.

and is subjective. This is in contrast to trait and factor theory, which emphasizes objective or outside measures of the self, for example, interest inventories and aptitude tests. Super's emphasis on the self-concept can be seen in his development of inventories that focus on evaluating roles and values that are important in the different stages of life.

As Betz (1994) and Bejian and Salomone (1995) show, defining self-concept is a very difficult task. Super (1990) wrote of constellations or systems of self-concepts. In developing his theory, Super was influenced by Kelly's (1955) personal construct theory, which examined bipolar constructs, such as *smart–stupid* and *kind–mean* that could be differentially important to various individuals. Herr (1997) stresses the importance of social constructivist theory (based on Kelly's work) in developing Super's theory further. Self-efficacy theory (Betz, 1994), described in Chapter 13, has had a long and active history (Bandura, 1997) as a means of defining the self-concept. Basically, *self-efficacy* refers to the "expectations or beliefs concerning one's ability to perform successfully a given behavior" (Betz, 1994, p. 35). A somewhat similar term, but less precise, is *self-esteem*, which refers to how good one feels about oneself, or to how certain or confident one is about aspects of one's life, such as school, work, and being liked. In Chapter 7, Gottfredson's theory examines children's self-concepts as they encounter societal expectations about men's and women's roles, the values of being in a specific occupation, and their societal expectations. For Super, self-concept served to organize varying roles that individuals played and their view of the roles as they changed across the life span. Increasingly, Super became interested in how the self-concept developed differently for women and for people from different cultures. An examination of his research shows a cross-cultural emphasis in his study of the roles that individuals value as they grow.

ROLES

A constant concept throughout Super's career development theory is the concept of role. Super describes six major roles: homemaker, worker, citizen, leisurite, student, and child. His Salience Inventory (Nevill & Super, 1986) measures the importance of all the roles, except that of child. In childhood, the roles of leisurite, student, and child are particularly important. The roles of worker, citizen, and homemaker (in the sense of responsibility for these roles) are minimal. In adolescence, citizen and worker may become more important roles, but they are generally limited. In adolescence, work is not often directly related to one's eventual career. It is in adulthood that one has more choice in life roles. Therefore, a full discussion of these roles is given in Chapter 9, "Late Adolescent and Adult Career Development."

Super's rainbow (Figure 6-2) shows how the roles may vary within the lifetime of one person. In this figure, each arc represents a role in life. The thicker the shaded area in each arc, the more important the role. As Super

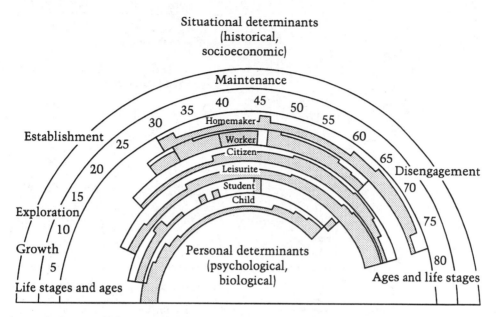

Figure 6-2   The life-career rainbow: Six life roles in schematic life space. *Source:* Adapted from *Career Choice and Development,* by D. Brown, L. Brooks, and Associates. Copyright © 1984 by Jossey-Bass, Inc. Reprinted by permission.

and Nevill (1986) explain, "The person portrayed in this rainbow finished college at the age of 22, went at once to work, married at age 26, became a parent at age 27, intermittently attended school part time until returning full time at age 47, suffered the loss of parents at age 57, retired at 67, was widowed at 78, and died at age 81" (p. 3). In conjunction with developmental stages, the concept of life roles may be useful in many career-counseling situations.

DEVELOPMENTAL STAGES

The notion of stages and substages is essential to Super's life-span theory. Figure 6-3 depicts the stages and substages associated with various ages. Chapter 7, "Career Development in Childhood," describes those tasks that take place during the growth stage. Chapter 8, "Adolescent Career Development," focuses on the development of interests, capacities, and values that takes place during the exploration stage. How and when interests and capacities emerge in career decision making is an aspect of career maturity that is a central part of Super's theory. Further exploration that may occur during late adolescence or early adulthood is described in Chapter 9, "Late

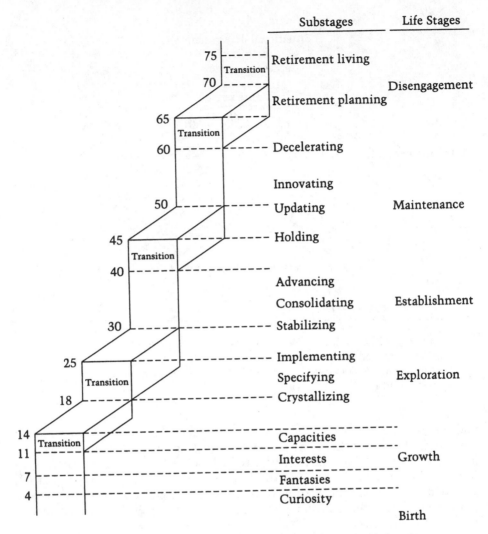

Figure 6-3 Life stages and substages based on the typical development tasks.
Source: Career Choice and Development, by D. Brown, L. Brooks, and Associates. Copyright © 1984 by Jossey-Bass, Inc. Reprinted by permission.

Adolescent and Adult Career Development." The exploration stage includes crystallizing: making an occupational choice, becoming more specific in the choice, and implementing it by finding and choosing a job. The other stages encompassed in Chapter 9 are establishing oneself in one's career, maintaining one's position, and disengaging from the world of work. A concept essential to the understanding of Super's theory is recycling. One may recycle through various stages at any time. For example, if someone at midlife desires to change his or her job, the individual is likely to reenter the exploration stage. Implied in the developmental stages is the interaction of the individual with the world of work.

THE ROLE OF OCCUPATIONAL INFORMATION AND TESTING

The use of occupational information and testing is an integral part of Super's theory. Emphasized particularly in Chapters 8 and 9, occupational information and testing are a focus of counseling. Further, the acquisition of occupational information plays a predominant role in career maturity, an important concept in adolescence. Super has developed more inventories to test his theories than any other career development theorist. By doing so, he has not only supported constructs of his own theory but has also provided useful instruments for counselors to use in their work.

APPLYING THE THEORY TO WOMEN AND CULTURALLY DIVERSE POPULATIONS

While Super (1957) was concerned about the career development of women, other theorists have focused more specifically on gender issues in career development. Gottfredson (1981, 1996) has dealt with the effect of gender-role stereotyping on career choice, which can occur early in the elementary school years. Her work, along with that of other researchers, is described more specifically in Chapter 7. Many researchers have documented the impact of gender-role stereotyping on the career choices of adolescent men and women. Chapter 8 describes how gender-role stereotyping affects the career choices of adolescents. Adult women (Chapter 10), because of choices about marriage and children, often have more varied career concerns than men. Because they are more likely to reenter and leave the workforce at different points in their lives, these factors are taken into consideration in a discussion of the applicability of Super's career development theory to women. During the course of their working lives, women may experience career crises not experienced as often by men: discrimination, disruption due to child-rearing, and sexual harassment. Methods for conceptualizing these issues are discussed in Chapter 10, "Adult Career Crises and Transitions."

Super (1957, 1990) was also concerned about the career issues facing a wide range of cultural groups, as illustrated by his investigations on work salience with colleagues throughout the world. It is difficult to present unified explanatory information for childhood, adolescent, and adult career development because of the variety of social contexts. However, information about career concerns of culturally diverse populations is discussed as it relates to Super's life-span theory. In Chapter 10, Atkinson, Morten, and Sue's (1998) model of minority identity development is presented to augment Super's life-span model. In discussing career crises that people from diverse cultures may encounter in their adult lives, Hopson and Adams's (1977) theory of adult transitions is applied.

SUMMARY

This introduction to developmental career concerns at varying times in the life span describes issues that will be explained in the next four chapters. Super's life-span theory will be used to show how life roles and developmental stages can assist the counselor to understand career development for individuals at all ages. Each of the following four chapters incorporates developmental stage issues for women and culturally diverse populations. Examples of approaches to counseling individuals at different life stages and crises will be given.

References

Atkinson, D. R., Morten, G., & Sue, D. W. (1998). *Counseling American minorities: A cross-cultural perspective* (5th ed.). New York: McGraw-Hill.

Bandura, A. (1997). *Self-efficacy: The exercise of control.* San Francisco: W. H. Freeman.

Bejian, D. V., & Salomone, P. R. (1995). Understanding midlife career renewal: Implications for counseling. *The Career Development Quarterly, 44,* 52–63.

Betz, N. E. (1994). Self concept theory in career development and counseling. *The Career Development Quarterly, 43,* 32–42.

Blustein, D. L. (1997). A context-rich perspective of career exploration across the life roles. *The Career Development Quarterly, 45,* 260–274.

Gottfredson, L. S. (1981). Circumscription and compromise: A developmental theory of occupational aspirations. *Journal of Counseling Psychology, 28,* 545–579.

Gottfredson, L. S. (1996). A theory of circumscription and compromise. In D. Brown & L. Brooks (Eds.), *Career choice and development: Applying contemporary theories to practice* (3rd ed., pp. 179–232). San Francisco: Jossey-Bass.

Herr, E. L. (1997). Super's life-span, life-space approach and its outlook for refinement. *The Career Development Quarterly, 45,* 238–246.

Hopson, B., & Adams, J. (1977). Towards an understanding of transition. In J. Adams & B. Hopson (Eds.), *Transitions: Understanding and managing personal change* (pp. 1–19). Montclair, NJ: Allenheld & Osmund.

Kelly, G. A. (1955). *A theory of personality: The psychology of personal constructs.* New York: Norton.

Nevill, D. D., & Super, D. E. (1986). *Manual for the Salience Inventory: Theory, application, and research.* Palo Alto, CA: Consulting Psychologists Press.

Savickas, M. L. (1997). Career adaptability: An integrative construct for life-span, life-space theory. *The Career Development Quarterly, 45,* 247–259.

Super, D. E. (1953). A theory of vocational development. *American Psychologist, 8,* 185–190.

Super, D. E. (1957). *The psychology of careers.* New York: Harper & Row.

Super, D. E. (1990). A life-span, life-space approach to career development. In D. Brown, L. Brooks, & Assoc. (Eds.), *Career choice and development: Applying contemporary theories to practice* (2nd ed., pp. 197–261). San Francisco: Jossey-Bass.

Super, D. E., & Nevill, D. D. (1986). *The Salience Inventory*. Palo Alto, CA: Consulting Psychologists Press.

Super, D. E., Starishevsky, R., Matlin, N., & Jordaan, J. P. (1963). *Career development: Self-concept theory*. New York: College Entrance Examination Board.

7

Career Development in Childhood

This chapter covers career-related issues that affect the child until the age of 12. The primary emphases of the chapter are the maturational activities in elementary school and Super's (1990) model of the bases of career maturity. This chapter also covers the development of gender role, the career development of children from different cultural backgrounds, and presentation of occupational information to children. Super's model of childhood career development deals only in general ways with gender issues. Gottfredson's (1981, 1996) theory is concerned with the development of gender-role stereotyping during childhood, making hypotheses about the relationship of gender-role stereotyping to career choice. Research on children of culturally diverse backgrounds is more limited than is research on gender issues and children, but there is information to assist the counselor in conceptualizing career issues for children from culturally diverse backgrounds.

When counselors work with vocational issues with young children, it is usually as a secondary issue in counseling or in organizing an occupational information program. In either event, occupational information is an essential aspect of career interventions. Counselors have an opportunity to influence the later career development of children in significant ways. However, the impact of counselors' interventions may not be recognizable until many years later. Implications of Super's career development theory for the communication of vocational information to children are discussed with suggestions. Super's theory also has implications for ways in which counselors can look developmentally at themselves in relationship to their clients. By using a developmental approach to occupations, testing, and counselor issues, counselors can establish a consistent framework within which to view their young clients.

SUPER'S MODEL OF THE CAREER DEVELOPMENT OF CHILDREN

This chapter describes Super's (1990, 1994) model of childhood career development as illustrated in Figure 7-1. A very basic drive in children is curiosity. Curiosity is often satisfied through exploration, an important career development activity that may never cease. This exploratory activity leads to the acquisition of information. Several views of how children process information are given. One important source of information is the key figure—a person whom a child may choose to imitate. Using information derived from exploratory activities and impressions of role models, interests are developed. During the maturational process, children develop ways to control their own behavior by listening to themselves and others. To make career decisions, children need to develop a time perspective, a sense of the future. This along with the development of a self-concept will eventually lead to planful career decision making. The development of a self-concept is an exceedingly important part of Super's life-span theory. The self-concept derives from the child's exploratory behavior, which leads to acquiring occupational information, imitating key figures, and developing interests. Each of these concepts is illustrated through counseling examples.

Curiosity

Curiosity is among the most basic of all needs or drives, being observed in animals as well as infants. Using Berlyne's (1960) work as a starting point for his discussion of exploratory behavior, Jordaan (1963) provides a useful approach to the understanding of exploration and curiosity in children. According to Jordaan (1963), curiosity may develop when there are changes in an individual's physical or social needs. For a child, curiosity may be prompted by hunger, thirst, loneliness, and a variety of other stimuli. When a child is uncertain or confused, the child may decide to resolve his or her perplexity. Also, boredom, a wish for excitement, or a desire for stimulation may produce curiosity. In relating curiosity to vocational development, Jordaan emphasizes more complex stimuli than did Berlyne (1960) in his study of animal and infant behavior. Curiosity may be observed in very young children with new objects, new people, and new concepts. Being exposed to puzzling new stimuli, the child must try to understand them or try out new behaviors. For example, a child seeing a toy horse in a playpen

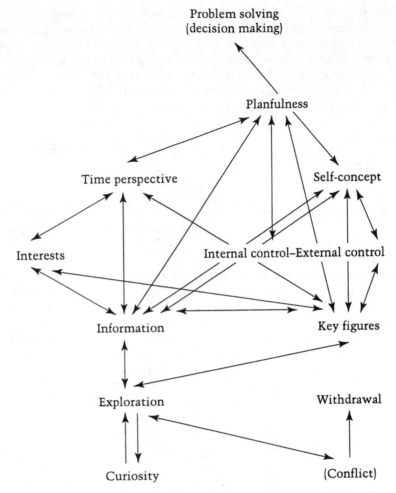

Figure 7-1 A person-environment interactive model of the bases of career maturity.
Source: Career Development in Britain, by A. G. Watts, D. E. Super, and J. M. Kidd (Eds). Copyright © 1981 by Hobson's Press. Reprinted by permission.

may try to ride it, fantasizing that he is riding a real horse. Another child may pick up a stick, pretending that it is a baseball bat and that she is a professional baseball player. Through curiosity, fantasized thinking may develop. Fantasy is the first stage of Ginzberg, Ginsburg, Axelrad, and Herma's (1951) theory of career development. Both Jordaan and Ginzberg et al. agree that curiosity and fantasy in the young child are important and should be encouraged, particularly in the early years of elementary school.

Although it is appropriate for elementary school guidance counselors to encourage curiosity as an acceptable goal of career development for young children, doing so is often not simple. Guidance counselors often see children because they are not doing what they are told to do by their teacher. A child who draws when he or she is expected to be reading or talks to another child when the teacher is talking may be expressing curiosity. In other words, being curious may often be disruptive. Reinforcing curiosity while discouraging disruptive behavior can be difficult. Encouraging the child to find ways to express curiosity in a positive sense may be one alternative to punishment as a means of dealing with disruptive behavior. Curiosity may lead to vocational exploration in later years; it is not important that curiosity have a career component at an early age.

Exploration

Being curious can lead to children's exploring their environment, home, school, and peer and parental relationships. Curiosity refers to the desire for knowledge or for something new or unusual, whereas exploration is the act of searching or examining. Curiosity is a need; exploration, a behavior. For children, play and playful activities are an expression of exploratory behavior and help to meet curiosity needs. Jordaan (1963) lists ten dimensions of exploratory behavior. These are combined here to give examples of important activities that make up exploration. The behavior may be intentional and systematic, or it may be accidental. For example, children may want to find out how a clock works by carefully disassembling the pieces and putting them back together (intentional), or they may find a broken clock and just start to play with it (accidental). Exploratory behavior can occur because others ask a child to do it or because a child seeks it out. Sometimes, a teacher requests that a child put a puzzle together, or the child may take the initiative to do it. In exploring, a child can use either current or past experience. Having played with a puzzle three weeks ago, a child may decide to play with a similar one now. Some exploratory behavior may benefit a child and help the child learn. Other behavior may just be for the enjoyment of the activity, such as writing one's name backward. Some exploratory behavior that is required can later turn out to be enjoyable. For example, being required to read does not mean that reading will always be a chore. Once the skill is partially mastered, children are likely to read on their own initiative. All these play behaviors are vocationally relevant only in an indirect sense. However, as the behaviors become more complex, they are likely to be more related to tasks required by various jobs.

When exploration is thwarted, the child may experience conflict and have less to do with peers, adults, and school subjects. (Note the arrow leading away from exploratory and planful behavior at the bottom of Figure 7-1.) When exploration is stifled, a child is likely to lose the motivation to study. His or her work may become less imaginative. The child is less likely to respond to teachers' questions or to initiate activities in the classroom, obtaining information only because of external factors. A truly withdrawn child will have difficulty developing vocational maturity, because interests and information about career-related activities will be missing. Naturally, most children are not at one end or the other of the ex-ploration-withdrawal continuum. Rather, they choose to explore some ac-tivities and not others.

Exploratory behavior builds on other exploratory behavior. To encour-age exploratory behavior of any type (that is not damaging to oneself or oth-ers) can have eventual positive consequences in terms of career develop-ment. Trusting the exploration process without forcing it can be a useful goal for counselors and teachers. For example, a third-grader may learn, in very general terms, how a phone works. Such learning will develop in so-phistication, both at a teacher's request and also perhaps on the child's own initiative in later years. As a fifth-grader, the child may draw on past ex-perience with the phone, as he or she learns more about the details of its operation. When counselors are talking to children about problems at school or at home, exploratory activity may play a minor role. However, there are times when reinforcement of this activity is helpful. For exam-ple, a young girl who is complaining about her unmarried mother's new boyfriend may feel some satisfaction and control in her life when she can talk about the new things she has learned while reading stories at home. Exploratory behavior is not a panacea for family or school problems. Rather, it is an activity that is likely to produce more exploratory behavior, lead-ing eventually to an increased likelihood of successful vocational planning. In the process of exploratory activity, the child obtains much information about the environment. How this information is learned and processed is the subject of the next section.

Information

Clearly, the learning of information is essential to a child's development and success as an adolescent and an adult. The focus in this section is on how theories of learning can be applied to occupational information for elementary school children. A point that is repeatedly stressed in the work of Jean Piaget is that children are not merely uninformed adults; rather, there are differences in how children process information through-out their development. Only a brief synopsis of the work of Piaget, Vy-gotsky, and Erikson will be given here so that different theoretical ap-proaches to the acquisition of knowledge by elementary school children can be compared.

Piaget (1977) describes four major periods of cognitive development: sensorimotor, preoperational, concrete operational, and formal operational. The sensorimotor stage occurs from birth to age 2, when infants attend to objects and events around them and then respond to these objects or events. *Attending* refers to the sensory acts of touching, seeing, smelling, and so on. *Responding* refers to such motor acts as biting, hitting, and screaming.

The preoperational thought period occurs from approximately ages 2 to 7. In this period, the child can learn to add and subtract and perform sim-ilar operations. Children before the age of 7 are characterized as being ego-centric. If a teacher announces that one child in a classroom will be selected to do a highly regarded task, each child is apt to think that he or she will be chosen. Further, it is difficult for young children to tell fantasy from reality. When war scenes are shown on the evening news, it may be hard for young children to have an idea of how far this occurrence is from their house. Another example of the egocentricity of the young child is the "internalization of action" that occurs when young children describe what they are doing out loud, apparently talking to no one.

The third stage, and the one of most interest here, is concrete operations. In this stage, occurring between about the ages of 7 and 11, children think in concrete terms. They do not have to see an object to imagine manipulating it, but they must be aware that it exists. They can imagine adding 3 elephants to 5 elephants, but they cannot add $3y$ to $5y$. This ability to think abstractly takes place in the final period, called *formal operations,* beginning about the age of 12. It is easier for children between the ages of 7 and 11 to learn what a dentist does—how he or she uses equipment, examines teeth, and so forth—than it is for them to sense how long eight years of post–high school training really is or what a $75,000 income means. It is hard, for example, for an 8-year-old to grasp what it means to "help others feel better about themselves," as a social worker does. This idea is more likely to be understood by adolescents.

Although somewhat critical of Piaget's approach, Vygotsky (1986), a Russian psychologist, has described a system similar to that of Piaget. He describes three stages, each characterized by a "leading activity" that is the main feature in the child's psychological development and the foundation for the next major feature. Further, in a "leading activity," particular mental functions emerge for the first time. For ages 1 through 3, the leading activity is object manipulation. During the preschool years, up to the age of 7, the leading activity is playing games. And for ages 7 through 11, it is learning. At the age of 7, children are ready to learn about the world of things and objective laws of reality. This system, although it differs from Piaget's, also emphasizes the importance of learning activities in the acquisition of occupational information for elementary-school-aged children.

A very different view, but one with somewhat similar conclusions, is that of Erik Erikson (1963). In his eight stages of psychosocial development, he lists as the fourth stage that of industry versus inferiority. This occurs between the ages of 6 and 11. Children at this age have the freedom to make things and to organize them. This can give them a sense of industriousness if they are successful and inferiority if they are unsuccessful. In this stage, children develop a sense of achievement by organizing, developing, and applying information, or they have a sense of failure if they do not master these skills. From an occupational information perspective, if elementary school students have an opportunity to make signs or drawings for an occupation or to use tools, such as an electrician's pliers, they may be able to experience a sense of success. The concrete completion of an activity will be appreciated. The emphasis on the concrete is not unlike that of Piaget's third stage of learning. As will be shown in the next section, having role models to imitate and observe is consistent with the emphasis on concrete thinking and industriousness.

Key Figures

Adults are important role models for children in learning about the world of work and the development of their own self-concept. Key figures for children are parents, teachers, public figures such as athletes and television personalities, and people with whom they come in contact in their own community, such as police officers or mail carriers. Thelen, Frautsh, Roberts, Kirkland, and Dollinger (1981) have found that children are likely to copy the behavior of others. Parents' impact on children's view of occupations is illustrated by Trice and Tillapaugh's (1991) finding that children's aspirations to their parents' occupations are influenced by their perception of how satisfied their parents are with their own work. For seventh- and eighth-grade girls, mothers can be extremely important key figures, with maternal education and mothers' attitudes toward women having strong influences on girls' career orientation (Rainey & Borders, 1997). The findings that emphasize the importance of parental influence are consistent with Bandura's (1997) view that a significant method of learning for children is imitation. Rich's (1979) study shows that children know best those occupations that are in their own communities. Support for this conclusion was found by Trice, Hughes, Odom, Woods, and McClellan (1995), who reported that, among boys, 42% of kindergartners, 40% of second-graders, 47% of fourth-graders, and 36% of sixth-graders knew someone holding a job similar to their career choice. Because of population density, rural children may be exposed to fewer occupations than urban children. People who work in occupations that children can observe have the potential of becoming key figures. As children imitate the behavior of important others, they may choose to adopt or discard those aspects of the individual that seem to fit themselves. This process is one aspect of the development of the child's self-concept.

Super's emphasis on key figures in the development of children's self-concept can be a useful reminder to the counselor to listen carefully to what a child learns from his or her observation of role models. For example, a child whose father is a long-distance truck driver may be impressed by the father's mastery of such a huge vehicle, entranced by the father's visiting distant places, or impressed by the father's ability to lift heavy objects. Depending on the parent–child interaction, any one of these impressions may have an impact on the child. If the person modeling truck driving is not the father, but an uncle or neighbor, the impact of the role model is likely to be different. Sometimes children's observation of role models are inaccurate. If there is an occasion to correct the misinformation, counselors can take advantage of that opportunity by describing the behavior of other key figures or different behaviors of the misperceived key figure. Key figures are likely to make a greater impact on children as they are more able to observe others, thus developing a greater amount of control over their own behavior.

Internal Versus External Control

Gradually, children begin to experience a feeling of control over their own surroundings. In a study of 28,000 nine-year-olds, Miller (1977) found that most of the children did not see themselves as responsible for their own behavior. Children are often used to doing what they are told to do by their teachers and parents. Rules are to be followed. Even in games that elementary school children devise, the following of rules is often quite important.

As children are successful in completing tasks and projects, they develop a feeling of autonomy and of being in control of future events. For counselors, children's "out-of-control" behavior is a frequent source of concern. The notion that self-control can have a direct impact on one's concept of oneself and also on one's ability to make career decisions (as shown in Figure 7-1) is an interesting one. Often, the counselor who is dealing with a child who has hit another child in the classroom or talked back to a teacher is concerned with controlling the situation. Helping to develop a balance between self-control and external control may be a counseling goal. Relating this goal to career maturity may never be in the counselor's thoughts. The notion that self-control has an eventual impact on career planning, however, is an important one, whether or not it is a conscious element of the counselor's thinking when working with a child. Being able to control their behavior can help children become more aware of their likes and dislikes.

Development of Interests

In time, children's fantasies of occupations are affected by information about the world, and they become interests. The child who wants to become a professional athlete may enjoy the activity, playing ball or gymnastics, and not just imagine himself or herself receiving the adulation of an audience. In the development of interests, the capacity of a child to actually become an athlete is immaterial. Young children often do not see any barriers to what they may want to do in their future. In Miller's (1977) study of 28,000 nine-year-olds, most of the children were able to state strong and weak interests (although fewer were able to state weak interests than strong interests). Nelson (1963) showed that third-grade children are often able to discard some occupations because they do not interest them. The development of interests is clearly an outgrowth of exploration. As the child tries new behaviors, some become attractive and some do not. The development of interests in activities in school and outside school becomes an important facet of decision making in adolescence.

Encouraging children's emerging interests is helpful in the development of their career maturity. Talking about those aspects of their life that are exciting can eventually be helpful in career planning. Because counselors of elementary school children are rarely concerned with career issues, it may seem unimportant to focus on interests. Further, the impact that counselors and other significant role models have may not be seen for many years. Talking to a child about an interest in baseball, an excitement about helping an injured animal, or the pleasure of a recent trip to a zoo may help the child to feel more important. This feeling of importance can contribute to the child's ability to develop a sense of what he or she is like, and of how he or she is different from others. This development of self-concept is essential to the later career selection process.

Time Perspective

To develop a time perspective is to develop a sense of the future, to have a real appreciation that six months is different from six years. For children under the age of 9, this is very difficult, if not impossible. For example, the child who says, "I want to be a boat captain so I can steer a boat now," has a sense only of the present. The notion of how long "later" is develops over time (Ginzberg et al., 1951). The implication of time perspective for counseling is that it is unrealistic to expect young children, particularly those below fourth grade, to think about planning future vocational or higher education. Rather, it is more important to examine jobs and job tasks now, to start to develop interests, and to reinforce exploratory behavior. As a future orientation develops, children are able to construct a sense of planfulness that will allow them to start to make educational choices in middle school that will have an impact on their eventual career choices. Developing a time perspective is an issue that is also important for adolescents. A guidance program designed to develop a future orientation in 15- to 17-year-olds and adults was effective in developing optimism about the future and a sense of continuity between past and future (Marko & Savickas, 1998).

Self-Concept and Planfulness

A sense of self begins to emerge in late childhood or early adolescence. By following through on the need to discover more about the environment and to explore objects and people in the environment, the child learns information that will be one basis for the development of a self-concept. The child learns how he or she is different from or similar to other people. Further, by observing important people in their lives, children learn occupational and other roles. Also, exploratory behavior leads to information and experience with key figures that will eventually help the child develop interests in some activities and a lack of interest in others. The child starts to have a clear profile in terms of interest and experience that separates him or her from others. As a sense of self develops, the drama and excitement of activity becomes less important, and the accomplishment of goals becomes more so. Children now are in a position where they can plan and make decisions. Naturally, not all children have the same experiences, and not all are able to develop a strong sense of self and an ability to plan. Differences in career maturity between individuals and the elements of career maturity are the focus of Chapter 8, "Adolescent Career Development."

The point of the preceding discussion is to emphasize the importance of those concepts that lead to a sense of self and a feeling of planfulness. To plan, children must have sufficient information, motivation in terms of interests and activities, a sense of control over their own future, and an idea of what that future will be (a time perspective). Although the development of interests, the acquisition of information, and the development of a time perspective are goals that can be achieved in counseling, they are not ends in themselves. They are important because they lead to the development of planfulness and a sense of self. As these important concepts are developing, it is not possible for children to make career choices that are planful. Rather, they may express an interest in an occupation because of information they may have or because of their experience with role models. Therefore, career counseling as it is done with adolescents and adults is inappropriate for children. An awareness of Super's model of the bases of career maturity can be helpful when discussing other issues with children in counseling.

USING SUPER'S MODEL IN COUNSELING CHILDREN

Common topics in counseling young children deal with school and family. Thomas (1989) describes the following as typical elementary school guidance problems: lack of academic progress; dyslexia; lack of reading achievement; problems having to do with intellectual ability, sight, or hearing; and disruptive behavior. Typical family problems that Thomas (1989) cites are child abuse, child neglect, and issues arising from single-parent families, divorce, unwed parents, stepfamilies, and working parents. Occasionally, in dealing with these issues, counselors have the opportunity to make comments that fit with Super's model of childhood career development. This might mean a discussion of the child's exploratory behavior, the reaction the child is having to experiences with school, or a positive or negative reaction to key figures. An awareness of a limited time perspective in children can help the counselor in not expecting planful behavior from them. Another area where Super's view can be useful is in the attention that the counselor pays to the development of interests. The following example shows how a counselor can incorporate a knowledge of Super's concepts while working with a child on a topic seemingly not related to career choice.

Arthur is a white fourth-grade student in a predominantly wealthy suburban school system. Both parents were raised in Toronto, Canada. A student who has received C's in his previous classes, Arthur is starting to fall behind the other children in his class in reading, and he senses it. He seems to have few social contacts with his peers and cries rather easily when frustrated by reading assignments. His teacher has referred Arthur to the counselor because the teacher is concerned about his behavior and suspects that Arthur may have a learning disability. This dialogue between Arthur and the counselor occurs rather late in their discussion:

CL: I hate reading! It's too hard.

CO: What do you like to do? [The counselor very much feels Arthur's frustration with reading and wishes to move to a topic where Arthur does not have a sense of failure. Later, they will return to the topic of reading.]

CL: I like baseball. My friends and I play after school. We trade cards, too.

CO: What teams do you collect? [The counselor, almost randomly, chooses to follow up on collecting baseball cards rather than playing baseball. Mainly, the counselor wants to follow up on an area of interest that Arthur has.]

CL: All kinds. I like the American League. I like new players' and pitchers' stats.

CO: You really seem to enjoy collecting cards. [The counselor notes that Arthur is starting to relax and sound more enthusiastic. Further, the counselor notes that Arthur is interested in an activity that requires reading but chooses not to comment about it; rather, the counselor follows Arthur's exploratory behavior.]

CL: Oh, yes. It's really great. I buy cards when my parents will give me money, and I trade with whatever kids I can find. People know I am a good trader and sometimes it's hard to find kids to trade with. I've got a box full of cards.

CO: Seems like that's something that you do well. [The counselor is concerned about Arthur's sense of failure, coming from his difficulty with reading, and wishes to reinforce his area of interests and strength. Arthur's self-concept is important. The collecting of baseball cards itself does not need to have direct occupational relevance.]

CL: Yeah. I know the cards, and I know the players. I like to watch them on TV. It's fun to see a player whose card I have. Sometimes, when I'm playing baseball, I pretend that I'm a player.

CO: Who would you like to be like? [In his fantasy, Arthur is influenced by a key figure. The counselor wants to hear more about it.]

CL: The center fielder for the Red Sox. He can really hit. I like to watch him. I want to hit just like him. I want to be a ballplayer like him. I want to hit home runs and have a high batting average. I want to play for the Boston Red Sox. I love to hit the baseball hard. I love to catch the balls.

CO: Sounds like great things to do. [The counselor is aware that Arthur's time perspective is vague. Arthur seems to see himself in a short time being a professional baseball player. Not wanting to push Arthur into developing a time perspective when he is not able to, the counselor reinforces Arthur's interest in and exploration of baseball. The counselor is aware that they are moving away from the reading issue, but the counselor feels it is important to spend some time on areas that will strengthen Arthur's concept of himself.]

In this example, the counselor has used Super's concepts to encourage exploratory behavior in Arthur and to help him feel better about himself. Although the goal of counseling is to help Arthur with his reading problem, and this discourse seems unrelated, it is likely that helping Arthur have a sense of success will make him feel less frustrated in general. At a later point in the interview, the counselor may be able to draw a parallel between reading baseball cards and reading schoolwork. The counselor does not introduce career issues in a forced sense but uses knowledge of Super's theory to respond helpfully in the context of the situation. This example uses a gender-stereotyped situation. It is one in which a boy is choosing a traditionally masculine activity. The issue of gender-role stereotyping is an important one in the development of occupational selection. It is dealt with extensively in the next section.

GENDER-ROLE STEREOTYPING AND GOTTFREDSON'S THEORY

Super (1957), having long been concerned about career development issues as they apply to women, identified seven career patterns of women. The major factors determining these patterns are the ways in which women deal with marriage and homemaking. His theory does not speak directly to gender issues related to the career development of boys and girls, whereas Gottfredson's theory does.

Gottfredson's Theory of Career Development

Gottfredson (1981, 1996) has articulated a life-stage theory of career development in childhood and adolescence that emphasizes the important part that gender roles and prestige play in making choices. This focus on gender and social class background is generally not an active part of other career development theories. Like other career development theorists, Gottfredson includes intelligence, vocational interest, competencies, and values in her theory. Essential to her theory are four stages of cognitive development that provide a way to view oneself in the world. The first stage, occurring between the ages of 3 and 5, is the orientation to size and power. In this stage, children grasp the idea of becoming an adult by orienting themselves to the size differences between themselves and adults. In the second stage, ages 6 to 8, they develop an orientation to gender roles, becoming aware of the different gender roles of men and women. Their career choices are influenced by their view of gender roles. In the third stage, approximately 9 to 13, they are affected by the abstract ideas of social class. At this point, prestige becomes an important factor in career choice. In the fourth stage, occurring after the age of 14, adolescents become more introspective and develop greater self-awareness and perceptiveness toward others. Adolescents develop a more insightful view of vocational aspirations as they are affected by their view of themselves, gender roles, and prestige. This section will focus particularly on the second stage, and on the role of gender stereotyping in young children.

Gottfredson (1996) cites many studies that support her proposition that gender-role stereotyping occurs during the ages of 6 to 8, when children develop *tolerable gender-type boundaries*, beliefs about which occupations are appropriate for their own sex and for the opposite sex. For example, a girl may see police officers on the street and on television and conclude that police officers are men and that she could not become a police officer. Looft (1971) asked second-grade boys and girls what they wanted to be when they grew up. For boys, the most frequent choices were football player and police officer, with doctor, dentist, priest, and pilot being less frequent. For girls, nurse and teacher were most frequently mentioned, followed by mother and flight attendant. In a study including first- to sixth-grade children done about eight years later, Biehler (1979) found that teacher and nurse were still important, but girls had included some nontraditional occupations in their choices as well. Professional athlete was still an important occupational choice for boys. Studies by MacKay and Miller (1982) and Umstot (1980) generally confirmed these findings. In most of these studies, boys showed a narrower range of traditionally stereotyped occupations than did girls. Trice et al. (1995) reported that fourth-grade girls were less likely than boys to make career choices based on money/status or danger/excitement. Girls were more likely than boys to base their career choices on specific abilities, parental influence, and helping others. Helwig (1998b) reviewed many studies and concludes that girls identify more occupational aspirations than boys, whereas this was less true in the 1960s and 1970s. These studies tend to support Gottfredson's (1981, 1996) proposition that gender-role stereotyping is an important factor in career choice in 6- to 8-year-olds.

Insight into why gender-role stereotyping is so strong is provided by Betz and Fitzgerald (1987) in their review of gender bias in education. They cite many studies that show how pervasive gender stereotyping is in schools. In children's reading and textbooks, Scott (1981) reports that boys and girls are pictured in stereotyped roles: girls are depicted as passive and dull, whereas boys are shown as problem solvers. Examining changes in pictures in children's literature over a 50-year period, Kortenhaus and Demarest (1993) report that girls are pictured and described more frequently now than in earlier years, but they are still shown in more passive activities than boys. For example, girls may be shown caring for a pet, while boys may be shown participating in sports. Another aspect of gender-role stereotyping in the schools is the key figures themselves. According to Betz and Fitzgerald (1987), teachers tend to be women, whereas principals tend to be men. This pattern further reinforces children's view of sex-role stereotypes. In the early 1970s, most schools had gender tracking systems. That is, girls tended to go into typing and home economics, whereas boys took courses in science. Although major changes have occurred in the participation rate of boys and girls in various classes since then, there is both direct and indirect support for Gottfredson's emphasis on gender-role stereotyping in the career development of children.

Two significant aspects of Gottfredson's (1981, 1996) theory are circumscription and compromise. In general, *circumscription* concerns the idea that various factors limit career choices at different ages; it is "the progressive elimination of unacceptable alternatives" (Gottfredson, 1996,

p. 187), leaving acceptable alternatives. More specifically, circumscription refers to the prediction that gender will influence occupational preferences from the age of 6 and up, and that social background, or prestige level, will influence preferences at 9 years and beyond. In this way, choices are circumscribed or limited. Henderson, Hesketh, and Tuffin (1988) found that gender type had more of an effect at ages 6 to 8 than did prestige when career choices were examined. After the age of 8, prestige had more of an effect on occupational choice than did gender. Studying second-, fourth-, and sixth-graders, Helwig (1998a, 2000) reported that children chose more socially valued occupations in the latter grades, supporting Gottfredson's view that prestige becomes more important for children 9 and older. Leung and Harmon (1990) and Lapan and Jingeleski (1992) support the importance of gender typing and prestige as issues that adolescents consider in career exploration. Also, Lapan and Jingeleski (1992) showed how self-efficacy, assertiveness, and emotional expressiveness can affect the circumscribing of career choices for eighth-graders.

Compromise refers to the necessity for an individual to modify her or his career choices because of the reality of limiting environmental factors such as a competitive job market or not having sufficient academic performance to enter an academic program. This means that they may have to accept less attractive career alternatives. To be more precise, the compromise portion of Gottfredson's (1981) theory concerns the prediction that the earlier a stage occurs, the more resistant it will be to change and the less willing an individual will be to compromise on issues related to that stage. Thus, Gottfredson hypothesizes that gender type, prestige, and interest will be compromised (or sacrificed) in such a way that, when making a change in career choice, individuals will give up their interests first, then prestige, and finally gender type. The hypothesis deals directly with why it seems so difficult to encourage girls and women to consider nontraditional careers. Hesketh and colleagues (Hesketh, Durant, & Pryor, 1990; Hesketh, Elmslie, & Kaldor, 1990) have found that interests are most important in career decision making, followed by prestige, and then by gender type. Studying 14- and 15-year-old Spanish students, Sastre and Mullet (1992) found that gender was the best predictor of occupational choice for girls, and that prestige and free time were the best predictors for boys. Hall, Kelly, and Van Buren (1995) reported that the degree to which 8th- and 11th-graders' interests were compromised, if any, depended on the area of interest, for example, scientific or business-oriented. Asian American college students were more likely to compromise gender type for prestige than prestige for gender type as hypothesized by Gottfredson (1996).

Gottfredson (1996) comments that the reasons for the variation in support for the compromise aspect of her theory may be explained, in part, by whether the compromises under investigation are major or minor or are real or artificial. As a way of making the issue of compromise less artificial and more practical, a workbook (*Mapping Vocational Challenges* [MVC]) has been designed to help middle school students understand factors that can limit (compromise) their career options (Lapan, Loehr-Lapan,

& Tupper, 1993). Two studies have been done that indicate initial support for the MVC (Gottfredson & Lapan, 1997).

Implications of Gottfredson's Theory for Super's Theory

Super's (1990) model of early career development, as shown in Figure 7-1, does not deal with gender bias. Gottfredson's (1981, 1996) theory is relevant to several of Super's important concepts. Consistent with both theories is the importance of career exploration unrestricted by gender-role stereotyping. Thus, children of both genders should be able to explore activities such as knitting, sewing, sports, and science. Further, information made available in the schools should not reinforce gender-role stereotypes. In general, publishers of textbooks have made strides in showing adults and children in pictures that do not reinforce traditional gender-role models. By providing information free of gender-role bias, educational systems are more likely to provide an atmosphere in which wide varieties of interests can develop, regardless of gender. If exploration and information are not gender-biased, the selection of key figures by children is also more likely to be unbiased. These concepts will ultimately affect the child's self-concept and ability to make career decisions.

Use of Gottfredson's and Super's Concepts in Counseling

When counseling children, counselors may introduce alternative information about occupational gender roles when discussing exploration, key figures, information, and interest. If a young girl enjoys studying and watching insects and has been told by someone that little girls don't do that kind of thing, the counselor can indicate that this may be a view of one individual and emphasize the young girl's pleasure in learning about insects. By doing this, the counselor is providing alternative information to the young girl about those activities that may lead to an interest in biology. Dealing with key figures, particularly parents, who provide gender-stereotyped examples or information is more difficult. In a direct challenge to an important key figure, the counselor is likely to lose, and the child is likely to believe or identify with the key figure. In the following example, a counselor deals with this issue.

Lucy is a white fifth-grader in a small city in Texas. She has recently turned 11 and has done well in her schoolwork. She has been referred to the counselor by one of her teachers, who talked briefly with Lucy about why she seemed to be less interested in her English, history, and science work. Lucy just shrugged and said that things weren't fun anymore. In talking with Lucy, the counselor learns that Lucy's mother, a practical nurse at a local hospital, has asked Lucy's father to move out of the house. Lucy's father is a self-employed electrician. Lucy describes him as yelling a lot at her mother and as throwing things around the room. In talking with Lucy, the counselor is trying to decide how best to intervene to help Lucy: whether to talk to one or both parents, to make suggestions to Lucy, and/or to help Lucy express her feelings about the events at home. The following dialogue takes place in the middle of the initial counseling session:

CL: My mom usually gets home right after I do because she works from seven in the morning 'til three. She doesn't talk to me the way she used to. I usually go to the refrigerator, and she may go to her room. It's not like it used to be.

CO: How did it used to be? [The counselor wants to learn more about what is happening to Lucy and how things have changed in the family.]

CL: She used to come home and talk with me. Sometimes she'd ask me about school, and sometimes she'd talk about her work.

CO: That felt good, to talk with her. [The counselor, in an attempt to learn more about the situation, is encouraging Lucy to talk about her relationship with her mother.]

CL: Yeah! Like sometimes she'd tell me funny things that happened at work. She doesn't like being a nurse. She tells me it's awful being told what to do all the time and taking care of sick people who yell at her. I wouldn't want to do that.

CO: What seems so bad about that? [Not wanting to reinforce nursing as an occupation for women and not wanting to reinforce Lucy's biased view of nursing, the counselor feels caught. Further, Lucy's mother is an obvious key figure. Challenging her is not likely to work. Thus, the counselor asks for Lucy's view.]

CL: I don't know. I like doing things for other people. I like to baby-sit my little sister. She's only 3 and kind of fun sometimes—a brat at other times—and likes to play with me, too.

CO: What do you like to do with her? [Wanting to follow Lucy's lead, the counselor asks Lucy about her work.]

CL: I like to pretend that I'm her mother, and I make her do things, like behave right or read her a story. I'd like to be a mother sometime. Mom says that's what she wishes she could be all the time and not have to work. I don't want to work.

CO: Why not? [The counselor is concerned about Lucy's attitude toward work, which is learned from a key figure, her mother, as well as the gender-role stereotyping Lucy may be learning that suggests the woman's place is in the home.]

CL: You have to do what everybody tells you to, and you get tired.

CO: Baby-sitting is work, and you seem to like that. [Hearing Lucy voice some of her mother's objections to work, the counselor gently confronts Lucy with her own positive experience of work, which is different from her mother's experience. The counselor wants Lucy to learn from her own exploratory behavior. Although baby-sitting is something that Lucy is required to do, the ways in which she does it are of her own choosing, and she seems to like them. To reply, "Not everyone has to take orders in their work. Some people enjoy helping and taking care of others," might work, but the counselor is afraid that it would be challenging Lucy's mother's view, and that Lucy would reject it.]

CL: Yes, it's fun to do different things with my baby sister. Sometimes we try to fix things like my father. We broke a lamp that way. I was in lots of trouble for a while.

CO: What do you like to fix? [Seizing the opportunity to move away from traditional female occupational roles, the counselor is pleased that Lucy
brings up a more traditionally male activity, fixing things, so that the
counselor can explore this.]

Clearly, the career issue is secondary to the more pressing problem of
helping Lucy with the crisis that has happened in her home. However,
though the career issue may be subtle, it is far-reaching. This brief career
intervention may have an impact on Lucy, allowing her to broaden her occupational possibilities, have a more positive attitude toward work, and
continue in exploratory activities. Hopefully, when she enters high school,
she will conceive of herself as someone who can listen to the input of others and will also be able to start to make her own decisions. It should be
noted that the counselor was aware of Lucy's developmental stage in terms
of processing information. Thus, the conversation stayed on a concrete
level and did not deal with abstract concepts. When she enters high school,
Lucy will be better able to deal with intangible issues.

CAREER DEVELOPMENT OF CHILDREN FROM CULTURALLY DIVERSE BACKGROUNDS

Within the study of the career development of children, very little research has been done on issues that confront children of culturally diverse
backgrounds in their career development. Miller (1977) found that more 9-
year-old white children than 9-year-old African American children were
able to list both their academic and personal strengths and weaknesses.
African Americans had fewer out-of-school learning experiences such as
piano and dancing lessons than did whites. Nine-year-old African American students were less likely than white children to see their career decisions as their own. Further, the 9-year-old African American children had
less occupational knowledge. As Slaney (1980) points out, it is difficult to
separate social class and racial effects when studying factors influencing
career development. Vondracek and Kirchner (1974) studied urban African
American children under the age of 11 in 51 day care centers. They found
that these children were less able than urban white children to see themselves in a future career. Further, the African American children had a
more limited view than white children of what types of work adults did.
Very little research has been done on children in other racial groups. Frost
and Diamond (1978) studied fourth-, fifth-, and sixth-grade children who
were Hispanic, African American, and white. They found that Hispanic
and white girls chose more nontraditional and higher-status occupations
than did African American girls. Further, Hispanic and white girls had a
more open and less stereotyped view of career behavior than did African
American girls. These studies are typical of the few studies investigating differences between white children and children of culturally diverse
backgrounds.

This research suggests that African American and Hispanic children may be impeded in their exposure to exploratory activities in finding information that would enhance their development. The implication for counselors is that it is particularly important to try to provide the same opportunities for all children. This platitude can become a possibility when counselors have an opportunity to work individually or in groups with children from culturally diverse backgrounds. Counselors can help such children develop effective role models so that they may learn more information about occupations and educational opportunities. Counselors can do this by talking with the child about parents and relatives and the work they do. Research suggests that people from some cultural backgrounds are being denied this opportunity (see Chapter 15). In the following section, suggestions are made about how occupational information can be used with children of all racial and ethnic groups to put them in a better position to make career decisions when they reach adolescence.

THE ROLE OF OCCUPATIONAL INFORMATION

Both Super's and Gottfredson's theories have implications for the delivery of occupational information to elementary school children. Most occupational information is provided not in the counseling office but in the classroom. The provision of occupational information through the educational system is called *school-to-work*. Rather than review the many programs for educating students about the world of work, this section will deal with theoretical implications for the use of occupational information in elementary school counseling and career education.

Occupational Information in Counseling

Suggestions for giving information to children about occupations can be taken from developmental theorists. Piaget's view of learning suggests that information given to children under the age of 12 should be concrete and clear. Erikson focuses on the importance of success and achievement for the young child. Learning about an occupation should not be overwhelming but can be done in small pieces. Because of the limited time perspective that younger children have, counselors should focus on what adults do now rather than on future occupational entry. Research such as that done by Miller (1977) suggests that children have vocational choices and are able to learn about these choices, but that planning ahead is more difficult. Gottfredson's theory is useful in reminding the counselor that information about occupations should be without gender bias. The actual discussion of occupational information between guidance counselor and child may be infrequent. However, when such a dialogue occurs, these suggestions may be helpful. More common is the provision of occupational information in classroom activities.

School-to-Work Programs Designed for Children

Because school-to-work programs are a curricular rather than an individual or group counseling function, full treatment is beyond the scope of this book. However, one activity of counselors is the development of, or consultation on, programs that integrate work and school activities. Because school-to-work is such an important part of the precareer decision-making process, discussion is warranted. This is due in part to President Clinton's signing the School-to-Work Opportunities Act in 1994. School-to-work programs have been developed at all educational levels including elementary. Funding for such programs exists at federal, state, and local levels. Recently, much attention has been focused on school-to-work programs. Business Publishers, Inc., releases a monthly School-to-Work Report that describes legislation and programming that deals with activities that incorporate work in the classroom or education in the work setting. School-to-work was the focus of a special issue of *The Career Development Quarterly* (1999, Number 4). In this issue, school-to-work programs were discussed from a social cognitive perspective, Krumboltz's perspective, Super's developmental perspective, and from a trait and factor point of view. The school-to-work initiative has been particularly effective in creating programs for those students who do not go on to 4-year college programs (Blustein, Juntunen, & Worthington, 2000; Blustein, Phillips, Jobin-Davis, Finkelberg, & Roarke, 1997; Olson, 1997; William T. Grant Foundation Commission, 1998).

Implementing school-to-work, formerly referred to as career education, can be done in three basic ways in the elementary school (Herr & Cramer, 1996). The first type is the infusion of occupational information into the classroom in the form of films, oral reports on occupations, or the development of interest centers in the classroom. A second and less formal approach in the classroom involves group activities such as writing a skit using terms from the world of work; crossword puzzles using occupational terms; and comparing lists of interests, abilities, and achievements with requirements of occupations. The third type is community involvement, which can mean taking students out of the classroom or bringing the community into the classroom. Examples include going to a factory and observing each aspect of a manufacturing process or having students follow workers on the job as they go through their daily activities. Herr and Cramer (1996) list 69 of these activities that can be helpful to counselors in designing programs in collaboration with teachers. Additionally, comprehensive programs have been developed for young children.

Super's theory of the career development of children can be applied to activity programming for young children to relate work to school. The Experiential Career Guidance Model (Kyle & Hennis, 2000) includes activities designed for preschool children. The program is sensitive to childrens' limited time perspective. Activities focus on the family and home and include a play store and library in which children learn by playing roles as customers, librarian, storekeeper, and so forth. Field trips to a children's museum can help children learn about communication, transportation, and other activities through hands-on play or observation. For 8- to 11-year-old children, Smith (2000) proposes a model called FOCUS (Finding Out the Child's Underlying Self) which emphasizes exploratory behavior and the development of the self-concept. FOCUS includes materials that assess children's interests, personality, and behaviors. Gamelike activities and age-appropriate questionnaires and books help children develop a sense of self. The Experiential Career Guidance Model and FOCUS are two examples of activities that consider the developmental progress and needs of children in career exploration. Developmental needs of children and issues that they may encounter can be applied to counseling children when career issues may be a part of the process.

Exercises can be structured in such a way that they are consistent with the learning stage of children and with their ability to process information. In general, the successful activities focus on concrete functions, not abstract ones. They are often visual, for example, using films of an occupation or using tools brought into class. Exposure to people in occupations gives an increased opportunity for modeling behavior, as well as an opportunity for the child to have more exposure to key figures. Being able to explore equipment in a factory or to explore dental tools can be very helpful to a child in acquiring information about the world of work. Having a veterinarian show animals and how he or she helps them is more useful and concrete than just talking about his or her daily work. Gottfredson's theory suggests the importance of being careful to avoid gender-role stereotyping in factory visits or choice of outside speakers. This is often difficult, as the counselor or teacher may have less control over these activities than over ones that they direct in the classroom.

THE ROLE OF TESTING

Because interests, capacities, and values are not sufficiently developed in elementary school children, assessment of them should be done carefully. Rather, the emphasis is on acquiring information about oneself, others, and occupations and the development of a self-concept. Children need to be able to see a future and to have a sense of how far away college or work is in time. The appropriate timing of career testing is a difficult issue and is discussed in Chapter 8, "Adolescent Career Development." Various tests of career maturity serve as a means of assessing this readiness.

However, some inventories have been changed so that they are appropriate for children, whereas others have been developed specifically for children. For example, Holland's Self-Directed Search has a form (Form E) that can be used for middle school students. The Murphy-Meisgeier Type Indicator assesses Myers-Briggs types and can be used for children ages 7 to 13. Personality inventories such as the Children's Personality Questionnaire have been designed to be used with preadolescents.

COUNSELOR ISSUES

Career counseling with young children can be challenging because children are at the very beginning of the career choice process, and counselors are usually in an establishment or maintenance phase. Counselors have gone through the process of making career decisions; assessing their abilities, capacities, and values; and acting on them. Children are far from this. They need to experience and acquire information long before they are able to make decisions. This gap in developmental stage makes patience on the part of the counselor particularly important. Piaget's (1977) reminder that children are not adults without information is quite helpful. Being aware of Super's explanation of the career development of children can aid the counselor in dealing with them.

SUMMARY

Counseling children on career issues is rarely thought of as a duty of counselors. The purpose of this chapter has not been to show that it should be an important activity, but that, when it does occur, there are effective ways of talking about career development with children. Super's model of the bases of career maturity is helpful in stressing how curiosity leads to exploration, which can lead to the acquisition of information and the development of interests. Further, Super emphasizes the importance of key figures in the development of the self-concept, along with the development of a sense of internal control and with a respect for parental and educational authorities. Gottfredson's model includes the role of gender and prestige in examining career development of young children. As the young child develops a sense of the future and a sense of self, he or she becomes ready to plan and decide. Recently, school-to-work has become an important initiative in the schools. Suggestions are described for school activities that are consistant with Super's and Gottfredson's theories in the next chapter.

References

Bandura, A. (1997). *Self-efficacy: The exercise of control.* San Francisco: W. H. Freeman.

Berlyne, D. E. (1960). *Conflict, arousal, and curiosity.* New York: McGraw-Hill.

Betz, E. L., & Fitzgerald, L. F. (1987). *The career psychology of women.* Orlando, FL: Academic Press.

Biehler, R. F. (1979). Unpublished study. California State University at Chico.

Blustein, D. L., Juntunen, C. L., & Worthington, R. L. (2000). The school-to-work transition: Adjustment challenges of the forgotten half. In S. D. Brown & R. W. Lent (Eds.), *Handbook of counseling psychology* (3rd ed.), New York: Wiley.

Blustein, D. L., Phillips, S. D., Jobin-Davis, K., Finkelberg, S. L., & Roarke, A. E. (1997). A theory-building investigation of the school to work transition. *The Counseling Psychologist, 25,* 364–402.

Erikson, E. H. (1963). *Childhood and society* (2nd ed.). New York: Norton.

Frost, F., & Diamond, E. E. (1978). Ethnic and sex differences in occupational stereotyping for elementary school children. *Journal of Vocational Behavior, 15,* 43–54.

Ginzberg, E., Ginsburg, S. W., Axelrad, S., & Herma, J. (1951). *Occupational choice: An approach to a general theory.* New York: Columbia University Press.

Gottfredson, L. S. (1981). Circumscription and compromise: A developmental theory of occupational aspirations. *Journal of Counseling Psychology, 28,* 545–579.

Gottfredson, L. S. (1996). A theory of circumscription and compromise. In D. Brown & L. Brooks (Eds.), *Career choice and development: Applying contemporary theories to practice* (3rd ed., pp. 179–232). San Francisco: Jossey-Bass.

Gottfredson, L. S., & Lapan, R. T. (1997). Assessing gender-based circumscription of occupational aspirations. *Journal of Career Assessment, 5,* 419–441.

Hall, A. S., Kelly, K. R., & Van Buren, J. B. (1995). Effects of grade level, community of residence, and sex on adolescent career interests in the zone of acceptable alternatives. *Journal of Career Development, 21,* 223–232.

Helwig, A. A. (1998a). Developmental and sex differences in workers' functions of occupational aspirations of a longitudinal sample of elementary school children. *Psychological Reports, 82,* 915–921.

Helwig, A. A. (1998b). Gender-role stereotyping: Testing theory with a longitudinal sample. *Sex Roles, 38,* 403–423.

Helwig, A. A. (2000). *Career development of a longitudinal sample of school children.* Paper presented at the American Counseling Association World Conference, Washington, DC.

Henderson, S., Hesketh, B., & Tuffin, K. (1988). A test of Gottfredson's theory of circumscription. *Journal of Vocational Behavior, 32,* 37–48.

Herr, E. L., & Cramer, S. H. (1996). *Career guidance and counseling through the life span* (5th ed.). New York: HarperCollins.

Hesketh, B., Durant, C., & Pryor, R. (1990). Career compromise: A test of Gottfredson's (1981) theory using a policy capturing procedure. *Journal of Vocational Behavior, 36,* 97–108.

Hesketh, B., Elmslie, S., & Kaldor, W. (1990). Career compromise: Alternative account to Gottfredson's theory. *Journal of Counseling Psychology, 37,* 49–56.

Jordaan, J. P. (1963). Exploratory behavior: The formation of self and occupational concepts. In D. Super, R. Starishevsky, N. Matlin, & J. P. Jordaan (Eds.), *Career development: Self-concept theory* (pp. 42–78). New York: College Entrance Examination Board.

Kortenhaus, C. M., & Demarest, J. (1993). Gender role stereotyping in children's literature: An update. *Sex Roles, 28,* 219–232.

Kyle, M. T., & Hennis, M. (2000). Experiential model for career guidance in early childhood education. In N. Peterson & R. C. Gonzalez (Eds.) *Career counseling models for diverse populations* (pp. 1–7). Pacific Grove, CA: Brooks/Cole Publishing.

Lapan, R. T., & Jingeleski, J. (1992). Circumscribing vocational aspirations in junior high school. *Journal of Counseling Psychology, 39,* 81–90.

Lapan, R. T., Loehr-Lapan, S. J., & Tupper, T. W. (1993). *Tech-prep careers workbook: Counselor's manual.* Columbia Department of Educational and Counseling Psychology, University of Missouri–Columbia.

Leung, S. A., & Harmon, L. W. (1990). Individual and sex differences in the zone of acceptable alternatives. *Journal of Counseling Psychology, 37*, 153–159.

Looft, W. R. (1971). Sex differences in the expression of vocational aspirations by elementary school children. *Developmental Psychology, 5*, 366.

MacKay, W. R., & Miller, C. A. (1982). Relations of socioeconomic status and sex variables to the complexity of worker functions in the occupational choices of elementary school children. *Journal of Vocational Behavior, 20*, 31–37.

Marko, K. W., & Savickas, M. L. (1998). Effectiveness of a career time perspective intervention. *Journal of Vocational Behavior, 52*, 106–119.

Miller, J. (1977). *Career development needs of 9-year-olds: How to improve career development programs.* Washington, DC: National Advisory Council for Career Education.

Nelson, R. C. (1963). Knowledge and interest concerning 16 occupations among elementary and secondary students. *Educational and Psychological Measurement, 27*, 741–754.

Olson, L. (1997). *The school-to-work revolution.* Reading, MA: Addison-Wesley.

Piaget, J. (1977). *The development of thought: Equilibration of cognitive structures.* New York: Viking Press.

Rainey, L. M., & Borders, L. D. (1997). Influential factors in career orientation and career aspirations of early adolescent girls. *Journal of Counseling Psychology, 44*, 160–172.

Rich, N. S. (1979). Occupational knowledge: To what extent is rural youth handicapped? *Vocational Guidance Quarterly, 27*, 320–325.

Sastre, M. T. M., & Mullet, E. (1992). Occupational preferences of Spanish adolescents in relation to Gottfredson's theory. *Journal of Vocational Behavior, 40*, 306–317.

Scott, K. P. (1981). Whatever happened to Jane and Dick? Sexism in tests reexamined. *Peabody Journal of Education, 58*, 135–140.

Slaney, R. B. (1980). An investigation of racial differences in vocational values among college women. *Journal of Vocational Behavior, 16*, 197–207.

Smith, T. L. (2000). FOCUS: Finding Out the Child's Underlying Self: A career awareness model for children. In N. Peterson & R. C. Gonzalez, *Career counseling models for diverse populations* (pp. 8–21). Pacific Grove, CA: Brooks/Cole Publishing.

Super, D. E. (1957). *The psychology of careers.* New York: Harper & Row.

Super, D. E. (1990). A life-span, life-space approach to career development. In D. Brown, L. Brooks, & Assoc. (Eds.), *Career choice and development: Applying contemporary theories to practice* (2nd ed., pp. 197–261). San Francisco: Jossey-Bass.

Super, D. E. (1994). A life-span, life-space perspective on convergence. In M. L. Savickas & R. W. Lent (Eds.), *Convergence in career development theories* (pp. 63–74). Palo Alto, CA: Consulting Psychologists Press.

Thelen, M., Frautsh, N., Roberts, M., Kirkland, K., & Dollinger, S. (1981). Being imitated, conformity, and social influence: An integrative review. *Journal of Research in Personality, 15*, 403–426.

Thomas, R. M. (1989). *Counseling and life-span development.* Newbury Park, CA: Sage.

Trice, A. D., Hughes, M. A., Odom, K. W., Woods, K., & McClellan, N. C. (1995).

The origins of children's career aspirations: IV. Testing hypotheses from four theories. *The Career Development Quarterly, 43,* 307–322.

Trice, A. D., & Tillapaugh, P. (1991). Children's estimates of their parents' job satisfaction. *Psychological Reports, 69,* 63–66.

Umstot, M. E. (1980). Occupational sex-role liberality of third-, fifth-, and seventh-grade females. *Sex Roles, 6,* 611–618.

Vondracek, S. J., & Kirchner, E. P. (1974). Vocational development in early childhood: An examination of young children's expressions of vocational aspirations. *Journal of Vocational Behavior, 5,* 251–260.

Vygotsky, L. S. (1986). *Thought and language.* Cambridge, MA: MIT Press.

William T. Grant Foundation Commission on Work, Family, and Citizenship. (1988). *The forgotten half: Pathways to success for America's youth and young families.* Washington, DC: Author.

8

Adolescent Career Development

Many career development theorists have focused their attention on adolescence, as it is the time when educational commitment to career choices is made. Life-stage theorists have been helpful in identifying developmental tasks that are important for individuals in the career selection process. This chapter first describes cognitive and emotional factors that bear on career decision making. Then, the emergence of interests, capacities, and values will be discussed in terms of Ginzberg, Ginsburg, Axelrad, and Herma's (1951) theory of the stages of adolescent career development. These theorists also explain the transition that takes place around the 12th grade to a realistic phase of decision making. Their stages are compared to those proposed by Super, who is more concerned with the development of self-concept than with the actual timing of stages. Research is cited that disputes some of the timing of the stages postulated by Ginzberg and his colleagues. More important, examples are given of how counselors can recognize the emergence of interests, capacities, and values. Perhaps the single most important contribution to adolescent career development has been the research on career maturity. A similar area of research is related to Erikson's writings on identity formation that is called vocational identity. In this chapter, Super's research on the Career Development Inventory

(Super, Bohn, Forrest, Jordaan, Lindeman, & Thompson, 1971; Thompson & Lindeman, 1981) is used as a formulation for a conceptual understanding of career maturity and James Marcia's work is used as a basis for understanding vocational identity. Although there are no theories that specifically address the career development of adolescent girls or adolescents from diverse cultural backgrounds, there is a wide body of research that explores this topic. As in other areas of career life-span theory, there has been much more research on the career development of Caucasian adolescent boys and girls than on other adolescents. However, that trend is changing. Counseling examples will demonstrate how Super's theory can be used with different groups.

FACTORS INFLUENCING ADOLESCENT CAREER DEVELOPMENT

Abstract thinking is a process that greatly facilitates career planning. According to Piaget (1977), adolescents start a gradual process of developing their ability to solve problems and to plan. With age, planning becomes more ordered, permitting adolescents to introspect and think about themselves in a variety of situations. At this point, adolescents can more accurately picture themselves working in occupations than they could a few years earlier. This ability, which occurs in the last of Piaget's (1977) four stages of cognitive development, is called *formal thought*. There are individual differences in when an adolescent develops the ability to think abstractly. Furthermore, there are differences across courses in the requirement to think abstractly. For example, a high school sophomore may be able to think abstractly in algebra class but not in biology. Ability to use logic develops gradually. As formal thought emerges, the egocentrism of the concrete operational thinking of childhood does not disappear quickly. Because adolescents have developed the ability to think logically, they are apt to be quite idealistic, expecting their world to be logical when it is not. The process of job entry and job selection can help young people become more realistic in their thinking (Inhelder & Piaget, 1958). Cognitively, the period of formal thought is likely to bring the adolescent into conflict with parents and teachers, as students are likely to think that they are right and others are wrong. Although overstated, this suggests that adolescent thinking is a more tumultuous process than the thinking that takes place in elementary school children.

Just as Piaget has identified adolescence as a time of mild turmoil, so Erikson (1963) has posited that, in terms of psychosocial development, adolescence is a time of identity and role confusion. No longer concerned with following rules and being productive, as in Erikson's (1963) earlier stage focusing on industry and accomplishment, adolescents question their world. Along with their physical development and their exposure to difficult sexual decisions (premarital sex, pregnancy, AIDS) come career decisions that may affect the rest of their lives. As early as middle school, adolescents need to decide whether they want a "vocational track," a "college track," or something else. Ability to deal with these decisions varies greatly among adolescents. Career theorists have studied those aspects of adolescent development that are pertinent to the career choice process, such as interests, capacities, and values.

GINZBERG'S TENTATIVE STAGE OF ADOLESCENT CAREER DEVELOPMENT

Ginzberg, Ginsburg, Axelrad, and Herma's book *Occupational Choice: An Approach to a General Theory* (1951) was one of the earliest significant contributions to life-span theory. Their approach was a multidisciplinary one. Eli Ginzberg was an economist, Sol Ginsburg was a psychiatrist, Sidney Axelrad was a sociologist, and John Herma was a psychologist. In their work, they intensively studied the career choice process (mainly of upper-middle-class white adolescents). Their research consisted of interviews with students and reviews of the existing literature. As they interviewed adolescents and children, they distinguished three periods in the choice process. The fantasy stage (up to age 12) involves play and imagination in thinking about future work. The tentative stage, described in detail in this chapter, concerns a recognition of one's interests, abilities, and values, as well as one's knowledge of work. The realistic stage, occurring after age 17, includes specifying and crystallizing occupational choice. Within the tentative stage, four periods have been identified: the development of interests, the development of capacities, the development of values, and the transition period. Following the progress of adolescents through these periods can help the counselor appreciate the readiness of an adolescent to make career decisions.

Ginzberg (1970, 1972, 1984) reformulated his theory, making several changes in the model proposed by Ginzberg et al. (1951). Although only his views of childhood and adolescent development are discussed here, Ginzberg acknowledged that vocational choice making continues throughout life. Earlier, Ginzberg had argued that vocational choices were irreversible. He modified this view to include aspects of reversibility or changing one's mind, but he still kept the idea that, when choices are made, such as choosing to study printing rather than welding, this choice, while reversible, may have many implications, including impediments in the person's career development (Ginzberg, 1984). In general, Ginzberg (1984) saw the process of choosing an occupation as one of optimization, weighing one's needs and desires against the constraints and opportunities occurring in the work environment. These views show the breadth of his model, although our discussion will focus on the development of interests, capacities, and values.

Development of Interests

Ginzberg et al. (1951) felt that, at about the age of 11, children cease to make fantasy choices and instead tend to base their choices on interests. In particular, Ginzberg et al. found that many choices of young boys were related in some way to their fathers' careers. Based on their current interests, 11-year-old boys would comment about whether they would like to be in an occupation like their father's. The children were quite aware that their interests might change and that they might make different choices. However, they were very vague about alternative choices and not concerned, because they knew that there was a lot of time to make choices. At this time, the ability to judge their competencies was limited and relatively unimportant to them. Using a sample of 478 elementary school boys and 471 girls, Trice, Hughes, Odom, Woods, and McClellan (1995) found support for Ginzberg's idea that interests are the major factor in the selection and rejection of career choices during childhood.

When talking to students who are ready to enter middle school, counselors may notice that the students can speak more clearly about what they like than about what they are able to do. Children may have some exposure through their community to a number of occupations. They may be interested in being a detective or a doctor after seeing these occupations portrayed on television. They may observe the roles of their parents and of the parents of friends. They are able to ask themselves: Is this something I may like to do? Participating in sports and childhood jobs such as lawn mowing and baby-sitting also permits them to test their interests. Children who have not yet developed the ability to judge their capacities may want to be, for example, professional athletes and are not able to consider the quality of their performance.

Development of Capacities

According to Ginzberg et al. (1951), the capacity period covers the ages of 13 and 14 (middle school). In their discussions with counselors, adolescents are more likely to assess their own abilities than they would have been two years before. They may be able to say, "Two years ago, I wanted to be a basketball player, but now I realize I will never be good enough" or, "I'm not sure that I could ever be an engineer like my father; you have to know so much difficult math." For 13- and 14-year-olds, the educational process becomes more important in their preparation for work. Two years before, they may have been less concerned about that process. It is at this point that their time perspective improves and they are able to have a more realistic view of themselves and their future (adapted from Ginzberg et al., 1951).

Recognizing an adolescent's ability to assess his or her own capacities can be useful to the counselor. It is difficult for children to make decisions about curricular choice in eighth grade if they are not able to assess their capacities. Their choices at this point are likely to be based on interests or what their parents have told them. Often, parents make decisions for their middle school children, partially because the children have not yet developed the ability to assess their own capacities.

Development of Values

At the ages of 15 and 16, adolescents are able to take their goals and values into consideration when making a career decision. They may not know how to weigh their interests, capacities, and values, but they have the necessary building blocks for choice. They are becoming aware that they must make choices so that they can fit into a very complex world. With their developed cognitive abilities, they may start to consider such abstract questions as: Is it better to make money or to help others? Weighing the satisfaction of helping others or contributing to environmental protection may be issues they had not thought about two years before. Making a contribution to the world and being a credit to society are factors that may now be considered. The issue of marriage and life plans may emerge, even though there is no marriage partner in mind. Such abstract conceptualization allows adolescents to continue to the next period.

Transition Period

At this point, reality conditions start to play an important role in career choice. This period usually occurs in the last year of high school, at age 17 or 18. Decisions about whether to go to college and, if college is the choice, what to major in—these are real, immediate questions. Adolescents are aware that they need to pay attention to issues such as job availability. They know that they may not be able to get into the college or the field of their choice. Often, adolescents at 17 or 18 are aware that they may not have to make a decision, such as one about medical school, for a few years, but they are aware of the imminence of the decision. They know that they can determine their own future and must take action to do so, even if they cannot do it immediately. Considering salary, the education required, and work conditions becomes more important in this period than it was two years before. This period directly precedes the realistic stage, which includes exploration, crystallization, and specification. The realistic stage is very similar to Super's exploration stage, which is discussed in Chapter 9.

Career guidance for 17- and 18-year-olds usually includes an assessment of their interests, capacities, and values. When hearing a student discussing the world of work and her or his own abilities and desires, counselors can feel that testing and in-depth counseling may be helpful. This topic is dealt with in great detail by Super and his colleagues in their discussion of career maturity. The previous discussion provides a starting place for a critique of Ginzberg's work, which will lead to an understanding of some of the factors that make up career maturity.

Comparison of Super's and Ginzberg's Stages

In general, the adolescent life stages of Super are very similar to those of Ginzberg. We can see this similarity by comparing the stages of each theorist and the ages at which adolescents are supposed to enter those stages. However, there are also important differences of emphasis between Super and Ginzberg et al. Also, since the time that Ginzberg and his colleagues developed their theory, there has been research that questions the timing of their stages.

By comparing Ginzberg's stages to those of Super in Figure 6-2, small differences can be ascertained. Inspection of Super's diagram shows that, in his formulation, interests are followed by capacities, which are followed by a transition to the exploration stage. Super does not include values in his overview. Perhaps the reason is that the issue of values is quite complex. According to Super (Super, Thompson, & Lindeman, 1988), different values may emerge and become more important at various times in the life span. Except for omission of the values stage, the two theories are similar in that they both place interests before capacities.

A number of important differences also exist. Because Super emphasizes recycling of stages, time guidelines are not important in the same sense that they are in Ginzberg's work. To Super, it is the adolescent's attitude toward careers and his or her knowledge of careers that are important. In general, Super believes adolescents enter these stages about two or three years earlier than the ages proposed by Ginzberg. This difference is not an important one from the point of view of the counselor, as a client may enter a stage at a different time than the guidelines described by Super or Ginzberg. Of interest is the research that describes when adolescents and children pursue the tasks of developing interests, capacities, and values.

In a study of 9-year-olds, Miller (1977) found that many were able to state interests in activities and occupations. Aubrey (1977) found that many children were able to say what they could and could not do, although girls were better able to do this than boys. The difficulty in making accurate self-estimates is raised by Tierney and Herman (1973). This is consistent with O'Hara and Tiedeman (1959), who observed that, during the high school years, adolescents had difficulty in accurately seeing their capacities. Westbrook, Buck, Wynne, and Sanford (1994) found that adolescents were most accurate in rating their scholastic aptitude and least accurate in rating specific or special aptitudes, which they tended to overrate. Regarding values, Kapes and Strickler (1975) found little consistency in the work values of high school students. They suggested that different high school curricula may bring about different changes in work values. In a contrasting study, Hales and Fenner (1972, 1973) found that attitudes toward work were present in 11-year-olds and continued through 11th grade. Even though their sample was a homogeneous one in terms of socioeconomic and geographic characteristics, they did find a wide variety in the value profiles of students. These studies do not support the use of age guidelines in expecting consistent patterns in development of interests, capacities, and values in adolescents. Rather, they reaffirm the importance of assessing the individual student. The theorists and the research, however, are consistent in predicting that, in most adolescents, the development of interests precedes that of capacities.

A Counseling Example

To show the usefulness of assessing the relative development of interests, capacities, and values, an example of a 14-year-old ninth-grade student will be used. She is an African American girl from an affluent Chicago suburb. Both parents work in the advertising field. Her father is an account executive with a Chicago firm, and her mother is a market researcher in another firm. Although Joan's grades through her first two quarters of school have been A's and B's, her parents are concerned by her lack of motivation for college and have asked that she talk with her guidance counselor. This section of the interview takes place toward the beginning of the hour with her counselor:

CO: Do you have any idea what you want to do when you finish high school? [This question is designed to get Joan started talking about her plans.]

CL: Well, I'm not sure, but I have some ideas.

CO: Go ahead. I'd like to hear them.

CL: Well, I think I'd like to go into advertising like my parents. They seem to know lots of people and have fun with the products. Sometimes they talk about the products on TV that they've worked with. Sometimes my father will show me a magazine ad that he worked on. But sometimes I think I might like to be an actress or a model, or an aeronautical engineer, like my friend's mother. Sometimes, I think I would like to be a teacher like Mrs. Morgan. I have her for English now, and she's great. Then, I've thought of writing, too. It would be fun to write for a magazine.

CO: Can you tell me more of what appeals to you about advertising? [Feeling bombarded, the counselor decides to concentrate on depth rather than on breadth. Returning to the first topic, because it was talked about in detail, the counselor inquires about advertising, wanting to hear more about Joan's interest.]

CL: I think that I'd like to write ads. It would be fun to do. Sometimes my dad talks about them at dinner. I'm not sure I'd like to do research on toilet paper, the way my mother does.

CO: You seem to enjoy English. [Wanting to follow up on Joan's interest in advertising, the counselor explores further.]

CL: Writing seems so much fun, especially with Mrs. Morgan. She's given us great assignments to do. For her, I like to do my homework.

CO: How is your work going? [This question may get at Joan's perception of her performance in English.]

CL: Oh, I'm doing OK; Mrs. Morgan likes me and my work, I think. But I don't know how I'm *really* doing.

CO: I'm not quite sure what you mean. [The counselor has an idea that Joan is making some distinction between school and occupational ability but is not sure.]

CL: Maybe I could do schoolwork OK, but doing what my father does seems really hard. You really have to be smart to get people to work with your company and give them good ads.

CO: It seems difficult for you to make plans about what you want to do. [Joan seems able to differentiate between ability needed at school and in an occupation. She seems to be aware that she doesn't know yet whether she has the ability needed in advertising.]

CL: Sometimes it seems too hard. I wish I were a psychiatrist.

CO: Tell me more about that, please. [Where did this come from? the counselor wonders. Joan's interests are varied and seem to have no end.]

CL: I really like to help people. I have seen psychiatrists on television programs and how they do it. It seems great.

CO: To help people? [Wanting to learn more about Joan's motivation, the counselor inquires further.]

CL: Yes, it's just so easy to sit there and talk and make a lot of money.

CO: Seems like fun to you. [What had started out as a possible value for Joan has turned into a rather naive interest.]

Joan's difficulty in establishing her capacities and values suggests that career counseling using tests may be premature. Although the use of a career maturity instrument (to be described in the next section) may be helpful, the counselor wishes to continue discussing Joan's interests, as they are varied and confused. This may lead to more suggestions as to how to proceed. Currently, the counselor's goal for counseling is to assess career maturity rather than to work on career selection, and to continue to conceptualize Joan's interests, capacities, and values.

CAREER MATURITY

Vocational maturity was described by Super (1955) as having the following five major components:

1. Orientation to vocational choice, which deals with concern about career choice and using occupational information
2. Information and planning about a preferred occupation, that is, the specific information that the individual has about the occupation he or she intends to enter
3. Consistency of vocational preference, concerned not only with stability of an occupational choice over time, but also with its consistency within occupational fields and levels
4. Crystallization of traits, including seven indexes of attitudes toward work
5. The wisdom of vocational preference, which refers to the relationship between choice and abilities, activities, and interests

This work of Super's was a major focus of the early monographs published by the Career Pattern Study, an in-depth study of a sample of adolescents followed into adulthood. Super and his colleagues further refined the concept of vocational maturity (Super et al., 1957; Super & Overstreet,

1960). This extensive work led to the development of the original Career Development Inventory (Super et al., 1971) and culminated in a revised edition of the Career Development Inventory (Thompson & Lindeman, 1981). The concepts that make up Super's definition of career maturity have been arrived at by studying the responses of boys and girls, and men and women, to various versions of the Career Development Inventory. These concepts are described in detail here.

Super's Conception of Career Maturity

Throughout the extensive research that Super and his colleagues have done with adolescents, they have been concerned with readiness of individuals to make good choices. They do not assume that, just because a student reaches ninth grade, he or she is ready to plan his or her future career. Not only do they see differences in career maturity among individuals, but they are also able to identify different components of career maturity. To understand Super's model, it is helpful to use the structure of the Career Development Inventory (Thompson & Lindeman, 1981). With Figure 8-1 as a guide, the five subscales that make up the Career Development Inventory will be explained: Career Planning, Career Exploration, Decision Making, World-of-Work Information, and Knowledge of the Preferred Occupational Group. Also, the Career Orientation Total, which is a combination of subscales, will be described. Another concept that is part of Super's definition of career maturity but that is not tested by the Career Development Inventory is realism. The concepts described in the following paragraphs can by used to guide client discussion, with or without the use of the Career Development Inventory.

Career Planning   This scale (and therefore the concept of planning) measures how much thought individuals have given to a variety of information-seeking activities and how much they feel they know about various aspects of work. The amount of planning that an individual has done is critical to this concept. Some of the activities that are included are learning about occupational information, talking with adults about plans, taking courses that would help one make career decisions, participating in extracurricular activities or part-time or summer jobs, and obtaining training or education for a job. In addition, this concept deals with knowledge of working conditions, education required, job outlook, different approaches to job entry, and chances of advancement. *Career planning* refers to how much a student *feels* that he or she knows about these activities, not how much he or she actually knows. The latter is covered by the World-of-Work Information and the Knowledge of the Preferred Occupational Group scales.

When talking with a student about career planning activities, it is helpful to know not only what the student has done, but also what the student *thinks* he or she has done. Discussion of future plans, including courses to be taken the following year, college selection, or ideas about a potential college major or postsecondary education, all contribute to career planning.

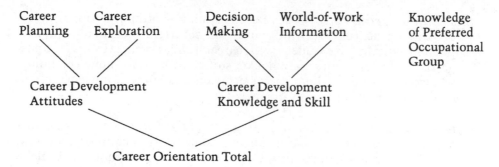

Figure 8-1 Relationship of the Career Development Inventory scales. (Modified and reproduced by special permission of the Publisher, Consulting Psychologists Press, Inc., Palo Alto, CA 94303, from *Career Development Inventory Volume 1: User's Manual,* by Albert S. Thompson and Richard H. Lindeman, with the collaboration of Donald E. Super, Jean Pierre Jordaan, and Roger A. Myers. Copyright© 1981 by Consulting Psychologists Press, Inc. All rights reserved. Further reproduction is prohibited without the Publisher's consent.)

Either a low score on the Career Planning scale of the Career Development Inventory or, in lieu of this, the counselor's assessment that the student has not given much thought to career plans suggests the next step in counseling. This step is to give more thought to experiences that may provide more information to serve as a basis for planning.

Career Exploration Willingness to explore or look for information is the concept basic to the Career Exploration scale. In this subscale (and concept), students' willingness to use resources such as parents, other relatives, friends, teachers, counselors, books, and movies is investigated. Besides willingness, career exploration also deals with how much information the student has already acquired from the source. Career exploration differs from career planning in that the latter concerns thinking and planning about the future, whereas the former deals with use of resources, but both focus on attitudes toward work. Combined, they are referred to by Super as career development attitudes, and a score for this concept is given on the Career Development Inventory.

Counselors may often find that students are reluctant, for various reasons, to use resources to get occupational information, sometimes because of a student's attitude that he or she does not need information. In such a case, the counselor can explore reasons for this thinking. Sometimes, students are hostile to authority figures and rule out certain valuable resources such as parents, teachers, or coaches. Other students may be afraid to use resources because they are apprehensive that teachers or relatives will not take them seriously. Encouraging career exploration can be an important activity prior to assisting a student with career selection. Giving the student a week, three months, or some specified period of time to talk to teachers and use books containing occupational information or some other resource and then to return for counseling is often a useful strategy. By focusing on attitudes toward work, the counselor can determine the next step in assisting the student with career development. However, a positive attitude toward work may not be sufficient to start career planning. Knowledge of how to make a career decision and some knowledge of occupational information is also important.

Decision Making   The idea that a student must know how to make career decisions is an important one in Super's concept of vocational maturity. This concept concerns the ability to use knowledge and thought to make career plans. In the Decision Making scale, students are given situations in which others must make career decisions and are asked to decide which decision would be best. An assumption is that, if students know how others should make career decisions, they will be able to make good career decisions for themselves.

Asking students how they plan to go about making a career decision can be useful. Some students will be unable to answer the question, or to say anything more than "I don't know; it will come to me." This is an opportunity for the counselor to explain portions of the career decision process. The counselor can focus on what the next steps may be for career decision making. If the counselor uses the Career Development Inventory, it would be helpful to go over that section of the test with the student, explaining why some of the student's answers were correct and others were wrong.

World-of-Work Information   This concept has two basic components. The first deals with knowledge of important developmental tasks, such as when others should explore their interests and abilities, how others learn about their jobs, and why people change jobs. The other portion of this concept (and subscale) covers knowledge of job duties in a few selected occupations, as well as job application behaviors. Super believes that it is important for individuals to have some knowledge about the world of work before effective career decision-making counseling can be done.

For the counselor, knowledge of the accuracy of the information that students have about work is helpful. Some students have misinformation about how to obtain a job and how to behave when they get a job. Others have little idea of the work that people such as doctors, lawyers, stockbrokers, and secretaries do. Often, some information is inaccurately gathered from television or films. Correcting students' inaccurate perceptions of the world of work may be a part of predecision-making counseling.

Knowledge of the Preferred Occupational Group   In the Career Development Inventory, students are asked to choose which of 20 occupational groups they prefer. Then, they are asked questions about their preferred occupational group. They are asked about duties of the job, tools and equipment, and physical requirements of the job. In addition, they are asked to judge their own ability (or capacities) in nine different areas: verbal ability, nonverbal reasoning, numerical ability, clerical ability, mechanical ability, spatial ability, motor coordination, English skills, and reading ability. They are also asked to identify the interests of the people in the preferred occupation. The interest categories that they choose from are verbal, numerical, clerical, mechanical, scientific, artistic/musical, promotional, social, and outdoor. This, then, constitutes a very thorough inquiry into students' knowledge of their preferred occupational group.

Information about students' knowledge of the occupation that they want to enter can be extremely helpful in determining what type of counseling should be offered. In talking to students about their knowledge of occupations, counselors can learn about their progress in career planning. For example, some students may have misinformation about their career choice. Some students may be quite naive, thinking that to be a veterinarian does not require more than an associate's degree. Others may believe that, to enter a business career, one needs a bachelor's degree in business. The assessment of knowledge of a preferred occupation is often a key aspect of counseling. If a counselor is not aware of a student's assumptions about his or her preferred occupation, the counselor may assume the student has made a good decision, when in fact that is not true. Assessing good decision making is related to another of Super's concepts: realism.

Realism   A concept that is part of Super's view of career maturity (Super, 1990), realism is not tested in the Career Development Inventory. Rather, Super describes it as a "mixed affective and cognitive entity best assessed by combining personal, self-report, and objective data as in comparing the aptitudes of the individual with the aptitudes typical of people in the occupation" (p. 213). Thus, to measure whether a choice of an individual is realistic, a counselor would need knowledge of the ability required in the occupation along with aptitude or grade information about the student.

The use of realism in career counseling has some dangers. It requires that the counselor be a very accurate judge of the student's aptitudes and the aptitudes required by the job. Inappropriate use of judging realistic choices can lead to the following: "My high school guidance counselor told me I could never make it to medical school, but I am in medical school now"; "My high school guidance counselor said I could never make it through college, and I graduated last year"; "My high school guidance counselor said I don't have the ability to go to college, so I guess I won't." Because students can misinterpret or misuse aptitude information, the concept of realism has to be used quite carefully. Inaccurate predictions can have an effect on an individual's later choice of occupation.

Career Orientation   *Career orientation* is a general term encompassing the concepts described previously. The Career Orientation Total score gives a single summary of the following scales: Career Planning, Career Exploration, Career Decision Making, and World-of-Work Information. It does not include the Knowledge of the Preferred Occupational Group score or the unmeasured concept, realism. Having a general sense of students' career maturity may be useful for the counselor before looking at the specific subscales. It may provide a summary of what to expect from the student in terms of orientation toward careers. However, the five subscales are likely to have more relevance for the counselor in deciding which areas of career maturity to explore with a student. Probably, the counselor will want to talk most about those in which the student scores low. The following is an example of how a counselor used both career maturity concepts derived from the Career Development Inventory and the inventory itself.

Using the Concept of Career Maturity in Counseling

Ralph is a white tenth-grade student in a Providence, Rhode Island, high school. His parents are second-generation Italian Americans. His father is a mail carrier and his mother is a waitress. Ralph has taken the Career Development Inventory along with the rest of his tenth-grade class in the early fall. He is talking about his schedule with his career guidance counselor in trying to decide what courses to take next year. Ralph has had C's in science and math and A's in English and social studies. He works after school in a fast-food restaurant and spends much of his weekends working with his older brother on his brother's car. Compared to other tenth-graders, Ralph's Career Planning and Career Exploration scores are at about the 15th percentile. His Decision Making score on the Career Development Inventory is at the 50th percentile, and his World-of-Work Information score is at about the 45th percentile. His scores on Knowledge of the Preferred Occupational Group and the Career Orientation Total are at about the 25th percentile. The transcript begins after the counselor and client have exchanged some introductory remarks:

CL: I know I need to think about next year and beyond, but I just haven't had time.

CO: Been very busy? [The counselor wants to know what life roles are important to Ralph. This is related to Super's concept of work salience, which was described in Chapter 6 and will be described in more detail in Chapter 9.]

CL: After school, I work at that fast-food place down the street, and then at night, I go out with my friends.

CO: Does it give you any time to think about what you want to do? [The counselor wants to inquire again about career planning that Ralph may have done. The counselor has Ralph's Career Development Inventory results. He has not shared these directly with Ralph at this point.]

CL: I really haven't thought about it much. It doesn't sound like fun. After work, I'm kind of tired, and I like to go home, have dinner. Then I like to go out. Sometimes I do some homework, but not too much.

CO: Have you had a chance to talk to anyone about what you might do? [The counselor, aware of Ralph's low scores on Career Planning and Career Exploration, wants to see if there is a possibility for Ralph to make progress in this area.]

CL: Not really. My parents don't seem to know much about what is available. They just think I should work hard and get a good, secure job that pays well. My friends don't seem to know anything serious anyway.

CO: Would you like to know more about what's available? [Possibly, Ralph's friends and relatives are limited sources of information. Maybe there are other sources that can help Ralph.]

CL: Yes, I know I should do more than I am doing. Where can I learn?

CO: Your teachers, the Career Center here at school, maybe friends of your parents.

CL: I know that our math teacher brought in an accountant, and I learned a little bit that way. But I certainly don't want to be an accountant.

CO: Sounds as if you've given some thought to possible occupations. [The counselor wants to reinforce the little career exploration that Ralph has done.]

CL: Actually, what seems more interesting to me—and it suprises me—is doing what my social studies teacher does.

CO: Surprises you? [Ralph is starting to think a bit about world-of-work information and is using a key figure—the importance of which is described in the previous chapter—in that exploration.]

CL: Yes. I never thought about doing anything like teaching. I always just thought that work was work, a real pain.

CO: Now it seems maybe work could be fun. You seem to be interested in teaching. [Wanting to note this change in attitude, the counselor emphasizes it.]

CL: Yes, I think I would like to help people learn things. My social studies teacher seems to really like what he's doing, and that's great. All I ever do at home is hear my parents complain about their work.

CO: You seem to be picking up some ideas about what teachers do, more than you have in past years. [Perhaps Ralph is starting to learn more world-of-work information because of a growing maturity. Even though he has been exposed to teachers for the last 11 years, he is just now starting to think about teaching as an occupation.]

By exploring ideas about career choice, the counselor is helping Ralph become more vocationally mature. As their counseling progresses, the counselor will make some decisions, as will Ralph. The counselor will decide when to share the Career Development Inventory scores with Ralph and how to help him learn from them. Further, the counselor will decide whether to do interest, aptitude, or values testing with Ralph. For Ralph, decisions about whether to continue thinking about career planning and the world of work will have to be made. By making use of Super's career maturity concepts, the counselor is able to make some assessment of Ralph's readiness for career decision making. Vocational maturity is one way of viewing adolescent career development, vocational identity is yet another. Erikson's view of identity formation has been modified by Marcia and applied to career development by Vondracek and others.

IDENTITY AND CONTEXT

Erik Erikson's (1963, 1968, 1982) theory of human development is broad, with several implications for career development. Influencing more career theorists than any other single developmental theory, Erikson's life-stage approach is frequently cited by Super as influential in his own theory. Of particular interest are his conceptualizations about adolescent identity issues. His identity stage is the fifth of eight stages and serves as a bridge between the four stages occurring in childhood and the three stages that arise in adulthood. The focus of this section will be on the identity stage and its relationship to other stages as they affect career development.

Compared to the attraction of career development theorists to Erikson's model, the direct application of Erikson's theory to career development issues has been minimal. An effort to apply Erikson's theoretical constructs to career development has been made by Munley (1977). Some research by Munley (1975) and others (Powers & Griffith, 1993; Savickas, 1985) has focused on the identity crisis. The most consistent research on vocational identity has been done by Fred Vondracek and his colleagues. These writers have attempted to define the concept of identity and to explain it through research and case studies. Although Erikson has written frequently on issues concerning the identity crisis, his work does not provide clear prescriptions for the counselor or psychotherapist. It could be said that Erikson presents an artistic rather than a scientific view of the identity crisis. Describing identity issues in the lives of clients can sometimes be difficult.

A significant effort has been devoted to studying Erikson's stages. For example, Zuschlag and Whitbourne (1994) studied three groups of college students, who were surveyed in 1967, 1977, and 1988, concluding that college seniors had more advanced emotional and cognitive development than younger students. Marcia, Waterman, Matteson, Archer and Orlofsky (1993) provide a handbook for investigating Erikson's psychosocial stages, especially identity and intimacy. Marcia (1989, 1998, 1999) has modified Erikson's work so that research can be done on important aspects of identity development. These are called statuses by Marcia and include achievement, moratorium, foreclosure, and diffusion.

Vondracek and his colleagues have preferred to use Marcia's diffusion, moratorium, foreclosure, and achievement statuses rather than vocational maturity as they believe that Marcia's statuses help to identify four levels of vocational identity within a specific context. These statuses can be measured through interviews or self-report questionnaires, including the Extended Objective Measure of Ego Identity Status (Adams, Bennion, & Huh, 1987) or survey questions like those from the Shell Youth Study (Jugendwerk der Deutschen Shell, 1992). In their work, Vondracek and his colleagues examine political and social issues that affect adolescents as well as individual issues.

Vocational identity can be viewed as four developmental statuses that many adolescents go through. *Diffusion* refers to having few clear ideas of what one wants and not being concerned about the future. A *moratorium* is a time, often more than several months, in which one explores options while wanting a direction, but not having one. *Foreclosure* refers to making a choice, often based on family tradition, without exploring other options. *Achievement* refers to knowing what one wants and making plans to attain an occupational goal. In some of their studies, Vondracek and his colleagues use single items to identify the vocational identity statuses.

Diffusion—I don't know what I want, what happens, happens.
Moratorium—I don't know what I want, but I want to find out.
Foreclosure—I know what I want and I follow established paths.
Achievement—I know what I want and have made plans already.

Source: Jugendwerk der Deutschen Shell (1992). Jugend 1992. Band 4. Methodenberichte-Tabellen-Fragebogen. (Youth 1992, Vol. 4: Methods, Tables, Questionnaires.) Opladen: Leske & Budrich.

Vondracek and his colleagues have examined identity development from several points of view. As individuals advance in their vocational identity development they tend to have positive attitudes and an openness to a variety of occupations. They are also more willing to explore occupations and feel more confident about being successful in their work (Vondracek & Skorikov, 1997). In studying occupational exploration of 13- to 19-year-olds, Schmitt-Rodermund and Vondracek (1999) found that those in the identity diffusion status explored activities in leisure, school, technology, and music areas the least and those in the achievement phase explored them the most. They also found that doing activities with parents predicted more exploratory behavior. Environmental exploration also predicts vocational identity in college students (Robitschek & Cook, 1999). Identity development has also been studied in domains other than the vocational one, such as religion, politics, lifestyle, and interpersonal relations. Vocational identity tends to precede the development of identity in the other domains, setting a tone for how the other aspects of identity will develop (Skorikov & Vondracek, 1998). The authors suggest that vocational development in early adolescence is particularly important as it influences other areas of identity development. Vocational identity is important in late adolescence as well as early adolescence and is related to age of the individual for all adolescents (Johnson, Buboltz, & Nichols, 1999).

Whereas most work on career maturity does not attend to the importance of environmental factors, Vondracek and his colleagues are concerned with the effect of social, political, and historical factors on individuals that influence them and their vocational identity. Examples of some of these factors are changes in the economy, local and federal social and educational policy, advances in technology affecting job performance, and job availability. This focus on the broader context of development is referred to as *developmental-contextual theory.*

Vondracek (Vondracek, Reitzle, & Silbereisen, 1999) stresses the importance of the timing of career choices within their specific contexts, as it can retard or advance vocational identity development. For example, adolescents in East Germany who grew up under a communist regime had fewer career choices available to them than those in West Germany, where there was a strong economy and many more choices. West German youth were slower to develop their vocational identity because they had many more choices and it was thus more difficult to choose than for East German youth (Reitzle, Vondracek, & Silbereisen, 1998; Vondracek & Reitzle, 1998). Comparisons of majority group and minority group high school students in Quebec also show the effect of context in vocational maturity (Perron, Vondracek, Skorikov, Tremblay, & Corbiere, 1998), with advancement in maturity depending on group membership, on the participants' age, and the time of measurement.

A Counseling Example

The following case illustrates how an identity issue may arise in counseling, creating both personal and career strains for an adolescent. Erikson and Marcia's conception of stage development helps us to understand issues and difficulties that arise from a crisis at a particular point in time.

Frank is a white college sophomore who has not yet declared his major. He is attending a large university in Boston. His father is a lawyer in New York City, and his mother is vice president of a large bank. Two younger sisters are still in high school. Frank has been wondering for some time what he is going to do with his future. He is confused about his career goals and feels that he is wasting time in college because he does not know what to major in or what career to prepare for. Returning from winter vacation, he decides to talk to a counselor about his dilemma. This dialogue occurs in the first session with the counselor:

CL: My friends seem to know what they are doing—they seem to have goals, ideas. My girlfriend is premed, studies a lot, and knows where she is going.

CO: And you?

CL: I don't know. Sometimes I feel real lost. I wonder if I belong here at school. Sometimes with my courses, I just do the work, but the courses don't seem to matter.

CO: There's no feeling of being there, of being a part of things. [The counselor notices immediately a lack of an overall feeling of identity.]

CL: I think I used to like to do things more than I do now.

CO: What kinds of things, Frank?

CL: Well, when I first got here, I played in the marching band—trumpet. I used to like that, but it didn't seem to matter after awhile, so I didn't join the band this year. The excitement of it seemed to wear off fast last year.

CO: Now things are just blah. [Again, Frank's lack of clarity seems apparent. This issue is similar to that of Marcia's diffusion status.]

CL: Yeah, "blah" is a good word for it. I don't know what I'm doing, and whatever it is I'm doing, I can't seem to do it right.

CO: That statement covers a lot of territory. Let me ask you about it. What can't you do right, Frank? [Frank seems to be talking about a lack of feeling of competency, leading the counselor to think that Frank may be advancing to the moratorium status where he can explore a variety of areas.]

CL: I did OK in high school, particularly music. I played in every band or orchestra that we had at school. I really liked the trumpet. I was always first chair, and that felt good.

CO: Something happened?

CL: Yes, I auditioned for a national competition between my junior and senior years in high school. I didn't get offered a position. At first, I was
very disappointed. Then, it was after that, like nothing seemed to matter
very much. I didn't care much about things after that.

CO: That seems to have been an important event for you. [The counselor
hears that this disappointment is a threat to Frank's sense of identity and
wonders if this alone could cause the feeling of depression that he seems
to be experiencing.]

CL: Well, I guess I didn't care, and no one else seemed to care either.

CO: Go on.

CL: Well, I think that my father always thought that the music was kid
stuff—fluff. You know?

CO: How did he react? [The counselor observes Frank's anger at his father, something that is not unexpected when there is a sense of a lack of identity.]

CL: It was like, "Well, so what else is new?" He has always seemed real
caught up in his work. He brings work home from the office. When I was
a kid I used to think that all he ever did was work.

CO: And work seemed unpleasant? [Thoughts about identification with his father and views of work occur to the counselor.]

CL: Nothing seemed fun at all. Actually, I guess fun was being at school. That
always seemed funny to me because most of my friends couldn't wait to
get out of school.

CO: It certainly had an effect on you. [Frank's father's commitment to work
seems to be having a negative effect on Frank. He doesn't want that same
feeling. Perhaps he sees that work can only be unpleasant.]

CL: It seemed that when I couldn't play the trumpet better than anybody else,
I was nobody. In college, the novelty of playing in a college band lasted
awhile, but it wore off.

CO: Real strong feelings, Frank. [Frank has experimented with exploration but
may need encouragement to make good use of a moratorium period.]

Frank and the counselor spend four sessions discussing his problems.
Frank is seeking a moratorium. He feels that he needs time to solve his
problems. Each semester, school seems to become more futile to him. He
is trying to look for meaning in his life, with school and with friends. He plans
not to continue school in the fall, preferring to work so that he can continue his search for meaning in his life. At appropriate points, the counselor
will introduce occupational information into the counseling process. When
to introduce occupational information and more testing is a future consideration. Occupational information and testing, as they pertain to Super's
theory and vocational identity theory, are the subject of the next sections.

THE ROLE OF OCCUPATIONAL INFORMATION

As may be apparent from the description of the Career Development Inventory, occupational information is critical to Super's theory. The Career
Planning subtest asks students how much thinking and planning they have

done about various educational and occupational opportunities. The Career Exploration scale asks students whom they have gone to, or whom they would go to, for occupational information. Implicit in the Decision Making scale is the integration of occupational information with career decision making. The World-of-Work Information and the Knowledge of the Preferred Occupational Group scales are measures of occupational knowledge. Clearly, Super's theory depends on the integration of self-concept and information about the world of work.

A concept described by two of Super's colleagues (Starishevsky & Matlin, 1963) provides another view of the relationship between self-concept and the world of work. Concepts of psychtalk and occtalk emphasize the relationship between occupation and self. *Psychtalk* refers to statements used to describe aptitudes, interests, and other characteristics of oneself. *Occtalk* refers to statements about occupations. Starishevsky and Matlin (1963) believe that occtalk and psychtalk statements can be translated from one to the other. For example, they state (p. 34) that wanting to be a lawyer may translate as being socially minded or being aggressive. A person who says that she will be a physician may also be saying, "I am intelligent, healthy, and concerned about others." Likewise, a person may say, "I am intelligent, healthy, and concerned about others (psychtalk); I could be a physician (occtalk)." The notion that discussion about occupations implies beliefs about self, and that beliefs about self can have implications for occupations, can be useful for counselors. The concepts of occtalk and psychtalk provide a convenient bridge in Super's theory between what could appear to be two very different concepts.

In the development of vocational identity, individuals gradually incorporate information from their environment into their sense of themselves. In the diffusion stage, individuals are likely to learn about their interests and abilities, but not incorporate this information into a sense of themselves. In the moratorium stage, adolescents experience leisure and work and start to develop a sense of self. In foreclosure, individuals may have information about an occupation but have not fully incorporated this information into a sense of themselves. In the achievement stage, adolescents make plans based on incorporating information about themselves and the world of work.

THE ROLE OF TESTING

Testing and assessment are a very important part of Super's developmental model. Testing of career maturity through the use of the Career Development Inventory has been discussed in detail in this chapter. Inventories measuring the importance of work roles, as well as the stages of late adolescent and adult development, are discussed in the next chapter. These stem directly from Super's life-span theory. In addition to these inventories, Super also advocates the use of inventories and tests that measure interests, capacities or abilities, and values. His Values Scale (Nevill & Super, 1989) is an example of the latter.

Super (1990; Osborne, Brown, Niles, & Miner, 1997) provide a very detailed and extensive model for career assessment, called the Career Development Assessment and Counseling (CDAC) model. Typical instruments that they recommend are the Adult Career Concerns, the Values Scales, and the Salience Inventory described in Chapter 9, the Strong Interest Inventory and the Career Development Inventory which are explained on pages 194–198. Hartung, Vandiver, Leong, Pope, Niles, and Farrow (1998) suggest that a measure of cultural identity should also be used as a part of this assessment. This model can be used for work-bound youth (Herr & Niles, 1997) as well as college-bound youth. Clients are not always ready for or open to an in-depth assessment, and counselors often do not have the time necessary. Sometimes, assessment in counseling can be done in groups; sometimes, it can occur over a period of months or even years. Super has developed a multitude of assessment techniques, and he advocates the use of many others. It is up to the counselor to decide how best to use these tests and inventories.

Assessment of vocational identity has received less attention than vocational maturity. Adams's (Adams, Bennion, & Huh, 1987) Extended Objective Measure of Ego Identity Status can be used to measure stages of diffusion, moratorium, foreclosure, and achievement. Frequently, counselors assess vocational identity by talking with their adolescent clients about the issues that are affecting their lives. Additional information about male and female adolescents and adolescents from diverse cultural backgrounds can influence the use of developmental assessment and theoretical concepts.

GENDER ISSUES IN ADOLESCENCE

Just as gender-role stereotyping has a limiting effect on the selection of occupations by children, it also does for adolescents. Research studies are cited here to give some idea of the effect that gender-role stereotyping has on occupational choice and aspirations for occupational success. In a study of 2000 Alabama seniors, Fottler and Bain (1980) found females tending to aspire slightly more than males to professional and technical occupations and aspiring slightly less than males to managerial occupations. Among lower levels of occupations, Fottler and Bain observed traditional patterns of females choosing clerical and service positions, and of males choosing craft and labor positions. Rojewski (1997) reported that female adolescents were more likely to aspire to lower levels and higher levels of occupations compared to males who aspired to mid-level occupations as determined by a measure of prestige. When McKenna and Ferrero (1991) compared 9th-grade boys and girls on how traditional their career choices were, they found that 77% of the boys and 45% of the girls said their choice was traditional. Additionally, they found that 52% of the boys and 85% of the girls thought it was acceptable to work in nontraditional occupations. For about a third of the tenth- and twelfth-grade girls whom they studied, Davey and Stoppard (1993) found that desired occupations were significantly less traditional than the occupations the girls actually expected to enter. As these studies show, stereotyping occupations according to gender continues to be an issue for adolescents.

Some studies have used less direct approaches to examine the effect of gender-role stereotyping on adolescents. In a study of high school juniors, Hurwitz and White (1977) found that women saw females in lower-paying and lower-status jobs than males. If high school girls were led to believe that the gender ratios in certain occupations would be balanced in the future, they expressed more interest in traditionally male occupations (Heilman, 1979). However, high school boys expressed less interest when they were told that the gender ratio would be more balanced in the future. These findings suggest that males preferred the dominant gender ratio and females were put off by occupations if they felt that other women were not going to be in them. Studying seventh-grade adolescents, Robison-Awana, Kehle, and Jenson (1986) asked their subjects to take a self-esteem inventory, both as themselves and as someone of the opposite sex. They found that both boys and girls believed that girls had lower self-esteem. Using Crites's Career Maturity Inventory as a measure of career maturity, Powell and Luzzo (1998) reported that males between the ages of 15 and 19 believed that they had more control over their career decision making than did women of comparable ages. To educate eighth- and eleventh-graders about choosing nontraditional occupations, Van Buren, Kelly, and Hall (1993) used videotape to model various occupations. They found that the boys' interest in social occupations increased. Van Buren et al.'s work represents an effort to make career information free of gender bias.

Social cognitive career theory described by Hackett and Betz (1981) suggests that, in certain situations, adolescent women, particularly college women, have less confidence in their abilities than do men. This theory, although not a developmental theory but a theory of social learning, has implications for the career development of adolescent women (see Chapter 13). Hackett and Betz believe that women lack strong expectations of their own personal efficacy in a number of occupational areas. They find that women often do not live up to their capabilities. Further, women have fewer opportunities for successful career behaviors, and they receive less encouragement than men in this process. These observations are confirmed in reviews by Lent and Hackett (1987) and Lent, Brown, and Hackett (1994).

Related to the finding that women often feel less competent than men in a number of career-related behaviors is the research on women's participation in math. Betz and Fitzgerald (1987) believe that girls stop taking math because of female socialization patterns that suggest that math is for men, and that women do not need to study math. Research suggests that math confidence is a better predictor of taking more math courses than are grades in math (Chipman & Wilson, 1985). In another study, Chipman, Krantz, and Silver (1992) found that math anxiety interfered with being interested in careers in science. In a report related to these findings, Monaco and Gaier (1992) found that adolescent females are less confident than males in a coeducational setting but perform better academically. Studying mathematics self-efficacy (a concept similar to career self-efficacy), Betz and Hackett (1983) found that college men had more confidence in their math ability than did college women. This study was one of the first of many studies to emphasize how women's beliefs ("Can I do math?") negatively affect women's interest in math, their intentions to enroll in math courses, and their performance in math courses (Lent, Lopez, & Bieschke, 1991, 1993; Multon, Brown, & Lent, 1991). A different model (Fassinger, 1990) also emphasizes the importance of math self-efficacy in career choices for women. O'Brien and Fassinger (1993) found that women valuing careers and work was related to liberal gender-role values, high math self-efficacy, and moderate attachment to and separation from their mothers.

Implications of Gender Research for Super's Theory

The research just cited has implications for how adolescent women deal with Super's career maturity concepts. In reviewing gender differences on the Career Development Inventory, Super (1990) states that girls tend to score slightly higher than boys on measures of career maturity, a finding supported by Hartung (1997) and Taveira, Silva, Rodriguez, and Maia (1998). However, the research cited earlier suggests that adolescent girls may have difficulty using occupational information about traditionally male-dominated occupations. Further, they may have less confidence in their ability to make certain career-related decisions. These are not factors that are directly measured by any of Super's career decision-making scales. Rather than refute Super's concepts of vocational maturity, the research seems to suggest additional constructs to be considered.

Implications for Counseling

It is important for the counselor to provide as many avenues as possible for girls in making career choices. With regard to career planning, it is helpful to encourage women to explore many sources of career information, such as books and working in a field of interest. The counselor may find it necessary to encourage and support girls in taking math and to help them reduce their math anxiety. With regard to career exploration, counselors may find it helpful to discuss information obtained from various resources. Sometimes, teachers, parents, relatives, and especially friends are the sources of gender-biased information about occupations. Magazines, movies, and TV shows sometimes perpetuate these stereotypes. The research cited earlier and Lent, Brown, and Hackett's (1994) social cognitive career theory suggest that, although adolescent girls may know how to make career decisions, they may lack self-confidence in decision making. Regarding Super's World-of-Work Information scale, the impact of gender-role stereotyping is such that it may be helpful, if the Career Development Inventory is not used, to inquire about the accuracy of the information that girls have acquired. The same can be said about the Knowledge of Preferred Occupations scale. Thus, awareness of the difficulties posed by gender-role stereotyping for adolescents can help the counselor use Super's life-span theory incisively. Following is an example of how a counselor can use Super's life-span theory while being sensitive to gender-role stereotyping in adolescent career development.

A Counseling Example

The following dialogue takes place between Lucy, a high school sophomore, and her guidance counselor. Lucy is the same student who appeared as an example in the last chapter. In the previous example, she was 11 years old and talking to a counselor about problems at home that were having an effect on her schoolwork. Now she is 15. Her current counselor does not have the benefit of information from the Career Development Inventory but is able to use Super's concepts of career development.

CL: I wanted to talk to you because I'm not sure what to do next year. I'm thinking of applying to a bunch of different schools in two years. Maybe I can get a scholarship. I'm not sure.

CO: What have you been thinking about?

CL: Well, I really would like to go to medical school, but I'm not sure I can afford it, and I'm not sure I can get into it.

CO: What makes you hesitant? [The counselor wants to know more about Lucy's uncertainty in questioning her career plans.]

CL: Well, my father would like me to go to work soon. He says to me that he doesn't want to support me forever. And my boyfriend says if I go to med school we'll never get married until we're 55.

CO: It's hard to separate out what you might want from what others want for you. [The counselor wants to relieve Lucy of some of the burdens put on her by others.]

CL: I know. I've given a lot of thought to this. Most people might think it's only a dream, but I've got A's and B's in my courses. I think I might be able to do it. I know you need B's in sciences, at least, and A's, too, to get into medical school. I know that it takes a lot of training. There are scholarships in college, and it is possible to get money for medical school. I could work for a while to earn money to go to medical school.

CO: You seem to have found out a lot about college. [Lucy certainly seems to have some knowledge of her preferred occupation and some information about the abilities required. Further, she seems to have some world-of-work information.]

CL: Yes, I've talked to my family doctor about medicine, and my cousin works for another doctor. He was really nice and took some time to talk to me. I think it seems fine, but I'm not sure. There are other medical occupations that don't take so long to get into and are easier to get into. Maybe I should just go into nursing like my mother. I know there's a nursing shortage. It would be easier.

CO: You seem to be questioning yourself. [The counselor is impressed again that Lucy has done considerable initial career exploration and has some knowledge of decision making. Noticing that Lucy's confidence is beginning to wane, the counselor focuses on her self-efficacy beliefs.]

CL: It seems that I am in this all alone. (*Lucy starts to cry*). Nobody seems to think I know what I'm doing. Sometimes, I think others want me to do things their way.

CO: You seem scared about doing it your way. [Lucy's lack of self-confidence seems to be quite strong.]

CL: I am scared. Do you think I'm making the right decision?

CO: It's hard to know what the right decision is. I really am impressed that you've talked to so many people and seem to have such good information about your future. It is just hard to do things when there's not a lot of support. [The counselor doesn't know the "right" decision for Lucy but does want to support her career exploration and information seeking, and to support her growing feelings of self-efficacy.]

Being knowledgeable about the career maturity concepts of Super and being aware of gender biases in the culture, the counselor is able to understand Lucy's struggle with her career choice. Even though Lucy is asking for limited help in career selection (not being sure about the right area of health science), counseling serves a valuable purpose. Lucy's decision making is being supported in part by the knowledge the counselor has of the important components of career maturity. The goal of counseling in this particular portion of the interview is to help Lucy regain her confidence in her career decision-making ability. This goal certainly is consistent with Super's theoretical propositions regarding career maturity and the concept of reinforcing beliefs of self-efficacy.

CAREER DEVELOPMENT OF ADOLESCENTS FROM DIVERSE CULTURAL BACKGROUNDS

One area of research with adolescents of diverse cultural backgrounds has been the study of the applicability of the concept of career maturity. Studying the career maturity of 90 economically disadvantaged rural youth, Rojewski (1994) found that those who scored low on measures of career maturity were more likely to be African American, educationally disadvantaged, male, and indecisive about their career choice. More vocationally mature students (scoring high on Crites's Career Maturity Inventory, were more likely to be white, not educationally disadvantaged, female, and decisive about their career choice. Studying African American high school students, Brown (1997) found that African American females scored higher on career maturity indices than males. In another study, Westbrook and Sanford (1991) found that white students scored higher on career maturity (on the Attitude Scale of the Career Maturity Inventory) than did African American students, but that the scores were not related to the appropriateness of the career choices of the African American students. Fouad and Kelly (1992) studied African American high school students and reported similar results. Compared to white students, Asian students scored lower in career maturity and indicated a stronger preference for a dependent style of decision making than did white students

(Leong, 1991). Discussing the career maturity of Asian students, Leong and Serifica (1995) questioned the applicability of Super's concept to Asian Americans, pointing out the effect of differing cultural values on developmental tasks. However, Mexican American ninth-grade students scored lower on the Decision-Making and World-of-Work Information scales of the Career Development Inventory than Anglo American ninth-graders, both are scales that focus on knowledge and skill rather than attitude (Lundberg, Osborne, & Miner, 1997). These studies suggest the need for more research on the use of Super's concept of career maturity with adolescents of diverse cultural backgrounds.

Another focus of research has been the vocational aspirations of adolescents from different cultural backgrounds. Arbona (1990) has pointed out that Hispanic/Latino and African American students often have aspirations that are more prestigious or desirable than the occupations that they actually enter. It may be that this gap results from expectations that do not match the availability of jobs, especially gender-stereotyped jobs (Arbona & Novy, 1991). For Hispanic/Latina women, aspirations to attend and stay in college were more likely to be achieved when the mother had more education and the student did not stereotype jobs by gender (Cardoza, 1991). In her study of white and Mexican American 11th- and 12th-grade students, McWhirter (1997) found that Mexican American students anticipated that there would be more barriers to attaining future goals than did Caucasians. Developing a model for understanding the career choice of Mexican American high-school-age girls, McWhirter, Hackett, and Bandalos (1998) found that culture had a greater influence on career choice than gender. They found that families' lack of support for pursuing prestigious occupations occurred more frequently in families that held traditional Mexican American values.

Aspirations and expectations of African American high school youth have also been explored. The top three occupational preferences for African American males were professional careers, professional sports, and business management; for African American females there was a greater preference for social careers such as teaching and social work (Brown, 1997). Studying the career aspirations of 11th- and 12th-grade African American inner-city males, Parmer (1993) found that 32% thought they were likely or very likely to become professional athletes in ten years. The chances of becoming a professional athlete are about 1 in 50,000 (Parmer, 1993). These studies provide detailed information for counselors to consider when discussing vocational aspirations with African American or Mexican American adolescents.

Case Example

Chad is a 15-year-old student whose parents fled Vietnam after the Vietnam War and who lives near Los Angeles with his parents, two younger brothers, and an older sister. His mother is currently unemployed and his father is a rental car clerk. Chad has been sent to talk to the counselor because he has been absent from school sporadically throughout the year and has recently missed a week of school. As Chad enters the counselor's office, she sees an attractive, average-size young man wearing jeans, a black T-shirt, and expensive sneakers. The counselor, to use the terms of Vondracek and his colleagues, is well aware of the context of the situation. The counselor has walked by Chad's home several times and many of the neighborhood children attend her school. The major employment of adolescents on Chad's street is in fast food, grocery stores, and illegal drugs. The counselor resists making hypotheses based only on Chad's appearance and wants to listen to him:

CL: (*Smiling*) Sorry, I haven't been in school as much as I should. I've been sick a lot.

CO: What's happening with you, Chad? [The counselor does not want to get into an argument with Chad, but neither does she want to show that she will take his story at face value.]

CL: Times are tough.

CO: Yes, can you tell me what's been happening?

CL: I've needed to make some extra money. My parents just don't have enough money for the kids.

CO: It's been hard for you. [The counselor doesn't want to challenge Chad immediately. Rather, she prefers to take his side.]

CL: Yes. My little brother broke his leg and my father doesn't make much money anyway. I've had to pick some up on the side.

CO: Selling drugs? [The counselor decides to get to the point. She believes that Chad knows that she can guess this anyway.]

CL: Yes. (*Defensively*) Not too much—just enough.

CO: What are you going to do? [The counselor asks a very broad, open question about Chad's future to see in what direction he will take it.]

CL: I don't know. Maybe get a job. I'm not sure.

CO: Some thoughts about what you'd like to do? [The counselor wants to know how developed Chad's interests are.]

CL: I like cars—fixing them, riding in them, racing them, anything to do with them. And I like TV and movies.

CO: Have you thought about doing more with working on cars? [The counselor picks the activity that has the most vocational relevance and asks about it.]

CL: I've thought about the vo-tech school, but I don't know. I don't think that mechanics make enough money.

CO: Do you know how much they make? [Not having access to the Career Development Inventory or other maturity inventories, the counselor asks about Super's concept of world-of-work information.]

CL: No.

CO: Let's find out.

As the counselor goes with Chad to look at information about auto mechanics, she has several thoughts running through her mind. Super's life-span rainbow flashes through her head for a moment. But it is not the rainbow in Figure 6-2; rather, it is a truncated rainbow, as shown in Figure 8-2.

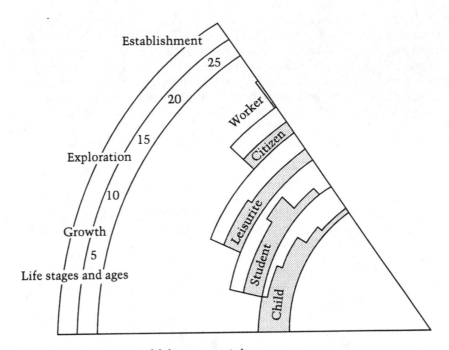

Figure 8-2   A truncated life-career rainbow.
(Adapted from *Career Choice and Development*, by D. Brown, L. Brooks, and Associates. Copyright © 1984 by Jossey-Bass, Inc. Reprinted by permission.)

The thicker the shaded area, the more important the role. Chad's role as child is most important (the role with the greatest shaded area). His role as worker has barely begun. Although she has not stated it at this point, the counselor believes that she is working with a life-or-death issue. If Chad continues to sell drugs, there is a chance that he may be killed or may kill someone. To Chad, being an auto mechanic may not be as attractive as selling drugs because of the excitement and the income. The counselor does not want to argue directly with Chad, feeling that she will lose. She is desperately trying to find a way for Chad to look into his future, so that his life will not end, as shown in Figure 8-2. Chad is not able (using Super's concept of decision making) to make appropriate decisions. The counselor hopes that she will be able to develop a relationship with Chad so that he will return, and so that she will gradually be able to make an impact. Chad's self-awareness and occupational awareness are limited. The counselor can look to the future, and she is scared.

Super's theory of life-span development for adolescents is not a panacea. It does provide guidelines for what to look for in career decision making. Sometimes, the context of a situation is so overwhelming that a theoretical conceptualization makes very little difference. It is possible in the case of Chad that the application of Super's concepts of career decision making will be just enough to keep Chad looking into a legitimate form of work. If the counselor is able to help Chad develop his interests in auto mechanics, find an auto mechanics program that he likes, and support his efforts, there may be a chance of his success. Or possibly, Chad and the counselor will arrive at some entirely different vocational goal. If Chad believes that the counselor is just some other adult who has a good income and for whom life is wonderful, then the counselor is likely to be discounted.

COUNSELOR ISSUES

A number of issues make counseling adolescents difficult. Earlier in the chapter, the notion (Piaget, 1977) that formal thinking brings with it a certain amount of egocentrism suggested that the client may think that he or she is right and the counselor is wrong. Further, Erikson's point that adolescents may be in an uncomfortable search for identity suggested that they need to separate themselves from adults and may be less likely to listen to them. In contrast, the counselor may be in a stage, according to Super's theory, of establishment or maintenance. Because the counselor has decided on a career, and has much information about that occupation and other occupations as well, the counselor's life situation is in marked contrast to that of the adolescent. These factors make it very important for the counselor to be empathic toward the client's decision-making issues. One of the frustrations of a counselor is that he or she can look ahead in terms of a client's occupational direction. Often, adolescents still have a limited time perspective and find it very difficult to see themselves in five or ten years. Super's life-stage theory makes it possible to see how vastly different the goals of the counselor can be from those of the client. This knowledge enables the counselor to structure limited goals consistent with the student's vocational maturity.

SUMMARY

Super and his colleagues offer concepts and inventories that can assist the counselor in working with adolescents. Being able to assess the development of interests, capacities, and values in a teenage client is quite helpful. Super's theory and the theory of Ginzberg, Ginsburg, Axelrad, and Herma are useful in this regard. Also helpful to the counselor are Super's concepts of career planning, career exploration, decision making, world-of-work information, and knowledge of the preferred occupational group. Vocational identity and the context in which it emerges is yet another useful view of adolescent career development. These concepts, used in combination, help the counselor assess the student's career orientation. Gender-role stereotyping and the obstacles confronting adolescents of culturally diverse backgrounds present additional problems. Knowledge of the context of the situation serves as a useful adjunct to Super's theory as it deals with conditions external to the individual. Since adolescence is such a critical time in the career decision-making process, applying Super's life-span theory can be very helpful.

References

Adams, G. R., Bennion, L., & Huh, K. (1987). *Objective Measure of Ego Identity Status: A reference manual.* Unpublished manuscript, Laboratory for Research on Adolescence, Utah State University, Salt Lake City.

Arbona, C. (1990). Career counseling research with Hispanics: A review of the literature. *The Counseling Psychologist, 18,* 300–323.

Arbona, C., & Novy, D. M. (1991). Career aspirations and expectations among Black, Mexican American, and White college students. *Career Development Quarterly, 39,* 231–239.

Aubrey, R. G. (1977). *Career development needs of thirteen-year-olds: How to improve career development programs.* Washington, DC: National Advisory Council for Career Education.

Betz, N. E., & Fitzgerald, L. F. (1987). *The career psychology of women.* Orlando, FL: Academic Press.

Betz, N. E., & Hackett, G. (1983). The relationship of mathematics self-efficacy expectations to the selection of science-based majors. *Journal of Vocational Behavior, 23,* 329–345.

Brown, C. (1997). Sex differences in the career development of urban African American adolescents. *Journal of Career Development, 23,* 295–304.

Cardoza, D. (1991). College attendance and persistence among Hispanic women: An examination of some contributing factors. *Sex Roles, 24,* 133–147.

Chipman, S. F., Krantz, D. H., & Silver, R. (1992). Mathematics anxiety and science careers among able college women. *Psychological Science, 3,* 292–295.

Chipman, S. F., & Wilson, D. M. (1985). Understanding mathematics course enrollment and mathematics achievement: A synthesis of the research. In S. E Chipman, L. R. Brush, & D. M. Wilson (Eds.), *Women and mathematics* (pp. 275–328). Hillsdale, NJ: Erlbaum.

Davey, F. H., & Stoppard, J. M. (1993). Some factors affecting the occupational expectations of female adolescents. *Journal of Vocational Behavior, 43,* 235–330.

Erikson, E. H. (1963). *Childhood and society* (2nd ed.). New York: Norton.

Erikson, E. H. (1968). *Identity: Youth and crisis.* New York: Norton.

Erikson, E. H. (1982). *The life cycle completed.* New York: Norton.

Fassinger, R. E. (1990). Causal models of career choice in two samples of college women. *Journal of Vocational Behavior, 36,* 225–248.

Fottler, M. D., & Bain, T. (1980). Sex differences in occupational aspirations. *Academy of Management Journal, 23,* 144–149.

Fouad, N. A., & Kelly, T. J. (1992). The relation between attitudinal and behavioral aspects of career maturity. *Career Development Quarterly, 40,* 257–271.

Ginzberg, E. (1970). The development of a developmental theory of occupational choice. In W. H. Van Hoose & J. J. Pietrofesa (Eds.), *Counseling and guidance in the twentieth century* (pp. 58–67). Boston: Houghton Mifflin.

Ginzberg, E. (1972). Restatement of the theory of occupational choice. *Vocational Guidance Quarterly, 20,* 169–176.

Ginzberg, E. (1984). Career development. In D. Brown & L. Brooks (Eds.), *Career choice and development: Applying contemporary theories to practice* (pp. 169–191). San Francisco: Jossey-Bass.

Ginzberg, E., Ginsburg, S. W., Axelrad, S., & Herma, J. (1951). *Occupational choice: An approach to a general theory.* New York: Columbia University Press.

Hackett, G., & Betz, N. E. (1981). A self-efficacy approach to the career development of women. *Journal of Vocational Behavior, 18,* 326–329.

Hales, L. W., & Fenner, B. (1972). Work values of 5th-, 8th-, and 11th-grade students. *Vocational Guidance Quarterly, 20,* 199–203.

Hales, L. W., & Fenner, B. (1973). Sex and social class differences in work values. *Elementary School Guidance and Counseling, 8,* 26–32.

Hartung, P. J. (1997). Rates and correlates of career development. *Journal of Career Assessment, 5,* 293–303.

Hartung, P. J., Vandiver, B. J., Leong, F. T. L., Pope, M., Niles, S. G., & Farrow, B. (1998). Appraising cultural identity in career-development assessment and counseling. *Career Development Quarterly, 46,* 276–293.

Heilman, M. E. (1979). Perception of male models of femininity related to career choice. *Journal of Counseling Psychology, 19,* 308–313.

Herr, E. L., & Niles, S. (1997). Perspectives on career assessment of work-bound youth. *Journal of Career Assessment, 5,* 137–150.

Hurwitz, R. E., & White, M. A. (1977). Effect of sex-linked vocational information on reported occupational choices of high school juniors. *Psychology of Women Quarterly, 2,* 149–156.

Inhelder, B., & Piaget, J. (1958). *The growth of logical thinking from childhood to adolescence.* New York: Basic Books.

Johnson, P., Buboltz, W. C., & Nichols, C. N. (1999). Parental divorce, family functioning, and vocational identity of college students. *Journal of Career Development, 26,* 137–146.

Jugendwerk der Deutschen Shell. (1992). Jugend 1992. Band 4. Methodenberichte-Tabellen-Fragebogen. (Youth 1992, Vol. 4: Methods, Tables, Questionnaires). Opladen: Leske & Budrich.

Kapes, J. T., & Strickler, R. T. (1975). A longitudinal study of change in work values between ninth and twelfth grade as related to high school curriculums. *Journal of Vocational Behavior, 6,* 81–93.

Lent, R. W., Brown, S. D., & Hackett, G. (1994). Toward a unified social cognitive theory of career and academic interest, choice, and performance. *Journal of Vocational Behavior, 45,* 79–122.

Lent, R. W., & Hackett, G. (1987). Career self-efficacy: Empirical status and future directions. *Journal of Vocational Behavior, 30,* 347–382.

Lent, R. W., Lopez, F. G., & Bieschke, K. J. (1991). Mathematics self-efficacy: Sources and relations to science-based career choice. *Journal of Counseling Psychology, 38,* 424–430.

Lent, R. W., Lopez, F. G., & Bieschke, K. J. (1993). Predicting mathematics-related choice and success behaviors: Test of an expanded social cognitive model. *Journal of Vocational Behavior, 42,* 223–236.

Leong, F. T. L. (1991). Career development attributes and occupational values of Asian American and White American college students. *Career Development Quarterly, 39,* 221–230.

Leong, F. T. L., & Serifica, F. C. (1995). Career development of Asian Americans: A research area in need of a good theory. In F. T. L. Leong (Ed.), *Career develop-ment and vocational behavior of racial and ethnic minorities* (pp. 67–102). Mahwah, NJ: Erlbaum.

Lundberg, D. J., Osborne, W. L., & Miner, C. U. (1997). Career maturity and per-sonality preferences of Mexican-American and Anglo-American adolescents. *Journal of Career Development, 23,* 203–213.

Marcia, J. E. (1989). Identity and intervention. *Journal of Adolescence, 12,* 401–410.

Marcia, J. E. (1998). Peer Gynt's life cycle. In E. E. A. Skoe & A. L. von der Lippe (Eds.), *Personality development in adolescence: A cross national and life span perspective: Adolescence and society.* (pp. 193–209). New York: Routledge.

Marcia, J. E. (1999). Representational thought in ego identity, psychotherapy, and psychosocial developmental theory. In I. E. Sigel (Ed.), *Development of mental representation: Theories and applications* (pp. 391–414). Mahwah, NJ: Erl-baum.

Marcia J. E., Waterman, A. S., Matteson, D. R., Archer, S. L., & Orlofsky, J. (1993). *Ego identity: A handbook for psychosocial research.* New York: Springer-Verlag.

McKenna, A. E., & Ferrero, G. W. (1991). Ninth-grade students' attitudes toward nontraditional occupations. *Career Development Quarterly, 40,* 168–181.

McWhirter, E. H. (1997). Perceived barriers to education and career: Ethnic and gen-der differences. *Journal of Vocational Behavior, 50,* 124–140.

McWhirter, E. H., Hackett, G., & Bandalos, D. C. (1998). A causal model of the ed-ucational plans and career expectations of Mexican-American high school girls. *Journal of Counseling Psychology, 45,* 166–181.

Miller, J. (1977). *Career development needs of 9-year-olds: How to improve career development programs.* Washington, DC: National Advisory Council for Ca-reer Education.

Monaco, N. M., & Gaier, E. L. (1992). Single sex versus coeducational environment and achievement in adolescent females. *Adolescence, 27,* 579–594.

Multon, K. D., Brown, S. D., & Lent, R. W. (1991). Relation of self-efficacy beliefs to academic outcomes: A meta-analytic investigation. *Journal of Counseling Psychology, 38,* 30–38.

Munley, P. H. (1975). Erik Erikson's theory of psychosocial development and voca-tional behavior. *Journal of Counseling Psychology, 22,* 314–319.

Munley, P. H. (1977). Erikson's theory of psychosocial development and career de-velopment. *Journal of Vocational Behavior, 10,* 261–269.

Nevill, D. D., & Super, D. E. (1989). *The Values Scale: Theory, application, and re-search* (2nd ed.). Palo Alto, CA: Consulting Psychologists Press.

O'Brien, K. M., & Fassinger, R. E. (1993). A causal model of the career orientation and career choice of adolescent women. *Journal of Counseling Psychology, 40,* 456–569.

O'Hara, R. P., & Tiedeman, D. V. (1959). Vocational self-concept in adolescence. *Journal of Counseling Psychology, 6,* 292–301.

Osborne, W. L., Brown, S., Niles, S., & Miner, C. U. (1997). *Career development, assessment, and counseling: Applications of the Donald E. Super C-DAC ap-proach.* Alexandria, VA: American Counseling Association.

Parmer, T. (1993). The athletic dream—but what are the career dreams of other African American urban high school students? *Journal of Career Development, 20,* 131–145.

Perron, J., Vondracek, F. W., Skorikov, V. B., Tremblay, C., & Corbiere, M. (1998). A longitudinal study of vocational maturity and ethnic identity development. *Journal of Vocational Behavior, 52,* 409–424.

Piaget, J. (1977). *The development of thought: Equilibration of cognitive structure.* New York: Viking Press.

Powell, D. F., & Luzzo, D. A. (1998). Evaluating factors associated with the career maturity of high school students. *Career Development Quarterly, 47,* 145–158.

Powers, R. L., & Griffith, J. (1993). The case of Rosie: Adlerian response. *The Career Development Quarterly, 42,* 69–75.

Reitzle, M., Vondracek, F. W., & Silbereisen, R. K. (1998). Timing of school-to-work transitions: A developmental-contextual perspective. *International Journal of Behavioral Development, 22,* 7–28.

Robison-Awana, P., Kehle, T. J., & Jenson, W. R. (1986). But what about smart girls? Adolescent self-esteem and sex role perceptions as a function of academic achievement. *Journal of Educational Psychology, 78,* 179–183.

Robitschek, C., & Cook, S. W. (1999). The influence of personal growth inituitive and coping styles on career exploration and vocational identity. *Journal of Vocational Behavior, 54,* 127–141.

Rojewski, J. W. (1994). Career indecision types for rural adolescents from disadvantaged and nondisadvantaged backgrounds. *Journal of Counseling Psychology, 41,* 356–363.

Rojewski, J. W. (1997). Characteristics of students who express stable or underrated occupational expectations during early adolescence. *Journal of Career Assessment, 5,* 1–20.

Savickas, M. L. (1985). Identity in vocational development. *Journal of Vocational Behavior, 27,* 329–337.

Schmitt-Rodermund, E., & Silbereisen, R. K. (1998). Career maturity determinants: Individual development, social context, and historical time. *Career Development Quarterly, 47,* 16–31.

Schmitt-Rodermund, E., & Vondracek, F. W. (1999). Breadth of interests, exploration, and identity development in adolescence. *Journal of Vocational Behavior, 55,* 298–317.

Skorikov, V., & Vondracek, F. W. (1998). Vocational identity development: Its relationship to other identity domains and to overall identity development. *Journal of Career Assessment, 6,* 13–15.

Starishevsky, R., & Matlin, N. A. (1963). A model for the translation of self-concept into vocational terms. In D. E. Super, R. Starishevsky, N. Matlin, & J. P. Jordaan (Eds.), *Career development: Self-concept theory* (pp. 33–41) (Research Monograph No. 4). New York: College Entrance Examination Board.

Super, D. E. (1955). Personality integration through vocational counseling. *Journal of Counseling Psychology, 2,* 217–226.

Super, D. E. (1990). A life-span, life-space approach to career development. In D. Brown, L. Brooks, & Assoc. (Eds.), *Career choice and development: Applying contemporary theories to practice* (2nd ed., pp. 197–261). San Francisco: Jossey-Bass.

Super, D. E., Bohn, M. J., Forrest, D. J., Jordaan, J. P., Lindeman, R. H., & Thompson, A. S. (1971). *Career Development Inventory.* New York: Teachers College Press, Columbia University.

Super, D. E., Crites, J. O., Hummel, R. C., Moser, H. P., Overstreet, P. L., & Warnath, C. F. (1957). *Vocational development: A framework for research.* New
York: Teachers College Press, Columbia University.

Super, D. E., & Overstreet, P. L. (1960). *The vocational maturity of ninth-grade
boys.* New York: Teachers College Press, Columbia University.

Super, D. E., Thompson, A. S., & Lindeman, R. H. (1988). *Adult Career Concerns
Inventory.* Palo Alto, CA: Consulting Psychologists Press.

Taveira, M.-D.-C., Silva, M. C., Rodriguez, M.-L., & Maia, J. (1998). Individual characteristics and career exploration in adolescence. *British Journal of Guidance
and Counselling, 26,* 89–104.

Thompson, A. S., & Lindeman, R. H. (1981). *Career Development Inventory: Vol.
1. User's manual.* Palo Alto, CA: Consulting Psychologists Press.

Tierney, R. J., & Herman, A. (1973). Self-estimates of ability in adolescence. *Journal of Counseling Psychology, 20,* 298–302.

Trice, A. D., Hughes, M. A., Odom, C., Woods, K., & McClellan, N. C. (1995). The
origins of children's career aspirations: IV. Testing hypothesis from four theories. *The Career Development Quarterly, 45,* 307–322.

Van Buren, J. B., Kelly, K. R., & Hall, A. S. (1993). Modeling nontraditional career
choices: Effects of gender and school location on response to a brief videotape.
Journal of Counseling Psychology, 20, 298–302.

Vondracek, F. W., & Reitzle, M. (1998). The viability of career maturity theory: A
developmental-contextual perspective. *Career Development Quarterly, 47,*
6–15.

Vondracek, F. W., Reitzle, M., & Silbereisen, R. K. (1999). The influence of changing contexts and historical time on the timing of initial vocational choices. In
R. K. Silbereisen & A. von Eye (Eds.), *Growing up in times of social change*
(pp. 151–169). New York: de Gruyter.

Vondracek, F. W., & Skorikov, V. B. (1997). Leisure, school, and work activity preferences and their role in vocational identity development. *Career Development
Quarterly, 45,* 322–340.

Westbrook, B. W. (1983). Career maturity: The concept, the instrument, and the research. In W. B. Walsh & S. H. Osipow (Eds.), *Handbook of vocational psychology* (Vol. 1, pp. 263–304). Hillsdale, NJ: Erlbaum.

Westbrook, B. W., Buck, R. W., Jr., Wynne, D. C., & Sanford, E. E. (1994). Career
maturity in adolescence: Reliability and validity of self-ratings of ability by
gender and ethnicity. *Journal of Career Assessment, 2,* 125–161.

Westbrook, B. W., & Sanford, E. E. (1991). The validity of career maturity attitude
measures among Black and White high school students. *The Career Development Quarterly, 40,* 198–208.

Zuschlag, M. K., & Whitbourne, S. K. (1994). Psychosocial development in three
generations of college students. *Journal of Youth and Adolescence, 23,* 567–577.

9

Late Adolescent and Adult Career Development

Super's life-span theory of late adolescent and adult career development makes use of two major concepts: life role and life stage. For Super, important roles for an individual are studying, working, community service, home and family, and leisure activities, as illustrated earlier in Figure 6-2. The importance, or salience, of these roles can be seen by a person's participation in an activity, commitment to the activity, or how much that activity is valued. Values are also significant in Super's theory, as can be seen by the development of several values inventories (Super, 1970; Super & Nevill, 1986, 1989).

In Super's theory, roles form the context within which to view the basic stages of career development: exploration, establishment, maintenance, and disengagement. The exploration stage includes the substages of crystallization, specification, and implementation. Next follows the establishment stage, which includes the tasks of stabilizing, consolidating, and advancing. The substages of holding, updating, and innovating make up the maintenance stage. Finally, the disengagement stage includes deceleration, retirement planning, and retirement living. A key aspect of Super's theory is that these stages are not entirely age-related. Individuals may recycle, or go through these stages, at many different times in life. Explanations and examples of counseling conceptualizations that can be useful in these stages are given in this chapter. Theorists and researchers have questioned whether these stages apply to women and to people from different cultures. Research on women suggests several factors to be considered. Atkinson, Morten, and Sue (1998) offer a series of developmental stages that people from diverse cultures may experience. This provides another dimension to Super's view of the life span. Developmental issues that arise for the counselor in dealing with people in various life stages will help to explain some of the issues that counselors face in counseling adults.

ROLE SALIENCE

Super (1990) believes that people differ in terms of the importance they assign to work in their lives. As shown by the research of Kanungo (1982), not everyone wants to work. Work can vary in importance to an individual at different points in that person's life. In fact, the normative data provided by Nevill and Super (1986) for the Salience Inventory show that people at different ages and across different cultures value work differentially. For example, high school students in the United States tend to value work, home, and leisure more than study and community service. In general, this is also true for college students. However, adults in the United States tend to value work and family life more than study, community service, or leisure. Not surprisingly, there are great individual differences across all age ranges.

In the Salience Inventory, Nevill and Super (1986) measure three aspects of life roles: commitment, participation, and value expectations. Another important aspect of work salience, but one not measured by the Salience Inventory, is knowledge of roles. The following pages describe first the life roles measured by the Salience Inventory (studying, working, community service, home and family, and leisure activities) and then different indicators of the salience of these life roles.

Life Roles

Studying   Studying includes a number of activities that may take place throughout the life span. During the school years, these include taking courses, going to school, and studying in a library or at home. We know that people may choose to continue education at any time during their lifetime. Newspapers show pictures of 80-year-old men and women receiving their high school diplomas or college degrees. Many people continue their education on a part-time basis at some stage during their lives for pleasure or to enhance their job advancement or success.

Working   Working may start in childhood, when children help their parents around the home, mow the lawn, or take jobs such as baby-sitting and delivering newspapers. It is common for adolescents to take a part-time job after school or during the summer. Many adults work at one or more jobs at various times during their lives. During retirement, jobs for pay or profit may be for fewer hours than they were during a person's younger years.

Community Service   Community service includes a broad range of voluntary service groups that may be social, political, or religious. Young people often participate in Boy or Girl Scouts, Indian Guides, or boys' or girls' clubs, which have as a part of their purpose either direct service to others or indirect service through the collection of money or goods. These groups, along with service fraternities and sororities, are available in various forms to adolescents. Activities may include literacy projects, environmental cleanup, or assistance in hospitals. Activity in these service groups, along with participation in political parties and trade unions, is available to adults throughout the entire life span.

Home and Family   This role can vary greatly depending on the age of the individual. A child may help out at home by taking care of his or her room or by doing the dishes or mowing the lawn. Adolescents may take on more responsibility by doing more complex tasks and ones with more responsibility, such as baby-sitting. For adults, responsibility for children and a home becomes much more important than it was in earlier years. Adults may have to take care not only of their own children but also of their aging parents. As adults enter their later years, their responsibility for home and family may increase or markedly decrease. For example, grandparents may live with their children and/or grandchildren, live in adult communities, or live alone.

Leisure Activities   The nature and importance of leisure are likely to vary considerably throughout the lifetime. Leisure is a particularly important and valued activity of children and adolescents. Often, this includes active participation in sports as well as more sedentary activities such as watching television and reading. The term *lifetime sports* refers to sports that are less physically demanding and require fewer participants, so they are easier for adults to participate in at various points in their lifetime. Contrast football and basketball with golf, tennis, and bowling. For adults, leisure activities may become more sophisticated and intellectual, such as attending the theater and museums or joining groups that discuss books, stocks and bonds, or religious issues.

Liptak (2000) considers leisure so important that he has outlined a leisure theory of career development. Often, leisure serves as a substitute for work and as a way of trying out new activities. Liptak's theory is based partly on the importance of play throughout the life span. His theory shows the significance of leisure in a variety of life stages. In early childhood parents are an important influence in the development of play and curiosity. At ages 6 to 12, school and after-school activities provide an opportunity to develop cognitive and motor skills through play or leisure activity. In adolescence, team and individual activities such as sports, clubs, and hobbies help individuals refine their interests and abilities. Between the ages of 19 and 25, individuals can develop leisure opportunities that may be related to work or educational pursuits. In adulthood, leisure may focus on work- or family-related activities. In retirement, leisure often becomes much more important than work as an outlet for interests and skills. From Liptak's perspective leisure can play a more important role in career development than work, especially in the beginning and end of the life span.

Indicators of the Salience of Life Roles

Not only does the importance of the roles change during a person's lifetime, but the nature of the involvement also changes. This involvement can be measured in terms of participation, commitment, knowledge, and value expectations.

Participation   Participation in a role can take a number of different forms. It can include spending time on something, improving a performance, accomplishing something, being active in an organization concerned with an activity, or just being active. A slightly less direct way of participating is through talking to people or reading about an activity. The concept of participation is particularly useful because it measures the actual behavior of an individual, not just what he or she says is important. For example, a person may say that he is committed to his religion but may never pray or go to church (participate).

Commitment   Commitment often concerns future plans. It may deal with a desire to be involved or be active. It also concerns the present: feeling proud of doing well or being personally committed. A less direct way of being committed is to admire people who are good at something.

Knowledge   Acquiring information about a role by experiencing the role either directly or by observing it brings about knowledge, a cognitive aspect of role importance. A child's knowledge may be limited to leisure and study. Knowledge of parental roles is gained by observation; only much later will the experience be direct. Knowledge of the worker role may be very different for a food service worker in high school and for that same individual employed as an engineer or physician 15 years later. The Salience Inventory does not measure knowledge. A measurement of knowledge is available only for the worker role in the Career Development Inventory, in the Decision Making, World-of-Work Information, and Knowledge of the Preferred Occupational Group subscales (see Chapter 8). However, when talking with clients about their study, leisure, or community service roles, the counselor may find assessing the client's knowledge to be helpful. For example, new college students often have little knowledge of the changing studying role that they will soon encounter. However, they are likely to be committed to the role and will soon participate in it. Knowledge, commitment, and participation, along with value expectations, are components of role salience.

Value Expectations   Similar theoretically to the concept of commitment, value expectations concern the opportunity for various roles to meet a variety of value needs. There are many values related to career issues. Values are measured by two of Super's instruments: the Values Scale (Super & Nevill, 1989) and the Salience Inventory (Nevill & Super, 1986). The Values Scale lists 21 different values; 14 of these are used in the Value Expectation Scale of the Salience Inventory. These 14 value expectations are described in the following paragraphs in terms of how they can be met in the five life roles. Reading through this list of values, the counselor can determine the relevance of the values for his or her clients and thus decide which of the many values to focus on when conceptualizing client issues.

Ability utilization: For some, an important value, regardless of the role performed, is using one's skills and knowledge. This may mean doing work or studying to develop one's ability. It also refers to applying one's skills in community service or being a good parent.

Achievement: Regardless of role, *achievement* refers to the feeling that one has produced good results. Individuals with this value set high standards for their work or study. If the role is leisure, achievement may mean a feeling of accomplishing something significant in sports or music.

Aesthetics: This value deals with finding beauty in the role that one chooses. It is often associated with artistic values, which are satisfied by creating a picture, a musical composition, or a poem.

Altruism: Referring to helping others with problems, the need for altruism can clearly be met in several roles. One can help people with personal problems in one's family and in one's career (social work). Also, there are many community organizations, such as the Red Cross, that are devoted to helping others. Athletic coaching is a way of helping others in the pursuit of leisure.

Autonomy: Some individuals value the opportunity to be independent and work on their own. They may want to make their own decisions about studying, about sports, about how to run their family.

Creativity: To be able to discover or design new things can be important in a variety of situations. Being able to try out new ideas in a hobby or in a community organization can be as important to some people as creating a new product at work.

Economic rewards: To have a high standard of living and the material things that one desires requires income derived from the working role. Although study may eventually lead to high income, and a wealthy family serves as a source of high income for a few people, the primary role for obtaining economic rewards is as a worker.

Lifestyle: To plan one's own activities, to live the way one wants to, can be an overriding issue for some people. Since studying is a solitary activity, studying the way one wants can sometimes be done rather easily.

Some leisure activities can be chosen without regard to other people's needs. However, working is most often a role done with others, and certainly community service and family life make it difficult to live life the way one wants, unless individuals can find people who feel the same way they do.

Physical activity: Although being physically active in studying is quite difficult, the other roles allow opportunity for physical activity. One can do community service by helping repair church or community center buildings. With one's family, one can choose to be active in taking trips, boating, or making things.

Prestige: Many roles provide the opportunity for individuals to be acknowledged for what they accomplish. Although prestige is ordinarily associated with the work role, teachers recognize good students, and local communities recognize the contributions that citizens have made to them. A wife, husband, or children can acknowledge the contributions of a parent or a spouse.

Risk: Some people like to have dangerous or exciting challenges in their lives. Leisure can provide that opportunity. Activities such as mountain climbing, wind surfing, and parachute jumping provide such an occasion. In work, logging, high-rise steel construction, and race car driving may provide another outlet. Risks taken in community service, studying, or home and family may be more psychological and less physical. In studying, taking risks could include trying a very challenging course, procrastinating until the night before an examination to study, or waiting until the last minute to write a paper. For home and family, taking risks may mean surprising someone with a gift or, to be more negative, having an affair.

Social interaction: Being with other people and working in a group can be accomplished in all roles. Some people prefer to study in a group, and some enjoy working as part of a team on a project. Certainly, community service provides that opportunity. Working with one's children and spouse to have a pleasant vacation or to paint a room can be enjoyable to some people. Leisure activity provides the opportunity for many types of social interaction, for example, parties, sports, and visiting friends.

Variety: Being able to change work activities is very pleasing to some people. Variety in other roles may mean changing the subject that one is studying or moving from one type of task at work to another. Being involved in many different sports or community organizations can also meet these needs. At home, one can spend time with children or various relatives, cook, clean, and socialize.

Working conditions: Having the proper light to study, a pleasing home, or the right equipment for sports activities can be necessary for some people. Also, working conditions, which would include lighting, pleasant temperature, and good equipment, can be important in work with community organizations or in the workplace itself.

When counseling using Super's theory, counselors will sometimes have the Salience Inventory available to them; at other times, they will not. Assessing which roles are important to a client and which value expectations are met by the roles can be extremely helpful. To do this, the counselor may want to make use of the Values Scale. Although the Minnesota Importance Questionnaire (see Chapter 3) could be used, Hackbarth and Mathay (1991) found only low to moderate correlations between similar scales of the two inventories. In addition to the concepts just listed, which are contained in but not measured by the Salience Inventory, the Values Scale includes the following: authority (telling others what to do); personal development (developing as a person); social relations (being with friends); cultural identity (being with people of the same race and religion); physical prowess (working hard physically); and economic security (having secure and regular employment). Reviews of the Salience Inventory (Goodnough & Niles, 1996; Nevill & Calvert, 1996) and the Values Scale (Goodnough & Niles, 1996; Nevill & Kruse, 1996) provide more evidence for the validity of these instruments, especially for culturally diverse populations. The authors also suggest counseling applications.

A counselor working with Super's concepts for the first time may wish to become comfortable with the five roles measured in the Salience Inventory. Also, incorporating values into the career stages described in the next section may be useful. Later, the counselor can memorize the values in the Values Scale for use in counseling sessions. To help the reader understand how the Salience Inventory's and the Values Scale's constructs can be useful, they will be integrated into examples demonstrating counseling issues in each of the four major adult life stages described in the next section.

ADULT LIFE STAGES

Super's (1990) concepts of life stages and substages can be confusing because they are both age-related and not age-related. They are age-related in the sense that there are typical times when people go through stages of exploration, establishment, maintenance, and decline or disengagement. However, it is also possible for an individual to experience a stage at almost any time during his or her lifetime. Further, one can be involved in several stages at one time. Super (1990) used the term *maxicycle* to describe the five major life stages. *Minicycle* is a term used to describe the growth, exploration, establishment, maintenance, and disengagement that can occur within any of the stages in the maxicycle. For example, a 42-year-old dentist could be in the establishment stage. She may become less concerned with stabilizing and advancing in her practice, explore ways to maintain herself in her practice, gradually disengage from the establishment stage, and grow into the maintenance stage. Or more dramatically, she could start to explore other career options and discover that she wants to become an artist and disengage from dentistry. Each of these is an example of a minicycle within a maxicycle. The concept of the minicycle highlights the dynamic nature of Super's theory. Throughout their lives, individuals are constantly trying out new ideas and activities as they make transitions to a new stage. For consistency and clarity, the stages and substages of the maxicycle will first be presented in the typical order in which the average person encounters them. Then, the concept of *recycling,* which refers to going through aspects of the stages at various times in one's life, will be discussed.

Super's life-stage theory has a long history. Beginning in 1951 with the Career Pattern Study (Super et al., 1957), the study of life-stage theory has continued ever since. Super's book *The Psychology of Careers* (1957) presented a more general exposition of his ideas. The work of Gribbons and Lohnes (1968), Crites (1979), and Super (Thompson & Lindeman, 1981) presents a vast array of studies on vocational maturity and measures that were developed to describe the concepts of maturity and life stages. After studying adolescents, Super paid considerable attention to developing instruments with which to measure and define adult development (Super & Kidd, 1979; Super & Knasel, 1979).

From this work, Super, Thompson, and Lindeman (1988) developed the Adult Career Concerns Inventory (ACCI), which assists in conceptualizing life stages. Confirmation of the validity of these stages can be seen in studies such as that of Smart and Peterson (1994), who found that 219 male and 238 female Australian adults could be classified accurately using the ACCI. Patterns of maintenance in an occupation, recycling, and innovating are important exploratory behaviors in adults and are a focus of the ACCI (Niles, Anderson, Hartung, & Staton, 1999). Using the ACCI as a basis for studying exploratory behavior has been a focus of research for Niles and his colleagues (Niles, Anderson, & Goodnough, 1998) and has led to the development of a version of the ACCI that is a behavioral response scale (Niles, Lewis, & Hartung, 1997), consistent with Super's stage concepts. These stages and their substages are described in more detail in the following pages.

Exploration

According to Super (1957), the exploration stage ranges from about 15 to 25 years of age. This stage includes the efforts that individuals make to get a better idea of occupational information, choose career alternatives, decide on occupations, and start to work. This stage includes three substages: crystallizing, specifying, and implementing.

Crystallizing   This is the stage in which people clarify what they want to do. They learn about entry-level jobs that may be appropriate for them, and they learn what skills are required by the jobs that interest them. Many high school students go through this stage. Much of what was described in the previous chapter in terms of the realization of abilities, interests, and values is applicable to this stage. Work experience and work knowledge help the person narrow his or her choices. When a person changes fields, as an adult may do at any time, he or she is likely to recycle through this stage to reexamine interests, abilities, and values.

Specifying   For college graduates, this stage occurs in their early twenties. For those who seek employment directly after high school graduation, specification occurs earlier. As these young people must choose their first full-time job, they are required to *specify* their preferences so they may find an employer. For those who go on to graduate school or specialized education, such as pediatric nursing or advanced electrical engineering, preferences must also be specified. While some must specify an occupation, others must specify a job within an occupation. They may wish to have part-time work or summer work in the occupation of their choice. For example, a student may work as a part-time nursing assistant in a hospital so that he or she may reaffirm that the choice is appropriate.

Implementing   This is the last phase prior to working. People at this point are making plans to fulfill their career objectives. They may be starting to network by meeting people who can help them get a job. Talking to a counselor in a university career-planning and placement office would be part of this phase. People may be writing resumés, having job interviews, or deciding between potential employers.

Example   This example illustrates the exploration stage. Incorporated into the example is the use of the Salience Inventory, the Values Scale, the Adult Career Concerns Inventory, and the Strong Interest Inventory. The Adult Career Concerns Inventory (Super et al., 1988) gives scores for each stage and substage. The counselor will use the scores from these inventories, as well as the concepts, to think about clients' issues using a counseling model similar to the Career Development Assessment and Counseling method (CDAC) (Hartung et al., 1998; Super, Osborne, Walsh, Brown, & Niles, 1992).

Ben is a white college junior in his second semester. His father is a stockbroker, and his mother is an airline ticket agent. He lives about 50 miles from the large city where he is enrolled in a major university as a business major. He has come to the counseling center because he is not sure whether or not to seek a business career, and if in business, he is not sure of the direction. In their first meeting, the counselor assigns the Adult Career Concerns Inventory, the Values Scale, the Salience Inventory, and the Strong Interest Inventory. The results, summarized in Table 9-1, show that Ben has considerable concern about the crystallization substage, the specification substage, and the implementation substage. About the other stages (establishment, maintenance, and disengagement) he has little or no concern. Regarding his scores on the Salience Inventory, Ben has high scores on leisure activities for participation, commitment, and values expectations. His scores for studying indicate moderate participation in commitment and low values expectations. Working also has moderate participation, commitment, and values expectations. The scores on the Community Service and the Home and Family scales are low to moderate, except for a high score on values expectations for home and family. On the Values Scale, Ben scores high on economic rewards, advancement, prestige,

Table 9-1   *Summary of Ben's Scores on Four Inventories*

Inventory	High Scores
The Adult Career Concerns Inventory	Crystallizing Specifying Implementing

The Salience Inventory	*Leisure*
	  Participation
	  Commitment
	  Values expectations
	Home and Family
	  Values expectations

The Values Scale	Economic rewards Advancement Prestige Risk

The Strong Interest Inventory	*Basic Interests*
	  Athletics
	  Sales
	  Law and politics
	Occupational Scales
	  Human resources director
	  Credit manager
	  Marketing executive

and risk. In brief, his Strong Interest Inventory reveals high interest in athletics, sales, and law and politics. He has high scores in the Occupational Scales cluster in several business occupations. He has interests that are similar to those of marketing executives, human resources directors, and credit managers. After having talked with the counselor once and having taken these inventories, Ben returns to talk about the results. Several segments of the discussion are used to illustrate a number of Super's concepts:

CL: Those were a lot of tests. I'm curious how I did.

CO: We'll go over as much as we can today, but we may not finish—in fact probably won't. [There is a lot of material to discuss and the counselor does not want to rush, as he realizes that Ben is at a critical point in his career decision making.]

CL: Well, OK. Those tests really got me thinking.

CO: What about?

CL: I really started to think about what I'm going to do. I graduate in another year, and I really haven't thought a lot about it. My friends and I talk some, but mainly we throw names of companies around and talk about who's going to have the nicest car—things like that.

CO: But you're concerned. [The counselor wonders about Ben's motivation for career counseling. However, he remembers Ben's high scores on the Adult Career Concerns Inventory, which would probably indicate that Ben is indeed concerned.]

CL: We joke about it, but sometimes it makes me nervous thinking about what happens in a year. It seems as if things will just end, and it's blank from there.

CO: Well, let's take a look at one of the inventories that you finished. [The counselor shows Ben his scores on the Adult Career Concerns Inventory.]

CL: High scores on all the exploration stages. What does that mean?

CO: You seem to be unsure of what you want to do, quite concerned about a job, and maybe wondering how to get one.

CL: Yes, all of those things, but I always thought of them as a big jumble, not as three different steps.

CO: Yes, it's hard to decide what you want to do and find a job all at once. [The counselor is pleased that Ben seems to be taking the process seriously and understands the need to take things one at a time.]

Ben and the counselor go on to talk further about the results of the Adult Career Concerns Inventory and its meaning for Ben:

CO: I also wanted to talk to you about the role of work in your life.

CL: I know that I have to work hard to make a lot of money.

CO: What would you like to do with your money if you made $100,000 your first year? [Wanting to see if Ben's role values are the same as those in the Salience Inventory, the counselor wants to know in what areas Ben would participate and where his commitment is.]

CL: I'd put a down payment on a boat and a sports car and get the best stereo you ever saw. I would really like to race motorcycles, so I would get a new one. I'd find as much time as I could to mess around.

CO: You certainly want to have fun. [Leisure activities come through loud and clear in terms of participation, commitment, and values expectations. The counselor is interested in Ben's commitment to studying and working.]

CL: Yes, school is a bore. I like summertime, when I can just work and take it easy. I'm a lifeguard at a hotel pool. It's a busy hotel, but the pool isn't very busy most times, so I get to relax, chat with people, have a good time. It's not much of a job, but the pay is OK.

CO: Pay seems important to you. [The counselor starts to explore Ben's work values.]

CL: Yes, it really is. I would like to have a nice home someday and to be able to have some free time to be with my family to do things. I'm not sure I want a family for awhile. But someday I would.

CO: Sounds like you're starting to think more and more about the future. [The counselor notes that, for home and family, values expectations come out high on the Salience Inventory, while participation and commitment do not. That seems to fit with Ben's statement, as home and family are not an immediate commitment for him but may be in future years.]

Ben and the counselor continue to discuss his plans and goals. They are getting ready to talk about the Strong Interest Inventory. Wanting to put the Strong Interest Inventory in context, the counselor talks to Ben about its purpose:

> CO: Let's look at your interest inventory results. It's helpful to talk about interests and careers in terms of the importance to you of working. [Not wanting to overstate the value of the Strong Interest Inventory, the counselor wants to establish a context for it.]
>
> CL: Well, I'm curious about what it has to say.
>
> CO: When we look at it, it may be helpful to remember that work seems to be a means to an end for you. You certainly want to get the things that work provides for you. This inventory will help you to understand how similar your interests are to those of people in different occupations.
>
> CL: As you talk, it does sound important. I've been thinking so much about what I want to do with what I will make. I've been less concerned about what I will do.
>
> CO: Some of your basic areas of interest seem to be in athletics and sales. [The counselor starts with the two highest scores on the Basic Interests scales.]
>
> CL: Yes, I really like to do fun things like play tennis, basketball, volleyball, and race boats and cars.
>
> CO: It would seem that way. The values test that you took seems to emphasize risk as well. [The counselor wants to integrate the test scores with each other and to form a clearer impression of Ben.]
>
> CL: Sales is interesting to me. I never thought about that. I think I would like it. It's a real challenge. One summer I spent trying to sell as much as I could in an appliance store. They gave me commissions. I really did a job.
>
> CO: You really seem to have gotten a lot of satisfaction from that accomplishment. [The counselor hears how important achievement is to Ben and reinforces it. At this point, the counselor is aware that Ben's values are very different from his own values. The counselor's values are more altruistic and creative, whereas Ben's are more toward achievement and economic rewards. The counselor does not want to devalue Ben just because their values are so different.]

In a counseling situation that uses four different inventories, it is impossible to give a good overview of the entire test interpretation process. However, the purpose of this illustration has been to show how the counselor can make use of Super's developmental concepts and inventories to help someone who is in the exploration stage. The issues that are important in the exploration stage are quite different from those in the establishment stage.

Establishment

The establishment stage generally ranges from the age of 25 to about 45. In general, *establishment* refers to getting established in one's work by starting in a job that is likely to mean the start of working life. In skilled, management, and professional occupations, this means work in an occupation that will probably be steady for many years. For those in semiskilled and unskilled occupations, *establishment* does not mean that a person will be established in a particular job or organization. Instead, it refers to the fact that the person will be working for much of his or her lifetime (Super et al., 1988). The substages of *stabilizing, consolidating,* and *advancing* refer to career behaviors that take place once working life has started.

Stabilizing   Getting started in a job requires a minimum amount of permanence. The individual needs to know that he or she will be in this job for more than a few months. Stabilization is concerned with settling down in a job and being able to meet those job requirements that will ensure that a person can stay in the field in which he or she has started. At this point, an individual may be apprehensive about whether he or she has the skills necessary to stay with the work. As persons become more comfortable, they start to consolidate their position.

Consolidating   Once a person has stabilized his or her position, often occurring in their late twenties and early thirties, consolidation can take place. The person starts to become more comfortable with her or his job or work and wishes to be known as a dependable producer, one who is competent and can be relied on by others. In this stage, individuals want bosses and coworkers to know that they can do the job well. Once they can consolidate their position and can feel secure, then they can consider advancement to higher positions.

Advancing   Occurring any time in the establishment stage, but usually after stabilizing and consolidating have taken place, advancing refers to moving ahead into a position of more responsibility with higher pay. Particularly in business, there is a concern with advancing to positions of higher authority. To do so, individuals often plan how to get ahead and how to improve their chances of being promoted. They want their superiors to know that they do well and are capable of handling more responsibility.

Example   Lucy, whose case was discussed in the two previous chapters, is now a 28-year-old physical therapist working with people who have spinal cord injuries. She lives in a large city, is unmarried, and works in a nationally known hospital on a staff with many physical therapists. Lucy has sought counseling because she has not been happy with her personal life or her work. She has recently ended a three-year relationship with a man and finds that she is lonely, having not attended to friendships when she was romantically involved. Though she had intended to go to medical school, she had been afraid that she could not finance her education, could not stay in school and study for four years after college, and needed income immediately. Now she is questioning that decision and trying to decide whether to apply to medical school. She is clear that her choice is within the field of health but is hesitant to apply to medical school. She feels frustrated in her work because she questions her supervisor's competence and

Table 9-2 *Summary of Lucy's Scores on Three Inventories*

Inventory	High Scores
The Salience Inventory	*Working*
	Participation
	Commitment
	Values expectations
	Leisure
	Participation
	Home and Family
	Commitment
	Values expectations
The Values Scale	Autonomy
	Lifestyle
	Social interaction
	Achievement
The Adult Career Concerns Inventory	Crystallizing
	Stabilizing

feels limited by the job duties of a physical therapist. She wonders if she would be happier if she had more responsibility for patients, just like the physicians do who work with her patients.

In counseling Lucy, the counselor decides to use the Salience Inventory, the Values Scale, and the Adult Career Concerns Inventory. The counselor hopes that these instruments will help Lucy understand the importance of work in her life, the values that are important to her, and the developmental concerns that matter most to her. There are differences between Lucy's participation scores on the Salience Inventory and her commitment and values expectations scores (Table 9-2). Lucy's participation is in working, followed by leisure activities, followed by home and family. Her high scores on the Values Scales are for autonomy, lifestyle, social interaction, and achievement. The Adult Career Concerns Inventory shows that Lucy has considerable concern about crystallization and great concern about stabilizing. Other stages of development are of little or some concern to her.

Having talked about her loneliness and worries about her social isolation during the first session, Lucy brings up her career concerns with the counselor at the beginning of their second session. The counselor has just shared the results of the Salience Inventory and the Adult Career Concerns Inventory with Lucy. They are discussing the results:

> CL: Work really is very important to me. I feel that I have accomplished some things just by being able to get a job in the hospital. I've shown others that I can take care of myself.

CO: Getting set and on your feet sounds important. [The counselor hears Lucy talking about stabilizing and sees the parallel between this discussion and her high score on the Stabilizing Scale.]

CL: Really, it is important to me. I think now it's even more important to me because Max and I have broken up. There were times when I thought that we really would get married. When he continued to back off from me, and finally when I found out that he had cheated on me, that did it. It seemed then as if work was all I had.

CO: It's scary now to think that being married and having a family seems so unknown. [Being aware of the salience of home and family, the counselor is aware of how deeply Lucy is affected. That role seems to be hard for her to imagine now.]

CL: It's been so hard. I seem so much more aware of what other people are doing at work now. I don't mean just with patients, but sometimes I think about what they do when they go home. When Max and I were living together, I never thought about that.

CO: A lot more thought about you, too, and what you're going to do. [Disruption in the participation in one salient role, a relationship leading to home and family, seems to have had the effect of causing questioning of other salient roles.]

CL: Even though I really like the people I work with and still enjoy being with them, I feel more removed from them. I look at where they're going and I look at where I'm going. I wonder if I'm going in the right direction.

CO: Sounds like we ought to talk more about medical school—you brought that up last time. [Lucy seems to want to recycle, in the sense that she wants to question her choices and return to the crystallizing stage. Further, Lucy values social interaction; her statement is confirmed by her high score on the Values Scale.]

CL: Yes, now that I'm learning a lot about physical therapists and physicians, much more than I ever knew before, I am questioning it.

CO: Sounds like you have a lot more practical experience than you got just from your internship. [The counselor hears how Lucy's world-of-work information has increased (concept discussed in the previous chapter) and how Lucy may wish to return to the question of occupational selection with new information.]

CL: I really don't want to have to depend on anyone. I want to do what I want to do.

CO: What is that? [Lucy's autonomy is apparent. She seems to have a strong sense of who she is and what she wants.]

CL: Being a physician, working with people who are badly hurt, has a great appeal to me. I think I can do it.

CO: You seem to want it but seem scared. [Understanding the wavering between the stabilizing and the crystallizing stages, the counselor sees Lucy as embarking on one career and starting to like it, but seeing another career with more potential. In some ways, a change from physical therapist to physician can be seen as advancing, rather than career change. If seen that way, it may be less traumatic. On the other hand, returning to school for several years is more than advancing.]

Using Super's instruments and concepts to help Lucy deal with her relationship and career issues provides an organizing format for the counselor. Being able to identify the life stage and the movement back and forth within it can be quite helpful in making sense of changes in a person's life. Furthermore, knowing that the role of work can change in one's life and seeing it in terms of other roles—home and family, leisure, community service, and studying—can be quite helpful. Lucy's values are very important in Lucy's decision making. Super's value concepts provide a way to label the important issues with which Lucy is struggling.

Although the establishment substages of stabilizing, consolidating, and advancing help in understanding the career issues that Lucy is faced with, problems occurring late in the establishment stage may not be addressed. Bejian and Salomone (1995) suggest that midlife stresses that occur in the early forties are not accounted for by either the establishment stage or the maintenance stage. They suggest another stage, "renewal," in which an individual confronts midlife crises, which include reexamining one's personal and career priorities, making changes based on this examination, and making different plans about the future. Their suggestions are based in part on the findings of Riverin-Simard (1988) and Williams and Savickas (1990), who found that the early forties is a time of personal turmoil for many of the individuals they studied. Lucy may face such issues when she is more established in her career, either as a physical therapist or as a physician.

Maintenance

Individuals from about the age of 45 to 65 may be in a situation where they are not advancing but maintaining their status in their work. This can vary from individual to individual, depending upon physical abilities, company policies, personal financial situation, and motivation. The substages of holding, updating, and innovating may be found in the maintenance stage in any chronological sequence. The concepts are useful to the counselor because they help expand on the meaning of the maintenance stage.

Holding   Now that some level of success has been attained, the individual is concerned with holding onto the position that he or she has. This may mean learning new things to adapt to changes that take place in the position, and being aware of activities that coworkers are involved in. In some companies, individuals may see forced early retirement or potential mass layoffs as a threat. This is enough motivation for an individual to hold his or her own.

Updating   In many fields, holding one's own is not enough. For example, health and education occupations often require that workers attend continuing education programs to maintain their status in that occupation. Attendance at these programs updates workers on changes in the field. Less formal activities than continuing education seminars include attending professional meetings, visiting with colleagues or customers to see new developments in the field, and meeting people who can update one's knowledge.

Innovating Somewhat similar to updating, *innovating* refers to making progress in one's profession. It may not be enough to learn new things (updating); it may be important to make new contributions to the field. To do so, an individual might need to develop new skills as a field changes. Sometimes, there are new ways to improve one's work or to find new areas of work to learn. Innovating may sound as if it contradicts the idea of maintenance. However, in most occupations, particularly higher-level occupations, if workers stop learning new things, they will not maintain themselves but will decline and be in danger of losing their position.

Example Having knowledge of Super's stages can be useful to counselors with or without Super's inventories. In the case described next, Richard is a 57-year-old insurance salesperson. He is talking to his physician about the general fatigue that he is experiencing, along with occasional low-back pain. The physician, while not familiar with Super's instruments, is familiar with Super's life-stage theory.

> *CL:* I seem to be tired much more than I used to be.
>
> *CO:* None of the tests, as we've discussed, has shown anything to be wrong. How is your life going? [The physician decides to take the time to listen to Richard and see if she can help out. Perhaps she will make a referral to a counselor, a psychologist, or a psychiatrist, or perhaps she will be able to help Richard herself.]
>
> *CL:* My twin boys are doing well in their new jobs, and my wife likes hers, so things are going well with them.
>
> *CO:* But how are things going with you?
>
> *CL:* At home things are fine—we have two new grandchildren, and that's great—but work is the same as it's always been.
>
> *CO:* And how is that? [The physician wants to learn more about Richard's working role, as he seems content with home and family.]
>
> *CL:* It's pretty drab. I have the same customers. I get some commissions for renewing their accounts. Customers refer friends to me, so I get new accounts that way. My business is pretty much established now, so I don't have to work the way I used to.
>
> *CO:* Richard, the way you describe it, it doesn't sound very interesting to you. [Questioning how Richard is dealing with the maintenance stage, the physician wonders whether Richard is even holding his own in the field, let alone updating knowledge or innovating.]
>
> *CL:* Yes, it is rather boring. They have seminars and I get materials all the time, but they seem like the same old stuff. I don't read half of them.
>
> *CO:* What keeps you from reading them? [The physician knows the value of updating knowledge and innovating. She is hopeful that she will be able to get this across to Richard.]
>
> *CL:* I don't know. There are all these people who seem brand new to the company, telling me what I ought to do and how I ought to do it. I've worked for them for 20 years.
>
> *CO:* You really seem to resent their telling you what to do, almost as if you don't feel respected. [The physician wants to explore the resentment that

Richard feels, believing that it may hold back his progress in his work and contribute to his overall feeling of tiredness.]

In this example, by having some idea of life stages, the physician is able to be sensitive to her patient and start to explore issues of concern. Later, she may decide to refer Richard elsewhere for counseling. For now, she has used her knowledge of adult career development and the importance of various life roles to diagnose a significant psychological issue for the client.

Disengagement

In the maintenance stage, if individuals do not update their knowledge of the field and make some effort to innovate, they are in danger of losing their job. In the previous example, Richard may be in that position. He may be starting to disengage from his work. Sometimes, the need to disengage comes from physical limitations. People in their fifties and sixties who have been involved in some kind of physical labor—for example, construction, painting, or assembly line work—may find that they are no longer able to work as long or as fast as they once were. Super (1957) originally referred to this stage as "decline" but changed his label because of its negative connotations for many people. Although people may be slowing down in their physical abilities and their ability to remember, this is also an age that is associated with wisdom. People can continue to use their mental capacities for growth and at the same time disengage from various activities. The substages of disengagement—decelerating, retirement planning, and retirement living—can be seen as tasks that older adults often, but not always, must consider.

Decelerating   Slowing down one's work responsibility is what is meant by *decelerating*. For some people, this may mean finding easier ways of doing work or spending less time doing work. Others may find that it is difficult to concentrate on things for as long as they did when they were younger. Drawing away from difficult problems at work and wanting to avoid deadline pressure are signs of decelerating.

Retirement Planning   Although some individuals begin their retirement planning early, almost all individuals must deal directly with retirement plans during their later years. This task includes activities such as financial planning and planning activities to do in retirement. Talking to friends, retirement counselors at work, and others will aid in this process. Some individuals may choose a new part-time job or volunteer work. In a sense, when they do this, individuals are returning to the crystallization stage and reassessing their interests, capacities (both physical and mental), and values.

Retirement Living   This stage is common for people in their late sixties, who often experience changes in life roles. Leisure, home and family, and community service may become more important, whereas work will become less significant. Important aspects of retirement living are the place in which one lives, one's friends, and use of the free time that may come with retirement.

As aging populations become larger (as of 2000, over half the U.S. population was over 50), there is a greater need to address the issues of individuals facing retirement. Suggestions for counseling such individuals is given in *Retirement Counseling: A Handbook for Gerontology Practitioners* (Richardson, 1993). Hanisch (1994) shows that, when individuals plan their retirement, the retirement is most successful. Those who retired for negative reasons, such as poor health, had lower life satisfaction scores than those who chose to retire voluntarily (Shultz, Morton, & Weckerle, 1998). Similarly, Robbins, Lee, and Wan (1994) found that early retirees who adjusted well to retirement had stable and meaningful goals to enhance their quality of life. In general, men were found to report slightly more satisfaction with retirement in a sample ranging in age from 50 to 72 than were women (Quick & Moen, 1998).

Recycling

Super recognizes that not everyone follows these stages in the neat order outlined here. Most do not. Many reassess their career plans at various points during their lifetime. When they do this, they reenter the exploration stage, reassessing their values, interests, and capacities. In a study of Australian men, Smart and Peterson (1997) confirm the concept of recycling, finding that men who were in the process of changing careers did show more concern with Super's exploration stage than men who did not change careers. On the Adult Career Concerns Inventory, Super (Super et al., 1988) uses one item to determine a person's recycling status. Because it so clearly describes the concept of recycling, the item is reprinted here:

> After working in the field for a while, many persons shift to another job for any of a variety of reasons: pay, satisfaction, opportunity for growth, shut-down, etc. When the shift is a change in field, not just working for another employer in the same field, it is commonly called a "career change." Following are five statements which represent various stages in career change. Choose the one statement that best describes your current status.
>
> 1. I am not considering making a career change.
> 2. I am considering whether to make a career change.
> 3. I plan to make a career change and I am choosing a field to change to.
> 4. I have selected a new field and I am trying to get started in it.
> 5. I have recently made a change and I am settling down in the new field.*

---

*From *Adult Career Concerns Inventory* by Donald E. Super, Albert S. Thompson, and Richard H. Linderman. Copyright © 1990. Reprinted by permission of Albert S. Thompson.

The following dialogue is part of an initial interview between Matthew, a 64-year-old journalist working for a newspaper in a midsized southwestern city, and the retirement counselor who is on the staff in the newspaper's personnel office. Matthew, a Mexican American who moved to Texas at the age of 12, has been on the staff of the paper for 37 years. For 25 years, the newspaper has had a pension plan that he has participated in. Matthew's job requires him to be mobile, interviewing politicians and police officers throughout the county. In the past 15 years, Matthew has gained considerable weight, and he had a heart bypass operation 3 years ago. He is finding that he does not have the stamina that he used to have and is extremely tired at the end of the day. He has been looking forward to retirement. The counselor and Matthew have been going over the financial aspects of his retirement plan, when the counselor asks Matthew what his plans are for retirement:

CL: I've really been looking forward to relaxing and sitting around taking it easy. This job is getting to me now. My health isn't what it once was. I just want to be able to take it easy. I'm planning to work a 30-hour workweek for the next nine months. My editor says that's fine and not to worry about it.

CO: And after that? [Using his knowledge of Super's life-stage theory, but not Super's inventories, the counselor recognizes that Matthew is discussing the deceleration substage of disengagement. His focus seems to be mainly on that stage and not on retirement planning or retirement living.]

CL: My home is all paid for, and my wife will be working for another few years. I'll just sit around and watch television.

CO: Does that seem enjoyable to you? [Expecting to go from an active work role to a very passive role with little activity may be unrealistic.]

CL: Well, that's not all that I'll do.

CO: And what else?

CL: Something that I've always wanted to do is work in the literacy program with adults who can't read and those who are having a hard time learning English. It really helped me when I was a boy to be able to learn English as quickly as I did. I remember, in high school, I got better grades in English than the Anglo kids, and it wasn't even my native language. I've seen so many people suffer here because they can't read or speak English.

CO: Sounds as if you've thought about it awhile. [Moving from an active work role to an active community service role seems to be a comfortable shift.]

CL: I think about it quite a bit when I have to interview someone for an article and they can't speak well or their English is lousy. I find myself more and more giving tips to the young guys coming up in the office.

CO: You seem to like teaching. [Identifying an interest that is different from those in Matthew's current work may be helpful as Matthew and the counselor recycle to the crystallization stage. It is not a dramatic recycling, as Matthew has had some opportunity to do a little bit of teaching and has given it some thought.]

CL: Well, I never have had much opportunity to teach, but I do it informally. I try not to be obnoxious about it. Most reporters have their own style, and they don't like being told what to do. It may seem strange to you,

> but I'd like to do something for other Mexican Americans who have not had it as good as I have.
>
> CO: Helping them sounds as if it will be very meaningful to you. [The values of altruism and cultural identity underlie Matthew's desire to change his role in a positive sense to community service.]

From this brief example, the utility of Super's life-stage and role salience concepts can be seen. Without them, the counselor would just be using his own intuitions as to what to look for in helping Matthew. He would not be taking advantage of the wide array of research and concept development that has been a part of the work of Super and his colleagues. It is not that Super's theory is the only theory; there are others, such as those of Levinson, Darrow, Klein, Levinson, and McKye (1978) and Erikson (1963). They have not generated as much research as Super's theory, and they are not related directly to career development. However, the use of any of the theories would probably be better than relying only on hunches.

LIFE STAGES OF WOMEN

Although Super's theory is often thought of as a theory for white middle-class males, Super has long been concerned about the career patterns of women. He proposed seven career patterns for women (Super, 1957):

1. *Stable homemaking career pattern:* Women marry shortly after they finish their education and have no significant work experience afterward.
2. *Conventional career pattern:* Women enter work after high school or college, but after marriage they cease work to enter full-time homemaking.
3. *Stable working career pattern:* After high school or college, women work continuously throughout their life span.
4. *Double-track career pattern:* This pattern characterizes those women who combine career and homemaking roles throughout their life span.
5. *Interrupted career pattern:* Women enter into work, then marriage and full-time homemaking, and later return to a career, often after children can care for themselves.
6. *Unstable career pattern:* In this pattern, women drop out of the workforce, return to it, drop out, and return—repeating the cycle over again.
7. *Multiple-trial career pattern:* In such a pattern, a woman works, but never really establishes a career. She may have a number of different unrelated jobs during her lifetime. (pp. 76–78)

Super (1990) points out that the career patterns for women that he described more than 40 years ago are probably quite different now. Many changes in society have taken place to allow women to enter a much broader spectrum of careers. In their review of women's career development, Phillips and Imhoff (1997) point out the many roles that women take on and suggest methods for planning for multiple roles. Women tend to see the importance of integrating work and family rather than a choice between them (Hallett & Gilbert, 1997). In a study of 105 women over a

14-year span, Vincent, Peplau, and Hill (1998) found that women's career behavior was predicted by their gender-role views and their views of the preferences that their boyfriends and parents had for them 14 years earlier. Research shows that women see themselves in many roles and that there are several reasons for these perceptions.

Several studies have focused on comparing how men and women deal with work-elated stress. Hughes and Galinsky (1994a) found that women with full-time employed spouses reported more psychological symptoms, less job enrichment, more household and child care burdens, and more job difficulties than did employed men. Barnett, Marshall, Raudenbush, and Brennan (1993) studied 300 white middle-class couples. Although both the men and women found that their work experiences contributed to psychological stress, the women reported greater overall stress levels than did the men. In two other studies, Hughes and Galinsky (1994b) and Barnett, Brennan, Raudenbush, and Marshall (1994) found that psychological stress at work had an effect on marital disagreements and problems at home for both men and women. Studying dual-earner couples, Barnett & Shen (1997) found that psychological distress was related to time spent in low-schedule-control tasks but not high-schedule-control tasks or total hours spent in housework. When both men and women had to work under time pressure and deal with conflicting demands, psychological distress increased (Barnett & Brennan, 1997).

Studies of gifted women show that they, too, encounter obstacles. A longitudinal study of gifted women showed that many had seen few obstacles to achievement as adolescents. At age 30, many reported experience with sex discrimination, resistance to their goal achievement from family members, and role conflicts (Hollinger & Fleming, 1992). In a study of 40 women growing up in the 1950s, 1960s, 1970s, and 1980s, Vermeulen and Minor (1998) reported that gender beliefs had an important role in their career decisions. Other factors affecting their career decision making were amount of career-related information, meeting others' expectations, work conditions, having a sense of empowerment, and their own values. These studies suggest that career patterns for women are more subject to psychological stress and external obstacles than are career patterns for men.

Several investigators have reviewed women's choices to enter or not enter science or technology careers. Comparing women who entered engineering (a traditionally closed area) with those entering math education (a traditionally open area), Brown, Eisenberg, & Sawilowsky (1997) found that the expectations that these women had of their success played an important role in their career choices. Helen Farmer did several longitudinal studies of women and their career development. Farmer (1997a) found that women experienced sexual harassment and discrimination in math and science courses, whereas men did not. In another study, several reasons for changing career aspirations from science to other fields were given (Farmer, 1997b): selecting a popular career without much thought, finding a career that better fit their interests and personality, having to overcome too many career obstacles, and experiencing one or more critical events that changed their career goals. Another study of women's choices of techno-logical careers concluded that women may not be avoiding technological courses, but rather choosing careers that have a higher degree of social in-volvement (Lightbody, Siann, Tait, & Walsh, 1997).

Bardwick (1980) examined the typical experiences of women at various points in their adult life. It is useful to compare these observations with Super's life stages. Where Super characterizes the establishment stage as a time to stabilize oneself in a career, consolidate one's gains, and prepare to advance in the profession, Bardwick suggests that many women between the ages of 30 and 40 who have been involved in a career are concerned with not wanting to delay having children any longer. She believes that many women are concerned about balancing their professional role and their feminine role. For some women, professional success at midlife did not seem to bring about independence, but increased dependence. Whereas Super describes the maintenance stage as a time to hold one's gains and to update and innovate one's career skills, Bardwick believes that many women between the ages of 40 and 50 (the late establishment and early maintenance stages) are starting to develop more autonomy and to become more independent. This is the time when those who gave up ca-reers so they could raise children may now return to a career. For women over 50, Bardwick sees a time not of maintenance, but of career accom-plishments. For some women, their husband's retirement or death may open up more opportunities for a creative and autonomous lifestyle. Bard-wick's observations of women's working patterns focus on women's con-cern about marriage and family and are based mainly on middle-class and upper-middle-class women. Bardwick's stages are contrasted with Super's stages to remind counselors of the importance of marriage and family to many women in their career decision making and planning.

Using Super's theory with women is made easier by the use of Super's five roles: work, community service, study, home and family, and leisure. In research for the Salience Inventory, Nevill and Super (1986) found that women in general placed a slightly higher value on family and home than on work. Super's life stages are likely to be less applicable to people for whom work is an unimportant role. Most of Super's substages are con-cerned with work-related activity. This suggests that the less a woman par-ticipates in work, is committed to work, and values work, the less applic-able Super's life stages will be.

The issue of the applicability of life-stage theory to women will prob-ably continue to be a problem for some time. Studies by Ornstein and Is-abella (1990) and Ornstein, Cron, and Slocum (1989) question the appro-priateness of stage models for women. Lippert (1997) reviews several life-stage issues for women at midlife and explains the difficulty of applying one theory to the diverse experiences of women at midlife. Drawing from several studies of graduates from Radcliffe College, Vandewater and Stew-art (1997) describe three different approaches to careers. Women with con-tinuous career commitments pursued stable and prestigious careers. They were as likely to be married as women in the other groups but had fewer children. Their lives were devoted to work and family. Women with alternative commitments took on traditional roles and pursued social values. Their occupations were traditional (for example, artists, nurses, social workers). Women with midlife career commitments took on traditional roles when they left college but pursued high-level careers as their children grew older. These patterns provide another view of women's ways of integrating family and work, and are somewhat similar to those of Bardwick (1980) and Super et al. (1992). Clearly, differences in men's and women's perceptions of the importance of life roles suggest that counselors need to recognize the complexity of life-span theory. The counseling examples given in this chapter all show counselors listening to the client and not trying to force life-span theory into their conceptualization of a client.

A case study that may be typical of adult women who return to college after raising a family may serve to illustrate how Super's theory can be applied. Jill is a 38-year-old white woman who is married to a truck driver. She has three teenage children in school. For the past four years, Jill has been attending classes at a local community college. She now wishes to go to a four-year college but is unsure as to whether she wants a teaching curriculum or one in business. She has a slight preference for teaching but is afraid that this curriculum will be longer, as some of her credits will not transfer, and that she will have more difficulty finding a job near home. Her husband tolerates her pursuit of higher education but complains about her lack of attention to the children, because he has to spend more time with them. Jill is tired of his pressure and cannot wait until she finishes school so he will not pester her. However, she really enjoys the studying that she is doing; her view of herself as a competent individual has grown.

From the point of view of Super's life-span theory, several comments can be made. First, Jill is juggling her participation in studying and in home and family because she is committed to work as well as to home and family. She values autonomy, personal development, prestige, and achievement. From a life-stage point of view, she is recycling through the crystallization phase. Unlike students 18 years younger than she, she has greater family commitment and responsibilities. She would benefit from some help in crystallizing her abilities, interests, and values. She does not fit Bardwick's (1980) description of 30- to 40-year-old women, as her children are teenagers. However, she somewhat resembles Bardwick's description of 40- to 50-year-old women. Using Super's theory may help her counselor focus on important life-role, life-stage, and value issues.

LIFE STAGES OF CULTURALLY DIVERSE ADULTS

Recently, research on college students and adults has focused on the career development of individuals from different cultural groups, especially African Americans. Valuing work was related to career maturity for African American university students. In general, these students valued home and family roles more strongly than work or study roles (Naidoo, Bowman, & Gerstein, 1998). Using a case study approach, Chung, Baskin, and Case (1999) show the importance of financial support and role modeling of fathers on African American males' career development. Even when fathers were not available as role models, other African American males provided positive role models for the sample of adult African American males. In an in-depth study of nine African American women and nine white women, Richie, Fassinger, Linn, Johnson, Prosser, and Robinson (1997) found that all of the women had a great drive to excel. The African American women were well aware of their minority status in their fields. They felt a sense of inter-connectedness with other African American women at their own level or with those aspiring to attain success in their own field. Comparing the attitudes of Mexican American men and women with regard to attitudes toward the role of women in the workplace and views of responsibility for child care for working parents, Gowan and Trevine (1998) reported Mexican American men were more likely to have traditional views than were Mexican American women. Studies such as these provide information that can be used to test existing theories of adult career development as they apply to individuals from different cultural backgrounds or to develop new theories.

Along with research studies, there have been efforts to apply theory, assessment techniques, and new approaches to culturally diverse populations. Super's Career-Development Assessment and Counseling (C-DAC) system has been expanded to include culturally sensitive interventions (Hartung et al., 1998). The C-DAC system includes attention to the interplay of universal, group (cross-cultural), and individual factors for clients. Also, the C-DAC model can include attention to the degree to which clients integrate their cultural background with the majority culture (acculturation). The C-DAC model also discusses collectivism, which is found in many non white cultures that value the group more than the individual. Other authors (McCollum, 1998) have taken a broader view of strategies for counseling African Americans, discussing, social, political, and cultural issues as well as specific issues such as the accessibility of career counseling to African American clients. Aware of barriers to entering the job market for African Americans, the Perceived Occupational Opportunity Scale and the Perceived Occupational Discrimination Scale were developed (Chung & Harmon, 1999). A career life-planning model for Native Americans considers issues such as connectedness, needs, roles, gifts, and values (McCormick & Amundson, 1997). All of these approaches are innovative in their application to culturally diverse populations. Of these applications, the C-DAC model is most closely related to Super's theory.

For each cultural group, it can be argued that there are aspects of that culture that make the application of career theory—in this case, life-stage theory—inappropriate. A good example of this line of thinking is that of Cheatham (1990), who contrasts "Africentrism" with "Eurocentrism." Cheatham argues that African American culture differs from majority American culture in that interdependence, communalism, and concern about others in the group are valued over autonomy and competitiveness. These concepts are similar to "collectivism" described previously in the C-DAC culturally sensitive model (Hartung et al., 1998). This difference may manifest itself in the fact that African Americans are overrepresented in the social and behavioral sciences, including many of the helping professions. Cheatham also states that Africentrism may explain differences in African Americans' management styles and relationships with coworkers. The work of Vondracek and his colleagues, as described in the previous chapter, emphasizes the social and historical context of individual development that can be considered when using Super's life-stage theory. Another approach is to look at developmental issues that affect all groups that are not in the majority culture.

Use of the minority identity development model (Atkinson et al., 1998) may help in the conceptual application of Super's theory to different populations. There has been very little research on the theory, yet it is included because of the balance that it provides to life-stage theory. Not being a career- or age-related theory, the minority identity development model is less specific in its use than other models or theories described in this book. Outlined in Table 9-3, the minority identity development model emphasizes the attitude toward self, toward others of the same minority, toward others of different minorities, and toward the dominant culture for an individual in a minority group. Atkinson, Morten, and Sue (1998) describe five stages that individuals go through in dealing with their attitude toward self and others. In the conformity stage, minority individuals generally prefer the values of the majority culture to the values of their own culture. In Stage 2, the dissonance stage, the minority individual, through information and experience, encounters conflict and confusion between the values of his or her minority culture and those of the dominant culture. In Stage 3, the resistance and immersion stage, an individual rejects the dominant culture and embraces the minority culture. In Stage 4, the introspection stage, the minority individual begins to question his or her total acceptance of the minority culture. In Stage 5, the synergetic articulation and awareness stage, minority individuals incorporate the cultural values of both the dominant group and other minorities. They develop a desire to abolish all forms of oppression.

When discussing this model, Atkinson et al. (1998) are clear that not all minorities start in Stage 1 or finish in Stage 5. Furthermore, not all stages are experienced in the order in which they are described in Table 9-3. However, being aware that these issues can take place among minority group members at virtually any time during their lifetime can add to the use of Super's developmental theory with minority group members.

To demonstrate integrating the minority identity development model with Super's life-span theory, some examples will be given for each of Super's basic career development stages. In the exploration stage, counselors

Table 9-3 *Summary of Minority Identity Development Model*

Stages of Minority Development Model	Attitude Toward Self	Attitude Toward Others of the Same Minority	Attitude Toward Others of Different Minority	Attitude Toward Dominant Group
Stage 1—Conformity	Self-depreciating	Group-depreciating	Discriminatory	Group-appreciating
Stage 2—Dissonance	Conflict between self-depreciating and self-appreciating	Conflict between group-depreciating and group-appreciating	Conflict between dominant held views of minority hierarchy and feelings of shared experience	Conflict between group-appreciating and group-depreciating
Stage 3—Resistance and immersion	Self-appreciating	Group-appreciating	Conflict between feelings of empathy for other minority experiences and feelings of culturocentrism	Group-depreciating
Stage 4—Introspection	Concern with basis of self-appreciation	Concern with nature of unequivocal appreciation	Concern with ethnocentric basis for judging others	Concern with the basis of group depreciation
Stage 5—Synergetic articulation and awareness	Self-appreciating	Group-appreciating	Group-appreciation	Selective appreciation

Source: Donald R. Atkinson, George Morten, and Derald Wing Sue, *Counseling American Minorities: A cross-cultural perspective* (5th ed.). Copyright © 1998 by McGraw-Hill, New York. All rights reserved. Reprinted by permission.

not only need to consider assessment of abilities, interests, and values, along with career information, but must also be aware of the attitudes of the individual toward self and others. For example, an individual in the conformity stage may have a self-depreciating attitude, which may make it difficult to appropriately assess abilities, interests, and values. Other individuals in the conformity stage may not attend to the existence of very real discrimination that may be operating in the world of work and may instead blame themselves for the problems that they encounter. Someone in the resistance and immersion stage may be unduly suspicious of the counselor's advice and information about the world of work. Also, implementing a career choice can be difficult if an individual is having to deal with employers who are in the dominant group. Having to make a place for oneself in an organization when one resists or is angry at colleagues and supervisors in the organization can be extremely difficult. Likewise, in the maintenance stage, when an individual has to update knowledge and innovate, not respecting the values of the organization with which one is working can create identity confusion. If an individual is in the dissonance stage or the resistance and immersion stage and going through Super's disengagement phase, this can be a traumatic process. One can feel quite isolated and not valued at the end of one's career. At any of Super's stages, an individual from a minority group who experiences dissonance will have more problems to contend with in terms of adjustment to his or her career and the majority culture values it supports than will a majority group member. Atkinson et al. (1998) provide a model that can add dimensionality to career issues for people from diverse cultures.

In reviewing theories and studies related to racial identity development, Bowman (1993) discusses the usefulness of the Atkinson et al. model. In a study of African American college students, Evans and Herr (1994) found that developing a positive racial identity was not significantly related to choosing a traditionally African American career. Comparing African American women at historically black colleges and universities (HBCU) with African American women at predominantly white colleges and universities (PWCU), McCowan and Alston (1998) found several differences. Seniors at HBCU did not differ in certainty about their career choices from first-year students, but had a significantly higher racial identity score. In contrast, senior women at PWCU were significantly more decided than first-year women, but did not differ in racial identity. The authors suggest that the experience as a minority at PWCUs may enhance the social adeptness of African American women, helping them to develop a strong sense of vocational identity. Comparing the racial identity of African American male college students with African American female college students, Jackson and Neville (1998) found that racial identity was more closely related to vocational identity for women than it was for men. Applying models of racial identity to various cultural groups should help to provide more information about the career development of older adolescents and adults.

COUNSELOR ISSUES

By focusing on the comparative life-span development of the counselor and the client, we can identify potential difficulties for counselors. For example, a counselor who has just completed graduate school and is in Super's implementation substage may be confronted with a client who is planning retirement. Both the counselor and the client may worry about the gap in age. The client may feel, "How can the counselor help me? He hasn't worked; he hasn't raised a family into adulthood. How can he possibly know what it's like to retire?" A beginning counselor may share those feelings. An answer to these concerns is the counselor's ability to understand the unique situation by listening to the content and the feeling of the client's concerns. Also, by having knowledge of the context of the situation, such as retirement benefits, pension plan information, and other concrete information, the counselor can react to this criticism. Furthermore, a knowledge of the life-span issues of people in the disengagement phase is likely to make the counselor feel more comfortable.

A different type of issue may arise when the counselor is in the disengagement stage and the client is in the exploration stage. Young clients may question whether a 65-year-old counselor can help them, because the client is just at the start of his or her career. Again, the counselor's understanding of the client's knowledge of career development issues and occupational information will help to cross the age barrier. Although the counselor may be in the disengagement phase in terms of life span, that does not mean that she or he will disengage from the client in counseling. One of the indications of a good counselor is the ability to put one's own life issues aside so that one's counseling can be effective. If life-role or life-stage issues impede the counselor's listening to and helping the client, then that counselor should get counseling and consider temporarily or permanently removing himself or herself from the role of counseling.

SUMMARY

Career development issues for adults may be exceedingly complex. Commitment to, participation in, and valuing the roles of studying, working, community service, home and family, and leisure may be much more difficult than in adolescence and childhood, when the majority of the time is spent in study and leisure. Throughout the life span, the importance of roles may change, varying with the stages. When one is first exploring the type of work that he or she would enjoy and trying to choose among occupations, the career concerns are very different from when one is trying to establish oneself in a job, trying to become a dependable worker, and learning how to advance in the profession. Likewise, maintaining a position in an organization, which includes updating knowledge and innovating new processes or ideas, may create a different type of stress and conflict from when one is exploring or establishing oneself. Also, the process of disengagement or retiring from a career forces individuals to look at their life roles differently from before. At any point, individuals may wish to, or may be forced to, consider change in their career or lifestyle. This may mean recycling through previous stages. For some people, this is traumatic and may be quite difficult. The career crisis or transition that occurs is the subject of the next chapter.

References

Atkinson, D. R., Morten, G., & Sue, D. W. (1998). *Counseling American minorities: A cross-cultural perspective* (5th ed.). New York: McGraw-Hill.

Bardwick, J. (1980). The seasons of a woman's life. In D. McGuigan (Ed.), *Women's lives: New theory, research, and policy* (pp. 35–57). Ann Arbor: University of Michigan, Center for Continuing Education of Women.

Barnett, R. C., & Brennan, R. T. (1997). Change in job condition, change in psychological distress, and gender: A longitudinal study of dual-earner couples. *Journal of Organizational Behavior, 18*, 253–274.

Barnett, R. C., Brennan, R. T., Raudenbush, S. W., & Marshall, N. L. (1994). Gender and the relationship between marital-role quality and psychological distress. *Psychology of Women Quarterly, 18*, 105–127.

Barnett, R. C., Marshall, N. L., Raudenbush, S. W., & Brennan, R. T. (1993). Gender and the relationship between job experiences and psychological distress: A study of dual-earner couples. *Journal of Personality and Social Psychology, 64*, 794–806.

Barnett, R. C., & Shen, Y. C. (1997). Gender, high- and low-schedule-control housework tasks, and psychological distress: A study of dual-earner couples. *Journal of Family Issues, 18*, 403–428.

Bejian, D. V., & Salomone, P. R. (1995). Understanding mid-life career renewal: Implications for counseling. *Career Development Quarterly, 44*, 52–63.

Bowman, S. L. (1993). Career intervention strategies for ethnic minorities. *Career Development Quarterly, 42*, 14–25.

Brown, M. T., Eisenberg, A. I., & Sawilowsky, S. S. (1997). Traditionality and the discriminating effect of expectations of occupational success and occupational values for women within math-oriented fields. *Journal of Vocational Behavior, 50*, 418–431.

Cheatham, H. E. (1990). Africentricity and career development of African Americans. *Career Development Quarterly, 38*, 334–346.

Chung, Y. B., Baskin, M. L., & Case, A. B. (1999). Career development of Black males: Case studies. *Journal of Career Development, 25*, 161–171.

Chung, Y. B., & Harmon, L. W. (1999). Assessment of perceived occupational opportunity for Black Americans. *Journal of Career Assessment, 7*, 45–62.

Crites, J. O. (1979). *Career Adjustment and Development Inventory*. College Park, MD: Gumpert.

Erikson, E. H. (1963). *Childhood and society* (2nd ed.). New York: Norton.

Evans, K. M., & Herr, E. L. (1994). The influence of racial identity and the perception of discrimination on the career aspirations of African American men and women. *Journal of Vocational Behavior, 44*, 173–184.

Farmer, H. S. (1997a). Gender differences in career development. In H. S. Farmer (Ed.), *Diversity and women's career development: From adolescence to adulthood. Women's mental health and development,* (Vol. 2., pp. 127–158). Thousand Oaks, CA: Sage.

Farmer, H. S. (1997b). Why women don't persist in their high school aspirations. In H. S. Farmer (Ed.), *Diversity and women's career development: From adolescence to adulthood. Women's mental health and development.* (Vol. 2., pp. 62–80). Thousand Oaks, CA: Sage.

Gowan, M., & Trevine, M. (1998). An examination of gender differences in Mexican American attitudes toward family and career roles. *Sex Roles, 38,* 1079–1093.

Gribbons, W. D., & Lohnes, P. R. (1968). *Emerging careers.* New York: Teachers College Press.

Hackbarth, J., & Mathay, G. (1991). An evaluation of two work values assessment instruments for use with hearing impaired college students. *Journal of the American Deafness and Rehabilitation Association, 24,* 88–97.

Hallett, M. B., & Gilbert, L. A. (1997). Variables differentiating university women considering role-sharing and conventional dual-career marriages. *Journal of Vocational Behavior, 50,* 308–332.

Hanisch, K. A. (1994). Reasons people retire and their relations to attitudinal and behavioral correlates in retirement. *Journal of Vocational Behavior, 45,* 1–16.

Hartung, P. J., Vandiver, B. J., Leong, F. T. L., Pope, M., Niles, S. G., & Farrow, B. (1998). Appraising cultural identity in Career-Development Assessment and Counseling. *Career Development Quarterly, 46,* 276–293.

Hollinger, C. L., & Fleming, E. S. (1992). A longitudinal examination of life choices of gifted and talented young women. *Gifted Child Quarterly, 36,* 207–212.

Hughes, D. L., & Galinsky, E. (1994a). Gender, job and family conditions, and psychological symptoms. *Psychology of Women Quarterly, 18,* 251–270.

Hughes, D. L., & Galinsky, E. (1994b). Work experiences and marital interactions: Elaborating the complexity of work. *Journal of Organizational Behavior, 15,* 423–438.

Jackson, C. C., & Neville, H. A. (1998). Influence of racial identity attitudes on African American college students' vocational identity and hope. *Journal of Vocational Behavior, 53,* 97–113.

Kanungo, R. M. (1982). *Work alienation.* New York: Praeger.

Levinson, D. J., Darrow, C. N., Klein, E. B., Levinson, M. H., & McKye, B. (1978). *The seasons of a man's life.* New York: Knopf.

Lightbody, P., Siann, G., Tait, L., & Walsh, D. (1997). A fulfilling career? Factors which influence women's choice of profession. *Educational Studies, 23,* 25–37.

Lippert, L. (1997). Women at mid-life: Implications for theories of women's adult development. *Journal of Counseling and Development, 76,* 16–22.

Liptak, J. J. (2000). *Treatment planning in career counseling.* Pacific Grove, CA: Brooks/Cole.

McCollum, V. J. C. (1998). Career development issues and strategies for counseling African Americans. *Journal of Career Development, 25,* 41–52.

McCormick, R. M., & Amundson, N. E. (1997). A career-life planning model for First Nations people. *Journal of Employment Counseling, 34,* 171–179.

McCowan, C. J., & Alston, R. J. (1998). Racial identity, African self-consciousness, and career decision making in African American college women. *Journal of Multicultural Counseling and Development, 26,* 28–38.

Naidoo, A. V., Bowman, S. L., & Gerstein, L. H. (1998). Demographics, causality, work salience, and the career maturity of African American students: A causal model. *Journal of Vocational Behavior, 53,* 15–27.

Nevill, D. D., & Calvert, P. D. (1996). Career assessment and the Salience Inventory. *Journal of Career Assessment, 4,* 399–412.

Nevill, D. D., & Kruse, S. J. (1996). Career assessment and the Values Scale. *Journal of Career Assessment, 4,* 383–397.

Nevill, D. D., & Super, D. E. (1986). *The Salience Inventory: Theory, application and research.* Palo Alto, CA: Consulting Psychologists Press.

Niles, S. G., Anderson, W. P., Jr., & Goodnough, G. (1998). Exploration to foster career development. *Career Development Quarterly, 46,* 262–275.

Niles, S. G., Anderson, W. P., Jr., Hartung, P. J., & Staton, A. R. (1999). Identifying client types from Adult Career Concerns Inventory scores. *Journal of Career Development, 25,* 173–185.

Niles, S. G., & Goodnough, G. E. (1996). Life-role salience and values: A review of recent research. *Career Development Quarterly, 45,* 65–86.

Niles, S. G., Lewis, D. M., & Hartung, P. J. (1997). Using the Adult Career Concerns Inventory to measure task involvement. *Career Development Quarterly, 46,* 87–97.

Ornstein, S., Cron, W. L., & Slocum, J. W., Jr. (1989). Life stage versus career stage: A comparative test of the theories of Levinson and Super. *Journal of Organizational Behavior, 10,* 117–131.

Ornstein, S., & Isabella, L. (1990). Age vs. stage models of career attitudes of women: A partial replication and extension. *Journal of Vocational Behavior, 36,* 1–19.

Phillips, S. D., & Imhoff, A. R. (1997). Women and career development: A decade of research. *Annual Review of Psychology, 48,* 31–59.

Quick, H. E., & Moen, P. (1998). Gender, employment and retirement quality: A life course approach to the differential experiences of men and women. *Journal of Occupational Health Psychology, 3,* 44–64.

Richardson, V. E. (1993). *Retirement counseling: A handbook for gerontology practitioners.* New York: Springer.

Richie, B. S., Fassinger, R. E., Linn, S. G., Johnson, J., Prosser, J., & Robinson, S. (1997). Persistence, connection, and passion: A qualitative study of the career development of highly achieving African American Black and White women. *Journal of Counseling Psychology, 44,* 133–148.

Riverin-Simard, D. (1988). *Phases of working life.* Montreal: Meridian Press.

Robbins, S. B., Lee, R. M., & Wan, T. T. H. (1994). Goal continuity as a mediator of early retirement adjustment: Testing a multidimensional model. *Journal of Counseling Psychology, 41,* 18–26.

Shultz, K. S., Morton, K. R., & Weckerle, J. R. (1998). The influence of push and pull factors on voluntary and involuntary early retirees' retirement decision and adjustment. *Journal of Vocational Behavior, 53,* 45–57.

Smart, R. M., & Peterson, C. C. (1994). Super's stages and four-factor structure of the Adult Career Concerns Inventory in an Australian sample. *Measurement and Evaluation in Counseling and Development, 26,* 243–257.

Smart, R. M., & Peterson, C. C. (1997). Super's career stages and the decision to change careers. *Journal of Vocational Behavior, 51,* 358–374.

Super, D. E. (1957). *The psychology of careers.* New York: Harper & Row.

Super, D. E. (1970). *Work Values Inventory.* Boston: Houghton Mifflin.

Super, D. E. (1990). A life-span, life-space approach to career development. In D. Brown & L. Brooks (Eds.), *Career choice and development: Applying contemporary theories to practice* (2nd ed., pp. 197–261). San Francisco: Jossey-Bass.

Super, D. E., Crites, J. O., Hummel, R. C., Moser, H. P., Overstreet, P. I., & Warnath, C. F. (1957). *Vocational development: A framework for research.* New York: Teachers College Press, Columbia University.

Super, D. E., & Kidd, J. M. (1979). Vocational maturity in adulthood: Toward turning a model into a measure. *Journal of Vocational Behavior, 14,* 255–270.

Super, D. E., & Knasel, E. G. (1979). *Specifications for a measure of career adaptability in young adults.* Cambridge and Hertford, England: National Institute for Careers Education and Counseling.

Super, D. E., & Nevill, D. D. (1986). *The Salience Inventory.* Palo Alto, CA: Consulting Psychologists Press.

Super, D. E., & Nevill, D. D. (1989). *The Values Scale: Theory, research, and application.* Palo Alto, CA: Consulting Psychologists Press.

Super, D. E., Osborne, W. L., Walsh, D. J., Brown, S. D., & Niles, S. G. (1992). Developmental career assessment and counseling: The C-DAC. *Journal of Counseling and Development, 71,* 74–80.

Super, D. E., Thompson, A. S., & Lindeman, R. H. (1988). *The Adult Career Concerns Inventory.* Palo Alto, CA: Consulting Psychologists Press.

Thompson, A. S., & Lindeman, R. H. (1981). *Career Development Inventory: Vol. 1. User's manual.* Palo Alto, CA: Consulting Psychologists Press.

VandeWater, E. A., & Stewart, A. J. (1997). Women's career commitment patterns and personality development. In M. E. Lachman & J. B. James (Eds.). *Multiple paths of midlife development* (pp. 375–410). Chicago: University of Chicago Press.

Vermeulen, M. E., & Minor, C. W. (1998). Context of career decisions: Women reared in a rural community. *Career Development Quarterly, 46,* 230–245.

Vincent, P. C., Peplau, L. A., & Hill, C. T. (1998). A longitudinal application of the theory of reasoned action to women's career behavior. *Journal of Applied Social Psychology, 28,* 761–778.

Williams, C. P., & Savickas, M. L. (1990). Developmental tasks of career maintenance. *Journal of Vocational Behavior, 36,* 166–175.

10

Adult Career Crises and Transitions

This chapter is concerned with crises and transitions in adult career development. From a stage-theory point of view, *transition* refers to movement from one stage to another. Transitions may be quite smooth, such as the transition from the establishment to the maintenance stage, provided an individual experiences relatively few abrupt changes in his or her career pattern. *Crisis* is a more negative term and refers to a situation in which a person has to develop new methods of dealing with a problem that has arisen rather suddenly. Definitions by Moos and Schaefer (1986) and Hill (1949) emphasize the suddenness and disorienting aspects of a crisis. The focus of this chapter is on career crises, disruptive situations that are likely to cause considerable consternation for the individual and may cause the person to seek counseling. Less dramatic transitions will also be covered. These crises and transitions are described in the context of Super's life-span stages.

There are several models of how individuals cope with crises or transitions. Although some will be described here, the model of Hopson and Adams (1977) will be used for conceptualizing reactions of clients to career crises and transitions. Examples will be used to identify clients in various stages of transition. Certain career crises tend to occur mainly with women and members of minority groups who experience discrimination. These special situations will also be examined in the context of Hopson and Adams's theory of transitions.

TYPES OF TRANSITIONS

Reviewing the literature on types of transitions, Schlossberg (1984) identified four: anticipated, unanticipated, "chronic hassles," and events that don't happen (nonevents). Anticipated events are ones that will happen in the life span of most individuals. Examples of these would be high school graduation, marriage, starting a job, and retiring. Unanticipated transitions are those that are not expected. Examples of these would be the death of a family member or being fired or transferred. Hopson and Adams (1977) refer to anticipated crises as predictable and unanticipated crises as not predictable. "Chronic hassles" are situations such as a long commute to work, an unreasonable supervisor, concern with deadline pressures, or physical conditions. A nonevent is something that an individual wishes to happen but that never occurs. For some, this may be a promotion that does not happen or a transfer to a desired community that does not take place. A common nonevent for women is being unable to enter or leave the workforce. Some women wish to leave and spend more time with family or other pursuits but do not do so because of financial conditions. Others may wish to enter the workforce as their children grow but may hesitate to do so because of continuing responsibilities at home or lack of confidence.

Another class of transitions mentioned by Hopson and Adams (1977) is voluntary and involuntary transitions. An example of a voluntary transition would be the decision to quit one's job as an accountant and become an actor. An involuntary transition would be being fired or laid off from one's job. An anticipated transition can be involuntary. For example, being given a new sale's territory may not be voluntary, but the individual may know about it for six months in advance. An unanticipated event can be voluntary. For example, making oneself available for an assignment, not knowing whether it will occur, can lead to being unsure about how such an assignment would affect one's life in the next few months. In general, crises tend to be unanticipated and involuntary. Examples would be being fired from a job, being given a radical shift in an assignment, or encountering a flood at work. These types of transitions can be sorted into useful categories.

CATEGORIES OF CAREER TRANSITIONS

In categorizing a variety of different strains on an individual's life roles, Schlossberg (1984) lists common life strains on a person's career, marriage, and parenthood. The career events are classified into three areas: nonnormative events, normative role transitions, and persistent occupational problems. Normative transitions tend to be anticipated and voluntary. Situations such as starting one's first full-time job or reentering the labor market after giving birth can be predicted weeks or months in advance. Many of these examples occur in Super's exploration stage. Another normative role transition is the loss of role. This may mean movement from an occupation to retirement. In terms of Super's theory, this could be construed as the movement (in terms of retirement) from the maintenance stage into the disengagement stage. Normative transitions tend to become crises only when they are not anticipated. For example, a person who ignores impending retirement and does not plan may be shocked by the change of roles forced by retirement.

Louis (1980a, 1980b) has created five categories of normative transitions that individuals experience in work roles: entering or reentering a labor pool, taking on a different role within the same organization, moving from one organization to another, changing professions, and leaving the labor pool. A prime example of entering the labor pool is the school-to-work transition, where understanding the transition process itself is helpful. A second transition may be less formal, as individuals move within a company, changing tasks, technologies, coworkers, and/or the actual physical surroundings. Dalton and Wimbush (1998) examine the implications of transferring from the perspective of the employer and employee. The third type of transition may cause greater stress as individuals make changes to a new employer, encountering new styles of work, tasks, and coworkers. A more dramatic change occurs when one leaves one profession for another; for example, an engineer becomes an entrepreneur, a lawyer, or a farmer. The fifth type of transition is the exit: leaving for retirement, pregnancy, a sabbatical, or being laid off or fired. Using a sample of 742 U.S. Navy officers, Bruce and Scott (1994) validated the applicability of Louis's typology as a useful way of categorizing career transitions.

Events and transitions that Louis describes are likely to be experienced in nontraditional ways. Mirvis and Hall (1994) and Sullivan (1999) describe the "boundaryless" career, in which there may be frequent job rotations, temporary assignments, and transfers from one part of a company to another, making the experience of transitions more frequent than in the past and occurring in more configurations than those described by Louis. A part of the evolution of the "boundaryless" career is the increase in complexity both in the nature of the work done and in relationships to coworkers (Lissack & Roos, 1999). Included in the idea of boundaryless careers are those individuals who work on their own but are consultants to a company (Cohen & Mallon, 1999). Such individuals may work at home, communicate over the Internet to colleagues, and work on several tasks with different colleagues. High degrees of conceptual flexibility and problem-solving competencies are required for such work (Sparrow & Daniels, 1999). Such changes are likely to heighten feelings of job insecurity. More involvement with family, community, and religious organizations may reduce the tensions that result from more frequent job transitions.

To assess how well individuals believe they have made career transitions, Heppner, Multon, and Johnston (1994) developed the Career Transitions Inventory. Its five subscales measure readiness, confidence, control, perceived support, and decision independence (Heppner, 1998). *Readiness* refers to how motivated an individual is to make a career transition. *Confidence* refers to an individual's sense of self-efficacy in being able to make a successful transition. *Control* refers to the degree to which individuals feel that they can make their own decisions. *Perceived support* refers to how much support individuals feel they get from family and friends. *Decision independence* refers to the extent to which individuals make the decisions based primarily on their own needs or whether or not they are considering the needs and desires of others. The Career Transitions Inventory may help counselors identify significant aspects of their clients' transitions which trouble or concern them. Specific variables, neuroticism and openness to experience, are both related to scores on the Career Transitions Inventory (Heppner, Fuller, & Multon, 1998), setting the stage for discussion and exploration of these issues. The subscales would seem to apply well to Louis's five categories of normative transitions. However, nonnormative transitions create special problems.

Nonnormative career events are far more likely to become crises than normative transitions. Perhaps the most common, as well as one of the most deeply disturbing, is loss of job. Being fired or laid off is for many people a devastating experience. However, if the work role is not a salient one, it is less likely to be devastating. If a person does not value work and relies on others or savings for income, then the family, leisure, or community service role is likely to fulfill that person's needs. However, for many people during the establishment and maintenance stage, the work role is highly valued. Stability is implied by the terms *establishment* and *maintenance*. When the essence of one's career is disrupted through job termination, this stability can turn into instability. If a person is fired at the very beginning of his or her career (the exploration stage) or six months before planned retirement (the disengagement stage), the disruptions may be easier to handle. Other nonnormative events are promotion, transfer, or demotion to another job. Although less dramatic than termination, these changes are likely to be most powerful in the establishment and maintenance stages. When these events are unanticipated, as they often are, the experience can be traumatic, more so than both normative and persistent occupational problems.

Persistent occupational problems are career problems that persist for a long period of time, causing a cumulative effect that can lead to a transition crisis. One example is an unpleasant physical working environment. This might include working in a very hot or cold building, in cramped quarters, or in hazardous conditions. Loggers, farm workers, and chemical workers are people who may have to continually face an unpleasant working environment. Another type of career problem that may persist is pressures on the job. These pressures may take the form of work deadlines such as those that journalists must meet, or there may be pressures to produce, for example, having to increase one's sales year after year. When rewards of the job decrease—in the form of a pay decrease, a smaller commission rate, fewer vacation days, a lack of recognition for performance by superiors, or being given less interesting work tasks—worrisome problems may arise. Another significant work problem that can start out small but fester to create a very major problem is work relations with colleagues and superiors. Not being able to get along with people that one must work with daily can create an emotional strain. If it continues, a worker must decide how to change the situation. If attempts at change fail, then the worker must decide whether to live with the stress or change to another job. Although longer in duration than nonnormative events, such as getting a termination notice, these persistent problems are most significant when the work role is extremely important to the individual. Furthermore, like nonnormative transitions, these are most disruptive during the establishment and maintenance stages. How people react to persistent, nonnormative, and normative transitions is the focus of the next section (adapted from Schlossberg, 1984).

MODELS OF TRANSITIONS AND CRISES

Reaction to a crisis or a transition takes place over a period of time. In their study of transition, Moos and Tsu (1976) identified two basic phases, the first directed toward dealing with and decreasing the stress that comes with the crisis, and the second directed toward attending to details of the crisis so that one can return to normal life. These observations would seem to summarize the general reaction of individuals to a crisis. A closer look at reactions of individuals to a career crisis will help to illustrate.

Studying the career transitions of 53 men whose jobs had been eliminated, Schlossberg and Leibowitz (1980) were able to categorize the process of transition in these men into five phases: disbelief, sense of betrayal, confusion, anger, and resolution. The men in the company that was studied were all subject to a planned reduction in employees. Most were surprised by this action on the part of the company and responded in disbelief. Some felt that it might not really be true or that something might happen to reinstate them in their jobs. At about the same time as the men experienced disbelief, they also felt betrayed by the company. Many felt they had been loyal to the company and the company was deserting them. Since the transition was unanticipated and involuntary, it was natural that they would experience confusion. Being surprised, they were unsure of what to do next. The company offered career assistance, which helped them mobilize their resources. Those who had difficulty resolving their confusion were angry at themselves and at the company. In fact, a sizable minority of the employees filed grievance complaints against the employer. The last phase was resolution. Three months after they had been notified of their job transition, some had been reassigned to other jobs in the company, and about half had found new jobs. Many were pleased by the eventual outcome, as some had found better jobs. In terms of Super's life-span theory, many of the men were in the maintenance stage and appeared to have a strong commitment to their role as workers.

Often, positive change and growth occur with involuntary work changes. Following 515 professionals who had been displaced involuntarily, Eby and Buch (1995) noted different reactions to this change in men and women. For the women, family flexibility in dealing with family, work, and other roles increased the chances that positive changes would occur with the involuntary change. For the men, positive growth was more likely to occur if they could avoid financial hardship and emotionally accept the job transition, as well as receive support from friends and family. Malen and Stroh (1998) observed that in their study of involuntarily unemployed managers, women seemed to have less confidence in their ability to seek and get a new job than did men. Being able to positively appraise oneself was an important factor in coping well with job loss as were problem-focused strategies such as searching for a job, seeking training, and relocating rather than focusing on symptom-focused strategies such as getting social support and finding financial help (Leana, Feldman, & Tan, 1998). Although positive growth may occur after involuntary work changes, severe reactions often take place, and individuals may seek the help of an outplacement counselor.

Outplacement counselors often have several functions. They help individuals deal with the shock and negative emotional impact of the career disruption. Also, they help individuals assess their current situation, abilities, values, and interests. From this information, they help their clients set career goals and develop strategies for a constructive job search. Depending on the clients' needs, the search may be for a job similar to the one that was lost, or it may lead to new training and education. Common skills that are taught by outplacement counselors are résumé writing, interviewing techniques, and locating job or educational opportunities. In some situations, outplacement counselors work directly for a firm or may be hired on a consulting basis by a firm. Less frequently, individuals may seek out the private services of an outplacement counselor to help them deal with involuntary transitions.

Most approaches to outplacement counseling do not follow a theoretical approach, although some have been influenced by Super's stages of adult career development (Aquilanti & Leroux, 1999). Contrasting cognitive-behavioral to behavioral individual approaches to outplacement counseling, Phillips (1999) found that the sample of unemployed professionals were more satisfied with the cognitive-behavioral approach. Earnings of those professionals receiving outplacement counseling have been found to be related to previous earnings, gender, and years working for the previous employer (Edwards et al., 1998). For individuals who have lost their job for a variety of reasons, outplacement counseling continues to be used as a means of helping with the transition to future employment.

HOPSON AND ADAMS'S MODEL
OF ADULT TRANSITIONS

No one model of coping with adult transitions fits every individual. One model that has been used by a number of psychologists has been that of Hopson and Adams (1977). Brammer and Abrego (1981) adopted this model in their strategies for coping with transitions. In terms of career transitions, Perosa and Perosa (1983, 1985, 1987, 1997) have found this model appropriate to the understanding of adult career crises. Hopson (1981) has slightly revised the earlier model of Hopson and Adams (1977). This revision, along with examples of its use as a conceptualization system in adult career crises and transitions, will be described in the following pages.

Figure 10-1 presents the seven stages of the model by showing the relationship of each stage or phase to mood and to time. Whether one is initially depressed or excited depends on the nature of the transition. Other phases are associated with varying degrees of depression or positive feeling. When describing each of the seven stages, we will use as a continuing example a man who has sought help from his minister because the company that he has been with for 23 years has gone bankrupt and closed its doors. A 55-year-old white male, John has worked hard as an inside salesperson, taking orders from people around the country for bicycle parts.

Immobilization

The initial shock that occurs when one finds out that one has been fired or laid off is an example of immobilization. The person is overwhelmed, unable to make plans, perhaps even unable to respond verbally. The time period of immobilization could be a few moments or a few months. How long the period lasts depends on the nature of the event and the psychological makeup of the individual.

When John first heard from his supervisor that the company was closing in two weeks, he was speechless. He kept repeating to himself, "I can't believe it; I can't believe it." He went back to his desk at 3:30 that afternoon. For the rest of the day, he answered the phones as usual, but he was just barely able to hear the customers. His voice was hollow; he did not engage in casual talk with some customers whom he had known for many years, nor did he ask them about their inventory of bike accessories or hardware, something that he would often do. After work, he went home and sat down on the sofa. This was very uncharacteristic of him. His wife, who had come home from work earlier, was surprised by the look on his face. Had the event been a happy one, such as being given a promotion or a coveted assignment, the feeling would have been elation, rather than despair (see Figure 10-1).

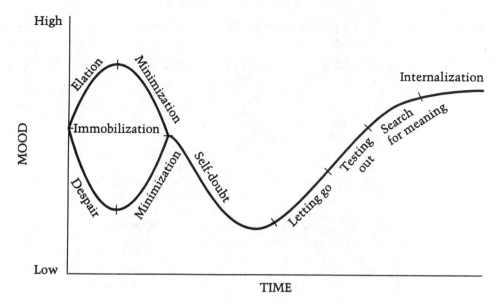

Figure 10-1 A seven-phase model of stages accompanying transition.
Source: Transition: Understanding and Managing Personal Change, by
J. Adams, I. Hayes, and B. Hopson. Copyright © 1977 by Sage Publications,
Inc., p. 38. Reprinted by permission.

Minimization

Minimization refers to the desire to make the change appear smaller than
it is. Often, an individual will deny that the change is even taking place or
will tell himself or herself that the event really does not matter, that things
will be perfectly fine anyway.

When John returned to work the next day, things were, in a physical
sense, as usual. The building was standing there; his desk was in the same
place. He talked to the salespeople whose desks were near him, but before
they had a chance to talk about the news, the phones started to ring. It was
a very busy day, and although John's job ordinarily provided little time to
talk to his coworkers, that morning he had no time at all to talk to them.
At noon, half the salespeople went to lunch, while the others covered the
phones. John went with them, and they talked about the closing. Most expressed surprise and said that the company was in good financial shape—
that there seemed to be plenty of inventory. They could not understand
why the company would be closing. A few said that perhaps they would
hear in a few days that the company was going to make it after all. John's
spirits were boosted; he felt a little bit better that others saw the situation
the way he did. Not only was John denying the plant's closing, but so were
some of his coworkers.

About 7 o'clock that evening, John received a call from his
minister. Knowing that his wife had called their minister during the

day, John was not surprised. A portion of their conversation went like this:

CL: I was shocked like everyone else yesterday. The company had done so well for so many years, I couldn't believe it.

CO: I'm sorry to hear it. That's terrible news for you. [Although the minister has several people in his congregation who have experienced the same layoff, the minister wants to focus on John's experience, noticing how the event has immobilized him.]

CL: Well, it may not be so bad. Maybe there's a chance that the company will be able to continue and someone will buy it out.

CO: Yes, that would feel a lot better to you. That's for sure. [Knowing that a company does not give two weeks' notice to employees without being very certain, the minister is not hopeful, as John is. He recognizes the denial, as he has experienced this many times with parishioners who have lost jobs or loved ones or have had other significant losses. He knows that this is not the time to argue with John about the likelihood of the plant's reopening.]

CL: I hope it will work. It would be a terrible disaster for me if things don't work out.

CO: I know, John, you put so much of yourself into your work. [The tragedy of this crisis is dramatically clear.]

CL: I have another 12 years to go before retirement, if only the company could hold on.

CO: You feel you need the company so much. [Staying with John's feelings of desperation seems really important to the minister now.]

Self-Doubt

Many different feelings can occur at this stage. A very common one is doubting oneself and one's ability to provide for oneself and for one's dependents. Other common reactions are anxiety due to not knowing what will happen, fear of the future, sadness, and anger.

For John, the principal emotion a few days later was anger. When John realized that plans were being made to liquidate inventory, the chances of the company's continuing began to appear very small to him. When John came home that night, he called his minister. Having known the minister for 15 years, he felt very comfortable with him and had been encouraged by him to call at any time.

CL: The company never gave me a chance. After all the hours I've put in for them, I didn't get a chance to even find out what was happening. They never told me until the last minute—what a bunch of jerks they are! I can't understand how they could do such a thing.

CO: You're so angry at them. I can hear it in your voice. [John is furious, yet he is toning his language down so as not to offend the minister.]

CL: I can't understand why they would do it. Such fools! It's like they don't care about anybody who has given them service and made them rich. I'm not the only one. A lot of others have been with the company a long time. It's a rotten thing to do.

CO: It feels as if they've betrayed you after all you've done for them. [The minister just wants to stay with the anger and not challenge it. He senses that John doesn't want to hear anything else.]

Letting Go

As can be seen in Figure 10-1, the individual next starts to let go of the angry, tense, frustrated, or other feelings. This is the time when the person accepts what is really happening to him or her. The individual detaches himself or herself from the original situation and starts to look at the future.

With each passing day, it becomes clearer that the company is going to close. John starts to think about what will happen to him next. He knows that a few of the workers in the plant are being kept on to close the plant down. There is no news that anyone will buy the plant. The company is giving each person two extra weeks of severance pay, but no other assistance. The money that John has accumulated in his pension will not be affected by the closing. As he goes home on Friday night, he starts to think about the future. In the evening, he goes through the want ads in his local paper. The next day, he goes out to buy newspapers from nearby cities. He plans to look for work on Monday. At home, he starts to think about what he can do and what he is good at. From Super's life-span point of view, John now recycles from the maintenance stage to the exploration stage. Although this was an involuntary, unpredictable event, John is letting go of his angry feelings and his desperate denial of the impending plant closing. John has hobbies that he has worked on from time to time. They now become potential career directions. Also, John thinks of the church work that he has done with poor families in his city. His leisure and community service pursuits can now become career possibilities.

Testing Out

At this point individuals may develop a burst of energy, a sense of "now I can handle it." In fact, sometimes people will describe the way things should be. They may have advice for others in the same situation. In a career situation, an individual may have thoughts about how he or she is going to network (talk to other significant people in the field) and move forward.

Sunday after church services, John talks very briefly with his minister, who inquires how John is doing:

CL: Things are looking up now. I have a number of avenues that I plan to explore this week. I am going to take a couple of days off and talk to some old friends. I have some ideas about opening up an auto garage or working as a salesman for machine parts. I haven't talked to anybody yet.

CO: Nice to hear your enthusiasm, John. [It is a relief to hear that John has moved away from his preoccupation with the company's closing. Some people stay in the denial stage or are extremely angry at the company for weeks. Yet John's newfound confidence does not sound real. It may fade quickly, but it is a start.]

CL: I do hope that I'll find something. It's been such a long time since I've thought about what I might do. I guess I never thought about being in this situation. When I think of new possibilities, it isn't so bad.

CO: It's good to hear you thinking about new possibilities. It's good to see that spark. [Encouragement is given for exploring new activities that will help John move on in his search, not only for a job, but also for his own peace of mind.]

Search for Meaning

In the search-for-meaning stage, an individual seeks to understand how events are different and why. This is a cognitive process in which people try to understand not only the feelings of others, but also their own.

Having finished his work with the company and having spent a week looking for work, John is busy following leads. He has contacted auto supply stores and hardware manufacturers for job leads. He had started out looking at the possibility of opening a gas station or car repair shop. As he learned more about this option, he felt he did not have the necessary experience or capital, nor was he prepared to work in someone else's shop. This felt as if it would be a step down not only in financial reward, but also in prestige. He is more comfortable using the skills that he has developed in his 23 years of experience as a bicycle parts salesperson. As John recycles through Super's exploration stage, he reconsiders his interests, capacities, and values. This is something that he has not done for many years. As he does this, he sees his job loss as a challenge and an opportunity to improve himself. His understanding of the reasons for the company's collapse is more apparent. Not only does he have more information now about the financial situation of the company, but he is also able to be more objective and less angry in his view of the actions that have taken place in the last three weeks.

Internalization

The final phase of dealing with transitions, *internalization*, implies a change in both values and lifestyle. The individual may have developed new coping skills and has grown emotionally, spiritually, or cognitively as a result of going through a difficult crisis.

Three months after being terminated from his job, John calls his minister to tell him of the progress that he has made:

CL: It took me over two months, but I finally got a job that I think will be an improvement, a step up for me. I started working a week ago for a very large auto parts distributorship. My work will be sales, like before, but also managing some other employees. That's something that I only did informally in my old job. I really want that opportunity now. Things are looking up.

CO: Sounds very much as if they are. It's great to hear such good news from you, John.

CL: It's been a rough few months. The second month that I was out of work was pretty depressing. I started to lose confidence in my ability to get a job. I wondered who would hire an old guy like me, but I really kept going at it, even though times got discouraging. My wife was really helpful, really encouraging.

CO: The ups and downs sound pretty tough. [John sounds quite different from a few months ago. The panic, anger, and tension are gone from his voice. He seems to have been fortunate in his resolution of the crisis.]

CL: Some days, I would be really excited about possibilities. Others, I might not. But I was able to think about what I was able to do and what I couldn't. I had dreamed of owning my own business, but it took a while for me to realize that I just couldn't handle it financially, and maybe I really wasn't able to commit the energy that I think it needs.

CO: You really have done a lot of thinking about yourself and your future. [John's *search for meaning* has not been an easy one, nor has that search been one that moved steadily upward; it has been full of fits and starts.]

CL: It's been rough, but when I think where I am now, I am a lot better off than I was three months ago. I feel more sure of myself. If this were to happen to me again, I think it would be easier the next time. Things that I was so afraid of before—like losing my job and then having to get a new one—don't scare me as much. I think I know more now what I can do than I did before.

CO: You sound terrific. [Hearing John talk this way feels very good. John has *integrated* this transformation into his life. As a result, he is feeling better about himself than he did prior to the crisis. He has moved past his fears and anxieties to an excellent resolution of his transition.]

Not all crises follow Hopson and Adams's (1977) seven-phase transition model as closely as this example does. John's case was presented to illustrate the sequence of the phases. Many people's situations, as will be shown by the examples in the next sections, do not fit the model so neatly. Clearly, not everyone is able to resolve a job crisis by finding a better job. Some people facing job crises have become physically ill, committed suicide, found only temporary and inferior work, or never found work again. The advantage of Hopson and Adams's model of transition is that the counselor has an idea of what to expect. For example, if during the second phase a client denies that his job is really important, Hopson and Adams's model is useful in helping the counselor accept this, without believing the client's statement to be one that will be true for a long period of time. Rather, the counselor accepts the denial as a phase. If a client's experience does not fit Hopson and Adams's model, there is no need to attempt to force it. The career-related crises that are especially applicable to women and to culturally diverse populations, which are described in the next sections, often do not fit smoothly into this model.

CAREER CRISES AFFECTING WOMEN

Three general types of career crises are far more likely to affect women than men. Women are much more likely than men to experience discrimination, to make decisions based on child-raising and family issues, and to face sexual harassment. Discrimination, when it occurs, is usually unanticipated and involuntary. The effects of discrimination are described in more detail in the example later in this section, and in Chapter 15 on sociological and economic theories of career development. The transitions out of and into the workforce or out of full-time and into part-time work are decisions that many women make at various times in their lives in consideration of children and family. In the previous chapter, Bardwick's (1980) views of child-raising and family issues at various points in a woman's life were described as they related to Super's life-span theory. Such transitions tend to be anticipated and voluntary. However, this is not always the case, and regardless of the type of transition, it can be a difficult crisis. A dramatic, unanticipated, and involuntary transition is that forced by sexual harassment. Having both severe personal and career consequences, this can be an extremely devastating experience. Betz and Fitzgerald (1987) and Fitzgerald and Ormerod (1993) describe in depth the research on discrimination, the effects of child-raising on workforce participation, and sexual harassment. The relationship between career and family and the effects of sexual harassment are described in the following pages in the context of Hopson and Adams's (1977) theory.

Temporary Reentry into and Leave-Taking from the Labor Force

Women may follow a large variety of patterns in going into and out of the labor force. For many women, leaving the workforce may be relatively easy. Some may participate in maternity leave programs that allow them to reenter their position. On the other hand, others may wish to stay out for a longer period of time than their position can be held for. They may have to go through the process of job hunting all over again. For some, a career that was satisfactory prior to leaving the workforce may no longer be fulfilling. Managing both marriage and career may mean limiting social relationships, increasing organization and delegation of home and other activities, and developing flexible jobs that allow part-time work and time at home. Morgan and Foster (1999) emphasize the importance of complex cognitive processes for women reentering the workforce in dealing with multiple roles and gender discrimination. In counseling women, using assessment instruments that examine barriers to women's career entry can be helpful (McWhirter, Torres, & Rasheed, 1998).

The greater the coping strategies, the more likely it is that few of the phases that are discussed by Hopson and Adams (1977) will be experienced. However, for some women, entry or reentry into the workforce can be traumatic. Particularly if reentry is due to divorce or the death of a husband, a woman can find herself in an uncomfortable and unfamiliar position with sole responsibility for her income and survival, as well as the survival of her family. A decision to return to school may bring about a crisis. With the possibility of increased income in the distant future, school can become a financial burden. For women deciding on a new career, new training, or a return to school means returning to Super's exploration stage. When talking with a woman who is reentering the labor force, counselors may determine whether or not there are changes in self-esteem during the transition.

For example, Mary had been an elementary school teacher for seven years prior to having children but then decided to raise her family and stay at home with two young children for a six-year period. When her children were 4 and 6, she decided to return to the school system. In February, she contacted the principal of the school she had worked at and made arrangements to teach again in September. Excited about returning to work, she made arrangements for her children to go to school and attend an after-school program.

Rachel, on the other hand, had worked as a teacher for 6 years prior to raising a family of four children. After 20 years of marriage, her husband died suddenly, leaving her with few financial resources and two children in high school and two in college. She had disliked teaching and had had no plans to return to the workforce. Rachel had two crises to deal with: the death of her husband and the requirement that she return to work. Rachel's period of immobilization lasted four weeks. She was in shock over the sudden death of her husband. She did not experience a period of denial or minimization; rather, she became depressed, seeing no reason for living. Relatives helped with her children, but some grew impatient. Finally, Rachel let go of her grief somewhat and started to plan for her children. She made some attempts to get work and finally settled for a job as a grocery cashier. At this point, she had no energy to use her interests, abilities, or values. After a year as a cashier, she sought career counseling to help her decide what it was that she wished to do. A year and a half after her husband's death, she was moving back and forth between the stages of letting go and testing out, until she finally began to search for what might be most appropriate for her. These two examples illustrate the wide range of reactions possible when women reenter the labor force.

Sexual Harassment

When it occurs, depending on its nature, sexual harassment may be an unanticipated, involuntary crisis that threatens one's career and psychological health. In this section, we will define sexual harassment and discuss the different perceptions that people have of it. We will also examine who the victims are, how sexual harassment affects them, and what the stages are of reacting to sexual harassment. Also, we will look at an example of dealing with sexual harassment in the workplace.

Sexual harassment is a form of sexual discrimination that includes sexual threats, sexual bribery, sexual jokes or comments, and touching that interfere with a person doing her job (Welsh, 1999). Are sexual innuendos or sexual jokes harassment? Till (1980) described five levels of harassment, which Fitzgerald and Shullman (1985) built on in developing the Sexual Experience Questionnaire. Listed in order of severity, these levels are helpful in defining the different types of sexual harassment that women may experience (Paludi, DeFour, Attah, & Betts, 1999).

Level 1: Gender Harassment. This refers to verbal remarks or nontouching behaviors that are sexist in nature. Examples would include being told suggestive stories or being required to listen to rude, sexist remarks.

Level 2: Seductive Behavior. Included here are inappropriate sexual advances. The individual may attempt to discuss a woman's sex life or may express sexual interest in the woman.

Level 3: Sexual Bribery. This refers to the request for sexual activity in return for some kind of reward. Often offered by a superior, the bribe may be a higher grade in a course, a raise in pay, or a promotion.

Level 4: Sexual Coercion. This is the opposite of sexual bribery in that an individual is coerced into sexual activity by threat of punishment. For example, if a woman is told that, if she does not engage in sexual activity, she will fail a course, lose a job, or be demoted, she is being coerced. All are potentially threatening to a woman's career.

Level 5: Sexual Assault: Such behavior includes forceful attempts to touch, grab, fondle, or kiss.

These definitions provide a useful way of viewing the different ways in which individuals perceive sexual harassment. Not surprisingly, males and females are likely to view sexual harassment quite differently (Fitzgerald & Ormerod, 1993). Men and supervisors, whether male or female, tend to blame the victim for sexual harassment more than do women coworkers or female victims. However, when sexual harassment is severe, both men and women are likely to agree that the behavior is harassment. When the behaviors are shown as being romantic or seductive, then both men and women may have difficulty determining if the activity is sexual harassment. Examining employee response to sexual harassment allegations, men and women did not respond differently as to the definitions of sexual harassment, but women were more likely to attribute company responsibility for it than were men (Plater & Thomas, 1998). Stockdale (1993) discusses the role of misperception theory in understanding how women's friendly behavior is sometimes perceived as sexual behavior by men, and how some types of sexual harassment can be accounted for by misperceptions. In related work, Pryor, LaVite, and Stoller (1993) found that men who have tendencies toward sexual harassment are likely to link sexuality and social dominance in their thinking. O'Hare and O'Donohue (1998) found that sexual harassment was more likely to occur in a work setting that was unprofessional, had a sexist atmosphere, and where there was little knowledge of formal grievance policies than in a more professional and regulated

environment. Several recent studies have added to the literature on perceptions of sexual harassment, showing that the issue is more complex
than this brief review would imply (Williams, Giuffre, & Dellinger, 1999).

Given the different factors influencing the variety of perceptions of the
definition of sexual harassment, it is difficult to determine the incidence
of sexual harassment. Welsh (1999) reports estimates of adult women being sexually harassed that ranges from 16 to 90%. Many studies report 25
to 50%. Not surprisingly, the most frequent types of harassment are at the
least severe level. For example, Gutek (1985) conducted a telephone interview study in which 53% of the participants said that they had been sexually harassed: 15% reported harassment that included insulting looks and
gestures; 20% reported insulting comments; 24% reported sexual touching;
11% believed socializing on the job was expected; and 8% believed sexual
activity was expected. A very different finding was reported in a study of
3, 169 women working in the telephone industry: only 3% agreed or strongly
agreed that sexual harassment was a problem at work (DeCoster, Estes, &
Mueller, 1999). In a study of female secretaries and college students about
one-third of each reported some level of sexual harassment (Chan, Tang, &
Chan, 1999). Those who reported harassment also stated that they had less
satisfaction with studies or college work. As this small sample of research
shows, reports of sexual harassment may vary widely depending on where
and how it is studied.

Given the frequency of sexual harassment, who is most likely to be harassed? Fitzgerald and Ormerod (1993) report that sexual harassment is
rarely reported by males, except at the least severe level. The incidence of
same-sex sexual harassment is also relatively uncommon. Women who
have experienced sexual harassment previously are more likely to label as
a form of sexual harassment behavior that they may not have classified as
sexual harassment before.

Regarding age, women of all ages report sexual harassment, and single
women report more harassment than married women (Fitzgerald &
Ormerod, 1993). Relatively little information is available regarding the differences in the incidence of harassment for women of color and homosex-
ual women. Both groups may be harassed for their color or their sexual
preference as well as for their gender. African American female college students report receiving sexual attention based on racial stereotypes or racially
based physical features (Mecca & Rubin, 1999). Shelton and Chavous (1999)
found that white women and African American women perceive sexual harassment differently when the perpetrator is African American rather than
white and the victim is African American and female.

A variety of studies have examined differences in the incidence of
sexual harassment in different occupational groups. In a sample of female
lawyers, 66% working in private practice and 50% in corporate or public agency settings reported experiencing or observing sexual harassment within a 2-year period (Laband & Lentz, 1998). Gold (1987) reported
that blue-collar tradeswomen were much more likely to report sexual
harassment than were women who worked as secretaries, lawyers, or

accountants. Interviewing 22 African American female firefighters, Yoder and Aniakudo (1995) found that 20 reported sexual harassment; of these, 16 reported unwanted sexual touching. Sexual harassment has been a significant problem in the United States military, prompting action at all levels of leadership. In a study of over 28,000 military personnel it was found that sexual harassment occurs less frequently when males are aware that sexual harassment will not be tolerated by superior officers (Fitzgerald, Drasgow, & Magley, 1999). Researchers report that it is not the number of males working at a job site that is related to the incidence of sexual harassment, but the degree to which the work group is male-dominated.

How do victims of sexual harassment respond to the event? Fitzgerald and Ormerod (1993) summarize reactions, dividing them into two major categories: internally and externally focused strategies. Internally focused strategies include those which Hobson and Adams observed, such as minimizing a behavior or denying that it is really offensive. Other internal strategies are to put up with the harassment, to excuse the offender ("He didn't really mean it"), or to take responsibility for the incident ("I should have been wearing different clothes"). Externally focused strategies include avoiding or placating the harasser. Other approaches are more assertive, such as confronting the harasser and telling him that the behavior is unwanted. Yoder and Aniakudo (1995) reported that about half of their sample of firefighters responded to sexual harassment with aggressive verbal remarks, and that a few responded physically, such as pushing the harasser up against a wall. Other external responses include getting support from the institution, such as an appropriate supervisor, and getting social support from friends or family. Such events tend to affect other work-related attitudes, including relationships with supervisors and coworkers and general work satisfaction (Reese & Lindenberg, 1999).

Gutek and Koss (1993) document how sexual harassment affects the careers of women as well as their physical and psychological well-being. A study by the U.S. Merit Systems Protection Board (1981) showed that over 36,000 federal employees quit their jobs or were transferred, reassigned, or fired after they reported sexual harassment. In 88 sexual harassment cases filed with the California Department of Fair Employment and Housing, half of the individuals were fired and 25% quit because of fear or frustration (Coles, 1986). Other studies show negative effects on relationships with coworkers and company loyalty. Gutek and Koss (1993) summarize studies that show that self-esteem and life satisfaction are negatively affected. Physical symptoms that were reported included stomach ailments, teeth grinding, nausea, and sleeplessness. Additionally, sexual harassment may contribute to posttraumatic stress disorder and depression (Gutek & Koss, 1993).

Sexual harassment is usually not a single event, but a series of events occurring over a period of weeks or months. Gutek and Koss describe four stages of reacting to sexual harassment that can occur over time.

Confusion and Self-Blame. Individuals may assume the responsibility for being harassed. They may be upset by their inability to stop the harassment, which may begin to worsen.

Fear and Anxiety. Fear for her career or safety may cause a woman to be afraid to drive home or to answer the phone and may affect her work performance. Her attendance at work and her ability to concentrate on her work may suffer.

Depression and Anger. When a woman recognizes that she is not responsible for the harassment, she may become less anxious and more angry. If charges are filed, the work situation may get worse, and the individual may feel despair over her progress on her job.

Disillusionment. The process of bringing charges against a harasser may be long and arduous and may not always have a successful outcome. Many organizations are not supportive of women who choose to follow through on harassment charges.

These stages bear some resemblance to those of Hopson and Adams. They differ in that they do not assume the organizational or social support of those of Hopson and Adams. Women often feel powerless when harassed by a supervisor or coworker and may feel little support from other coworkers or superiors in their organization. When predicting which women would report sexual harassment, Adams and Barling (1998) found that assertiveness behavior and perceptions of a just reporting system were important factors. For individuals wishing to prevent and deal with sexual harassment in the workplace, manuals by Paludi and Barickman (1998) and Reese and Lindenberg (1999) should prove helpful. In the following example, the client reacts to a sexual harassment situation assertively and with power. Because she negotiates the situation well, her process of working through the incident pertains more to the optimistic model of Hopson and Adams than to the more pessimistic model of Gutek and Koss.

Roberta is a 30-year-old lawyer working in a large New York City law firm. One of five children from a poor Puerto Rican family in New York, Roberta has worked her way through college and law school with the help of scholarships that she has earned. Specializing in tax matters, Roberta has been pleased with her training and is looking forward to the opportunity to advance in this firm, which she joined six months ago. She worked for a smaller law firm for three years after graduation but felt limited. She was offered a substantial pay raise to come to her new firm. One day, as she is bending over to pick up a pencil that fell off her desk, her immediate supervisor, the head of the tax law department, pats her buttocks. She is shocked by what has happened and continues with her work, growing angrier and angrier as the day goes on. When she is leaving at the end of the day, her superior says to her, "Let me help you on with your coat." Before she has a chance to respond, he helps her with her coat, brushing his hand against her breast. She says to him coldly, "Don't do that. Get your hands away from me." He responds, "Don't complain. I didn't mean anything." Shaking as she leaves work, she goes home to her apartment, quickly calling a respected friend who is an affirmative action officer at the university that she attended as an undergraduate:

CL: I can't believe what happened today. I've got to talk to you about it. My boss, who has said hardly anything to me since I've been here, touched me twice today—on my backside and on my breast. Can you believe that!?Then the stupid jerk has the nerve to say to me, "Don't complain!" Who does he think he is?

CO: What a terrible thing! Absolutely awful. [Having dealt with situations like this before, her friend knows this is not the time to make suggestions, although she knows methods of dealing with such situations. Recognizing that Roberta has gotten over the shock, is not minimizing what has happened, and is very angry, not depressed, she wants to listen. The fact that Roberta's reaction does not fit neatly into Hopson and Adams's theory of transition is unimportant.]

CL: I never expected that to happen. That fool—who does he think he is, that he can touch me like that!

CO: I've never heard you so angry—really, really furious. [Being aware of Roberta's anger, the counselor listens to her, knowing that, when it is time to move from this phase, Roberta will determine it.]

At the end of the 45-minute conversation, Roberta finally says, "I know I've got to do something about this. Can I call you back later tonight? I just need to sit down." Her friend agrees, and later that night, they do discuss possible actions. They talk about how to confront the supervisor, who else to talk to in the law firm, and how to proceed. By doing this, Roberta is letting go of her reaction to the situation so that she can deal with it. Being strongly committed to the role of working and being at the beginning of the establishment stage, Roberta, rather than starting to stabilize her career, now has to deal with an extremely destabilizing event. Ideally, she will be able to deal with it in such a way that her superior will be punished and his behavior will desist. However, the possibility exists that Roberta could lose her job and face a lengthy suit against her law firm. The potential ramifications of such an incident may affect not only her career mobility, but also her self-esteem. Being fired could lead to much self-questioning on her part, even though the situation was not of her making.

CAREER CRISES AFFECTING CULTURALLY DIVERSE POPULATIONS

Discrimination is well documented as a major problem for members of minority groups in their career development. Thomas and Alderfer (1989) present a thorough review of the effect of discrimination on culturally diverse adults in organizations. Discrimination is discussed in more detail in Chapter 15 in terms of the social structure of the U.S. labor market. Particularly when one is in the establishment or maintenance phase of one's career and work is important to one's self-esteem, discrimination can be quite damaging. An interesting approach to this concern was taken by Burlew and Johnson (1992), who contrasted barriers to movement toward career success among African American women. They reported that African American women in traditional occupations such as counseling and teaching experienced fewer barriers to success, such as race and gender discrimination, marital discord, and colleagues' doubt about their competence, than did African American women who were in nontraditional occupations such as law, engineering, and medicine. McWhirter, Torres, and Rasheed (1998) discuss how career barriers can be approached with an East Indian American Muslim woman. Barriers to choice can present a variety of crises that are affected by diverse cultural issues.

Discrimination takes many forms. Overhearing a customer in a department store say "nigger" to another customer, even though it is not directed at the African American salesperson, is offensive. Being denied promotion, attractive assignments, raises, or other advantages because of racism can be devastating to an individual. When discrimination occurs, a person is likely to experience a crisis, as described by Hopson and Adams. How the individual deals with that crisis will depend in some part on the situation, the supervisor, and the individual's own temperament. The model proposed by Atkinson, Morten, and Sue (1998), as outlined in Table 9-3 in the previous chapter, may describe how an individual deals with a job-related crisis caused by discrimination. For example, an individual in Atkinson et al.'s Stage 1, conformity, may blame himself or herself when faced with discrimination by a white superior, whereas someone in Stage 3, resistance and immersion, may lose self-control and respond angrily in dealing with a white superior. In Stage 5, synergetic articulation and awareness, an individual may be able to effectively confront his or her superior—and others, if need be—to remedy the discriminatory situation.

These individuals may go through Hopson and Adams's stages very differently. The person in Atkinson et al.'s Stage 1 may be stuck in Hopson and Adams's Phases 1 and 2 for some time: being shocked by the discrimination and then minimizing it—in essence, denying its importance. The person in Atkinson et al.'s Stage 3 may move quickly to Hopson and Adams's third phase of self-doubt and experience a great deal of anger. He or she may not move beyond that stage. In contrast, individuals in Stage 5 may move rather quickly through, or may skip entirely, Hopson and Adams's phases of immobilization, minimization, and self-doubt and may proceed to letting go and testing out. Ultimately, they may have a better sense of themselves for having handled the discriminatory situation positively. However, the nature of discrimination is such that, no matter how articulate and aware people from minority groups may be, the "dominant group" may exert its power destructively.

For an example of discrimination as a crisis, let us return to Roberta. If we use Roberta as an example, the notion of "double jeopardy" can be illustrated. *Double jeopardy* refers to the fact that women from minority groups may face occupational barriers both because they are women and because they are culturally different.

Roberta was able to handle the situation with her sexist superior in a positive way. She discussed her experience with one of the law partners who had hired her. Three weeks after the incident, the supervisor left the firm. Roberta had heard rumors that similar incidents had happened to two other women in the firm. No forthright explanation was ever given of what had happened.

Roberta continued to work for the firm, being given more and more responsible tasks and being put in charge of the tax portion of large corporate accounts and for wealthy clients. When a senior member of the tax department left to join another firm, her accounts were divided among the members of the department. Two weeks after being put in charge of the tax aspect of one of the firm's largest accounts, the Doe Corporation, Roberta was told that it would be given to someone else. When she asked her new superior why that was, he became embarrassed and talked about how another member of the department had expertise that she lacked. Roberta knew that the individual mentioned did not have more expertise than she had in that matter and that the Doe Corporation had a reputation of being conservative and discriminatory.

Her immediate reaction was shock when she realized what was happening. Having experienced racism several times during her life because she was Puerto Rican, she was surprised that it would occur among people whom she believed to be philanthropic and intelligent. Having gone through the stages described by Atkinson, Morten, and Sue (1998) and having arrived at Stage 5, synergetic articulation and awareness, she did not minimize the situation, nor would she take responsibility for it by doubting herself or being depressed. She had observed hypocrisy in large corporations that stated that they had an affirmative action policy but did not act as if they did. Roberta was able to talk with her superior about different strategies for handling the situation. She talked with him about not making the switch and leaving the account in her hands. He accepted her advice and returned to a representative of the Doe Corporation to discuss it. She felt empowered by how she had handled the situation and by her superior's appreciation of her advice.

COUNSELOR ISSUES

Two major issues confront counselors when dealing with clients in a career crisis or transition. The first concerns the counselor's own experience with his or her own past transitions. The second concerns counseling when one is in a crisis oneself. Regarding the first, counselors need to remember that each individual experiences a crisis differently. Even though a counselor may have experienced being laid off from work at one time, the counselor may have been in a different life-span stage from the client's. Experiencing different phases of the transition and valuing different life roles would make the counselor's response different from the client's. One helpful idea that counselors can learn from their experiences with transitions is that no one can move a person through phases; a person in crisis works through phases at his or her own pace.

The second issue deals with how counselors respond when they are themselves in crisis. Crises and transformations can consume much energy and time. A counselor going through a divorce or job loss may be able to think of little else. Seeking counseling is often extremely helpful. Sometimes, that is not sufficient, and the counselor temporarily or permanently removes himself or herself from the counseling situation. It is particularly the first three phases of Hopson and Adams's model that require much self-preoccupation. The phases of letting go, testing out, search for meaning, and internalization lend themselves to less preoccupation than do the first three phases.

SUMMARY

Career crises and transitions tend to be most difficult to handle when they are unanticipated and involuntary. Further, if they are experienced at a time when work-role salience is high for an individual and that person is in the establishment and maintenance stages as described by Super, then considerable trauma may occur. Hopson and Adams (1977) offer a seven-phase model for understanding crises that can be applied to career transition. Women and people from different cultures may experience discrimination as a type of adult life transition or crisis that white males do not experience. Further, women may encounter difficult situations in terms of reentering or leaving the world of work because of child-raising issues. Also, sexual harassment can be devastating to a woman's career development and sense of self at whatever time in the life span it occurs. Responding to a wide variety of career-related transitions is a fairly common occurrence for counselors or therapists who counsel working adults.

References

Adams, R. J., & Barling, J. (1998). Predicting the decision to confront or report sexual harassment. *Journal of Organizational Behavior, 4,* 329–336.

Aquilanti, T. M., & Leroux, J. (1999). An integrated model of outplacement counseling. *Journal of Employment Counseling, 4,* 177–191.

Atkinson, D. R., Morten, G., & Sue, D. W. (1998). *Counseling American minorities: A cross-cultural perspective* (5th ed.). New York: McGraw-Hill.

Bardwick, J. (1980). The seasons of a woman's life. In D. McGuigan (Ed.), *Women's lives: New theory, research, and policy* (pp. 35–57). Ann Arbor: University of Michigan, Center for Continuing Education of Women.

Betz, N. E., & Fitzgerald, L. F. (1987). *The career psychology of women.* Orlando, FL: Academic Press.

Brammer, L. M., & Abrego, P. J. (1981). Intervention strategies for coping with transitions. *The Counseling Psychologist, 9* (2), 19–35.

Bruce, R. A., & Scott, S. G. (1994). Varieties and commonalities of career transitions: Louis' typology revisited. *Journal of Vocational Behavior, 45,* 17–40.

Burlew, A. K., & Johnson, J. C. (1992). Role conflict and career advancement among African American women in nontraditional professions. *The Career Development Quarterly, 40,* 291–301.

Chan, D. K. S., Tang, C. S. K., & Chan, W. (1999). Sexual harassment: A preliminary analysis of its effects on Hong Kong Chinese women in the workplace and academia. *Psychology of Women Quarterly, 4,* 661–672.

Cohen, L., & Mallon, M. (1999). The transition from organizational employment to portfolio working: Perceptions of "Boundaryless." *Work, Employment and Society, 13,* 329–352.

Coles, F. S. (1986). Forced to quit: Sexual harassment complaints and agency response. *Sex Roles, 14,* 81–95.

Dalton, D. R., & Wimbush, J. C. (1998). Employment transfer: Review and research agenda. In G. R. Ferris (Ed.), *Research in personnel and human resources management,* (Vol. 16, pp. 331–358). Stanford, CT: Jai Press.

DeCoster, S., Estes, S. B., & Mueller, C. W. (1999). Routine activities and sexual harassment in the workplace. *Work and Occupations, 26,* 21–49.

Eby, L. T., & Buch, K. (1995). Job loss as career growth: Responses to involuntary career transitions. *The Career Development Quarterly, 44,* 26–42.

Edwards, J. M., Rudisill, J. R., Champney, T. F., Hershberger, P. J., Polaine, V. H., & Archambault, D. L. (1998). Outplacement: Client characteristics and outcomes. *Consulting Psychology Journal: Practice and Research, 50,* 173–180.

Fitzgerald, L. F., Drasgow, F., & Magley, V. J. (1999). Sexual harassment in the armed forces: A test of an integrated model. *Military Psychology, 11,* 329–343.

Fitzgerald, L. F., & Ormerod, A. J. (1993). Breaking silence: The sexual harassment of women in academia and the workplace. In F. L. Denmark and M. A. Paludi (Eds.), *Psychology of women: A handbook of issues and theories* (pp. 553–581). Westport, CT: Greenwood.

Fitzgerald, L. F., & Shullman, S. L. (1985). *The development and validation of an objectively scored measure of sexual harassment.* Paper presented at the convention of the American Psychological Association.

Gold, Y. (1987). *The sexualization of the workplace: Sexual harassment of pink-, white-, and blue-collar workers.* Paper presented at the annual conference of the American Psychological Association, New York.

Gutek, B. (1985). *Sex and the workplace.* San Francisco: Jossey-Bass.

Gutek, B. A., & Koss, M. P. (1993). Changed women and changed organizations: Consequences of and coping with sexual harassment. *Journal of Vocational Behavior, 42,* 28–48.

Heppner, M. J. (1998). The Career Transitions Inventory: Measuring internal resources in adulthood. *Journal of Career Assessment, 6,* 135–145.

Heppner, M. J., Fuller, B. E., & Multon, K. D. (1998). Adults in involuntary career transition: An analysis of the relationship between the psychological and career domains. *Journal of Career Assessment, 6,* 329–346.

Heppner, M. J., Multon, K. D., & Johnston, J. A. (1994). Assessing psychological resources during career change: Development of the Career Transitions Inventory. *Journal of Vocational Behavior, 44,* 55–74.

Hill, R. (1949). *Families under stress.* New York: Harpers.

Hopson, B. (1981). Response to papers by Schlossberg, Brammer, and Abrego. *The Counseling Psychologist, 9* (2), 36–39.

Hopson, B., & Adams, J. D. (1977). Towards an understanding of transitions: Defining some boundaries of transition. In J. Adams, J. Hayes, & B. Hopson (Eds.), *Transition: Understanding and managing personal change* (pp. 1–19). Montclair, NJ: Allenheld & Osmun.

Laband, D. N., & Lentz, B. F. (1998). The effects of sexual harassment on job satisfaction, earnings, and turnover among female lawyers. *Industrial and Labor Relations Review, 51,* 594–607.

Leana, C. R., Feldman, D. C., & Tan, G. Y. (1998). Predictors of coping behavior after a layoff. *Journal of Organizational Behavior, 19,* 85–97.

Lissack, M., & Roos, J. (1999). *The next common sense: Mastering corporate complexity through coherence.* London: Nicholas Brealey Publishing.

Louis, M. (1980a). Career transitions: Varieties and commonalities. *Academy of Management Review, 5,* 329–340.

Louis, M. (1980b). Surprise and sense-making: What newcomers experience in entering unfamiliar organizational settings. *Administrative Science Quarterly, 25,* 226–251.

Malen, E. A., & Stroh, L. K. (1998). The influence of gender on job loss coping behavior among unemployed managers. *Journal of Employment Counseling, 35,* 26–39.

McWhirter, E. H., Torres, D., & Rasheed, S. (1998). Assessing barriers to women's career adjustment. *Journal of Career Assessment, 6,* 449–479.

Mecca, S. J., & Rubin, L. J. (1999). Definitional research on African American students and sexual harassment. *Psychology of Women Quarterly, 23,* 813–817.

Mirvis, P. H., & Hall, D. T. (1994). Psychological success and the boundaryless career. *Journal of Organizational Behavior, 15,* 365–380.

Moos, R. H., & Schaefer, I. A. (1986). Life transitions and crises: A conceptual overview. In R. H. Moos (Ed.), *Coping with life crises: An integrated approach* (pp. 3–28). New York: Plenum Press.

Moos, R. H., & Tsu, V. (1976). Human competence and coping: An overview. In R. H. Moos (Ed.), *Human adaptation: Coping with life crises* (pp. 3–16). Lexington, MA: Heath.

Morgan, B., & Foster, V. (1999). Career counseling for reentry dual career women: A cognitive development approach. *Journal of Career Development, 26,* 125–136.

O'Hare, E. A., & O'Donohue, W. (1998). Sexual harassment: Identifying risk factors. *Archives of Sexual Behavior, 27,* 561–580.

Paludi, M. A., & Barickman, R. B. (1998). *Sexual harassment, work, and education: A resource manual for prevention* (2nd ed.). Albany State University of New York Press.

Paludi, M. A., DeFour, D. C., Attah, K., & Betts, J. (1999). Sexual harassment in education and the workplace: A view from the field of psychology. In M. A. Paludi (Ed.), *The psychology of sexual victimization: A handbook* (pp. 119–149). Westport, CT: Greenwood.

Perosa, S., & Perosa, L. (1983). The mid-career crisis: A description of the psychological dynamics of transition and adaptation. *Vocational Guidance Quarterly, 32,* 60–79.

Perosa, S., & Perosa, L. (1985). The mid-career crisis in relation to Super's career and Erikson's adult development theory. *International Journal of Aging and Human Development, 20* (l), 53–68.

Perosa, S., & Perosa, L. (1987). Strategies for counseling mid-career changers: A conceptual framework. *Journal of Counseling and Development, 65,* 558–561.

Perosa, L. M., & Perosa, S. L. (1997). Assessments for use with mid-career changers. *Journal of Career Assessment, 5,* 151–165.

Phillips, W. E. (1999). The effectiveness of a cognitive behavioral stress reduction program in outplacement counseling. *Dissertation Abstracts International: Section A: Humanities and Social Sciences, 59* (8-A): 2871.

Plater, M. A., & Thomas, R. E. (1998). The impact of job performance, gender, and ethnicity on the managerial review of sexual harassment allegations. *Journal of Applied Social Psychology, 28,* 52–70.

Pryor, J. B., LaVite, C. M., & Stoller, L. M. (1993). A social psychological analysis of sexual harassment: The period situation interaction. *Journal of Vocational Behavior, 42,* 68–83.

Reese, L. A., & Lindenberg, K. E. (1999). *Implementing sexual harassment policy: Challenges for the public sector workplace.* Thousand Oaks, CA: Sage.

Schlossberg, N. K. (1984). *Counseling adults in transition.* New York: Springer.

Schlossberg, N. K., & Leibowitz, Z. B. (1980). Organizational support systems as buffers to job loss. *Journal of Vocational Behavior, 17,* 204–217.

Shelton, J. N., & Chavous, T. M. (1999). Black and White college women's perceptions of sexual harassment. *Sex Roles, 40,* 593–615.

Sparrow, P. R., & Daniels, K. (1999). Human resource management and the virtual organization: Mapping the future research issues. In C. L. Cooper & D. M. Rousseau (Eds.), *Trends in organizational behavior: Vol. 6. The virtual organization* (pp. 45–61). Chichester, England: John Wiley & Sons, Ltd.

Stockdale, M. S. (1993). The role of sexual misperceptions of women's friendliness in an emerging theory of sexual harassment. *Journal of Vocational Behavior, 42,* 84–101.

Sullivan, S. E. (1999). The changing nature of careers: A review and research agenda. *Journal of Management, 25,* 457–484.

Thomas, D. A., & Alderfer, C. P. (1989). The influence of race on career dynamics: Theory and research on minority career experiences. In M. A. Arthur, D. T. Hall, & B. S. Lawrence (Eds.), *Handbook of career theory* (pp. 133–158). New York: Cambridge University Press.

Till, F. (1980). *Sexual harassment: A report on the sexual harassment of students.* Washington, DC: National Advisory Council on Women's Educational Programs.

U.S. Merit Systems Protection Board. (1981). *Sexual harassment of federal workers: Is it a problem?* Washington, DC: U.S. Government Printing Office.

Welsh, S. (1999). Gender and sexual harassment. *Annual Review of Sociology, 25,* 169–190.

Williams, C. L., Giuffre, P. A., & Dellinger, K. (1999). Sexuality in the workplace: Organizational control, sexual harassment, and the pursuit of pleasure. *Annual Review of Sociology, 25,* 73–93.

Yoder, J. D., & Aniakudo, P. (1995). The responses of African American women firefighters to gender harassment at work. *Sex Roles, 32,* 125–137.

PART THREE
Special Focus Theories

Several theories have been developed that represent different ways of viewing the career selection process. Many of these theories have taken psychological theory and applied it to career development. In Chapter 11, personal construct psychology and narrative counseling are applied to career development. Both are constructivist approaches that emphasize understanding clients' perceptions of their world. Chapter 12 describes attempts to predict occupational choice from parents' child-raising styles, as well as examines the effect of attachment to parents on career decision making and how parents can be involved in career counseling with their children. Anne Roe's occupational classification system is also described. Learning theory and behavioral approaches in psychology have also had an impact on career development theory. These are described in Chapter 13 in Krumboltz's social learning theory of career development, which focuses on a systematic approach to career decision making, as well as career social cognitive theory, which features the role of self-efficacy. In Chapter 14, three different career decision-making theories are described. Tiedeman describes a developmental approach that can be applied to career counseling. Counselors who take a spiritual approach emphasize personal values and beliefs in making career decisions. In contrast, cognitive information processing theory examines how individuals can improve their career decision making by understanding and changing their thought processes. Differing from psychological approaches, Chapter 15 illustrates the contribution of sociology and economic theory to the labor market and to career development issues. Each of these chapters provides important perspectives that may be useful in counseling.

Constructivist Approaches to Career Development

Constructivism is a psychological approach that has developed out of a philosophical position, *postmodernism*, which believes that individuals construct or perceive their own reality or truth, and that there is no fixed truth (Neimeyer & Stewart, 1998). Postmodernism is a reaction to *modernism*, which takes a *rationalist* approach that emphasizes scientific proof and is a reflection of advances in technology and science. Postmodernism reflects a multiculturally diverse world in which psychologists, counselors, philosophers, and others have recognized that different individuals can have their own construct or view of what is real for them.

Related to postmodernism is *constructivism*. Constructivists view individuals as creating their own views of events and relationships in their lives. Constructivist counselors attend not only to the meanings that their clients' give to their own problems, but also help clients see problems as meaningful options that are no longer helpful. Constructivist counselors deal with the ways in which their clients' impose their own order on their problems and how they derive meanings from their experiences with others.

Constructivist theories of counseling and therapy owe their beginnings to the work of George Kelly (1955). Kelly believed that personal constructs are ways that individuals interpret and view their lives. He felt that individuals' careers are a major means of giving one's life role clarity and meaning. Extending this focus, constructivists not only look at how people fit into the world of work, but how the world of work fits into individuals' lives (Savickas, 1993, 1994).

Much of the work on constructivist approaches to career counseling has been done since the 1980s. One reason for this is that the structure of occupations has changed since the 1970s. There was a time in which individuals might have an occupation and spend their whole life in that occupation and job. Now, there is less loyalty by companies to employees, more "downsizing," and more workers who are hired part-time or as consultants. As Savickas (1997) points out, the notion of matching people with positions is no longer as attractive as it once was, as individuals are changing occupations more frequently. Rather than corporations being managers of people's careers, individuals themselves must manage their careers. Counselors can be helpful to clients by helping them draw meaning from their own lives, not just by understanding an organization. In the post modern age, careers now take twists and turns that they did not prior to the 1970s. The career counselor then focuses on careers not as lifetime employment, but as a way of providing meaning to individuals.

This chapter will describe two different constructivist approaches to career counseling. Each of these approaches (personal construct psychology and narrative counseling) shares an emphasis on understanding clients' values or constructs (the way they see the world). Personal construct counseling is based on Kelly's approach to understanding ways in which clients view their reality, particularly as it applies to occupational selection. In the narrative approach the client is seen as an active player in a story. Cochran's seven-episode counseling method shows how clients can actively understand their own career story and apply this understanding to actively constructing the future of their careers. The organization and development of this chapter is based on Savickas's (1997) conceptualization of constructivist career counseling methods.

PERSONAL CONSTRUCT PSYCHOLOGY

Of the two approaches to constructivist theory that are described in this chapter, personal construct psychology is the one based most closely on the work of George Kelly (1955) and his 1,200 page book, *The Psychology of Personal Constructs*. Basic to Kelly's theory is that individuals view the world differently from each other, a concept called *constructive alternativism*. To make sense of their world, individuals develop constructs or theories toward viewing people and events. In essence, individuals behave as scientists predicting events by advancing theories about them and then testing the theories. Individuals have unique sets of constructs that are continually being modified to enhance their predictions. The more predictive a set of constructs are, the more likely they are to be stable.

Constructs are bipolar-reflecting opposites, such as smart versus stupid. Not all constructs are applied to all events. Rather, constructs have a range of convenience, meaning they apply to some events and not others. Constructs are arranged in terms of how meaningful they are to individuals. Some constructs may be used rarely, others frequently. Additionally, individuals vary in the number of constructs they use and in the rate of developing new constructs.

Constructs can be grouped into themes, as constructs apply to all areas of human life. For our purposes the phrase "vocational construct system," which Kelly (1955) described, includes constructs related to the work role and to vocational choice. The vocational construct system helps individuals to find a purpose in work, control how they work, evaluate the choices they make and the work they do, and develop a sense of identity through work.

Vocational construct systems change as individuals develop. As individuals learn more about themselves and occupations, their constructs may become clearer and they may become more aware of them. When life transitions such as marriage, graduating college, taking a new job, or being laid off occur, then these concepts are subject to change. The vocational construct system then changes as individuals cope with new issues in their lives. In the course of normal development or in reaction to a crisis or transition, differentiation and integration may occur.

Differentiation refers to an increasing number of constructs, which are different from each other and diverse. For example, the more constructs there are within a vocational construct system, the more likely an individual is to develop deeper understanding of areas related to career choice and work. Fine distinctions may exist between one's view of mathematical abilities or the role of statisticians. As the vocational system becomes more complex, it provides more value and function to individuals. However, the larger or more differentiated construct systems become, the greater need there is to organize them.

Integration refers to the organization of a system by relating the constructs to each other. In this way constructs are grouped in themes (Cochran, 1977). For example, an individual may have a theme of vocational abilities that may include constructs dealing with mathematical, English, and other abilities. Another theme may deal with the individual's academic value system that may include valuing mathematics and English. As the individual is exposed to new information, these two themes, academic ability and academic value, may be reformulated or changed. Integration refers not to the acquiring of information, but to the reorganizing of new constructs into themes (Savickas, 1997). As individuals integrate new constructs into themes and the themes change, their view of themselves and the world of work change.

Too much differentiation or integration can cause problems for individuals. If individuals develop many constructs without organizing them, this can lead to confusion and indecision. If individuals integrate constructs into too many themes, then confusion can result. Further, it can be difficult to integrate new constructs into themes if the system is already very complexly organized. Integration and differentiation are concepts that help individuals develop a flexible view of the world of work and of themselves in relationship to it. Constructivist counselors may work to help individuals understand the constructs that they use to relate to their world. They also help individuals to learn about new constructs that help them to find perceptions of themselves and the world of work. Integrating these constructs into useful themes can be another aspect of constructivist career counseling. Counselors can also help clients to see values that are inherent in their constructs and to relate interests that are not constructs to them.

Values and Interests

Constructs are not events, but perceptions of events. These perceptions can be viewed as values because they represent judgments and evaluations that individuals have about themselves and their world. These values help individuals cope with their world. How people value aspects of their world varies widely. For example, some individuals may view the occupation of funeral director with constructs such as depressing–happy, boring–interesting, emotionally draining–exciting. The individual's value system of funeral director may include sad, boring, and emotionally–draining. Certainly, not all individuals who do not want to be funeral directors will use the same constructs in their perception of that occupation. Funeral directors themselves, may have a different set of constructs such as helping others–hurting others, energizing–boring, and helping the community–self-centered. Thus, some funeral directors may use these constructs, valuing that occupation as helping others, energizing, and serving the community.

In contrast to values, interests are not perceptions that lie within the person, rather they are a connection between the individual's perceptions and social situations (Savickas, 1997). For example, funeral directors may be interested in roles where they help others, are energized, and serve the community. They may have interest in being a funeral director, but also social work, and counseling as they represent connections between the individuals' values of constructs and actual situations. The values of helping others, being energized, and serving the community are not restricted to occupations. Individuals may apply these values to develop interests in church activities or volunteer work with children. In a sense, constructs are more flexible than interests because they can be applied to many different activities and events. Interests, on the other hand, refer to specific situations, such as "I enjoy skating," "I enjoy reading the newspaper," "I enjoy teaching small children."

Although individuals can have a great variety of values that lead to the development of interests, this chapter will focus on vocational values or constructs. Constructs can be studied not only in terms of the ways that they can be differentiated into more constructs, and integrated into themes, but also into ways that they develop. In the next section, we will examine a way of differentiating developmental stages in vocational construct systems.

Developmental Stages of Vocational Construct Systems

Greg Neimeyer and his collegues (Neimeyer, 1988; Nevill, Neimeyer, Probert, & Fukuyama, 1986) have described four stages in the development of a vocational construct system. This system uses knowledge of dichotomous constructs, differentiation, and integration, as well as an understanding of human development to provide a way of viewing vocational development from a constructivist point of view. Although focusing on the development of constructs, their view has similarities to the life stages of Super (1957) (Chapter 9) and the decision-making stages of Tiedeman and O'Hara (1963) (Chapter 14). Stages of the development of vocational construct systems are useful not only in further understanding a personal construct approach to career development, but in helping counselors see the type of interventions that may be useful in counseling clients as they move from one stage to another.

Stage 1   In this stage individuals have relatively few vocationally related constructs and have not integrated them to a great degree. In other words, there is low differentiation with low integration of constructs. At this point individuals do not have a sufficient number of constructs for understanding themselves in terms of the world of work. Their values need to be developed so that they can more fully expand their interests, and they may need to increase their knowledge of occupational information. Values clarification exercises and inventories may be helpful to them in further developing vocational constructs.

Stage 2   Individuals develop more constructs and their vocational themes are more clearly organized than in the previous stage. They are developing more constructs dealing with abilities and values as well as specific occupations. Clients who are in this second stage may focus on organizing their vocational construct systems. Classification systems with relatively few categories, such as Holland's RIASEC hexagonal model (Chapter 4) and Roe's field-and-level occupational classification system (Chapter 12), may prove particularly useful. These methods provide a way of organizing interests and constructs regarding occupations.

Stage 3   With increased differentiation come new constructs. Individuals develop more specific information about themselves and occupations. For example, they may be able to differentiate constructs that describe occupations such as purchasing agent, buyer, and assistant buyer. If this information is not integrated into new themes, then individuals may experience some anxiety. Counselors may find it helpful to show clients how to explore occupations by talking to people at their work site, taking specific courses, or finding relevant part-time jobs or volunteer work. Such experiences will further differentiate the vocational construct system.

Stage 4   At this stage, new concepts have been developed, and a new organization of constructs that are systematically related is now present. Constructs are highly differentiated and very well integrated into a system so that individuals can specify occupational choices and appropriate alternatives. At this point, counselors may encourage clients when they describe the choices that they have made. They may also talk further with clients about implementing their choices.

The four stages of the development of vocational construct systems of Neimeyer and his colleagues are based on constructs and their differentiation and integration. This system of developmental stages differs from that of Super and Tiedeman (Chapter 14) because of the emphasis on the development of dichotomous constructs. Super focuses more on work roles and Tiedeman on career decision making. These four stages provide a context for viewing techniques that constructivist career counselors use in assessing and counseling their clients.

Assessment and Counseling Strategies

In constructivist career counseling, the counselor is learning about and working with the client's career theory. As the counselor and client use various techniques to explore the client's constructs, the constructs are likely to develop, becoming more specified and more diverse. Techniques that help to assess clients' perceptions of constructs about themselves and the occupational world are likely to lead to new constructs and the development of themes. Whereas in trait and factor theory, some counselors may make a specific differentiation between assessing client interest, ability, and values and then giving clients information about their traits. Constructivist counselors typically interact in a very collaborative way with their clients, making it difficult to separate the assessment process from the counseling process. Although the three techniques discussed in this section, the reptest, laddering, and the card sort, are assessment techniques, use of these techniques helps clients move from Stage 1 to Stage 3 of the developmental stages of the vocational construct systems. In this sense, these techniques are part of the counseling process.

The Vocational Reptest

The most widely used instrument within personal construct theory has been the "Role Construct Repertory Test," which is known as the *reptest*. It has been widely adapted for a variety of purposes by both counselors and researchers. Neimeyer (1992) has adapted the reptest for career purposes. The reptest differs from standard interest inventories and values scales because the client provides much of the information used in the reptest.

In the version that Neimeyer (1992) provides, clients describe constructs that relate to 10 occupations. There is nothing magic about the number ten; 8 or 12 could be used, perhaps more, but that might be unwieldy. Although occupations are used, other aspects of career-relevant experience would also be appropriate, such as majors, people that the client knows, or famous people. All would be valuable in developing an understanding of the client's construct theory. In fact, there may be occasions when the counselor may wish to use the reptest with occupations and then again with a list of 10 famous people.

When the vocational reptest is presented to a client, the client is asked to compare and contrast various sets of items. When occupations are used, three occupations are presented at a time and the client is asked to "indicate any way in which you see two of these occupations as alike in some way, but different from the third" (Neimeyer, 1992, p. 165). A client may say that two occupations "require a lot of education," whereas the third "requires little education." This discrimination ("requires a lot versus little education") is a vocational construct. It serves as a basis for perceiving, discriminating, or evaluating a wide range of possible occupations. After eliciting this construct, the counselor may present the client with three different constructs and again ask him or her to "indicate any way in which two of these are alike, but different from the third." Two occupations may be seen as "working with people" and the third as "working alone," and this procedure is continued until a set of ten vocational constructs are elicited. Each pair of differences represents a personal construct that can be used to evaluate other occupations.

When the individual has finished comparing occupations, then he or she may be asked to rate or rank each occupation according to each construct, using some method of rating (such as a 7-point rating scale) or ranking (such as from 1 to 10). As the client develops these evaluations, the counselor begins to understand important constructs that the client uses. Neimeyer gives an example of a vocational reptest, describing how it is used with Jean, a 19-year-old woman who has a variety of dimensions and unique constructs. In describing Jean's reptest (Figure 11-1), Neimeyer states:

> Because the positive side of each construct is placed to the left of its more negative counterpart we can also see Jean's own preferences. She values indoor over outdoor work, for example, jobs that don't require "much education" (despite the fact that she is in college!) over ones that do, greater freedom over lots of rules and regulations, and so on.
>
> By scanning down the columns of her occupational ratings, we can also see how she views specific occupational alternatives. Farming, for example, garners eight out of twelve negative ratings, in contrast with being a lawyer, which has only two negative ratings associated with it. These perceptions represent Jean's own constructions, of course, and may or may not reflect "reality," or the ways in which the people in the field experience their own professions. Their value is in providing a window into the person's own framework for construing the world of work, and therefore furnishing the counselor with

Figure 11-1 A sample vocational Reptest. (From "Personal Constructs in Career Counseling and Development" by Gregory J. Neimeyer in *Journal of Career Development*, pp. 163–174. Copyright © 1992. Reprinted by permission of Kluwer Academic/Plenum Publishers and the author.)

Positive Side (+3 +2 +1)	Artist	Life Insurance Salesperson	Lawyer	Office Worker	Accountant	Public School Teacher	Social Worker	Physician	Physicist	Architect	Machine Operator	Farmer	Negative Side (0 −1 −2 −3)
Indoors a lot	0	+3	+3	+3	+3	+3	+1	+3	+3	+2	−3	−3	Outdoors a lot
Don't need much education	+3	−2	−3	−1	−3	−2	+1	−3	−3	−3	+2	+2	Need a lot of education
More freedom	+3	−2	+3	−1	−3	+2	+3	−3	−2	+2	−2	+1	A lot of rules & regulations
Nonrestricted job	+3	−2	0	−2	−3	+1	+3	−3	−2	+2	−2	+3	Restricted job
A lot of money	−3	+2	+3	0	+3	−2	−2	+3	+2	+1	−2	−2	Little money
Teaches more	0	−2	−3	−2	−2	+3	−3	−3	−2	−2	−2	−2	Helps more
Interesting (something new every day)	+3	−2	+3	−3	−3	+3	+3	+3	+2	+2	−3	−2	Boring (same stuff every day)
Investigative	−3	−3	+3	−2	−2	+2	+3	+1	+3	−3	−3	−3	Not investigative
Works with many people	+1	+3	+3	−2	−2	+3	+3	+3	−2	−2	−2	−2	Doesn't work with many people
Doesn't deal with families	−1	−3	+1	+3	+3	−2	−3	−3	+3	+3	+3	+2	Deals with families
Creativity involved	+3	−3	+2	−3	−3	+2	+1	−3	−2	+3	−3	−2	Not much creativity involved
Not much manual labor	+2	+3	+3	+3	+3	+3	+3	+3	+3	−3	−3	−3	Involves manual labor

286

an ethnographic and phenomenological assessment (Hoshmand, 1989) from the perspective of the client's unique worldview.

In addition to determining her occupational preferences, we can also quickly glean the basis for these preferences. The only drawbacks she sees to becoming a lawyer, for instance, is that it requires a lot of education, and that it would involve more "helping" than "teaching," whereas she values the latter over the former. (Neimeyer, 1992, pp. 166, 168)

By viewing Figure 11-1, you can see that Jean is ambivalent about most occupations and rates many with both positive and negative features. This shows that she is not idealizing most occupations, although she gives high ratings to "lawyer." This might possibly reflect an idealization of the occupation.

As Neimeyer (1992) states, completing the vocational reptest is helpful to the counselor in organizing clients' constructs and also in helping clients articulate their own occupational values. Thus, Jean and the counselor discuss the constructs that Jean has developed as they apply to Jean's value system. They look for occupations that may fit with the positive side of the constructs.

Laddering Techniques

A means of determining which constructs are most important to clients, laddering can be used in the context of counseling. The reptest, in contrast, requires time devoted to writing, ranking, and scoring. Whereas the reptest may show which constructs are important to clients, laddering can help clients identify the relative importance of the constructs within their system of constructs. Laddering starts with choosing three occupations (other categories can be used) and then developing constructs by asking questions about them. The counselor continues to focus on questions about constructs as he or she moves up the "ladder." This technique is best described by Neimeyer (1992), who uses the technique with Jean.

I initiated the laddering procedure by asking her to "choose the first three occupations that come to mind for you." She chose a teacher, a paramedic, and musician. Then I asked her to think about these three occupations for a minute and then tell me any way in which two of them are alike, but different from the third. I emphasized that there are no right or wrong answers, but what mattered most was what she thought, how she viewed the occupations. She responded that she saw the teacher and the musician as more alike in that they are both "more creative," in contrast to the paramedic who is "more technical." I then wrote down the two ends of her construct dimension (creative versus technical), as depicted on the bottom of Figure 11-2.

The next step involved asking her which she preferred, "an occupation that was more creative or one that was more technical?" She preferred a more creative job, so I placed a plus sign (+) for "creative," and then asked her "Why?" "Because a creative job lets you express yourself," was her response, which she contrasted with a more technical job which "just lets you get better and better along certain predetermined lines." I then entered this construct into the

PERSONAL CONSTRUCT LADDERING TECHNIQUE

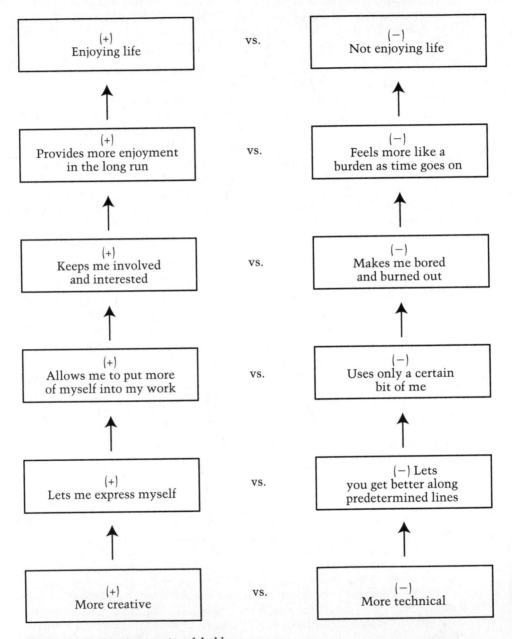

Figure 11-2 Jean's vocational ladder.
(From "Personal Constructs in Career Counseling and Development" by Gregory J. Neimeyer in *Journal of Career Development*, pp. 163–174. Copyright © 1992. Reprinted by permission of Kluwer Academic/Plenum Publishers and the author.)

ladder (lets you express yourself versus get better along predetermined lines), and again asked her, "which of these would you prefer?" In response, she indicated that she preferred a job that would let her be more expressive. When I asked why, she reflected for a moment, and said, "Because I could put more of myself into my work." "Would you prefer to put more or less of yourself into work," I asked. She responded, "More of me because that way I am always involved and interested instead of being bored and burned out." "It sounds kind of silly to ask you this," I queried, "but I assume that you would prefer to be interested and involved, over being bored and burned out. Why is that?" She thought still longer and finally responded by saying, "I guess I feel that if I am more involved, then I will enjoy my work more in the long run, for life, rather than feeling like it is a burden as time goes along." This construct was again entered on her ladder and I risked one more assessment, asking her if she could articulate why she would prefer enjoying work or experiencing it as a burden. Her answer was that "enjoying life is what it's all about in the end, I guess," suggesting that she had reached the ceiling of her construct hierarchy. (pp. 169, 171)

Jean's vocational ladder is shown in Figure 11-2. Using this technique for only a few minutes, Neimeyer was able to establish important constructs for Jean and to establish an order of importance. He starts with a discrimination between creative and technical occupations and moves up toward a very important construct-enjoying life. Neimeyer notes that the laddering technique can be helpful when clients are resisting pressure for a specific occupational alternative.

Resistance toward a given occupational alternative often can be clarified with a laddering exercise such as this. In this case, for example, Jean's parents were lobbying hard for her consideration of a technical career since, from their perspective, "she's so good at math and sciences." Jean's resistance in this regard can be clarified by seeing the implications that a technical career carries for her personally, within her own career framework. Her resistance is based less on her perceived incompetence or frustration with technical skills than with her fear that it would lead her to ultimate alienation from her work and burn out in her career. (p. 171)

Neimeyer states that laddering can be useful not only in understanding clients' constructs but also in helping them clarify their own feelings. By using this exercise, Jean develops an understanding of some of the constructs or values that are important to her in career choice. Furthermore, she is able to differentiate her own work values from those of her parents. Although in this example Neimeyer used three occupations to get started, personalities associated with various professionals or the use of specific people, such as your wife, your brother, and yourself could be used (Waas, 1984).

Vocational Card Sort

The Vocational Card Sort (VCS) was developed by Tyler (1961) and then refined by Dolliver (1967). Basically, the VCS is a group of 100 cards with the name of an occupation on one side and information about the occupation, such as a description and entry requirements, on the other side. Some counselors have developed their own card sorts using just occupational titles or other information. Typically, these card sorts include 60 to 100 cards. Clients are asked to sort the cards into three piles: occupations one would consider or find acceptable, those that one would not choose, and those that the client is uncertain about. Some counselors may use the card sort technique to choose from a group of occupations to consider for a possible career. However, Cochran (1997) uses the card sort to derive constructs or values for the client and counselor to consider.

In using a constructivist approach to the card sort, the counselor asks the client to first divide the pile into accept, maybe, and reject. Then, working either with the accept or reject pile, the counselor asks the client to divide that pile into as many piles as he or she wants, which reflects a common reason for rejection (or acceptance). When the client has divided the cards into piles, the client is asked what the jobs in each pile have in common. Then the clients are asked, "What is it about these jobs that you reject (or accept)?"

When the client describes the reason for rejecting or accepting a pile of occupations, the counselor may ask more questions or summarize what the client has said. The counselor is attempting to determine the values or constructs that are important to the client. This procedure is followed with both the accept and the reject pile. Cochran (1997, p. 45) gives some examples of constructs that he has obtained as a result of using this process:

Be your own person, more individualistic
    versus
Too much conformity, too controlling

Confident in practical work with mechanics and electricity
    versus
Lack talent in artistic work

Authority and prestige, being looked up to
    versus
Restricted, being looked down on

Being able to take credit for good results
    versus
Fear of being held accountable for bad results

Using the card sort this way, the counselor and client can discuss the constructs that were developed as a result of using this procedure. They may also wish to discuss the occupations in the accept or reject pile and how they fit with the constructs. Thus, the client learns about jobs and also learns about him- or herself.

The purpose of constructivist career counseling is to help clients articulate their values and make meaning for their life as a whole. The exercises described previously (the reptest, laddering, and the card sort) are different methods for determining which constructs are important to individual clients. Certainly, other methods can be used which include un-structured or structured exercises that are based on personal construct psychology. Forster's (1992) program entitled *Goals Review and Organizing Workbook,* designed to be used with groups, is an elaborate method for determining constructs. More conventional tasks and inventories can also be used and constructs can be integrated with interest and value inventory interpretation.

The four-stage model of Neimeyer and his colleagues that was previously discussed shows how counselors can gradually help clients to develop and integrate constructs and themes as they reexamine themselves. In the latter two stages of this model, counselors are likely to help their clients take action on their realization of significant constructs that make up their perceptions of themselves and the world of work.

NARRATIVE COUNSELING

In narrative counseling, clients narrate or tell about their past career development, present career development, and construct their future career. Listening to the clients describe their lives and how they enact the work role helps the counselor assist the clients in future career decision making. This is an active approach that attends to how clients intentionally interact with their world and learn about it through these interactions (Young, Valach, & Collin, 1996). The narrative model differs from the personal construct system in that it focuses on the story of clients' lives rather than on constructs. The narrative model is more similar to that of a play or psychodrama, in which individuals enact their lives. The career is seen as a story.

Seeing a career as a story, Jepsen (1992) and Cochran (1991, 1994, 1997) suggest that the metaphor of viewing a client's career as a story is an excellent metaphor for counseling. Meaning can be derived from these stories by attending to what clients feel is important or unimportant in their description of their life or career. Like stories, careers contain two important elements: action and time. The client acts or interacts with his or her environment within a time frame.

Viewing the client's career as a story, or possibly even a novel, allows the application of concepts from literary criticism (Jepsen, 1992). The narrator or author of the story (the client) is referred to as the *agent.* There is a *setting* in which the story occurs, much like the background or scenery in a play. However, the setting also includes important people such as family, friends, and colleagues at work. Like a play or a story, there is *action* that is designed to reach a goal that will satisfy the needs of the agent (client). The agent then uses an *instrument* to reach the goal. Instruments can include one's abilities, friends, family, or employers. This is similar to a novel where characters interact with each other to achieve a goal, and action takes place as the protagonist (major character) interacts with others in the environment (the setting) to achieve a goal. From Jepsen's point of view, problems arise when the instruments and goals do not match, the actions and goals do not match, or the client (agent) and the goals do not match.

When there are problems in the career story, difficulties in decision making, such as career indecision, often occur. From a narrative perspective, indecision can be seen positively, as a sign that the client is in the process of making change. Clients are losing a sense of where they are in their story of their life, but do not have a clear idea of where they are going and their goals. By examining the indecision and sensing the meaning that takes place before acting (choosing an occupation), clients can get a fuller sense of their career pattern. Career indecision is seen actively, not as something that happens to the client in a passive manner. Cochran (1991) uses the term *wavering*. When clients waver back and forth they are moving toward finding meaning in their career path. This presents an opportunity for counselors to help clients clarify their needs, values, and aspirations. To put this another way, there is a pause in the story and the counselor's role is to help the client determine the future direction of this story and to clarify the plots within the story. This may mean a change in setting (another career or job, a move to another location) and a plan of how to reach this setting or situation.

Storytelling

In narrative counseling, both client and counselor learn from the client's narration of the story. Like a story, the client's narration has a beginning, middle, and end. In the beginning, the difficult or troubling situation is described. This provides the motivation for the middle and end of the story. In the middle of the story, the client describes the obstacles and instruments that may be used in working toward reaching a personal goal. In the end, the counselor and client work together to develop solutions that will help to provide satisfaction and to reach a goal that will satisfy the client. In using this approach, there are some goals that are implicit in the narrative approach.

Goals of Assessment in Narrative Counseling

The counselor listens through much of the story, sorting out significant data. A guideline is needed for the counselor to know what data are important and what data are of less importance. In a sense, the counselor is like an editor, putting together the significant parts of the story in order, emphasizing some, and deleting others. This story will include an emphasis on the client's past life, the present way the client sees him- or herself, and future plans or desires. As an editor, the counselor has several goals in assessing the client's life patterns.

One goal in listening to a narrative is to identify a pattern in the individuals' lives. The counselor focuses not on a chronology of events, but on the meaning of those events. For example, a chronology might say, "Started work in a hardware store November 3, 2000. Left job April 17, 2001." In contrast, a story might say, "Started job in hardware store November 3, 2000. Liked my coworkers, but not my boss. Was fired for stealing ammunition from the ammo locker April 17, 2001." In the very brief story, much more information is told than is implied in the chronology. The stealing and not liking the boss connect having the job with being fired from the job. Still, there is a need for more information. Thus, the stories explain the meaning and events. This brief story would be one of many that the counselor would listen to in order to identify the pattern in an individual's life. There are likely to be many plots besides the brief one described here.

Another goal of assessment is for the client and counselor to form a sense of the client's identity. The client's identity consists of both the story that the client tells and the client's approach to telling the story. The client is active in the story and is the protagonist, or focus of the story. The counselor learns about the client by the way the client tells the story: Is it brief and choppy? Does the client put herself down? Or does she make excuses for herself? Listening to clients describe their stories and listening to the unfolding of the story helps the counselor to get a sense of who the client is—the client's identity.

Another goal in listening to the narrative and assessing it is to learn about the client's goals for the future. When counseling is done, the plot line should be extended beyond the past and present into the future. To do this, counselors need to help clarify the choices that clients have. Tasks are likely to include generating alternative choices and explaining decisions to be made. Tools that may be helpful in this process are describing occupational daydreams, writing one's future biography, and writing one's own obituary (Savickas, 1991). At this point the focus on assessment changes to that of counseling. Certainly, some aspects of counseling occur during the assessment phase, as clients are learning more about themselves, their skills, interests, abilities, and desires through the assessment phase.

Narrative Career Counseling

As clients tell their stories, counselors listen to the narratives and the patterns of living implied in the narratives. They may ask questions that will help restore order to the narrative or reduce confusion. Several choices about future events may come up during the course of the narrative. All are related to the pattern within the narrative. The counselor's role is to clarify the narrative and help the client make career decisions.

In working with a life story, Young, Valach, and Collin (1996) believe counselors should listen for three important elements in a story: coherence, continuity, and causality. For a story to be coherent, it should make sense chronologically or in terms of the sequence of events. For a story to have continuity, it should be able to be seen in terms of action that is directed toward a goal. Causality in a story refers to being able to explain events. Clients should be able to see the purpose behind their actions. By emphasizing coherence, continuity, and causality, the counselor places the client in an active role. The client can be seen as an agent who is active in a plot, not reactive or passive. As an active agent, the client makes decisions, rather than listens to the counselor's suggestions for completing the client's story.

Cochran's Narrative Career Counseling

In order to understand the application of narrative counseling to career counseling, I will explain Cochran's (1997) approach, which is described in his book *Career Counseling: A Narrative Approach*. In his book, Cochran describes seven "episodes" or phases in career counseling using a narrative point of view. The first three episodes emphasize making meaning out of the career narrative: elaborating a career problem, composing a life history, and founding a future narrative. Episodes four through six focus on enactment or being active: constructing a reality, changing a life structure, and enacting a role. The seventh episode refers to the crystallization of a decision. To illustrate Cochran's narrative career counseling approach I will use the case of Dennis.

A 25-year-old white male, Dennis has sought career counseling because he is dissatisfied with his current employment. He is an assistant manager in a grocery store where he has worked on and off since high school. When he graduated high school at the age of 18, Dennis entered the Navy, where he worked in radio communications. He left the Navy at the age of 22. At first, Dennis thought joining the Navy would be fun and he would get a chance to see the world. However, he was not prepared for what he believed was much routine work as a communications technician. He had some regrets about not entering an officer's training program, but then decided he was ready to leave the Navy. After leaving the Navy and returning to his home in Iowa City, Dennis went back to the supermarket where he had been employed as a high school student. He spends most of his spare time racing cars and preparing them for races in the local area. He has thought that he might want to go to college so that he can enter into a management position in the supermarket or retail field, but he is not sure. Because narrative counseling is a very thorough approach, only parts of his interaction with the counselor can be illustrated here.

Elaborating a Career Problem   The first step is to clarify the client's concern. The gap between what the current situation is and what the client wants it to be is the start of counseling (Cochran, 1985). Not only must there be a gap between the ideal and the actual, but the client must also want to do something about this discrepancy. Also, the client should be uncertain about how to bridge the gap. If the client were certain, then there would be no need for counseling. To elaborate a career problem, the counselor and client work to fill in the middle between what is actually happening and the ideal.

There are a number of ways to elaborate on the problem and fill in the middle. The counselor's interest in the client's story shows that he or she

cares about the client and the problem that the client shares with the counselor. Although ordinary conversation is a primary way of elaborating the
career problem, there are others. The vocational card sort, described on
page 289, helps the counselor and client understand the constructs that the
client uses in viewing his own life. Another approach, construct laddering,
described on page 287, also helps develop the range of constructs that the
client sees as important, and then ladders them in increasing levels of importance. In essence, laddering provides a way for understanding the client's
career theory or way of viewing his career pattern. Cochran (1997) also suggests that interest inventories, value inventories, and ability tests may be
useful in providing information about the client that can be integrated with
information gathered from other sources.

Another technique is that of drawing. This is an intuitive approach that
usually starts with having the individual relax or use guided meditation
(Dail, 1989). The client can be instructed to draw pictures or symbols that
represent *What I am*, a representation of the actual situation the client is
dealing with currently. Two other pictures, *What I'd like to be* and *What
hinders me*, represent the middle of the story. The fourth picture, *What
will overcome the obstacle*, can be used to see the ending of the story, how
the client would like to be in the future. This approach fits very closely
with Cochran's (1997) narrative approach to assessment.

A technique that fits in well with the narrative approach is that of
anecdotes. These are short stories that individuals tell that help the counselor understand aspects of clients' lives. The client may tell an anecdote,
followed by the counselor and client working together to see its importance and how it fits in to a career pattern. In interpreting this story, the
counselor wants to be as precise as possible and not just make a generalization. The following is an example of Dennis describing an anecdote to
his counselor.

CL: When I get home from work at the store, my father always has some wise
guy thing to say.

CO: Oh, tell me more about that. [The counselor wants to hear this story,
even though it is short.]

CL: Well a few days ago after I came home from work, he says to me "How
are all the rotten apples."

CO: Sounds like that had several meanings for you.

CL: Yeah. He doesn't think much of the people I work with. He hears me talk
about these 40-year-old men and women who are still working in the produce or other sections and he doesn't think that they did much with their
lives. He is also talking about one guy, I think, who was in prison for
awhile and now is working at the store. On top of all that, he likes to
tease me about the quality of the vegetables and fruits themselves. He
can really be a pain.

CO: You get tired of hearing his negative comments about your work and your
colleagues.

CL: I sure do. It's happened again and again. It makes me think that he has
no confidence in me, no confidence in my ability to do well in life.

CO: That really hits home for you, a real sore spot. [The counselor is aware that Dennis has some of the same feelings himself and it bothers him to have that theme touched on by his father.]

CL: Yes, you know I am concerned that I am not advancing, that I am not doing more with my life. To hear my father make comments about what I am doing sometimes distracts me by getting me angry at him instead of working on what I need to do with myself.

There are many anecdotes like this that Dennis shares with his counselor. Together, Dennis and the counselor work to see how such incidents are woven together and fit in with a theme. Using techniques such as the vocational card sort, construct laddering, drawing, testing, and anecdotes, the counselor helps clients elaborate their career problems. This helps the client prepare for the next step, which is putting a life history together.

Composing a Life History   Exploring a client's life history has two basic intentions. One, which is similar to the first stage of trait and factor theory, is to gather information about clients' interests, values, abilities, and motives. A second intention is different from that of most other theories. It is to attend to the way individuals select and organize their life stories. Counselors listen to the way in which individuals describe their previous activities and the kind of people they are. Perhaps the most common way to obtain a life history is to ask individuals to describe important events in their lives and to discuss their meaning. Often the counselor might ask the client to present it from a third-person perspective, as if he or she is talking about someone else. But if this is done, it is important to also use a first-person approach, as it may add more meaning to the story.

Cochran (1997) suggests several ways in which counselors can help clients add more meaning to their stories. In telling a story, counselors can point out, when appropriate, either positive or negative meanings for the client. This is done to help put together a pattern of experiences. Cochran also suggests that counselors emphasize strengths, as clients too often dwell on their weaknesses. When clients express desires that they have for the future, it is particularly helpful for counselors to comment on them. A method that is effective and stimulates effect is that of dramatization. In this method, the counselor becomes the narrator of the story and may refer to the client in the third-person. The counselor may do that with Dennis, for example:

There is this eight-year-old boy walking home from school. The neighborhood bully, Wally, is looking for him and beats him up about a block from his house. Going home should feel like a safe haven. It doesn't, he's worried what will happen when his father comes home. Will he get mad or criticize him? So he watches television; he fantasizes about the cartoons and the programs he watches. He forgets himself, but not totally. When the commercials come on he worries about what will happen with Wally tomorrow and what his father will say when he comes home tonight.

By talking about Dennis in the third-person, the counselor is emphasizing the emotional aspect of this event and sets it up to be related to other events so that a pattern can be determined. Other aspects of composing a life history deal with the continuity of the character and personal causality. The counselor attends to qualities of the individual that are likely to be found in most events. This provides a pattern or a theme for the client and counselor to attend to. The client is the protagonist responsible for events, rather than a passive victim.

In addition to asking clients to describe their life histories, there are several techniques that counselors can use in composing a life history. Three of these techniques include success experiences, lifelines, and life chapters. To develop a list of strengths, or success experiences, a counselor asks a client to make a list of activities that were enjoyable and in which the client felt a sense of accomplishment. Strengths could include basic abilities, skills, special knowledge, or character traits such as being honest. In using the list of strengths, a counselor may wish to keep a chart to see if the strengths are similar to or different from each other and to find a pattern in them. In the lifeline, an individual draws a line lengthwise across a piece of paper. The client is then asked to record important life experiences and put them in chronological order on the paper. Each dot is labeled to represent a particular event. This lifeline may include not only the events, but thoughts and emotions related to the events. In life chapters, the client can be told to imagine that his life is a book and that he is to come up with titles for important chapters in his life. He is told not to use common terms like *preschool, elementary school,* and *military training.* Rather these should be titles that are distinctive to the client. For Dennis, the titles may be "Wally the Bully," "Running to Escape," "My First Love," and other titles which have meaning to the client and to the counselor. Then the counselor can ask questions about each chapter or period of the client's life having to do with conflict, goals, significant influences, interests, and skills. All of these exercises focus on past history, and to a limited extent on current events.

Eliciting a Future Narrative   In constructing a future narrative, clients consider their strengths, interests, and values as they may appear in the future. The focus in this stage is on evaluation of one's strengths, interests, and values. Several of the techniques that are used are an extension of those needed when composing a life history. These include success experiences, lifeline, and life chapters. In these success experience exercises, clients can project what would constitute success in their future lives. They can also examine strengths in past events and project activities that they may best use these strengths in. For the lifeline exercise, individuals can extend their lifeline into the future and place experiences that they would like to have that would make their life complete. These experiences would be a reflection of current desires, strengths, and resolution of conflict.

A similar approach can be taken with the life chapters exercise. Clients develop chapter titles that represent important accomplishments for them. If clients use negative chapter titles, they can be reworded in a positive way. For example, if Dennis has as a chapter "Not Experienced Enough to Be Promoted," this could be rephrased as "Learning Enough to Be Promoted." For Dennis, chapter titles might include "Managing the Department," "Managing the Store," "Managing My Father's Tantrums," and "Having a Home." These titles provide an opportunity for the counselor and client to explore them and to attach meaning to them.

A technique that is often used in eliciting a future narrative is that of guided fantasy. Guided fantasies can be descriptive, evaluative, or some combination of each. Often, guided fantasies represent an end point. For example, the counselor may present a fantasy of an award ceremony, a retirement ceremony, or going to one's funeral. The purpose of the fantasy is, in part, to help the client reflect on accomplishments that he or she would like to have. When using this procedure (Cochran, 1997, p. 88), counselors are likely to help clients relax first, then narrate a fantasy as the client imagines the narration, filling in parts of the fantasy. The fantasy can also be interpreted.

In addition to guided fantasy and other exercises, Cochran (1997) also recommends a written and narrative outline. The written report is constructed in collaboration with the client. There are five sections: mission, strengths, work needs, vulnerabilities, and possibilities. The mission statement encapsulates the client's goals for the future. This is followed by a list of strengths, usually in clusters reflecting the clients own expressions of accomplishments. The work needs section reflects the client's work values and focuses on what clients need to facilitate their performance. This section is followed by one which focuses on client vulnerabilities—what is likely to sidetrack the client from meeting goals. Finally, the client is presented with a list of occupational possibilities or descriptions of relevant fields.

When the client receives the report, he is given an opportunity to read it and to ask questions about it or comment on it. This can be followed by the counselor's verbal description of the report. When doing this, counselors ask questions such as, "Did I portray your values accurately?" "Do you think I was accurate in discussing your vulnerabilities?" "Would there be any other vulnerabilities that you might add?" In this way, the process is collaborative and not limited to the counselor's impressions or views.

When a written and narrative report are concluded, then the counselor and client can move into a more active process, which is called "actualizing the narrative." To end counseling with the written report would be to describe goals, values, interests, abilities, strengths, and weaknesses and not proceed further. In the three types of enactment, clients construct reality, change a life structure, and enact a role.

Reality Construction   Action is a significant component of narrative career counseling. Whether the problem is work adjustment or making a career decision, individuals need to enact a script; that is, they need to try out a variety of actions. The more active the exploration, the better. Reading a description of a job is a good beginning, but it is not as rich as talking to people within a field or interviewing them to get work information. More active than reading is volunteer work, job visitations, discussions with friends, spending a day on a job with a friend, and so forth. There are three major purposes to active exploration. First, it immerses the client in the real world. The client has to get things done and check things out. Second, individuals get information from a variety of sources and are able to evaluate the information as they talk to many sources. Third, as individuals talk to people about, and in a variety of, occupations, they can imagine themselves in an occupation. They now have a clearer idea about than they did when they started talking to and interviewing people.

For Dennis, reality construction meant going beyond familiar people he knew in his store. A friend of his worked at a large home improvement store and had arranged for him to talk with the manager there. Banking had also been a consideration, and he wanted to learn about customer service and being a loan officer. He arranged to talk to the assistant manager and a manager at the branch office where he banked. Also, he talked to his father's accountant about his work and the accountant's relationship with customers. What was new to Dennis was the amount of activity that he participated in. Previously, he would just go home after work and watch television, occasionally call a few friends. By talking to so many different people, he developed a sense that he had more control over the direction of his life.

Changing a Life Structure   When seeking career counseling, clients expect some type of change. Usually there is change to the situation, oneself, or both. For work adjustment counseling, clients often expect to make a positive change in the way they work or who they work with. For career decision-making counseling, clients expect to be in a new setting unlike one that they are in currently. With change comes new opportunities such as training, salary increase, or being appreciated. Also with change comes more negative aspects, such as fear of failing, anxiety about doing a poor job, and so forth.

When changing a life structure, there is often a theme that emerges. Cochran (1992) describes a *career project*. Individuals perform many different tasks that are indirectly or directly related to their career. They make friends, take exams, pay bills, and so forth. These can be seen as unrelated tasks. However, there may be themes that emerge in the way that individuals go about these tasks. If individuals feel good about the ways they interact with others, manage their finances, and so forth, then they are likely to have a positive sense of meaning about what they do.

For Dennis, there was a certain amount of caution in which he approached activities. He wanted to make sure that he understood what he was supposed to do at his job before he did it. More cautious than most, he might ask more questions than his coworkers. With friends, he wanted to have a sense that they were interested in him and that he could depend on them. With his finances, Dennis was careful to pay his bills on time and not to overspend. His *career project* could be tentatively surmised as a caution that suggests concern about vocational adequacy. Eliciting more events and more information would help to clarify or alter what may be his personal theme or *career project*.

Enacting a Role   Trying things out or enacting a role is a way of trying to make one's desired goal possible. In doing so, individuals try out activities that are meaningful and enjoyable. Sometimes it is not clear what activity would be best, so several activities will be tried. Also, some activities may not be immediately attainable. Individuals cannot start out as successful athletes. People work toward achieving a role and may or may not meet with success.

Often individuals start with a small role, and that role develops into other opportunities for more enactment. For example, Dennis used to work out at the YMCA after work in the evenings. He had become friendly with the director, as they had helped some children learn how to use equipment. The director asked him if he wanted to help organize activities for 9- to 12-year-old boys. Dennis thought that would be fun and did some part-time volunteer work organizing some sports events for the boys. One evening, he was talking to the father of one of the boys about the activities that the boys were involved in. The father asked Dennis if he would like to help with soccer coaching on some weekends. Dennis thought that would be fun and tried it out for a season. By enacting one role, going to the YMCA, Dennis put himself in a position to enact other roles. He uncovered possibilities that existed through his actions, that he could not plan. This may or may not have a direct impact on Dennis's later career development.

Crystallizing a Decision   Crystallization occurs when a gap between a client's career problem and the ideal or possible solutions diminishes. Sometimes crystallization takes place when clients experience the previous six episodes. Choosing among occupations may not be a deliberate process, but one that comes from being active in ways described in the six previous episodes.

Not all decisions need to focus on making a specific choice. For some individuals, exploring occupational possibilities is sufficient. For example, freshmen at college may be in the position of exploring opportunities rather than having to decide immediately on majors or occupational alternatives. Other problems may be related to work adjustment, such as finding ways to get along with a boss.

Cochran (1997) believes that crystallization can be facilitated in three ways: identifying and eliminating obstructions, actualizing opportunities, and reflecting on career decisions. Sometimes there are internal obstructions to crystallizing a choice, such as lack of confidence in being able to obtain a job. Other times, there are external factors, such as pressures from parents to enter a certain occupation. Obstructions such as these represent an opportunity to start a new story and remove oneself from the old story. By actualizing a choice, individuals are taking advantage of new roles and new opportunities. Counselors can encourage clients to accept new challenges in their work.

Clients can often reflect on their experience of choosing occupations. Neimeyer's (1992) explanation of the reptest (p. 284) can be used to facilitate this process. This way clients can see if there are conflicts among their values or constructs when considering occupational choices. Discussing the narrative career counseling process is an excellent way to put career choice issues into perspective.

In crystallizing a career choice, Dennis addressed both internal and external obstructions. An external barrier for Dennis was his father's comments about Dennis's unlikelihood of succeeding in an occupation other than his current one. Dennis also had similar feelings, when presenting internal obstructions, which brought him to consider whether or not he could handle higher-level administrative abilities. When he thought of his ability in managing others at work, and the types of management responsibilities that he encountered in his interviews, he believed that he could be successful in accomplishing such administrative tasks. By discussing this with a counselor, Dennis could see that much of his self-doubt came from his father's criticism and that when he was actually in a management position, he could handle the responsibilities well. Review of the six previous episodes involved in narrative counseling helped Dennis to have a new perspective on his career choices. He was now excited about taking college courses that would lead to a business degree and looking for new work that would lead to more administrative responsibility.

Cochran's (1997) approach to narrative career counseling focuses on the client's active role in telling his or her story. For Cochran, the counseling process includes seven "episodes." In the first three episodes, clients see meaning in their lives by actively elaborating their career problems, tell stories about their lives (composing a life), and look into their future (constructing a future narrative). After telling a story about their past and constructing stories about their future, clients can then move into the three enactment episodes: constructing reality, changing a life structure, and enacting a role. With these three episodes completed, individuals can then move toward crystallizing a decision.

THE ROLE OF TESTING

Standard interest inventories, values inventories, and tests of ability and achievement play a minor role in constructivist career counseling. Because constructivist counselors are interested in how their clients see reality, applying inventories or tests that are used for all individuals may not help in an understanding of the perceptual world of the client. Counselors who use personal construct approaches are likely to use the reptest, which is not subject to validation or reliability in the same way as other tests, because each reptest will be different for each client. Such counselors may integrate traditional testing with personal constructs that are derived from the reptest, laddering, or a vocational card sort. In narrative career counseling, Cochran (1997) shows how traditional testing can be integrated with constructivist methods such as the reptest, construct laddering, and drawing, in the first episode, elaborating a career problem. Because constructivist career counselors are focused on understanding the client's perception of their career problems and the constructs that they use to see their world, constructivist career counselors are cautious about using instruments that impose a test developer's set of constructs on the client.

THE ROLE OF OCCUPATIONAL INFORMATION

Constructivist career counselors are concerned not only with the constructs that individuals use to see themselves, but also with the constructs that they use in viewing the world around them. Each of the two approaches discussed in this chapter have similar but slightly different perspectives on integrating occupational information into career counseling. The integration of occupational information and personal constructs can be seen in the three instruments that were described in that section: the reptest, laddering, and the vocational card sort. In the reptest, individuals apply their constructs to ten occupations. When laddering techniques are used, counselors are likely to initiate this process by asking clients to choose the first three occupations that come to mind (Neimeyer, 1992). Many vocational card sorts include not only the name of the occupation, but also a brief description of the occupation. Constructs are derived by asking the client to take preferred occupations and nonpreferred occupations, and then sort them into piles based on their similarity. This integrates the individuals' perception of themselves with the world of work. As clients learn more occupational information, they clarify their occupational constructs.

Cochran (1997) emphasizes the importance of action on the part of the client. After clients tell their stories, they are involved in three enactment episodes. All three involve active exploration and occupational research. It is not enough for the client to just read about occupations. In the reality construction episode, clients may do volunteer work, visit people at work, interview workers, or discuss occupations with relatives or friends. In the changing a life structure episode, clients focus on the work that they do, studying the effects on their lives. As clients try out new activities, their lives change, and they can examine how they react to different occupational tasks. When enacting a role, clients live out roles that they are interested in exploring. On page 300, an example was given of how Dennis tried different supervisory assignments and tasks. This increased his knowledge of relevant occupational information.

APPLYING THE THEORIES TO WOMEN AND CULTURALLY DIVERSE POPULATIONS

From a constructivist point of view, culture and gender interact within the context of client actions (Young, Valach, & Collin, 1996). Thus, stories or histories exist within a cultural context. How one views an action can have varying cultural interpretations. For example, putting an arm around a coworker can be seen as friendly encouragement or sexual harassment. One's cultural background may influence how one interprets such an event.

Both gender and culture guide how individuals develop attitudes, skills, and values (Cochran, 1997). For example, in North America there are cultural stereotypes that suggest that women do not do well in math. Other cultural narratives may guide certain views, such as "Asians prefer science." Cochran cautions that cultural narratives are only one aspect of what individuals learn. Some cultural systems are closely related to vocational expectations. For example, caste systems in India are often linked with certain types of occupations, whether they be custodial, small business, or other occupations.

Cochran (1997) suggests that cultural narratives do not keep up with the times, that these expectations are not particularly valid when applied to individuals. First, narratives often conflict. Lee and Cochran (1988) give an example of a conflict between Western emphasis on self-fulfillment and Chinese emphasis on family obligation. These two cultural narratives may conflict for an individual raised in a Chinese culture and working in North America. Second, there are career experiences that do not have adequate cultural narratives. There is no narrative to guide a male worker in dealing with a female supervisor. Third, some narratives may be distorted or inaccurate. Examples are "A woman's place is in the home" and "Be loyal to your employer." These cultural narratives can interfere with career development as they may conflict with development of other personal constructs.

Constructivist career counselors attend to cultural components of stories as well as stories about culture. Such constructs can help counselors understand their clients' value systems. Each client's story, whether referring to gender, culture, or some other topic, provides a way of perceiving clients' construction of reality.

COUNSELOR ISSUES

Because the focus of constructivist approaches to career counseling is on understanding the way clients view reality, it is important for counselors to be aware of their own construction of reality and its relationship to significant constructs of clients. For example, if the prestige of an occupation is irrelevant to the counselor, but relevant to the client, it is important that the counselor's values do not interfere with the client's valuing of prestige.

There are some differences in counselor issues between the two constructivist approaches discussed in this chapter. Personal construct theory focuses most directly on ways of helping clients understand their way of viewing reality. Counselors are likely to be quite aware of their own value system when working with personal construct theory. When using the narrative approach to career counseling, counselors are focused on the client's story. When listening to the client's history, counselors may be reminded of their own history and see differences between the two. Seeing these differences can be advantageous or disadvantageous to the counselor depending on how they affect the counselor's perception of the clients' stories.

SUMMARY

This chapter has focused on two different approaches to constructivist career counseling. Both have in common their attention to clients' perceptions of reality. Two different approaches to understanding client constructs are explored in this chapter: personal construct theory and narrative career counseling.

Personal construct career counseling is based on George Kelly's construct theory. Individuals' constructs are ways of orienting themselves to others and to events. Basically, constructs represent individual value systems. Three ways of assessing clients' constructs have been shown: the reptest, laddering, and the vocational card sort. All are ways of ascertaining important constructs that are related to occupations. Also, a four-stage process of personal construct career counseling was described. Each stage helps to further refine constructs that clients have about themselves and the world of work. The final stage moves toward crystallizing or choosing occupational alternatives.

The narrative approach to career counseling views the client's story as the focus of career counseling. In this approach, the client is seen as an active player, someone responsible for making changes in their environment. Cochran describes seven "episodes" that counselors use in working with clients. The first three involve the construction of career narratives: elaborating a career problem, composing a life, and founding a future narrative. The next three episodes emphasize enactment: constructing a reality, changing a life structure, and enacting a role. The final episode is crystallizing a career decision.

Both approaches provide different ways of viewing the career counseling process. A significant feature of these approaches is specific assessment and career counseling techniques for counselors to use to help clients construct their reality. Differences between the two approaches tend to focus on ways of assessing clients' perceptions of their value or construct systems and ways to help clients use this information to make career decisions.

References

Cochran, L. (1977). Differences between supplied and elicited constructs: Consideration in career evaluation. *Social Behavior and Personality, 5*, 241–247.

Cochran, L. (1985). *Position and nature of personhood*. Westport, CT: Greenwood Press.

Cochran, L. (1991). *Life-shaping decisions*. New York: Lang.

Cochran, L. (1992). The career project. *Journal of Career Development, 18*, 187–197.

Cochran, L. (1994). What is a career problem? *Career Development Quarterly, 42*, 204–215.

Cochran, L. (1997). *Career counseling: A narrative approach*. Newbury Park, CA: Sage.

Dail, H. (1989). *The lotus and the pool*. Boston: Shambhala.

Dolliver, R. (1967). An adaptation of the Tyler Vocational Card Sort. *Personnel and Guidance Journal, 45*, 916–920.

Forster, J. R. (1992). Eliciting personal constructs and articulating goals. *Journal of Career Development, 18*, 175–185.

Hoshmand, L. L. S. (1989). Alternative research paradigms: A review and teaching proposal. *The Counseling Psychologist, 17*, 3–80.

Jepsen, D. A. (1992, March). Understanding careers as stories. In M. L. Savickas (Chair), *Career as story*. Symposium conducted at the American Association for Counseling and Development.

Kelly, G. A. (1955). *The psychology of personal constructs*. New York: Norton.

Lee, C., & Cochran, L. (1988). Migration problems of Chinese women. *Canadian Journal of Counseling, 22*, 202–210.

Neimeyer, G. J. (1988). Cognitive integration and differentiation in vocational behavior. *The Counseling Psychologist, 16*, 440–475.

Neimeyer, G. J. (1989). Applications of repertory grid technique to vocational assessment. *Journal of Counseling and Development, 67*, 585–589.

Neimeyer, G. J. (1992). Personal constructs in career counseling and development. *Journal of Career Development, 18*, 163–174.

Neimeyer, R. A., & Stewart, A. E. (1998). Constructivist psychotherapies. *Encyclopedia of mental health* (Vol. 1, pp. 547–559). New York: Academic Press.

Nevill, D. D., Neimeyer, G. J., Probert, B., & Fukuyama, M. A. (1986). Cognitive structures in vocational information processing and decision making. *Journal of Vocational Behavior, 28*, 110–122.

Savickas, M. L. (1991). Improving career time perspective. In D. Brown & L. Brooks (Eds.), *Techniques of career counseling* (pp. 236–249). Boston: Allyn & Bacon.

Savickas, M. L. (1993). Career counseling in the postmodern era. *Journal of Cognitive Psychotherapy: An International Quarterly, 7*, 205–215.

Savickas, M. L. (1994). Vocational psychology in the postmodern era: Comment on Richardson (1993). *Journal of Counseling Psychology, 41*, 105–107.

Savickas, M. L. (1997). Constructivist career counseling: Models and methods. *Advances in Personal Construct Psychology, 4*, 149–182.

Super, D. E. (1957). *The psychology of careers*. New York: Harper.

Tiedeman, D. V., & O'Hara, R. P. (1963). *Career development: Choice and adjustment*. New York: College Entrance Examination Board.

Tyler, L. (1961). Research explorations in the realm of choice. *Journal of Counseling Psychology, 8*, 195–201.

Waas, G. A. (1984). Cognitive differentiation as a function of information type and its relation to career choice. *Journal of Vocational Behavior, 24,* 66–72.

Young, R. A., & Valach, L. (1996). Interpretation and action in career counseling. In M. L. Savickas & W. B. Walsh (Eds.), *Handbook of career counseling theory and practice* (pp. 361–375). Palo Alto, CA: Davies-Black.

Young, R. A., Valach, L., & Collin, A. (1996). A contextual explanation of career. In D. Brown, L. Brooks, & Associates (Eds.), *Career choice and development* (3rd ed., pp. 477–512). San Francisco, CA: Jossey-Bass.

12

Parental Influence Theories

Career development researchers have been interested in the questions: What impact do parents and others have on the occupational choice of children? And what impact does the child-raising experience have on the career choices and decision-making styles of children? Most theorists who have studied influences that others have on the career development of children have focused on parental influence. The impetus for the study of parental impact on career development comes from the work of Sigmund Freud and his influence on psychodynamic explanations of personal development. Although parental influence is the focus of this chapter, reference is also made to the impact on a child's development made by other family members as well as by some nonfamily members. The role of teachers, peers, and broader social influences on career choices is dealt with in the Chapter 7 discussion of Gottfredson and in the Chapter 15 discussion of studies on the effect of the work environment on the individual and of status attainment theory.

Some of this chapter is devoted to the systematic work of Anne Roe in trying to predict the occupational entry of individuals, but discussions of newer ideas from attachment theory and family therapy are also included. For more than 50 years, Anne Roe investigated the influence of parental child-raising styles on individual occupational choice. In the process, she developed a widely used occupational classification system that is explained in this chapter. More recently, theories about the impact of children's attachment to their parents have also been applied to career choice. Also, family therapists have developed some concepts and practical approaches that can be applied to career counseling. These family-focused theories are the subject of this chapter.

ROE'S PERSONALITY DEVELOPMENT THEORY

Anne Roe developed a theory to predict occupational selection based on individual differences, which are biological, sociological, and psychological. More specifically, she focused on predicting occupational selection based on the psychological needs that develop from the interaction between children and their parents. She wanted to be able to show that people in certain occupations have a common background in terms of the way they were raised. To build this theory, she needed to develop an occupational classification system so that she could relate parent–child relationships to specific occupational groupings. The classification system that she developed in this process has been supported by research and has become useful to counselors, whether or not it is used in the context of her theory. Because this classification system has been used so widely and can be used for counseling conceptualization, it will be examined in some detail. Another prerequisite for Roe's theory was Maslow's hierarchy of needs. Both the hierarchy itself and its relationship to Anne Roe's theory of vocational choice will be described.

Roe's Occupational Classification System

In her book *The Psychology of Occupations* (1956), Anne Roe describes her occupational classification system in great detail. She lists the job duties and abilities required by many occupations, characterized in the 48 cells of her 8 × 6 classification system. The system has eight groups and six levels, as presented in Table 12-1. The eight groups are listed across the top of the table. The groups that adjoin each other are the closest to each other in job duties, while those that are farthest apart are least similar; this is a circular system in that Group 1 and Group 8 are similar to each other and should be regarded as adjoining. The six rows of the system represent six different levels of complexity and responsibility for each occupation. Roe's work in developing this system is described not only in *The Psychology of Occupations*, but also in Roe (1972), Roe and Klos (1972), and, more recently, Roe and Lunneborg (1990) and Meir, Rubin, Temple, and Osipow (1997). As will be shown, this classification system has been used in the development of interest inventories and has applications to counseling.

The Eight Occupational Groups   The development of the eight occupational groups represents years of careful work by Roe, followed by research
validating her system. Roe (Roe & Lunneborg, 1990) describes her early
work as being influenced by research on interests, some of which was done
by early developers of interest inventories (Kuder, 1946; Strong, 1943). Considering this research, she selected eight groups that were suggested by
many of the studies that served to identify a primary occupational characteristic. She thought of this grouping as a circle, as shown in Figure 12-1
on page 312. Support for Roe's system comes from six studies showing that
about two-thirds of job changes occur within the same group (Roe & Lunneborg, 1990, pp. 83, 98).

The groups are described as follows (Roe & Klos, 1972, pp. 202–203):

1. *Service:* This involves one person doing something for another person. Occupations include clinical psychologist, social worker, career counselor, nurse,
waiter, and servant.

2. *Business contact:* People in this group are involved in persuading others,
possibly selling products. Examples include public relations work, car sales, insurance sales, and door-to-door sales.

3. *Organization:* Management is the primary activity. It may be government
on a federal, state, or local level, or it may refer to management in a privately
owned company. Examples are senator, accountant, and secretary.

4. *Technology:* This category includes making, producing, maintaining, and
transporting products. Included in this category are engineers, production managers, pilots, electricians, and heavy-equipment operators.

5. *Outdoor:* Protection of the environment and production of crops and forest
products are included in this group. Also included is work with natural resources,
such as oil and coal, as well as those found in lakes, rivers, and streams. Examples
of such occupations are corporate farm manager, landscape architect, fish and game
warden, miner, and lumberjack.

6. *Science:* These occupations concern the development and application of science in many areas: natural science, physical science, social science, and so on. Scientific careers include university professor, pharmacist, medical technician, and lab
technician.

7. *General culture:* People in this group tend to be interested in human activity and culture. This group includes communicating and preserving culture (the humanities). Fields included are law, ministry, history, and education. Principals and
teachers may be found in this group, but university science teachers would be in
Group 6 and art professors in Group 8. Examples of occupations are lawyer, editor,
elementary school teacher, and radio announcer.

8. *Arts and entertainment:* This group includes those who perform for the public or create. Areas include music, art, writing, and athletics. Examples of careers
in this category are music conductor, museum curator, music critic, interior designer, football player, and stagehand.

Tracey and Rounds (1994) have found Meir's (1970, 1973) arranging
of the eight groups to be superior to that of Roe's. They examined the relative fit using a factor analysis and suggest the arrangement described in

Table 12-1 *Roe's Classification of Occupations*

Level	I Service	II Business Contact	III Organization	IV Technology	V Outdoor	VI Science	VII General Cultural	VIII Arts and Entertainment
1	Personal therapists. Social work supervisors. Counselors.	Promoters.	U.S. president and cabinet officer. Industrial tycoon. International bankers.	Inventive geniuses. Consulting or chief engineers. Ships' commanders.	Consulting specialists.	Research scientists. University, college faculties. Medical specialists. Museum curators.	Supreme Court justices. University, college faculties. Prophets. Scholars.	Creative artists, performers (great). Teachers (university equivalent). Museum curators.
2	Social workers. Occupational therapists. Probation, truant officers (with training).	Promoters. Public relations counselors.	Certified public accountants. Business and government executives. Union officials. Brokers (average).	Applied scientists. Factory managers. Ships' officers. Engineers.	Applied scientists. Landowners and operators (large). Landscape architects.	Scientists, semi-independent. Nurses. Pharmacists. Veterinarians.	Editors. Teachers (high school and elementary).	Athletes. Art critics. Designers. Music arrangers.
3	YMCA officials. Detectives, police sergeants. Welfare workers. City inspectors.	Salespeople: auto, bond, insurance. Dealers, retail and wholesale. Confidence men.	Accountants (average). Employment managers. Owners, catering, drycleaning, and so on.	Aviators. Contractors. Foremen (DOT I). Radio operators.	County agents. Farm owners. Forest rangers. Fish, game wardens.	Technicians: medical, X-ray, museum. Weather observers. Chiropractors.	Justices of the peace. Radio announcers. Reporters. Librarians.	Ad writers. Designers. Interior decorators. Showmen.

Level	I Service	II Business Contact	III Organization	IV Technology	V Outdoor	VI Science	VII General Cultural	VIII Arts and Entertainment
4	Barbers. Chefs. Practical nurses. Police officers.	Auctioneers. Buyers (DOT I). House canvassers. Interviewers, poll.	Cashiers, clerks, credit, express, and so on. Foremen, warehouse. Salesclerks.	Blacksmiths. Electricians. Foremen (DOT II). Mechanics (average).	Laboratory testers, dairy products, and so on. Miners. Oil well drillers.	Technical assistants.	Law clerks.	Advertising artists. Decorators, window, and so on. Photographers. Racing car drivers.
5	Taxi drivers. General house workers. Waiters. City firefighters.	Peddlers.	Clerks, file, stock, and so on. Notaries. Runners. Typists.	Bulldozer operators. Delivery people. Smelter workers. Truck drivers.	Gardeners. Farm tenants. Teamsters. Cow-punchers. Miners' helpers.	Veterinary hospital attendants.		Illustrators, greeting card. Showcard writers. Stagehands.
6	Chambermaids. Hospital attendants. Elevator operators. Watchmen.		Messengers.	Helpers. Laborers. Wrappers. Yardmen.	Dairy hands. Farm laborers. Lumber-jacks.	Nontechnical helpers in scientific organizations.		

Source: Adapted from *The Psychology of Occupations*, by Anne Roe. Copyright © 1956, John Wiley & Sons, Inc.

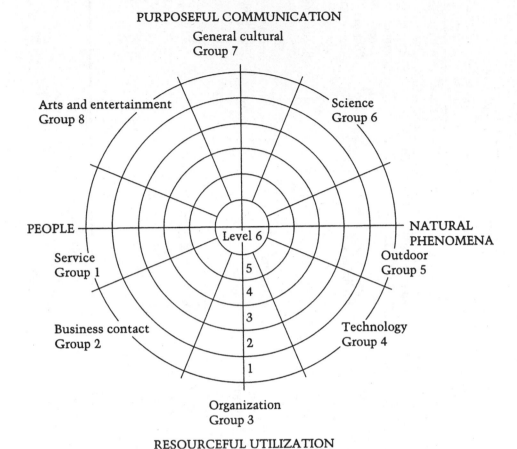

PURPOSEFUL COMMUNICATION

General cultural
Group 7

Arts and entertainment
Group 8

Science
Group 6

PEOPLE

Level 6

NATURAL
PHENOMENA

Service
Group 1

Outdoor
Group 5

5

4

Business contact
Group 2

3

Technology
Group 4

2

1

Organization
Group 3

RESOURCEFUL UTILIZATION

Figure 12-1 Diagram of levels and groups in Roe's classification system. *Source:* From "Early Determinants of Vocational Choice," by Anne Roe, 1957. *Journal of Counseling Psychology, 4,* pp. 212–217. Copyright© 1957 by the American Psychological Association.

Figure 12-2 on page 313. This statistical procedure provides a way of determining which categories are most similar to each other and thus belong next to each other in a circular or other arrangement. In Roe's system, the categories, as arranged, are not as similar to each other as in Meir's system. Contrast the arrangement of Roe's system in Figure 12-1 with Meir's grouping. Tracey and Rounds (1994) suggest that it would be useful for counselors to explain occupations to clients using Meir's grouping, as it is a more accurate arrangement than Roe's and would seem to update and improve on her classification system.

The Six Levels of Occupations Classification by level is based on the amount of responsibility and ability that is required by the occupation. Responsibility (Roe & Klos, 1972, p. 206) is particularly important and refers

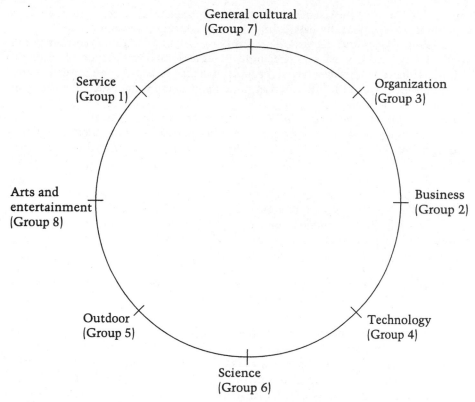

Figure 12-2 Diagram of Meir's (1970) grouping of Roe's eight groups. Roe's group numbers have been put in parentheses for comparison to Figure 12-1. The diagram is based on information from Meir (1973).

to the difficulty and complexity of decisions along with the variety of problems that people encounter in their work. Levels of occupations can be viewed as being on a continuum, and separating occupations into such categories is often difficult. Originally, Roe developed eight levels but then condensed them into six. Figure 12-1 is useful in showing that those at the lowest levels are most similar to each other, at the center of the circle. It is easier to move from one group to another at the lower levels of occupations than at the higher levels. Because lower levels of occupations require relatively few skills, changes between groups are likely to be more frequent at lower levels than at higher levels. The six levels are described as follows (Roe & Klos, 1972, pp. 208–209):

1. *Professional and managerial 1:* Independent responsibility. This category includes those who have the highest level of responsibility within a group. Their responsibilities tend to be very important and varied. They may make policy decisions that affect many people through government, education, health, or private

companies. Those in the sciences and many in the general cultural group often have a doctorate. Others usually have a high level of education in their group.

2. *Professional and managerial 2:* Similar to Level 1 but differs in that the individual may have less independence or fewer or less important responsibilities. Often, individuals at this level have a bachelor's degree or possibly a master's degree. They may be involved in interpreting policy and making important decisions for themselves and others.

3. *Semiprofessional and small business:* Only a moderate level of responsibility for others, such as the responsibility of police sergeants for other police officers, or of retail businesspeople for their salesclerks. Often, only a high school education is required, but many people have degrees from technical schools or four-year institutions.

4. *Skilled:* Training is required, whether in the form of an apprenticeship or vocational education, at either a technical school or a high school.

5. *Semiskilled:* On-the-job training and some special schooling may be required. For example, truck drivers may receive training from their union or a special school. Taxi drivers may receive very brief training before being given assignments.

6. *Unskilled:* Little special training is required. Individuals need only to follow basic directions. No specific education is required.

Testing and Occupational Classification   Roe's classification system has been helpful in interest measurement. Four interest inventories were developed through the use of Roe's classification system. Perhaps the most well known is the Career Occupational Preference System Interest Inventory. It is also known as the California Occupational Preference System (COPS; Knapp & Knapp, 1985). The COPS not only provides scores for each Roe group but also includes scales for more than one level per group. For example, science, organization, arts and entertainment, and service each have scales on two levels, and technology provides scores on three levels. The Vocational Interest Inventory (VII; Lunneborg, 1981) is a forced-choice inventory designed for high school and college students that controls for sex bias. Another inventory uses activities described in the fourth edition of the *Dictionary of Occupational Titles* (DOT). This inventory was developed for women college graduates (Lunneborg & Wilson, 1982). Meir developed two interest inventories for use in Israel (Meir, 1975; Meir, Rubin, Temple, & Osipow, 1997). One of them contains a list of occupational titles (RAMAK). The other, Courses, contains a list of 64 college-level courses. In addition to the eight occupational groups, RAMAK provides scores on three levels: professional, semiprofessional, and skilled. These inventories can be helpful to the counselor who uses Roe's conceptual classification system by providing objective information as to the occupational groups a client may wish to consider. They may also be helpful in differentiating levels, although those inventories that do differentiate levels mainly use two or three broad levels rather than six. However, it is not necessary to use one of these inventories to use Roe's classification system in counseling.

Maslow's Hierarchy of Needs

Central to Roe's theory of personality development and career choice is the concept of needs. Roe found that Maslow's (1954) list of needs fit her viewpoint best. Maslow's theory focuses on human needs, rather than needs derived from research on animals. These needs, involuntary or unconscious, range from the most basic to the most complex. Although Roe's theory, as will be described later, has biological and sociological underpinnings, it is the psychological motivations of individuals that are most important in her theory. These are emphasized in the later stages of Maslow's hierarchy.

The needs Maslow identified are listed in the following paragraphs in order of their strength. The physiological needs are listed first, as they must be satisfied before other needs can be met. Individuals must satisfy their physiological hunger before they can be concerned about shelter, love, or information. Although there are exceptions, in general the needs at the beginning of the list must be satisfied before the others can be satisfied. People do not need to satisfy all needs. In fact, Maslow would claim that self-actualization (the last need listed) is realized by relatively few people. The needs are described here along with their relationship to occupational choice and entry (Roe & Siegelman, 1964):

1. *Physiological needs:* These are the most basic needs, as they are required for survival. They differ from other needs in that they can be localized in the body. For example, thirst is felt in the mouth and throat. When physiological needs are not met, they become the dominating force. If you are very hungry or thirsty as you read this book, you will not be able to concentrate on the subject matter, nor will you care, until you satisfy those needs. Work provides an income used to satisfy these needs. Agriculture and hunting are a direct way of satisfying these needs.

2. *Safety needs:* These needs are met through shelter, good health, and avoidance of danger. Except in emergency, safety needs are usually met for adults. Children are more likely to be frightened by strange events than are adults. Usually, toddlers react very strongly and loudly if their safety needs are not met. For adults, during wartime and times of famine, safety and physiological needs may not be met. When these needs become predominant, the remaining needs become quite minor. From an occupational point of view, safety needs can be translated into security needs (Roe, 1956, p. 32). Some people will choose security over working with cooperative colleagues or other benefits, as security meets safety needs more than needs for belongingness.

3. *The needs for belongingness and love:* Caring for and being cared for are the most basic needs after safety and physiological needs. Psychological problems develop in children and adults when needs for belongingness and love are not met. Sexuality is a physical need, but its expression as affection belongs in this category. In a work setting, the need for belongingness is met through relationships with one's colleagues. Occupations vary in the extent to which they offer opportunities for satisfactory coworker relationships. For many people, this is one of the most important aspects of a successful career.

4. *Esteem needs:* People need to feel important and respected by themselves and by others. One often develops self-respect by feeling respected by others. One of the main reasons for seeking counseling is low self-esteem that is not affected

by positive feelings that others may have for the individual. Feeling weak and inferior to others is a common reason for entering counseling or psychotherapy. An example is people who are unemployed and therefore feel bad about themselves, perceiving themselves to be inferior to those who are working. In contrast, the respect that people receive from colleagues and superiors when they perform well does much to develop self-esteem. Self-esteem is likely to be greatest in the higher occupational levels of Roe's classification system, as there is a greater degree of responsibility in these occupations, which brings about more self-respect and respect from others.

5. *The need for information:* People have a need for information to understand their own personal and cultural history, to understand the environment around them, and to understand themselves. Children often want to know how things work, why things are done, and what will happen next. To perform all jobs, there is a need for information. At the highest levels of Roe's classification system, people may work for years achieving an M.D. or a Ph.D. degree to acquire the information needed for a specific occupation. Most of the occupations at Levels 1 and 2 of Roe's system require that the individual master a great deal of information.

6. *The need for understanding:* We need not only to have information about our world and our career, but also to have a way to process and understand this information. Those in the higher levels of Roe's classification system must understand and interpret great amounts of information.

7. *The need for beauty:* Although this seems to be a need one can do without meeting, it is an important experience for many people. For those in the arts and entertainment field (Group 8), it is essential. Often, the need for beauty may be the most important need for creative painters, writers, and musicians.

8. *The need for self-actualization:* This is the need to be all that one can be. The more an individual is able to do, the more he or she must do. To be self-actualized, one must meet the other needs first. However, Roe differs from Maslow in that she would put self-actualization prior to the need for information, as it seems so basic to her. Work, certainly that in the higher levels as described by Roe, gives individuals an opportunity for self-actualization. For those whose abilities go beyond what is required by their occupations, self-actualization may be impeded.

Maslow's (1954) hierarchy of needs provides a platform for Roe's personality development theory and can be, by itself, valuable in career counseling (Sackett, 1998). As shown here, work meets many needs, but in different ways. In general, the higher the level of occupation, the more likely it is that higher-level needs will be met. Various occupational groupings meet needs, such as those for information, beauty, and understanding, in vastly different ways. The driving force for Roe, however, was to try to understand how needs develop in children and to predict career entry from this development.

Propositions of Roe's Personality Development Theory

Roe's theory is a very broad one, based not only on Maslow's hierarchy of needs, but also on genetic and sociological factors that affect career choice. In addition, Roe tried to predict the development of interests and abilities.

She also discussed the important determinants of interest. Her theory also made statements about how needs develop into motivation. Her basic propositions are elaborated on in the following paragraphs (Roe & Lunneborg, 1990).

Development of Interests and Attitudes   The study of the development of interests and attitudes has been an important aspect of Roe's theoretical research. Interests and attitudes were considered an excellent subject for study because Roe believed that they are relatively unaffected by genetic predisposition. The development of interests and attitudes is involuntary. Individuals don't choose parents, teachers, or many of the situations that they encounter. Even friends are chosen only to a limited degree—from the neighborhood or the classroom. Roe feels that interests and attitudes are determined by early patterns of satisfactions and frustrations. This is the most important element of Roe's theory, as it is the focus of much of her research.

Determinants of Interests   Interests are determined in large part by the degree of need satisfaction. The energy that results from a partially met need may develop importance for the individual. For example, a student who wishes to satisfy his or her need for information about the human eye may develop that interest if a teacher presents material about the eye that stimulates that interest. If the student is very frustrated by the difficulty of the information or does not have the ability to grasp it, then this activity will not develop as an interest. Studying the eye is an involuntary activity. When first learning biology, the student does not say, "I choose to become interested in the study of the eye and biology." The interest develops gradually and without awareness.

Development of Needs into Motivators   The more intense the needs, the more intense the need to become successful. As the need for information and understanding about the eye increases, the student will work harder to learn more about it. As he or she is rewarded for meeting this need, basic needs such as feeling loved, respected, and important may be realized. Parents may offer praise; teachers may assign high grades. In this way, needs develop into motivators.

Roe's emphasis on the development of needs and her interest in psychological factors focus her work on parent–child interaction. Being particularly interested in how the attitudes of parents frustrate or fulfill the needs of their children, Roe interviewed artists, scientists, and others to learn more about how they had been motivated by their parents. She was particularly interested in the child-raising attitudes of her subjects' parents. Much of her research was retrospective; that is, she asked adults what had happened to them as children. Retrospective research has been criticized because of the unreliability of recall over 20 or more years. Direct observation or testing of children is the preferred research method.

Roe's Model of Parent–Child Interaction

Anne Roe (1957) classified early parent–child relationships into three types, each with two subclassifications. Roe was more interested in the attitudes of parents toward their children than in the specific ways in which parents behaved toward their children. Her classification system deals with the attitude toward (or away from) the child. In this section, the predictions that Roe made about categories of occupations to be selected depending on child-raising practices will be illustrated. Research on Roe's predictions and their implications for counseling practice will be discussed. A case study dealing with career choice and style of parenting will help the reader to understand the depth and complexity of Roe's theory.

The Three Types of Parental Attitudes   For Roe, parents exhibit one of the following three types of attitudes toward their children:

Concentration on the child: Roe describes two types of emotional concentration on the child. The first is overprotection. An *overprotective* parent encourages dependence in the child and restricts curiosity and exploration. An *overdemanding* parent may request perfection from the child, asking for excellent performance and setting high standards of behavior. If the child does not meet these standards, the parent may punish the child. Roe shows that it is quite possible for parents to have different styles of behavior with each of their children. For example, she states that parents of a first child may be anxious and rather overprotective but may be more relaxed with less emotional concentration on the second child.

Avoidance of the child: Roe suggests two different methods of avoidance: rejection and neglect. An *emotionally rejected* child may be criticized or punished by his or her parents and not given love and affection. A *neglected* child may be ignored for a myriad of reasons, such as parents' concern with their own problems, other children, and work.

Acceptance of the child: Parents encourage independence rather than dependence and do not ignore or reject their child, creating a relatively tension-free environment. *Casual acceptance* refers to a low-key attitude of the parent, offering a minimum of love. *Loving acceptance,* on the other hand, shows a warmer attitude of the parent toward the child, while not interfering with the child's resources by fostering dependency.

Parental Attitudes and Maslow's Hierarchy   Maslow's hierarchy of needs can be used to describe, in general terms, how certain needs are met or not met, depending on parental style. In homes where there is an emotional concentration on the child, the emphasis may be on the gratification of low-level needs. Meeting the needs for belongingness, love, and esteem may be contingent on the child's conforming to the parents' wishes. Needs for information and understanding may be limited by the parents' overprotectiveness or overdemandingness. Parents who avoid the child through either emotional rejection or neglect may meet mainly physiological and safety needs. Rejecting the child, or withholding love, can have a strong negative effect in terms of children's learning to avoid interaction with others. Needs for information and understanding may develop irrespective of the parents. What provides the possibility of all the needs' being gratified is the accepting parent. Through acceptance, children are likely to feel loved and to develop an independent style that will encourage the search for information, understanding, beauty, and self-actualization. The three basic styles of parenting are shown in the second innermost ring in Figure 12-3. The subtypes of parental understanding are shown in the third ring.

Orientation Toward or Away from People Roe believed that the variety of parental attitudes just described bring about certain types of personalities in the child. These are outlined in the next-to-outermost ring in Figure 12-3. Roe felt that children brought up in overprotective or overdemanding homes are likely to become self-centered in that they are aware of the views of others about themselves and wish to be in a strong position in relationship to others. Children brought up in rejecting homes are likely to develop attitudes against, rather than toward, people. They may be aggressive or defensive, preferring working with data or things rather than with people. Those children brought up by accepting parents are likely not to be aggressive or defensive and are likely to be interested in people rather than data or things. Roe then related these attitudes toward people or away from people to general patterns of relating in each of the eight occupational groups.

Relationship of Parental Style to Occupational Selection Roe made predictions about the occupational selections of individuals who she felt would develop certain attitudes toward or away from people depending on the child-raising approach of their parents. One can follow these predictions by examining Figure 12-3, moving from the outside of the circle to the inside. For example, people in Group 1, Service, are likely to have a major orientation toward themselves or others. They may have been brought up in a home where they were overprotected or in one in which they felt loving acceptance from their parents. In contrast, those who select Science (Group 6) may prefer things or data to people and may have been ignored or rejected by their parents. Roe recognized that each parent within a family constellation may have a different style of parenting, and that parents may alter their styles at various times in their lives. However, she was referring to the most dominant style of child-raising when she made her predictions. To do this, she developed A Parent–Child Relations Questionnaire (PCR I) based on the classification system that was described earlier (Roe & Siegelman, 1963). The questionnaire results were categorized into three basic factors: loving versus rejecting, casual versus demanding, and overt attention. These factors can be related directly to the parenting styles described earlier.

Research Support Because of the difficulty of making predictions about adult behavior from early childhood behavior and parental child-raising strategies, many complex research problems were posed by Roe's theory.

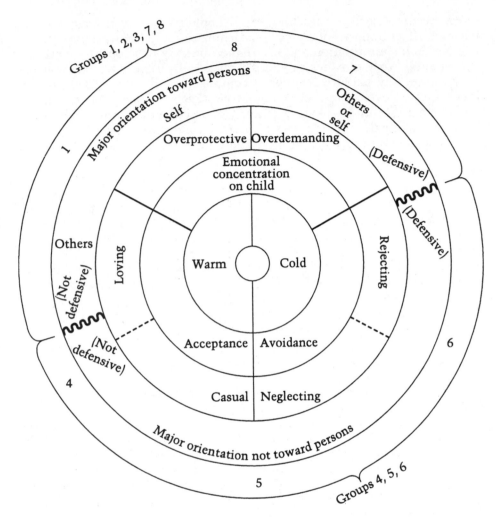

Figure 12-3 Hypothesized relations between major orientation, occupational choice, and parent–child relations. (Adapted from "Classification of Occupations," by A. Roe and D. Klos. In J. H. Whiteley and A. Resnikoff (Eds.), *Perspectives on Vocational Development*, p. 213. Copyright © 1972 ACA. Reprinted with permission. No further reproduction authorized without written permission of the American Association for Counseling and Development.)

Much of the research was conducted by asking people about their memories of their childhood experiences. As mentioned earlier, this retrospective data can be faulty because of selective and distant memory. Although there were many studies investigating the child-raising backgrounds of engineers, scientists, artists, ministers, homemakers, and many other occupations, the samples were quite small (Osipow, 1983). Also, the research did not deal with differences in child-raising techniques between parents or those that may have changed with time.

After reviewing the research in detail, Osipow and Fitzgerald (1996) and Roe and Lunneborg (1990) concluded that the research does not support the theory. There is no evidence that early child-raising patterns predict later occupational entry. However, both Roe and Lunneborg (1990) and Osipow (1983) did cite evidence that the work activity chosen by people within highly narrow fields of interest does reflect attitudes related to the experiences of early childhood (Roe & Lunneborg, 1990, p. 86). Thus, there is evidence that, within an occupation, people may select activities that indicate an orientation either toward or away from people. For example, a park ranger (Group 5, Outdoor) who experienced little concern or attention (avoidance–neglect) from her parents may prefer activities that take her away from people, such as protecting wildlife or monitoring forests for fires or other damage. On the other hand, a park ranger who experienced love and acceptance from her parents may prefer to deal with the public through tours, assistance, or rescue operations. In summary, the research suggests a very limited application of Roe's theory in counseling. In fact, Roe (Roe & Lunneborg, 1990) is quite clear in stating that her theory was never designed for counseling application. A recent review of Roe's theory (Brown, Lum, & Voyle, 1997) suggests that flaws in past research have lead to an inaccurate appraisal of her theory. Roe's theory along with views of children's attachment to parents provide interesting perspectives of parental influence on the career choice of children.

ATTACHMENT THEORY

Just as Roe has tried to make predictions based on parent–child interactions, attachment theorists have had similar intentions. Briefly, attachment theory studies the role that attachments (primarily parental) play in shaping the life of an individual (Cassidy & Shaver, 1999). Attachment theory grew out of object relations theory, a development of psychoanalysis (Sharf, 2000), which emphasizes the relationship that the infant has with others, particularly the mother. Bowlby (1969/1982, 1973, 1980), the most well-known attachment theorist, studied the importance of attachment, separation, and loss in human development. Unlike object relations theorists, who are interested in mother–child relationships in early childhood and their effect on psychiatric illness, some attachment theorists have studied the effect that attachment has on children not diagnosed with psychiatric problems. Other attachment theorists have focused on the entire life span. Bowlby was particularly interested in how individuals' sense of being worthwhile and views of their own competence develop along with their views of others. Of great importance in this development, according to Bowlby, is the role of "attachment figures," such as the mother and the father. To study attachment, Ainsworth (Ainsworth, Blehar,

Waters, & Wall, 1978) used the "strange situation" method to observe the attachment behavior of young children. This involves making unobtrusive observations of children when the mother comes and goes, when a stranger enters, and when the child is alone. From these observations, three types of responding were found: the secure pattern, the anxious-ambivalent pattern, and the avoidant pattern.

> *Secure Pattern.* The infant responds to the caregiver easily and is able to continue exploratory behavior (an important feature for career development, as described in Chapter 7). The security experienced by infants allows them to interact well with people and things in their world.
>
> *Anxious-Ambivalent Pattern.* Because the infant experiences the caregiver as being inconsistent, the child becomes anxious. Also, the child's view of herself or himself is one of uncertainty, as is the child's view of others. Such anxiety and uncertainty often result in decreased exploratory behavior.
>
> *Avoidant Pattern.* In this pattern, the infant ignores or rejects care that is offered by an adult. Ainsworth et al. (1978) saw that such children would develop a sense of being alone in the world and of being unable to trust others.

A large amount of research has shown that these patterns are stable during the first six years of life and are different from infant moods or temperament (Cassidy & Shaver, 1999). Attachment patterns are less consistent in families with high stress than in those with low stress. Other researchers have modified these attachment patterns and added one or two others. Suggested by patterns of attachment is the idea that children who have a secure pattern of attachment in their first six years of life are more willing to explore relationships with others and more willing to play with objects or animals, activities leading eventually to greater familiarity with their world and the world of work. However, there is no direct evidence to support this conjecture because, like Roe's theory, attachment theory has the very difficult task of trying to predict behavior over a long period of time. Longitudinal studies of this type are rare. Also, the parental attitudes of the father, as opposed to the mother (Roe's theory), and different kinds of attachment to the mother and the father may also be significant variables.

Reviewing nonlongitudinal studies, Blustein, Prezioso, and Palladino Schultheiss (1995) have shown how attachment theory can be useful in understanding career development. Of particular importance is the relationship between attachment and exploration that is related to learning. Being secure, the adolescent and adult can more freely explore his or her world and thus develop social competence throughout life that is related to job satisfaction (Lucas, 1999). Puffer (1999) found that when female college students were attached to parents who were committed to encouraging independence the students had a stable sense of vocational identity and minimal anxiety or indecision about career choice. Blustein et al. (1995) make a point that secure and close relationships are important not only in childhood but also in late adolescence, when career exploration is a prominent activity.

Recent research adds information about the relevance of separation–attachment concepts to vocational development. O'Brien (1996) reported that attachment and emotional closeness to the mother and attitudes that were similar to those of both parents were predictive of confidence in career decision making and in being realistic about career choices. In a study of college students, Ketterson and Blustein (1997) reported that parental attachment was associated with increased exploration of one's environment. They note that, in general, older students tended to engage in more career exploration than younger students. In studying attachment, attachment to the mother, but not the father, appeared to contribute to fuller career exploration (Felsman & Blustein, 1999). Not only was attachment to mother important, but also attachment to peers was related to increased exploration of one's environment and greater progress in committing to career choices. Tyson (1999) found that ratings of attachment to the mother and father were related to different styles of career indecision that included anxiety about career choice, general indecisiveness, need for career information, and need for more knowledge about one's self. In a study of employed adults, Hardy and Barkham (1994) reported that employers who revealed anxious–ambivalent attachments were also anxious about their performance at work and in work-related relationships. These studies suggest that the concepts of separation and attachment can add to knowledge of the career development process, but the findings are not specific enough to make concrete suggestions to counselors.

Using an attachment perspective, Susan Phillips and her colleagues (Christopher, Phillips, Lisi, Groat, & Carlson, 1999; Lisi, Phillips, Christopher, Carlson, & Groat, 1999; Phillips, 1997) have tried to identify different career decision-making strategies. Phillips and her colleagues have identified three themes that reflect relationships with others (actions of others, recruitment of others, and pushing others away) and categories within these themes. Actions of others refers to the involvement that a decision maker has with other individuals. The categories within this theme are on a continuum from nonactive support through forced guidance and criticism. Recruitment of others concerns the process that individuals use in enlisting others in their decision making. The categories include being cautious, seeking advice, seeking information, and using others as a sounding board. The third theme is pushing others away, which describes those decision makers who do not involve others in their decision making and may show systematic or confident independence in their approach. Although these themes and categories are still in the process of being developed, they show counselors how career decision making can be viewed by examining how clients incorporate (or do not incorporate) other people in their career choice process.

When applied to career development, attachment theory does not make specific predictions about career choices, as does Roe's theory. Because the research is limited and predictions are only partially related to career development, the suggestions for counseling application are general. Blustein et al. (1995) believe that understanding individuals' relationships with others in terms of separation and attachment is useful in working with career choice and career adjustment concerns. Particularly, discussing issues of separation from and attachment to parents that are causing problems in an adolescent's life may help individuals develop a sense of security so that they can deal with career exploration and choice issues that are causing anxiety. When working with clients who are anxious about their career choice, counselors may find it helpful to ask about current or past strains in parental relationships. For example, if her or his parents are in the process of getting a divorce or were divorced earlier, the client may feel unsure of herself or himself in deciding about how to deal with parents, siblings, and educational or career decision making. Some investigators have studied the role of parental relationships in career decision making by observing or investigating the ways in which parents and their adolescent children talk about career choice issues.

PARENT–CHILD CAREER INTERACTIONS

A relatively recent focus of research has been the work of Richard Young and his colleagues on the influence of parents on the career development of young people. They refer to this research, which studies conversations between parent(s) and child, as "Joint Action." Their focus is on how parents and children perceive career decision making and their areas of agreement and disagreement. This emphasis on the perceptions of parents and children reflects the social constructivist point of view described in Chapter 11. In studies of 14 videotaped parent–adolescent career conversations Young and his colleagues (Young, Paseluikho, & Valach, 1997; Young, Valach, et al., 1997) focused on the feelings and emotions that arose from parent–adolescent conversations. They show how parents and children try to establish a common ground or area of agreement in their conversations. As families talk, they may establish closeness or a sense of separateness depending on the nature of the agreements and disagreements. These investigators identified the importance of exploration, struggle, and negotiation as parents and their high-school-age students address the career choice of the students. The investigators studied both short-term goals, such as continuing an open discussion between parent and child, and long-term goals, such as selecting a career direction. In another study of the conversations of adolescents and their parents, Young, Antal, Bassett, Post, DeVries, and Valach (1999) examined the way adolescents talked to their parents to reach goals such as educational planning, career selection, and their future. Processes that take place in these conversations included exploring ideas, formulating plans, validating plans, and challenging ideas. When asked about the role of parental influence, adolescents saw that parental influence was appropriate in developing short-term goals, especially if the adolescents' decisions may have negative moral consequences

(Bregman & Killen, 1999). Unlike the work of Roe and attachment theorists who have studied career development, Young and his colleagues analyze actual parent–child conversations. This work has helped in the development of a specific approach to involving parents in the career counseling process.

A five-step method of including parents and children in career counseling, Parent Involved Career Exploration (PICE) Counseling Process has been designed by Amundson and Penner (1998). This method includes an introduction, pattern identification exercises, discussion of school preferences and performance, a perspective on education and labor market possibilities, and planning the next step. In this process, which is designed for students between the ages of 14 to 18, two students and their parents are involved in the counseling sessions. In the first step, the process is introduced so that students and parents can understand how counseling can be helpful to them. In the second step, the Pattern Identification Exercise (PIE) is used so that students may identify their strengths and weaknesses that are related to their career development. They are asked to talk about a leisure activity that went well, and to discuss a time when it did not work out so well. By doing this, students can see some patterns of weaknesses and strengths. Students consider the patterns that are suggested by this information and how these patterns can affect their career choice. Then parents are asked for additional comments. In the third step, School Preferences and Performance, the students talk about what they like about their courses and how well they are doing. After the students illustrate their views with examples, the parents are asked for feedback. In the fourth step, Perspectives on Educational and Labor Market Opportunities, they discuss labor market trends, the need to be flexible in choices, how school and work activities relate, the need to talk with others for information, admissions standards, and so forth. Their parents are asked to contribute to this discussion and provide their own information about the labor market strategies that they might find useful. The fifth step, Setting the Next Step, occurs at the end of the session and includes time for the counselor to give students and parents information about resources in the school and the community.

Typically, PICE is done in one session. Amundson and Penner (1998) suggest that PICE is an adjunct counseling approach that will work best when both student and parent are interested and motivated to explore careers. This innovative approach highlights the importance of the role of parents in the career exploration of their children.

FAMILY SYSTEMS THERAPY

In general, family therapists and marriage counselors have paid little attention to career counseling. However, a few studies have described the effect of family relationships on career development. Of particular interest to researchers on family processes have been the enmeshed and the disengaged family (Goldenberg & Goldenberg, 2000). Basically, an enmeshed family is one in which the responsibilities in the family are unclear. For example, the mother and the father may give an eleventh-grade student different advice about choosing a career. Her younger sister may tease her about being stupid because she has no career plans. In contrast, in a disengaged family, an eleventh-grade student may be told by his father to make plans to study engineering because there are good-paying jobs in that field. The relationship between father and son is authoritarian, with the father telling the son, but not listening to him. Penick and Jepsen (1992) found that family relationships, such as enmeshment or disengagement, were stronger predictors of career development than gender, socioeconomic status, or educational achievement. In another study, Gordon (1991) found that problems in family functioning are related to the working style of employed adults, adults who experienced divorce or the loss of a family member in childhood being more likely than others to become innovative problem solvers. In a study comparing college students whose parents were divorced with those who were not, students from intact families shared more career decidedness than those whose parents were divorced, especially when parents were recently divorced (Scott & Church, 1999). These types of studies are infrequent, and more research along these lines needs to be done.

One approach that family therapists use with their clients can be applied to career counseling. When working with clients who are trying to choose an occupation, it may be helpful to discuss family career patterns. McGoldrick and Gerson (1985) describe the use of the genogram as a way of drawing relationships in a family and indicating important information about them.

Okiishi (1987) and Okocha (1998) describe how genograms can be used in career counseling. They encourage client self-disclosure, organize relevant information about the attitudes of the family toward work, and reveal how the work patterns of family members affect the client. To construct a genogram, Okiishi (1987) suggests using a large piece of newsprint or paper so that relevant information about the family can be listed (an abridged version is illustrated in Figure 12-4). When occupational information about the family is included, many issues of the client's view of himself or herself, others, and the work world can be explored. Counselors can find out from their clients how different family members served as role models for attitudes toward work and further education. For example, did certain relatives stereotype careers by gender, or did they especially value certain occupations, such as medicine or the ministry? Did the family members have different attitudes toward obtaining more education after high school? Discussing such topics helps clients better understand the origin and the content of their own attitudes toward career decision making. The use of the genogram is illustrated in the following case.

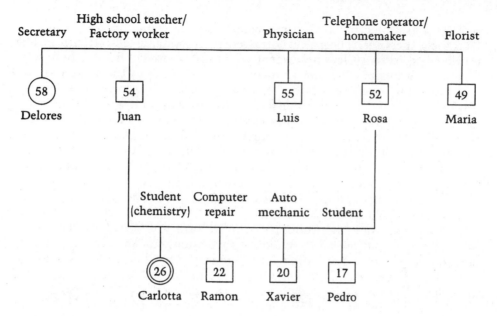

Figure 12-4 Genogram of Carlotta's family, including ages and occupations.

USING PARENTAL INFLUENCE THEORIES IN COUNSELING

It is difficult to be specific in the application of parental influence theories in counseling. Although Roe's theory makes specific predictions, they have not been confirmed by research. Neither attachment theory nor family systems theory has been sufficiently tested with career issues, nor has it been clearly shown how their hypotheses can be applied to career counseling. Rather, these theories emphasize the importance of examining parental influences. In the following case the counselor makes use of Roe's emphasis on parent–child interaction and on parental attitudes toward children, attachment theory's focus on closeness to and separation from parents, and the genogram in exploring these issues.

Carlotta is a 26-year-old single female whose parents were born in Cuba and emigrated to the United States when Carlotta was 5 years old. In Cuba, Carlotta's mother had been a telephone operator and her father had been a high school teacher. Both were fluently bilingual, and Carlotta grew up speaking both English and Spanish. Carlotta is the oldest of four children, having three younger brothers, each about two years apart. Carlotta's mother was protective of Carlotta when she was young. However, as Carlotta's brothers were born, Carlotta received less and less attention. Her mother tended to neglect her except when she wanted child care help with Carlotta's brothers. The family income after coming to the United States was quite low. Carlotta's father had to find a job in a local shoe factory. Carlotta's relationship with her father had always been warm and loving. Although it experienced some strain when they moved to the United States, the relationship essentially remained close. When Carlotta was 12, her mother was injured severely in an auto accident that considerably limited both her physical and mental functioning. At this point the relationship between Carlotta's parents deteriorated greatly. Carlotta's father was not understanding of his wife's difficulties, and they communicated little, although they lived in the same house.

Throughout her high school years, Carlotta was torn between caring for her family and pursuing school. An excellent science student, she received the praise of her biology and chemistry teachers. They supported her desire for further education. On graduation from high school, Carlotta attended a community college, where she received all A's. She had been working part time at a clothing store and continued to do so full time for two more years after receiving an associate's degree. She then entered a local university to complete a bachelor of science degree in chemistry. She worked for one year in a pharmaceutical laboratory as an assistant to a scientist and then returned to graduate school at a city far from home. Her intention was to receive a doctorate in chemistry and to become a professor of chemistry.

In discussing Carlotta's family, the counselor used a genogram, illustrated in Figure 12-4. Females are represented by circles, males by squares. The client is indicated by a double circle (or, if male, a double square). In this abridged version of the genogram, the occupations of Carlotta's brothers, parents, and their parents' brothers and sisters are also listed. In a larger genogram, cousins, spouses of parents' brothers and sisters, and grandparents would be included. With the genogram (Figure 12-4), the counselor had a clear approach to a discussion of the impact of Carlotta's father's changing from a high school teacher to a factory laborer, and of how his resulting dissatisfaction was played out in the family. Furthermore, the genogram was a basis for examining how her mother's career change from telephone operator to homemaker and her auto accident had affected her attitude toward herself and Carlotta. Using the genogram, the counselor was able to ascertain how Carlotta's mother (and others) had served as role models for Carlotta's career ambitions. Additionally, the counselor and Carlotta discussed the fact that her education was much more extensive than other family members (except her Uncle Luis, a physician). Her brother Xavier, an auto mechanic, resented her further education, and it had been a source of tension between the two of them.

When Carlotta entered counseling, she had been enrolled in a doctoral-level chemistry program for one year. She was in a panic. She was now questioning her desire to be a chemist, which she had not questioned for six years. She found the material very difficult and the professors demanding. She was questioning her ability to complete her thesis and dissertation and then continue in an extensive research program. During her first year of graduate school, Carlotta had taught a laboratory section of an undergraduate chemistry course. She had very much enjoyed teaching and was looking forward to teaching in her career. She was not sure, however, that she would be able to finish a doctoral degree. Her entire family was supportive and had become increasingly so as her brothers became older and more independent.

Her counseling dealt with several issues concerning her family relationships. Carlotta explored her relationship with her mother. She recalled times when she was 14 or 15 when she had been quite angry at her mother for not being more helpful. Now she felt some guilt about that, as she thought back to the times when her mother had been in pain from her automobile accident. She remembered very fondly good times with both parents before her adolescence. She talked of returning home occasionally on vacations and how she had played the role of peacemaker. Much of the counseling dealt with her feeling nurtured by her parents and later reversing roles to nurture both parents and brothers. In this process, she felt that her mother had withdrawn her caring from Carlotta. She recalled a profound feeling of separation from her mother when she was about 14. Perhaps as a result, helping others had become a very important role for her. It was natural for her to enjoy teaching. When she had worked in the clothing store, assisting customers in the selection of items was the part of her work that she enjoyed the most; the rest bored her. Carlotta was still fascinated by chemistry. She enjoyed her courses but was apprehensive about the coming year, when she would be working more independently with a research team. Counseling served to help her reconcile her scientific interest and her nurturing needs. It also helped to bolster her self-confidence in her ability to accomplish difficult assignments.

A follow-up contact with Carlotta ten months later revealed that she had changed the content of her research. She had changed advisers, switching to a smaller research team whose goals were more concrete and less demanding. Carlotta could see herself clearly as a chemistry teacher in a small college, where the emphasis would be on teaching and on student contact, rather than on research. She was planning to take a research assistantship the following year outside the chemistry department and in the university's program that provided help to new graduate assistants and faculty in their teaching skills.

While Roe's theory does not directly describe the occurrences in this case, the issues in the case are similar to those that concerned Roe. Parental and family relationships had an influence on Carlotta's later choices. The crisis that Carlotta faced about her future had to do with the conflict between her academic interest in chemistry and her orientation toward people and toward helping others, which had developed in her family. Furthermore, attachment theory alerts the counselor to deal with issues of

Carlotta's attachment to her mother, followed by an unwanted forced separation. Although this case study may not be typical, it illustrates the relationship of parent–child interactions to occupational choice. Carlotta was willing to explore the relationship between her current crisis and family issues; not all clients are willing to do so.

APPLYING THE THEORIES TO WOMEN AND CULTURALLY DIVERSE POPULATIONS

Roe (Roe & Lunneborg, 1990) was concerned that her occupational classification system did not account for women whose careers are interrupted by caring for a family. There really is no category in Roe's system for homemakers. She felt that her classification system was quite adequate for those who enter occupations and stay in the labor force.

Regarding her theory of personality development and career choice, Roe developed a specific formula to predict career choice that included cultural background and gender. Although it was not dealt with in this chapter because it has little application for counselors, the formula does show that Roe considered cultural and gender factors quite carefully. Race is incorporated into family background as a part of her formula, and the gender of the individual had a prominent place in her formula. Because her theory relating child-raising approaches to career choice has little applicability and her research predictions were not found to hold, the theory's application to women and culturally diverse populations is moot.

With regard to attachment theory, there are few, if any, gender differences reported in early childhood in attachment styles, and few differences have been found in studies relating attachment to career development (Blustein et al., 1995). Investigations on attachment have been carried out in England, Uganda, the United States, and other countries, providing a multicultural approach to this work. From a broader perspective, psychoanalytic writers such as Chodorow (1996) have discussed the impact of different social roles of men and women on child-raising. However, Chodorow and other writers have provided observations that are more speculative than research that investigates attachment theory. She has not focused on career development, or on issues related to cultural diversity.

Recently, much attention has been paid to gender and multicultural issues in family therapy, as shown by Goldenberg and Goldenberg (2000) and Sharf (2000). These authors provide an overview of how the two genders and different cultural groups vary in their child-raising strategies. Sinacore, Healy, and Hassan (1999) note that parents' advice to children about career concerns often differs depending on the child's gender. Although family therapists do not focus on career development issues, their observations of the role of culture and gender in career adjustment and decision making would appear to be consistent with the research on women and culturally diverse populations discussed in Chapters 7, 8, and 9.

SUMMARY

Anne Roe has contributed to career development research since the publication of her first paper (Roe & Brown, 1927). Her classification system, consisting of six levels and eight groups of occupations, is quite helpful in classifying both occupations and career choices. The occupational groups have been shown to have a meaningful relationship to each other in terms of their placement in her system. Her predictions about the effect of child-rearing practices on later occupational choice have not been borne out. However, she has pointed out the importance of meeting needs through occupational choice and has heightened counselors' awareness of the role of parenting styles in childhood development. Further insights into parental roles in career development come from attachment theory and family systems theory. This work is recent, presenting interesting questions about family influences on career choice, as well as some issues to be considered in counseling, such as discussing parental relationships as they affect confidence and exploration regarding career decision making and involving parents in the career counseling session. A practical application of the importance of parental influence is a counseling approach that includes two students and their parents.

References

Ainsworth, M. D. S., Blehar, M. C., Waters, E., & Wall, S. (1978). *Patterns of attachment: A psychological study of the strange situation.* Hillsdale, NJ: Erlbaum.

Amundson, N. E., & Penner, K. (1998). Parent involved career exploration. *Career Development Quarterly, 47,* 135–144.

Blustein, D. L., Prezioso, M. S., & Palladino Schultheiss, D. P. (1995). Attachment theory and career development: Current status and future directions. *The Counseling Psychologist, 23,* 416–432.

Bowlby, J. (1973). *Attachment and loss: Vol. II. Separation.* New York: Basic Books.

Bowlby, J. (1980). *Attachment and loss: Vol. III. Loss.* New York: Basic Books.

Bowlby, J. (1982). *Attachment and loss: Vol. I. Attachment.* London: Tavistock. (Original work published 1969.)

Bregman, G., & Killen, M. (1999). Adolescents' and young adults' reasoning about career choice and the role of parental influence. *Journal of Research on Adolescence, 9,* 253–275.

Brown, M. T., Lum, J. L., & Voyle, K. (1997). Roe revisited: A call for the reappraisal of the theory of personality development and career choice. *Journal of Vocational Behavior, 51,* 283–294.

Cassidy, J., & Shaver, P. R. (Eds.). (1999). *Handbook of attachment theory: Theory, research, and clinical applications.* New York: Guilford.

Chodorow, N. J. (1996). Theoretical gender and clinical gender: Epistemological reflections of the psychology of women. *Journal of the American Psychoanalytic Association, 44,* 215–238.

Christopher, E. K., Phillips, S. D., Lisi, K., Groat, M., & Carlson, C. (1999, August). *Correlates and consequences of relational career decision-making strategies.*

Paper presented at the meeting of the American Psychological Association, Boston, MA.

Felsman, D. E., & Blustein, D. L. (1999). The role of peer relatedness in late adolescent career development. *Journal of Vocational Behavior, 54,* 279–295.

Goldenberg, H., & Goldenberg, I. (2000). *Family therapy: An overview* (6th ed.). Pacific Grove, CA: Brooks/Cole.

Gordon, V. Z. (1991). Successful careers and cognitive style: A follow-up study of childhood family discontinuity. *Psychological Reports, 69,* 1071–1074.

Hardy, G. E., & Barkham, M. (1994). The relationship between interpersonal attachment styles and work difficulties. *Human Relations, 47,* 263–281.

Ketterson, T. U., & Blustein, D. L. (1997). Attachment relationships and the career exploration process. *Career Development Quarterly, 46,* 167–178.

Knapp, R. R., & Knapp, L. (1985). *California Occupational Preference System: Self-interpretation profile and guide.* San Diego, CA: Educational and Industrial Testing Service.

Kuder, G. F. (1946). *Manual to the Kuder Preference Record.* Chicago: Science Research Associates.

Lisi, K. L., Phillips, S. D., Christopher, E. K., Carlson, C., & Groat, M. (1999, August). *Understanding the role of others in career decision making.* Paper presented at the meeting of the American Psychological Association, Boston, MA.

Lucas, C. (1999). Predicting at-risk adolescent work adjustment: An application and extension of attachment theory. *Dissertation Abstracts International, 59* (7B): 3747.

Lunneborg, P. W. (1981). *The Vocational Interest Inventory (VII) manual.* Los Angeles: Western Psychological Services.

Lunneborg, P. W., & Wilson, V. M. (1982). *To work: A guide for women college graduates.* Englewood Cliffs, NJ: Prentice Hall.

Maslow, A. H. (1954). *Motivation and personality.* New York: Harper & Row.

McGoldrick, J., & Gerson, R. (1985). *Genograms in family assessment.* New York: Norton.

Meir, E. I. (1970). Empirical test of Roe's structure of occupations and an alternative structure. *Journal of Counseling Psychology, 17,* 41–48.

Meir, E. I. (1973). The structure of occupations by interests—A small space analysis. *Journal of Vocational Behavior, 3,* 21–31.

Meir, E. I. (1975). *Manual for the RAMAK and Courses interest inventories.* Israel: Tel Aviv University, Department of Psychology.

Meir, E. I., Rubin, A., Temple, R., & Osipow, S. H. (1997). Examination of interest inventories based on Roe's classification. *Career Development Quarterly, 46,* 48–61.

O'Brien, K. M. (1996). The influence of psychological separation and parental attachment on the career development of adolescent women. *Journal of Vocational Behavior, 48,* 257–274.

Okiishi, R. W. (1987). The genogram as a tool in career counseling. *Journal of Counseling and Development, 66,* 139–143.

Okocha, A. A. G. (1998). Using qualitative appraisal strategies in career counseling. *Journal of Employment Counseling, 35,* 151–159.

Osipow, S. H. (1983). *Theories of career development* (3rd ed.). Englewood Cliffs, NJ: Prentice Hall.

Osipow, S. H., & Fitzgerald, L. (1996). *Theories of career development* (4th ed.). Needham Heights, MA: Allyn & Bacon.

Penick, N. I., & Jepsen, D. A. (1992). Family functioning and adolescent career development. *Career Development Quarterly, 40,* 208–222.

Phillips, S. D. (1997). Toward an expanded definition of adaptive decision making. *Career Development Quarterly, 45,* 275–287.

Puffer, K. A. (1999). A study of collegians' family activities, roles, and interpersonal relations and their vocational identity, career choice commitment and decision making: An application of the development contextual framework. *Dissertation Abstracts International, 59* (12-A): 4370.

Roe, A. (1956). *The psychology of occupations.* New York: Wiley.

Roe, A. (1957). Early determinants of vocational choice. *Journal of Counseling Psychology, 4,* 212–217.

Roe, A. (1972). Perspectives on vocational development. In J. M. Whiteley & A. Resnikoff (Eds.), *Perspectives on vocational development* (pp. 61–82). Washington, DC: American Personnel and Guidance Association.

Roe, A., & Brown, C. F. (1927). Qualifications for dentistry: A preliminary study. *Personnel Journal, 6,* 176–181.

Roe, A., & Klos, D. (1972). Classification of occupations. In J. M. Whiteley & A. Resnikoff (Eds.), *Perspectives on vocational development* (pp. 199–221). Washington, DC: American Personnel and Guidance Association.

Roe, A., & Lunneborg, P. W. (1990). Personality development and career choice. In D. Brown, L. Brooks, & Assoc. (Eds.), *Career choice and development: Applying contemporary theories to practice* (2nd ed., pp. 68–101). San Francisco: Jossey-Bass.

Roe, A., & Siegelman, M. (1963). A Parent–Child Relations Questionnaire. *Child Development, 34,* 355–369.

Roe, A., & Siegelman, M. (1964). *The origin of interests.* Washington, DC: American Personnel and Guidance Association.

Sackett, S. J. (1998). Career counseling as an aid to self-actualization. *Journal of Career Development, 24,* 235–244.

Scott, D. J., & Church, A. T. (1999, August). *Separation attachment theory and career development: Effects of parental divorce.* Paper presented at the meeting of the American Psychological Association, Boston, MA.

Sharf, R. S. (2000). *Theories of psychotherapy and counseling: Concepts and cases* (2nd ed.). Pacific Grove, CA: Brooks/Cole.

Sinacore, A. L., Healy, P., & Hassan, S. (1999). Parent connection: Enlisting parents in career counseling. *Canadian Journal of Counseling, 33,* 317–335.

Strong, E. K., Jr. (1943). *Vocational interests of men and women.* Stanford, CA: Stanford University Press.

Tracey, T. J., & Rounds, J. (1994). An examination of the structure of Roe's eight interest fields. *Journal of Vocational Behavior, 44,* 279–295.

Tyson, T. S. (1999). The relation of parental attachment to career indecision subtypes of college students. *Dissertation Abstracts International: Section B: The Sciences and Engineering, 59* (9-B): 5115.

Young, R. A., Antal, S., Bassett, M. E., Post, A., DeVries, N., & Valach, L. (1999). The joint actions of adolescents in peer conversations about career. *Journal of Adolescence, 22,* 527–538.

Young, R. A., Paseluikho, M. A., & Valach, L. (1997). The role of emotion in the construction of career in parent–adolescent conversations. *Journal of Counseling and Development, 76,* 36–44.

Young, R. A., Valach, L., Paseluikho, M. A., Dover, C., Matthes, G. E., Paproski, D. L., & Sankey, A. M. (1997). The joint action of parents and adolescents in conversation about career. *Career Development Quarterly, 46,* 72–86

13

Social Learning and Cognitive Theory

The study of human learning makes up a significant portion of research in theoretical, experimental, and educational psychology. Bandura (1969, 1977, 1986, 1997) has reviewed and compiled research that supports a social learning view of human behavior based on both reinforcement theory and observational learning. Bandura believes that individuals' personalities grow from their learning experiences more than from their genetic or intrapsychic processes. Bandura (1986) acknowledged the role of behavior in learning but also recognized the importance of thoughts and images in psychological functioning. He referred to the interaction of the environment, personal factors (such as memories, beliefs, preferences, and self-perceptions), and actual behavior as a *triadic reciprocal interaction system*. In this system, each of the three factors affects the other two. As shown in this chapter, Bandura valued the importance of learning by observation. Regulating these three factors is a self-system of cognitive structures and perceptions that determines individual behavior (Bandura, 1987). How individuals regulate their behavior depends on their view of how well they can deal with difficult tasks in life, a concept that Bandura (1986, 1997) refers to as *self-efficacy*. Two significant theories of career development are based on his views and are the subject of this chapter: Krumboltz's social learning theory and social cognitive career theory, formerly referred to as self-efficacy theory.

John Krumboltz and his colleagues have developed a theory of how individuals make career decisions that emphasizes the importance of behavior (action) and cognitions (knowing or thinking) in making career decisions. It differs from most other theories in this book in that it focuses on teaching clients career decision-making techniques and helping them use these techniques effectively in selecting career alternatives and dealing with unexpected events. The theory also focuses on helping the counselor conceptualize issues. A general overview of this theory is presented here that considers genetic endowment, environmental conditions, learning experiences, and task-approach skills. With this background, important client cognitive and behavioral skills that are needed to make career decisions are explained. Behavioral counseling skills, such as reinforcement and modeling, are important tools for determining and correcting problematic beliefs about the career decision-making process that counselors are likely to find helpful. Cognitive and behavioral techniques and skills can be used by the client and the counselor in dealing with many career concerns and in encountering unplanned situations.

Another approach, with a stronger emphasis on thinking processes than on behavioral processes, is social cognitive career theory. Started about 20 years ago, and first known as career self-efficacy theory, social cognitive career theory focuses on the strength of individuals' belief that they can successfully accomplish something. This belief in oneself has been viewed as playing a more powerful role in career choice than interests, values, or abilities. Generating many research studies that have investigated the role of self-efficacy in the career choices of women, its developers, Steven Brown, Gail Hackett, and Robert Lent, expanded the original concepts into a detailed theory of career and academic interests, choice, and performance. The cognitive concepts of self-efficacy, outcome expectation, and goal selection are significant factors in academic and career decision making. Although not emphasizing application as much as does Krumboltz's social learning model, this approach gives suggestions for helping clients make academic and career choices by helping them raise the level of their belief in their own effectiveness.

Although these approaches to explaining career development vary somewhat (as will be discussed later), both rely on the writings of Albert Bandura; Krumboltz's theory uses Bandura's early work and social cognitive career theory, which emphasizes his later work. More than almost all other theories discussed in this book, social learning approaches to career decision making are directly related to psychological research into the human learning process.

KRUMBOLTZ'S SOCIAL LEARNING THEORY

Why do people choose the occupations they do? Why do they choose one major rather than another? Why choose one college and not another college? Krumboltz's social learning theory attempts to answer these questions by examining four basic factors: genetic endowment, environmental conditions, learning experiences, and task-approach skills. Each of these factors plays an important part in the eventual selection of a specific career alternative, and all four are diagrammed in Figure 13-1. The way they interact with each other is shown here. Although many other theories of career development focus on inherited abilities and environmental events, no other theory emphasizes the importance of learning experiences and task-approach skills as social learning theory does. Each of the four components of career decision making will be described in the following paragraphs, but learning experiences and task-approach skills will receive the most attention in this section. (These are described in more detail in Mitchell and Krumboltz, 1996, and briefly in Krumboltz, 1994b.)

Genetic Endowment

Genetic endowment refers to those aspects of the individual that are inherited or innate rather than learned. These include physical appearance, such as height, hair color, and skin color; a predisposition to certain physical illnesses; and other characteristics. Additionally, some individuals are born with special abilities in the arts, music, writing, athletics, and so on. In general, the greater an individual's innate genetic abilities, the more likely he or she is to respond to learning and teaching. For example, an individual with limited musical ability (e.g., tone deafness) is unlikely to respond well to musical instruction no matter how long it is done and how well. The individual may improve but is not likely to become a skilled musician. The issue of how much of a particular ability is inherited and how much is learned is a difficult one. Social learning theory does not deal directly with this issue; rather, it focuses on learning and enhancing skills and abilities, where appropriate, as well as considering them in the career decision-making process.

Environmental Conditions and Events

A vast array of conditions affects individuals. These factors are generally outside the control of the individual. These include social, cultural, political, and economic considerations. Factors such as climate and geography also affect an individual in significant ways. Living in a polluted environment or an environment subject to earthquakes or extremely cold weather certainly has an impact on an individual's career choices. Mitchell and Krumboltz (1996) describe several conditions and events, categorized as social, educational, and occupational, that affect an individual's career decision making. Such factors may be planned or unplanned, but they are usually beyond the control of the individual.

Social Factors   Changes in society have had a great effect on the available career options. For example, technological developments such as improved medicine and changes in transportation (e.g., faster cars and planes) create new jobs. The use of computers to process and store information in a wide

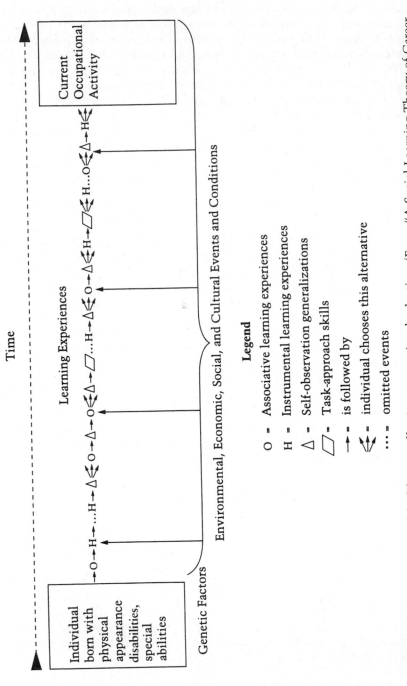

Figure 13-1 General model of factors affecting occupational selection. (From "A Social Learning Theory of Career Decision Making," by J. D. Krumboltz, p. 32. In A. M. Mitchell, G. B. Jones, & J. D. Krumboltz (Eds.), *Social Learning and Career Decision Making.* Copyright © 1979 by Carroll Press. Reprinted with permission.)

variety of fields has also had great impact on the labor market. Abuses of technology, which lead to jobs in environmental engineering and waste management, are also important. Related to the abuse of the environment is the continuing demand for natural resources, such as oil, that require new techniques to find and remove from the earth. Social organizations, like the Social Security system, programs for military personnel, and welfare programs, affect how people finance or seek careers and also require a staff to manage them, thus creating jobs. On another level, communities vary greatly in the occupations that they require. For example, a plains region may require ranchers and farmers, while a city requires merchants and salespeople. Social conditions also affect the availability of and the demand for educational resources.

Educational Conditions   The availability of education is influenced by both social and personal factors, for example, the degree to which a person's parents value higher education and have the ability to lend financial assistance. Related to that is the school system that an individual attends and the effect of the teachers and the resources in that system on the development of the individual's interests and abilities. Furthermore, training opportunities vary. Universities, technical schools, military service, and apprenticeship programs provide a variety of opportunities. Financial assistance also varies greatly among these institutions. The ability to get the necessary education to undertake a career is just one of several occupational considerations.

Occupational Conditions   There are a number of factors affecting jobs and the job market over which individuals have little control. One of the most important is the number and nature of job opportunities. Jobs may be seasonal; limited by geographical considerations, such as logging and fishing; or may be affected by changing economic conditions. Educational requirements vary: some jobs require certification, licensure, a college degree, or other prerequisites to entry. Some jobs may require a college degree or other training when it may not really be necessary for performance of the job. Further, the salary and the prestige of jobs differ, depending on supply, demand, and cultural value. Also, labor laws or union rules may limit the number of people in a given occupation. Safety and other requirements may also affect the availability of certain occupations.

Learning Experiences

One's career preferences are a result of her or his prior learning experiences. An individual may have millions of prior learning experiences that will eventually influence his or her career decisions. Hundreds of times during a day, a schoolchild is exposed to bits of information, which he or she responds to and may feel good about, confused by, discouraged by, and so on. Because the variety of experience is so great, each individual's learning experience is different from another's. There are two basic types of learning experiences—instrumental (H) and associative (O)—that are important in career choice (see Figure 13-1).

Instrumental Learning Experiences (H)   An instrumental learning experience has three components: antecedents, behaviors, and consequences. *Antecedents* refers to almost any type of condition, including genetic endowment, special abilities and skills, environmental conditions or events, and tasks or problems. People then respond to the antecedent with behaviors. The *behavior* may be quite obvious or it may be subtle. Likewise, the *consequences* of the behavior may be obvious or subtle. Further, the behavior may have an impact on others or it may not. Perhaps the key to understanding the instrumental learning experience is the focus on the behavior of the individual. Examples of an instrumental learning experience include taking an exam, studying for an exam, reading about an occupation, or talking to someone about his or her work. If the consequences of the behavior are positive, the individual is more likely to repeat it or similar behaviors. For example, if an individual receives an A on an exam, he or she is more likely to continue studying in that field and to take more courses in the same subject area than if he or she does poorly.

Associative Learning Experiences (O)   When an individual pairs a situation that was previously neutral with one that is positive or negative, an associative learning experience occurs. Two types of associative learning experiences are observation and classical conditioning. Classical conditioning is an associative learning experience that occurs when an event is generalized to a category of experiences. For example, an individual who gets caught between floors for half an hour in an elevator may develop a fear of all elevators. Future uneventful elevator rides will help to change the fear, and it is likely that the individual will return to former neutral associations with elevators. Less dramatic associative learning may occur through observing others, for example, watching a mail carrier or teacher perform his or her occupation. More passive associative experiences come about through reading and hearing. Reading occupational information and hearing a discussion about occupations are frequent ways of learning occupational information. Occupational stereotypes may develop from powerful associative experiences. For example, if a child hears that "dentists like to hurt people" or "bankers want to steal your money," inaccurate information may be learned.

Task-Approach Skills

Understanding how an individual approaches a task is critical to career decision making. For the purpose of this chapter, task-approach skills include goal setting, values clarification, generating alternatives, and obtaining occupational information. Interactions among genetic endowment, environmental conditions, and learning experiences lead to skills in doing a variety of tasks. One's study skills, work habits, ways of learning, and ways of responding emotionally are a result of genetic character-istics, special abilities, environmental conditions, and instrumental and associative learning experiences. How an individual approaches a task de-pends on previous experience and influences the outcome of the task. For example, how an individual studies a French assignment depends on her innate ability, how she was taught French, and how much she has already learned. These factors, combined with how she prepares for the French exam, will affect the outcome (her grade). Certain task skills are particu-larly important in career decision making. These include setting goals, clarifying values, predicting future events, generating alternatives, and seeking occupational information. The development of these task-approach skills is a major emphasis of Krumboltz's social learning ap-proach to career decision making.

Thoughts and beliefs arise from the four influencing factors just dis-cussed. Thoughts and beliefs about the self and the environment arise from genetic endowment, environmental conditions, learning experiences, and task-approach skills. The ways in which individuals develop beliefs and act on them is the subject of the next section.

Client Cognitive and Behavioral Skills

How individuals apply their prior learning experience and innate abilities has a direct effect on career choice and other career issues. Individuals may make observations about themselves and their environment that they will then use to make career decisions. Observations about self include obser-vations about capacities or abilities, interests, and work values. General-izations about the world include the world of work as well as other events outside oneself. Task-approach skills are related to the manner in which in-dividuals approach the career decision-making process. Implicit in social learning theory is the idea that more experience provides an opportunity to make better career decisions.

Self-Observation Generalizations about Abilities   People make observa-tions about their ability to perform tasks adequately based on prior experi-ence and information that they may have acquired about themselves. A student may observe that she is good in math but poor in music. Or she may observe that she is skillful in dealing with young children but awk-ward in dealing with elderly people. For many people, making accurate gen-eralizations about their own competencies is quite difficult. People may tend to understate or overstate their abilities. Further, some students would regard a B as a high grade, others as a failure. Similarly, students who re-ceive scores on the SAT or ACT that put them at the 50th percentile com-pared to other students may either be very disappointed or overjoyed. A person's view of his singing abilities may be quite different from the view of his audience. Thus, the accuracy of generalizations about one's own abil-ities is often derived from comparing one's view of one's capacities with others' views.

Self-Observation Generalizations About Interests   Just as individuals make observations about what they are good at, they also generalize about what they like or do not like. If a person in a biology class did not like dissecting animals, was bored by studying anatomy, and disliked learning about plants, he may generalize that he does not like biology. Interests can be very general or very specific. For example, an individual may enjoy eighteenth-century European history but may not be as interested in other aspects of history. Interest inventories are helpful in assessing generalizations that individuals have about interests derived from learning experiences. However, interest inventories do not assess specific interests, such as an interest in eighteenth-century European history. Furthermore, interest inventories are not likely to separate an interest in chemical engineering from an interest in electrical engineering. However, they are of particular use when an individual has difficulty in identifying interests that have arisen from a large number of prior learning experiences.

Self-Observation Generalizations About Values   People make judgments about the desirability of certain behaviors or events. From these judgments, they develop both personal and work values. Personal values may include a desire to be politically active or a desire to be involved in religious activity. Other personal values may include a deep love of art, music, or the natural beauty of the environment. Work values may include the desire to achieve or advance in one's profession. Other common work values include security, prestige, and high income. Some work values may be more difficult to state because they may be different from the work values that others hold. For example, a desire to persuade others by selling them a product may be more difficult to observe in oneself than the wish to help small children. Views of one's capacities, interests, and values contrast with perceptions of the world outside oneself.

Generalizations About the World   As people make observations about themselves, they also make observations about the world in which they live and the people around them. Generalizations about occupations may come from both instrumental and associative learning experiences. Some generalizations may come from a great deal of actual experience. For example, a student who has worked in many retail businesses after school and during the summer may be able to make generalizations about retail sales work based on her experience. However, if her experience has not included training and management experience or exposure to managers, she may not be able to make accurate generalizations about the work of retail store managers. Some students may make generalizations based on very few associative learning experiences. For example, it is common to hear people stereotype the career of funeral director based on jokes or movies. Frequently, they have little accurate information about the job duties of a funeral director. The purpose of occupational information and experience is to provide an opportunity for people to make generalizations about the world.

Task-Approach Skills Used in Career Decision Making   Often, individuals apply to career decision making the task-approach skills that they have learned in studying or working. Because career decision making requires one to make many generalizations about oneself and the world, previous task-approach skills may not be sufficient. Further, the accuracy of an individual's worldview and self-observation generalizations may need to be questioned. The accuracy of these observations may be determined by a combination of the quantity of experiences, the representativeness of the experiences, and the task-approach skills that an individual uses in evaluating these. Mitchell, Levin, and Krumboltz (1999) describe an approach to planned happenstance, which emphasizes using learning strategies to cope with unexpected events. In the following section, behavioral and cognitive techniques are described to assist clients in learning new skills and challenging troublesome beliefs.

Counselor Behavioral Strategies

While many behavioral techniques have been developed by psychologists to deal with a vast variety of problems, this section will explain four procedures that follow from social learning theory and are directly related to career issues in counseling: reinforcement, the use of role models, role playing, and the use of simulation in counseling. Reinforcement is the most important technique, with the broadest use, having an application in all phases of career decision-making counseling. In addition, the use of role models and simulation (trying out an occupation) can be particularly helpful when assisting clients in expanding their worldview generalizations.

Reinforcement   Many times during the day, individuals are positively reinforced for their actions. Positive reinforcement increases the occurrence of a response. For example, a student may be thanked for helping with the breakfast dishes, taking out the trash, and doing well on a history exam. Having been rewarded (thanked), the student is more likely to continue the behavior than if the student had not been rewarded. These experiences of positive reinforcement are cumulative. As suggested earlier, they influence an individual's observations of his or her capacities, interests, and values. Mitchell and Krumboltz (1996) review a number of studies that support the importance of positive reinforcement in career decision-making activity. For example, Baird (1971) suggests that junior college students who seek additional education do so because of reinforcement for their academic work. Osipow (1972) and Mansfield (1973) demonstrate the importance of positive reinforcement in task preference. Positive reinforcement in terms of verbal praise is shown to be a valuable tool in career decision-making counseling (Krumboltz & Schroeder, 1965; Krumboltz & Thoresen, 1964; Oliver, 1975).

By reinforcing various aspects of a client's behavior, the counselor can assist in the accomplishment of career counseling goals such as selecting an appropriate occupational alternative or dealing with difficult problems on the job. To reinforce a client's skills, the counselor needs to be viewed as a reinforcer. In most cases, this is automatic. Clients seek out counselors for help because they value their expertise. Thus, a counselor's positive reinforcement of an activity may have greater value than that of a client's friend or acquaintance. Positive reinforcement can include expressions of approval, positive excitement, and appreciation by the counselor. A brief example will illustrate:

> CL: Last week after we talked, I read about what sales managers do in the *Occupational Outlook Handbook*. It really gave me a pretty good idea. Then I went out and talked to my uncle's friend, who is a sales manager at a local paint distributorship.
>
> CO: That's great! You really made progress in finding out about an important career possibility for you.
>
> CL: Both the article and my uncle's friend helped me to get a better idea of the difference between being a salesperson and being a sales manager.
>
> CO: That puts you in a better position to make an informed decision.

Both of the counselor's statements positively reinforce the client. The second statement is more subtle and less exuberant than the first. Sometimes, it is helpful for a counselor to reinforce an activity that has already been reinforced:

> CL: I just got an A on my Latin exam.
>
> CO: That's terrific! I know how important it was to you.
>
> CL: It makes me feel as if I can go on to college, and to a real good one.
>
> CO: It makes you feel good about what you can accomplish academically.

The counselor reinforces an important event for the client, even though the A on the Latin exam is itself reinforcing. By doing this, the counselor is assisting the client in developing accurate self-observation generalizations about her ability. Positive reinforcement can be given for both self-observation generalizations and worldview generalizations.

Role Models   Through the use of role models, clients can have a valuable associative learning experience. Mitchell and Krumboltz (1990) list several studies that support the effectiveness of role models as an aid in working with career concerns (Almquist, 1974; Fisher, Reardon, & Burck, 1976; Pallone, Rickard, & Hurley, 1970; Thoresen, Hosford, & Krumboltz, 1970). These studies evaluate the effectiveness of peer, parental, and other role models in helping students decide among occupational alternatives.

Counselors can assist clients both by acting as role models and by providing role models for them. By describing appropriate ways to deal with career issues, counselors become role models for the client. It is likely that a client will think of the counselor's strategies when approaching future career concerns. Furthermore, a counselor who follows a social learning framework is likely to act in an organized and decisive manner, thus providing a role model for the client. Counselors can provide other role models for clients by making available audiotapes, or possibly videotapes, of people describing their decision-making process. For group career counseling, the counselor can invite employed persons or recent graduates to discuss their career development with the group. Besides being role models for dealing with career concerns, individuals can also be role models for specific occupations. Audiotapes or videotapes of individuals who describe their occupation can be useful, as can referrals to job sites. There a client can watch and/or talk to a worker in a particular field.

Role Playing   In role playing, several strategies can be used to help clients learn new behaviors. Sometimes the counselor can play the role of the client and the client can play the role of another person. For example, the counselor may model an information-seeking interview by asking the client about something she is familiar with such as writing computer programs. The counselor can also model job interviewing skills by playing the role of the client and have the client be a manager wishing to hire a computer programmer. After playing the role, the counselor may ask the client for feedback on strategies the counselor used to effectively request information or answer questions. By identifying strategies, the client can then try them out with a counselor.

By changing roles, the counselor can play the part of the person who has information the client wants, the role of a job interviewer, or a number of other roles. The client can play herself and practice new strategies. Sometimes it is helpful for the client to practice a portion of an interview several times. After each role-play the client can discuss aspects of her behavior that seemed effective and others that need to be improved. The counselor may positively reinforce assertive and other effective behavior that the client demonstrates. Role playing may continue until the client and counselor believe that new skills have been learned.

Audio- or videotaping the role playing can be an effective technique. Rather than recalling behavior from memory, the client and counselor can observe the behavior and discuss the client's strengths. Counselors are likely to use positive reinforcement as often as appropriate and to use criticism or point out problems as infrequently as possible. Reinforcement is likely to increase the chances that clients will use the behavior in actual situations. Counselors who use taping are likely to stop the tape and discuss a situation when behavior seems to warrant discussion. In some instances the counselor may suggest that the client role-play a situation with a friend of the client's.

Simulation   By doing some of the tasks that an individual in a particular occupation must perform, a client can simulate a career experience. Kits designed to help high school students experience jobs were researched in several investigations (Krumboltz, 1970; Krumboltz, Baker, & Johnson, 1968; Krumboltz, Sheppard, Jones, Johnson, & Baker, 1967). The purpose of the job experience kits (Krumboltz, 1970) was to give students a chance to experience success in tasks that are common in a specific occupation. Care was taken to be certain that the initial task would not be frustrating to the client. Research done by the investigators just listed showed that students who used the job experience kits expressed more interest in that occupation than students who received written or filmed occupational information.

To some extent, job simulation is provided by high schools and vocational technical schools when they offer introductory courses to various craft and trade professions, such as carpentry, metalworking, or welding. However, often such courses do not describe an occupation to a student; rather, they just provide the student an opportunity to learn simple tasks associated with that occupation. For counselors who do not have access to job experience kits, suggestions of volunteer, part-time, or summer jobs for clients sometimes provide a simulated job experience. However, there is often the danger that an individual who seeks such work will end up doing menial tasks. For example, a student who desires to find out what it is like to be a chef could end up in a part-time job washing dishes.

Cognitive Strategies for Counseling

There is a much greater variety of cognitive than behavioral strategies for career decision-making counseling. Many of these strategies are adaptations of cognitive psychotherapeutic approaches. They will be mentioned only briefly here, as a full description is beyond the scope of this book.

Mitchell and Krumboltz (1996) and Krumboltz (1996) describe several strategies for determining and changing inaccurate thoughts and generalizations regarding career issues. These suggestions are concrete and are excellent illustrations of a cognitive approach to career concerns.

An interesting point that Mitchell and Krumboltz make is that, although many beliefs may be erroneous, some will be quite unimportant and not worth changing. The counselor must decide which of the client's faulty beliefs are interfering with the career decision-making process. Methods for assessing and changing inaccurate beliefs and generalizations follow:

Goal Clarification   According to Krumboltz (1996), for individuals to learn necessary skills to apply to a variety of career issues, it is important that goals be clear and identifiable. Often, the counselor makes goals explicit so that the client and the counselor agree on what issues will be explored, what choices may be made, and/or what skills may be learned. Sometimes clients expect that the counselor will tell them what to do or that a test will tell them what occupation to seek. Counselors may wish to restate goals so that mutually agreeable goals can be arrived at between counselor and client. For example, the counselor may say, "I want to work with you to help you explore occupational alternatives. This may or may not lead to an actual choice on your part at the conclusion of our work." The counselor and client can then explore the acceptability of this proposed goal.

Often it is helpful to break down goals into smaller goals so that the client does not feel overwhelmed. For example, the counselor might say,

"One of the first steps that we will take in trying to find possible future occupations is to examine activities and aspects of jobs you have enjoyed." This makes the problem of examining occupational alternatives seem more attainable, as steps are taken one at a time.

In clarifying goals it is helpful to reinforce open-mindedness. When a client says "There is so much to do, so many occupations to choose from, I don't know where to start," the counselor can view this as open-mindedness. Open-mindedness means that the client is willing to explore options and is open to suggestions and learning new information. Such an attitude helps in seeing goals as attainable and something that the client can implement in the not too distance future.

Counter a Troublesome Belief   Clients may often make generalizations that are inaccurate or that may inhibit them from career exploration. One example is "You have to know someone to get a job in that field." This statement can be challenged; there are other ways of getting jobs besides having a friend in the occupation. Further, there are ways to get to know people. The client's statement illustrates an inaccurate assumption. Another example of a troublesome belief may be a belief about oneself. For example, a client may say, "I am not smart enough to go to medical school." Instead of accepting that assumption, a counselor can ask for evidence for that belief. A freshman in college may not have sufficient course grades to support that belief. Furthermore, a senior with all C's may not be able to compete well with other applicants to medical school, as candidates often need a B average and better to be selected to medical school. That is different from saying, "I am not smart enough." This method of dealing with a troublesome belief is referred to as *reframing.* The counselor may respond to the senior: "Just because you may not be able to compete with other applicants for medical school now, does not necessarily mean you are 'not smart enough.' There may be other explanations for your C grades."

Look for Inconsistencies Between Words and Actions   Clients may say that they realize that they need to spend time talking to people in different fields, but they may spend their time doing something else. Pointing out the difference between the behavior of a client and the intention may be helpful. In general, when clients state that they will do something, such as look at occupational information on given occupations, and then fail to follow through, there is an inconsistency between words and actions.

Cognitive Rehearsal   Sometimes it is not sufficient to counter a troublesome belief. Individuals may need to practice or rehearse statements that are positive, which replace negative thoughts that they have about themselves. Individuals are often prone to focus on negative criticism rather than positive feedback. Sometimes the negative criticisms of others turn into negative beliefs about oneself. Counselors may encounter beliefs that clients seem to be quite persistent about. Having them mentally rehearse positive statements that dispute the negative statement is often quite helpful.

CL: Throughout my life, my parents have either implied or told me that maybe college is not for me. Now that I'm a sophomore at Washington High School I keep running into teachers who knew my older brother, who's now a freshman in college. They all tell me how well he did in school and I know I didn't do so well last year.

CO: These comments from your parents and teachers make it hard for you to believe that you can actually go to college. We have talked about courses that you have done well in before and there is plenty of evidence to show that you are capable of going to college. Furthermore, you told me how much you want to learn.

CL: I know I do want to learn and I know that we have talked about my good grades in English and in math.

CO: When you find yourself feeling like you won't be able to go to college, you can say to yourself, "I have done well in English and math and I really do want to go to college."

CL: Do you think that will help?

CO: Yes I do. In fact, I want you to say those words to yourself silently now five times.

CL: OK. I did that.

CO: How do you feel when you say that to yourself?

CL: Much better. Repeating that makes me feel I can do it, not so discouraged.

Cognitive rehearsal helps strengthen clients' positive beliefs. When used in career counseling, it helps clients expand upon options that they have. It also helps to ensure that when clients encounter opportunities in the future, they will not automatically dismiss them. In the previous example, the client would be encouraged to use this positive self-statement throughout the week. At the next meeting, the counselor may ask the client how often she used the positive self-statement and how well it worked. If the client did not use it, the counselor may encourage the client to do so.

In their writings, Krumboltz and his colleagues (Krumboltz, 1996; Mitchell & Krumboltz, 1996) have suggested many behavioral and cognitive techniques that counselors may use in helping their clients. These methods focus on coping with assumptions that they make about themselves or their world that interfere with their career goals. In this section I have described how reinforcement, role models, role playing, and simulation are techniques that assist clients in exploring their interests, abilities, and values, as well as their world around them. These techniques have focused on activities that clients can do rather than the way they think about themselves. Cognitive strategies are designed to help clients change their thinking about themselves and their environment. One strategy is related to the goal of career counseling: goal clarification. Other methods focus on dealing with beliefs that interfere with career goals. These including countering a troublesome belief and looking for inconsistencies between words and actions. Cognitive rehearsal is a method for actively dealing with interfering beliefs. There are many more cognitive and behavioral techniques that can be used in career counseling. I just presented techniques that appear to arise more commonly when using behavioral and cognitive strategies for assisting clients with career issues.

Social Learning Theory Goals for Career Counseling

The factor that distinguishes the goals of Krumboltz's social learning theory from other theories described in this book is the emphasis on learning. Krumboltz (1996) states that, "The goal of career counseling is to facilitate the learning of skills, interests, beliefs, values, work habits, and personal qualities that enable each client to create a satisfying life within a constantly changing work environment" (p. 61). The emphasis in this statement is on learning about self and the environment rather than making a choice. It is not that choosing is unimportant, it is that learning is the focus of social learning.

When applying principles of learning to career counseling, Krumboltz does not limit goals of career counseling to the selection of an occupation. Career counseling includes work adjustment as well as career choice issues. For example, Krumboltz (1993) suggests that clients are often concerned about obstacles, such as finances and family responsibilities, that interfere with achieving career goals. Often, discouragement and motivation are concerns of clients when they have lost a job or are seeking a job and feel they are being rejected by potential employers. Job dissatisfaction may result from problems with supervisors and colleagues or other aspects of the job, such as a commute or problems in one's company. For many individuals, planning a family and planning a career are interrelated issues. Both men and women often need to decide when and if they will work part time, full time, or devote full time to child care responsibilities. For older workers, retirement planning is an issue requiring the consideration of abilities, interests, values, financial responsibilities, and physical condition. Krumboltz (1993) believes that social learning theory has much to offer clients who have concerns in any of these areas.

A theme that emerges out of Krumboltz's recent work (Krumboltz 1996; Mitchell & Krumboltz, 1996; Mitchell, Levin, & Krumboltz, 1999) is an emphasis on change within the individual and the individual's environment. Krumboltz and his colleagues believe that individuals need to be prepared to make changes as their abilities and interests change and the social, educational, and occupational environment change. Krumboltz (1996) describes three criteria that influence goals of career counseling.

1. *People need to expand their capabilities and interests, not base decisions on existing characteristics only.* Krumboltz states that self-observation generalizations about abilities, interests, and values are subject to change. Also, some individuals have limited knowledge on which to base these self-observations. Thus, answers to an interest inventory may be based on an individual's lack of knowledge of certain aspects of the working world. This may make the interest inventory of limited use, as it may discourage an individual's development of new interests. Encouraging individuals to explore new hobbies and occupations is an important part

of career counseling. Trying new educational, occupational, or other experiences is likely to help the client make better judgments about career selection as well as deal with new events that the client encounters in his or her life.

2. *People need to prepare for changing work tasks, not assume that occupations will remain stable.* In his theory of social learning, Krumboltz emphasizes the importance of social, educational, and occupational conditions as they affect individuals' learning experiences. In particular, Krumboltz (1996) notes how there are many factors that are changing rapidly in the change from an industrial society to an informational one. Because of this, individuals' generalizations about the world need to be based on rapidly changing information. Workers often need to be flexible to complete several tasks rather than to follow a written job description that may remain in place for several years.

In Chapter 10, the concept of "boundaryless" work is described. There are fewer and fewer task specifications. Individuals are expected to deal with tasks that were not originally described to them when they applied for a job. An example of rapid changes in the environment is the Internet and new approaches to commerce that have developed as a result of easier access to the Internet. As individuals see the need to improve their own abilities in order to cope with new occupational demands, they are likely to experience more stress.

3. *People need to be empowered to take action, not merely to be given a diagnosis.* From Krumboltz's (1996) point of view, trait and factor theory focuses on giving individuals a diagnosis. He believes that trait and factor theory helps individuals to make decisions based on their interests, values, and abilities, but does not help them to deal with changes that they may encounter as they look for work, experience work, or deal with others in relationship to work. Because of changes that are occurring both in the individual and in the world of work, Krumboltz believes that it is the counselor's role to help the individual take action as well as to decide on a course of action.

According to Krumboltz (1996), career counseling should not end when a person has decided on a course of action. Rather, the individual is going to have to look for jobs, experience rejection perhaps, deal with positive and negative aspects of a job, and have to deal with new unforeseen problems and possible crises that may arise in following through on a plan of action. Krumboltz believes that counselors should follow up with their clients as they implement their job hunting or changing.

In our current society, individuals need to be able to respond to new and unexpected events that occur in their lives. Individuals should be able to respond in a positive way that will help them improve their lives when unexpected events occur. This positive approach is referred to as planned happenstance by Mitchell, Levin, and Krumboltz (1999). This recent work has focused on how counselors can help their clients deal with unplanned events.

Applying Planned Happenstance Theory to Career Counseling

Krumboltz (Mitchell, Levin, & Krumboltz, 1999) recognizes the importance of chance events in individuals' lives. As described on pages 337 to 339, unpredictable social factors, educational conditions, occupational conditions, as well as one's genetic endowment influence one's life. From Krumboltz's point of view, individuals need to capitalize on the events that occur in their lives. Taking advantage of such events is called *planned happenstance,* an idea first put forth and developed by Kathleen Mitchell. In using this theory, the counselor helps clients recognize and incorporate chance events into their lives. Counselors also help clients generate such events so that they may work with them. In many ways, the more chance events that clients have in their lives, the more opportunities there are to take advantage of them. Of course, not all such events are likely to lead to positive outcomes. Illnesses and deaths of loved ones are examples of events that may require coping skills but do not typically lead to positive career development.

Planned happenstance theory is positive and encouraging. It replaces *indecision* with *open-mindedness.* When clients have difficulty making a choice, this then becomes an opportunity to look at a number of different paths and chances that they can take. Rather than help a client make a decision quickly, the counselor can help the client see that this is an opportunity to explore alternatives. The client may say, "I'm not sure what I'm going to do when I graduate high school. I'm really worried about it." The counselor may respond, "One thing we can do now is to help you to become more comfortable with being undecided."

In planned happenstance theory, five skills are helpful in dealing with chance career opportunities. These skills are curiosity, persistence, flexibility, optimism, and risk taking (Mitchell, Levin, & Krumboltz, 1999).

Curiosity is used to explore new learning opportunities and to follow up on options that result from chance events.

Persistence is learned when there are setbacks in one's experience. For example, if a client is not offered a job and keeps trying, and finally a job interview results in an offer, the client may learn persistence.

Flexibility is learned when dealing with many chance events. Individuals are often flexible in changing their attitudes when dealing with different circumstances such as different employers in different job interviews.

Optimism comes from pursuing new opportunities and finding that actions can pay off.

Risk taking occurs when there are unexpected new events. Clients learn that taking risks (for example, having an interview for a job in which the client does not feel sufficiently qualified) can result in a positive outcome. The outcome may not be a job offer, but rather another job lead.

According to Mitchell et al. (1999), a model of planned happenstance should be integrated into career counseling. By doing this, clients can be prepared for a counseling process in which a discussion of unplanned events is a part of the process. This process deals with clients' anxiety about their future and problems they may encounter. It also helps clients understand that they may need to make many decisions when faced with unexpected events. The goal of counseling in dealing with planned happenstance is to initiate a learning process that encourages curiosity and helps clients take advantage of unplanned events. Mitchell et al. (1999) described four steps, which will be explained in more detail:

Step 1: Normalize planned happenstance in the client's history.
Step 2: Assist clients to transform curiosity into opportunities for learning and exploration.
Step 3: Teach clients to produce desirable chance events.
Step 4: Teach clients to overcome blocks to action.

In the following example, Xavier's career concerns are used to illustrate the application of planned happenstance theory. Xavier is a high school senior whose father repairs kitchen appliances. His mother is an assembly line worker at a local car manufacturing company near Tucson, Arizona. Xavier was a star linebacker on his high school team and was having an excellent year when he broke his leg in the fourth game. Aspiring to be a professional football player, he has not let go of these aspirations, and is frustrated by not being able to finish his senior year on the football team. Although Xavier would really like a career in football, he is aware that he would need to do well in college for four years and that the competition is extremely stiff. Now he has the time to consider other options, although unwillingly. He discusses possibilities with his guidance counselor, who makes use of planned happenstance theory.

Step 1: Normalize planned happenstance in the client's history. Using planned happenstance theory, the counselor integrates finding out about Xavier's background with happenstance-related questions. The counselor wants to know about Xavier's interests both in and out of school as well as how well he has done in courses. The counselor also inquires about Xavier's experience in both part-time and volunteer work. Knowing Xavier's parents' aspirations for themselves and Xavier is also helpful.

However, in addition to these questions, the counselor wants to know how the client has dealt with chance experiences in his life. The counselor will try to make the client aware of how the client's own choices or actions have contributed to educational and career opportunities. In this first step, the counselor will try to help Xavier identify examples of happenstance and how he has taken advantage of happenstance through actions that he has taken. Xavier will be helped to realize how he has been able to benefit from events that occurred by chance.

CL: Since I broke my leg in that football game a month ago, things haven't been the same.

CO: How has breaking your leg affected you and what you might do now? [The counselor wants to find out about how Xavier is responding to having broken his leg and being out of football—a chance event.]

CL: It's been really tough. Especially the first few weeks were bad. There was a lot of pain. Now that my leg is better, it's not so bad.

CO: You have a lot more time now than you used to. [The counselor is setting up an opportunity for Xavier to talk about how he has used his time and what other events may have occurred in his life.]

CL: Yes, I have. In a way it turned out to be good timing.

CO: What do you mean?

CL: Well, my brother, who is in the eighth grade, got in trouble. He was caught about three weeks ago breaking windows at his school. That really turned things around at home. Were my parents ever angry!

CO: It sounds like your brother's trouble has had an impact on you too.

CL: It sure has. My brother isn't allowed out of the house and my parents are really concerned about his poor grades. So that means that I have to help him.

CO: Help him with his studies? [Xavier's brother's problem becomes an opportunity for Xavier.]

CL: Yes, I have to help him on his English and math. It really isn't something I've ever done before. I kind of like it.

CO: What is it that you like?

CL: I like the tutoring and teaching. I'd never really thought about teaching, but maybe the idea of coaching or teaching might be something that I could do.

CO: Xavier, this is great. You've taken two real difficult situations that happened beyond your control, your broken leg and your brother's trouble, and turned them into something positive. You've learned that maybe teaching might be something that you will do later on. Chance events can be something that you learn from and can take advantage of. It seems you've really been able to benefit from these unplanned events. [The counselor reinforces and normalizes random events in Xavier's recent history.]

The counselor and Xavier can continue to discuss Xavier's history and other chance events that have occurred in his life. As they discuss these events, the counselor can point out how Xavier can learn about himself and the world of work from events that occur in his life.

Step 2: Assist clients to transform curiosity into opportunities for learning and exploration. Chance events become an opportunity for the client to indulge his curiosity. Future possibilities can be thought of and explored. Sometimes the learning may be self-observations about abilities, interests, values, or the world. These unexpected events give clients a larger platform from which to make decisions and to deal with new unexpected events.

In the following example, Xavier and the counselor discuss how helping his brother, Raoul, has helped Xavier learn.

CO: Xavier, can you tell me more about your thoughts about considering teaching after you worked with your brother?

CL: Sure. I really liked showing him how to do things. It really made me think about how I could help others by teaching. It was a really good feeling.

CO: Sounds like it made you want to learn more about teaching. [The counselor notes that Xavier is curious about teaching and excited about it. He wants to help Xavier take advantage of his curiosity.]

CL: But there's this problem with teaching. Teachers don't make any money. I mean their salaries are really low.

CO: How do you know that? [The counselor is trying to counter a troublesome belief. She believes that Xavier may not have accurate information about teaching.]

CL: Well, I don't exactly. I just hear teachers grumble about not making money.

CO: Here. Let's look at information in this booklet about teaching.

The counselor and Xavier take a few minutes to look at salary information about teachers and discuss benefits that come with teaching.

CL: Teachers make more money than I thought. Plus they have the summers off. I think I can live with that.

CO: It seems now that we've addressed that issue you can continue thinking about teaching. It's not that teaching has to be definite now, but you're curious about it and it's great to take advantage of that now.

The counselor finds out how Xavier's curiosity is increased by his learning experience. She helps him to deal with a troublesome belief that interferes with his curiosity. Two unfortunate events, his brother's trouble and his broken leg, have become opportunities for learning and exploration.

Step 3: Teach clients to produce desirable chance events. Clients not only can respond positively to chance events, they can plan that if they encounter chance events, they will respond positively in the future. In Xavier's case, he didn't plan to respond positively to these two incidents, he just did so. When unplanned events occur, there are many things that individuals can do to take advantage of them. For example, Xavier may wish to talk to his teachers about what it's like to teach. He may do some volunteer tutoring or literacy work. Since he is a senior, he may wish to explore opportunities for elementary and secondary teaching by reading college catalogs. So far, the example has focused on teaching, simply to be clear about the application of happenstance theory. However, the counselor is likely to use many other examples besides the one that we have been discussing.

CO: Xavier, we've been talking a lot about teaching your brother, but I'm also wondering what kind of chance event you would like to happen to you?

CL: Well, I guess I would like to win two million dollars in the lottery.

CO: OK. Let's say that does happen. [The counselor is hoping for a more realistic example, but this will do.]

CL: I guess I'd want to pay for my college education and my brother's. I think I'd like to get a new house for my parents, too.

CO: I understand how this would change your life financially, but how else would it change your life? [The counselor is interested in finding out about how Xavier would respond to new opportunities and deal with fewer financial restrictions.]

CL: I would like to have more opportunity to watch sports and to read.

CO: What kind of reading would you do? [The counselor wants to know how Xavier might produce desirable chance events.]

CL: I read the newspaper now. But I'd have much more time to learn about local politics. I'd like to be more involved in that; it seems fun.

CO: It seems like you would be able to make a lot of opportunities for yourself. That seems important to you. Can you do that if you don't get two million dollars? [Since winning two million dollars is not likely, the counselor wants to follow up on Xavier's curiosity.]

CL: You know, I could. My uncle works in the office of a councilman. I think

> I'll talk to him and ask him about what he does. I know he is coming over to help my father with some stuff this weekend.

CO: Sounds like a great idea. Here your uncle is coming over and you're going to make it something that will be helpful to you. You would enjoy his visit anyway, but this will help you learn some. [By talking to his uncle, Xavier may generate unexpected information which then may lead to other opportunities, such as visiting his uncle at work.]

The counselor uses positive reinforcement to encourage Xavier to explore opportunities related to Xavier's career development. Talking about what he would do with $2 million leads Xavier to talking about his uncle and then sets up the possibility of learning more about politics from his uncle. Furthermore, that may lead to visiting his uncle at his office or going with his uncle to a political event. In this way, clients can be taught to produce chance events that are likely to have desirable consequences.

Step 4: Teach clients to overcome blocks to action. Encouraging clients to engage in positive actions is important. It is not sufficient to just discuss possible actions. Sometimes there are blocks to beliefs. A small example of a block was Xavier's inaccurate information about teaching. The counselor wants to take opportunities to promote curiosity, persistence, flexibility, optimism, and risk taking, qualities discussed earlier on page 351. Clients sometimes become overwhelmed or discouraged in pursuing career-related issues. They may be afraid of what other people think and not wish to pursue new skills or ideas. In the following example, Xavier talks about politics as a possible career.

CL: I know that my uncle is pretty good with words. He has lots of friends and they really respect him. I think he may run for political office sometime soon. I hope he does. I'd like to see him get elected. He deserves it.

CO: You really seem to admire him. You like what he is doing.

CL: I really do. I think he has really helped other people in his community a lot in the last few years. I think I would like to do that, but I could never do it.

CO: You seem to think you would be blocked from ever becoming a politician because of your skills. [Xavier's beliefs are being directly challenged.]

CL: I just don't think I could talk to people as well as my uncle.

CO: You seem to think you wouldn't be able to develop the skills that your uncle has. [The counselor challenges some of Xavier's self-observation generalizations about his skills.]

CL: Well, I guess I could. If I had four years of college like my uncle does, I would know a lot more.

CO: So you think it would be possible to develop those skills?

CL: Yes, I guess I could. I know I get along with people now. It's just that I don't know enough about how to work with people in a political way. I guess I could learn that from people like my uncle.

CO: As you talk about how you can learn from talking to people, from going to college, from being with your uncle, I can see how you are learning how to overcome blocks that get in the way of your taking advantage of events that you may encounter in your life that can help you do things that you may enjoy, like politics.

In this case, the counselor's challenge to Xavier helps him to overcome a block to action. The counselor lets Xavier reflect on different options he has to learn new skills that can take advantage of opportunities that may occur should he choose to become more involved in local politics.

The four steps described here may overlap at times, but they are designed to help clients take advantage of many events that happen in their lives over which they have little control (such as a broken leg). Because unexpected events continue to happen in an individual's life, Krumboltz and his colleagues want to assist clients in making the most of these opportunities through their description of planned happenstance theory. Within this theory, interests, abilities, values, and personal styles can be discussed, but they are done in an active way to promote the client's curiosity, persistence, flexibility, optimism, and risk taking. In working with planned happenstance, attending to clients' beliefs is important.

Krumboltz (1988) has developed the Career Beliefs Inventory that assesses many of the career beliefs that are potential problems for clients. The Career Beliefs Inventory contains 25 scales that measure a wide variety of beliefs, relating to such issues as experimenting with jobs, self-improvement, and learning to overcome obstacles. These 25 scales have been organized into five categories (Krumboltz, 1994a): my current career situation, what seems necessary for my happiness, factors that influence my decision, chances I am willing to make, and effort I'm willing to initiate. Many of these groups of scales emphasize empowering clients to take advantage of unexpected events that may occur in their lives. In social learning theory, there is an emphasis in learning about one's interests, skills, and values, as well as to take advantage of unpredictable events.

SOCIAL COGNITIVE CAREER THEORY

Like Krumboltz's theory of career development, social cognitive career theory (Brown & Lent, 1996; Lent & Brown, 1996; Lent, Brown, & Hackett, 1994; Lent & Hackett, 1987, 1994) is based on Bandura's social learning theory. Although both Krumboltz's theory and social cognitive career theory make use of Bandura's concepts, they emphasize different versions of his theory in their work. Both theories make use of Bandura's triadic reciprocal interaction system, focusing on the environment, personal factors, and behaviors. Both also emphasize the role of instrumental and associative learning experiences in career decision making and career development. Both also view thoughts and cognitions, which include memories, beliefs, preferences, and self-perceptions, as a part of the career decision-making and career development process.

However, they differ in several important respects. Social cognitive career theory emphasizes cognitive processes (such as self-efficacy) that moderate or regulate actions, more than does Krumboltz, who focuses on learning behaviors related to a variety of career concerns. Social cognitive career theorists have developed a model of career development that is more specific and complex than Krumboltz's (Figure 13-1), which focuses primarily on how prior learning experiences affect later learning experiences, and ultimately career choices. Social cognitive career theorists emphasize individuals' belief systems that affect their behaviors rather than concentrating on the behaviors themselves, as does Krumboltz.

Because social cognitive career theory is relatively recent (starting in the early 1980s), Hackett and Betz's (1981) focus has been on the development of a theory and providing research evidence to support it. However, the theory has application for counselors, and I will illustrate some applications after describing the theory itself (Brown & Lent, 1996). First, I will examine three important cognitive concepts that regulate the career decision-making process and that are essential to social cognitive career theory: self-efficacy, outcome expectations, and personal goals. To illustrate these concepts, we will examine Sharon's career decision-making behavior. Sharon is a 15-year-old African American who attends a large high school in San Francisco, where she is in the spring of her junior year.

Self-Efficacy

Bandura (1986) has described self-efficacy as "people's judgments of their capabilities to organize and execute courses of action required to attain designated types of performances" (p. 391). How individuals view their abilities and capacities affects academic, career, and other choices. Individuals with a low sense of self-efficacy may not persist in a difficult task, they may have thoughts that they will be unable to do the task well, and they may feel discouraged or overwhelmed by the task. Self-efficacy is a changing set of beliefs about oneself that varies, depending on the context of the situation. Some of the factors include the nature of the task, the people and surroundings that an individual has contact with, and success on similar tasks. As Lent, Brown, and Larkin (1986) have shown, there is only a moderate relationship between individuals' views of their own ability and objective measures of ability such as grades or scores on standardized exams.

Sharon is very worried about school. She doesn't like her math class and feels stupid when she's there. Although her grade for the year is a B— so far, Sharon just believes that she can't do the algebra assignments well enough: "I never will be able to know what I'm doing in math, and the teacher seems to make it seem as if this is so easy." Some of her friends share her views, and they talk about how hard math is and how glad they will be when they are done with it. Her friends' beliefs reinforce Sharon's own sense of self-efficacy as it applies to math. There is clearly a difference between Sharon's grades in math and her sense of self-efficacy regarding math. Sharon's sense of self-efficacy about math refers to the concept of academic self-efficacy, which is different from, but related to, the concept of career self-efficacy (Lent et al., 1994). Sharon's view that she isn't very good at math is likely to affect her plans for future education and the career alternatives that she will consider.

Outcome Expectations

When individuals estimate what the probability of an outcome would be, this is referred to as *outcome expectations*. Examples are "If I play basketball, what will happen?" "If I play well, what will happen?" "If I apply to Harvard University, what will happen?" and "If I ask Mrs. Brown for a reference, what will happen?" In contrast, self-efficacy beliefs are concerned with "Can I do this activity?" Examples are "How well can I play basketball?" "Can I get into Harvard?" and "Will someone evaluate my job performance effectively?" Thus, outcome expectations refer to what may happen, and self-efficacy is concerned with estimates of the ability to accomplish something. Bandura (1986, 1997) has written about several types of outcome expectations, including the anticipation of physical, social, and self-evaluative outcomes. An example of a physical outcome expectation would be getting paid for working, a social outcome might be approval from your father for having done well at school, and a self-evaluative outcome might be being satisfied with your own performance in a class. In making judgments, individuals combine both outcome expectations ("If I do this activity, what can happen?") and self-efficacy ("Can I do this activity?"). In general, Bandura finds that self-efficacy is often more important in determining a behavior than outcome expectations. Depending on the situation, either self-efficacy or outcome expectations may be more important than other expectations. Examples from Sharon's situation will help to illustrate.

Sharon is considering the possible outcome of her next math exam. She wonders whether, if she does the homework and discusses her questions with the teacher, perhaps her math grade will be an A or A−. However, her sense of self-efficacy with regard to math is low, so that she is not sure that she can do these activities, and therefore, her sense of self-efficacy may be a more powerful determinant of her eventual math performance than is her outcome expectation. Thus, it is possible that she will not do her homework or ask the teacher or other students questions, and her math performance will be poor. Another factor that may influence her performance is her goals.

Goals

Individuals do more than just respond to the events and the environment around them. They set goals that help them to organize their behavior, and to guide their actions over various periods of time. For example, a freshman in college who decides to be a lawyer must set subgoals and choose behaviors that will help her reach the goal. The reinforcement of being a lawyer will not occur for another seven years. Goals are self-motivating, and the satisfaction that comes with meeting goals, such as graduation, is highly significant. Goals, self-efficacy, and outcome expectations are related to each other and affect each other in a variety of ways.

Sharon has a goal to be a store manager. Her outcome expectation is that, if she goes to college, works part-time in the mall, and enters a training program with a department store, she can reach this goal. Her self-efficacy beliefs cause her to think that she is a poor math student, will not be able to do math in high school, and therefore cannot do math in college. These beliefs will directly affect her outcome expectations and may cause her to revise her goal.

The Social Cognitive Model of Career Choice

The social cognitive career model of career choice is quite complex, involving interactions between self-efficacy, outcome expectations, goals, choice, outcome, and environmental factors. Related to the model of career choice are the models of interest development and performance, which are described elsewhere (Lent et al., 1994). All of these models are circular, in that concepts indirectly or directly affect each other and continue to do so throughout most of the life span. The model of self-efficacy career choice behavior is diagrammed in Figure 13-2, and the paths of interaction among the concepts are described here.

To illustrate the self-efficacy model of career choice, it will be useful to continue our example of Sharon's academic and career concerns. The following paragraphs explain and illustrate the paths that are a part of this model. The factors that are described here are those that social cognitive career theorists consider the most significant, but not the only ones, in career selection. The model starts out with those concepts that are key in career choice and the selection of occupations.

Self-Efficacy ⎯ 1 ⎯→ Interest

Outcome Expectations ⎯ 2 ⎯→ Interest

Bandura (1986) believes that interests that are likely to persist across time arise from activities that people feel they are effective in completing and in succeeding in. As individuals try out activities, such as sports, they may feel that they are not very good at them and may lose interest. Likewise, when they feel that the outcome of the activity, such as sports, will not be successful, they tend to lose interest. Sharon believes that she can't learn math well, and further, she expects that the outcome on her math exam will be poor. Both of these factors contribute to her lack of interest in math.

Interest ⎯ 3 ⎯→ Choice Goals

Individuals' interests affect their intent to do certain activities and their goals that relate to activities. Sharon has lost interest in math. She intends not to study, and she chooses other goals besides math. Because she

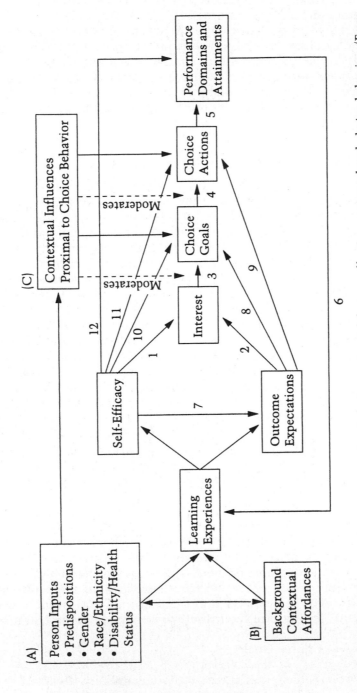

Figure 13-2 Model of person, contextual, and experiential factors affecting career-related choice behavior. (From "Toward a Unified Social Cognitive Theory of Career and Academic Interest, Choice, and Performance," by R. W. Lent, S. D. Brown, and G. Hackett, *Journal of Vocational Behavior*, Vol. 45, 1994, pp. 79–122. Copyright © 1993 by Academic Press, Inc. Reprinted by permission.)

believes that she is an excellent soprano and her expectations that she will do well are strong, based in part on being asked to be a soloist in church several times, her interest in singing (Paths 1 and 2) has grown. Therefore, her goals for singing become much stronger than those for math.

Goals —— 4 ——➤ Choice Actions

The goals that individuals choose affect the actions that they take to achieve the goals. Sharon chooses to improve her singing and takes actions, such as singing lessons and more practice, to become more expert as a singer. Math becomes a relatively unimportant goal, and she spends only 10 minutes a day on math homework.

Choice Actions —— 5 ——➤ Performance Outcomes

The actions that individuals choose greatly affect the outcome of their performance. Sharon's singing improves, and her math performance decreases.

Performance Outcomes —— 6 ——➤ Learning Experiences —— 7 ——➤ Self-Efficacy/Outcome Expectations

The outcome of the performance that individuals experience affects their learning experiences in general, which in turn affect beliefs in self-efficacy and outcome expectations. Sharon has positive learning experiences in her chorus and as a soloist. Her beliefs about her singing ability increase, as does her expectation regarding her ability to get offers to sing. In contrast, her negative performance on math exams affects her experience of learning, and therefore, she believes that she is not a good math student (self-efficacy) and will do poorly on future math tests (outcome expectations).

Social cognitive theorists make clear that there are other factors that affect learning and performance. Boxes A and B in Figure 13-2 show the importance of personal and background factors. Biological predisposition, gender, ethnicity, disabilities, and other factors such as parental background have an impact. For example, Sharon has a strong, excellent voice, which contributes to her positive performance outcomes and positive learning experiences and thus to her sense of self-efficacy as a singer. With regard to math, Sharon has heard that women are not good at math (a background contextual affordance), which negatively affects her learning experience and sense of math self-efficacy.

Outcome Expectations —— 8 ——➤ Choice Goals

Outcome expectations may have a direct effect on the way individuals perceive goals. If Sharon can find no opportunities to sing professionally, this will affect her goal to be a professional singer. Although Sharon values the goal of professional singer, her expectation of a positive outcome is not great.

Self-Efficacy
- 1 → **Interest**
- 11 → **Choice Actions**
- 12 → **Performance Outcomes**

One's belief in oneself is a major force that directly affects one's career goals, choice actions, and performance outcomes. For example, Sharon's lack of belief in her math ability not only affect her interests, her goals, and her choices related to occupations, but also her eventual occupational choice.

Contextual influences, or factors outside an individual's control, also moderate or have an impact on career choices, as seen in Box C in Figure 13-2. For example, the fact that there are few jobs for singers and Sharon has few financial resources for further singing training are likely to moderate or have an impact on her choice to be a singer.

Figure 13-2 diagrams important factors in an individual's career choice. Although self-efficacy and outcome expectations are significant factors in this process, Lent et al. (1994) do not ignore either past biological, social, or environmental influences (Box A) or current contextual factors (Box C). These authors note that, as individuals get older, it becomes more difficult to change interests, goals, and performance outcomes, as these are affected by past behaviors. This conceptualization of the choice process gives counselors a useful perspective from which to view their clients.

Counseling Example

Although there has been relatively little work on the application of social cognitive career theory to counseling, Betz (1992) and Brown and Lent (1996) make several suggestions that are of use to counselors. As she did in her earlier work, Betz (Hackett & Betz, 1981) focuses on counseling women. She recognizes the importance of environmental forces which affect women's beliefs about both their ability to master particular content areas, such as math and science, and their ability to enter particular career areas. Betz suggests that counselors help women understand that low self-esteem with regard to math and other areas is part of their socialization as women. Such suggestions can also be applied to people from a variety of cultures, who may be the victims of discrimination or stereotyping. Exploring how low self-esteem negatively affects the development of certain interests can be useful to clients. Observing role models in the feared area may also help to encourage the client to pursue nontraditional academic courses or actual work. Reinforcing clients' beliefs in their underused capabilities may be quite helpful, for example, encouraging women to persist with difficult math assignments. Sometimes, it may also be useful to reduce the anxiety that surrounds the notion of taking math or science courses. Social cognitive career theorists recognize the negative impact of social biases and discrimination on women and culturally diverse people. Thus, they have been particularly interested in developing a theory that would explain the career choices of all people, especially women and minorities.

   A somewhat similar point of view is taken by Brown and Lent (1996) as they apply social cognitive career theory to both men and women. They suggest that counselors help clients identify instances when they foreclose on options because of low or inaccurate self-efficacy beliefs or low outcome expectations. In Sharon's case, they would attend to Sharon's beliefs about her ability to learn math and her goals for math. These beliefs may become barriers for Sharon as she proceeds through high school. Even if Sharon did not have low self-efficacy beliefs about math, she might see barriers to pursuing a goal for a math or science career due to finances or other reasons. The counselor could help Sharon to remove or reduce these barriers. Helping Sharon have new positive experiences related to math (and science) may become a goal of counseling.

   The following example shows how Sharon is helped with both academic and career choice issues by a counselor using social cognitive career theory as a conceptual basis. Sharon has come to see her high school guidance counselor about picking courses for her senior year of high school. She is unsure about both her future career goals and the specific courses she will take. Furthermore, she is unsure about whether to apply to colleges.

   CL: I am not sure what to take next year or what I'm going to do. Math is really getting to me. It stinks.

   CO: Tell me more about math, Sharon.

   CL: I just can't do it. It's getting too hard and too much boring stuff. I don't see why I should have to do it. It's a real pain.

   CO: It's really frustrating. Sounds as if you try hard to do the work, but it doesn't come. [The counselor believes that Sharon is frustrated by not getting results from her work.]

   CL: Well, I guess I could have tried harder to do my homework, but I guess I kind of gave up.

   CO: Gave up?

   CL: Yeah, I just don't think math is for me. After all, the guys in class seem to do well in it, but not the women.

   CO: Sharon, you might be surprised by how many women are able to do well in science and in engineering. Many of them do very well in math. In fact, there have been a number of women who have left our school to go to college in math. [The counselor gives Sharon information that contradicts her perception of how others have done, so as to prevent Sharon from foreclosing on a goal too quickly.]

   CL: Well, I have done pretty well in math, but now I'm getting tired of it.

   CO: Yes. I see that you've got B's in math. You really have done well in math before. That's great. [The counselor reinforces Sharon's math performance, hoping to influence both her math self-efficacy and outcome expectations.]

   CL: Well, now it seems that the teacher is just going too fast. I've been busy with singing, which is going great, but neither the math teacher nor I seem to have time to work on this.

   CO: I'm sure that Mr. Aldo would be glad to help you with some of your algebra. Continuing with math really increases your options. You seem to have done well and liked it before. It would be great if it doesn't slip away. [The counselor is working to help Sharon boost her sense of math self-efficacy, knowing that it can affect her interest, and ultimate goals, both for academic subjects and for her career choice.]

CL: (*not convinced*) Well, I could do that, but I'd really like to be a singer. Things are going great at church. I was asked to sing at a wedding, and I can't wait.

CO: Singing seems like it could lead to an occupation that you like.

CL: I'd love to do it, but I just know how difficult it is. There're some people in our neighborhood who have been singing in a group for years, and they never went anywhere.

CO: Having several skills, math, music—That can really increase your options. [The counselor is well aware of the job market for singers and wants to help Sharon develop her abilities and competencies as much as possible. By doing so, Sharon can develop and broaden her goals, which will in turn give her more choices and will increase her chances of good performance. By reinforcing Sharon's interest in math, the counselor helps her to expand her career options.]

In future sessions, the counselor may help Sharon to learn more about the importance of math. If Sharon is anxious, she may show her ways to use relaxation techniques and positive self-talk to improve her confidence. The counselor may also introduce her to women who are using math in their careers. Books and pamphlets on minority mathematicians and scientists may also prove helpful as a way to reduce barriers to considering new career goals. Because the counselor recognizes the negative effect of biases about math for women, she uses many techniques to help Sharon increase her sense of self-efficacy.

THE ROLE OF OCCUPATIONAL INFORMATION

Accurate occupational information is essential to the application of social learning theory. Rather than just saying that occupational information is important, Krumboltz (1970) has designed Job Experience Kits to be used to simulate occupations that provide exercises that are similar to tasks done by people working in the occupations. More recently, Krumboltz (personal communication, November 23, 1999) has developed computer simulations of occupations, such as advertising, in which the client plays the role of an employee in the profession, interacts with simulated colleagues, and learns about the profession. Furthermore, in research that he and his colleagues have done on career decision making, they have used occupational information seeking as a criterion for effective career planning. More than most theorists, Krumboltz has emphasized the importance of learning occupational information in the career decision-making process. Social cognitive career theorists tend to focus more on explaining the career development process than on procedures for career counseling. However, Betz (1992) describes the importance of having career information that is accurate and unbiased, featuring women and culturally diverse people in nontraditional occupations. Brown and Lent (1996) show how occupational information can remove barriers to career exploration.

THE ROLE OF TESTING

Although testing is not featured in social learning and cognitive theories as it is in some other career development theories, it is still useful. Values inventories may be particularly helpful in clarifying values when dealing with planned happenstance. Interest inventories and ability and aptitude tests may be useful in the application of both social learning theories. In using Krumboltz's theory, counselors provide information from outside the individual, so that clients can make accurate self-observation generalizations. Since client beliefs are an integral part of Krumboltz's model, the Career Beliefs Inventory (Krumboltz, 1994a) may be of considerable help in most stages of career decision making.

In social cognitive career theory, both interest and performance are important aspects of the model, and tests and inventories provide information for the client to use in making career decisions. Further, the tests give the counselor information, so that he or she may reinforce and strengthen self-efficacy beliefs and discuss outcome expectations. Brown and Lent (1996) believe that discrepancies between measured interests and abilities in a specific area, such as biology, may point to low self-efficacy beliefs about biology. When there are discrepancies between work-related needs or values and interest measures, clients may be experiencing faulty outcome expectations. The Career Decision-Making Self-Efficacy Scale (Betz & Luzzo, 1996; Taylor & Popma, 1990) has also been used, but primarily for research purposes. It contains five-to-ten item subscales that measure career choice competencies: goal selection, gathering occupational information, problem solving, planning for the future, and accurate self-appraisal. Taylor and Betz (1983) report reliability and other information that relate this instrument to career decision making.

APPLYING SOCIAL LEARNING AND SOCIAL COGNITIVE CAREER THEORIES TO WOMEN

Mitchell and Krumboltz (1996) discuss the application of their social learning theory to women in the context of four basic components of their theory: genetic endowment and special abilities, environmental conditions and events, learning experiences, and task-approach skills. They note that, although women do not have control over their gender, they do have some (limited) control over environmental forces, and more control over their learning experiences and task-approach skills. Mitchell and Krumboltz comment on the gender stereotyping that creates traditional and nontraditional occupations for men and for women. Relatively little research has been done on Krumboltz's social learning theory as it applies to women. Almquist (1974) found that women who selected nontraditional careers were likely to have been influenced by female role models. When women were shown a videotape of other women who were being reinforced for making nontraditional career choices, the viewers of the videotape made more nontraditional career choices than did women who had not seen the videotape (Little & Roach, 1974). More recently, Williams, Soeprapto, Like, Touradji, Hess, and Hill (1998) have shown the importance of unplanned events in the lives of prominent women in counseling psychology. Williams et al. show that the five skills (curiosity, persistence, flexibility, optimism, and risk taking), which Mitchell et al. (1999) identify as important factors in dealing with chance events, were helpful to the women in the study in taking advantage of unplanned events in their lives. By calling attention to the importance of learning experiences in career issues for women, Mitchell and Krumboltz and colleagues hoped that their emphasis would alert counselors to the need to enhance opportunities for women, who have been denied these because of discrimination.

Whereas career development issues for women have played a minor role in Krumboltz's social learning theory, they have been a major focus in the development of social cognitive career theory. In their original article on career self-efficacy, Hackett and Betz (1981) proposed that career self-efficacy beliefs would play a stronger role than interests, values, or abilities in restricting women's career choices. Since this article was written, over 25 investigations have been carried out to test their propositions. Almost all of these studies have addressed self-efficacy as it relates to women's academic, career, and other choices. Because this research is so extensive, only general findings arising from the results of these studies can be presented here. Lent et al. (1994) summarize research evidence that relates to specific propositions that are a part of social cognitive career theory. Multon, Brown, and Lent (1991) have conducted a meta-analysis of self-efficacy beliefs as they are related to academic outcomes. Also, Hackett (1995), Betz and Hackett (1997), and Solberg (1998) have summarized much of the research that relates to career self-efficacy issues as they relate to women. The information that is presented here is drawn from these sources, as well as more recent research.

A number of studies have examined the general topic of the relationship of self-efficacy to career-related choices (Hackett, 1995). Early research (Betz & Hackett, 1981) showed that college men's occupational self-efficacy was relatively constant across occupations, but that women scored significantly lower on occupational self-efficacy for nontraditional occupations, and significantly higher for traditionally female occupations. Other studies have shown that occupational self-efficacy predicts interest and career choice. Further, there are gender differences in occupational self-efficacy in different groups of college students for different occupational choices, job tasks, and work activities. However, gender differences in self-efficacy are usually not reported in samples that are quite similar to each other, such as high-achieving students. When adults were studied across all six Holland types (21 occupations were included), minimal gender differences were found for self-efficacy (Betz, Borgen, Kaplan, & Harmon, 1998). When tasks are particularly gender-stereotyped, differences in self-efficacy between men and women may be found. Stereotypes about how women should behave are likely to undermine women's self-esteem regarding the choice of a nontraditional career. A conclusion reached about this research is that, if women eliminate nontraditional career opportunities because of low self-efficacy beliefs, they are limiting their opportunities to find satisfying and well-paid jobs after college. Although most studies have been done on college students, research on high school students also shows gender differences in occupational self-efficacy.

Besides studying the relationship of career self-efficacy to career-related choices, researchers have found relationships between self-efficacy and the choice of a college major, career interests, and career decision-making processes. Since many women are often fearful of math or not confident in their math ability, many researchers have studied the role of math self-efficacy, showing that it is of greater importance in predicting career choice behavior than are ability and past experience. However, when women are engineering majors and presumably have confidence in their math ability, few differences are found between male and female engineering majors in levels of math self-efficacy as well as persistence in engineering (Schaefers, Epperson, & Nauta, 1997). The social cognitive career model is not limited to predictions about math and science, but the model has also been predictive in areas of study in art, English, and social studies in college students (Smith & Fouad, 1999).

Other investigations have shown that the higher the level of self-efficacy beliefs, the greater the interest expressed in a specific occupational area. Although several studies have shown that both interest and self-efficacy predict the range of career options that students consider, self-efficacy has frequently been found to be a stronger predictor of academic achievement and persistence. Hackett points out that beliefs about the ability to make a career decision are only moderately related to which occupations are being considered. However, research has also shown that the more confidence individuals have in their ability to make decisions, the more likely they will be to search for occupational information. Additionally, Nauta, Epperson, and Kahn (1998) report that ability, self-efficacy, role models, and role conflict influence higher levels of career aspirations of women in science, math, and engineering majors. Swanson and Woitke (1997) have shown how social cognitive career theory can help women deal with perceived career barriers and environmental factors in career choice.

Social cognitive career theory is probably the most active area of current career-related investigations. Although the research has broadened since its original focus on women's lack of confidence in their academic and career choices, this still remains a major focus of research. The large number of research studies has been important in developing and confirming a model of academic interest, career choice, and career performance (Lent et al., 1994). As research has expanded in this area, more attention has been given to understanding the role of self-efficacy in individuals from diverse cultural groups.

APPLYING SOCIAL LEARNING AND SOCIAL COGNITIVE CAREER THEORIES TO CULTURALLY DIVERSE POPULATIONS

In their application of social learning theory to culturally diverse populations, Mitchell and Krumboltz (1996) discuss the importance of environmental conditions. They comment that some cultures glamorize one occupation, while other cultures may favor another. Further, some cultures may value income as opposed to spirituality or educational success. Such values may reinforce certain occupations for people from different cultures. Racial discrimination is another environmental barrier to culturally diverse people, who may encounter obstructions in trying to follow through on a career choice. Although it is difficult to do so, the environment can be changed through collective action that leads to the passing of laws such as those dealing with racial discrimination and affirmative action. By emphasizing the importance of social learning, Mitchell and Krumboltz (1990) point out that counselors can assist in developing a proactive approach to career concerns and can help culturally diverse clients deal with discrimination that might otherwise limit their career opportunities.

Although some studies have shown the importance of role models for culturally diverse clients, very little research has applied Krumboltz's social learning theory to culturally diverse groups. For social cognitive career theorists, gender differences have been the central focus. However, a number of studies have examined self-efficacy issues for people from different cultural groups. In general, the gender differences found among white Americans tend to be found in men and women in other countries (Hackett, 1995). For both male and female African American students, Post, Stewart, and Smith (1991) have found that occupational self-efficacy predicts interest in math and science occupations. African American college students' interest in math activities increased when they believed that they had skills in math and that having these skills would help them in their education and future career (Gainor & Lent, 1998). Studying Native American students, Lauver and Jones (1991) found that those living on reservations were much less likely to have the opportunity to develop self-efficacy than were other students. Hackett, Betz, Casas, and Rocha-Singh (1992) found lower levels of self-efficacy for engineering careers in Mexican American students, which was due primarily to differences in academic preparation. Weiss (2000) found that the greater the perceived likelihood of career barriers, the lower the career decision-making self-efficacy among African American, Asian American, and Caucasian college students. These studies represent some of the efforts that have been made to apply self-efficacy theory to the academic and career choices of culturally diverse people. Bingham and Ward (1997) show the importance of considering self-efficacy in a four-step process for career assessment for culturally diverse women.

Just as women must deal with myths about their ability that negatively affects their sense of self-efficacy, so must people of different cultures. Individuals from cultures that have been negatively stereotyped in a society may find it difficult to believe that they, as members of that culture, can achieve academically or occupationally. Furthermore, some individuals may be isolated from other members of society, as are many Native Americans who live on reservations, which limit educational and occupational information that may enhance their opportunities and enable them to develop stronger self-efficacy beliefs.

COUNSELOR ISSUES

Krumboltz views the counselor's role from a social learning point of view. He believes it is important that the skills, interests, and values of the counselor be appropriate to the client. The counselor may have her own ways of dealing with unexpected events. Such social learning strategies may or may not be appropriate for the client. Listening to the client's description of how he deals with unexpected events allows the counselor to apply appropriate cognitive or behavioral techniques to the client's learning system without depending on the counselor's personal social learning system.

In determining whether to work with a client, a counselor must decide whether the client's problem fits within the interests, competencies, and ethical standards of the counselor (Krumboltz, 1964). If counselors specialize in a type of population (for example, older adults or college students) or a specific counseling technique (such as behavioral counseling), it is important that they be certain that the needs of the client are within their areas of expertise. Furthermore, if the client has a goal that seems unethical or inappropriate to the counselor, the counselor is bound to tell the client and either not work with the client or help the client redefine his or her goal. For example, if a client says to a counselor, "I want you to guarantee me that I can get a job in business," the counselor must decline or must change the client's goal. When applying the planned happenstance approach to clients, it is particularly important for counselors to listen to concerns that may not necessarily fit in with the planned happenstance steps. For example, if a client is grieving over the death of a parent, the counseling should be flexible enough so that the counselor can assist the client with his grief. Since the concept of self-observed generalizations of abilities, interests, and values is quite broad, the counselor should be open to a discussion of experiences that may at first appear to be unrelated to career concerns.

Social cognitive career theorists focus on cognitive processes that interact with behaviors. Self-efficacy, outcome expectations, and goals are important aspects of social cognitive career theory. It is important that counselors be aware of their own issues or stereotypes that may interfere with helping their clients. Unrecognized biases about race and gender directly interfere with helping clients develop career self-efficacy beliefs. As counseling evolves, counselors may become aware of the differences between their clients' outcome expectations and their own views of educational and career possibilities for their clients. Similarly, as counselors help their clients to develop self-efficacy beliefs, they may find that they are developing goals for their clients different from the goals their clients develop for themselves. When they are aware of their own values and views of their clients, counselors can help clients to make their own career decisions without interfering in the decision-making process.

SUMMARY

Krumboltz's social learning theory presents a model that emphasizes a behavioral orientation, with some cognitive components. The theory stresses the importance of genetic endowment, environmental conditions, learning experiences, and task-approach skills. Krumboltz and his colleagues provide both conceptualization skills and counseling techniques to help clients deal with future unexpected events. The behavioral and cognitive counseling techniques that they suggest include reinforcement, modeling, role playing, and simulation. Their cognitive strategies include goal clarification, countering troublesome beliefs, and cognitive rehearsal. These techniques are used at various points throughout career counseling. A four-step approach to dealing with planned happenstance is illustrated in this chapter.

Starting with the work of Hackett and Betz (1981), who proposed that career self-efficacy plays a more important role than interests, values, and abilities in restricting women's choices, social cognitive career theory has developed into a widely researched theory of career development. Emphasizing cognitive concepts more than behavioral ones, social cognitive career theory has focused on the importance of self-efficacy, outcome expectations, and goals as variables in academic and career choices. As a result of a significant body of research, social cognitive career theorists have been able to describe a detailed process of career development. Familiarity with this model can be useful for counselors in attending to and reinforcing the self-efficacy beliefs of their clients.

References

Almquist, E. M. (1974). Sex stereotypes in occupational choice: The case for college women. *Journal of Vocational Behavior, 5,* 13–21.

Baird, L. L. (1971). Cooling out and warming up in the junior college. *Measurement and Evaluation in Guidance, 4,* 160–171.

Bandura, A. (1969). *Principles of behavior modification.* New York: Holt, Rinehart & Winston.

Bandura, A. (1977). *Social learning theory.* Englewood Cliffs, NJ: Prentice Hall.

Bandura, A. (1986). *Social foundations of thought and action: A social cognitive theory.* Englewood Cliffs, NJ: Prentice Hall.

Bandura, A. (1987). Reflections on self-efficacy. In S. Rachman (Ed.), *Advances in behavior research and therapy* (Vol. 1, pp. 237–269). Oxford: Pergamon Press.

Bandura, A. (1997). *Self-efficacy: The exercise of control.* San Francisco: W. H. Freeman.

Betz, N. (1992). Counseling uses of career self-efficacy theory. *The Career Development Quarterly, 41,* 22–26.

Betz, N., Borgen, F. H., Kaplan, A., & Harmon, L. W. (1998). Gender and Holland type as moderators of the validity and interpretive utility of the Skills Confidence Inventory. *Journal of Vocational Behavior, 53,* 334–352.

Betz, N. E., & Hackett, G. (1981). The relationship of career-related self-efficacy expectations to perceived career options in college women and men. *Journal of Counseling, 28,* 399–410.

Betz, N. E., & Hackett, G. (1997). Applications of self-efficacy theory to the career assessment of women. *Journal of Career Assessment, 5,* 383–402.

Betz, N. E., & Luzzo, D. A. (1996). Career assessment and the Career Decision-Making Self-Efficacy Scale. *Journal of Career Assessment, 4,* 413–428.

Bingham, R. P., & Ward, C. M. (1997). Theory into assessment: A model of women of color. *Journal of Career Assessment, 5,* 403–418.

Brown, S. D., & Lent, R. W. (1996). A social cognitive framework for career choice counseling. *The Career Development Quarterly, 44,* 354–366.

Fisher, T. J., Reardon, R. C., & Burck, H. D. (1976). Increasing information-seeking behavior with a model-reinforced videotape. *Journal of Counseling Psychology, 23,* 234–238.

Gainor, K. A., & Lent, R. W. (1998). Social cognitive expectations and racial identity attitudes as predictors of math choice intentions in Black college students. *Journal of Counseling Psychology, 45,* 403–413.

Hackett, G. (1995). Self-efficacy in career choice and development. In A. Bandura (Ed.), *Self-efficacy in changing societies* (pp. 232–258). Cambridge, England: Cambridge University Press.

Hackett, G., & Betz, N. (1981). A self-efficacy approach to the career development of women. *Journal of Vocational Behavior, 18,* 326–339.

Hackett, G., Betz, N. E., Casas, J. M., & Rocha-Singh, I. (1992). Gender, ethnicity, and social cognitive factors predicting the academic achievement of students in engineering. *Journal of Counseling Psychology, 39,* 527–538.

Krumboltz, J. D. (1964). Parable of the good counselor. *Personnel and Guidance Journal, 43,* 118–124.

Krumboltz, J. D. (Ed.). (1970). *Job experience kits.* Chicago: Science Research Associates.

Krumboltz, J. D. (1979). A social learning theory of career decision making. In A. M. Mitchell, G. B. Jones, & J. D. Krumboltz (Eds.), *Social learning and career decision making* (pp. 19–49). Cranston, RI: Carroll Press.

Krumboltz, J. D. (1988). *Career Beliefs Inventory.* Palo Alto, CA: Consulting Psychologists Press.

Krumboltz, J. D. (1993). Integrating career and personal counseling. *Career Development Quarterly, 42,* 143–148.

Krumboltz, J. D. (1994a). The Career Beliefs Inventory. *Journal of Counseling and Development, 72,* 424–428.

Krumboltz, J. D. (1994b). Improving career development theory from a social learning perspective. In M. L. Savickas & R. W. Lent (Eds.), *Convergence in career development theories* (pp. 9–32). Palo Alto, CA: Consulting Psychologists Press.

Krumboltz, J. D. (1996). A learning theory of career counseling. In M. L. Savickas & W. B. Walsh (Eds.), *Handbook of career counseling theory and practice* (pp. 55–80). Palo Alto, CA: Consulting Psychologists Press.

Krumboltz, J. D., Baker, R. D., & Johnson, R. G. (1968). *Vocational problem-solving experiences for stimulating career exploration and interests: Phase II.* Washington, DC: U.S. Office of Education.

Krumboltz, J. D., & Schroeder, W. W. (1965). Promoting career planning through reinforcement and models. *Personnel and Guidance Journal, 44,* 19–26.

Krumboltz, J. D., Sheppard, L. E., Jones, G. B., Johnson, R. G., & Baker, R. D. (1967). *Vocational problem-solving experiences for stimulating career exploration and interest.* Washington, DC: U.S. Office of Education.

Krumboltz, J. D., & Thoresen, C. E. (1964). The effect of behavioral counseling in groups and individual settings on information-seeking behavior. *Journal of Counseling Psychology, 11,* 324–333.

Lauver, P. J., & Jones, R. M. (1991). Factors associated with perceived career options in American Indian, White, and Hispanic rural high school students. *Journal of Counseling Psychology, 38,* 159–166.

Lent, R. W., & Brown, S. D. (1996). Social cognitive approach to career development. An overview. *The Career Development Quarterly, 44,* 311–321.

Lent, R. W., Brown, S. D., & Hackett, G. (1994). Toward a unified social cognitive theory of career and academic interest, choice, and performance. *Journal of Vocational Behavior, 45,* 79–122.

Lent, R. W., Brown, S. D., & Larkin, K. C. (1986). Self-efficacy in the prediction of academic performance and perceived career options. *Journal of Counseling Psychology, 33,* 165–169.

Lent, R. W., & Hackett, G. (1987). Career self-efficacy: Empirical status and future directions. *Journal of Vocational Behavior, 30,* 347–382.

Lent, R. W., & Hackett, G. (1994). Sociocognitive mechanisms of personal agency in career development: Pantheoretical prospects. In M. L. Savickas & R. W. Lent (Eds.), *Convergence in career development theories: Implications for science and practice* (pp. 77–101). Palo Alto, CA: Consulting Psychologists Press.

Little, D. M., & Roach, A. J. (1974). Videotape modeling of interest in nontraditional occupations for women. *Journal of Vocational Behavior, 5,* 133–138.

Mansfield, R. (1973). Self-esteem, self-perceived abilities, and vocational choice. *Journal of Vocational Behavior, 3,* 433–441.

Mitchell, L. K., & Krumboltz, J. D. (1990). Social learning approach to career decision making: Krumboltz's theory. In D. Brown, L. Brooks, & Assoc. (Eds.), *Career choice and development: Applying contemporary theories to practice* (2nd ed., pp. 145–196). San Francisco: Jossey-Bass.

Mitchell, L. K., & Krumboltz, J. D. (1996). Krumboltz's learning theory of career choice and counseling. In D. Brown, L. Brooks, & Assoc. (Eds.), *Career choice and development* (3rd ed., pp. 233–280). San Francisco: Jossey-Bass.

Mitchell, K. E., Levin, A. S., & Krumboltz, J. D. (1999). Planned happenstance: Constructing unexpected career opportunities. *Journal of Counseling and Development, 77,* 115–124.

Multon, K. D., Brown, S. D., & Lent, R. W. (1991). Relation of self-efficacy beliefs to academic outcomes. A meta-analytic investigation. *Journal of Counseling Psychology, 38,* 30–38.

Nauta, M. M., Epperson, D. L., & Kahn, J. H. (1998). A multiple-groups analysis of predictors of higher level career aspirations among women in mathematics, science, and engineering majors. *Journal of Counseling Psychology, 45,* 483–496.

Oliver, L. W. (1975). The relationship of parental attitudes and parent identification to career and homemaking orientation in college women. *Journal of Vocational Behavior, 7,* 1–12.

Osipow, S. H. (1972). Success and preference: A replication and extension. *Journal of Applied Psychology, 56,* 179–180.

Pallone, N. J., Rickard, F. S., & Hurley, R. B. (1970). Key influences of occupational preference among black youth. *Journal of Counseling Psychology, 17,* 498–501.

Post, P., Stewart, M. A., & Smith, P. L. (1991). Self-efficacy, interest, and consideration of math/science and nonmath/science occupations among college freshmen. *Journal of Vocational Behavior, 38,* 179–186.

Schaefers, K. G., Epperson, D. L., & Nauta, M. M. (1997). Women's career development: Can theoretically derived variables predict persistence in engineering majors? *Journal of Counseling Psychology, 44,* 173–183.

Smith, P. L., & Fouad, N. A. (1999). Subject-matter specificity of self-efficacy, outcomes expectations, interests, and goals: Implication for the social-cognitive model. *Journal of Counseling Psychology, 46,* 461–471.

Solberg, V. S. (1998). Assessing career search self-efficacy: Construct evidence and developmental antecedents. *Journal of Career Assessment, 6,* 181–193.

Swanson, J. L., & Woitke, M. B. (1997). Theory into practice in career assessment for women: Assessment and interventions regarding perceived career barriers. *Journal of Career Assessment, 5,* 443–462.

Taylor, K. M., & Betz, N. E. (1983). Applications of self-efficacy theory to the understanding and treatment of career indecision. *Journal of Vocational Behavior, 22,* 63–81.

Taylor, K. M., & Popma, J. (1990). An examination of the relationships among career decision-making self-efficacy, career salience, locus of control, and vocational indecision. *Journal of Vocational Behavior, 22,* 63–81.

Thoresen, C. E., Hosford, R. E., & Krumboltz, J. D. (1970). Determining effective models for counseling clients of varying competencies. *Journal of Counseling Psychology, 17,* 369–375.

Weiss, K. I. (2000). *The social cognitive model of career choice: A cross-cultural analysis.* Unpublished dissertation.

Williams, E. N., Soeprapto, E., Like, K., Touradji, P., Hess, S., & Hill C. E. (1998). Perceptions of serendipity: Career paths of prominent women in counseling psychology. *Journal of Counseling Psychology, 45,* 379–389.

Career Decision-Making Approaches

14

There have been many different approaches to the study of career decision making. Some early models follow an organizational decision-making approach. This approach suggested that there is a right way of making decisions in organizations and if individuals would apply it to their own career decisions, they would be able to make good choices. Other early approaches did not rely on an organizational model, but tried to model an effective way to make career decisions. These models have had relatively little following. Of more recent interest has been a focus on understanding the process of career decision making and understanding the role of thought processes and decision making.

In this chapter two categories of decision-making models are explained: descriptive and prescriptive. Descriptive theories describe or explain the choices that an individual makes when deciding on career choices. In contrast, prescriptive decision-making theories focus on an ideal approach to decision making. Descriptive theories tend to be based on studies of adolescent or adult decision making. On the other hand, prescriptive theories originate with psychological decision-making theory or observations of cognitive decision-making processes. These two categories lead to two very different ways of viewing career decision making.

In this chapter, two descriptive approaches will be presented, followed by a prescriptive approach. One descriptive model is that of David Tiedeman which is a developmental one that explains four phases of anticipating a choice. These phases deal with exploration, crystallization, clarification, and the choice process itself. Tiedeman also explains how individuals go through a process in adjusting to a choice once they have taken a job. Another prescriptive approach is that of Anna Miller-Tiedeman whose model could be described as spiritual. Miller-Tiedeman explains that life and career are totally related, and titles her theory Lifecareer® Process Theory. To further explain a spiritual approach to career counseling, I have integrated seven spiritual concepts that relate to career choice and work adjustment that have been described by Bloch and Richmond: change, balance, energy, community, calling, harmony, and unity. The spiritual approach to counseling shows how individuals can transcend their ordinary lives and connect with inner meanings found deep within themselves.

In contrast to the process approach of Tiedeman and the spiritual approach of Tiedeman-Miller and Bloch and Richmond is the cognitive information processing approach of Gary Peterson and his colleagues. In their model, which is based on cognitive science, Peterson and his colleagues examine how decision-making skills can be used to help clients integrate information about self and occupations and make good career choices. A central aspect of their model is a career decision-making approach which starts with communicating the problem, analyzing information, synthesizing alternatives, evaluating or valuing alternatives, and executing action plans.

The process model of Tiedeman was developed in the 1960s and has had some initial research investigation into its conceptual formation. Spiritual approaches to career decision making have become more popular in recent years, but have relatively little research related to their concepts. The cognitive information processing approach of Peterson and his colleagues is also relatively new, being initiated in the early 1980s, and relatively little research has been applied to this model. All three provide interesting views of career decision making, although there is less research to support these models than many others described in this text.

TIEDEMAN'S PERSPECTIVE ON THE PROCESS OF CAREER DECISION MAKING

In his thinking about career decision making, David Tiedeman was influenced strongly by White's (1952) individualistic approach to the study of human lives and the striving toward competence. Furthermore, Erikson's (1959) study of ego development and description of the stages of psychosocial development had an impact on Tiedeman's articulation of career decision-making stages. In addition, Tiedeman was influenced by the developmental approach to career choice as described by Super (1957) and Ginzberg, Ginsburg, Axelrad, and Herma (1951). Tiedeman's early work with Robert O'Hara shows both the influence of these theorists and a unique approach to career decision making, evident in the model of Tiedeman and O'Hara (1963). In an ambitious research project, Tiedeman applied his career decision-making paradigm to the development of a computer-assisted guidance system (Tiedeman, 1979). Tiedeman's early work is characterized by his concern about the uniqueness of the individual and the complexity of the decision-making process.

The process of career decision making deals with the gradual development of, and commitment to, a choice. As described by Tiedeman and O'Hara, the two major stages are anticipating and adjusting to a choice. Anticipating a choice has four phases: exploration, crystallization, choice, and clarification. Adjusting to a choice refers to adjusting to work when one has a job. These phases are induction, reformation, and integration.

Anticipating a Choice

Tiedeman and O'Hara (1963) divide the anticipating stage of decision making into four basic developmental phases: exploration, crystallization, choice, and clarification. These phases are not always sequential, nor are they age-related. Furthermore, one can be at various phases for several different career decisions at a particular point in time.

These phases can be guides for the counselor in understanding the decision-making process and the nature of the individual's internal cognitive and affective processes. To illustrate these phases, an example will be given of a student who is in her senior year of high school and trying to decide whether to get a job, attend college, or join the armed forces. Susan, whose parents are both Polish, is in a quandary as to what to choose. To make matters more difficult, her mother is suffering from terminal cancer, and Susan is not sure how long she will live. In this example, the counselor will help Susan to decide among her alternatives by working through the phases of exploration, crystallization, choice, and clarification. For purposes of this situation, the flow will be from each phase to the next higher phase. In other situations, progress may be made much more slowly and with less directionality than in this example.

Exploration   In the exploration phase, individuals may follow leads in an unsystematic way. They may imagine themselves in different situations, try out certain behaviors, fantasize about later career goals, worry about their deepest fears, and follow avenues of choice in systematic or unsystematic ways. How they explore will reflect their own style. The counselor may help to clarify and strengthen the client's self-knowledge but does not impose a structure from outside. There is a need to take action or make a decision, but the process may not be felt clearly.

> CL: Here it is December, and I don't know what to do. I graduate in May, and
> · I don't know what to do.
>
> CO: So many choices. [The counselor recognizes Susan's need to explore. He wants to help her to do that to the best of her ability.]

CL: It's just so hard. I don't know what to do. I've thought about school, going to college, getting a degree. I don't know how I would pay for it. I don't know what I would study. It feels so unknown. Maybe I should just get a job at home.

CO: So much pressure on you right now. You can relax a bit, and we can talk about it. [Susan seems to be paralyzed by the huge responsibility that she is feeling for the decision.]

CL: It's just so hard to relax. I feel so bad. Every time I go home, I see my mother. Sometimes, she's had a chemotherapy treatment and she's really sick. I feel so scared then. I know I should help her. I know I should take care of her, but I should take care of myself, too.

CO: Seeing your mother sick like that—it's so hard. She's on your mind so often. [Recognizing Susan's caring and sense of responsibility for her mother, the counselor wants to help Susan explore that aspect of the decision making further.]

CL: Sometimes when I'm with her, my mind wanders. I think of her. I think of me. I've thought about me being stationed in Europe with the army. Being over there with other American soldiers. Ever since I was a little girl, I've liked to do things like march and salute. Stuff like that. My father was a policeman. When I think of him now—and he's not a policeman any longer—I think of him in his blue uniform. I was always in awe of him then. He looked so strong. Maybe that's why. But I've always enjoyed military movies, war games, all kinds of stuff like that.

CO: It seems freeing to let your imagination run like that. [Letting Susan's exploration follow her inner feelings and her imagination seems appropriate to the counselor.]

CL: Yes, I worry about my mother so. It's nice to take a break from that. It's hard, too. She's often cranky because she hurts. It's so hard for me to see her hurt. [crying] She's been so good to me.

CO: Her illness brings you back to what you have to do each day. [The counselor is aware of how difficult it is for Susan to explore when she feels such responsibility right now for her mother.]

The dialogue between counselor and client moves along this way for two more sessions. Susan moves back and forth between her responsibility for her mother and her desire to make plans. As best he can, the counselor helps Susan search within herself for the various paths that she wants to explore. He helps her to explore them and not run away from them, even though they are frightening, such as the fear of her mother's dying. Gradually, and without the counselor's immediate awareness, Susan's choices start to crystallize.

Crystallization   According to Tiedeman and O'Hara (1963), "Crystallization normally represents a stabilization of thought" (p. 41). Thoughts and feelings may start to be more orderly. The advantages and disadvantages of various choices may start to emerge. Temporary choices may emerge and may be challenged and changed. Awareness of the choice may be clear, vague, or nonexistent. But more definition is found in this phase than in the exploratory phase.

At this point, Susan is in her third counseling appointment. She has been able to speak more about her fears about her mother's health with the counselor. She further explores options of working in a retail store at home, joining the army, or applying for admission to her state university.

CL: I've talked to the army recruiter in town. He was real nice to me. He was flexible about when I could enter and what I would do. He seemed to understand the situation about my mother. I guess I was kind of surprised about that, and I appreciated it.

CO: He seemed to make you feel good about yourself, as if to give you more options to do what you might want. [The counselor takes the opportunity to comment on a growing sense of self, a sense that Susan may be feeling that she can take care of herself.]

CL: I guess I want to know that I'm not stuck, that I can make different choices at different times. For a while, it felt as if I had to do one thing or the other, but I couldn't do more than one. I still don't know about school. I don't know whether I want to go to college. I really have been getting B's and C's and don't like school too much. Gosh, I don't know what I would study. Maybe English, science, math—I don't think so. I don't know.

CO: Tell me more about what you like at school. [The counselor senses Susan moving back from crystallizing some options to still exploring her likes about academic subjects. If assigning an interest inventory or values inventory will help her explore this area, then he will do so.]

CL: I like history. I like learning about different cultures, different people. I really like learning about how this country was settled. When the events seem to take place in my mind I can imagine the Revolutionary War or things like that; it's fun. I like geography, too.

CO: Can you tell me more about that? [The counselor wants Susan to continue her exploration.]

CL: I like geography because I can picture different countries. I can imagine what they would be like. I think I'd really like to travel. I'd like to help people travel. That's what I think part of the fun is about being stationed overseas. It's so different. If I were over there with the army, I'd have a free trip. I have often liked to travel with my parents. We visit relatives all over the place. I love it.

Susan continues to explore some interests while her more pressing choices are tending to crystallize in terms of what she may do in the immediate future. She is moving closer to the choice of college, the army, or home, but not an eventual career goal.

Choice   As crystallization develops, a choice may occur. The person may have varying degrees of confidence about that choice. Choices vary in terms of their clarity and complexity. Sometimes, they emerge with conscious awareness, and sometimes, without.

Four weeks have passed since Susan's initial conference with the counselor. Susan is moving closer to a decision about what she plans to do in the summer.

CL: I really think that I need to be here with my mother, as long as I can. She's been getting worse. I really worry for her. I don't know how long she will live. It scares me terribly; we've been so very close. I feel as if I can join the army after that—maybe travel some. I know about possibilities for schooling. Having the army help me out—things like that. I think that might work.

CO: You seem to have things clearer in your mind. The choices seem to be falling into place. [The counselor notes how Susan has prioritized her choices in terms of time.]

CL: Yes. I've thought about it a lot. I just feel that I need so much right now to be with my mother. My father seems to need me, too; so does my younger sister. It's strange; I'm not used to that. My father was always gruff. He's such a big guy, and someone who's quiet a lot. I see him sad, crying sometimes. It's awful.

CO: I know it's really hard for you. This has been a tough time. [Susan's life and career decisions are intimately intertwined; moving back and forth from one issue to another seems natural.]

CL: It's so hard for me now. But sometimes, when I think that I can go into the army and then I can do more things that I want to do—come out and go to school, or work in a travel agency, or work for an airline—then things seem OK, but not always for long.

CO: You're really doing some thinking about the future. [The counselor is surprised to hear some career choices emerge. He is patient and feels no need to develop them at the moment.]

Clarification   When individuals make a decision, they ordinarily act on it. However, they may experience doubt between the time the decision is made and when it is acted on. Time gives an opportunity to reassess the choice and to clarify the options. If the choice is questioned, the individual may return to explore, crystallize, and choose all over again. Miller-Tiedeman (1977) found that ninth-graders often leaped from exploration to choice and, depending on outcome, tended to recycle back through crystallization and clarification.

Susan continued to experience doubt about her decision. Sometimes, she felt she should just stay at home with her family and, no matter what happened with her mother, not leave them. Being with her friends and hearing about their plans would reinforce her feeling about following her inner wishes. She wanted to take a trip to visit a friend several hours away. That was a particularly meaningful experience to her, as it allowed her to develop her sense of self. She could feel stronger about herself, making her own plans for the trip and spending time with her friend on an equal basis. She felt relieved not to be taking care of someone. Telling the counselor about this helped her become more aware of her goals. Taking that trip seemed to clarify her own notion of what was important to her.

The phases of anticipating a choice—exploration, crystallization, choice, and clarification—lead to the implementation of and adjustment to a choice. Once a choice has been made and is about to be acted on, the second of Tiedeman's two major stages—adjusting to a choice—begins.

Adjusting to a Choice

Acting on a choice is an important part of Tiedeman's conceptualization of decision making. He does not feel that the decision-making process is over once the choice has been made. Tiedeman and O'Hara (1963) outline three phases of adjustment: induction, reformation, and integration. These phases deal with carrying out the decision. Interaction with others is required. There may be teachers, bosses, or others whom one needs to deal with in order to carry out the decision. As an illustration of these phases, we will follow Susan in her progress through them.

Induction   In this phase, a person implements his or her choice. The choice may be to go to college, take adult education courses, start a new job, or work a second part-time job. As an individual is inducted into his or her new choice, a certain amount of change will take place in response to the commitment that has been made.

Susan continued her schoolwork. When she graduated, she started to work for a pharmacy in town as a cashier and a stock clerk. She continued to discuss her plans with the army recruiter. This gave her a sense of being transitory, an awareness that her current goal (career choice) was not permanent. Throughout the summer, she had to take time off from work as her mother grew weaker. In October, her mother died, leaving Susan in shock. She felt the need to stay at home to be with her younger sister and her father. She had made friends at work who were supportive of her and who helped her in her crisis. In June of the following year, she entered the army. She had been looking forward to this experience for some time. Induction into this goal felt less transitory and more like a choice that would help her feel that she was moving in a positive direction. She felt excited, knowing that she was doing something that she had wanted to do for some time.

Reformation   The introduction of a new member into a group and the reception of that individual by other members constitute reformation. Often, in this phase an individual is hesitant to join or feel a part of the group at first but may later become an advocate of the group.

For Susan, boot camp was not unexpected. She had talked to friends about basic training and was prepared. She actually enjoyed it, particularly liking the feeling of comradeship that she experienced with other members of her group. After basic training, she was assigned to the infantry. She enjoyed learning about the equipment and how to clean and operate rifles, machine guns, and such. This experience gave her a sense of belonging and excitement.

Integration   In integration, the newness wears off, and the group and the individual accept each other. The excitement about the new choice may diminish and become an integral part of the individual.

As new individuals joined and left Susan's infantry group, her feeling about them and herself changed. When one of her closest friends left, she felt somewhat lonely and unsure of herself. However, when someone else entered, she enjoyed the excitement of the new discovery of this individual. After two years in the army, Susan began to give more thought to whether to reenlist, move back home, or enter college. As she did this, she reentered the exploratory phase.

As Susan went through the stages of anticipation and adjustment in her career decision-making process, her sense of self developed. She had a sense of herself not as a military person, a bereaved daughter, a friend, or a potential college student, but as a whole person. The counselor, who dealt with her in the anticipation aspects of a portion of her career decision making, also saw her as a whole person. He did not differentiate between career choice and other life choices. The counselor helped her develop her decision but did not suggest what to do. This emphasis on the individual is consistent with the work of Tiedeman.

Research on Tiedeman's Process Perspective

Though not a frequent object of study, the Tiedeman and O'Hara (1963) paradigm has stimulated some behavioral research. Basically, there are two types: research that tests the theory directly in terms of the accuracy of the stages of decision making and research that has studied instruments designed to measure decision-making styles.

Miller-Tiedeman and Tiedeman (1990) report two studies that bear directly on the four phases of anticipation of Tiedeman and O'Hara (1963): exploration, crystallization, choice, and clarification. Miller-Tiedeman (1977) reports that adolescent learners first make a decision; after experiencing negative consequences, return to the crystallization phase; and then go on to choose a second time. If that doesn't work, they go to the crystallization phase and then to the clarification phase before making a final choice. Thus, deciders worked in a more complex manner than predicted by Tiedeman and O'Hara (1963). In another study of adolescents, Jepsen and Grove (1981) found that rather than following the order of exploration, crystallization, choice, and clarification, the participants reversed the last two phases and choice followed clarification. Naturally, not all students respond in this way. Miller-Tiedeman (1989) points out that it is the individual style of decision making that is particularly important, not the decision-making style of a group of individuals.

In addition to research on career decision-making stages, several investigators have attempted to develop a scale to measure career decision making. Most notable is the work of Harren (1979), who originated the Assessment of Career Decision Making. In general, research on this inventory has supported the concepts of Tiedeman and O'Hara. The Assessment of Career Decision Making, as developed by Buck and Daniels (1985), corresponds only partially to the theory of Tiedeman and O'Hara. This inventory includes scales that measure three decision-making styles: rational, intuitive, and dependent.

Rational: In this approach, individuals are able to plan when making a decision. They pay attention to both their feelings and their knowledge of their abilities, interests, and values when making a career-related decision.

Intuitive: Making a decision based on feelings rather than thoughts about what one wants to do would be intuitive. Intuitive decisions may be quite appropriate, but they can be supplemented by an analysis of one's own strengths, for example, one's abilities and interests. Certain occupational choices tend to be made on the basis of feelings. Deciding to be a minister, priest, or rabbi may be based on a spiritual feeling rather than on a cognitive decision-making process. The desire to become a stage or movie actor with full knowledge of the limited and competitive job market is an example of making a decision based on the fact that the career choice feels right.

Dependent: A person who complies with the plans of another lets that person make the decision for him or her. The classic example is the child whose parents want him or her to become a doctor when the child does not want to enter medicine. Sometimes, individuals are compliant because they are passive and, at other times, because they feel coerced by an authority figure.

In addition to these decision styles, Buck and Daniels measure school adjustment, consisting of three subscales (Satisfaction with School, Involvement with Peers, and Interaction with Instructors). Also, they measure two decision-making tasks, Choosing an Occupation and Choosing a Major, on separate scales. These last scales do not correspond directly to the stages of Tiedeman and O'Hara (1963), although these scales represent critical decisions in Tiedeman and O'Hara's theory. Earlier versions of the Assessment of Career Decision Making are more closely allied to the Tiedeman and O'Hara paradigm. Miller-Tiedeman and Tiedeman (1990) cite research on the earlier version that supports the concepts in the Tiedeman and O'Hara theory.

A SPIRITUAL PERSPECTIVE ON DECISION MAKING

A number of counselors and authors have taken a spiritual approach to work and decision making about work. These writers see work not as a mundane task or as a job that one has to do, but rather as a place in which one's spirit can be nourished and one can develop oneself. From this perspective, individuals' *spirit* can greatly affect their lives, their choices, and the type of individuals they will become. *Spirit* can be seen as an essential principle that gives life to physical being (Savickas, 1997). Individuals can be seen as trying to become more complete and more whole as they develop their spiritual self. Individuals' motivations provide a direction for them in their lives and their decision making. Spiritual energy and motivation is often expressed in work through needs, values, and interests. Counselors and writers using a spiritual perspective often are implicit rather than explicit in their discussion of needs, values, and interests.

A spiritual approach to career decision making may or may not include a religious point of view. Many writers take a very broad, nonreligious view of spirituality. However, other writers integrate their theological beliefs with their views of career decision making. For example, Huntley (1997) and Rayburn (1997) illustrate how Christianity provides a framework for helping clients understand their careers and career decision making. Stoltz-Loike (1997) uses Judaism as a perspective to understand careers and career decision making. In this section, a broad spiritual perspective will be presented rather than one using specific theological views. Unlike most career development theories, a spiritual perspective has not been developed using objective criteria. I have combined the general overview of Miller-Tiedeman (1997, 1999) with seven spiritual concepts as explained by Bloch and Richmond (1998).

Perhaps the best-known author writing about spirituality is Miller-Tiedeman (1988, 1989, 1992, 1997, 1999). As the founder of the Lifecareer® Foundation, Miller-Tiedeman has focused on the importance of viewing life-as-career. From her perspective, life is one's career; a career is not a job. Her view can be characterized as valuing the intelligence and experience of individuals.

Miller-Tiedeman's point of view is referred to as Lifecareer Theory. In this theory, she shows how individuals should accept themselves, their feelings, and beliefs, and approach decision making in a way that reduces stress and increases motivation. Rather than be afraid of change, they should appreciate the surprise and newness that comes with change. Rather than focus on right and wrong answers, they should appreciate information that comes from different aspects of choosing. The counselor's role is not to advise or direct, but to help individuals listen to themselves and appreciate their intelligence and experience by using their intuition. This focus is very present-oriented, rather than dwelling in the past or speculating on the future.

Lifecareer Theory

In Lifecareer Theory, individuals are seen as being able to process information and make decisions in a process that flows. Using a perspective similar to that of constructivist theorists (Chapter 11), Miller-Tiedeman sees each individual as his or her own theory maker. Implicit in this view is deep respect for the individual and the individual's life process. From this point of view, you are not looking for a career, you have one. Life is our career. By trusting inner wisdom that comes from your intellectual ability, previous experiences, and intuition into past experiences, you can experience your career. Because one's life is one's career, you can flow with it, not fight it or work against it. In essence, you are doing what you want to do, not what others think is best for you. In emphasizing the importance of listening to one's self, Miller-Tiedeman distinguishes between personal and common realities.

Personal and Common Realities

Reality concerns the awareness of one's career decision making (Miller-Tiedeman & Tiedeman, 1990). The question of whether a decision or act is realistic is a matter of opinion. The question is: Realistic to whom? Tiedeman and Miller-Tiedeman (1979) specify two types of reality: personal and common. *Personal reality* refers to an individual's sense of what is right. It is a feeling that the decision or direction to be taken is correct and appropriate to the decision maker. On the other hand, *common reality* is what others say the individual should do; for example, "You would be a good teacher," "You can get a better job than that," and "You can't get anywhere without a college degree." Common reality also includes the opinions of experts.

Spirituality

When individuals experience the wholeness of living, they experience spirituality. Thus, spirituality is not brought into one's life, rather it develops. Understanding yourself and your whole being can also help you to relate to others in a nonviolent and effective way. In doing so, individuals reduce stress in their lives and become more relaxed.

Lifecareer is *the dynamic lived-in-the-moment process defined by each person in individual moments* (Miller-Tiedeman, 1997). In Lifecareer Theory, the client determines what works and what doesn't, not the counselor. Individuals experience their feelings, thoughts, physical self, and spiritual self in a harmonious way. Clients are helped to reflect on their lives in a very serious and deep way. They are shown how trusting in one's life helps to develop a career naturally and in a relaxed manner. In doing this, counselors can listen for themes or issues that are important in clients' lives.

In their book, *Soul Work*, Bloch and Richmond (1998) have described seven themes that individuals can use to better understand their lives and the career decisions that are a part of their lives. These seven themes reflect a spiritual approach to career decision making. They include: change, balance, energy, community, calling, harmony, and unity.

Change   Change is inevitable, occurring at many times throughout one's life career. When change occurs by chance or through seemingly unconnected events, it can be called *synchronicity*. Being open to changes that occur in work can give individuals opportunities that they previously had not considered.

Change can be internal or external. Internal changes may occur through anxiety or dissatisfaction with aspects of a job. On the other hand, when one feels excited by aspects of one's work and seeks new challenges, then that is a positive internal change. In contrast, external events may force change on people, whether they desire it or not. The classic example is being fired or losing a job because a company is going out of business. Change may come about through the experience of a loss of a loved one or losing a valued coworker.

Regardless of whether change is internal or external, there are likely to be many feelings and emotions. Being able to identify and be aware of feelings is important for individuals coping with change. Sometimes change brings about disruptions in physical being. Working the night shift can clearly bring about changes in sleeping and other physical functions.

Individuals often cope with change by keeping current in their field or by attending workshops. From a spiritual point of view, another way of coping with change is through identifying strengths and acting on them. Strengths may be physical, interpersonal, emotional, verbal, analytic, or moral. All of these strengths provide ways of coping with distress or the surprise of change.

Balance   Sometimes individuals seek a balance in their lives, and other times it is a natural inclination to maintain a balance between work, play, and other activities. Individuals often seek out a balance in relationships with others. An excellent example of this is the dual-career family, in which individuals seek to achieve at work while having a good relationship with their partner. Circumstances in our lives cause us to seek a balance among the many roles that we may play such as that of child, spouse, homemaker, parent, citizen, and worker. Super's roles that were discussed in Chapter 6 describe more aspects of balancing circumstances in our lives. Another area of balance, is that of one's relationship with self. Are interests and values being met? Are only a few of them being met and the others ignored? Individuals often ask themselves these questions to develop balance in their lives.

Bloch and Richmond (1998) suggest some ways to bring about more balance in life. They state that by changing one's view of time, one may be able to stop procrastinating and experience the moment. Weighing the importance of the different tasks that we work on may help in doing this. Sometimes changing views of authority, parents, supervisors, and teachers may help to balance the demands that are placed on us. By changing the way we talk and the messages we give ourselves, we may be able to change our views of authority and our views of how we will spend our time. Changing from "I can't do that" to "I can do that" can change the balance in life. Likewise, changing the way we behave, whether it is in our relationship with others or in doing tasks at work, can also change the balance in life, bringing about a greater feeling of equanimity.

Energy   In order to bring about change and balance in one's life, there must be energy. Energy exists throughout the universe. Physics and biology observe energy in different ways. The way individuals approach their careers can be measured or viewed by the amount of energy that they generate in their work.

For individuals there are many different sources of energy. Some individuals are energized by being with others, whereas some individuals are energized by being alone. For some, music, painting, theater, film, and books generate energy. Sports and physical activity can be yet another source of energy. When individuals love their work, the work generates energy. Individuals who approach work in such a way that they are totally involved are often said to be "in the flow." When they are "in the flow" they are doing what they can to the best of their ability, fully enjoying it, and fully immersed in their work. In this way energy often brings about more energy rather than tiredness.

Community   Bloch and Richmond (1998) identify three types of communities that individuals are likely to participate in: communities of companionship, communities of culture, and the cosmic community. The community of companionship includes immediate and extended family as well as close friends. The community of culture may include neighbors, classmates, coworkers, and individuals one shares leisure or professional interests with. Cosmic communities are those which concern large ideas such as the environment, the dying poor, the homeless, taxation, and many others. Not only are there many different types of communities, but there are many different ways in which individuals connect with them.

Individuals have many different styles of relating with each other. For example, Chapter 5 contrasts the way extraverts and introverts deal with the external and the internal world. Individuals vary in their need to be included or recognized by others. Some have strong needs for belonging and contact, whereas others do not. For some, being in control of others and influencing others is important, whereas others are content to listen and to follow the suggestions of authorities. Individuals also differ in their need for support, warmth, and love. Work is a means of interacting with one's community. Certainly, work provides the opportunity to feel included, to be in control, and to feel needed and cared for.

Calling   "Calling is about hearing your own song and singing it out loud and clear" (Bloch & Richmond, 1998, p. 128). Although traditionally used to mean to be called by God to a religious occupation, calling refers to finding one's ideal work. Finding one's calling is to recognize one's interests, skills, values, and abilities and apply them to productive work. When individuals find their calling, they find much joy in their work. However, some individuals are not aware of how much joy they find in their work until they stop doing it, either for a vacation or for a transfer to a new occupation. When people have found their calling, they are truly absorbed by their work and are "in the flow." Trait and factor theorists refer to matching interests, abilities, and values with an occupation; career counselors who take a spiritual point of view may help individuals find their calling.

Harmony   Whereas calling refers to knowing your ideal work through knowing yourself, harmony refers to finding the work that will bring about a true sense of appreciation and understanding. Searching for information about education and occupations helps individuals to find harmony. But this is not enough; individuals must know that their work and their current career is producing harmony by meeting their interests, values, and abilities.

Harmony not only comes from work but from meditation or stillness. Individuals find harmoniousness when they have a sense of meaningfulness in their life and a way of knowing that comes from quiet self-examination. Bloch and Richmond believe that through meditation individuals will find harmony between their internal search for their interests, values, and abilities and their external search for information about occupations.

Unity   To believe in unity is to trust the universe. To trust the universe is to be prepared to deal with changes that occur and to believe that the universe is one whole. For most religions, unity is a goal—a sense of union with a higher power. Bloch and Richmond refer to ways that individuals can achieve unity of career, of spirit, of energy, and with others. Unity of career refers to feeling a sense of flow or being totally involved in one's work, to be a part of the work not apart from it. Unity of energy can be seen by the feeling of being connected to one's work and one's world and to intentionally bring about changes in one's career to increase harmoniousness. Unity of spirit refers to feeling connected with oneself (being fully aware), being connected with one's partner and friends, feeling a sense of belonging with one's community, to have a sense of connection with ones' culture, and to have a sense of being connected to the universe. Interpersonal unity comes from involvement with others.

These seven concepts provide a spiritual way of viewing how individuals can achieve job satisfaction and satisfaction in their lives. The concepts of change, balance, energy, community, calling, harmony, and unity are ways that counselors can view their clients' struggles with their lives and their careers—Lifecareer. How counselors can help clients by using a spiritual point of view is the subject of the next section.

A Spiritual Approach to Career Counseling

A spiritual approach to career counseling may seem vague and unclear. However, Miller-Tiedeman (1997) makes several suggestions that can be helpful to counselors in working with clients using the Lifecareer Theory. These suggestions reflect her profound respect for the client and the client's role in decision making that affects his or her life career.

- Let clients know that they have a career and that it is their life. Listen to their narration of their life career and provide information where helpful. Help clients respect their lives and process their decisions. Decreasing their anxiety through relaxation techniques or meditation may be helpful.
- Let clients know that they are the best judge of whether something is working or not working, rather than the counselor. In other words, emphasize the importance of personal rather than common reality. Not only does the counselor not judge the client's reality, the counselor encourages clients not to pass judgment on their own reality. Rather, they should accept what they have done so they can discover their potential to do more.

- Encourage students to learn through their experience and to assess this experience. This assessment may lead to developing three or four plans that can be modified each semester so that individuals can apply their decision making to important events.
- When using tests and inventories be careful that tests and inventories (common reality) do not interfere with students' exploration of educational or occupational opportunities.
- Help clients set intentions without placing time restrictions on them. Intentions or desires may change from time to time. Some may be stable and some may disappear. If clients want to track their intentions they can write "intention" on one side of the paper and "date completed" on the other side. This way they can follow what their intentions are and keep track of their decision making. On the other hand, they may wish to just jot down ideas and look at them from time to time to see if they merge into a direction to follow.
- If you are enthusiastic about change, your clients are less likely to feel afraid to change and more likely to feel excitement in making career decisions. This focus on change will help students take action and worry less about the outcome of their decisions. Thus, the focus should be on taking action now rather than worrying about the outcome. In this way, the counselor concentrates on the present, not the future or the past.

These suggestions value the client and the client's Lifecareer. The counselor assists clients with the flow of their careers and does not interpret or judge. The counseling approach is to help clients be less judgmental and to be more self-aware. As they become more self-aware they can focus on understanding changes in their lives, creating balance, being aware of their energy, understanding their relationship with their communities, developing a calling, and being at harmony with this calling. In following this spiritual approach, they can strive to achieve unity in their lives. A case example will serve to show how a counselor might apply a spiritual approach to career counseling.

A Case Example of Spiritual Counseling

Bonnie is an 18-year-old high school senior whose father is Caucasian and mother is Japanese. At the suggestion of her parents, Bonnie has come to talk to her high school guidance counselor about her future plans. An excellent student with A's in most courses, Bonnie had originally planned to stay at her home in Madison, Wisconsin, and attend the University of Wisconsin at Madison. Her excellent grades in science and math suggested to her parents that a career in engineering or medicine might be appropriate for her. However, Bonnie disagrees. She has been active in student government and in the honor society. But her first love has been acting. She has had major roles in high school productions over the past three years. Furthermore, she has appeared in the chorus and in minor roles in community productions in Madison.

Conflict has developed between Bonnie and her parents about her future plans. Bonnie would like to go to Hollywood to try to get a job in acting or modeling. Her parents are frightened that Bonnie will be taken advantage of or that harm will come to her when she leaves home. They much prefer to see her stay at home and enter the University of Wisconsin. The following dialogue is an excerpt of a conversation between Bonnie and her counselor. The counselor is using a model that is consistent with Lifecareer Theory.

CL: My parents are really bugging me at home. I can't stand it. They drive me crazy. They're always telling me what will happen to me next year if I leave home.

CO: Tell me more. [The counselor wants to learn more about how Bonnie perceives the current situation.]

CL: I love acting. I know that this is what is going to be my future. I've been acting for the last five years. I just get this wonderful feeling when I am out there in front of an audience. Even when I am auditioning and rehearsing it's great. It's like this is me. This is what I am going to be and what I am now.

CO: You feel so energized by acting, it's such a fulfilling experience. [The counselor is struck by Bonnie's energy and reflects this back to her.]

CL: Yeah. We did *Guys and Dolls* and I played the role of the Salvation Army woman. It was great. I got to sing, dance, act, and work with a demanding director. That's what I look forward to. I sure don't look forward to math class.

CO: Right now acting is just what you want to do. It's for you. [At this moment, now, Bonnie sees her calling. It is clear that it is acting. Whether this will be her calling in the future is unclear. But now the counselor honors her decision about acting.]

CL: Yeah. It seems great to me, but not to my parents. My mother is always saying to me "You should be a doctor."

CO: How does that fit for you? [The counselor wonders whether that is an occupation that would create harmony for Bonnie. Right now, she wants to focus on Bonnie's views, not her mother's.]

CL: I don't know. How can I tell? My mother keeps bugging me.

CO: Well, let's take a look and examine this. [The counselor is trying to help Bonnie achieve harmony, to be open to change, and to examine her interests, values, and abilities.]

CL: I really don't like biology and I don't like being with sick people. Of all the courses that I have, I probably like biology the least. I mean I like figuring out problems, don't get me wrong. That's fun. But trying to deal with sick people and all their ailments is not something that I want to do.

CO: It's really clear that medicine does not interest you now. It seems like this is also creating problems between you and your mother. [The counselor observes the disharmony between medicine and Bonnie and between Bonnie and her mother.]

CL: This is really difficult. My mom and I used to get along real well. Now there is tension. I don't like being home the way I use to like it. When I am at school in the evening working on plays, it is a relief for me.

CO: It's so hard for you to be at odds with your mother now.

> *CL:* It really is. (*crying*) I miss her. I miss my mother. I miss the closeness that we had, I don't know what to do. This is really tearing me apart that we can't talk the way we use to.
>
> *CO:* This dilemma is eating at you so. You want so much to be with your mother and at the same time have her agree with your choice. [The counselor frames the problem for Bonnie and is aware of the lack of balance that this is creating in her life.]
>
> *CL:* It's so hard to do what I want, to try out acting the way I want to.
>
> *CO:* The way you want to?
>
> *CL:* Yes. I really don't want to go to college next year. I want to try acting and see what I can do; maybe later I will go to college, but I don't want to now.
>
> *CO:* Trying acting would give you the feeling that you were doing what is best for you. [The counselor is encouraging Bonnie to try something out and is not making a judgment about her success or potential.]
>
> *CL:* Yes. I know it is difficult to get a job acting. I really want to try. I know I might fail. But, that's possible, people may not hire me. I may not get an agent.
>
> *CO:* You're willing to try. You know that your choice may work or may not work. [The client is encouraged to continue and her plan, her life career, is supported. The counselor does not take sides or interfere with Bonnie's perception of her internal reality.]
>
> *CL:* But then there is my mother. I keep worrying about her. She means so much to me. She worries about me so.
>
> *CO:* I know you're worrying. I wonder if you have impressed your mother with the strength of your passion for acting and your willingness to consider something else only if it doesn't work out.

This example may cause some discomfort to parents and counselors. It illustrates the emphasis that counselors, using a spiritual model, particularly that of Miller-Tiedeman, put on the client in making decisions in his or her life. The counselor is patient and continues to discuss with Bonnie the dilemma between doing what it is that she wants to do with her career now and the potential of hurting her mother. When the counselor sees Bonnie again, Bonnie's perception of her personal reality may have changed. The counselor does not pass judgment, but encourages Bonnie to look at her inner self and to make decisions that she is comfortable with.

The essence of spiritual approaches to career development is seen through the work of Miller-Tiedeman and Bloch and Richmond. In Miller-Tiedeman's view of career development, life is career. There is a strong emphasis in her work on the value of the human being in making decisions and appreciating a person's ability to decide for him- or herself. Many of Miller-Tiedeman's strategies for helping students in career decision making are to support and encourage them to take action, and to listen to their inner selves. Bloch and Richmond provide another dimension to a spiritual approach by describing themes of change, balance, energy, community, calling, harmony, and unity. These themes can provide useful ways of mapping the direction of the decision making. Most of these themes are not typically used by other theorists in their discussion of career choice and work adjustment. These themes emphasize the importance of the human spirit in career development.

A COGNITIVE INFORMATION PROCESSING APPROACH

Whereas Miller-Tiedeman and her colleagues emphasize the importance of the human spirit in career decision making, other theorists have focused on a cognitive approach to choosing careers and making career decisions. Starting in the early 1980s, Gary Peterson, James Sampson, Robert Reardon, and Janet Lenz, all professors and practitioners at Florida State University, turned their attention to how individuals think about careers and how their thought processes affect their career decision making. They were concerned not only about helping individuals to learn about their interests, abilities, and values, as well as the world of work, but also to help individuals understand the way that they think and how that influences their career decision making. They believe that individuals can profit from questioning their belief system about themselves and occupations and learning effective strategies for making career decisions. In their work, Peterson and his colleagues (1996) are influenced by research in cognitive science, the study of human thinking processes.

The early work on cognitive information processing (how people think) was done in the 1970s. Peterson and his colleagues were particularly influenced by the work of Hunt (1971); Newell and Simon (1972); and Lackman, Lackman, and Butterfield (1979). In their study of how individuals learn and process information, Peterson and his colleagues studied the learning involved in mathematics, physics, verbal analogies, and approaches used in taking intelligence tests. All of these subjects have in common the study of the learning process when there is a specific correct answer. In career development, the client and counselor must work out an appropriate strategy when often a "correct answer" is unclear. In *Career Development and Services: A Cognitive Approach* (Peterson, Sampson, & Reardon, 1991), research from cognitive information processing is applied to a theory of career development. This approach can best be summarized by the following question, "What can we do as career counselors to enable individuals to acquire self-knowledge, occupational knowledge, career decision skills, and metacognitions to become effective and responsible career problem solvers and decision makers?"

Assumptions of a Cognitive Information Processing Approach

Unlike Tiedeman who takes a developmental or process approach that describes career decision making and theorists who take a spiritual approach that also describes a point of view of decision making, Peterson and his colleagues take a prescriptive point of view. In other words, they prescribe or suggest ways that individuals can think about career decision making that will improve their ability to make good career decisions. From Miller-Tiedeman's perspective, they are helping individuals incorporate "common reality" information into "personal" career decision-making concerns. The four assumptions that Peterson and his colleagues make about applying career information processing theory to career concerns reflect this prescriptive approach.

1. Both affect and cognitive processing are important components of career decision making. Anxiety, confusion, depression, and other emotions may be part of the decision-making process for many individuals. Peterson and his colleagues do not deny the importance of emotions in career decision making, rather they examine how human emotions interact with information processing.
2. To make adequate career decisions, individuals must not only know themselves and the world of work, but they should also have information about thinking and how it affects decision making. Knowledge of career decision making helps individuals to recognize, to find, and to analyze occupational information as well as information about themselves. This then allows them to formulate and evaluate career choice possibilities (Peterson et al., 1996).
3. Information about self and the world of work is continually changing. There are cognitive structures such as schemas (ways of grouping and networking learned information) that develop and grow throughout the life span.
4. By improving one's information processing capabilities, clients can improve their career problem-solving abilities. Individuals' career decision-making abilities will improve if they can develop specific decision-making skills as well as higher-level executive control processes, which deal with acquiring, storing, and retrieving information about self, occupations, and other areas.

These four assumptions can help in understanding the pyramid of information processing that is the core of the cognitive information processing approach. This pyramid describes the important relationship between knowledge about self and occupations and decision-making skills.

The Pyramid of Information Processing

Cognitive information processing theory's approach to career development is best illustrated through the pyramid of information processing. This pyramid is based on Robert Sternberg's (1980, 1985) approach to understanding human intelligence. Figures 14-1 and 14-2 illustrate this pyramid. Figure 14-1 shows the theoretical components of cognitive information processing theory. Figure 14-2 shows how these components translate into a client's thinking.

The three basic components of cognitive information processing are knowledge domains, decision-making skills domain, and the executive processing domain. The knowledge domain consists of knowing oneself and knowing about occupations and the world of work options. In the decision-making skills domain individuals learn about how to make decisions. In the executive processing domain, clients become aware of how their

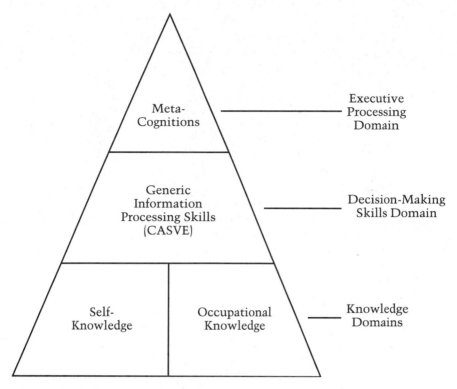

Figure 14-1 Pyramid of information processing domains in career decision making. (From "A Cognitive Approach to Career Services: Translating Concepts into Practice" by J. P. Sampson, Jr., G. W. Peterson, J. Lenz and R. C. Reardon in *Career Development Quarterly,* pp. 67–74. Copyright © 1992. Reprinted by permission of National Career Development Association.)

thoughts influence their decisions. In describing the pyramid, we will first focus on the base of the pyramid, the knowledge domain, and go next to the decision-making domain, and finally to the executive processing domain. To illustrate the cognitive information processing approach to career development we will use a case example.

Parnell is an African American college freshman from Cincinnati, Ohio. He is attending a small predominantly African American, religiously affiliated college near Nashville, Tennessee. Parnell is a son of middle-class college-educated parents. Both are accountants and work together in their own accounting firm. Both parents are active in Parnell's church and have supported the church through financial gifts and service in various capacities. Parnell has a younger sister who is completing eighth grade and is talented musically. When at church functions, Parnell has often heard about how his parents are both upstanding citizens and have done so much for their community. Parnell has felt the pressure to be a model citizen and to follow in his parents' footsteps in the church. Although his parents have

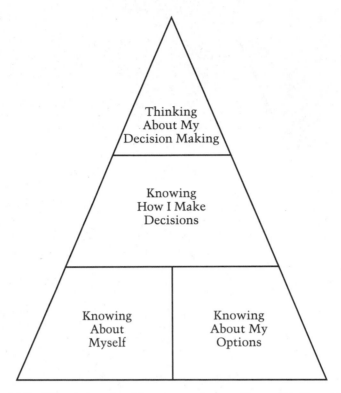

Figure 14-2 What's involved in career choice. (From "A Cognitive Approach to Career Services: Translating Concepts into Practice" by J. P. Sampson, Jr., G. W. Peterson, J. Lenz and R. C. Reardon in *Career Development Quarterly*, pp. 67–74. Copyright © 1992. Reprinted by permission of National Career Development Association.)

not pushed Parnell to go into accounting, they have shown him how well that profession has improved their own lives and how it has provided a good home for the family.

When Parnell started college, he thought that he might go into accounting like his parents. He started off with economics and accounting courses in his freshman year. Because he had done well in all of his subjects in high school, he thought that this would be a very practical career. Living at the college and taking the courses, boring though they seemed, was going along relatively smoothly for Parnell. However, the weekend before he was to go home for Thanksgiving vacation, he went off campus with some of his friends. They were at a party, where they had been drinking when Parnell had joined them. In the past, Parnell had only had a drink or two, but this time was an exception. When he got back to college and went into the student lounge, he was inebriated and in good humor. As friends would walk into the lounge, he would greet them by heaving a chair in their direction, and purposely missing them. Although he did not do any damage to individuals, he damaged the walls of the lounge. When his parents found out they were furious. This was the first time that he had truly provoked their anger. He was to meet with a counselor to discuss both his career direction and his inappropriate behavior when he returned from Thanksgiving break.

Self-Knowledge   In describing knowledge about self, Peterson et al. (1996) present different ways that information is stored in individuals' memories. For individuals to learn about themselves, they must both interpret events and reconstruct them. To interpret events they must match their sensation of present events with episodes stored in memory. These episodes contain subjects, actions, feelings, objects, and outcomes. Episodes related to present events are linked across time to help us have a view of ourselves. Reconstruction involves interpreting past events to put them into a current social context. Sometimes individuals may look at past events in order to compare these events with new information. This provides a new look at ourselves or an embellishment to our self-concept. Self-knowledge comes from information about previous school performance, previous work performance, interactions with other individuals, and observations about past events. From a career development perspective, the self-knowledge domain may include scores on interest inventories, ability tests, grades, as well as reactions to school and work.

For Parnell, the pertinent information in the self-knowledge domain is dislike of economics and accounting. From a more positive perspective, it included his enjoyment as a day camp counselor in working with young children and playing tennis and soccer. Good grades in school and strong religious beliefs are also part of this domain.

Occupational Knowledge   Throughout their lives individuals acquire information about the educational system and occupations. They structure and organize this information into related concepts. "Schemas" are ways of organizing information that is relevant to occupations so that meaningful connections can be made. When individuals learn new information about occupations they are continually combining new information with old. On one hand, they may acquire new information that more specifically describes an occupation, such as accounting, or, on the other hand, they may learn information that ties occupations together, such as "economist" and "accountant." These are two processes important in acquiring occupational knowledge.

For Parnell, occupational knowledge was somewhat limited. He heard much about his parents' work, as they would sometimes describe it at dinner. He learned that accounting was not just numbers, but also consulting with others and helping them in difficult situations. He also seemed to have a clear idea about roles of ministers and teachers through his exposure to them at school and at church. However, his knowledge of science, health, the trades, and other areas of the world of work was quite limited.

The two knowledge domains that have been discussed (self and occupational) correspond directly to trait and factor theory. Self-knowledge corresponds directly to Step One in trait and factor theory (Chapter 2), gaining self-understanding. The occupational knowledge domain corresponds to Step Two of trait and factor theory, obtaining knowledge about the world of work. It is the decision-making skills domain of cognitive information processing theory that sets it apart from trait and factor and other theories.

Decision-Making Skills   The capabilities that enable individuals to process information about themselves and occupations are referred to as generic information processing skills (Peterson et al., 1996). These skills are known by the acronym CASVE (Communication, Analysis, Synthesis, Valuing, Execution). These skills are outlined in a cycle and represent the skills that Peterson and his colleagues believe represent good decision making. Figure 14-3 shows the five skills in relationship to each other. Figure 14-4 shows how each of these skills is represented in the way clients think about themselves and occupations when making good decisions. These five skills are described in some detail below, and instances of how they may occur in counseling with Parnell are given.

1. *Communication.* When individuals get input from within themselves or from the environment, the communication process starts. Individuals become in touch with internal or external information signals. This is when they become aware of a problem, such as one they may have previously denied the existence of. Individuals start to examine themselves, their environment, and the problems that exist. They become aware that they need to act on information or to make a choice.

In Parnell's case the signals were rather clear. One blatant external signal to Parnell was the letter from the Dean of Students placing him on probation for damaging the dormitory lounge. If that signal were not enough, his mother's angry phone call was another. Regarding his career development, the internal signal of his dissatisfaction and boredom with accounting and economics was yet another. These signals communicated to Parnell that he needed to make a choice, to do some things differently. In talking to his counselor, the communication phase emerged in the following way:

CL: When I first came to college, I thought no problem. I'll just go into accounting like my parents. That's easy. They have a great business and I can work with them.

CO: But then some things happened. [The counselor gets a hint of some strong internal communication messages.]

CL: I was just aware that things weren't working out.

CO: Can you tell me more about that, Parnell? [The counselor wants to learn more about problems emerging in the communications stage.]

CL: I admitted to myself that accounting was really boring. The exercises that we had to do, the class assignments, the classes themselves, everything.

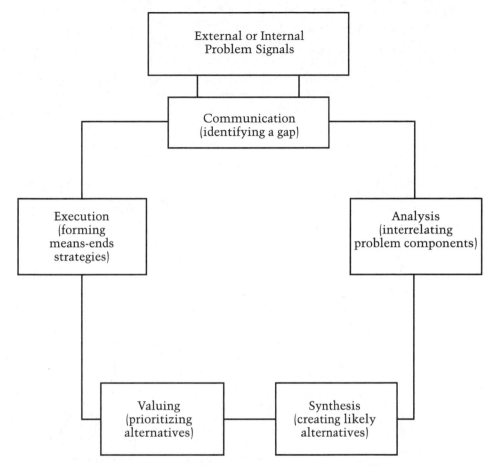

Figure 14-3 The five stages of the *CASVE* (*C*ommunication, *A*nalysis, *S*ynthesis, *V*aluing, *E*xecution) cycle of information processing skills used in career decision making. (From "A Cognitive Approach to Career Services: Translating Concepts into Practice" by J. P. Sampson, Jr., G. W. Peterson, J. Lenz and R. C. Reardon in *Career Development Quarterly*, pp. 67–74. Copyright © 1992. Reprinted by permission of National Career Development Association.)

     At first this scared me, I didn't like it. I mean I wanted to like accounting. I didn't like the fact that I didn't like accounting.

CO: It sounds like somewhere you said to yourself that you needed to rethink your career choice.

CL: Yes. I need to figure out something else. What else can I do? I need to know that.

CO: We can work together to help you figure out alternative career choices. [The communication stage focuses on becoming fully aware of the problem and starting to do something about it.]

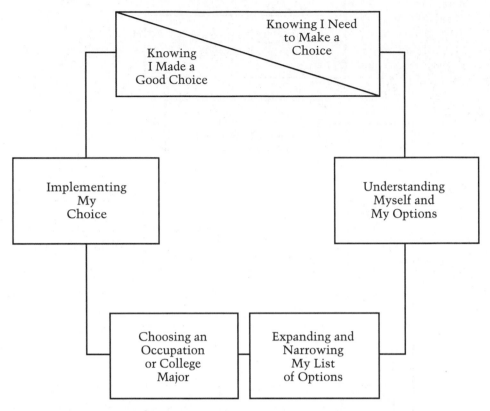

Figure 14-4 A guide to good decision making. (From "A Cognitive Approach to Career Services: Translating Concepts into Practice" by J. P. Sampson, Jr., G. W. Peterson, J. Lenz and R. C. Reardon in *Career Development Quarterly*, pp. 67–74. Copyright © 1992. Reprinted by permission of National Career Development Association.)

The short dialogue on the previous pages is consistent with the major goal of the communication stage. Peterson et al. (1996) suggest there are two particularly important questions for clients at this stage: "What am I thinking and feeling about my career choice at this moment?" and "What do I hope to attain as a result of career counseling?" (p. 436).

2. *Analysis.* Examining the self-knowledge and occupational knowledge domain is a part of the analysis phase. Individuals attend to causes of the problem and reflect on the problem. Reexamining values, interests, skills, and family situations may be a part of the phase. Learning new occupational information and reexamining old information might also be a part. Additionally, clients can consider their approach to making decisions and understand how positive and negative thoughts might influence their decision making (Sampson et al., 1999).

In Parnell's case the analysis phase included examining his interests and skills. Parnell was eager to take the Strong Interest Inventory. As he examined the results that indicated interests in social service and teaching occupations, he could understand why his interests would match those of teachers and social workers. The low score on Accounting surprised him at first, because he was so familiar with the occupation. When the counselor pointed out that the low score represented lack of interest in doing those types of activities that accountants do, he understood the score had to do with likes and dislikes, not familiarity. The scores helped him understand why he was currently undecided. He had to look at different aspects of himself than he had before and to consider different occupational information.

CL: I thought it was interesting that I scored so high on teaching.

CO: What was interesting about that? [The counselor is interested in how Parnell analyzes information in the self-knowledge domain.]

CL: Well, it got me thinking about teaching I had done. I guess I haven't done formal teaching. But I really like teaching the kids at the day camp how to swim and how to play sports.

CO: You seem excited when you talk about teaching the children. [The counselor is aware that emotional excitement can be a part of the analysis phase, it may not be purely an intellectual process.]

CL: Yes, it was lots of fun because I felt a sense of reward in helping children learn things that they felt good about, like how to play baseball.

CO: Sounds like as we talk about this, you're learning more about yourself. [In more technical terms, the counselor is referring to Parnell's analyzing his self-knowledge domain.]

Counseling with Parnell may include many discussions of various aspects of his interests, abilities, and values. By examining these areas, Parnell is analyzing his self-knowledge and occupational knowledge domains and how they relate to each other.

3. *Synthesis.* When information is analyzed, then individuals can pursue courses of action. Thus, they are taking information and synthesizing it through elaborating or crystallizing what they have analyzed. Elaboration refers to creating many possible solutions, even unlikely ones. Individuals may brainstorm or create metaphors so that they can generate many possible actions without having reality considerations limit the possibility of interactions. There is time for reality constraints later. Crystallization is the opposite of elaboration in that it refers to narrowing potential options through the application of reality constraints such as finances and ability (Sampson et al., 1999).

Parnell's synthesis occurred after considerable analysis. At first he was somewhat reluctant to explore options other than accounting and credit managing. Parnell explored options such as psychiatry, psychology, occupational therapy, and others. By elaborating on the information that he had analyzed, Parnell was able to examine occupations he had not previously considered. The counselor reassured Parnell that whether he could actually enter the occupation or get good enough grades to go to graduate school was to be considered later, not now. After generating so many opportunities, the counselor and Parnell could crystallize or narrow options. Parnell felt that as a freshman he did not want to limit his options too much. He thought that he could do well enough to go to graduate school in education or social work, but was not sure. In this way, Parnell was limiting possible courses of action and thus being consistent with the synthesis stage.

4. *Valuing.* As potential options are crystallized or narrowed, the client can evaluate or value possible actions or career directions. The client can then evaluate occupational or other choices in terms of first choice, second choice, and so on. In essence, the client is asking what is the best choice for me now? How will it affect my future life and the people who I care about? In some cultures, the relationship between a career option and spiritual and cultural values is also important. This may refer to specific occupational possibilities, job areas, or even specific positions, depending on the nature of the question the client seeks to answer (Sampson et al., 1999). In valuing, clients consider both the self-knowledge and the occupational knowledge domain. This phase may include considering job opportunities, qualifications, job duties, costs of schooling, and so forth.

For Parnell, the valuing stage gave him an opportunity to consider many of his actions. He evaluated not only his career concerns but also previous actions.

CL: I don't know if I'm ever going to live down that chair flinging thing.
CO: It really has had a big impact on you. You've done a lot of thinking about yourself since that happened. [The counselor is aware of the evaluation process that Parnell is going through.]
CL: Yes. It's not just that my mother has brought it up each time I talk to her. Really embarrassing. It's also that I know that if I do something like that again, I may never be able to go to graduate school and that's something that I really want to do.
CO: It's good to hear how you're thinking about that incident. [The counselor comments on the valuing that Parnell is doing.]
CL: I have to be careful, at least somewhat, so I can do those things that are important to me.

5. *Execution.* Once choices have been evaluated or have undergone the valuing process, then a plan or strategy can be formulated to implement the choice. This is done by taking small and intermediate steps. Individuals examine how they can try out a choice and see if it fits for them. Sometimes executing refers to finding volunteer work, part-time work, or taking specific courses. At other times, deciding where to send résumés or spending time with someone doing a specific job may be appropriate (Sampson et al., 1999). Depending on an individual's career concern, very different types of actions may be appropriate. For individuals who are upset about the way they are being treated in their current job, possible actions might include strategies for talking to coworkers or supervisors, or possibly hiring a lawyer.

Parnell, near the end of counseling, had decided that he was really interested in doing parole or probation work. The counselor helped Parnell find out more about probation work in the local community. After doing that, Parnell was able to talk to a probation counselor about his work and to see how he processed case reports in his office.

The CASVE process does not end here. Individuals may then act on or execute a particular choice, with actions resulting from this choice. They may have problems with following through on their plan or unanticipated results may follow. They then recycle through the CASVE cycle, beginning with the communication phase and examining their exploration experiences.

In Parnell's case he did have an interview with a probation counselor. He felt disappointed that the work seemed more routine than Parnell thought it would be. He reasoned that he wanted to have an option to work with younger people or at least have more of an impact on them than he thought he could as a probation counselor. This caused Parnell to reenter the CASVE cycle and reconsider his second choice of becoming an elementary school teacher.

The Executive Processing Domain

The top section of the pyramid (Figures 14-1 and 14-2) refers to higher-order functions. This is called executive processing because individuals examine how they think and how they act. Peterson et al. (1996) and Sampson et al. (1999) describe three major ways of thinking about decision making. These include self-talk, self-awareness, and monitoring and control.

Self-Talk   Similar to expectations that we have of ourselves, self-talk refers to the internal messages that we give ourselves about career choice and other issues. Self-talk can be positive or negative. Positive self-talk includes thoughts like "I can make good career decisions" or "I can find the information that I need about an occupation." Similarly, positive self-talk can refer to academic performance, such as "Although I did poorly on the last exam, I can study more effectively this time and do better." Negative self-talk is associated with difficulties in making decisions. It can include comments such as "I never do anything well," "I won't be able to get a job as a teacher," and "No one will want to hire me." If individuals use positive self-talk in their decision making (communication, analysis, synthesis, valuing, and execution), they are able to make career decisions better than if they use negative self-talk.

When Parnell thinks about his career decision making, he uses both positive and negative self-talk. The first two comments reflect positive self-talk; the last two reflect negative self-talk.

> I can explore many alternatives to accounting as a possible occupation for me to choose.
> I can control my drinking in a party situation.

I will never be able to be a social worker.
I have been in trouble once, I will probably be in trouble again.

Self-Awareness   Individuals can be more effective problem solvers when they are aware of what they are doing and why they are doing it. Being aware of one's career decision-making strategy and process is much more helpful than not being aware of it. When one is aware of one's decision making, negative self-talk can be labeled and then changed. Also when self-aware, individuals can more easily follow the CASVE process by being aware of what they think and feel about their current situation, how they are analyzing information about their choices, how they are synthesizing alternatives, how they prioritize and value alternatives, and execute their plan by taking action.

The following brief dialogue indicates self-awareness on Parnell's part.

> CL: I wouldn't have thought it, but since I got put on probation for the study lounge incident, it's changed my outlook on how I choose careers.
> CO: That's interesting. Tell me more about how that incident has changed your career decision-making thoughts. [The counselor picks up that this is an indication of Parnell being self-aware and wants to reinforce and follow up on his self-awareness.]
> CL: I guess it made me more aware that I could have control of myself. I could choose when to drink and when not to drink or how much to drink. I could choose which occupations to explore and which occupations not to explore. I could choose to be scared of what my mother might think if I am not an accountant or I could choose not to be.
> CO: That's a great way that you put it. You are aware of the choices that you make and the types of choices that you could make in the future.

Monitoring and Control   Individuals are able to monitor the way in which they go through the CASVE process and control how much time they give to each of these stages or phases. When clients can monitor and control accurately, then they know how much information they need to analyze about a career choice before moving to the synthesis stage. They then will know how much time to synthesize information in order to create alternatives, and then how much information and time is needed to evaluate (valuing alternatives). They can then move to an action plan and execute the decisions that they have made. Clients who are not able to monitor and control their decision-making skills may spend too much or too little time in any one of the five stages. For example, individuals who are anxious or indecisive may spend much time gathering data (analysis), but feel unsure in synthesizing this information and be reluctant to move toward making a career choice. Counselors can help clients by providing encouragement and support in their monitoring and controlling of how they go through the CASVE process.

Focusing particularly on Parnell's career decision-making skills, his counselor was able to help him move from one phase to another. Parnell was anxious about not having enough information to make a list of alternatives (analysis). His counselor was able to help him decrease his anxiety by pointing out the positive decisions that he had made in the past. As Parnell proceeded in the career decision-making process he developed more and more confidence in his ability to monitor his own decision making and to execute his career plans by talking to teachers and counselors.

To review the pyramid of information processing domains in career decision making, it may be helpful to start at the top—the executive processing domain. Individuals can control the way they make decisions through the way they talk to themselves, through self-awareness, and through monitoring and controlling their career decision-making process. This career decision-making process includes communicating the problem, analyzing information or data, synthesizing the data and creating alternatives, valuing the information by prioritizing alternatives, and executing a plan by taking a variety of actions. The information that is used in the decision-making skills domain is that of self-knowledge and occupational knowledge. This entire process provides a view of career decision making.

Career Decision Making

Consistent with their approach to career decision making, Peterson and his colleagues have developed a system of classifying individuals into three major categories with regard to decision making: decided, undecided, and indecisive. Some individuals are decided and need to get information to confirm their decision, others need to implement it through action, and yet others have made a decision to hide the fact that they are undecided, being reluctant to acknowledge it. Some undecided individuals may need more information to make a choice, others are lacking self or occupational information to make a decision, and yet others have many talents and interests that make choosing difficult. In contrast, the indecisive individual is one who has a maladaptive approach to career decision making and usually has considerable anxiety (Peterson et al., 1996).

Parnell's career decision making could best be categorized as undecided–developmental. In other words, he needed more information about himself and occupations in order to make a career decision. As he gathered this information through the counseling process, he moved to "decided-implementation," meaning that he was still needing some help in implementing his career decision making.

The Career Thoughts Inventory

To help counselors in dealing with thoughts about career decision making, Sampson, Peterson, Lenz, Reardon, and Saunders (1996a) have developed three scales that make up the Career Thoughts Inventory: Decision-Making Confusion, External Conflict, and Commitment Anxiety. They have also developed a workbook that can be used with the Career Thoughts Inventory (1996b).

Decision-Making Confusion indicates the difficulty that individuals have in initiating or sustaining career decision making. This may be due to anxiety or other emotions related to career decision making, or it may be due to a lack of understanding about how career decisions are made. The Decision-Making Confusion Scale relates to difficulties involved in the CAS steps in the CASVE cycle.

External Conflict refers to the difficulty in balancing one's own views of information about self and occupations with the views of others. When individuals have difficulty in balancing the input of self and others, they may be reluctant to be responsible for career decision making. The External Conflict Scale relates to difficulty in the valuing phase of the CASVE cycle.

Commitment Anxiety refers to the fear or anxiety that comes with the difficulty in implementing a career choice and addressing problems in moving from the valuing phase to the execution phase.

The Career Thoughts Inventory workbook uses the scores from each of these scales and helps individuals deal with negative career thoughts that might interfere with the career decision-making process. The five sections of the workbook show one way in which cognitive information processing theory can be implemented in career choice issues.

Section 1. Identifying the extent of negative career thoughts.
Section 2. Identifying the nature of negative career thoughts.
Section 3. Challenging and altering negative career thoughts and taking action.
Section 4. Improving one's ability to make good decisions.
Section 5. Making good use of support from other people.

Counselors who use the Career Thoughts Inventory may find the workbook to be helpful in dealing with individuals with negative career thoughts that impede the decision-making process (Sampson, Peterson, Lenz, Reardon, & Saunders, 1998). The Career Thoughts Inventory and the workbook can be used within a seven-step service delivery sequence.

Seven-Step Service Delivery Sequence

Peterson et al. (1996) recommend a seven-step approach to cognitive information processing. The seven steps represent a structured model for career counseling that is more organized than most of the other approaches described in this text:

Step 1: Initial interview. Information is gathered about the context of the client's career problem. Rapport is established with the client and the pyramid of the information processing domain and the CASVE cycle is explained.

Step 2: Preliminary assessment. A screening instrument such as the Career Thoughts Inventory is given to a client and readiness for counseling is assessed.

Step 3: Define problem and analyze causes. The problem is clarified and defined so that counseling goals can be developed.

Step 4: Formulate goals. Together, counselor and client establish goals for career counseling. Goals become the basis for an individual learning plan (ILP).

Step 5: Develop individual learning plan. Together, counselor and client develop an ILP that lists the activities that are to be completed by the client in order to achieve his or her goals.

Step 6: Execute individual learning plan. With the help of a counselor, clients follow through on the individual learning plan which is integrated with the CASVE cycle.

Step 7: Summative review and generalization. After the client has completed the ILP, client and counselor discuss progress toward reaching counseling goals.

In following this seven-step model, counselors may use a variety of counseling techniques. Many of these may be cognitive in nature. They include questions that challenge clients' beliefs. Also, statements that challenge and support clients may be used. When individuals are anxious, relaxation or guided imagery may be used. Not all counselors who use the cognitive information processing model will choose to use this seven-step process.

THE ROLE OF OCCUPATIONAL INFORMATION

For each of the three decision-making theories that have been discussed, occupational information is used in different ways. In Tiedeman's stage of anticipating a choice, occupational information needs to become more specific and detailed as one moves through the stages. In exploration, occupational information may be obtained in a rather haphazard or random way. When one begins to crystallize thoughts about an occupation, information about it becomes more specific and individuals need to know job duties, qualifications, employment outlook, and so forth. When individuals move to the choice and clarification phases they obtain occupational information through commitment to a specific occupation, job interviews, or part-time or volunteer work.

When a spiritual approach is applied to career choice, occupational information is an important aspect of it. However, the occupational information may be obtained through a variety of sources. Individuals not only use occupational libraries, but also their own job experience, discussions with other people, and job interviews. Career theorists taking the spiritual point of view emphasize the role of the client in evaluating the opinions of others.

In cognitive information processing theory, occupational information plays a very significant role, as it is covered in the occupational knowledge domain at the base of the pyramid of information processing. When individuals analyze and synthesize information that is related to career decision making, they are weighing information related to occupations as well as information related to self. Classification systems, such as those described in Chapter 2, may help individuals organize occupational information so they can synthesize and evaluate it.

THE ROLE OF TESTING

As with occupational information, the three different decision-making approaches take three different views of testing. Testing can be very helpful as individuals move through the anticipating a choice stage of Tiedeman. Interest inventories, value inventories, and ability tests can help individuals as they explore career options and start to crystallize them. These are the two stages in which individuals are most likely to find testing to be helpful. Perhaps the inventory that most closely measures concepts that are similar to the theoretical constructs of Tiedeman are the scales of the Assessment of Career Decision-Making Inventory. The rational, intuitive, and dependent styles of decision making can help the counselor understand how clients approach phases of adjusting to a choice.

Career counselors who use a spiritual approach to helping individuals with career choice and work adjustment problems may find tests and inventories to be helpful. However, they are very careful to help their clients rely on their own views of test results and not be overwhelmed by what appears to be expert advice. Counselors using this approach may use nontechnical terms to explain the limitations of tests (reliability and validity). For such counselors, testing is likely to play a relatively minor role.

Career counselors who use cognitive information processing theory are likely to find that tests are helpful in this process. The Career Thoughts Inventory may be used as a measure of attitude toward career decision making. Assessing confusion about decision making, anxiety about committing to a choice, and reluctance to assume responsibility for decision making can help counselors decide how to work with clients as they progress through the CASVE cycle. Tests and inventories are likely to be widely used in helping clients learn about themselves (the self-knowledge domain).

APPLYING THE THEORIES TO WOMEN AND CULTURALLY DIVERSE POPULATIONS

In general, career decision-making theories do not offer different recommendations for women or people from culturally diverse populations. In their development of the anticipating a choice stage of decision making, Tiedeman and O'Hara (1963) did not consider gender and diversity issues. Their phases of exploration, crystallization, choice, and clarification would seem to be broadly applicable. However, in cultures where family members or others make career decisions for individuals, this theory would be less applicable. In a process theory such as theirs, the ability to have opportunities to explore and crystallize would be very significant. From this perspective, it would be important to make sure that clients have access to testing and occupational information and are not discriminated against.

Counselors using a spiritual approach to career counseling are aware of wide differences in spiritual values of clients. Religious values and theological considerations may influence the way that clients respond to comments by the counselor. Although counselors who use a spiritual approach are aware that concepts such as change, balance, energy, community, calling, harmony, and unity are useful constructs to apply to many clients, they are likely to be flexible and not force clients into this conceptual framework. Miller-Tiedeman, in particular, emphasizes the importance of considering the individual and not have societal norms unduly pressure clients. Understanding and responding to relevant issues related to gender and culture are likely to be an important part of a spiritually based approach to career counseling.

Counselors who use cognitive information processing theory may apply it to all clients. However, counselors should be aware that the CASVE model represents a Western "scientific" point of view. In the CASVE cycle of knowing there is a need to make a choice through understanding self and occupations, expanding and narrowing a list of occupations, choosing an occupation or major, and implementing that choice. However, Peterson and his colleagues (Sampson et al., 1998) understand that clients often are constrained in their career choice by prejudice and stereotyping. As clients discuss information about self and occupations (the knowledge domain), counselors are able to respond to clients' concerns about discrimination.

Because relatively little research has been done with regard to gender or cultural diversity on any of these theories, it is difficult to provide more information about gender and diversity issues. Tiedeman's process approach to career development has not attracted much recent interest. Research on a spiritual approach to career development is sparse and difficult to do because of the complexity of concepts and the difficulty in defining them. Because the cognitive information processing approach to career development is relatively new, little information exists with regard to gender and diversity. However, there is potential for research in this area.

COUNSELOR ISSUES

When applying Tiedeman's process approach to counseling clients, counselors need to be patient. Having successfully negotiated the exploration, crystallization, choice, and clarification stages of adjusting to a choice, counselors have clarity about their own choices. Clients differ very much in ways of deciding about occupations and may spend much time in various phases of adjusting to a choice. Being familiar with the phases of decision making can help counselors not push clients prematurely to make choices. Typically, counselors are in the integration phase of adjusting to a choice. Clients may not be ready to adjust to a choice or to be in the induction or reformation phase. Awareness of the process of adjusting to a choice can help counselors understand the difficulties that clients may have in adjusting to work.

When using the spiritual approach to career counseling, counselors focus on the client's internal decision-making process. Often counselors will be aware of how different their own decision-making process is from that of their clients. The counselor does not want to encumber the client with "shoulds" that will interfere with the client's making the decisions that are best for him or her. Furthermore, if the counselor's own personal decision-making reality is so strong that it interferes with the client's decision making, the counselor's effectiveness will be limited. Miller-Tiedeman (1997) cautions counselors not to impose their own view of the "common reality" onto clients, but rather attend to clients "personal reality."

In cognitive information processing theory, counselors may wish to avoid imposing too much structure on clients. Some counselors might find the seven-step service delivery sequence (Peterson et al., 1996) to be useful for some clients, but may modify it for others. Deciding which inventories to use to assess client readiness, or whether to assess it at all, are issues that counselors may need to consider. In a cognitive information processing approach, there is an emphasis on listening for clients' negative thinking.

SUMMARY

Three types of career decision-making theories have been compared: a process approach, a spiritual approach, and a cognitive information processing approach. The process perspective of Tiedeman has a developmental focus that includes four phases of anticipation of a choice: exploration, crystallization, choice, and clarification. Unique to Tiedeman's theory is his stages of adjusting to a choice, once a job has started: induction, reformation, and integration.

In presenting a spiritual approach to career choice and work adjustment, I have focused on Miller-Tiedeman's Lifecareer Theory. To further illustrate a spiritual approach to career counseling, I have explained the seven spiritual concepts that have been described by Bloch and Richmond: change, balance, energy, community, calling, harmony, and unity. All of these approaches focus on the client's view of decision making and "personal reality" that describes the decision-making process.

In contrast, the cognitive information processing approach to career development takes a prescriptive approach to career decision making by describing a method of choosing careers that will improve client decision-making ability. The cognitive information processing approach emphasizes understanding decision making and developing decision-making skills in order to process self-knowledge and occupational knowledge. This chapter has presented an emphasis on career decision making that other chapters have not.

References

Bloch, D. P., & Richmond, L. J. (1998). *Soul work: Finding the work you love, loving the work you have.* Palo Alto, CA: Davies-Black.

Buck, J. N., & Daniels, M. H. (1985). *Assessment of Career Decision-Making manual.* Los Angeles: Western Psychological Services.

Erikson, E. H. (1959). Identity and the life cycle [Whole issue]. *Psychological Issues, 1.*

Ginzberg, E., Ginsburg, S. W., Axelrad, S., & Herma, J. (1951). *Occupational choice: An approach to a general theory.* New York: Columbia University Press.

Harren, V. A. (1979). A model of career decision making for college students. *Journal of Vocational Behavior, 14,* 119–133.

Hunt, E. B. (1971). What kind of computer is man? *Cognitive Psychology, 2,* 57–98.

Huntley, H. L. (1997). How does "God-Talk" speak to the workplace: An essay on the theology of work. In D. P. Bloch & L. J. Richmond (Eds.), *Connections between spirit and work in career development* (pp. 115–136). Palo Alto: CA: Davies-Black.

Jepsen, D. A., & Grove, W. M. (1981). Stage order and dominance in adolescent decision-making processes: An empirical test of the Tiedeman-O'Hara paradigm. *Journal of Vocational Behavior, 18,* 237–251.

Lackman, R., Lackman, J. L., & Butterfield, E. C. (1979). *Cognitive psychology and information processing.* Hillsdale, NJ: Erlbaum.

Miller-Tiedeman, A. L. (1977). Structuring responsibility in adolescents: Actualizing "I" power through curriculum. In G. D. Miller (Ed.), *Developmental theory and its application in guidance programs: Systematic efforts to promote personal growth* (pp. 123–166). Minneapolis, Minnesota: Minnesota Department of Education.

Miller-Tiedeman, A. L. (1988). *LIFECAREER: The quantum leap into a process theory of career.* Vista, CA: Lifecareer Foundation.

Miller-Tiedeman, A. L. (1989). *How NOT to make it . . . and succeed: Life on your own terms.* Vista, CA: Lifecareer Foundation.

Miller-Tiedeman, A. L. (1992). *LIFECAREER®: How it can benefit you.* Vista, CA: Lifecareer Foundation.

Miller-Tiedeman, A. L. (1997). The Lifecareer® process theory: A healthier choice. In D. P. Bloch & L. J. Richmond (Eds.), *Connection between spirit and work in career development* (pp. 87–114). Palo Alto, CA: Davies-Black.

Miller-Tiedeman, A. L. (1999). *Learning, practicing, and living the new careering.* Philadelphia, PA: Accelerated Development.

Miller-Tiedeman, A. L., & Tiedeman, D. V. (1990). Career decision making: An individualistic perspective. In D. Brown, L. Brooks, & Assoc. (Eds.), *Career choice and development: Applying contemporary theories to practice* (2nd ed., pp. 308–337). San Francisco: Jossey-Bass.

Newell, A., & Simon, H. (1972). *Human problem solving.* Englewood Cliffs, NJ: Prentice Hall.

Peterson, G. W., Sampson, J. P., Jr., & Reardon, R. C. (1991). *Career development and services: A cognitive approach.* Pacific Grove, CA: Brooks/Cole.

Peterson, G. W., Sampson, J. P., Jr., Reardon, R. C., & Lenz, J. G. (1996). Becoming career problem solvers and decision makers: A cognitive information processing approach. In D. Brown & L. Brooks, & Assoc. (Eds.), *Career choice and development* (3rd ed., pp. 423–475). San Francisco, CA: Jossey-Bass.

Rayburn, C. A. (1997). Vocation as calling: Affirmative response or "wrong number." In D. P. Bloch & L. J. Richmond (Eds.), *Connections between spirit and work in career development* (pp. 163–184). Palo Alto, CA: Davies-Black.

Sampson, J. P., Jr., Lenz, J. G., Reardon, R. C., & Peterson, G. W. (1999). A cognitive information processing approach to employment problem solving and decision making. *The Career Development Quarterly, 48,* 3–18.

Sampson, J. P., Jr., Peterson, G. W., Lenz, J. G., Reardon, R. C., & Saunders, D. E. (1996a). *Career Thoughts Inventory manual.* Odessa, FL: Psychological Assessment Resources.

Sampson, J. P., Jr., Peterson, G. W., Lenz, J. G., Reardon, R. C., & Saunders, D. E. (1996b). *Career Thoughts Inventory workbook.* Odessa, FL: Psychological Assessment Resources.

Sampson, J. P., Jr., Peterson, G. W., Lenz, J. G., Reardon, R. C., & Saunders, D. E. (1998). The design and use of a measure of dysfunctional career thoughts among adults, college students, and high school students: The Career Thoughts Inventory. *Journal of Career Assessment, 6,* 115–134.

Savickas, M. L. (1997). The spirit in career counseling: Fostering self completion through work. In D. P. Bloch & L. J. Richmond (Eds.), *Connections between spirit and work in career development* (pp. 3–26). Palo Alto, CA: Davies-Black.

Sternberg, R. J. (1980). Sketch of a componential subtheory of human intelligence. *Behavioral and Brain Science, 3,* 573–584.

Sternberg, R. J. (1985). Instrumental and componential approaches to the nature of training on intelligence. In S. Chapman, J. Segal, & R. Glaser (Eds.), *Thinking and learning skills: Research and open questions.* Hillsdale, NJ: Erlbaum.

Stoltz-Loike, M. (1997). Creating personal and spiritual balance: Another dimension in career development. In D. P. Bloch & L. J. Richmond (Eds.), *Connections between spirit and work in career development* (pp. 139–162). Palo Alto, CA: Davies-Black.

Super, D. E. (1957). *The psychology of careers.* New York: HarperCollins.

Tiedeman, D. V. (1979). *Career development: Designing our career machines.* Schenectady, NY: Character Research Press.

Tiedeman, D. V. (1992). Yes . . . but . . . , and . . . , so? Comments on Callanan and Greenhaus (1992). *Journal of Vocational Behavior, 41,* 232–238.

Tiedeman D. V., & Miller-Tiedeman, A. L. (1979). Choice and decision processes and career revisited. In A. M. Mitchell, G. B. Jones, & J. D. Krumboltz (Eds.), *Social learning and career decision making* (pp. 160–179). Cranston, RI: Carroll Press.

Tiedeman, D. V., & O'Hara, R. P. (1963). *Career development: Choice and adjustment.* New York: College Entrance Examination Board.

White, R. W. (1952). *Lives in progress.* New York: Holt, Rinehart & Winston.

15

The Labor Market: Sociological and Economic Perspectives

Counselors must not only help clients assess interests, personality, values, and abilities but also have information about occupations and the labor market. In this chapter, an overview of the labor market is given that includes the trends of growth in industries and occupations as they affect adults and youth. The fields of sociology and economics study various aspects of the labor market as well as specific occupations. As a result of research, some models or theories have been developed that point out inequities or obstacles in the labor market that may affect the earnings or success of different individuals. When thinking about the U.S. labor market (and the markets of some other countries), individuals have often held the view "Each person has an equal opportunity to succeed or fail on his or her own." Often, this assumption is oversimplified and false. A number of factors are beyond the control of individuals that may affect their eventual career choice and success. Losing out to another individual when applying for a job or a promotion may have a significant impact on individuals' lives. Furthermore, being taught to value an education and having consistent helpful parenting and financial support to pay for schooling occur in some people's lives, but not in others'. Discrimination because of gender or race is another variable that greatly affects individuals' career choices and financial and personal success. After describing some basic facts about the U.S. labor market, we will examine each of these factors as they influence how individuals deal with the labor market.

THE UNITED STATES LABOR MARKET

A labor market, basically, serves to fulfill the needs of citizens of a state, a nation, or the world. Job availability is related to the demand of individuals for food, shelter, clothing, health services, transportation, entertainment, fire and police protection, and so forth. The information about the U.S. labor market in Table 15-1 describes the broad occupational groups in which individuals were employed in 1998 and their predicted increase. Employment change is also shown in Table 15-1, with professional specialties being the group that is likely to increase the most.

Further information about general occupational trends can be obtained by examining growth and replacement needs. Growth refers to the need for new workers to meet demands of an occupation beyond the needs that are met by replacing existing workers. Workers leave occupations for a variety of reasons: transferring to other occupations, retiring, returning to school, assuming household duties, or choosing not to work. Of the 55 million job openings estimated between 1998 and 2008, about 63% will be due to replacement needs. As Figure 15-1 shows, growth will be greatest in professional specialty areas that include teachers, counselors, librarians, computer programmers, mathematicians, and nurses and physicians. Because of

Table 15-1 *Employment (in Millions) in Broad Occupational Groups, 1998 and Projected Change, 1998–2008*

		1998–2008
Occupational Group	*1998 Employment*	*Percentage Change*
Total, all occupations	141	14
Executive, administrative, and managerial	15	16
Professional specialty	20	27
Technicians and related support	5	22
Marketing and sales	15	15
Administrative support, including clerical	24	9
Services	23	17
Agriculture, forestry, and fishing	4	2
Precision production, craft, and repair	16	8
Operators, fabricators, and laborers	19	9

Source: Occupational Outlook Quarterly, U.S. Department of Labor, Bureau of Labor Statistics, Washington, DC (1999–2000), pp. 10, 11.

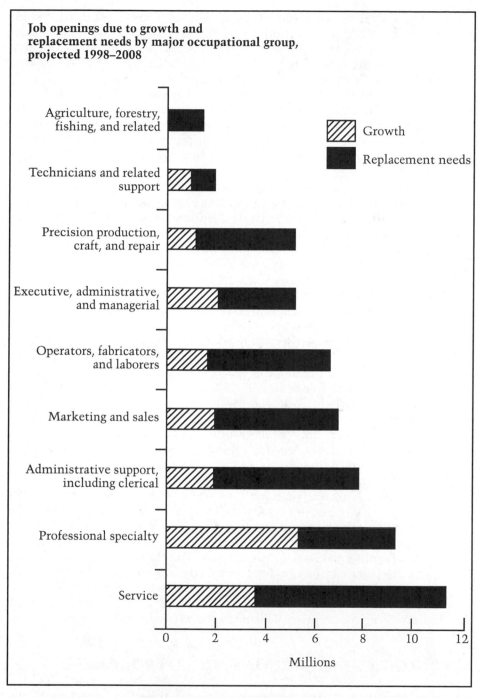

Figure 15-1 Projected growth in industries, 1998–2008. (From *Occupational Outlook Handbook*, U.S. Department of Labor, Bureau of Labor Statistics, Washington, DC, 2000, p. 6.)

turnovers, as well as other replacement factors, service occupations are projected to have the largest number of job openings (11.1 million). In general, replacement needs are greatest in occupations with relatively low pay and limited training requirements. Some occupations, such as clerical ones, may have limited growth due to office automation.

Much increase in numbers of jobs in the United States to 2008 is projected to occur in occupations that do not require a college education. As Figure 15-2 shows, 6 of the 10 occupations with the most projected increase require a high school education or less. Computer systems analysts (first), general managers and top executives (fourth), and registered nurses (seventh) usually have a four-year bachelor's degree. Occupations such as janitor, salesperson, and cashier often have high turnover. Individuals leave them for a variety of reasons: to find a better-paying job, to return to school, to care for children, and so forth. Thus, the increase reflects the need to replace these workers as well as to add new positions (*Occupational Outlook Quarterly*, 1999–2000). The 20 occupations listed in Figure 15-2 represent 39% of the projected total employment increase in occupations in the United States; the other 480 occupations surveyed by the Bureau of Labor Statistics represent the rest. Nine of the 20 occupations that are listed in Figure 15-2 are in the lowest quartile of earnings, a factor related to having high replacement needs.

Clearly, the amount of education is closely related to income. Figure 15-3 shows the vast differences in annual salary in 1997 between those with only a high school education ($26,000) and those with a doctorate ($62,400) or professional degree ($71,700), such as in law or medicine. Individuals with a bachelor's degree ($40,100) earn, on average, twice as much as individuals who do not graduate from high school ($19,700). These data emphatically point out the economic value of an education.

In this brief overview of the U.S. labor market, only the most important features are mentioned. In general, there is considerable predicted increase for occupations that require technical skills such as systems analysts and registered nurses. However, there will also be a great need for service workers such as retail salespersons, cashiers, and clerks. Salary continues to be greatly affected by the type and amount of education that individuals have. More information on the employment of women and African Americans and Latinos is presented later in the chapter. Additional information about local labor markets can be obtained from State Occupational Information Coordinating Committees. With so much information available to counselors from so many sources, it is important to present only highly relevant information to clients, so they will not be overwhelmed by the data.

SOCIOLOGICAL AND ECONOMIC APPROACHES

Whereas psychology is primarily concerned with the study of individual behavior, sociology and economics emphasize the study of social organizations. All other chapters in this book are concerned with how individuals

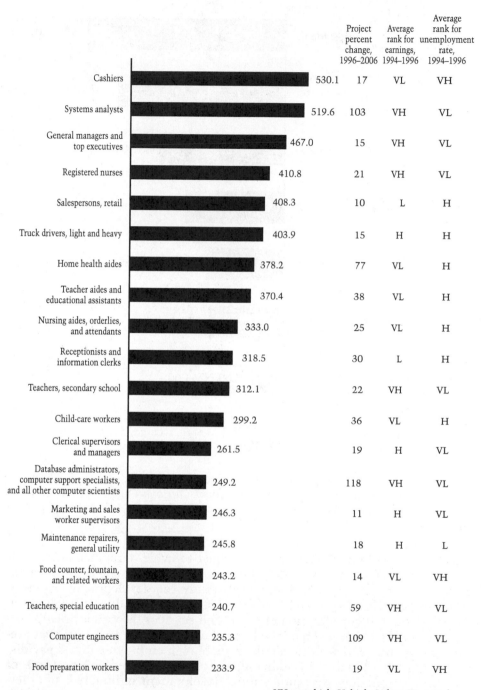

	Project percent change, 1996–2006	Average rank for earnings, 1994–1996	Average rank for unemployment rate, 1994–1996
Cashiers	530.1	17 VL	VH
Systems analysts	519.6	103 VH	VL
General managers and top executives	467.0	15 VH	VL
Registered nurses	410.8	21 VH	VL
Salespersons, retail	408.3	10 L	H
Truck drivers, light and heavy	403.9	15 H	H
Home health aides	378.2	77 VL	H
Teacher aides and educational assistants	370.4	38 VL	H
Nursing aides, orderlies, and attendants	333.0	25 VL	H
Receptionists and information clerks	318.5	30 L	H
Teachers, secondary school	312.1	22 VH	VL
Child-care workers	299.2	36 VL	H
Clerical supervisors and managers	261.5	19 H	VL
Database administrators, computer support specialists, and all other computer scientists	249.2	118 VH	VL
Marketing and sales worker supervisors	246.3	11 H	VL
Maintenance repairers, general utility	245.8	18 H	L
Food counter, fountain, and related workers	243.2	14 VL	VH
Teachers, special education	240.7	59 VH	VL
Computer engineers	235.3	109 VH	VL
Food preparation workers	233.9	19 VL	VH

VH=very high; H=high; L=low; VL=very low

Figure 15-2 Numerical and percent growth by occupation (in thousands), projected for 1998–2008. Earnings are described by quartiles. (From *Occupational Outlook Quarterly*, U.S. Department of Labor, Washington, DC, 1999–2000, p. 15.)

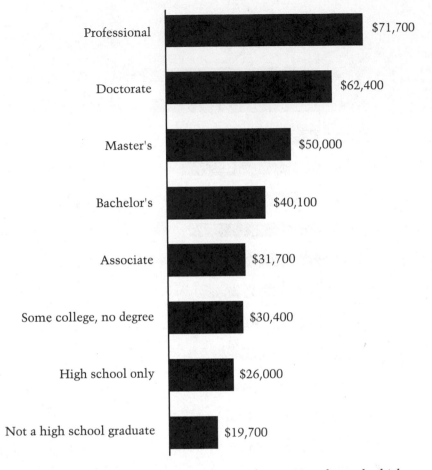

Figure 15-3 Mean annual earnings for people age 18 and over by highest level of education, 1997. (From *Occupational Outlook Quarterly,* U.S. Department of Labor. Bureau of Labor Statistics, Washington, DC, 1999, p. 40.)

make career choices and decisions or adjust to career circumstances. Sociologists and economists approach the question of career choice from an entirely different perspective. Sociologists study the development, organization, and operation of human society. Economists study the production, distribution, and consumption of goods and services. More specifically, sociologists have examined family, cultural, and other social factors that predict career choice as well as variables such as unemployment and pay distributions by industry. In addition, they have studied the patterns of customs, interactions, and professional development of hundreds of different legal and illegal occupations. Economists have investigated factors such as unemployment, pay distribution by industry, job title, gender, and race, which are all factors directly related to a person's career development. For both economists and sociologists, ability, interests, values, and career decision making, among other variables, are studied when trying to predict labor market or work behavior. Because the focus of sociologists and economists is on social organizations and the focus of counselors is counseling individuals, not organizations, the application of sociological and economic theories is indirect.

Both psychologists and sociologists have studied how societal factors and pressures affect adolescents, whether working part time or full time. In general, psychologists examine how the individual shapes and alters the environment through job choice or work adjustment. A sociological perspective on unemployment, part-time employment, and underemployment of youth provides an interesting view on entry into the workforce. Several sociologists and economists have suggested ways in which the workplace changes the individual. This different frame of reference provides new insights into both the worker and the workplace.

Several theories have been the subject of a large number of research investigations. A theory that has prompted study by many sociologists is the status attainment model, which predicts the prestige level of a person's job from an individual's social (particularly family) background. The primary economic theory related to career development is human capital theory. Human capital theory suggests that individuals invest in their own education and training in order to achieve a higher-paying job with more prestige. Criticism of this model has led to the development of a dualistic theory of labor markets: primary and secondary. In the primary labor market, work is steady, organizations are large, and a prospect of promotion exists. In contrast, the secondary labor market is made up of low-paying jobs that offer little chance of advancement.

Related to status attainment and human capital theory is the study of the organizational and societal treatment of women and minorities, which critiques and elaborates on these theories. Much research has documented that women and minorities hold different types of jobs from white males, are paid less, and have less chance of advancement. Although these theories and the resulting research do not provide a method of conceptualizing career counseling, they do yield insights into the world of work that a counselor can apply in both career choice and work adjustment counseling.

YOUTH EMPLOYMENT

Providing an overview of youth employment is difficult, as youth are not a homogeneous group (Barling & Kelloway, 1999). When discussing youth, the ages of 15 to 24 are often used, but not uniformly. Not surprisingly, different issues impact younger and older "youth." When attention is paid to high school students, it is observed that over 60% of North American students work part time (Desmarais & Curtis, 1999). Not all youth stay in school, some leave to get full-time employment and start a career, others may leave school with no specific employment in mind. Not only are there differences in age, but there are differences in gender. Even in part-time jobs, young women tend to make 70 to 75% of the male wage even though they may work about the same hours after school and when employed full time (Desmarais & Curtis, 1999). Motivation of youth toward work may also depend on socioeconomic status. Some youth may work to supplement the income of their parents or to pay for their future education, whereas others may seek employment for spending money for cars or entertainment. These differences in motivation provide different attitudes toward work.

A recent concern has been not only the quantity (number of hours) of work, but also the quality of employment (Loughlin & Barling, 1999). Many jobs for young workers are in the lower-level service industries such as food service and retail work. Fewer jobs are available to youth in public administration, health, social service, and education. One reason is the entry-level or job requirements in the latter area. Studies on part-time work (Loughlin & Barling, 1999) indicate that it can have both positive and negative effects on future employment. For example, working too many hours per week for high school students can lead to problem behavior in school, minor delinquent acts, and alcohol use. This is particularly true when individuals work more than 20 hours per week. However, there are examples of individuals working more than 20 hours per week who develop a sense of mastery and improved school behavior. Some jobs lead to more personal satisfaction and better attitudes toward work, while others may be routine or even expose individuals to dangerous work conditions. For individuals with a better attitude toward school, and no substance abuse, working many hours after school can still be related to higher post–high school occupational attainment for both men and women (Frone, 1999). The work-related attitudes that youth learn can have an impact on their later attitudes toward full-time work.

Part-time work can be secure in giving students a sense of autonomy. Because part-time jobs often pay at a lower hourly rate than full-time jobs, employers may prefer part-time workers. With part-time work, individuals also have more control over their jobs, often having input into when they work, thus reducing employee turnover. Jobs can also offer individuals an opportunity to use and develop job skills and to become more responsible in their work and their relationships with coworkers (Loughlin & Barling, 1999).

Youth are more likely than adults to be underemployed. Older individuals who have more experience or on-the-job training are able to get better jobs. Sometimes employers may perceive youth as being more likely to quit, less responsible, and less productive than older workers. Rosenbaum (1999) notes that employers may not trust youth, particularly low-income and minority youth, to work effectively. Miller and Rosenbaum (1997) have found that although employers may have information about young workers, they may distrust it and rely on impressions during job interviews. Thus, young people may suffer from a type of "age discrimination" based on stereotypes of their work attitudes and abilities, and face underemployment.

Sociologists have paid particular attention to youth of low socioeconomic status. Osterman (1989) found that jobs for low socioeconomic adolescents are acquired by chance encounters, such as openings in the neighborhood. Referrals are made by friends or parents to a job that they happen to know about. The adolescents whom Osterman studied were more interested in adventure seeking, sex, and peer-group activities than in work. Osterman referred to the ages of 18 to 25, when many adolescents are not concerned with their career, as a moratorium. After this time, unemployment becomes less frequent, and the length of time on a job increases.

Different problems and issues affect young men as opposed to young women. Werner (1989) found that adolescent women who did not go to college had a shorter period of delay before taking on family or work responsibilities than did men. Many of the women made early commitments to both work and family. Studying 2,954 white youth, Koenigsberg, Garet, and Rosenbaum (1994) found that young women with children who enter the labor force considered parenting, rather than providing financially for their family, their major responsibility, whereas young men with children reported the opposite. In another study of 3,828 young men and women, Pirog and Magee (1997) found that both men and women can suffer in terms of reduced educational attainment, earning capabilities, and ability to support their children when they take on parental responsibilities. In a general overview of the different experiences of young men and women in the job market, Lowe and Krahn (1999) state that young men who have not completed secondary education face many difficulties in the labor market, whereas young women face such challenges but may have additional ones because of household and family roles. They highlight the importance of improving the quality of jobs to prevent underemployment for such individuals.

For counselors, this information suggests the importance of discussing attitudes toward work and actual work demands with their young clients. It is helpful to discuss what individuals expect to get from their work. Is it just income, or is there an opportunity to explore new areas of interest? When discussing students' work experience, it can be helpful to ask about employer attitudes, relationships with coworkers, new skills learned, and advancement opportunities for both part-time and full-time workers.

THE EFFECT OF THE WORK ENVIRONMENT ON THE INDIVIDUAL

Just as an individual has an effect on his or her work—for example, producing a good performance or performing effectively—so does the work have an effect on the individual. The impact of the work on the individual has been the focus of two lines of research. Kohn and Schooler (1983) and Schooler (1998) have studied the effect that work and the individual have on each other. Rosenbaum (1976, 1989) and Tharenou (1997) have suggested a tournament approach to understanding the impact of the organization on the individual: There are winners and losers in organizational competition for promotion. Both winners and losers are affected by the organizational environment. These two sociological approaches to career development are discussed further in the following paragraphs.

The work of Kohn and his colleagues shows that having an unchallenging job may lead to a loss of intellectual skills (Mainquist & Eichorn, 1989; Schooler, Mulatu, & Oates, 1999). Kohn and Schooler (1978) studied "substantive complexity," which they defined as "the degree to which the work requires thought and independent judgment" (p. 30). They found that the intellectual demands of a job had influenced workers' intellectual ability more than workers' ability had affected how they approached their work. In a follow-up study, Kohn and Schooler (1982) found that job conditions affect an individual's psychological functioning more than an individual's psychological functioning affects his or her job. Applying this theory to workers, unemployed individuals, and those doing housework in the Ukraine and Poland, Kohn, Zaborowski, Mach, Khmelko, Heyman, and Podobnik (1999) found that complexity in any of the tasks done by these individuals was related to intellectual flexibility, self-directedness of orientation, and a sense of well-being. In a national longitudinal study of employed men and women in the United States, Schooler et al. (1999) confirm that substantive complexity of work significantly increased levels of intellectual functioning in the sample. This was especially true in the older half of the sample. The following example will illustrate the effects of work on an individual.

For four years, Pedro has worked in a factory, where he has assembled computer hardware. He has been promoted to a supervisor's job. This assignment requires that he use writing and mathematical skills that he has not used since high school graduation. As a result, his reading ability has improved. His job requires independent decision making based on reading manuals and talking to workers. At work, he must improve on skills that he has not used since high school. In a sense, the demands of Pedro's job require that he become more intelligent. He had to struggle at first to improve his math and writing skills. Not all organizations provide individuals such opportunities to develop their skills.

Some organizations make it difficult for individuals to develop skills because unknown or arbitrary rules keep individuals from advancement. The tournament system of Rosenbaum (Rosenbaum, 1989; Tharenou, 1997) illustrates how an organizational system may affect individuals. In tournaments the best candidates are chosen for positions through a series of selective competitions. Much as in a tennis tournament, the winners advance to the next round; the losers stop competing in that tournament but may decide to enter another tournament. However, there is a significant difference between Rosenbaum's career system tournament and a tennis tournament. Rosenbaum's tournament is like a tennis tournament without rules. For example, imagine a tennis tournament where the rules for each match are different; the players don't know how many sets they will need to win a match or how many players they will have to face to win the tournament. Rosenbaum believes that individuals often do not know the organizational rules that will result in promotion or in getting a job. Early selection in a career for specific positions may determine how far and where an individual will rise on the corporate ladder. For example, failure to obtain a promotion early in a career may affect an individual's entire career by limiting job promotion possibilities (Rosenbaum, 1984). Rosenbaum also found a bias toward promoting younger employees; those over 40 are often at a marked disadvantage. These findings can be considered "rules" that employees may not know. Rosenbaum recognizes that the tournament model does not apply to all systems. For example, there are job ladders on which everyone is promoted and caste systems in which no one can be promoted. Further, there are situations such as door-to-door sales where past success is not related to future success. In general, tournaments are more likely to be found in large organizations, where there are many people competing for positions and there are a variety of career options. The tournament concept points out the impact that the environment has on the individual.

Rosenbaum (1976) has also applied his theory to the tracking of students in the educational system. As Osterman's (1989) research and Barling and Kelloway's review (1999) suggest, students who drop out of school or enter dead-end jobs are making decisions that will affect their later decisions. In a sense, they have lost in the early rounds of a tournament and will have difficulty finding tournaments that are likely to lead to high income or job satisfaction.

The research just cited suggests several factors that may interfere with individual choice. In the example below, Paul, a 35-year-old white male truck driver, is discussing his job dissatisfaction with a counselor. Paul is married, has no children, and has not completed high school. Through discussion, Paul realizes the effect that his work is having on him:

CL: I've been driving now for three years for a large trucking company. I got into it by working with my brother-in-law some. He owns his own truck, and sometimes I'd help him out by driving for him. I didn't mind it then, but it's not right for me now. I don't like it.

CO: Can you tell me more about it? [The counselor wants to learn more about Paul's response to his environmental conditions.]

CL: Well, I'm kind of confused. I was working in an auto plant for two years. Then I got laid off. I thought truck driving would be good—sitting, driving, listening to the radio. It's not that way.

CO: What way is it, Paul? [Again, the counselor wants to hear more about Paul's work environment.]

CL: Part of it's the boredom. I'm driving a trailer truck on the highway for thousands of miles. Just more and more roads. It makes me so depressed. When I get home, I'm down; I snap at my wife. She notices the difference. She says that I'm different since I took this job.

CO: That boredom is taking a toll on you. [Paul has changed because of his work. He is sad; there is a feeling of hopelessness.]

CL: It's not as if this job will go anywhere. (*Smiling*) Yes, I know I go everywhere all the time. That's not what I mean. I could be doing this for the rest of my life. I have no sense that I'll get anywhere. I sure didn't think about it much when I left school in the tenth grade. I had no idea I could be like this. I was pretty carefree back then.

CO: You're not carefree now.

CL: No. When I was in school, I wanted to get out of school. Now, I want to learn. I feel dumber than I ever have in my life.

The counselor notes that Paul is being deeply affected by his job environment. Paul has become upset that his intellectual functioning is not improving, and he is tense. From Kohn's point of view, he is losing intellectual capabilities because of the lack of intellectual demands of his work. Furthermore, because of Paul's education and his job choice, he is in an environment where he has, in Rosenbaum's sense, lost the tournament. To receive more training or schooling may put him into a tournament that he can win. By focusing on the effect that Paul's job has on him, the counselor can look for ways in which Paul can change, or perhaps for ways in which the job can change.

STATUS ATTAINMENT THEORY

Status attainment theory concerns issues regarding the relative role of achievement and social status in influencing occupational selection. Most research on status attainment theory has been on intergenerational change, sometimes called vertical mobility, and has focused on predicting an individual's occupational role from the father's occupations. Of particular note is the early work by Blau (1956) and Blau and Duncan (1967). They, along with other researchers, found that they could predict the socioeconomic status of an individual's first job, which would then predict a current job, from the father's occupation and education.

As research continues on the status attainment model, it becomes more and more complex. A basic overview of status attainment theory is provided by Hotchkiss and Borow (1990) and will be followed in this discussion. Figure 15-4 outlines the path of prediction leading from variables concerning family status and cognitive functioning to the eventual prediction of occupational attainment. Family status includes the father's occupational and socioeconomic status, income, and education. Occupational status is determined by measures of prestige assessed both in the United States and throughout the world (Fredrickson, Lin, & Xing, 1992). A second group of variables measures educational performance (e.g., aptitude tests and school grades). These variables affect social-psychological processes, which include the educational and occupational aspirations of adolescents, the amount of parental and teacher encouragement to attend college, and peers' plans to attend college. These social-psychological processes then act to predict educational attainment, which is measured by the number of years of schooling. The number of years of schooling then leads to the prediction of occupational attainment measured by the status or prestige levels of the career. The statistical processes used to come to

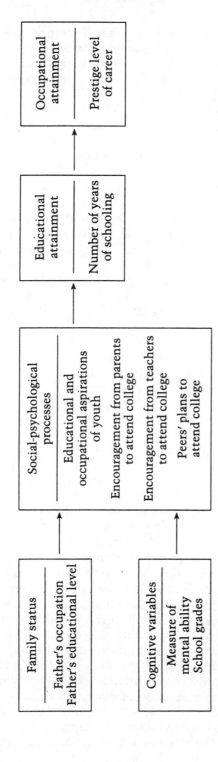

Figure 15-4 Abridged outline of an early version of the Wisconsin model of status attainment. [From "Sociological Perspectives on Work and Career Development," by L. Hotchkiss and H. Borow, in *Career Choice and Development*, (2nd ed.), by D. Brown, L. Brooks, and Assoc. Copyright © 1990 by Jossey-Bass, Inc. Reprinted by permission.]

these conclusions are known as *path analyses,* a method by which variables are graphed so as to indicate their causal effect on each other (Babbie, 1973). Wilson (1989) emphasizes the influence that an adolescent's view of his or her future has on persistence in school: "Staying [in school] is the strongest known determinant of subsequent career" (p. 71).

An area that has received a considerable amount of recent attention is family influences on career choice and occupational status. Recent work shows the importance of knowing the mother's occupation in predicting the child's later occupational attainment. Khazzoom (1997) surveyed 4756 individuals and found mothers' occupations were especially helpful in predicting daughters' occupational attainment, but also useful in predicting sons' attainment as well. Studying sixth-graders, Castellino, Lerner, Lerner, & vonEye (1998) found that mothers' employment and education predicted the academic competence, career aspirations, and gender-role attitudes of adolescents. Following the educational plans of ninth-grade students, Hossler and Stage (1992) reported that parental educational expectations had a stronger influence than did the parents' level of education, student achievement, or student involvement in school activities. Examining family functioning, Biblarz and Raftery (1993) found that divorce and separation increase the probability that individuals will be in the lowest-status jobs rather than the highest. Similarly, Li and Wotjkiewicz (1992) showed that living in a mother-only or mother–stepfather family lowers a child's socioeconomic attainment. Also, domestic violence can contribute to lower status attainment of women and lower earnings (Lloyd, 1997). For men who were already employed, Lai, Lin, and Leung (1998) demonstrate the importance of family, friendships, and work relationships in status attainment of adults. These studies point out the influence of family expectations and functioning on the career plans and concerns of young people and adults.

Culture has also been studied as a factor in status attainment theory. Studying 76 high-level African American executives, Collins (1993) reported that their high level of attainment was due to employment practices that were affected by the politics of race rather than deracialization in the labor market, suggesting that employers may have hired them because they were required to hire African Americans based on corporate policy, not because the firms were fully integrated. Studying 6,885 new entries to the job market, Waight (1998) reports that African Americans and women do not attain the same levels of occupational status as white men, due to race and gender. Shu and Marini (1997) note that when males of both races enter the workforce their aspirations tend to be lowered. Applying status attainment theory to Japanese women, Imada (1998) notes that childbirth and child-rearing limit women's occupational attainment. In Kenya, cultural factors affect how long children are enrolled in school and their later occupational attainment (Buchmann, 1998). These include expectations for children contributing to family income and views of discrimination toward women in the workplace. Such studies provide information about how cultural factors affect educational and occupational planning.

Several investigators have shown how status attainment can be affected by societal factors and timing. In Poland, during socialism (before 1989), status attainment was stable but after socialism the amount of education predicted increases in earnings and occupational prestige (Krymkowski & Domanski, 1997). In the Netherlands, fathers' occupational status was less predictive for individuals who were late entrants into the labor market and for those who had considerable work experience (Hendrickx & Ganzeboom, 1998). In contrast, in Japan data from 1975 to 1985 show that fathers' occupations continue to be a good predictor of children's occupational attainment (Kanomata, 1998). Contrasting African American and white education expectations in the United States, Morgan (1998) reports that white high school seniors had lower educational expectations than African American seniors in the 1970s but that in the 1980s the educational expectations of both groups were close to each other. Differences in these studies emphasize the importance of societal factors and culture in examining predictions of status attainment theory.

Although status attainment theory has been useful in predicting occupational attainment, it has also been the subject of criticism. Sonnenfeld (1989) states that status attainment theory has been unable to adequately explain later status changes once an individual has begun employment. He criticizes status attainment theory for failing to use recent data and for not looking at changes in occupational status within a career. Further, status attainment theory has not paid attention to changing social values that have led to less agreement on the definition of a successful career. Most important, he believes that status within a firm should be measured, rather than occupational attainment. These comments notwithstanding, status attainment theory is relevant to career decision making and work adjustment counseling.

Status attainment theory calls attention to important variables that psychological theories tend to omit. Of the theorists discussed in this book, only Gottfredson (1996) deals with sociological variables in career development theory. The variables that status attainment theory emphasizes are the importance of prestige, the status of the family, and encouragement to seek higher education. Although the United States is considered a land of equal opportunity, status attainment theory says that, in reality, one's occupational position is determined to a great extent by one's family's status (and until recently, one's father's status). This knowledge may help a counselor who is working with a client from a low socioeconomic background think about some of the factors that are necessary for the client to attain an occupation that is much higher in status than that of his or her family. As shown previously, one of the factors related to status is lack of parental encouragement to succeed. Adolescents from a low socioeconomic background may lack parental, peer, and teacher encouragement to seek higher education. Furthermore, this background may inhibit accurate occupational aspirations.

The challenge for the counselor is to provide support and information that will help a client counter sociological processes that may interfere with making full use of her or his intellectual abilities. Status attainment theory does not say how to do this. Rather, status attainment theory underscores the importance of making special efforts to open areas of the labor market to clients that they may otherwise have considered closed. An example of a counselor dealing with an individual from a low socioeconomic background is given next.

Betty is a 15-year-old African American high school sophomore, living in Chicago. Her mother is unmarried and works for a large industrial cleaning firm in the downtown section of Chicago. Betty has two younger sisters who are still in school. Her older sister is enrolled in a nursing program. Betty has been working after school for a fast-food chain. Now, as she approaches the age of 16, she is considering dropping out of school and working full time for the restaurant. In this brief excerpt, she is discussing her plans with her guidance counselor:

CL: Since I've been working at this job, I've finally been able to buy some of the clothes that I always wanted. My mother needs some of the money, too, so she takes some.

CO: Sounds as if that's made you feel useful. [The counselor comments on Betty's sense of productivity.]

CL: Yeah, feels like I'm doing something that makes sense with my life, not just sitting around in school reading stuff that seems boring.

CO: School doesn't make sense to you? [The counselor wants to challenge Betty's sweeping view of school.]

CL: Well, I guess it does. I have learned to read pretty much. I've gotten A's and B's. I thought everybody learned to read. Some of the kids I work with can barely write their names. They can hardly read the menus.

CO: Does that limit what they can do? [The counselor wants Betty to assess her own view of the relationship between schooling and advancement.]

CL: It sure does. It looks as if they'll never make more than five or six dollars an hour at that rate.

CO: How much do you think you can make at this job? [The counselor starts to examine the limitations of fast-food counter work as a full-time job.]

CL: Maybe $300 a week.

CO: That's about $15,000 a year. Does that seem like much to you?

CL: No, not really.

CO: How much would you like to earn? [The counselor is helping Betty start to think about the type of future she would like to have.]

CL: A lot more than that. My mother earns about $18,000 a year, and that's terrible.

CO: What do you think you would have to do to earn more?

CL: Everybody tells me that to earn money, you need to go to college. I could never do that.

CO: Why not? [The counselor wants to question Betty's negative assumptions about her abilities and her potential future.]

CL: We don't have any money to go to college, that's for sure.

CO: There are scholarships available. Students from this school with no support from their parents have gone on to do well in college. Something I can do to help you is to show you how you can get financial aid and to make suggestions about school. Your work is good in school—your grades

show it and your teachers say it. I can help you figure out what you want
to do and where you can go to school. [The counselor offers direct support and encouragement to help Betty make positive steps toward her future choices. Betty is unaware of the alternatives available to her. The
counselor will help.]

CL: You think I can do this?
CO: Yes, I do. I want to show you how and help you with it.

Having a plan to follow will help Betty's counselor counter Betty's discouragement. The counselor will empower Betty to look at her options.
Having established contacts with local colleges and having obtained information about financial aid, the counselor is in a position to suggest how
Betty can find an alternative to a job that does not sufficiently use her
abilities.

HUMAN CAPITAL THEORY

The basic idea behind human capital theory is that individuals invest in
their own education and training so that they will receive increased lifetime earnings (Becker, 1964; Wachter, 1974). Career earnings are seen as a
function of ability, education, and training, combined with the effort to
produce effectively (Sharda, 1998). Education is viewed as an investment
that, when combined with appropriate job experience, will produce a desired income. Individuals (and their families) invest money in college or
other training at an early point in an individual's career. This investment
is realized some years later, when an individual starts to receive pay for his
or her work. For example, in a study of 2087 Colombian workers,
Psacharopoulos and Velez (1992) found that education had a positive impact on individuals' earnings, even when ability was controlled for. However, Tomaskovic-Devey (1998) points out that the salaries and benefits offered by employers can have a great impact on influencing individuals to
stay with a job rather than investing over time in a long-term goal, especially for better educated workers. In human capital theory, the individual
is viewed somewhat as a firm or a company: If health care and moving ex-
penses will help improve earning power, then these, like educational ex-
penses, can be seen as investments in one's eventual lifetime earnings.

An application of this theory to high school jobs by Stern and Nakata
(1989) may help to illustrate human capital theory. Stern and Nakata found
that jobs that teenagers do, which are primarily in services, sales, and labor, differ in quality. Like Greenberger and Steinberg (1986), they find that
many jobs of adolescents provide immediate income but do little to develop abilities that can be used in more complex occupations. From a long-
term point of view, Stern and Nakata believe that high school students will
be better off after graduation if they can find jobs in high school that teach
skills required in full-time occupations. They believe that schools should
teach problem-solving and other high-level skills that can be used after

graduation. Stern and Nakata are concerned that individuals with relatively low academic abilities will choose high school jobs that will not give them an opportunity to improve their skills, and that this choice will lead to a poor long-term investment with relatively little economic payoff. Additionally, communities with a large percentage of low-skill jobs do not reward education and thus do not create incentives for students to continue or complete their education (Stallman, Johnson, Mwachofi, & Flora, 1993).

In some ways, human capital theory can be seen as an endorsement of trait and factor theory. Like trait and factor theory, human capital theory emphasizes the role of the assessment of interests and abilities in selecting an occupation. Human capital theory differs from trait and factor theory in that it emphasizes career choice as a long-term process and investment and focuses on income.

Counselors may use information culled from human capital theory to comment on an individual's choice of part-time or summer work in terms of how it will help that individual develop income over a lifetime. Furthermore, individuals who do not have sufficient income to pay for investment in the type of education they want may view immediate work as an investment. For example, an individual who wishes to become a physician but cannot pay for the education that is necessary may choose to go to college for two years, work as an emergency medical technician for two years, return to college for a year, work as a technician for two years, finish college in one year, work as a registered nurse for three years, and then go to medical school. In terms of human capital theory, this process could be viewed as a carefully planned long-term investment. However, the older an individual is when his or her education is completed, the less time there is to collect on the investment.

Human capital theory has been criticized because its goal is a monetary reward. Often, individuals have other goals, such as being elected to political office, helping others, or having leisure time. It is possible, but more difficult, to think of work as an investment that will have nonmonetary payoffs such as these. When an individual has multiple goals, such as a high income and helping others, investing in his or her abilities, preferences, and values toward this goal becomes much more complex. Thus, one of the advantages of occasionally thinking about the client in terms of human capital theory is that long-term investment is emphasized, and the individual's future development is considered. In this aspect of planning, human capital theory resembles the developmental work of Donald Super (1990).

Human capital theory assumes that the labor market is open equally to all workers. This assumption has generated much criticism and has been partially responsible for a vast amount of research demonstrating the oversimplification of human capital theory. For example, Duncan, Prus, and Sandy (1993) have shown that, although human capital theory may explain a woman's decision to work, it does not explain her occupational choice. Women who are out of the workforce for family or other reasons tend to be penalized more than males if they are working in traditionally female occupations, as they have lower starting wages (Duncan & Prus, 1992). Female pharmacists earn less than male pharmacists because they move in and out of the labor force and thus are employees rather than managers or owners of pharmacies (Tanner, Cockerill, Barnsley, & Williams, 1999). Kilbourne, Farkas, Beron, Weir, and England (1994) found that women earn less in occupations that employ a large percentage of women or that require nurturing social skills. Bayley (1997) reports that African American college-educated women tend to defer having families more than white college-educated women. In doing so, African American women are earning capital from their investment in their education as predicted by human capital theory. These observations about the complexities of the labor market will form the rationale for the rest of the chapter. Human capital theory does not consider job discrimination against women and people from different cultural backgrounds in predicting individual earnings. Also, some research has focused on inequalities in different types of organizations. This work is related to research that is often referred to as *dual-economy theory*.

DUAL-ECONOMY THEORY

Human capital theory assumes that all individuals have an equal opportunity to compete in the labor market. Sociologists and economists have long recognized that this is not true. Disadvantaged and underprivileged groups, particularly, tend to enter different types of jobs from those who are more privileged (Berger & Piore, 1980). Dual-economy theory classifies both firms and labor markets into two groups: primary (core) and secondary (peripheral). Although originally used to describe two different types of labor markets, dualistic theory gradually evolved into a way of seeing a variety of discontinuous segments in the labor market. Originally, primary employers were seen as holding a monopolistic or oligopolistic market share, as using advanced technology, and as being nationally or internationally involved in commerce (Brand, 1997). These large firms offered higher wages, job stability, and more chances for advancement than did those in the secondary labor market. Retail sales and fast-food businesses are examples of the secondary labor market. These jobs usually pay minimum wage or a little more, offer little chance of advancement, and have a relatively high turnover. It was hypothesized that workers who were a part of the primary labor market were not likely to move to the secondary labor market, and vice versa.

Some studies have revealed a more complex structure in the labor market than that suggested by dualistic theory. Piore and others (Berger & Piore, 1980; Piore, 1975, 1979; Piore & Sable, 1984) suggest three levels of the labor market. They categorize secondary work as situations that have low pay, poor working conditions, and low social status. Little security or advancement is available in these jobs, and little skill is required of the worker. Relationships with supervisors tend to be personal and informal.

Members of this labor force tend to be women, adolescents, and migrants, and the turnover is frequent.

Piore and others divide the primary sector into two tiers. The lower tier of the primary sector is more substantial than the secondary market. There is more status, better working conditions, more chance for advancement, and better pay. More skill is required of the workers, and more formal training is necessary. Relationships between workers and supervisors may be informal or may be controlled by more formal union relationships. Wages are likely to be set through collective bargaining, rather than by the employer. In contrast, the upper tier of the primary market consists of managerial and professional occupations. These jobs offer higher pay, status, prestige, security, and opportunities for advancement. They require more education before employment than do jobs in the lower tier. In general, the worker has more autonomy than in the lower tier, and relationships between supervisors and workers are less important and less formal than in the lower tier.

Not all jobs fit into the primary or secondary labor markets. Piore and colleagues have stated (Berger & Piore, 1980) that craft jobs are hard to classify. They tend to fall between the upper and lower tiers of the primary sector. Although craft work may be similar to the work done by those in the lower tier, because it is often learned on the job and formal relationships between workers and supervisors exist, craftspeople tend to work independently. In that sense, their work is more like that of workers in the upper tier. Craft work includes occupations such as master plumber, electrician, and pipe fitter. One focus of research has been to discover how work is learned and how that learning is applied in each of the four strata of the job market.

How adolescents gain entry into various sectors of the labor market is explained by Osterman (1989). His research used a simple classification of primary and secondary jobs rather than the tier system proposed by Piore and others. In his study, he found that adolescents employed in the secondary labor market tended to work for small retail or contracting concerns. These firms tended to develop a reputation for hiring young people. Adolescents often heard about job openings in this sector through their friends. In contrast, jobs that were found in primary firms came more often through relatives who worked in the primary firm than through friends.

Recent investigations have studied the dual economy in countries outside the United States. In Israel, immigration of foreign workers tended to reinforce the dual-economy system, with immigrating workers taking secondary level employment (Bartram, 1998). The immigration of Peruvian women to Spain, who worked as domestic servants, seemed to reinforce the secondary labor market in Spain rather than bridge the gap between primary and secondary markets (Escriva, 1997). In South Africa a high unemployment rate and a tradition of racial segregation under apartheid tended to accentuate the dual labor market there, as African blacks are usually found in the secondary sector and whites in the primary (Kenny, 1998).

For counselors, the value of a dualistic labor market theory is its emphasis on factors external to the client. The primary emphasis of the psychological theories that are discussed in all of the other chapters of this book is on the individual and individual choice. Dualistic theory calls attention to basic differences in broad segments of the working world. Whether the counselor thinks of the labor market in terms of two, three, four, or more sectors is not as important as the fact that counselors should be aware that there are broad differences in hiring practices, work relationships, advancement possibilities, and earnings in various categories of jobs. This information is particularly helpful to those who counsel adolescents, who are beginning their encounter with the labor market and are likely to start in the secondary labor market. This information is helpful in counseling, so that the client and the counselor can examine how to move to better (primary labor market) work situations. Counselors can help teenagers become aware that many jobs (primary) will not be available to them without more education and experience. However, experience gained on jobs will help develop personal skills such as reliability and cooperation.

An awareness of occupational information about local employers is helpful to the counselor. Such information includes detailed knowledge about specific jobs, hiring practices, pay scales, and so on of major local employers. Dual-labor-market theory provides a rationale for assessing such information. Counselors can get information that they can give to clients about wages, job stability, chances for advancement, and turnover. This information, which is useful in separating primary from secondary labor markets, will help clients understand the long-range implications of taking relatively dead-end (secondary labor market) jobs, which pay low salaries and have a rapid turnover and little chance of advancement.

WOMEN AND DISCRIMINATION IN THE WORKPLACE

Sociologists have studied the effect of gender on career outcomes. Much of this research has been in the context of status attainment theory, human capital theory, and dual-labor-market theory. Research examining the effect of gender has shown that discrimination leads to lower pay, less advancement, and occupational segregation, which results in working in occupations with lower prestige than those of men.

In describing discrimination in hiring and promotion, Browne (1999) and England and Farkas (1986) list four determinants of discrimination: taste discrimination, monopoly, error, and statistical generalization. Becker (1957) discusses *taste discrimination* as a preference not to employ members of a particular group. If employers do not hire women, fewer jobs will be available to them, and therefore, wages will be lower. The *monopoly model of discrimination* occurs when an organized group agrees to exclude another group from positions. For example, an all-male trade union's deciding not to allow women into the union is an example of the "monopoly" model of discrimination. *Error discrimination* refers to employers who do not have discriminatory taste but may underestimate the ability of women to perform the same work as men. *Statistical discrimination* happens when an employer applies generalizations about a group of people to an individual. England and Farkas (1986) give this example: "If employers correctly observe that, on average, women have less mechanical knowledge than men, they may decide not to hire any women in positions requiring mechanical knowledge, screening out even those atypical ones with extensive mechanical skills" (p. 160). Whatever the form of discrimination, it acts to limit women's attainment in many ways.

To understand the employment issues of women in the workplace, it is helpful to examine unemployment data, the distribution of women in various occupations, and the salaries of women. As Table 15-2 shows, women tend to have similar unemployment rates to men. Note that U.S. Bureau of Labor Statistics employment rates include only those individuals who are actively looking for work and receiving unemployment benefits. These rates exclude individuals who are able to work but are not interested in doing so and individuals who would like to work but are discouraged because they believe they will not be able to find work. Unemployment rates appear to differ markedly more by race than by gender. Although men's and women's unemployment rates are similar, women tend to move in and out of the labor force more frequently than men and may be involved in family responsibilities that require them to temporarily drop out of the labor force. When they do look for work, they may accept work that men would not consider. For these reasons, the types of occupations that women enter tend to pay less and to have less prestige than those that are typically male-dominated. Eccles (1995) and her colleagues find that women are less likely to enter prestigious occupations in the physical sciences or in math both because they have less confidence in their math and science abilities and because they place less subjective value on these occupational fields. As Table 15-3 illustrates, women have less than 30% of the high-paying, high-prestige professional jobs, such as engineer, physician, and lawyer, and have more than 75% of lower-paying, less-prestigious professional jobs, such as registered nurse and elementary and high school teacher. In nonprofessional occupations, women represent 93% of secretaries and 83% of maids and house cleaners. Men dominate the higher-paying nonprofessional occupations such as truck driver, mechanic, and repairer. For women to enter the trades or become mechanics often means to enter occupations where they may encounter discrimination. Characteristics of such women include a sense of innate ability, self-esteem, a wish to be independent, and having good role models (Greene & Stitt-Gohdes, 1997).

In general, the wages of women are between two-thirds and one-half of those of white men (see Table 15-4). Analyzing gender-based earning inequalities, Anderson and Tomaskovic-Devey (1995) find that gender inequalities are lowest when specific rules are formulated about earnings and promotions. They find that exclusion from traditionally male and high-skill or authority jobs is part of the reason for unequal pay for women. An-

Table 15-2 *Unemployment Rates in Percentages by Demographic Group, 1998*

Age	White Male	White Female	Black Male	Black Female	Hispanic Male	Hispanic Female	All
16–17	17.1	12.4	33.9	33.2	29.0	26.4	17.2
18–19	12.1	9.8	27.9	20.9	16.4	20.2	12.8
20–24	6.7	6.3	18.0	15.7	8.9	10.1	7.9
25–54	2.9	3.2	6.2	7.1	4.7	6.6	3.5
55–64	2.8	2.2	4.5	3.4	5.3	5.4	2.6
Total	3.9	3.9	8.9	9.0	6.4	8.2	4.5

Source: Data from the U.S. Department of Labor, *Employment and Earnings* (January 1999), Table 3 (pp. 168–171).

Table 15-3 *Employed Persons by Selected Occupation, Sex, Race, and Hispanic Origin, 1998*

Occupation Center	Total Employed (in Thousands)	Percentage of Total		
		Women	Black	Hispanic
Engineers	2,052	11.1	4.1	3.8
Physicians	740	26.6	4.9	4.8
Registered nurses	2,032	92.5	9.3	3.2
Managerial and professional	38,957	49.0	7.6	5.0
Teachers, college	910	42.3	5.8	3.6
Teachers, except college	4,962	75.3	10.0	5.4
Lawyers	912	28.5	4.0	3.0
Counseling, educational, and vocational	230	68.8	13.2	5.5
Sales occupations	15,850	50.3	8.9	7.4
Secretaries, stenographers, and typists	3,599	92.6	9.6	7.0
Food preparation workers	6,071	56.5	11.8	17.0
Nursing aides and orderlies	1,913	89.0	34.0	9.8
Janitors and cleaners	2,233	34.8	21.7	19.6
Maids and house cleaners	653	82.8	26.7	25.0
Mechanics and repairers	4,527	4.0	8.0	10.5
Truck drivers	3,012	5.3	14.9	12.0
Bus drivers	471	50.4	20.3	11.7

Source: Data from the U.S. Department of Labor, *Employment and Earnings* (January 1999), Table 1 (pp. 68–78).

other issue is organizational culture, such as patriarchal views toward women, unequal promotion practices, and evaluating jobs in terms of gender. For example, women make up a large portion of clerical workers and have family situations that influence their interaction with the labor force, such as having to take time off from work to care for a sick child (Browne, 1999).

A detailed analysis of women's role in the labor force revealed several interesting findings. Studying the values of 7436 full-time workers from 12 different nations, Rowe and Snizek (1995) found no differences between men and women in how much they valued high income, security from being fired, free time, advancement, and a feeling of accomplishment. Rather, differences in valuing these variables depended on age, education, and occupational prestige. Studying young workers, Witkowski and Leicht (1995) report that men tend to benefit economically as they assume more family roles, but women's earnings are reduced as they assume family roles. They suggest that employers of married mothers do not value the mothers' prior

Table 15-4   *Earnings as a Percentage of White Male Earnings for Full-Time Workers Over 18 Years Old, 1996*[a]

Women	Dollars	
African American	21,000	60%
Mexican origin	17,000	49%
Puerto Rican	22,000	63%
Cuban	22,000	63%
Central and South American	18,720	53%
Other Latino	18,300	52%
White[b]	25,000	71%
Men		
African American	26,000	74%
Mexican origin	19,900	57%
Puerto Rican	25,000	71%
Cuban	28,000	80%
Central and South American	20,000	57%
Other Latino	26,000	74%
White[b]	35,000	100%

[a]Earnings in real (1996) dollars.
[b]White, non-Hispanic.
Source: U.S. Department of Commerce, U.S. Department of Census, 1998. *Current Population Survey—March 1997*, Washington, DC. *Hispanic Population of the United States Current Population Survey—March 1997*. Detailed Tables. Table 1.

work experience because they do not believe it has an impact on how long the women will continue working. This uncertainty may make employers reluctant to hire women for jobs that require administrative or other responsibilities. The authors stress the importance of family responsibilities as they affect the hiring and advancement of both men and women. Investigating the impact of societal messages on women's career development, Levine and Zimmerman (1995) found very little relationship between the occupations women aspired to and the occupations they entered. They reported that women who had selected traditional occupations as their goal had had more success than women who had selected nontraditional occupations as their goal, concluding that societal stereotypes about gender continue to affect women's career choices. Jacobs's *Gender Inequality at Work* (1995) explores these issues in greater depth.

Although discrimination against women in the labor force continues, a gradual gender desegregation of occupations has taken place since the mid-1960s. One reason is the growth in the service sector, which has caused men to enter occupations that have traditionally been women's occupations, such as nursing and teaching (Browne, 1999). Cotter, DeFiore, Hermsen, Kowalewski, and Vanneman (1995) suggest that women's entering traditionally male occupations will be a stronger force in occupational desegregation than men's entering traditionally female occupations. Cotter et al. also suggest several other reasons for continuing occupational desegregation: As occupations grow in the numbers needed, both men and women are likely to seek entry, thus desegregating a particular field. Equal employment legislation continues to have an impact on reducing gender discrimination, particularly in public service jobs. Also, because women are generally paid less than men, employers have an economic incentive to hire more women. Kaufman (1999) points out that employment growth by itself does not necessarily lead to better jobs for women as women and minority groups continue to have restricted access to better jobs. Thus, several economic and sociological forces point toward continued gender desegregation in the labor force.

The above description discusses discrimination from an economic and sociological, rather than from a psychological, point of view. In Chapter 7, Gottfredson's contribution to the role of gender discrimination in the career development of young children is explained. She feels that children develop an orientation to gender roles between the ages of 6 and 8 that has an important influence on their career choices for the rest of their lives. In that chapter, studies of gender-role stereotyping among children and within the educational system are discussed. In Chapter 8, there are examples of the effect of gender-role stereotyping of adolescents in the social and educational systems. Some of the difficulties that women have in dealing with labor force expectations at various times in their adult lives are examined in Chapter 9 from the point of view of Super (1990), and others. In explaining some of the career crises that women are likely to experience in their adult lives, Chapter 10 illustrates the potential problems of leaving and reentering the workforce, sexual harassment, and discrimination. These chapters describe the effect of gender-role stereotyping and discrimination at various stages in women's lives. In contrast, sociological and economic research demonstrates the effect of discrimination on occupational attainment and earnings.

Counselors may find it difficult to use the information about gender-role stereotyping and gender discrimination in terms of earnings and occupational attainment. Social cognitive career theorists (Chapter 13) emphasize the importance of being attuned to women's lack of confidence in academic areas, such as math and science, and in pursuing nontraditional careers. Challenging self-limiting assumptions and reinforcing women's strengths help to increase career self-efficacy beliefs. Career counselors can help female clients by examining traditional gender roles and the effects of society on these roles. Learning about the actual differences between men and women in earnings and occupational attainment may also be of value. Sometimes, counselors are in a position to influence the educational or social system in their setting. For example, high school guidance counselors may be able to identify teachers or counselors in the high school who are suggesting educational or career paths to students based on their sex. The counselors may then take action to correct this problem. Successful women can be excellent role models for other women, as Krumboltz (Chapter 13) suggests in describing the importance of modeling in social learning theory.

Although the above ideas may be helpful, even more basic in counseling women on career issues is the identification of one's own bias. Because counselors have also been raised in a society that treats men and women quite differently, they may unconsciously have developed societal values that affect their counseling. Recognizing one's gender bias without becoming upset with oneself is valuable for counselors. In the example below, a counselor uses an internal dialogue to recognize stereotyping.

Judy has been working as a secretary at the same company since she graduated from high school seven years ago. Now 25, she is married, without children, and has sought counseling because she feels limited in her job. Judy is fashionably dressed, and her appearance shows that she has spent time and effort to make herself look attractive.

CL: The people I work with are so nice to me, and it's so much fun talking with them, but I'm not sure that I like my work anymore. I'm doing the same thing each day. In fact, I'm doing more typing than I ever have before. My boss keeps giving me more and more tapes to transcribe.

CO: Can you tell me a little bit more about what is happening at work?

CL: Well, my boss is a sales manager with lots of salespeople under him. I am always busy taking calls from the salesmen and relaying messages to my boss. Then I have plenty of typing to do. I do pretty well. My boss is always telling me how well I do. He's given me pretty good pay raises. I don't get anything like the salesmen, but I guess, compared to other secretaries, I do pretty well. When the work eases up some, I certainly like it better, but maybe there is something else I'd like.

CO: What other options have you considered? [Counselor to self: "I wonder what she's complaining about? She's got a good job. She's making pretty good money. Why would she want to leave? Wait, what am I thinking? Why am I making assumptions for her? It is not my role to determine what's best for her. I am making assumptions about her role as a secretary, that it's a good one for her. Watch it!"]

CL: I'm not sure, but I've thought of being a salesperson like the men who work in our company. I think I could do that, but the company seems to hire just men.

CO: [To self: "Let me get back on track now."] We can consider a number of fields, including becoming a salesperson in your company. If there are barriers, we can look at ways to cross them. For now, let's not close any options. [The counselor is aware that before her last statement Judy has used the term *salesmen* and perhaps she sees their type of work as not being open to her.]

Because gender-role stereotyping is so pervasive in so many cultures, it is important to be alert to how such values affect the counselor. In the example above, the counselor became aware of the biases before they affected the client. Unless counselors can eliminate their own bias, their other efforts to help female clients will be limited.

CULTURALLY DIVERSE INDIVIDUALS AND DISCRIMINATION IN THE WORKPLACE

Just as discrimination is a barrier to occupational attainment and earnings for women, so it is for culturally diverse populations. Because many studies in sociology and economics rely on large samples for their research, most work in the United States has focused on the largest minority group, African Americans. Most of the discussion in this section examines the amount and nature of discrimination against African Americans. In general, the arguments against the effectiveness of human capital theory and status attainment for women given in the previous section also apply to African Americans.

The racial discrimination that African Americans and Latinos (Hispanics) experience is reflected in employment and wage statistics. As Table 15-2 shows, the unemployment rate for African Americans and Latinos in 1999 was much greater than the rate for whites. For African American youth, 16 to 17, the rate was extremely high—about one-third were unemployed. Not only is unemployment higher for African Americans and Latinos, but the types of occupations they work in differ greatly. As Table 15-3 shows, Hispanics and blacks tend to make up a relatively small proportion of the workers in high-skill jobs (at the top of Table 15-3) and a much larger proportion of the workers in semiskilled and unskilled jobs (at the bottom of the table). Furthermore, the salaries of African Americans and individuals from different Latin American countries tend to be from about one-half to one-quarter less than those of white males (Table 15-4). Analyzing the effect of race on earnings in the United States, Ashraf (1995) notes differences within occupations and reports that African Americans earn about 54% less than whites in the South but earn about a third less than whites in the rest of the country. Explaining differences in unemployment and wages has been the task of many sociologists and economists.

Many investigators have examined a variety of factors preventing people from different minority groups from attaining high-status jobs, high wages, and lower unemployment rates. Wilson, Tienda, and Wu (1995) have analyzed the racial gap in unemployment and have found that African American men are more likely than white men to be unemployed because of firings and layoffs. Also, the lower average education of African American men affects their unemployment rate, as there are fewer opportunities for less-educated workers. Browne (1999) shows that one reason for the high unemployment of less-educated young African American men is the shift in the labor market away from manufacturing, a segment of the labor market that has traditionally employed less-educated young African Americans, into the service sector. Williams (1987) reports that African American adolescents tend to move in and out of the labor force more frequently than whites; they also receive fewer job offers per time period than whites. Williams found support for the hypothesis that lower participation in the labor force results from a lack of information about jobs and other aspects of the job attainment process. Browne (1999) summarizes several studies that show that when African Americans and white adolescents or adults with similar resumés look for jobs, African Americans experience more discrimination. In a study of employers in Atlanta, Browne and Kennelly (1999) reported that African American women were often stereotyped negatively. A prominent stereotype was that African American women were single mothers whose child care responsibilities interfered with job performance. Their data show that white women reported about the same amount of work–child care conflicts as African American women. In coping with racism, avoidance was used more often than problem solving or seeking social support by African American college students (Utsey, 1998).

Discrimination is not limited to less-educated African Americans. Wilson, Tienda, and Wu (1995) reported that college-educated black men had higher unemployment rates than college-educated white men, because of having difficulty entering occupations that had traditionally been closed to African Americans, and because of entering occupations where the turnover is traditionally high, such as certain sales occupations. In a survey of professional and managerial African American women, Higginbotham and Weber (1999) reported that many of the women felt that they were treated differently because of their race and that these views had an effect on their career plans. One effect was that African American women saw a greater need for further education than did white women so that they could advance in their work.

Some writers have examined a variety of political and economic variables affecting the progress of African Americans in the United States. Reviewing writings on the experience of young African American men in the labor market, Skinner (1995) criticizes human capital theory, concluding that the payoff of investments in high school and college education is declining for young African American men. He urges that attention be given to discrimination in housing, hiring, and job promotion, along with an effort to promote full employment and improved urban housing. Skinner also finds support for a dual labor market, with a large proportion of young African American men working for service employers (in the secondary labor market) in large urban cities. Piore (1979) uses the dual-labor-market theory to explain differences in the participation of African American and white youth in the labor market. His view is summarized by Osterman (1989):

> The first generation of black migrants from South to North accepted poor quality, secondary Northern jobs because their frame of reference was conditions in the rural South. From this perspective the Northern jobs were not so bad, and in any case, many of these migrants expected to return south. However, many of them remained in the North, and their children found themselves expected to accept the same secondary work. The children's frame of reference was the North. In this context, and with sensitivities heightened by the Civil Rights Movement, the jobs were not acceptable. The consequence was either outright rejection of the work or behavior patterns that rendered them an undesirable labor force. (p. 239)

Ogbu (1989, 1993, 1997) has found that African American children's orientation to society is unlike that of white children. Furthermore, he has differentiated the cultural orientation of minority children who are of immigrant origins, and those, like African Americans, who are an involuntary minority group, having been brought to the United States as slaves. He believes that African American children's view is a product of the collective experience of African American people in the workforce, both currently and in the past. Furthermore, he feels that this heritage applies to middle-class African Americans as well as to lower-class African Americans. This sociological observation is different from the usual explanation for lack of participation in the labor market, which is that African Americans receive education that is inferior to that of whites (Smith, 1981).

Another view expressed by Ogbu (1989, 1993, 1997) is that the experience of African Americans, as an involuntary minority group, in looking for work has led them to believe that getting ahead is important. However, this belief has not led to concentration on academic work or academic effort. He believes that African Americans perceive a job ceiling (being denied entrance to high-paying jobs). This perception in turn has led to a negative perception of the value of education. He believes that African American youth perceive school learning as a threat to their sense of identity and security, rather than as an opportunity for advancement. His research suggests a sense of disenfranchisement and a distrust of white Americans. He reports somewhat similar observations of Mexican Americans. Werner (1989) studied minority groups in Hawaii and suggested that the views of native Hawaiians, whom she considered similar to a castelike minority, had attitudes similar to the African Americans of Ogbu's (1989) study (a captive minority group). Filipino and Japanese youth had attitudes that were more like those of the voluntary immigrants in Ogbu's study.

As stated by Hotchkiss and Borow (1990, 1996), African Americans may already have high educational expectations. The issue is how to help African Americans (and other minority groups) to realize their goals. They suggest that strengthening work-related attitudes and information is helpful. Furthermore, they suggest using community, school, and parental resources to help minority adolescents develop attitudes that will be effective in the labor market. The challenge to counselors is great because nonwhite people are, in general, less likely than whites to have access to counseling resources.

Just as there are stereotyped attitudes in the United States toward women, so is there prejudice toward different cultural groups. It is difficult for people, counselors included, not to be exposed to and incorporate prejudices and discrimination. It is important for counselors to recognize and cope with any of their own attitudes that will prevent effective counseling of culturally diverse people. Sometimes, reactions are visceral rather than conscious, as the following example shows.

Brian is an African American freshman at a large Midwestern university. He has been recruited on an athletic scholarship to play football. He is a large man—6 feet, 3 inches, weighing 260 pounds. Like many other freshmen, he has found the transition from high school to college difficult. His football coach, sensing that Brian is unsure about his major and his course performance, recommends counseling. This dialogue starts with the beginning of the counseling interview:

CO: How can I help you, Brian?

CL: Coach sent me here because he knows that I might be headed for some trouble.

CO: Can you tell me more about this? [Since walking with Brian from the waiting room, the counselor has been aware of a feeling right in the middle of the stomach. There is a sense of fear, but there seems to be no reason for it. Brian is pleasant and friendly. The counselor becomes aware that the fear is not due to Brian; rather, it comes from old feelings of prejudice based on skin color and body size. Being aware of these feelings reduces the counselor's physical sense of anxiety. The counselor starts to relax and focus away from old feelings and toward Brian.]

CL: I received a D in math and a D in science, and I'm worried.

CO: It feels really bad for you to get those grades now. I want to see what I can do to help you. [As the counselor's upper body moves slightly toward Brian, so does the counselor's attention. The counselor is now genuinely interested in Brian, and personal distractions have diminished.]

Not all counselors become aware of their feelings so quickly; some never become aware of them. If the counselor is to continue to feel tension or negative feelings toward the client because of prejudice, the effectiveness of counseling will be greatly diminished. If the counselor believes that African Americans are better in some professions than in others, the counselor will be doing a disservice to clients. Feelings and beliefs of prejudice are likely to undermine counseling, no matter what else the counselor does.

In addition to identifying their own prejudices, counselors often need to help their clients deal with the discrimination that they encounter in the job application process or in the workplace. Familiarity with affirmative action guidelines and legal procedures that address grievances is helpful. However, counselors may find assertiveness techniques useful in dealing with job discrimination. Examples of dealing with discrimination are given in Chapter 10.

SUMMARY

Unlike the others in this book, this chapter has focused on the labor market and the influence of social and economic factors on the individual's career development. Different sociological and economic theoretical positions provide different views of the labor market. Of particular interest to counselors is the effect of unemployment and underemployment on youth. Some sociologists have studied how the environment affects the individual, an approach quite dissimilar to that of psychologists, who are concerned with individuals' making choices and influencing their environment. An area much studied by sociologists is status attainment theory, which emphasizes the importance of parental and aspirational variables in occupational attainment. A theory developed by economists, human capital theory views individuals as investing in themselves, their education, and training, to increase their lifetime earnings. The theory of dual labor markets opposes human capital theory, suggesting that there are core and peripheral labor markets that provide different pay rates, opportunities for advancement, and working conditions. The study of discrimination, which has been well documented for both women and people from nonwhite cultures, also addresses the oversimplification of human capital theory. Each theory, as well as research on the discrimination against women and minorities in the United States, provides insights that counselors may use in their work.

References

The American work force: 1992–2005. (1993). *Occupational Outlook Quarterly, 37,* 4–44.

Anderson, C. D., & Tomaskovic-Devey, D. (1995). Patriarchal pressures: An exploration of organizational processes that exacerbate and erode gender earnings inequality. *Work and Occupations, 22,* 328–356.

Ashraf, J. (1995). The effect of race on earnings in the United States. *Applied Economics Letters, 2,* 72–75.

Babbie, E. R. (1973). *The practice of social research.* Belmont, CA: Wadsworth.

Barling, J., & Kelloway, E. K. (1999). Introduction. In J. Barling & E. K. Kelloway (Eds.), *Young workers: Varieties of experience* (pp. 1–16). Washington, DC: American Psychological Association.

Bartram, D. V. (1998). Foreign workers in Israel: History and theory. *International Migration Review, 32,* 303–325.

Bayley, L. J. (1997). Using higher education for aspirational attainment: An American perspective. *International Studies in Sociology of Education, 7,* 213–227.

Becker, G. S. (1957). *The economics of discrimination.* Chicago: University of Chicago Press.

Becker, G. S. (1964). *Human capital.* New York: Columbia University Press.

Berger, G. S., & Piore, M. J. (1980). *Dualism and discontinuity in industrial societies.* New York: Cambridge University Press.

Betz, N. E., & Fitzgerald, L. F. (1987). *The career psychology of women.* Orlando, FL: Academic Press.

Biblarz, T. J., & Raftery, A. E. (1993). The effects of family disruption on social mobility. *American Sociological Review, 58,* 97–109.

Blau, P. M. (1956). Social mobility and interpersonal relations. *American Sociological Review, 21,* 290–295.

Blau, P. M., & Duncan, O. D. (1967). *The American occupational structure.* New York: Wiley.

Brand, H. (1997). Global capitalism and the decay of employment policy. *Dissent, 44,* 56–62.

Browne, I. (1999). Employment and earnings among Latinas and African American women. In I. Browne (Ed.), *Latinas and African American women at work* (pp. 1–31). New York: Russell Sage Foundation.

Browne, I., & Kennelly, I. (1999). Stereotypes and realities: Images of black women in the labor market. In I. Browne (Ed.), *Latinas and African American women at work* (pp. 302–326). New York: Russell Sage Foundation.

Buchmann, C. (1998). *Family background, parental perceptions and labor demand: The determinents of educational inequality in contemporary Kenya.* Paper presented at the International Sociological Association.

Bureau of Labor Statistics. (2000). *Occupational outlook handbook.* Washington, DC: U.S. Department of Labor.

Castellino, D. R., Lerner, J. V., Lerner, R. M., & vonEye, A. (1998). Maternal employment and education: Predictors of young adolescent career trajectories. *Applied Developmental Science, 2,* 114–126.

Collins, S. M. (1993). African Americans on the bubble: The vulnerability of black executives in white corporations. *Sociological Quarterly, 34,* 429–447.

Cotter, D. A., DeFiore, J., Hermsen, J. M., Kowalewski, B. M., & Vanneman, R. (1995). Occupational gender desegregation in the 1980s. *Work and Occupations, 22,* 3–21.

Desmarais, S., & Curtis, J. (1999). Gender differences in employment and income experiences among young people. In J. Barling & E. K. Kelloway (Eds.), *Young workers: Varieties of experience* (pp. 59–88). Washington, DC: American Psychological Association.

Duncan, K. C., & Prus, M. J. (1992). Starting wages of women in female and male occupations: A test of the human capital explanation of occupational sex segregation. *Social Science Journal, 29,* 479–493.

Duncan, K. C., Prus, M. J., & Sandy, J. G. (1993). Marital status, children and women's labor market choices. *Journal of Socio-Economics, 22,* 277–288.

Eccles, J. S. (1995). Understanding women's educational and occupational choices. *Psychology of Women Quarterly, 18,* 585–609.

England, P., & Farkas, G. (1986). *Household, employment, and gender: A social, economic, and demographic view.* New York: Aldine.

Escriva, A. (1997). Control, composition and character of new migration to South-West Europe: The case of Peruvian women in Barcelona. *New Community, 23,* 43–57.

Fredrickson, R. H., Lin, J. G., & Xing, S. (1992). Social status ranking of occupations in the People's Republic of China, Taiwan, and the United States. *The Career Development Quarterly, 40,* 351–360.

Frone, M. R. (1999). Developmental consequences of youth employment. In J. Barling & E. K. Kelloway (Eds.), *Young workers: Varieties of experience* (pp. 89–128). Washington, DC: American Psychological Association.

Gottfredson, L. S. (1996). Gottfredson's theory of circumscription and compromise. In D. Brown, L. Brooks, & Assoc. (Eds.), *Career choice and development* (3rd ed., pp. 179–232). San Francisco: Jossey-Bass.

Greenberger, E., & Steinberg, L. D. (1986). *When teenagers work.* New York: Basic Books.

Greene, C. K., & Stitt-Gohdes, W. L. (1997). Factors that influence women's choices to work in the trades. *Journal of Career Development, 23,* 265–278.

Hendrickx, J., & Ganzeboom, H. B. G. (1998). Occupational status attainment in the Netherlands, 1920–1990. A multinomial logistic analysis. *European Sociological Review, 14,* 387–403.

Higgenbotham, E., & Weber, L. (1999). Perceptions of workplace discrimination among black and white professional-managerial women. In I. Browne (Ed.), *Latinas and African American women at work* (pp. 327–353). New York: Russell Sage Foundation.

Hossler, D., & Stage, F. K. (1992). Family and high school experience influences on the postsecondary educational plans of ninth-grade students. *American Educational Research Journal, 29*, 425–451.

Hotchkiss, L., & Borow, H. (1990). Sociological perspectives on work and career development. In D. Brown, L. Brooks, & Assoc. (Eds.), *Career choice and development* (2nd ed., pp. 262–307). San Francisco: Jossey-Bass.

Hotchkiss, L., & Borow, H. (1996). Sociological perspectives on work and career development. In D. Brown, L. Brooks, & Assoc. (Eds.), *Career choice and development* (3rd ed., pp. 281–334). San Francisco: Jossey-Bass.

Imada, S. (1998). Status attainment of women: Closed hierarchical space. *International Journal of Sociology, 28*, 66–91.

Jacobs, J. A. (Ed.). (1995). *Gender inequality at work*. Thousand Oaks, CA: Sage.

Kanomata, N. (1998). Trends in inequality and solidification of socioeconomic status in Japan. *International Journal of Sociology, 28*, 11–32.

Kaufman, R. L. (1999). *Queing, labor market segmentation and the sorting of black females, black males, white females, and white males into labor market positions*. Paper presented at the American Sociological Association.

Kenny, B. (1998). *The South African labour market in transition: Flexibility and the changing nature of work*. Paper presented at the International Sociological Association.

Khazzoom, A. (1997). The impact of mothers' occupations on children's occupational destinations. *Research in Social Stratification and Mobility, 15*, 57–89.

Kilbourne, B. S., Farkas, G., Beron, K., Weir, D., & England, P. (1994). Return to skill, compensating differentials, and gender bias: Effects of occupational characteristics on the wages of white women and men. *American Journal of Sociology, 100*, 689–719.

Koenigsberg, J., Garet, M. S., & Rosenbaum, J. E. (1994). The effect of family on the job exits of young adults: A competing risk model. *Work and Occupations, 21*, 33–63.

Kohn, M., & Schooler, C. (1978). The reciprocal effects of the substantive complexity of work and intellectual flexibility: A longitudinal assessment. *American Journal of Sociology, 84*, 24–52.

Kohn, M. L., & Schooler, C. (1982). Reciprocal effects of job conditions and personality. *American Journal of Sociology, 87*, 1257–1286.

Kohn, M. L., & Schooler, C. (1983). *Work and personality*. Norwood, NJ: Ablex.

Kohn, M. L., Zaborowski, W., Mach, B. W., Khmelko, V., Heyman, C., & Podobnik, B. (1999). *Complexity of activities and personality under conditions of radical social change: A comparative analysis of Poland and Ukraine*. Paper presented at the American Sociological Association.

Krymkowski, D. H., & Domanski, H. (1997). Social change and status attainment among men and women in contemporary Poland. *Social Science Information/Information sur les Sciences Sociales, 36*, 641–666.

Lai, G., Lin, N., & Leung, S. Y. (1998). Network resources, contact resources, and status attainment. *Social Networks, 20*, 159–178.

Levine, P. B., & Zimmerman, D. J. (1995). A comparison of the sex-type of occupational aspirations and subsequent achievement. *Work and Occupations, 22,* 73–84.

Li, J. H., & Wotjkiewicz, R. A. (1992). A new look at the effects of family structure on status attainment. *Social Science Quarterly, 73,* 581–595.

Lloyd, S. (1997). The effects of domestic violence on women's employment. *Law and Policy, 19,* 139–167.

Loughlin, C., & Barling, J. (1999). The nature of youth employment. In J. Barling & E. K. Kelloway (Eds.), *Young workers: Varieties of experience* (pp. 17–36). Washington, DC: American Psychological Association.

Lowe, G. S., & Krahn, H. (1999). Re-conceptualizing youth unemployment. In J. Barling & E. K. Kelloway (Eds.), *Young workers: Varieties of experience* (pp. 201–234). Washington, DC: American Psychological Association.

Mainquist, S., & Eichorn, D. (1989). Competence in work settings. In D. Stern & D. Eichorn (Eds.), *Adolescence and work* (pp. 327–367). Hillsdale, NJ: Erlbaum.

Miller, S. R., & Rosenbaum, J. E. (1997). Hiring in a Hobbesian world: Social infrastructure and employers' use of information. *Work and Occupations, 24,* 498–523.

Morgan, S. L. (1998). Adolescent educational expectations: Rationalized, fantasized, or both? *Rationality and Society, 10,* 131–162.

Occupational outlook quarterly (1999–2000). U.S. Department of Labor, Bureau of Labor Statistics, Washington, DC.

Ogbu, J. (1989). Cultural boundaries and minority youth orientation toward work preparation. In D. Stern & D. Eichorn (Eds.), *Adolescence and work* (pp. 101–140). Hillsdale, NJ: Erlbaum.

Ogbu, J. (1993). Differences in cultural frame of reference. *International Journal of Behavioral Development, 16,* 483–506.

Ogbu, J. (1997). African American education: A cultural ecological perspective. In H. P. McAdoo & H. Pipes (Eds.), *Black families* (3rd ed.), (pp. 234–250). Thousand Oaks, CA: Sage.

Osterman, P. (1989). The job market for adolescents. In D. Stern & D. Eichorn (Eds.), *Adolescence and work* (pp. 235–256). Hillsdale, NJ: Erlbaum.

Piore, M. J. (1975). Notes for a theory of labor market stratification. In R. L. Edwards, M. Riech, & D. M. Gordon (Eds.), *Labor market segmentation* (pp. 125–150). Lexington, MA: Heath.

Piore, M. J. (1979). *Birds of passage: Migrant labor and industrial societies.* New York: Cambridge University Press.

Piore, M. J., & Sable, C. F. (1984). *The second industrial divide: Possibilities for prosperity.* New York: Basic Books.

Pirog, M. A., & Magee, C. (1997). High school completion: The influence of schools, families, and adolescent parenting. *Social Science Quarterly, 78,* 710–724.

Psacharopoulos, G., & Velez, E. (1992). Schooling, ability, and earnings in Colombia, 1988. *Economic Development and Cultural Change, 40,* 629–643.

Rosenbaum, J. E. (1976). *Making equality: The hidden curriculum of high school tracking.* New York: Wiley-Interscience.

Rosenbaum, J. E. (1984). *Career mobility in a corporate hierarchy.* New York: Academic Press.

Rosenbaum, J. E. (1989). Organization career systems and employee misperceptions. In M. B. Arthur, D. T. Hall, & B. S. Lawrence (Eds.), *Handbook of career theory* (pp. 329–353). New York: Cambridge University Press.

Rosenbaum, J. E. (1999). Institutional networks and informal strategies for improving work entry for youths. In W. R. Heinz, (Ed.), *From education to work: Cross-national perspectives* (pp. 235–259). New York: Cambridge University Press.

Rowe, R., & Snizek, W. E. (1995). Gender differences in work values: Perpetuating the myth. *Work and Occupations, 22,* 215–229.

Schooler, C. (1998). Environmental complexity and the Flynn effect. In U. Neisser, (Ed.), *The rising curve: Long-term gains in IQ and related measures* (pp. 67–79). Washington, DC: American Psychological Association.

Schooler, C., Mulatu, M. S., & Oates, G. (1999). The continuing effects of substantively complex work on the intellectual functioning of older workers. *Psychology and Aging, 14,* 483–506.

Sharda, B. D. (1998). Labour markets and status allocation. *Sociological Bulletin, 47,* 17–31.

Shu, X., & Marini, M. M. (1997). *Occupational aspirations and opportunities: Coming to terms with life's limitations.* Paper presented at the American Sociological Association.

Skinner, C. (1995). Urban labor markets and young black men: A literature review. *Journal of Economic Issues, 29,* 47–65.

Smith, E. J. (1981). The black female adolescent: A review of the educational, career, and psychological literature. *Psychology of Women Quarterly, 6,* 261–288.

Sonnenfeld, J. A. (1989). Career system profiles and strategic staffing. In M. B. Arthur, D. T. Hall, & B. S. Lawrence (Eds.), *Handbook of career theory* (pp. 202–224). New York: Cambridge University Press.

Stallman, J. I., Johnson, T. G., Mwachofi, A., & Flora, J. L. (1993). Labor market incentives to stay in school. *Journal of Agriculture and Applied Economics, 25,* 82–94.

Stern, D., & Nakata, Y. F. (1989). Characteristics of high school students' paid work, and employment experience after graduation. In D. Stern & D. Eichorn (Eds.), *Adolescence and work* (pp. 189–233). Hillsdale, NJ: Erlbaum.

Super, D. E. (1990). A life-span, life-space approach to career development. In D. Brown, L. Brooks, & Assoc. (Eds.), *Career choice and development* (2nd ed., pp. 197–261). San Francisco: Jossey-Bass.

Tanner, J., Cockerill, R., Barnsley, J., & Williams, A. P. (1999). Gender and income in pharmacy: Human capital and gender stratification theories revisited. *British Journal of Sociology, 50,* 97–117.

Tharenou, P. (1997). Explanations of managerial career advancement. *Australian Psychologist, 32,* 19–28.

Tomaskovic-Devey, D. (1998). *Organizational resources and earnings: The nonspurious results of loose coupling.* Paper presented at the American Sociological Association.

Utsey, S. O. (1998). Racism and discrimination, coping, life satisfaction, and self-esteem among African Americans. *Dissertation Abstracts International Section A: Humanities and Social Sciences, 59* (2-A): 0425.

Wachter, M. L. (1974). Primary and secondary labor markets: A critique of the dual approach. *Brookings Papers on Economic Activity, 3,* 637–693.

Waight, J. (1998). Income stratification at retirement: Continuity or change? *Research in Social Stratification and Mobility, 16,* 271–287.

Werner, E. E. (1989). Adolescents and work: A longitudinal perspective on gender and cultural variability. In D. Stern & D. Eichorn (Eds.), *Adolescence and work* (pp. 159–187). Hillsdale, NJ: Erlbaum.

Williams, D. R. (1987). *Labor force participation of black and white youth.* Ann Arbor, MI: UMI Research Press.

Wilson, A. B. (1989). Dreams and aspirations in the status attainment model. In D. Stern & D. Eichorn (Eds.), *Adolescence and work* (pp. 49–73). Hillsdale, NJ: Erlbaum.

Wilson, F. D., Tienda, M., & Wu, L. (1995). Race and unemployment: Labor market experiences of black and white men, 1968–1988. *Work and Occupations, 22,* 245–270.

Witkowski, K. M., & Leicht, K. T. (1995). The effects of gender segregation, labor force participation, and family roles on the earnings of young adult workers. *Work and Occupations, 22,* 48–72.

PART FOUR
Theoretical Integration

Counselors rarely use one theoretical orientation to career development without at least making some use of other theories. Being able to combine theories when working with a client may make a counselor more flexible in meeting a wide range of client needs. These needs may include career choice, work adjustment, and placement counseling as well as others. Some theories meet the needs of certain types of clients more than do others; for example, some are better than others for adolescent clients. It is the purpose of Chapter 16 to describe the many ways that theories can be used in combination.

Theories in
Combination

16

The previous chapters have each explained how a particular theory or theories can be used in counseling. These chapters have looked at theories in isolation. However, it is possible to combine theories to fit both one's theoretical counseling orientation and the work setting. Much of this chapter concerns the appropriateness of different combinations of career development theories for individuals in specific age ranges.

Throughout this book, the emphasis has been on using career development theory in individual counseling. This focus has been used to illustrate the application of theory. However, counselors are often in situations where there is not sufficient time for individual counseling or where other methods may seem more appropriate. This chapter addresses those situations. Noncounseling uses of career development theory, such as in administering self-help and computer materials, will be described. Some counselors work with career groups, either by choice or because career groups are an efficient way of providing career services to large numbers of clients. Career group counseling will be discussed.

Two special applications of theory have not yet been addressed. The first is using career development theory when career counseling issues are not the presenting problem. The second concerns the implication of career development theory for job search or placement strategies. Since most of this book has focused on career choice and work adjustment, it is fitting to also include information about implications for job search strategies. Although most career development theories have not addressed this issue directly, giving job search assistance is a very important role for many counselors.

Topics that have been covered throughout this book have included the roles of testing and occupational information, the career development of women and culturally diverse populations, and the counselor issues raised by specific theories. For each of these topics, comparisons will be made among theories.

COMBINING THEORIES

To discuss how theories can be used with each other in counseling, it will be helpful to categorize them into three groups: trait and factor theory, life-span theory, and career decision-making theories. The trait and factor theories include general trait and factor theory (Chapter 2), Lofquist and Dawis's work adjustment theory (Chapter 3), Holland's typology (Chapter 4), and Myers-Briggs type theory (Chapter 5). With regard to life-span theory, the focus will be mainly on the work of Super (Chapters 6–9), but will also include that of Gottfredson (Chapter 7), Erikson (Chapter 8), Atkinson, Morten, and Sue (Chapter 9), and Hopson and Adams's theory of transitions (Chapter 10). The career decision-making theories include Krumboltz's social learning theory (Chapter 13), as well as the developmental perspective of Tiedeman, a spiritual approach to career decision making, and the cognitive information processing perspective, all from (Chapter 14). Parts of some of these theories have been drawn on by Hansen in developing her integrative life planning (ILP) tasks, which are described in this chapter.

Four types of theories that do not fit neatly into any of these categories are those of constructivist approaches (Chapter 11), parental influence theories (Chapter 12), social cognitive career theory (Chapter 13), and the sociological and economic theories of career development (Chapter 15). There are very different reasons for not including these theories in this section on combining theories. The constructivist theories focus on the subjective perceptions of the client. Personal construct psychology and narrative counseling attend to the clients' stories of their lives. These approaches are more subjective than trait and factor theory, decision-making theories, or developmental theories, and are therefore hard to compare. Regarding parental theories of personality development, only some evidence has been found to support their hypotheses. Thus, it may be inappropriate to use them in discussions of counseling conceptualization. However, Roe's eight occupational groupings have been found useful by counselors and test developers alike. They are discussed further in the section on occupational information. Applications of social cognitive career theory have not been well developed, but its emphasis on increasing self-efficacy in counseling is useful. Sociological and economic theories of career development provide informative insights into the labor market, especially for counseling women and culturally diverse populations. However, because of their emphasis on the working environment rather than the individual, they are limited in providing an overall conceptualization of career counseling. Because these theories do have much to offer, they will be alluded to in later sections of this chapter.

Combining Life-Span Theory with Trait and Factor and Career Decision-Making Theories

Because it encompasses the entire life span, Super's life-span theory has received considerable attention. Super's theory is compatible with theories such as trait and factor and career decision-making theories. Such theories focus on career choice or work adjustment at a particular point in time. Therefore, it is helpful to examine which trait and factor theories and career decision-making theories are most useful at which stage in the life span. Such an approach is compatible with Super's (1990) suggestions for counseling, which incorporate Holland's model as well as trait and factor approaches. Figure 16-1 examines eight theories in terms of their appropriateness for different age groups according to Super's life stages. The solid line shows when, in an individual's lifetime, the theory is likely to be most useful. The dotted line shows when it is likely to be helpful, but not as pertinent. In the following pages we will discuss the applicability of nonlife-span theories to life-span theories in relation to childhood, early adolescence, late adolescence and adulthood, and adult career transitions.

Childhood   The developmental models of Ginzberg, Ginsburg, Alexrad, and Herma (1951), Super (1990), and Gottfredson (1996) provide information about the career development of children. Trait and factor and career decision-making theorists have little to say about this period. Ginzberg and his colleagues emphasize the development of interests, capacities, and values. Gottfredson's focus on orientation to size and power, gender roles, social class variables, and self-awareness provides an interesting insight into the development of career choice. Super's (1990) emphasis on the development of curiosity, exploration, and information leading to the development of interests, an accurate time perspective, and a self-concept is yet another helpful view of the career development process of children. Since career selection and work adjustment are inappropriate at this age, developmental life-span theories provide useful information for the counselor that is not provided by trait and factor and career decision-making theories.

Early Adolescence   At this point, the convergence of life-span theory and other theories becomes murky. The work of Super (1990) emphasizes the importance of career maturity, which is desirable before career selection takes place. Super's concepts of career planning, which include career exploration, decision making, world-of-work information, and knowledge of

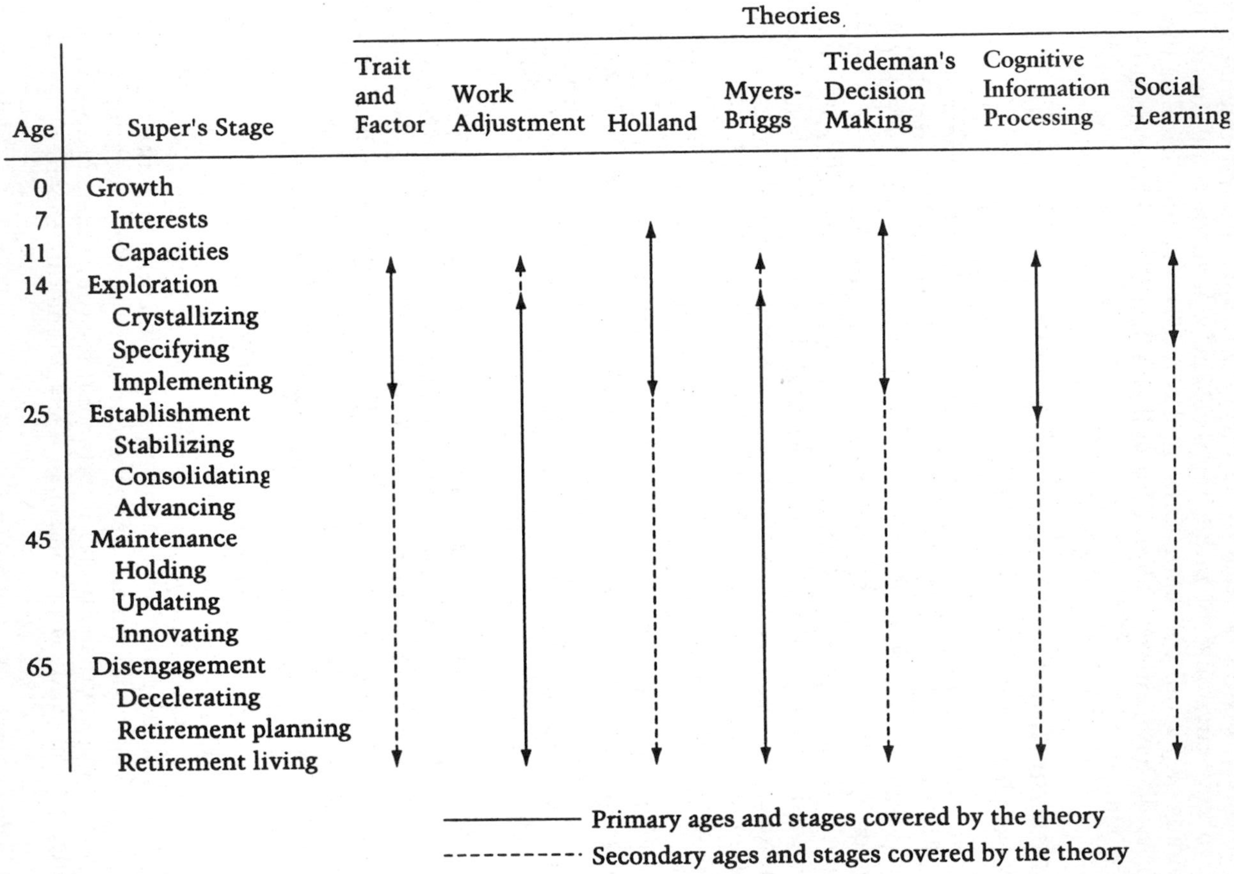

Figure 16-1 How various career development theories relate to Super's life-span stages.

preferred occupation, focus on the readiness of the individual. Erikson's theory of identity has also been applied to vocational identity by Vondracek and his colleagues and provides concepts that describe vocational readiness. According to developmental theorists such as Super, it is at the point of vocational readiness (or some approximation thereof) that trait and factor and career decision-making theories are useful. For trait and factor theorists, with the possible exception of Holland, readiness for self-assessment is not a focus. For Tiedeman, who has devised developmental models of career decision making, readiness would be more of a concern than for spiritual perspectives, cognitive information processing, or Krumboltz (Mitchell & Krumboltz, 1990), who do not incorporate developmental concepts in their approaches. The age group that is the focus of concern for the concept of readiness for career selection is adolescence from the eighth grade through the twelfth grade. The Career Development Inventory (Super et al., 1971; Thompson & Lindeman, 1981) was developed to determine maturity and readiness to explore careers. Often, trait and factor and career decision-making theories are used with this age group without measures of readiness. Whether students who may be only partially ready to explore career alternatives can benefit from trait and factor theory or career decision-making approaches is unknown.

Late Adolescence and Adulthood   In high school and college, counseling for career choice is common. With regard to trait and factor theories, some counselors use a variety of tests measuring interests, abilities, personality, and/or values that follow the general trait and factor model. Others find the six personalities and environments of Holland to be quite useful. Because the concepts of the Myers-Briggs theory are rather complex, that theory is rarely used with high school students. The work adjustment theory of Lofquist and Dawis can be used with high school students but rarely is. To benefit from the use of work adjustment theory, the client should have experience and knowledge of work-related values and needs. Most high school students have had limited work experience. In terms of decision-making theories, most are applicable to high school students, as well as college students. Cognitive information processing and Krumboltz's social learning theory, which emphasize faulty beliefs, may be appropriate for high school students, who may have many misconceptions about career selection. These views about correcting inaccurate information in order to make career decisions is somewhat similar to Super's notion of having accurate occupational knowledge and information about career decision making.

Adult Career Development   Super's stages of adult career development as described in Figure 16-1 provide a way to view trait and factor and decision-making theories. The stage of exploration, which includes the substages of crystallizing, specifying, and implementing, is the stage in which trait and factor and decision-making theories are most likely to be used. However, Super's concept of recycling would suggest that exploring one's career can occur at almost any age for adults. Certainly, general trait and factor theory, as well as the theories of Holland and Myers-Briggs, can be useful in career selection, as work adjustment theory can be. The decision-making theories of Tiedeman's social learning theory, spiritual approaches, and cognitive information processing fit Super's exploration phase. Also, the anticipating stage of Tiedeman's theory is somewhat similar to the crystallizing substage of Super's exploration stage. The adjusting stage of Tiedeman is in many ways comparable to the specifying and implementing substages of exploration (Super, 1990). In social learning theory, task-approach skills are likely to be used in Super's crystallizing and specifying substages of exploration. In spiritual approaches to career decision making, many of the processes described by Miller-Tiedeman (1999) concern understanding oneself and committing to this understanding, consistent with Super's crystallizing and specifying substages of exploration. In cognitive information processing theory, the communication and analysis phases of the CASVE cycle would correspond with the crystallizing subphase. Synthesis and valuing might most resemble the specifying substage, and execution is comparable to the focus of the substage of implementing. All of these theories, including Super's, provide a means to understand adult career decision-making processes.

In the establishment, maintenance, and disengagement stages, work adjustment is an important issue. Although Holland's theory and general trait and factor theory may address this issue, the work adjustment theory of Lofquist and Dawis and the Myers-Briggs typology are specifically concerned with ways of helping individuals adjust to work concerns. Work adjustment theory does this by attending to the congruence between the needs, values, and abilities of the client, on the one hand, and the reinforcers offered by the job, on the other. Myers-Briggs type theory examines work adjustment by attending to the judging and perceiving patterns of the client in comparison to those of his or her colleagues and other aspects of the work environment. These approaches are appropriate to retirement issues as well as problems that arise at work. The decision-making theorists provide a model that is helpful not only in career choice, but in decision making in general as well. Therefore, the approaches of Krumboltz, Tiedeman, Miller-Tiedeman (spiritual approaches), and cognitive information processing contain elements that can be used at any phase of the career adjustment process, such as when a worker experiences conflicts with his or her superior and must decide how to resolve them.

Also related to the establishment, maintenance, and disengagement stages is the approach to crises and transitions proposed by Hopson and Adams (1977). They recognize that problems arising from being fired or laid off, sexual harassment, and other crises can be very serious for an individual. This appears to be particularly true for those individuals who see their role as worker as being very important, and who are in the establishment or maintenance stages as described by Super. Hopson and Adams suggest that individuals react to crises in this sequence: shock and immobilization, minimization and denial, self-doubt, letting go, testing options, searching for meaning, and integration. For some counselors, it may be helpful to look at issues such as job loss from the point of view of Hopson and Adams's transition theory, work adjustment theory, and the perceiving and judging style of the Myers-Briggs typology. For example, whether an individual deals more in the inner world or the outer world (introversion/extraversion) and senses or intuits may be related to how he or she deals with the initial shock of job termination and the minimization phase. Often, several different theoretical points of view will add to the counselor's understanding of a career crisis.

Combining Trait and Factor Theories

Can a counselor use more than one trait and factor theory without being confused or possibly confusing the client? Briefly, the answer is yes. A lengthier answer can be arrived at by examining Table 16-1. Each trait and factor theory emphasizes certain traits and factors more than others. For example, general trait and factor theory allows the counselor to emphasize aptitudes, interests, values, and personality in any way that he or she wishes to do so. Many tests and inventories are available in each of these categories (Table 16-1 provides a sample of some of these). It is up to the counselor to emphasize those tests and inventories that seem most appropriate. Holland's system emphasizes use of either the Self-Directed Search or the Vocational Preference Inventory, measures of interests and self-estimates of competencies. Work adjustment theory stresses measurement of aptitudes and values with the General Aptitude Test Battery and the Minnesota Importance Questionnaire. For career selection purposes, the Myers-Briggs typology is an incomplete trait and factor theory, focusing on personality measurement. Because these theories emphasize different traits, it is quite possible to use them in combination.

For example, using Holland's Self-Directed Search with the Myers-Briggs Type Indicator provides information about work personality as measured by interests and self-estimated competencies (Self-Directed Search) and perceiving and judging style (the Myers-Briggs Type Indicator). Similarly, either or both of these theories could be used with the work adjustment theory. As more theories are used, the addition of more concepts may create confusion for both client and counselor. In general, however, there seems to be little overlap in the approaches of general trait and factor theory, Holland's theory, work adjustment theory, and the Myers-Briggs typology.

Combining Career Decision-Making Theories

Unlike trait and factor theories, which tend to differ from each other because they measure different characteristics of individuals, career decision-making theories tend to describe the same process. Therefore, it is unlikely that a counselor would wish to use more than one career decision-making theory in counseling. Krumboltz's social learning theory uses behavioral

Table 16-1 Tests and Inventories Associated with Specific Career Development Theories

Theory	Test Type					
	Aptitude	Interest	Values	Personality	Decision Making	Maturity and Development
Trait and factor theory*	Scholastic Assessment Test	Kuder Career Search	Study of Values	California Psychological Inventory		
	Differential Aptitude Tests	Strong Interest Inventory	Values Scale	Sixteen Personality Factor Questionnaire		
	General Aptitude Test Battery	California Occupational Preference Survey				
	Armed Services Vocational Aptitude Battery					
Holland's typology		Self-Directed Search Vocational Preference Inventory				

Theory	Tests and Inventories
Myers-Briggs typology	Myers-Briggs Type Indicator
Work adjustment theory	General Aptitude Test Battery; Minnesota Importance Questionnaire
Super's life-span theory	Values Scale; Salience Inventory; Career Development Inventory; Adult Career Concerns Inventory
Cognitive Information processing theory	Career Thoughts Inventory
Krumboltz's social learning theory	Career Beliefs Inventory

*Trait and factor theory can make use of many tests and inventories. Examples are presented here.

and cognitive interventions, as does cognitive information processing theory. In contrast, the developmental perspective of Tiedeman and the spiritual approach of Miller-Tiedeman and others emphasize the subjective experience of the client. Tiedman's stages of exploration, crystallization, choice, and clarification are guidelines rather than prescriptions for the counselor to follow. Likewise, the stages of induction, reformation, and integration are ways of implementing and adjusting to a choice. Furthermore, the Myers-Briggs typology can be seen as a theory of career decision making because it focuses on making perceptions about events and then judging or deciding about those events. If a counselor does decide to use a career decision-making theory in counseling, it is important that the theory fit the counselor's orientation as well as the client population.

An Integrative Approach to Life Planning

Sunny Hansen (1997, 2000) has developed an approach that includes many subjects covered in this book. Her integrative approach has suggestions for counselors to consider in career counseling, as well as an overview of career development. Her model focuses on ways to make society a better place while helping individuals with their career concerns. Hansen has traveled widely to countries such as Australia and Japan, showing how the Integrative Life Planning approach represents a worldview of career development. Reflecting her interests in gender and multicultural issues, Hansen looks at changes in the workplace, families, and in society as they affect each other. In her approach, she integrates the work of many of the theorists discussed in this text, but focuses on the societal context for change and change in life roles. In her approach she identifies six critical life tasks. I will describe these tasks briefly and indicate which chapters of this text relate to Hansen's six tasks.

Task 1: Finding Work That Needs Doing in a Changing Global Context

Increasingly, clients and counselors will find it helpful to have a worldview that goes beyond looking at just the local job market or even that of their country, but includes an awareness of changes in societal and economic conditions in the world. There is a need for individuals to understand technology and the use of computers and information processing. Along with this emphasis on technology, Hansen stresses a value system that emphasizes the need to understand cultural and gender diversity, to reduce violence, to reduce poverty, and to advocate human rights. Chapters 2 and 15 of this text emphasize changes in the world labor market and changes in work. All chapters deal with Hansen's emphasis on cultural and gender diversity.

Task 2: Weaving Our Lives into a Meaningful Whole

Hansen emphasizes the roles of men and women that go beyond their working life. She believes that counselors working with career concerns need to help their clients integrate work and their personal lives. This reflects her emphasis on values such as treating others with respect, being flexible in relationships, and considering social, intellectual, physical, spiritual, and emotional roles of clients. Like Super, Hansen sees work as one of several important roles, believing that all roles should be woven together and considered as interrelated. Similar to Super (Chapters 6–9), Hansen's approach is integrative of life roles. Like Anna Miller-Tiedeman and Bloch and Richmond (Chapter 14), Hansen emphasizes the spiritual aspect of career development.

Task 3: Connecting Family and Work   Hansen believes that an important integrative life planning task is to help clients understand how family relationships impact work. In career counseling, counselors may attend to a number of family issues and concerns such as attitudes toward child care, importance of work and family to both partners, sharing tasks at home, marital satisfaction, stress, and power in the marital relationship. In the 1970s Hansen developed BORN FREE to study and to address gender-role issues across cultures. An important aspect of BORN FREE studied the effect of gender-role stereotypes on individuals and on work. Suggestions to employers as to how they can assist in helping individuals connect family and work include creating more flexible work arrangements, varied scheduling and time outs from a career, more home-based work, and viewing a person's work–family choice as flexible, rather than as a one-time decision. Hansen stresses that the family must not always fit around work, but work can fit around the family. In this text, Chapter 12, "Parental Influence Theories," describes some contributions to understanding the role of families and parents as they relate to work.

Task 4: Valuing Pluralism in Individuality   Hansen believes that an important aspect of career development that both counselors and clients should attend to is the valuing of cultural diversity. She believes that counseling professionals need to truly understand the importance of valuing diversity and at the same time understand their own biases and attitudes. As they expand their worldview, clients are likely to develop a worldview that will allow them to function in a multicultural environment. Hansen challenges traditional assumptions about career development. Recognizing that not all individuals have many choices in their lives due to racism or sexism can help clients and counselors work with both individual and societal limitations. A population that she believes is often neglected is that of immigrants and refugees. With such individuals, it is particularly important to attend to cultural diversity. Hansen's emphasis on pluralism and inclusivety is covered in this text's sections on gender and cultural diversity, and emphasized by the spiritual approaches to career development described in Chapter 14.

Task 5: Exploring Spirituality and Life Purpose   For Hansen, exploring spirituality is an important and critical task that is central to the lives of many individuals. Often it can mean a yearning for a higher power, something larger than one's self, or it can mean an acknowledgment of others and their importance. For example, individuals who explore their spirituality and value it highly may be involved in doing volunteer work with the homeless, with children, or with older individuals. This can provide a sense of connectiveness with others and an internal sense of the value of life. In discussing this task, Hansen emphasizes Asian values such as *Zen* meditation, which provides an opportunity to reach higher levels of consciousness, as well as other methods for doing so. By exploring one's life purpose, work can become more meaningful. This task fits well with the philosophical position of the spiritual theorists described in Chapter 14 of this text.

Task 6: Managing Personal Transitions and Organizational Change   Individuals need to be aware that there are many transitions that take place in life—graduation, marriage, layoffs, new jobs, and so forth. For example, Hansen sees the growth of outplacement counseling as an indication of the abundance of transitions that are currently occurring in the workplace. Individuals must deal not only with details of transitions, but the stress and effects that these transitions have on families. Counselors can assist clients in managing the many wanted and unwanted transitions in their lives. Both clients and counselors can be aware that even when decisions are made purposefully by clients about transitions, these may be rational, intuitive, or a combination. Clients in a rapidly changing world are often dealing with uncertainty in their decisions. Thus, societal changes can influence the degree to which a career decision is emotionally and rationally based. Hansen's emphasis on personal transitions is explained in more detail in Chapter 10. Also, Krumboltz's concept of planned happenstance, Chapter 13, is consistent with Hansen's emphasis on ways that individuals can capitalize on unanticipated events.

In her Integrative Life Planning approach, Hansen shows how many important life concepts are tied together. She sees individuals as exploring their identity, which is affected by their ethnicity, gender, social class, disabilities, and so forth. This exploration is related to social, intellectual, physical, spiritual, as well as career development concerns that are related to each other. These factors impact life roles such as romantic and family relationships, work, learning, and leisure. Like Fred Vondracek (Chapter 9), Hansen sees the exploration of identity as fitting into the social context of families, organizations, and society.

Given this broad view, Hansen suggests that counselors be informed about changes in work and work patterns. As this text does, Hansen emphasizes the importance of considering gender and cultural diversity issues when dealing with clients. From a social context point of view, Hansen feels counselors can help influence organizations to develop flexibility in the workplace and to develop flexible and humane leadership models. Thus, Hansen encourages counselors to take a holistic and humanistic approach to career counseling.

The Counselor's Choice

Each of the theories described in the preceding pages has been supported by varying amounts of research. In general, these theories are clear and concise. For the counselor, they offer a tested approach to understanding and helping clients with career problems. Whether a counselor uses one theory or several in the conceptualization of client issues is a personal decision. There is no information to suggest the most appropriate number of theories to use.

NONCOUNSELING APPLICATIONS OF THEORIES

Practical considerations, such as a large caseload and little time available for career counseling, often require counselors to look for other methods besides individual counseling to help their clientele with issues of career selection. Some noncounseling interventions can serve as a way of identifying those individuals who might profit from further counseling. In some cases, noncounseling materials are offered as the only career selection aid. Three noncounseling applications of theories are described here: screening methods, paper-and-pencil materials, and computerized guidance systems.

Screening Methods

Some theorists have developed tests or inventories that screen for the clients who will benefit most from counseling. Another use of screening is to separate clients into groups by test scores so that appropriate counseling interventions can be offered. An excellent example of a screening instrument is Super's Career Development Inventory (Super et al., 1971). For example, depending on how a student scores on this instrument, he or she can be referred either to counseling for career choice or to information that will increase the level of his or her vocational maturity, so that he or she can then be assigned to a career-selection intervention. Holland's Self-Directed Search can be used in a similar manner. Those students who are not able to arrive at a series of acceptable career alternatives through the Self-Directed Search can be scheduled for individual or group career counseling. Although many other inventories and tests are not normally used in this manner, it may be possible to do so.

Paper-and-Pencil Materials

Most theories do not offer materials designed to be used in lieu of counseling. Holland's Self-Directed Search is a notable exception. Holland (1997) believes that help in selecting an occupation can be provided through easy-to-use inventories and supplemental materials, so that, in many cases, counseling will be unnecessary. The Self-Directed Search is designed so that individuals can score the inventory themselves as well as interpret it.

Professionals should not be necessary, except in situations where the results of the Self-Directed Search are confusing or incomplete. In addition, Holland developed *The Occupations Finder*, which lists hundreds of careers sorted by Holland's three-letter codes. Thus, a student can look up in *The Occupations Finder* the three-letter code that he or she received on the Self-Directed Search and locate careers that exactly, or nearly, match that code. Also, Holland (1985) has written an easy-to-read eight-page booklet called *You and Your Career* that advises students how to understand the Holland six-type system and how to make career decisions. Many educational systems have used these instruments to provide career assistance to their students. Counselors wishing to use these materials need to consider the cost effectiveness of these relatively inexpensive materials and the merits of a system that does not stress a counseling approach to career selection.

Computerized Guidance Systems

Since the early 1970s, computer-assisted guidance systems have become an integral part of career counseling. Although these systems are designed to be used as an adjunct to counseling, they are occasionally used similarly to Holland's Self-Directed Search. For example, a computerized guidance system can be assigned to individuals so that they may select appropriate careers. If this method is not sufficient for an individual, then counseling may be offered. Two systems are particularly well known and have been highly developed: DISCOVER and SIGI PLUS. Both systems follow the trait and factor method in that they help individuals assess their abilities, interests, and values. Then, the systems provide occupational and educational information for the people using the system. A match is made between the self-assessment of the individual and occupational information. Clients then go on to select the occupations that would fit them best. SIGI PLUS emphasizes the values aspect of self-assessment, whereas DISCOVER uses some portions of Super's developmental life-span theory in its approach.

These descriptions do not do justice to the sophisticated interactive nature of these programs. Both are available for many computers and have large databases of occupational information. Their self-assessment sections are, in many ways, similar to paper-and-pencil assessments of interests, self-estimated competencies, and values. Other computer systems are also available. Evaluating SIGI PLUS and DISCOVER, Peterson, Ryan-Jones, Sampson, and Reardon (1994) found no practical differences in effectiveness between the systems. Studying SIGI PLUS, Lenz, Reardon, and Sampson (1993) reported that, as students' scores on Holland's Enterprising and Social categories increased, their rating of SIGI PLUS's contribution to their own knowledge of self and of occupations decreased, a finding suggesting that students responded differently to SIGI PLUS depending on their personality type. Kratz (1998) studied the use of SIGI PLUS and found that SIGI PLUS was assigned after an interview with a client, but often there was no counseling provided after the client had completed SIGI PLUS. Kratz questions the appropriateness of using SIGI PLUS in this manner.

SPECIAL COUNSELING ISSUES

A number of counseling issues have implications for career development theories. One important concern is group counseling. Sometimes because of preference, and often because of limited time, counselors choose to use career group counseling rather than individual counseling. Most of the theories that have been discussed in this book lend themselves to the group approach. Another issue that arises is career counseling as a related concern. Some counselors work in a setting where they deal with personal or family problems to which career issues are related. For example, they may rarely do counseling for career choice and more often do work adjustment counseling as a part of other issues. Selecting a career development theory to use in that case may be different than if one's chief responsibility is career counseling. Another issue that occasionally faces counselors is changing the career development theories that one uses when one changes work setting. For example, if a counselor changes from a job in which he or she has worked with children to one in which he or she is working with adults, the career development theory that the counselor uses may be different in the two settings. Another duty of counselors is placement and job search counseling. The theories that have been discussed in this book have implications for helping people locate a job once they have decided about the career that they wish to pursue. Although these issues do not apply to all counselors, they do arise for many.

Group Career Counseling

The concepts and materials that career development theorists provide for counselors can be applied in most group settings. In his review of career group counseling, Kivlighan (1990) found that most studies of career groups revealed that a primary purpose was imparting information to clients. Other purposes included helping clients in vocational exploration and in developing self-efficacy (Sullivan & Mahalik, 2000). Some features of group counseling that are not available in individual counseling are motivation from peers, an opportunity to learn from the experience of peers, and the opportunity to help and be helped by people who are in a similar situation. Also, groups can be designed for specific populations, such as those with disabilities (Zunker, 1998), Asian Americans (Pope, 1999), and displaced homemakers (McAllister & Ponterotto, 1992). Herr and Cramer (1996) make similar recommendations. They find that role-playing certain situations and using a board game such as the Life Career Game, in which people can play different roles, are excellent group career counseling techniques. Whether the goal of group career counseling is career selection or work adjustment, career groups can fulfill many of the functions of individual career counseling.

Trait and factor theory can be adapted rather easily to a group counseling format. If using general trait and factor theory, the counselor must select the tests and inventories that will be used for the group. Interpretation of tests can be done in a group, with the counselor suggesting meanings of the test results, and other group members adding input. Similarly, the materials developed by Holland can be used in a group setting. Because they are particularly easy to understand, they can be used with clients with a wide range of ages and abilities. The Myers-Briggs Type Indicator is used widely in group settings, with both career and other issues or in structured exercises (Tieger & Barron-Tieger, 1992). In discussion, group members can give feedback to each other about their views of the person's type. Discussion of the kind of work setting that would fit a particular individual's type can be instructive. Although Lofquist and Dawis's work adjustment theory is often thought of in terms of individual vocational rehabilitation counseling, it, too, can be used in career groups. Administering the General Aptitude Test Battery and the Minnesota Importance Questionnaire for discussion and interpretation in a group may be quite conducive to exploration. However, the counselor needs to be prepared to make suggestions to the group as to which occupations would match their abilities and values.

Developmental theory can be used in several different ways in group counseling. With adolescents, career maturity issues, which include career planning, career exploration, and finding out about the world of work, can be a focus. Further, Super's (1990) rainbow enables adolescents to examine where they have been and what they might expect in the future. Looking behind and looking ahead can also apply to adults. Adults who are contemplating making career changes or are experiencing work adjustment problems may find it helpful to examine the importance of various roles in their life, such as worker, leisurite, citizen, and student. Looking at life roles in the context of the stages of exploration, establishment, maintenance, and disengagement can help clients see how they compare to other members of the group in terms of the similarity and the dissimilarity of their life situations, a process that will give them a sense of understanding about their life situation. Super's theory also supplies a context for understanding career crises such as firings and layoffs.

Career decision making is often used in a group format. Krumboltz's social learning theory has been used in a group format called DECIDES (Krumboltz & Hamel, 1977). Tiedeman's developmental approach can be applied to anticipating a choice or adjusting to a choice. For the anticipating a choice phase, career maturity and interest inventories could help in exploration and crystallization subphases. A one- or two-session group might be helpful for new workers who were going through the induction or reformation phase of adjusting to a choice. In a spiritual approach to group career counseling, group members can discuss their feelings about career choice and encourage each other to freely explore career options. Cognitive information processing theory has been used at Florida State University as a structure for a course that uses group procedures that are oriented toward student career development (Reardon, Lenz, Sampson, &

Peterson, 2000). Krumboltz's social learning theory and cognitive information processing have manuals that group leaders can use that follows a structured format.

Career Counseling as a Related Issue

For counselors who do career counseling infrequently or have clients who present work adjustment problems, certain theories may be particularly appropriate. In terms of trait and factor theories, the Myers-Briggs typology and Lofquist and Dawis's work adjustment theory may be particularly helpful. The former emphasizes perceiving and judging styles, whereas the latter emphasizes abilities and work-related values that directly correspond to job issues. These theories may provide useful insights into work adjustment difficulties, such as problems with colleagues or superiors and difficulties with job requirements. Another theory that is particularly helpful for working with career issues when they are a related concern is that of Super. By assessing how important the work role is in comparison to that of student, citizen, leisurite, and family member, the counselor can put career issues into a useful perspective. The career stages of Super also provide a way of understanding the kinds of work-related problems that adults experience. For children, Super's and Gottfredson's developmental theories can be particularly valuable, since they can be used to examine exploratory gender-role behavior that other theories do not (see Figure 16-1 for a comparison).

Changing Work Settings

The ages and ability levels of the clients may determine the type of theory that the counselor chooses. For example, if a high school guidance counselor who has used Super's concepts of vocational maturity along with Holland's typology moves to a community college setting, in which he or she is dealing with returning adult students, his or her choice of theory may change. The counselor may wish to use Myers-Briggs typological theory in addition to Holland's theory or may wish to replace Holland's theory with the work adjustment theory of Lofquist and Dawis. In general, counselors may be less likely to change their theory of counseling and/or psychotherapy when they move from one work setting to another, than to modify the career development theory that they use.

Placement Counseling

Most career development theorists have been more concerned with career selection and career adjustment than they have been with issues of finding a job. However, many authors have written job search books to help individuals find employment. Most notable of these is *What Color Is Your Parachute?* (Bolles, 2001). This book, which is updated each year, is designed for adult job hunters and career changers. It deals with issues such as finding out about the labor market, where jobs are, how to get leads, writing résumés, and conducting oneself during job interviews. Many writers, such as Bolles, emphasizes the importance of developing a network of people who can help in the job search. However, most advice is practical and not related to theory.

One exception is the work of Azrin and Besalel (1980), who have developed the concept of the "job club." This approach is based on the behavioral principle of positive reinforcement. Focusing on professionals who had lost jobs, Azrin developed a structured approach so that members of the job club could reinforce each other's progress in job seeking. The effectiveness of this approach has been shown by Black, Tsuhako, and Mc-Dougall (1998) with young adults with modest cognitive impairments, with unemployed older workers (Rife & Belcher, 1994), and with unemployed professional workers (Coxford, 1998). The action-oriented approach of Azrin to getting a job once one has lost a job contrasts with the approach of Hopson and Adams (1977), which emphasizes understanding the stages of a crisis. Although these approaches are very different, they are not incompatible. Hopson and Adams provide a way of understanding a crisis that may help in knowing when the best time is to implement an action-oriented program such as that of Azrin.

The focus of Azrin is on looking for work when one has experienced a job crisis. The career development theories discussed in this book offer a way of viewing both crises and more normal transitions that occur when individuals graduate from high school or college and then look for work.

One approach to finding a job can be extrapolated from Holland's theory. Often, people who are looking for work are encouraged to sell themselves to employers, to develop a network of contacts that can help them find a job, and to be assertive in their job search. This type of behavior is most similar to that of the Enterprising individual, who often enjoys persuading others and selling. The assertive approach recommended by many job search strategists may be more difficult for Realistic, Conventional, and Investigative types to employ. A counselor, when assisting a client in the job search process, may wish to consider his or her client's Holland type and how that person can develop an appropriate job search strategy.

Using the Myers-Briggs typology, individuals who deal with the outer world (extraversion) may be more comfortable in using assertive job search strategies than those who deal with the inner world (introversion). Similarly, those individuals who take a sensing approach to finding information about job openings may have a very different style from those who take an intuiting approach. For example, those who acquire information about the job market based on intuition may exaggerate the difficulties that they are facing.

Super's concept of role salience can be helpful in career placement counseling. Clients vary as to how much they value the worker role in contrast to that of student, leisurite, citizen, or homemaker. This notion of role provides an opportunity to put the entire context of the job search into perspective. The stage theory of Super also provides a broader context within which to view job search strategies. The job search process itself fits within the specifying and implementing substages of the exploration stage.

Career decision-making theory offers yet another perspective on job search strategies. The adjustment stage of Tiedeman and O'Hara (1963) provides an interesting subjective view of the job search process. The first substage, induction, highlights the importance of change in an individual's life and the uncertainty surrounding the change that occurs during the job search process. Reformation concerns not the job-hunting process, but the initial reaction to the job once one has been hired. This phase deals with adjustment to work and to new colleagues. Finally, the integration substage describes moving away from the newness of a job to other aspects in one's life and other career possibilities.

In contrast to the developmental perspective of Tiedeman are the social learning and cognitive information processing approaches. Since the job-hunting process is often seen by an individual as a process of many rejections, these cognitive and behavioral approaches can be useful. Reinforcing the job search process itself, rather than its outcome, is an important part of a behavioral approach. Because individuals may be discouraged as they start to look for work, attending to inaccurate beliefs and correcting them is part of the role of the counselor using social learning theory or cognitive information processing. These perspectives and those of other career development theorists offer an interesting approach to the job search process that is different from the pragmatic approach of most job search books.

TEST USE IN THEORIES

Career development theories vary as to the importance of tests in the conceptualization of client career problems. In general, trait and factor theories rely more heavily on test use than does life-span theory, which in turn uses tests more than career decision-making theories. A comparison of test use is provided in Table 16-1, listing the trait, factor, or characteristic measured for theories described in this book. Part of the success of trait and factor theory relies on the ability of test developers to accurately measure traits and factors such as aptitudes, interests, values, and personality. General trait and factor theory requires that career counselors select tests that are reliable and valid. Matching the measured traits and factors of a client with characteristics of a job is the essence of applying trait and factor theory. Holland's typological theory also measures traits and factors but categorizes them into six types that are then matched with environmental types. There are several inventories, such as the Strong Interest Inventory, that provide scores for the six types. In addition, Holland's Vocational Preference Inventory and Self-Directed Search are designed to provide scores for the six types so that matching can occur with occupational environments. The Myers-Briggs Type Indicator gives information to the counselor about the personality type of the client. Those counselors who use the Myers-Briggs type theory in their work rely heavily on the Myers-Briggs Type Indicator to assess personality style. Perhaps the most precise use of testing occurs in work adjustment theory. Client scores on the General

Aptitude Test Battery and the Minnesota Importance Questionnaire are matched with the ability patterns and needs and values reinforcer patterns of over 1700 occupations. It is fair to conclude that, without accurate measurement of traits and factors, there would be no trait and factor theory.

For life-span theory, testing serves the purpose of identifying important developmental issues that individuals must face. Super's Career Development Inventory assesses the developmental phase of career maturity. Super's Adult Career Concerns Inventory assesses the extent to which adults are concerned about issues relating to the exploration, establishment, maintenance, or disengagement stage, or to any of the substages. In general, inventories that measure developmental tasks or stages are less precise than those that measure traits and factors. The reason is that life-span issues are broader and less predictable than measurements of aptitudes or interests. However, such instruments can still be useful in conceptualizing career concerns.

Career decision-making theory focuses on the process of selecting occupations. Although testing is often a part of this process, it is a secondary focus, whereas for trait and factor theory it is a primary focus. The developmental approach of Tiedeman is more concerned with the client's internal experience of decision-making issues than with more objective methods of measuring the process. The Assessment of Career Decision-Making Scale (Buck & Daniels, 1985) measures some of the concepts of Tiedeman and O'Hara's (1963) theory of decision making. However, this instrument is quite different from the approach taken by Miller-Tiedeman (1999) in her work on LIFECAREER®, and that of other career counselors who use a spiritual approach to career counseling. Although tests can be used by counselors using a spiritual approach, they are used cautiously so as not to detract from the individuals' self-assessment and career development. In cognitive information processing theory, the Career Thoughts Inventory is used to assess client confusion and anxiety about making career decisions, as well as to assess how individuals balance their own views with outside information. For Krumboltz, values inventories can help individuals in the process of clarifying values. Aptitude tests and interest inventories can help in identifying alternatives and in discovering probable outcomes of these alternatives. In addition, the Career Beliefs Inventory provides assistance in assessing inaccurate beliefs that clients may have that interfere with the career decision-making process. Thus, for career decision-making theories, as well as for other theories of career development, the purpose of the theory and the role of testing are highly related.

OCCUPATIONAL CLASSIFICATION SYSTEMS AND CAREER DEVELOPMENT THEORIES

The development of classification systems for occupations has been associated with trait and factor theory because occupations must be classified so that they can be matched with measured traits and factors of individu-

Table 16-2   *Comparison of Holland's Classification System to Three Other Systems**

Roe's Groups	Dictionary of Occupational Titles	Guide for Occupational Exploration
Service (S, R)	Professional, technical, and managerial occupations (A, E, I, S)	Artistic (A)
Business contact (E)		Scientific (I, R)
Organizations (E, C)	Clerical and sales occupations (C, E)	Plants and animals (I, R)
Technology (R, I)		
Outdoor (R, I)	Service occupations (S, R)	Protective (S, R)
		Mechanical (I, R)
Science (I, R)	Agricultural, fishery, forestry, and related occupations (R)	Industrial (R)
General cultural (A)		
		Business detail (E)
Arts and entertainment (A)	Processing occupations (R)	
		Selling (E)
	Machine trades occupations (R)	Accommodating (S, E, R)
	Benchwork occupations (R)	Humanitarian (S)
	Structural work occupations (R)	Leading-influencing (E)
		Physical-performance (A)
	Miscellaneous occupations	

*Letters in parentheses represent the Holland code that roughly corresponds to the occupational grouping: (R) Realistic, (I) Investigative, (A) Artistic, (S) Social, (E) Enterprising, and (C) Conventional.

als. The focus of various classification systems differs widely. For comparison, Table 16-2 lists the groupings used in three classification systems (Roe's, the *Dictionary of Occupational Titles*, and the *Guide for Occupational Exploration*) and cross-classifies them by Holland's system. This provides an opportunity to see how the four systems relate to each other. Roe's eight groupings are somewhat similar to those of Holland, with some overlap. The 12 categories of the *Guide for Occupational Exploration* represent a more detailed categorization system than Holland's. The 17,000 occupations listed in the *Dictionary of Occupational Titles* have as their primary classification the eight categories listed in Table 16-2. The predominance of Realistic occupations in this first level of the *Dictionary of Occupational Titles* categorization is indicative of the large number of Realistic occupations in the definitions. The O*NET's (Occupational Information Network) nine categories are very similar to those of the *Dictionary of Occupational Titles* and therefore are not listed in Table 16-2. The *Dictionary of Holland Occupational Codes* provides a Holland code identification for each of the occupations listed in the *Dictionary of Occupational Titles*. How career development theories make use of classification systems is the subject of this section.

As previously stated, classification systems are essential for use in trait and factor theory. Those counselors who use a general trait and factor theory can choose from classification systems that fit the tests and inventories they wish to use in counseling. For Holland's theory, it is essential to use his classification system. Although Roe's personality system may not be viewed as a trait and factor theory, the part of the theory that describes the classification system does fit with trait and factor theory. The California Occupational Preference Inventory, for example, uses Roe's classification system, as do several other inventories. On the other hand, work adjustment theory categorizes occupations according to the system of the *Dictionary of Occupational Titles*. In general, the theories or tests that counselors select are likely to dictate the classification system that the counselor will use.

For life-span theory, classification systems become important when career selections are to be made. When that occurs, life-span theorists incorporate developmental concepts as well as trait and factor theory. Therefore, life-span theorists are likely to make use of classification systems in the same way as trait and factor theorists.

For career decision-making theorists, the selection of tests and inventories, which may be a secondary part of counseling, will determine the occupational classification system to be used. The classification of occupations is not a major emphasis of career decision-making theorists.

HOW THEORIES APPLY TO CAREER DEVELOPMENT ISSUES OF WOMEN

Much of the information about the career development of women has come from life-span theory rather than from trait and factor or career decision-making theory. It is life-span theory that draws attention to gender-role issues that affect career development in childhood, adolescence, and adulthood. Knowledge of gender-role stereotyping and gender-role issues of women in various stages of their lives can help in work adjustment and career selection. In contrast, the information available from trait and factor and career decision-making theories about gender differences is minimal. However, the recent research on social cognitive career theory as it affects women is a notable exception.

With regard to trait and factor theory, some research shows differences in the interests and abilities of men and women. It is often difficult to separate learned from genetic characteristics. For example, if women do more poorly than men in math, is that poor performance due to a lack of innate ability or to socialization that women should not be as good in math as men are? Research reviewed in Part Two suggests that it is the latter. Similarly, in Holland's typology, women predominate in the Social and Artistic areas. This is a reflection of socialization rather than misclassification in using Holland's system. This information should not be used to suggest that women whose personalities are Realistic or Investigative are in some way aberrant and should be considering other occupations. There are some differences between the scores of men and women on the Minnesota Importance Questionnaire, which is an important component of work adjustment theory. Lofquist and Dawis suggest that it is the individual's needs that are important, not those of women or men in general. A similar conclusion can be reached about the Myers-Briggs typology. Although women tend to predominate in the feeling category and men in the thinking category (Myers, McCaulley, Quenk, & Hammer, 1998), this fact may have few implications for individual counseling. The fact that men and women, in general, may differ on various traits and factors cannot be generalized to the individual client, who may have interests, aptitudes, and personality patterns that are atypical of those of other women.

With regard to career decision-making theories, there are some findings useful in the counseling of women. In his social learning theory, Krumboltz emphasizes the importance of role models for women. He points out that, although groups such as women may have limited control over environmental conditions, there are ways through collective action that cultural biases such as gender discrimination can be changed. Social cognitive career theory, investigates how environmental factors affect the way women learn about their academic and career competencies in the process of making career choices. The developmental approach of Tiedeman and spiritual career decision-making perspective focus on the individual's own developmental process or subjective experiencing rather than emphasizing issues of gender role. That is not to say that these theorists consider gender-role stereotyping unimportant.

Examining the life-span development of women was a major focus of the chapters in Part Two. Gottfredson's attention to the impact of gender role on career choice at ages 6 to 8 has been instrumental in emphasizing that the career choices that men and women make in their adolescence and adulthood are different. Gottfredson's concepts of circumscription and compromise are useful in highlighting these differences. Chapter 8 explains the impact of the educational system on gender-role stereotyping of adolescent women. In adulthood, the career development of women is often more varied than that of men, with family and child care considerations leading to varied patterns of leaving and reentering the labor force. In addition to these concerns, women are far more likely than men to face sexual harassment issues in the workplace. Knowledge of these issues can help counselors provide an enlightened approach to working with women who have career choice or work adjustment problems.

HOW THEORIES APPLY TO CULTURAL DIVERSITY ISSUES IN CAREER DEVELOPMENT

In general, there has been less research on the career development of nonwhite people than on women. One reason is that there are a large number of cultural groups. In the United States, much research has focused on differences between African Americans and whites. Trait and factor theory, as well as career decision-making theory, has provided relatively little information about varying characteristics of nonwhite populations. One difficulty in interpreting the research in trait and factor theory is that it is important not to apply generalizations about the interests, aptitudes, and personalities of a group to an individual client. Social learning theory emphasizes environmental influences on the importance of role models who have the same cultural background as the client. Social cognitive career theory focuses on concerns about self-efficacy that can affect the career development of people from diverse cultural backgrounds as well as women. Other career decision-making theories do not focus on cultural background.

Perhaps the life-span perspective has the most to say about issues affecting culturally diverse populations. In general, minority children may be prevented from, or may have limited access to, exploratory activities that help them acquire information that leads to career maturity. In the United States, nonwhite adolescents with high aspirations may be thwarted from achieving them because of limited access to educational and occupational opportunities. Research discussed in Chapter 15 suggests that nonwhite adolescents are more likely to find jobs in the secondary labor market and to encounter job discrimination. Negative attitudes toward work can be the result of a historical pattern of experiencing discrimination from one generation to another. The work of Vondracek and his colleagues emphasizes the importance for counselors of being aware not only of the individual's vocational identity but also of the context of the individual's historical and social situation. The minority identity development model of Atkinson, Morten, and Sue (1998) can be helpful to counselors in understanding how people from culturally diverse populations may react to a variety of work situations. Their model suggests that minority group members may start in a stage of conformity and move through dissonance, resistance, emergence, and introspection to a stage of synergetic articulation and awareness. This theory is useful in understanding how minorities relate to their own group as well as to the majority group. Although not a model of career development, it has direct applicability to issues of job selection and work adjustment.

The need for counselors to attend to issues of women and culturally diverse populations in career development is highlighted by the research of sociologists and economists. They document, over and over again, that women and nonwhite employees in the United States receive less pay than white men for equal work and are often denied access to jobs that are likely to lead to advancement and higher pay. The sociological and economic theories of career development draw conclusions about broad groups from their studies of large numbers of people. The importance of attending to gender and cultural diversity is strongly emphasized in Hansen's Integrative Life Planning approach. However, for the individual counselor, the research is a reminder to look for attitudes within oneself that may hinder the career development of a client who is female or of another ethnic group.

COUNSELOR ISSUES

Career development theories not only provide a means of conceptualizing the client's concerns but also suggest a perspective on client–counselor issues. From a trait and factor point of view, it is often helpful to look at the traits and factors of the client and compare them to those of the counselor. In a life-span perspective, a contrast between the counselor's life stage and that of the client can be helpful in counseling situations. With regard to decision-making theories, being aware of the contrast between the decision-making style and progress of the client and that of the counselor can be instructive.

Trait and Factor Theories

In general, when using trait and factor theory, it is helpful for the counselor to be aware that the abilities, aptitudes, personality, values, and interests of the client are likely to be very different from those of the counselor. Appreciating a wide range of interests, abilities, and values can be helpful to the counselor in working with many problems.

From the point of view of Holland's typology, the less congruent the counselor's type is with the client's type, the more likely it is that the counselor will have to deal with a value conflict. For example, a counselor who is primarily Social in orientation may not enjoy organizing and working with numbers as does a person who is Conventional.

With regard to the Myers-Briggs typological theory, researchers (Yeakley, 1983) point out the importance of using a communication style that is similar to that of the client. For example, if the counselor's primary way of perceiving is through sensing and the client's way of perceiving is through intuiting, each will be looking at events from a different point of view. It is important for the counselor to adapt to or understand the client's communication style.

Lofquist and Dawis, in their theory of work adjustment, view the client and the counselor as serving as environments for each other. As environments, they reinforce each other and meet each other's needs in different ways. Being aware of both his or her own needs and those of the client can help the counselor in offering appropriate reinforcers for the client. For example, if the client has a need for responsibility, it may be helpful for the counselor to let the client act independently and make little acknowledgment of the counseling process in order to achieve a satisfactory result. This may mean sacrificing the counselor's own altruistic needs. Although trait and factor theory is generally not thought of as encompassing approaches that have an impact on the client–counselor relationship, it is clear that all of these theories can be viewed in this manner.

Life-Span Theories

Life-span theory draws attention to the different roles and stages of the client and the counselor. For example, a 65-year-old person who is counseling a 15-year-old is working with someone whose interests, exploratory behavior, and self-concept are at relatively early stages. For the counselor, focusing on the client's issues and not on his or her own will cross the large generational gap. Similarly, counselors often work with clients in crises. Knowing that each individual in each crisis is different will help the counselor to refrain from applying his or her own experience with a crisis to that of the client. Also, being aware of gender-role issues when the client is of the other gender can help the counselor focus on the needs and issues of the client. For example, being aware of a client's early experiences with gender bias in school may affect how the counselor assists the client with career selection issues.

Career Decision-Making Theories

Implications of career decision-making theories for counselors vary. Krumboltz and Baker (1973) point out that counselors using social learning theory should be careful that their counseling skills match the needs of the client. Further, they believe it is important for client and counselor to have mutually agreeable goals. If a counselor is expert in working with a specific type of client but chooses to work with a very different type of client, that behavior may be unethical. A counselor who uses a spiritual approach to career development should be clear about the subjective experience of career decision making of the client, which may be vastly different from that of the counselor. Appreciating the client's unique individuality is one of the main goals of the spiritual perspective on career decision making. In contrast, the cognitive information processing approach can be quite structured, so the counselor should be certain that the structure does not preclude discussion of atypical matters affecting career choice.

Sociological and Economic Approaches

The implications of sociological and economic perspectives on career choice are quite different from those of the psychological approaches. Sociological and economic research on career development factors points out the many inequalities that exist for culturally diverse populations and women as they deal with the labor market. Rather than assume that these apply to each client, the counselor can use this information as background from which to evaluate the client's individual issues. Further, the research of sociologists and economists into cultural and gender issues can serve as a guide to evaluating one's own values and prejudices.

CONCLUSION

The theories that have been discussed in this book provide useful approaches to problems of career choice and work adjustment. In many cases, the theorists and many of their colleagues have spent 20, 30, or more years developing, evaluating, and refining their theories. Through research and evaluation, they have modified and strengthened their work, at the same time providing new and better tests and inventories for counselors to use. In addition, recent theorists have developed perspectives and insights into the career-development-choice process that provide new ways for counselors to view their clients. The continuing research into, and the development of, revised and new theories is evidence that career development theory will continue to offer new and better tools and ideas for counselors to use. Implicit in the work of these theorists and researchers is the importance that they attribute to careers and career problems. They have great respect for the role of the counselor, whose work can significantly improve the client's satisfaction with his or her life.

References

Atkinson, D. R., Morten, G., & Sue, D. W. (1998). *Counseling American minorities: A cross-cultural perspective* (5th ed.). Boston: McGraw-Hill.

Azrin, N. H., & Besalel, V. A. (1980). *Job club counselor's manual: A behavioral approach to vocational counseling*. Baltimore: University Park Press.

Black, R. S., Tsuhako, K., & McDougall, D. (1998). Job club intervention to improve interviewing skills of young adults with cognitive disabilities. *Journal for Special Needs Education, 20*, 33–38.

Bolles, R. N. (2001). *What color is your parachute?* (31st ed.). San Francisco: Ten Speed Press.

Buck, J. N., & Daniels, M. H. (1985). *Assessment of career decision-making manual*. Los Angeles: Western Psychological Services.

Coxford, L. M. (1998). The role of social support in the job seeking behaviors of unemployed professionals. *Dissertation Abstracts International*, Vol. 59 (4-A): 10,076.

Ginzberg, E., Ginsburg, S. W., Axelrad, S., & Herma, J. (1951). *Occupational choice: An approach to a general theory*. New York: Columbia University Press.

Gottfredson, L. S. (1996). A theory of circumscription and compromise. In D. Brown, L. Brooks, & Assoc. (Eds.), *Career choice and development: Applying contemporary theories to practice* (3rd ed., pp. 179–232). San Francisco: Jossey-Bass.

Hansen, L. S. (1997). *Integrative life planning: Critical tasks for career development and changing life patterns.* San Francisco: Jossey-Bass.

Hansen, L. S. (2000). Integrative life planning: A new worldview for career professionals. In J. Kummerow (Ed.), *New directions in career planning and the workplace.* Palo Alto, CA: Consulting Psychologists Press.

Herr, E. L., & Cramer, S. H. (1996). *Career guidance through the life span* (5th ed.). New York: HarperCollins.

Holland, J. L. (1985). *You and your career.* Odessa, FL: Psychological Assessment Resources.

Holland, J. L. (1997). *Making vocational choices: A theory of vocational personalities and work environments* (3rd ed.). Odessa, FL: Psychological Assessment Resources.

Hopson, B., & Adams, J. D. (1977). Towards an understanding of transitions: Defining some boundaries of transition. In J. Adams, J. Hayes, & B. Hopson (Eds.), *Transition: Understanding and managing personal change.* Montclair, NJ: Allenheld & Osmun.

Kivlighan, D. M. (1990). Career group therapy. *The Counseling Psychologist, 18,* 64–79.

Kratz, L. E. (1998). The use of the SIGI PLUS computer-assisted career guidance system as a career counseling intervention. *Dissertation Abstracts International:* Vol. 59 (3-A): 0737.

Krumboltz, J. D., & Baker, R. D. (1973). Behavioral counseling for vocational decision. In H. Borow (Ed.), *Career guidance for a new age* (pp. 235–284). Boston: Houghton Mifflin.

Krumboltz, J. D., & Hamel, D. A. (1977). *Guide to career decision-making skills.* New York: Educational Testing Service.

Lenz, J. G., Reardon, C., & Sampson, J. P. (1993). Holland's theory and effective use of computer-assisted career guidance systems. *Journal of Career Development, 19,* 245–253.

McAllister, S., & Ponterotto, J. G. (1992). A career group program for displaced homemakers. *Journal for Specialists in Group Work, 17,* 29–36.

Miller-Tiedeman, A. L. (1988). *LIFECAREER: The quantum leap into a process of career.* Vista, CA: Lifecareer Foundation.

Miller-Tiedeman, A. L. (1989). *How to NOT make it . . . and succeed: The truth about your LIFECAREER.* Vista, CA: Lifecareer Foundation.

Miller-Tiedeman, A. (1999). *Learning, practicing, and living the new careering.* Philadelphia: Accelerated Development.

Miller-Tiedeman, A. L., & Tiedeman, D. V. (1990). Career decision making: An individualistic perspective. In D. Brown, L. Brooks, & Assoc. (Eds.), *Career choice and development* (2nd ed., pp. 308–377). San Francisco: Jossey-Bass.

Mitchell, L. K., & Krumboltz, J. D. (1990). Social learning approach to career decision making: Krumboltz's theory. In D. Brown, L. Brooks, & Assoc. (Eds.), *Career choice and development* (2nd ed., pp. 308–337). San Francisco: Jossey-Bass.

Myers, I. B., McCaulley, M. H., Quenk, N. L., & Hammer, A. L. (1998). *MBTI Manual: A guide to the development and use of the Myers-Briggs Type Indicator* (3rd ed.). Palo Alto, CA: Consulting Psychologists Press.

Peterson, G. W., Ryan-Jones, R. E., Sampson, J. P., & Reardon, R. C. (1994). A comparison of the effectiveness of three computer-assisted career guidance systems: DISCOVER, SIGI, and SIGI PLUS. *Computers in Human Behavior, 1,* 189–198.

Pope, M. (1999). Applications of group career counseling techniques in Asian cultures. *Journal of Multicultural Counseling and Development, 27,* 18–30.

Reardon, R. C., Lenz, J. G., Sampson, J. P., & Peterson, G. W. (2000). *Career development and planning: A comprehensive approach.* Pacific Grove, CA: Brooks/Cole.

Rife, J. C., & Belcher, J. R. (1994). Assisting unemployed older workers to become reemployed: An experimental evaluation. *Research on Social Work Practice, 4,* 3–13.

Sullivan, K. R., & Mahalik, J. R. (2000). Increasing career self-efficacy for women: Evaluating a group intervention. *Journal of Counseling and Development, 78,* 54–62.

Super, D. E. (1990). A life-span, life-space approach to career development. In D. Brown, L. Brooks, & Assoc. (Eds.), *Career choice and development* (2nd ed., pp. 197–261). San Francisco: Jossey-Bass.

Super, D. E., Bohn, M. J., Forrest, D. J., Jordaan, J. P., Lindeman, R. H., & Thompson, A. S. (1971). *Career Development Inventory.* New York: Teachers College, Columbia University.

Thompson, A. S., & Lindeman, R. H. (1981). *Career Development Inventory: Vol. 1. User's manual.* Palo Alto, CA: Consulting Psychologists Press.

Tiedeman, D. V. & O'Hara, R. P. (1963). *Career development: Choice and adjustment.* New York: College Entrance Examination Board.

Tieger, P. D., & Barron-Tieger, B. (1992). *Do what you are: Discover the perfect career for you through the secrets of personality type.* Boston: Little, Brown.

Yeakley, F. R. (1983). Implications of communication style research for psychological type theory. *Research in Psychological Type, 6,* 5–23.

Zunker, V G. (1998). *Career counseling: Applied concepts of life planning* (5th ed.). Pacific Grove, CA: Brooks/Cole.

Appendix: Tests and Their Publishers

Test or Inventory	Publisher or Distributor
ACT Assessment Program: Academic Tests	American College Testing Program
Adult Career Concerns Inventory	Consulting Psychologists Press
Armed Services Vocational Aptitude Battery	U.S. Military Entrance Processing Command
Assessment of Career Decision Making	Western Psychological Services
California Occupational Preference Survey	Educational and Industrial Testing Service
California Psychological Inventory	Consulting Psychologists Press
Career Beliefs Inventory	Consulting Psychologists Press
Career Decision Scale	Psychological Assessment Resources
Career Development Inventory	Consulting Psychologists Press
Career Thoughts Inventory	Psychological Assessment Resources
Differential Aptitude Tests	Psychological Corporation
General Aptitude Test Battery	U.S. Employment Service

Test or Inventory	Publisher or Distributor
Kuder Career Search	National Career Assessment Services, Inc.
Minnesota Importance Questionnaire	Vocational Psychology Research
Minnesota Job Description Questionnaire	Vocational Psychology Research
Minnesota Multiphasic Personality Inventory	National Computer Systems
Minnesota Satisfaction Questionnaire	Vocational Psychology Research
Minnesota Satisfactoriness Scales	Vocational Psychology Research
Myers-Briggs Type Indicator	Consulting Psychologists Press
Rorschach	Psychological Assessment Resources
Salience Inventory	Consulting Psychologists Press
Scholastic Assessment Test	Educational Testing Service
Self-Directed Search	Psychological Assessment Resources
Sixteen Personality Factor Questionnaire	Institute for Personality and Ability Testing
Strong Interest Inventory	Consulting Psychologists Press
Study of Values	Houghton Mifflin
Thematic Apperception Test	Harvard University Press
Values Scale	Consulting Psychologists Press
Vocational Interest Inventory	Western Psychological Services
Vocational Preference Inventory	Psychological Assessment Resources

PUBLISHERS' ADDRESSES

American College Testing Program, P.O. Box 168, Iowa City, IA 52243

Consulting Psychologists Press, 3803 East Bayshore Road, Palo Alto, CA 94303

Educational and Industrial Testing Service, P.O. Box 7234, San Diego, CA 92107

Educational Testing Service, P.O. Box 6736, Princeton, NJ 08541–6736

Harvard University Press, 79 Garden Street, Cambridge, MA 02138

Houghton Mifflin Company, One Beacon Street, Boston, MA 02108

Institute for Personality and Ability Testing, P.O. Box 188, Champaign, IL 61820–0188

National Career Assessment Services, Inc., 601 Visions Pkwy., P.O. Box 277, Adel, IA 50003

National Computer Systems, P.O. Box 1416, Minneapolis, MN 55440

Psychological Assessment Resources, P.O. Box 998, Odessa, FL 33556

Psychological Corporation, 555 Academic Court, San Antonio, TX 78204–2498

Science Research Associates, 155 North Wacker Drive, Chicago, IL 60606

U.S. Employment Service, Division of Program Planning and Operations, Employment and Training Administration, U.S. Department of Labor, 601 D Street N.W., Washington, DC 20213

U.S. Military Entrance Processing Command, Testing Directorate, 2500 Green Bay Road, North Chicago, IL 60064

Vocational Psychology Research, Department of Psychology, University of Minnesota, 75 East River Road, Minneapolis, MN 55455

Western Psychological Services, 12031 Wilshire Boulevard, Los Angeles, CA 90025

Name Index

Abeles, R. P., 56
Abrego, P. J., 258
Achter, J. A., 86
Ackerman, P. L., 32, 36
Adams, J. D., 152, 160, 252, 253, 258, 259, 263, 264, 268, 269, 271, 273, 452, 456, 457, 468
Adams, G. R., 200, 205
Adams, R. J., 269
Adler, T., 30
Ainsworth, M. D. S., 321, 322
Alderfer, C. P., 270
Almquist, E. M., 344, 366
Alston, R. J., 246
Alvarado, I. Y., 146
Alvi, S. A., 111
Amundson, N. E., 243, 325
Anderson, C. D., 432
Anderson, P. E., 144
Anderson, W. P., Jr., 226
Aniakudo, P., 268
Antal, S., 324
Aquilanti, T. M., 257
Arbona, C., 112, 114, 210
Archambault, D. L., 257
Archer, S. L., 200
Asama, N. E., 109, 115
Ashraf, J., 438
Astin, A. W., 31
Atkinson, D. R., 18, 152, 159, 220, 244, 245, 246, 271, 272, 452, 474
Attah, K., 266
Aubrey, R. F., 26
Aubrey, R. G., 191
Austin, J. T., 114
Axelrad, S., 152, 164, 170, 186, 188, 189, 191, 213, 375, 453
Axelson, J. A., 18, 58
Azrin, N. H., 468

Babbie, E. R., 424
Bain, T., 205
Baird, L. L., 343
Baker, R. D., 345, 476
Bandalos, D. L., 59, 210
Bandura, A., 153, 156, 168, 335, 336, 356, 357, 358, 359
Bardwick, J., 241, 242, 264
Barger, N. J., 141, 145, 146
Barickman, R. B., 269
Barkham, M., 323

Barling, J., 269, 417, 418, 421
Barnett, R. C., 240
Barnsley, J., 429
Barrineau, P., 146
Barron-Tieger, B., 141, 466
Barton, M., 32
Bartram, D. V., 430
Baskin, M. L., 243
Bassett, M. E., 324
Bates, M., 141
Bayley, L. J., 429
Becker, G. S., 427, 431
Bedeian, A. G., 114
Bejian, D. V., 156, 234
Belcher, J. R., 468
Benbow, C. P., 86
Bennion, L., 200, 205
Bents, R., 143
Berenson, B., 8
Berger, G. S., 429, 430
Berlyne, D. E., 163
Beron, K., 429
Besalel, V. A., 468
Betsworth, 57
Betts, J., 266
Betz, E. L., 113, 174
Betz, N. E., 56, 57, 113, 144, 156, 206, 207, 264, 357, 362, 364, 365, 366, 367, 368, 370
Biblarz, T. J., 424
Biehler, R. F., 174
Bieschke, K. J., 207
Bingham, R. P., 369
Bizot, E. B., 82
Black, R. S., 468
Blain, M. D., 87
Blake, R., 109
Blau, G., 143
Blau, P. M., 422
Blehar, M. C., 321, 322
Bloch, D. P., 375, 383, 384, 385, 386, 387, 390, 408, 461
Blumenfeld, P., 57
Blustein, D. L., 154, 180, 322, 323, 324, 330
Bohn, M. J., 187, 194, 455, 463
Bolles, R. N., 467, 468
Borders, L. D., 168
Borgen, F. H., 58, 75, 76, 88, 113, 367
Borow, H., 422, 423, 440
Bowlby, J., 321

Bowman, S. L., 89, 242, 246
Boyd, C. U., 114
Bradley, P., 36
Brammer, L. M., 258
Brand, H., 429
Breeden, S. A., 82
Bregman, G., 325
Brennan, R. T., 240
Bretz, R. D., Jr., 82
Briggs, K. C., 16, 19, 120–150, 181, 452, 454, 455, 456, 457, 459, 466, 467, 468, 469, 473
Broadbent, D. E, 7
Brogan, D. R., 57
Brooks, L., 5, 155, 157, 158, 212, 423
Brown, C., 209, 210
Brown, C. F., 331
Brown, D., 5, 155, 157, 158, 212, 423
Brown, M. T., 321
Brown, S., 205
Brown, S. D., 32, 109, 206, 207, 227, 336, 356, 357, 359, 360, 362, 363, 365, 366, 367
Browne, I., 431, 434, 435, 438, 439
Bruce, R. A., 254
Buboltz, W. C., 201
Buch, K., 257
Buchmann, C., 424
Buck, J. N., 381, 382, 470
Buck, R. W., Jr., 191
Burck, H. D., 344
Burlew, A. K., 270
Butterfield, E. C., 391

Calvert, P. D., 225
Camp, C. C., 109
Campbell, V. L., 28
Card, J. J., 56
Cardoza, D., 210
Carkhuff, R. R., 8
Carlson, C., 323
Carskadon, T. G., 146
Carson, A. D., 32, 146
Casas, E., 146, 368
Case, A. B., 243
Cassidy, J., 321, 322
Castellino, D. R., 424
Champney, T. F., 257

Chan, D. K. S., 267
Chan, W., 267
Chartrand, J. M., 109
Chavous, T. M., 267
Cheatham, H. E., 243, 244
Chipman, S. F., 57, 206
Chodorow, N. J., 330
Christopher, E. K., 323
Chung, Y. B., 243
Church, A. T., 82, 326
Claiborn, C. D., 37
Clinton, President W. J., 180
Cochran, L., 280, 281, 290, 291, 292, 294–301, 302, 303, 304
Cockerill, R., 429
Cohen, L., 254
Cole, N. S., 96
Coles, F. S., 268
Collin, A., 291, 293, 303
Collins, R. C., 57, 112, 113
Collins, S. M., 424
Conneran, J. M., 110
Conoley, C. W., 109
Constantine, M. G., 110
Cook, S. W., 201
Corbiere, M., 202
Cotter, D. A., 435, 436
Coxford, L. M., 468
Cramer, S. H., 114, 180, 465
Crites, J. O., 193, 206, 209, 226
Cron, W. L., 241
Croteau, J. M., 2
Curtis, J., 417, 418

Daiger, D. C., 108
Dail, H., 295
Dalton, D. R., 259
Daniels, K., 254
Daniels, M. H., 381, 382, 470
Darrow, C. N., 239
Davey, F. H., 205
Davidson, S. L., 2
Davidson, J. P., 59
Dawis, R. V., 5, 17, 19, 61, 65, 66, 67, 68, 69, 71, 72, 74, 75, 76, 80, 87, 88, 89, 90, 91, 452, 455, 456, 466, 467, 473, 475
Day, D. V., 113, 117
DeCoster, S., 267
DeFiore, J., 435, 436
DeFour, D. C., 266
DeFruyt, F., 109
Dellinger, K., 267
Demarest, J., 174
Desmarais, S., 417, 418
DeVries, N., 324
Diamond, E. E., 57, 178
Dohm, T. E., 75
Dollinger, S., 168
Dolliver, R., 289
Domanski, H., 425
Dover, C., 324
Downs, F. S., 4
Drasgow, F., 268
Duncan, K. C., 428, 429
Duncan, O. D., 422
Durant, C., 175

Eby, L. T., 257
Eccles, J. S., 57, 432
Edwards, J. M., 257
Eftekhari-Sanjoni, E., 86
Egan, G., 8, 9
Eggerth, D. E., 87
Eichorn, D., 420
Eisenberg, A. I., 240
Elmslie, S., 175
England, P., 65, 429, 431, 432
Epperson, D. L., 56, 367
Erickson, D. B., 147
Erickson, E. H., 110, 166, 167, 179, 186, 187, 199, 200, 202, 213, 239, 375, 452, 455
Escriva, A., 430
Estes, S. B., 267
Evans, K. M., 246

Farh, J., 114
Farkas, J., 429, 431, 432
Farmer, H. S., 240
Farr, J. M., 40, 41
Farrow, B., 205, 227, 243, 244
Fassinger, R. E., 59, 207, 243
Fawcett, J., 4
Feldman, D. C., 257
Felsman, D. E., 323
Fenema, E., 56
Fenner, B., 191
Ferrero, G. W., 205
Finkelberg, S. L., 180
Fischer, A. R., 109
Fisher, T. J., 344
Fitzgerald, L. F., 5, 56, 57, 89, 174, 206, 264, 266, 267, 268, 321
Fleming, E. S., 240
Flint, P. L., 80
Flora, J. L., 428
Ford-Richards, J. M., 113
Forrest, D. J., 187, 194, 455, 463
Forster, J. R., 291
Foster, V., 264
Fottler, M. D., 205
Fouad, N. A., 57, 112, 113, 209, 367
Frautsh, N., 168
Fredrickson, R. H., 422
Freud, S., 307
Fritzsche, B. A., 101, 112, 113
Frone, M. R., 418
Frost, F., 178
Fukuyama, M. A., 383
Fuller, B. E., 255
Fuqua, D., 59
Furnham, A., 144

Gade, E. M., 59
Gaier, E. L., 206
Gainor, K. A., 368
Galinsky, E., 240
Gallivan, M. J., 80
Ganzeboom, H. B. G., 425
Garden, A., 144
Garet, M. S., 419
Gay, E. G., 89
Gerson, R., 326

Gerstein, L. H., 243
Gilbert, L. A., 2, 239
Ginsburg, S. W., 152, 164, 170, 186, 188, 189, 191, 213, 375, 453
Ginzberg, E., 152, 164, 170, 186, 188, 189, 191, 213, 375, 453
Giuffre, P. A., 267
Glassman, R. B., 7
Gold, J. M., 2
Gold, Y., 267
Goldenberg, H., 326, 330
Goldenberg, I., 326, 330
Goldenson, R. M., 28
Goldman, S. H., 82
Gomez, M., 59
Goodnough, G., 225, 226
Gordon, J., 7
Gordon, V. Z., 326
Gore, R. A., Jr., 109
Gottfredson, G. D., 101, 112
Gottfredson, L. S., 26, 59, 95, 110, 152, 159, 162, 173–178, 179, 181, 182, 307, 425, 436, 452, 453, 473
Gough, H., 36, 143
Gowan, M., 59, 243
Greenberger, E., 427
Greene, C. K., 432
Gribbons, W. D., 226
Griffith, J., 200
Grant, W. T., 180
Groat, M., 323
Grove, W. M., 381
Gustafson, S. A., 89
Gutek, B. A., 267, 268, 269

Haagestad, E. D., 32, 36
Hackbarth, J., 225
Hackett, G., 32, 57, 59, 206, 207, 210, 336, 356, 357, 359, 360, 362, 366, 367, 368, 370
Hales, L. W., 191
Halford, G. S., 7
Hall, A. S., 175, 206
Hall, D. T., 254
Hallett, M. B., 239
Hamel, D. A., 466
Hammer, A. L., 121, 124, 130, 131, 132, 134, 135, 136, 137, 139, 141, 142, 143, 145, 147, 148, 473
Hanisch, K. A., 237
Hankinson, G. L., 110
Hansen, J.-I. C., 57, 109, 112, 113
Hansen, L. S. (Sunny), 452, 460, 461, 462, 475
Hanson, W. E., 37
Hanzel, J., 4
Hardy, E. G., 323
Harmon, L. W., 113, 175, 243, 367
Harmon, V., 32
Harold, R. D., 57
Harren, V. A., 381
Hartman, B. W., 110
Hartung, P. J., 205, 207, 226, 227, 243, 244

Harvey, R. J., 144
Hassan, S., 330
Haverkamp, B. E., 113
Hayes, I., 259
Healy, C. C., 132, 144
Healy, P., 330
Heilman, M. E., 206
Heinen, J. R., 4
Helms, J. E., 58
Helwig, A. A., 174, 175
Hendel, D. D., 89
Henderson, S., 175
Hendrickx, J., 425
Henley, G. A., 67, 68
Hennis, M., 180
Heppner, M. J., 255
Herma, J., 152, 164, 170, 186, 188, 189, 191, 213, 375, 453
Herman, A., 191
Hermsen, J. M., 435, 436
Herr, E. L., 154, 156, 180, 205, 246, 465
Hershberger, P. J., 257
Hesketh, B., 89, 175
Hess, S., 366
Heyman, C., 420
Higgenbotham, E., 439
Hill, C. E., 366
Hill, C. T., 240
Hill, R., 252
Hirsch, S. K., 141
Hoeglund, T. J., 109
Hogan, R., 109
Holland, C. L., 143
Holland, J. L., 14, 16, 19, 39, 41, 61, 94–116, 181, 283, 366–367, 452, 453, 454, 455, 456, 457, 458, 463, 464, 466, 467, 468, 469, 471, 472, 473, 475
Hollinger, C. L., 240
Holmberg, K., 101, 110
Hopke, W. E., 15
Hoppock, R., 15
Hopson, B., 19, 152, 160, 252, 253, 258, 259, 263, 264, 268, 269, 271, 273, 452, 456, 457, 468
Hosford, R. E., 344
Hoshmand, L. L. S., 287
Hossler, D., 424
Hotchkiss, L., 422, 423, 440
Hughes, D. L., 240
Hughes, M. A., 168, 174, 189
Hughey, K. F., 115
Huh, K., 200, 205
Hummel, R. C., 193, 226
Hunt, E. B., 391
Huntley, H. L., 383
Hurlburt, G., 59
Hurley, R. B., 344
Hurwitz, R. E., 206

Imada, S., 424
Imhoff, A. R., 239
Impara, J. C., 27
Inhelder, B., 187

Isabella, L., 241
Ivey, A. E., 8
Ivey, D., 58, 113
Ivey, M. B., 8

Jackson, C. C., 246
Jackson, C. R. S., 75
Jacobs, J. A., 435
Jenson, W. R., 206
Jepsen, D. A., 291, 326, 381
Jingeleski, J., 175
Jobin-Davis, K., 180
Johnson, J., 243
Johnson, J. C., 270
Johnson, P., 201
Johnson, R. G., 345
Johnson, T. G., 428
Johnston, J. A., 115, 255
Jones, G. B., 338, 345
Jones, R. M., 368
Jordaan, J. P., 154, 163, 164, 165, 187, 194, 195, 455, 463
Joyner, J. W., 144
Juarez, R., 59
Judge, T. A., 82
Jung, C. G., 19, 120, 121, 122, 127, 144, 153
Juntunen, C. L., 180

Kahn, J. H., 367
Kaldor, W., 175
Kanomata, N., 425
Kanungo, R. M., 220
Kapes, J. T., 28, 191
Kaplan, A., 113, 367
Karesh, D., 143
Katz, L., 144
Kaufman, A. S., 113
Kaufman, R. L., 436
Kehle, T. J., 206
Keirsey, D., 141
Kelloway, E. K., 417, 421
Kelly, G. A., 156, 279, 280, 281, 304
Kelly, K. R., 175, 206
Kelly, T. J., 209
Kennelly, I., 439
Kenny, B., 430
Kerr, B., 37, 56
Ketterson, T. U., 323
Khazzoom, A., 424
Khmelko, V., 420
Kidd, J. M., 164, 226
Kilbourne, B. S., 429
Killen, M., 325
Kirby, L. K., 141, 145, 146
Kirchner, E. P., 178
Kirkland, K., 168
Kivlighan, D. M., 465
Klein, E. B., 239
Klos, D., 308, 309, 312, 313, 320
Knapp, L., 314
Knapp, R. R., 314
Knasel, E. G., 226
Koenigsberg, J., 419
Kohn, M. L., 419, 420, 422
Komarraju, M., 114
Kortenhaus, C. M., 174

Koss, M. P., 268, 269
Kowalewski, B. M., 435, 436
Krahn, H., 419
Krantz, D. H., 57, 206
Kratz, L. E., 464, 465
Krumboltz, J. D., 2, 19, 180, 277, 335, 336–356, 357, 364, 365, 366, 368, 369, 370, 436, 452, 455, 456, 457, 459, 462, 466, 467, 470, 473, 476
Kruse, S. J., 255
Krymkowski, D. H., 425
Kuder, G. F., 309
Kummerow, J. M., 141
Kutner, N. G., 57
Kuvlesky, W. P., 59
Kyle, M. T., 180

Laband, D. N., 267
Lackman, J. L., 391
Lackman, R., 391
Ladany, N., 110
Lai, G., 424
Lapan, R. T., 175, 176
Laribee, S. F., 145
Larkin, K. C., 357
Latona, J. R., 109
Lattimore, R. R., 58
Lau, S., 59
Lauver, P. J., 368
LaVite, C. M., 266
Law, K., 114
Lawson, L., 67, 71, 80
Leana, C. R., 257
Lease, S. H., 57
Lee, C., 303
Lee, R. M., 237
Leibowitz, Z. B., 256
Leicht, K. T., 434
Leman, N., 31
Lent, R. W., 32, 57, 206, 207, 336, 356, 357, 359, 360, 362, 363, 365, 366, 367, 368
Lentz, B. F., 267
Lenz, J. G., 107, 111, 115, 116, 391, 395, 396, 398, 399, 400, 401, 403, 404, 407, 408, 464, 466
Leong, F. T. L., 59, 114, 205, 210, 227, 243, 244
Lerner, J. V., 424
Lerner, R. M., 424
Leroux, J., 257
Leung, S. A., 58, 109, 110, 113, 175
Leung, S. Y., 424
Levin, A. S., 343, 349, 350, 351, 366
Levine, P. B., 435
Levinson, D. J., 239
Levinson, M. H., 239
Lewis, D. M., 226
Li, J. H., 424
Lightbody, P., 241
Like, K., 366
Lin, J. G., 422
Lin, N., 424

Lindeman, R. H., 187, 191, 194, 195, 226, 227, 231, 237, 455, 463
Lindenberg, K. E., 268, 269
Linn, S. G., 243
Linnehan, F., 143
Lippert, L., 241
Lips, H. M., 58
Liptak, J. J., 221, 222
Lisi, K., 323
Lissack, M., 254
Little, D. M., 366
Little Soldier, L., 146
Lloyd, S., 424
Lock, R. D., 41
Loehr-Lapan, S. J., 175
Lofquist, L. H., 17, 19, 61, 65, 66, 67, 68, 69, 71, 72, 74, 75, 76, 80, 87, 88, 89, 90, 91, 452, 455, 456, 466, 467, 473, 475
Lohnes, P. R., 226
Looft, W. R., 174
Lopez, F. G., 207
Lorr, M., 144
Loughlin, C., 418
Louis, M., 254, 255
Love, R., 110
Lowe, G. S., 419
Lubinski, D., 86
Lucas, C., 322
Lucas, M. S., 2
Ludden, L., 40, 41
Lum, J. L., 321
Lundberg, D. J., 146, 210
Lunneborg, P. W., 308, 309, 314, 317, 321, 330
Luzzo, D. A., 57, 206, 365

MacDaid, G. P., 145
MacDonald, D. A., 144
MacGregor, J. N., 7
Mach, B. W., 420
MacKay, W. R., 174
Magee, C., 419
Magley, V. J., 268
Mahalik, J. R., 465
Maia, J., 207
Mainquist, S., 420
Malen, E. A., 257
Mallon, M., 254
Mangin, P., 40, 41
Mansfield, R., 343
Marcia, J. E., 187, 199, 200, 202
Maresh, S., 56
Marini, M. M., 424
Markham, S. E., 144
Marko, K. W., 170
Marlow, D. B., 143
Marshall, N. L., 240
Martin, R. P, 58
Maslow, A. H., 153, 308, 315–316, 318–319
Mastie, M. M., 28
Mathay, G., 225
Matlin, N. A., 16, 154, 204
Matteson, D. R., 200
Matthes, G. E., 324

Maximovich, T. M., 80
Mayo, E., 26
McAllister, S., 465
McCaulley, M. H., 121, 124, 130, 131, 132, 133, 134, 135, 136, 137, 139, 141, 142, 143, 144, 145, 147, 148, 473
McClellan, N. C., 168, 174, 189
McCollum, V. J. C., 243
McCormick, R. M., 243
McCowan, C. J., 246
McDougall, D., 468
McGoldrick, J., 326
McKenna, A. E., 205
McKye, B., 239
McLean, J. E., 113
McWhirter, E. H., 59, 210, 264, 271
Mecca, S. J., 267
Meir, E. I., 308, 309, 312, 313, 314
Melchiori, L. G., 82
Meldahl, J. M., 57
Melincoff, D. S., 110
Mervielde, I., 109
Miller, C. A., 174
Miller, G. A., 7
Miller, J., 169, 178, 179, 191
Miller, S. R., 418
Miller-Tiedeman, A. L., 375, 383, 384, 387, 390, 391, 392, 407, 408, 456, 460, 461
Millon, 113
Miner, C. U., 146, 205, 210
Minor, C. W., 240
Mirvis, P. H., 254
Mitchell, A. M., 338
Mitchell, K. E., 343, 349, 350, 351, 366
Mitchell, L. K., 337, 343, 344, 346, 348, 349, 365, 366, 368, 455, 470
Moen, P., 237
Moos, R. H., 252, 256
Morgan, B., 264
Morgan, S. L., 425
Morten, G., 18, 159, 220, 244, 245, 246, 271, 272, 452, 474
Morton, K. R., 152, 237
Moser, H. P., 193, 226
Muchinsky, P. M., 57
Mueller, C. W., 267
Mulatu, M. S., 420
Mullet, E., 175
Multon, K. D., 207, 255, 366
Munley, P. H., 200
Murphy, L. L., 27
Murray, J. B., 144
Murray, W. D., 144
Mwachofi, A., 428
Myers, I. B., 16, 19, 120–150, 181, 452, 454, 455, 456, 457, 459, 466, 467, 468, 469, 473
Myers, K. D., 130, 133, 142
Myers, P. B., 130, 133, 142
Myers, R. A., 195
Myors, B., 87

Naidoo, A. V., 242
Nakata, Y. F., 427, 428
Nauta, M. M., 56, 367
Neimeyer, G. J., 283, 284, 285, 286, 287, 288, 289, 291, 301, 302
Neimeyer, R. A., 279
Nelson, R. C., 169
Nevill, D. D., 156, 157, 204, 219, 220, 223, 225, 241, 283
Neville, H. A., 246
Newell, A., 391
Nichols, C. N., 201
Nieberding, R., 28
Niles, S. G., 115, 205, 225, 226, 227, 243, 244
Norris, D. S., 37
Novy, D. M., 210
Nuby, J. F., 146

O'Brien, K. M., 207, 323
O'Donohue, W., 266
O'Hara, R. P., 191, 283, 375, 376, 377, 380, 381, 382, 406, 469, 470
O'Hare, E. A., 266
Oates, G., 420
Odom, C., 168, 189
Odom, K. W., 174
Ogbu, J., 440
Okiishi, R. W., 326
Okocha, A. A. G., 326
Okun, B. F., 8
Oliver, L. W., 343
Olson, L., 180
Orlofsky, J., 200
Ormerod, A. J., 264, 266, 267, 268
Ornstein, S., 241
Osborn, D. B., 146
Osborn, T. N., 146
Osborne, W. L., 146, 205, 210, 227
Osipow, S. H., 5, 109, 308, 314, 321, 343
Osterman, P., 419, 421, 430, 439
Overstreet, P. L., 193, 226
Oxford, R. L., 146
Ozone, S. J., 113

Palladino Schultheiss, D. P., 322, 330
Pallone, N. J., 344
Pallone, M. A., 266, 269
Paproski, D. L., 324
Parmer, T., 210
Parsons, F., 25, 26, 27, 67
Paseluikho, M. A., 324
Patterson, L. E., 8
Pazy, A., 109
Penick, N. I., 326
Penner, K., 325
Peplau, L. A., 240
Perosa, L. M., 258
Perosa, S. L., 258
Perron, J., 202

Peterson, A. C., 144
Peterson, C. C., 226, 237
Peterson, G. W., 375, 391, 392, 395, 396, 398, 399, 400, 401, 403, 404, 407, 408, 464, 466
Peterson, J. H., Jr., 59
Philips, S., 7
Phillips, S. D., 180, 239, 323
Phillips, W. E., 257
Piaget, J., 166, 167, 179, 182, 187, 213
Pieper, W. A., 143
Piore, M. J., 429, 430, 439
Piper, R. E., 58
Pirog, M. A., 419
Pittenger, D. J., 144
Plake, B. S., 27
Plater, M. A., 266
Podobnik, B., 420
Polaine, V. H., 257
Ponterotto, J. G., 465
Pope, M., 205, 227, 243, 244, 465
Popma, J., 365
Posey, A. M., 146
Post, A., 324
Post, P., 368
Powell, A. B., 101, 112, 113
Powell, D. F., 206
Power, P. G., 108
Powers, R. L., 200
Prezioso, M. S., 322, 330
Prince, R. A., 144
Probert, B., 283
Prosser, J., 243
Provost, J. A., 141
Prus, M. J., 428, 429
Pryor, J. B., 266
Pryor, R., 175
Psacharopoulos, G., 427
Puffer, K. A., 322
Pusateri, M. L. R., 110

Quenk, N. L., 121, 124, 130, 131, 132, 134, 135, 136, 137, 139, 141, 143, 145, 147, 148, 473
Quick, H. E., 237

Raftery, A. E., 424
Rainey, L. M., 168
Rasheed, S., 264, 271
Raudenbush, S. W., 240
Rayburn, C. A., 383
Read, B. K., 57
Reardon, R. C., 107, 111, 115, 116, 344, 391, 395, 396, 398, 399, 400, 401, 403, 404, 407, 408, 464, 466
Rees, A. M., 113
Reese, L. A., 268, 269
Reitzle, M., 201, 202
Resnikoff, A., 320
Rich, N. S., 168
Richards, J. M., Jr., 95, 96
Richardson, E. H., 59
Richardson, V. E., 327
Richie, B. S., 243

Richmond, L. J., 375, 383, 384, 385, 386, 387, 390, 408, 461
Rickard, F. S., 344
Rife, J. C., 468
Riverin-Simard, D., 234
Roach, A. J., 366
Roarke, A. E., 180
Robbins, S. B., 237
Robert, S., 59
Roberts, M., 168
Robinson, S., 243
Robison-Awana, P., 206
Robitschek, C., 201
Rocha-Singh, I., 368
Rodriguez, J., Jr., 59
Rodriguez, M. A., 59
Rodriguez, M-L, 207
Roe, A., 19, 277, 283, 307, 308–321, 322, 323, 325, 327, 329, 330, 331, 452, 471, 472
Rogers, C., 8, 26
Rojewski, J. W., 205, 209
Roos, J., 254
Rosen, D., 101, 110
Rosenbaum, J. E., 418, 419, 420, 421, 422
Rounds, J. B., 67, 68, 72, 89, 113, 309, 312
Rowe, R., 434
Rubin, A., 267, 308, 314
Rudisill, J. R., 257
Ryan-Jones, R. E., 464
Rytting, M., 144

Sable, C. F., 429
Sackett, S. J., 316
Salomone, P. R., 156, 234
Salvendy, G., 7
Sampson, J. P., Jr., 391, 395, 396, 398, 399, 400, 401, 403, 404, 407, 408, 464, 466
Sandy, J. G., 428
Sanford, E. E., 191, 209
Sankey, A. M., 324
Sastre, M. T. M., 175
Saunders, D., 145
Saunders, D. E., 403, 404, 407
Savickas, M. L., 154, 170, 200, 234, 280, 281, 282, 293, 382
Sawilowsky, S. S., 240
Scanlon, C. R., 2
Schaefer, I. A., 252
Schaefers, K. G., 56, 367
Scheel, M. J., 109
Schlossberg, N. K., 253, 256
Schmidt, D. B., 86
Schmidt, F. L., 26
Schmitt-Rodermund, E., 201
Schneider, P. L., 58
Schonegevel, C., 114
Schooler, C., 419, 420
Schroeder, W. W., 343
Schultheiss, D. P., 322, 330
Scott, D. J., 326
Scott, K. P., 174
Scott, S. G., 254

Seaman, N., 144
Sears, S., 3
Sekaran, U., 114
Serifica, F. C., 210
Sewell, T. E., 58
Sharda, B. D., 427
Sharf, R. S., 15, 321, 330
Shaver, P. R., 321, 322
Shelton, J. N., 267
Shen, Y. C., 240
Sheppard, L. E., 345
Sherman, J. A., 56
Shu, X., 424
Shullman, S. L., 266
Shultz, K. S., 237
Siann, G., 241
Siegelman, M., 315, 319
Silbereisen, R. K., 201, 202
Silva, M. C., 207
Silver, A., 57
Silver, R., 206
Simmons, G., 146
Simon, H. A., 7, 391
Sinacore, A. L., 330
Skinner, C., 439
Skorikov, V. B., 201, 202
Slaney, R. B., 178
Slocum, J. W., Jr., 241
Smart, R. M., 226, 237
Smith, E. J., 440
Smith, P. L., 113, 367, 368
Smith, T. L., 181
Snizek, W. E., 434
Snow, R. E., 4
Soeprapto, E., 366
Solberg, V. S., 366
Sonnenberg, R. T., 109
Sonnenfeld, J. A., 425
Sparrow, P. R., 254
Spencer, B. F., 59
Spokane, A. R., 2
Stage, F. K., 424
Stalikas, A., 146
Stallman, J. I., 428
Starishevsky, R., 16, 154, 204
Staton, A. R., 206
Stead, G. B., 114
Steel, L., 56
Steinberg, L. D., 427
Stern, D., 427, 428
Sternberg, R. J., 392
Stewart, A. E., 279
Stewart, A. J., 241
Stewart, M. A., 368
Stitt-Gohdes, W. L., 432
Stockdale, M. S., 266
Stoller, L. M., 266
Stoltz-Loike, M., 383
Stoppard, J. M., 205
Strickler, R. T., 191
Stroh, L. K., 257
Strong, E. K., Jr., 309
Subich, L. M., 2, 109
Sue, D. W., 18, 59, 152, 159, 220, 244, 245, 246, 271, 272, 452, 474
Sullivan, K. R., 465
Sullivan, S. E., 254

Super, D. E., 14, 15, 16, 19, 151,
    152, 153–160, 162, 163–173,
    176–178, 179, 180, 182, 186,
    187, 190, 191, 193, 194, 195,
    197, 200, 203, 204, 205, 207,
    208, 209, 210, 211, 212, 213,
    219, 220, 223, 224, 225, 226,
    227, 231, 235, 236, 237, 239,
    241, 242, 243, 244, 246, 252,
    254, 257, 261, 262, 264, 265,
    273, 283, 284, 375, 385, 428,
    436, 452, 453, 454, 455, 456,
    459, 461, 463, 464, 466, 467,
    468, 470
Suzuki, L., 58, 113
Swaney, K., 113
Swanson, J. L., 57, 109, 112,
    113, 367

Tait, L., 241
Tan, G. Y., 257
Tang, C. S. K., 267
Tang, M., 113
Tanner, J., 429
Taveira, M.-D.-0C., 207
Taylor, F., 26
Taylor, K. M., 365
Temple, R., 308, 314
Tharenou, P., 419, 420
Thelen, M., 168
Thiel, M. J., 2
Thomas, D. A., 270
Thomas, R. E., 266
Thomas, R. M., 171
Thompson, A. S., 187, 191, 194,
    195, 226, 227, 231, 237, 455,
    463
Thompson, C. E., 59
Thompson, J. M., 87
Thoresen, C. E., 343, 344
Thorne, A., 143
Thorne, B. M., 146
Tiedeman, D. V., 191, 277, 283,
    284, 375–382, 384, 391, 405,
    406, 407, 408, 452, 454, 455,
    456, 460, 466, 469, 470, 473
Tieger, P. D., 141, 466
Tienda, M., 438, 439
Tierney, R. J., 191
Till, F., 266
Tillapaugh, P., 168
Tinsley, H. E. A., 5, 75, 76, 88
Tischler, L., 143, 144
Tokar, D. M., 109
Tomaskovic-Devey, D., 427,
    432

Torres, D., 264, 271
Touradji, P., 366
Tracey, T. J., 58, 309, 312
Tremblay, C., 202
Trevine, M., 243
Trevino, M., 59
Trice, A. D., 168, 174, 189
Truax, C. B., 8
Tsagarakis, C. I., 144
Tsu, V., 256
Tsuhako, K., 468
Tuel, B. D., 144
Tuffin, K., 175
Tupper, T. W., 176
Twillman, B., 146
Tyler, L., 289
Tyson, T. S., 323

Umstot, M. E., 174
Utsey, S. O., 439

Valach, L., 291, 293, 303, 324
Van Buren, J. B., 175, 206
Van de Water, E. A., 241
Vandiver, B. J., 205, 227, 243,
    244
Vanneman, R., 435, 436
Velez, E., 427
Vermeulen, M. E., 240
Vincent, P. C., 240
Vondracek, F. W., 110, 152, 199,
    200, 201, 202, 211, 244, 455,
    462, 474
Vondracek, S. J., 178
vonEye, A., 424
Voyle, K., 321
Vygotsky, L. S., 166, 167

Waas, G. A., 289
Wachter, M. L., 427
Waight, J., 424
Wall, S., 321, 322
Walsh, D., 241
Walsh, D. J., 227
Walsh, W. B., 109
Wan, T. T. H., 237
Ward, C. M., 369
Ware, R., 144
Warnath, C. F., 193, 226
Watanabe, N., 58
Waterman, A. S., 200
Waters, E., 321, 322
Watkins, C. E., Jr., 28
Watson, J., 114
Watts, A. G., 164
Weathers, P. L., 59

Weber, L., 439
Weckerle, J. R., 237
Weir, D., 429
Weiss, D. J., 65, 67, 68, 75, 76,
    88, 89
Weiss, K. I., 368
Welfel, R. E., 8
Welsh, S., 266, 267
Werner, E. E., 419, 440
Westbrook, B. W., 191, 209
Whitbourne, S. K., 200
White, M. A., 206
White, R. W., 375
Whiteley, J. H., 320
Whitfield, E. A., 28
Whitney, D. R., 96
Wickelgren, W. A., 7
Wierschke, A., 143
Wigfield, A., 57
Williams, A. P., 429
Williams, C. L., 267
Williams, C. P., 234
Williams, D. R., 438
Williams, E. N., 366
Williamson, E. G., 26
Wilson, A. B., 424
Wilson, D. M., 206
Wilson, F. D., 438, 439
Wilson, V. M., 314
Wilson, W. H., 7
Wimbush, J. C., 254
Windham, G. O., 59
Witkowski, K. M., 434
Woitke, M. B., 367
Wong, A. K., 59
Woods, K., 168, 174, 189
Woodward, G. A., 144
Worthington, R. L., 180
Wotjkiewicz, R. A., 424
Wu, L., 438, 439
Wynne, D. C., 191

Xing, S., 422

Ye, N., 7
Yeakley, F. R., 147, 475
Yoder, J. D., 268
Young, R. A., 291, 293, 303, 324,
    325
Yu, J., 111

Zaborowski, W., 420
Zimmerman, D., 435
Zin, R., 109
Zunker, V. G., 37, 465
Zuschlag, M. K., 200

Subject Index

Ability
definition, 67
General Aptitude Test Battery
measured, 68
matching values and
reinforcers with, 77–82
patterns, 75, 76–77, 83
self-observation
generalizations about, 341,
349, 369
test definition, 28
tests, 67
utilization, 76, 223
work adjustment theory, 66,
67–68, 77–82
Ability Profile, 68
Absenteeism, 66
Abstract thinking, 173, 187, 190
Academic achievement
measurement, 30, 31
Acceptance of child, 318, 319
Achievement(s)
definition, 30
Marcia, 200, 210
Minnesota Job Description
Questionnaire, 76
occupational information,
204
quantitatively measuring, 31
Super, 223
testing role and, 205
tests available for different
kinds of work, 31
trait and factor theory, 28,
30–31
types of, 30
Vondracek, 201
work adjustment theory, 69,
70
Achievement Scale, 80
ACT Assessment Program:
Academic Test, 28, 29, 30,
341
Action plan, DECIDES, 466
Activeness, 77, 80
Actuarial counseling, 26
Adjusting to a choice, stage,
376, 380–381
Adjusting to job, counseling for,
82–84
Adjustment problems, work
adjustment theory, 67,
82–84

Adjustment style, 67, 77, 80
Adolescence
abstract thinking, 187, 190
capacities development, 188,
189–190
and career decision-making
theories, 196
career development, 186–218
career maturity, 193–199
combination of theories, 453,
455
context, 199–203
counseling example, 192–193
counselor issues, 213
culturally diverse
backgrounds, 209–213
employment, 417–419
factors influencing career
development, 187–188
gender issues, 205–209
Ginzberg's tentative stage of
career development,
188–193
identity issues, 187, 199–203
interests, 188, 189
occupational information,
196–197, 203–204
realism, 197
role confusion, 187
Super's and Ginzberg's stages
comparison, 191–192
testing, 204–205
transition period, 188, 190
values, 188, 190
work, 196
Adult Career Concerns
Inventory (ACCI), 205, 226,
227, 232, 237, 459, 470
Adult career crises and
transitions, 252–276
Adult development, 219–251
combined theories, 455–457
counselor issues, 246–247
disengagement, 236–237
establishment, 230–234
exploration, 226–230
life roles, 220–222
maintenance, 234–236
recycling, 237–239
role salience, 220–225
summary, 247
women, 239–242

Adults and combined theories,
455–457
Advancement, 76
Advancing, 219, 231
Aesthetics (Super), 223
African American. *See*
Culturally diverse
populations
Africentrism, 243, 244
Agent in narrative counseling,
291, 292
Agreeableness, 109
Alternatives, generating, 341
Altruism
Super, 223
valuing, 61
work adjustment theory, 69,
70, 90
American College Testing (ACT)
Assessment Program:
Academic Test, 28, 29
Analysis phase, 397, 398–399
Anecdotes, 295–296
Antecedents, 340
Anticipated transitions, 253,
254
Anticipating a choice, 376–379
Anxious-ambivalent pattern,
322, 323
Aptitude
abilities and, 67
tests, 28–30, 31
Armed Services Vocational
Aptitude Battery (ASVAB),
28, 29, 30, 52, 458
Army General Classification
Test (AGCT), 26
Artistic, 98
Arts and entertainment (Roe),
309, 310, 311, 312, 313
Asian Americans. *See* Culturally
diverse populations
Assessment of Career Decision-
Making Scale, 381, 382,
406, 470
Assessment of traits, 25–26
Associative learning, 340, 342
Attachment theory, 321–324,
327
Attending skills, 9, 166
Attitudes, Roe's theory, 317
Attitudes toward work, 196

Authority
  Minnesota Job Description
    Questionnaire, 76
  parental, 326
  Super, 225
  work adjustment theory, 70
Autobiographies, 296–297
Autonomy
  Super, 223
  work adjustment theory, 69, 71
Auxiliary process, 131–132
Avoidance of child, 318
Avoidance pattern, 322

Balance and spirituality, 385
Ball Aptitude Battery, 32
Basic Interests Scales (SII) of
    Strong Interest Inventory,
    32, 33
Basic skills, 41
Beauty, need for, 316
Behavioral strategies for
    counseling, 343–346
  cognitive, 257
  reinforcement, 343–344
  role models, 344–345
  role playing, 345
  simulation, 345–346
Beliefs, counter troublesome,
    347
Belongingness, need for, 315
Biographical information form
    work adjustment theory,
    87
BORN FREE, 461
Boundaryless career, 254, 350
Business contact (Roe), 309, 310,
    311, 312, 313

C Index, 77
California Occupational
    Preference Survey (COPS),
    32, 33, 314, 458, 472
California Psychological
    Inventory (CPI), 28, 35, 36,
    458
Calling and spirituality, 386
Capacities stage, 188, 189–190,
    191, 192
Card sorts, 289–291
Career Attitudes and Strategic
    Inventory (CASI), 111–112
Career definition, 3
Career Beliefs Inventory, 356,
    459, 470
Career change stages, 237
Career choice
  definition, 3
  steps in, 394
Career counseling
  adjustment example, 139–142
  decision-making example,
    134, 135, 136, 137–139,
    403
  genograms usage, 326–327,
    328
  goals, 16–17, 108

group, 465–467
narrative, 293–301
occupational information,
    179
personal nature of, 2
placement, 467–469
related issue, 467
sessions purpose, major,
    103
social learning theory,
    349–356
special issues, 465–469
spiritual approach, 387–391
Career crises and transitions,
    252–276
Career Decision Making, 194,
    196, 197, 204, 210, 212,
    222
Career Decision-Making Self-
    Efficacy Scale, 365
Career decision–making
    theories, 374–410
  and adolescents, 196
  and childhood, 453
  classification of occupations,
    472
  combined, 457, 460
  counselor issues, 476
  culturally diverse populations,
    474
  example, 134, 135, 136,
    137–139
  and group counseling, 466
  job search strategies, 469
  testing, 469, 470, 472
  theories and life-span theory,
    453–457
  trait and factor theory,
    453–457
  women, 473
Career determinants archway
    figure (Super), 155
Career development
  adolescent, 186–218
  childhood, 162–185
  children from culturally
    diverse backgrounds,
    178–179
  late adolescent and adult,
    219–251
Career Development
    Assessment and Counseling
    model (CDAC), 205, 227,
    243, 244
Career Development Inventory,
    14–15, 186–187, 194, 195,
    196, 197, 198, 199, 203, 204,
    205, 207, 208, 210, 222, 455,
    459, 463, 470
Career Development Quarterly,
    39, 108, 180
Career development theory(ies),
    3, 4
  chunking, 7–8
  client population, 6
  counselor's use of, 5–8
  evaluating, 4–5

occupational classification
    systems, 470–472
  relating of, 16
  tests, 469
Career education. *See*
    School-to-work
Career Exploration, 194,
    195–196, 197, 204
Career maturity, 154, 193–199
  components, 193
  counseling usage, 198–199
  culturally diverse adolescents,
    209–210
  Super's conception of,
    194–198
Career Maturity Inventory, 206,
    209
Career Occupational Preference
    System Interest Inventory,
    28, 35, 458
Career Orientation Total, 194,
    197–198
Career Pattern Study, 193,
    226
Career patterns, women, 239
Career Planning, 194, 195, 197,
    203
Career self-efficacy theory. *See*
    Self-efficacy theory
Career Thoughts Inventory,
    403–404, 406, 459, 470
Career Transitions Inventory,
    255
Casual acceptance, 318
CASVE. *See* Cognitive
    information processing
    skills
Celerity, 71, 74
Center for the Application of
    Psychological Type, 121
Change and spirituality,
    384–385
Changing work settings, 467
Child development, 162–185
  counseling issues, 171–173,
    182
  culturally diverse
    backgrounds, 178–179
  curiosity, 163, 164–165
  exploration, 165–166
  exposure to occupations, 1
  gender-role stereotyping and
    Gottfredsons' theory,
    173–178
  information, 166–168
  interests, 169–170
  internal versus external
    control, 169
  key figures, 168
  occupational information role,
    179–181
  planfulness, 170–171
  self-concept, 170–171
  summary, 182
  Super's model, 163–173
  testing role, 181
  time perspective, 170

Childhood and career decision-making theories, 453
Children's Personality Questionnaire, 181
Choice stage, 378–379, 381
Choosing a Vocation, 25
Chronic hassles, 253
Chunking, 7–8, 33, 122
Circumscription, 174–175
Clarification, 379, 381
Classical conditioning, 340
Classification systems, 39–47, 48–51
   Dictionary of Occupational Titles (DOT), 40, 41, 42–43, 46, 471, 472
   Guide for Occupational Exploration (GOE), 47, 48, 471
   Holland, 39, 41, 471
   O*NET, 40, 41, 44–46, 472
   Roe, 471
   Standard Occupational Classification Manual (SOC), 47, 49–51
Clerical ability, 68, 89
Client cognitive and behavioral skills, 341–343
Client population, 6
Closed-ended questions, 9
Cochran's narrative career counseling, 294–301
   changing life structures, 299–300
   composing life history, 296–297
   crystallizing a decision, 300–301
   elaborating career problem, 294–296
   eliciting future narrative, 297–298
   enacting a role, 300
   reality construction, 298–299
Cognitive abilities and men versus women, 89
Cognitive-behavioral approach, 257
Cognitive development, 166
Cognitive information processing approach, 375, 391–405
   assumptions, 391–392
   career decision making, 403
   Career Thoughts Inventory, 403–404
   combining theories, 452
   counselor issues, 408
   culturally diverse populations, 407
   executive processing domain, 401–403
   group counseling, 466
   late adolescence and adulthood, 455
   occupational information role, 405

pyramid of, 392–401
   service delivery sequence, 404–405
   testing role, 406
   tests and inventories associated with, 459
   women, 407
Cognitive information processing skills (CASVE), 393, 396–401, 402
   adult career development, 456
   analysis, 397, 398–399
   communication, 396, 397, 398
   execution, 397
   monitoring and control, 402–403
   self-awareness, 402
   synthesis, 397, 399–400
   testing role, 406
   valuing, 397, 400
   as Western point of view, 407
Cognitive rehearsal, 347–349
Cognitive strategies, 346–349
Cognitive theories of psychotherapy and career counseling, 346–349
College Board Scholastic Assessment Test (SAT), 28, 29, 30, 86, 341, 458
Combination of theories, 7, 451–479
Comfort, work adjustment theory, 69, 70
Commitment, 220, 222
Commitment Anxiety Scale, 404
Common reality, 384, 392
Communication skills, 396, 397, 398
Community and spirituality, 386
Community service as life role, 221
Company policies and practices, 70, 76
Compensation, 70, 76
Competencies. See Abilities
Compromise, 174, 175
Computer-assisted guidance systems, 464–465
   DISCOVER, 16, 54, 464
   SIGI PLUS, 16, 54, 464, 465
   Tiedeman's career decision-making paradigm, 376
   trait and factor theory and, 54
Computer simulations, 364
Concentration on child, 318
Concrete operations stage, 166, 167
Concurrent validity, 14
Confidence and career transition, 255
Conflict between themselves and job, dealing with, 80
Conformity, 244, 245
Confusion and transition, 256

Congruence, 103–104, 116
   condition for change, 8
   counseling implications, 103
   counselor issues, 115
   defined, 103
   example of, 103–104
   research, 109, 110
   women, 112
Conscientiousness, 109
Consequences, 340
Consistency, 106–107
Consolidating, 219, 231
Construct validity, 14
Constructive alternativism, 280
Constructivist approaches to career development, 279–306, 452
   assessment and counseling strategies, 284
   counselor issues, 303–304
   culturally diverse populations, 303
   definition, 279
   narrative counseling, 291–301
   occupational information role, 302
   personal construct psychology, 280–291
   purpose of, 290
   summary, 304
   testing role, 301–302
   women, 303
Content reflection(s), 10, 54, 60
Content validity, 14
Continuation responses, 10–11
Control
   career transition and, 255
   monitoring and, 402–403
Conventional
   client behavior, 101
   environment, 100
   personality types, 100–101
   placement counseling and, 468
Counselor issues
   adolescence, 207–209, 213
   adult development, 246–247
   career decision-making theories, 407–408, 476
   changing work settings, 467
   children, 171–173, 182
   congruence, 103, 115
   constructivist career development, 303–304
   crisis, 272–273
   decision-making theories, 475
   differentiation, 105, 115–116
   dual-economy theory, 430–431
   flexibility, 90
   group career counseling, 465–467
   Holland, 114–116, 475
   life-span theories, 476
   Myers-Briggs, 132–142, 147, 475
   placement counseling, 467–469

Counselor issues (*continued*)
prejudice, 440–441
social learning theory,
369–370
sociological and economic
approaches, 476–477
special, 465–469
spirituality, 387–391, 476
status attainment theory,
425–426
theories, 475–477
trait and factor theories,
60–61, 475–476
transition, 272–273
women on career issues,
436–437
work adjustment theory, 90,
475–476
youth employment, 419
Counselor needs, 52
Counselor skills, 8–16
*Counselor's Guide to Career
Assessment*, 28
Counselor's use of career
development theory, 5–8
Courses, 314
Creativity, 71, 76, 223
Crises
anticipated, 253
culturally diverse populations,
270–272
definition, 252
and transitions, 252–276
unanticipated, 253
women, 264–270
Cross-functional skills, 41
Crystallization stage
adult career development, 456
elaboration versus, 399
Ginzberg, 190
Super, 192, 219, 226, 456
Tiedeman, 377–378, 381
Crystallizing a decision,
300–301
Cultural identity, 225
Culturally diverse populations
adolescents, 209–213
adult development, 242–246
attitudes, 245
career decision-making
theories, 406–407, 474
career development, 18,
178–179, 209–213, 242–246
children, 178–179
conformity stage, 244, 245
constructivist career
counseling, 303
crisis, 270–272
discrimination, 245, 270–272,
368, 438–441
disengagement phase, 246
dissonance stage, 244, 245,
246
dual economy theory, 439
Holland, 58, 113–114
human capital theory, 438,
439

identity development model,
474
interest inventories, 58
introspection, 244, 245
life-span theories, 474
life stage of, 242–246
maintenance stage, 246
Myers-Briggs, 145–147
occupational information, 59
parental influence theories,
330
resistance and immersion,
244, 245, 246
role models for, 243
self-efficacy, 368, 369, 474
sexual harassment, 267
social learning and cognitive
career theories, 368–369, 474
status attainment theory, 424,
425, 438
Strong Interest Inventory, 58
Super's life-span theory,
159–160
synergetic articulation and
awareness, 244, 245
theories application, 474–475
trait and factor theory, 58–60,
474
unemployment rates, 433, 438
wages, 435, 438
work adjustment theory, 67,
88–90
Culture and status attainment
theory, 424
Curiosity, 163, 164–165, 351,
353, 354, 355

Decelerating, 219, 236
DECIDES, 466
Decision crystallization,
300–301
Decision independence, 255
Decision making
career, 403
guide to, 398
perception or judgment, 126
spiritual perspective, 385,
382–391
task-approach skills in, 343
Decision-making approaches,
374–410
Decision-Making Confusion
Scale, 404
Decision-making skills domain,
392, 393, 396–401
Decision-making strategies,
381–382
Decline, 236–237, 246
Denial, 456
Dependent decision-making
strategy, 382
Descriptive theories, 374,
375–382
Developmental contextual
theory, 201
Developmental stages (Super),
157–159

*Dictionary of Holland
Occupational Codes*, 101,
110
*Dictionary of Occupational
Titles (DOT)*, 40, 52, 88,
101, 314, 471, 472
key to codes, 40
occupational divisions 2–digit
codes, 42–43
Differential Aptitude Tests
(DAT), 28, 29, 30, 458
Differentiation, 104–106
constructs, 281, 282
counseling implications, 105
counselor issues, 115–116
definition, 104, 281
example of, 105–106
Diffusion, 200, 201, 204, 205
Directive counseling, 26
Discouragement stage, 219
DISCOVER, 16, 54, 464
Discrimination
culturally diverse populations,
270–272, 368, 438–441
determinants, 431
error, 431–432
monopoly, 431
racial, 368
statistical generalization,
431
taste, 431
women, 264, 431–437
working adjustment theory,
89–90
youth, 418
Disengaged family, 326
Disengagement, 236–237, 246
Dissatisfaction with job, 1
Dissonance, 244, 245, 246
Dominant process, 131–132
Double jeopardy, 271–272
Drawing, 295, 302
Dual economy theory, 429–431
culturally diverse populations,
439
foreign countries, 430
labor market, 417
occupational information,
431
research, 430

Earnings, 435
Economic and sociological
perspectives, 411–447
counselor issues, 476–477
Economic rewards, 223
Economic security, 225
Education and income, 414,
416
Education requirements, 41
Educational conditions, 339
*Educational Opportunities
Finder*, 101, 110
Egocentrism, 167, 187, 213
Emotionally rejected child, 318
Empathy as condition for
change, 8

Employment in occupational groups and projected change, 412
Encyclopedia of Careers and Vocational Guidance, 15
Endurance, 71, 74
Energy and spirituality, 385–386
Enmeshed family, 325, 326
Enterprising
  client behavior, 100
  environment, 99–100
  personality type, 100
  placement counseling, 468
Environment Fit model, Person-, 5
Environmental conditions and events, 337, 338, 339
Environmental Identity Scale (EIS), 112
Erikson
  combining theories, 452
  identity stage, 200, 213
  life stage approach, 199–200
  theory applied to career development, 199–203
Error discrimination, 431–432
Establishment stage, 219, 230–234, 255
Esteem, need for, 315–316
Eurocentrism, 243
Executive phase, 397, 400
Executive processing domain, 392, 393, 401–403
Expected utility model
Experience requirements, 41
Experiential Career Guidance Mode, 180, 181
Explanatory constructs, 102–108
Exploration
  behavior dimensions of, 165
  decision-making theories, 455
  environmental, 201
  as goal for children, 165–166
  thwarting, 165
  trait and factor theory, 455
Exploration stage
  Ginzberg, 190
  Super, 165–166, 219, 226–230, 254, 262, 265
  Tiedeman, 376–377
Exposure to occupations, 1
External Conflict Scale, 404
External versus internal control, 169
Externally focused strategies and sexual harassment, 268
Extraversion, 109, 127, 131, 132, 134, 143
Eye-hand coordination, 68, 89

Factor definition, 25
Falsification of type, 146–147
Family
  background exploration, 12
  disengaged, 326
  enmeshed, 325, 326

influences on career choice, 424
lack of support by, 210
problems, typical, 171
systems therapy, 325–327
Fantasy creation, 298
Fantasy stage, Ginzberg, 164, 188, 189
Faulty generalizations, 341–342
Feeling
  finding reason behind, 54
  judgement, 123, 124
  intuition and, 124–125
  reflections, 54, 60
  sensing and, 124
  work situations effect of, 136
Finger dexterity, 68, 89
Flexibility, 77, 80, 90, 351, 355, 420
FOCUS, 181
Foreclosure, 200, 201, 204, 205
Form perception, 68, 89
Formal operational stage, 166 167
Formal thought, 187
Future narrative elicitation, 297–298

Gender
  adolescence issues, 205–209
  Gottfredson, 173–178
  harassment, 266
  role stereotyping, 173–178
General Aptitude Test Battery (GATB), 28, 29, 30, 52, 53, 81, 458, 459, 469–470
  abilities measured by, 68
  ability requirements, 75
  counseling example using, 72–74
  group counseling and, 466
  job adjustment counseling and use of, 82–83
  men versus women, 89
General learning ability, 68
Genetic endowment, 337, 338, 351
Genogram, 12, 326–327, 328
Genuineness as condition for change, 8
Ginzberg's theory
  capacities development, 188, 189–190, 192
  comparison to Super's stages, 191–192
  counseling example, 192–193
  fantasy stage, 188
  interests development, 188, 189, 192
  realistic stage, 188, 190
  tentative stage of adolescent career development, 188–193
  transition period, 188, 190
  values development, 188, 190

Goals
  of career counseling, 16–17, 53, 107
  clarification, 346–347
  explicit, 17
  implicit, 17
  narrative counseling assessment, 292–293
  open-mindedness, 347
  setting, 341
  social cognitive career theory, 358–359, 360, 361
  social learning theory, 341, 346–347, 349–350
Gottfredson
  career development theory, 173–176
  childhood, 453
  combining theories, 452
  gender role stereotyping and theory of, 173–178
  implications of theory for Super's theory, 176
  use of with Super's concepts in counseling, 176–178
Group career counseling, 99, 465–467
Guide for Occupational Exploration, 41, 47, 48, 471

Happenstance theory, planned, 343, 350–356, 365
Harassment. *See* Sexual harassment
Harmony and spirituality, 386–387
Helping skills, 8–12
  attending, 9
  continuation responses, 10–11
  family background exploration, 12
  information giving, 11
  questions, 9
  reflections, 10
  reinforcement, 11–12
  statements, 10
  test and inventory interpretation, 12
Hispanics. *See* Culturally diverse populations
Holding, 219, 234
Holland's theory of types, 23, 33, 41, 94–119
  Artistic, 98
  classification system, 16, 39, 471
  combination of types, 101–102
  combining theories, 452
  congruence, 103–104, 109, 110
  consistency, 106–107
  constructs, 102–108
  Conventional, 100–101
  counselor issues, 114–116
  culturally diverse populations, 113–114
  daydreams, 107
  differentiation, 104–106

Holland's theory of types (*continued*)
Enterprising, 99–100
explanatory constructs, 102–108
identity, 108, 109, 110
Investigative, 97–98
Myers-Briggs Type Indicator (MBTI) and, 144
NEO Five-Factor Inventory (FFM) and, 109
occupational information role, 110–111
personality, 95, 96, 97, 989
Realistic, 95, 96–97
relationship among types, 96
research on, 108–110
Social, 99
stereotypes, 94
summary, 116
testing role, 111–112, 181
tests and inventories associated with, 458
theories that go with, 7, 457
types, 95–101
women, 112–113
Home and family, 221
Human capital theory, 417, 427–429, 438, 439

Identity
adolescence, 199–203
confusion, 187
and context, 199–203
counseling example, 202–203
cultural, 201–202, 225
Holland's theory of types, 108, 109, 110
minorities, 202, 474
vocational, 200–201
Immersion, 244, 245, 246
Immobilization, 258, 456
Implementing, 219, 227
Improved Career Decision Making through the Use of Labor Market Information, 40
Income and education, 414, 416
Inconsistencies between words and actions, 347
Independence, 76
Induction stage, 380
Industry versus inferiority stage, 167
Inferior function, 139
Inflexibility Scale, 80
Information. *See also* Occupational information
biased, 11
giving of, 11
need for, 316
organizing, 395
processing pyramid, 392–401
Super's model of career development of children and, 166–168

Information integration about oneself and world of work, 53–56
Innovating, 219, 235
Instrumental learning, 340, 342
Integration
adult career development, 457
constructs, 281, 282
definition, 281
stage, 380–381
Integrative life planning (ILP), 452, 460–462
Interests
career decisions and, 175
children development of, 169–170
combining scales for, 33
constructs, 282–283
determinants of, 317
development of, 169–170, 188, 189, 192, 317
Ginzberg, 188, 189, 191, 192
Holland, 41
inventory examples and their scales, 33
occupational, 32
self-observation generalization about, 342, 349, 369
Strong Interest Inventory, 32, 33
Super, 191
traits and factor theory, 32–33
work adjustment theory, 66, 71–72
Intergenerational change, 422
Internalization, 262–263, 268
Internal versus external control, 169
Internet, 350
Interviewing, 257
Introduction, 1–22
Introspection, 244–245
Introversion, 127, 131, 132, 134, 143
Intuition, 122, 123
counselors discussing, 143
and feeling, 124–125
and thinking, 124, 125
work situations effects of, 135
Intuitive decision-making strategy, 382
Inventory
definition, 13
interpretation, 12
Investigative
client behavior, 97
environment, 97–98
personality type, 97
placement counseling and, 468
Involuntary transitions, 253, 256, 257, 265

Job
adjustment counseling, 82–84
club, 468
definition, 3

dissatisfaction, 1, 82
hunting, 469
youth, 417–419
Job Experience Kits, 345–346, 364
Journal of Psychological Type, 121
Judging, 132
decision making and, 126
perception and, 122–126
ways of, 123–124
work situations and effect of, 137
Judging-perceiving in work situations, effects of, 137
Judgment perception, 126
Jungian theory, 7

Key figures, 168, 176, 181
Knowledge
of decision making, 392, 393
occupational, 393, 395–396
requirements, 41
of roles, 222–223
of self, 393, 395
Knowledge obtaining about world of work, 38–53
classification systems, 39–47, 48–51
counselor needs to know, what, 52
example of, 52–53
trait and factor requirements, 47, 51–52
types of occupational information, 38–39
Knowledge of the Preferred Occupational Group, 194, 196–197, 204, 207, 222
Krumboltz's social learning theory, 336–356
combining theories, 452
environmental conditions and events, 337, 339
genetic endowment, 337, 338
group counseling and, 466
high school students, 455
learning experiences, 337, 339–340
task-approach skills, 337, 340–341
tests and inventories associated with, 459, 470
women, 366, 473
Kuder Career Search (KCS), 32, 33, 39, 55, 56, 458
Kuder DD, 32

Labor market
primary, 417, 429, 430
secondary, 417, 429, 430, 431
sociological and economic perspectives, 411–447
tiers, 430

United States, 412–414, 415, 416
Laddering techniques, 287–289, 295, 302, 421
Late adolescent development. *See* Adult development
Leading activity, 167
Learning
  experiences, 337, 339–340
  Krumboltz, 337, 339–340
Leisure activities, 221–222
Letting go, 261, 265, 456
Lifecareer® foundation, 383, 470
Life Career Game, 465
Lifecareer Process Theory, 375, 383, 384, 387, 408
Life career rainbow, 157, 211–212
Life history composing, 296–297
Lifeline, 297
Life roles
  commitment to, 222
  community service, 221
  home and family, 221
  indicators of salience of, 222–225
  knowledge of, 222–223
  leisure activities, 221–222
  participation in, 222
  studying, 220
  value expectations, 223–225
  working, 220–221
Life-span theories, 151–276
  adolescence career development, 186–218
  adult career crises and transitions, 252–276
  and career decision-making theories, 153–161, 453–457
  career development in children, 162–185
  classification systems, 472
  combining theories, 452
  counselor issues, 475, 476
  culturally diverse populations, 474
  late adolescent and adult career development, 219–251
  Super's life-span theory, introduction to, 153–161
  testing, 156, 459, 469, 470
  and trait and factor theories, 156, 453–457, 472
  women, 472, 473
Life stages and substages, 158
  adult, 225–239
Life structure changing, 299–300
Life style, 223–224
Lifetimes sports, 221
Love, need for, 315
Loving acceptance, 318

Maintenance stage, 219, 234–236, 246, 255, 257, 270
Manual dexterity, 68

Maslow's hierarchy of needs, 308, 315–316, 318–319
Mathematics
  self-efficacy, 207
  women and, 206, 207, 240, 367, 432, 436, 473
Maxicycle, 225, 226
MBTI Career Report, 145
MBTI Expanded Analysis, 145
Measurements reliability, 14. *See also* Validity and testing
Memory, 7. *See also* Chunking
Midlife stresses, 234, 241
Minicycle, 225
Minimization, 259–260, 456
Minnesota Importance Questionnaire (MIQ), 67, 68, 70, 71, 75, 77, 80, 86, 88, 91, 225, 459, 470
  counseling and use of, 82
  counseling example using, 72–74
  differences between men and women, 88
  grid for, 87–88
  group counseling and, 466
  job adjustment counseling and use of, 82
  needs scale, 69
  sample report form, 78–79, 81
  women, 473
  work adjustment theory, 457
Minnesota Job Description Questionnaire (MJDQ), 75, 76, 77, 86
Minnesota Multiphasic Personality Inventory-2 (MMPI), 35, 36
Minnesota Occupational Classification System (MOCS), 76, 77, 81, 84–85, 88, 89
Minnesota point of view, 26
Minnesota Satisfaction Questionnaire (MSQ), 86, 87–88
Minnesota Satisfactoriness Scale, 87
Minority, 18
Minority identity development model, 244, 245
Misperception theory, 266
Modernism, 279
Monitoring and control, 402–403
Monopoly, discrimination, 431
Moral values, 70, 76
Moratorium, 200, 201, 204, 205
Motivators and needs, 317
Murphy-Meisgeier Type Indicator, 181
My Vocational Situation (MVS), 108, 109–110
Myers-Briggs type theory, 23, 120–150
  abbreviations used in, 130
  books on, 141–142

career adjustment counseling example, 139–142
career decision-making counseling example, 134, 135, 136, 137–139
combining theories, 452
counseling examples, 125–126
counseling use of, 132–142
counselor issues, 147
culturally diverse populations, 145–147
development of, 120–121
dominant and auxiliary processes, 131–132
men, 144, 145
occupational information, 16, 142–143
perceiving and judging, 122–126
as personality theory, 121
sixteen type combinations, 127–131
summary, 147–148
testing, 143–145
tests and inventories associated with, 459
and trait and factor theory, 121, 142
women, 145–147
Myers-Briggs Type Indicator (MBTI), 120, 121, 122, 131, 135, 138, 140, 141, 143–145, 148, 457, 459, 466, 469
Myers-Briggs types
characteristics associated with, 128–129
extraversion, 127, 134, 143
extraversion-introversion in work situations, effects of, 134
feeling judgment, 123, 124
introversion, 127, 132, 134, 143
intuition, 122, 123, 128, 129
intuition and feeling, 124–125
intuition and thinking, 124, 125
judging, 123–124, 132
judging-perceiving in work situations, effects of, 137
Jungian theory and, 7, 120
occupation choices made by each type, 133
perceiving, 122–123, 132, 134
perceiving and judging, 122–126
sensing, 122, 123, 128, 129, 132, 143
sensing and feeling, 124
sensing and thinking, 124
sensing-intuition in work situations, effects of, 135
thinking, 123, 132, 143
thinking-feeling in work situations, effects of, 136
weaker functions example, 139–142

Narrative counseling, 280, 291–301, 452
  assessment goals, 292–293
  Cochran's, 294–301
  counseling, 293–294
  defined, 291
  storytelling, 292
National Career Development Association, 3, 39
National Occupational Information Coordinating Committee (NOICC), 47
National Vocational Guidance Association, 39
Native Americans. *See* Culturally diverse populations
Needs
  for beauty, 316
  Maslow. *See* Maslow's hierarchy of needs
  and motivators, 317
  work adjustment theory, 66, 67, 68, 69, 76
Neglected child, 318
NEO Five Factor Inventory (FFM), 109, 144
Neuroticism, 109, 144
Noncounseling application of theories, 451, 463–465
Nondirective counseling, 26
Nonevents, 253
Nonnormative events, 253, 254, 255, 256
Normative role transitions, 253, 254, 255
Norms and testing, 13
Numerical ability, 68

O*NET (Occupational Information Network), 40, 41, 52
  descriptors, 40–41, 46–47
  Dictionary of Occupation Titles and, 472
  sections and groupings of, 44–46
Observation, 340
Occtalk, 16, 204
Occupation(s)
  definition, 3
  measuring requirements and conditions of, 74–77
  requirements, 41
Occupation-specific requirements, 41
Occupational Ability Patterns, 75, 76, 77, 80, 88, 91
Occupational characteristics, 41
Occupational classification systems
  and career development theories, 470–472
  Holland, 16, 471
  Roe, 308–314, 471
  trait and factor theory, 470
Occupation conditions, 339

Occupational groups. *See* Roe's occupational groups
Occupational information
  adolescence, 203–204
  career decision-making approaches, 405
  and career development theory, 166–168
  childhood, 166–168, 179–181
  cognitive information processing theory, 405
  computer simulations, 364
  constructivist career counseling, 302
  in counseling, 179
  culturally diverse populations and lack of, 59
  dual economy theory, 431
  Holland, 16, 110–111
  important types of, 15
  infusion into classroom of, 180
  knowledge of, 38–53
  Myers-Briggs, 16, 142–143
  providing, 15–16
  social learning theory, 341, 364–365
  sources of, 15–16
  spiritual approach, 405
  Super's life-span theory and, 159
  Tiedeman, 405
  trait and factor theory, 38–39
  types of, 38–39
  work adjustment theory and role of, 88
Occupational Information Network. See O*NET, 40, 41, 52
Occupational knowledge, 393, 395–396
Occupational Outlook Handbook (OOH), 15, 39, 52, 81
Occupational Reinforcer Patterns, 75, 76, 77, 80, 81, 88, 91
Occupational selection and parental style, 319
Occupations (Roe), levels of, 312, 313–314
Occupations Finder, The, 101, 110, 116, 464
Open-ended questions, 9, 12, 54
Open-mindedness and goals, 347, 351
Openness to Experience, 109
Opinion, information giving instead of, 11
Optimism, 351, 355
Organization (Roe), 309, 310, 311, 312, 313
Organizational context, 41
Orientation
  away from people, 319
  to gender roles, 173
  to self-awareness, 173

to size and power, 173
to social class, 173
toward people, 319
to vocational choice, 193
Outcome expectations, 358, 359, 360, 361
Outdoor (Roe), 309, 310, 311, 312, 313
Outplacement counselor, 257
Overdemanding parent, 318, 319
Overprotective parent, 318, 319

Pace, 71, 74
Paper-and-pencil materials, 463–464
Parent-child career interactions, 324–325
Parent-Child Relations Questionnaire (PCR I), 319
Parent Involved Career Exploration Counseling Process (PICE), 325
Parental attitudes, 318–319
Parental influence theories, 307–334
  attachment theory, 321–324
  counseling use of, 327–330
  culturally diverse populations, 330
  family systems therapy, 325–327
  Maslow's hierarchy of needs, 308, 315–316, 318–319
  occupational selection and, 319
  Roe, 308–321
  summary, 331
  women, 330
Participation, 220, 222
Part-time or volunteer work, 55
Path analysis, 424
Pattern Identification Exercise (PIE), 325
Patterns
  ability, 75, 76, 77
  value, 75–77
Patterns of attachment
  anxious-ambivalent, 322, 323
  avoidant, 322
  secure, 322
Perceiving, 122–123, 132, 134
  and career transitions, 255
  combinations of judging and, 124–125
  counseling examples, 125–126
  decision making and, 126
  and judging, 122–126
  ways of, 122–123
  work situations and effect of, 137
Performance outcomes, 361, 362
Perseverance, 77, 80
Persistence, 351, 355
Persistent occupation problems, 253–254, 255–256

Person-environment-
correspondence theory, 90
Person-Environment Fit model,
5, 114
Person-environment interactive
model of bases of career
maturity, 164
Personal concerns, 2
Personal construct psychology,
280–291, 452
assessment and counseling
strategies, 284
bipolar, 281
counselor issues, 304
development stages of
vocational construct
systems, 283–284
differentiation, 281, 282
integration, 281, 282
laddering techniques, 287–289
values and interests, 282–283
vocational card sort, 289–291
vocational construct system,
281
vocational reptest, 284–287
Personal development, 225
Personal identity, 2
Personal issues, 2
Personal reality, 384, 392
Personality development theory,
Roe's. See Roe's theory
Personality
difficulty of inventories, 36
inventories and their scales
example, 35
style, 66, 67, 71, 77
trait and factor theory, 35, 36
Perspective, 189
Phases. See Stages
Physical activity, 224
Physical prowess, 225
Physiological needs, 315
Placement counseling, 467–469
Planfulness, 170–171
Planned happenstance theory,
343, 350–356, 365
Position Classification
Inventory, 112
Postmodernism, 279
Predicted skills, 67
Prediction(s)
aptitude test scores and, 30
future events, 341
Predictive validity, 14
Preoperational thought stage,
166–167
Prescriptive approach, 374, 375,
391–392
Prestige, 70, 173, 175, 224, 425
Primary labor market, 417, 429,
430
Process skills, 41
Professional and managerial
occupation level, 313–314
Psychological Types, 120, 121
Psychology, role of theory in,
4–5

Psychometric instruments, 86
Psychometric measures, 27, 67,
87
Psychosocial development, 167,
187
Psychtalk, 16, 204
Pyramid of information
processing, 392–401

Questions, 9
close-ended, 9
open-ended, 9, 12, 54

Rainbow, 156–157, 466
RAMAK, 314
Rational decision making, 382
Rationalist approach, 279
Reactiveness, 77, 80
Reactiveness Scale, 80
Readiness and career transition,
255
Realism, 194, 197
Realistic
client behavior, 96–97
environment, 95
personality type, 95, 96
placement counseling and,
468
Realistic stage, 188, 190
Reality construction, 298–299
Reality principle, 384
Recognition, 76
Recycling (Super), 158–159, 191,
226, 237–239
Reentering workforce, 254,
264–265
Reflections, 10, 12
Reformation stage, 380, 469
Reinforcement, 11–12, 343–344
Reinforcer patterns, 75, 77, 82,
83, 90
Reinforcers, abilities, and values
matching, 77–82
Related issues, career counseling
as, 467
Reliability and testing, 13–14
Renewal, 234
Replacement needs as job
openings, 412, 413, 414
Reptest, 284–287, 301, 302
Research
cornerstone of, 8
Holland's constructs, 108–110
Roe, 319, 320–321
testing theories and, 4, 5
Tiedeman, 381–382
Resistance, 244, 245, 246
Responding skills, 166
Responsibility, 71, 76, 90
Résumés
outplacement counselors and,
257
writing and MBTI, 144
Retirement
adjusting to, 84–86
career counseling versus, 85
case study, 85–86

counselors, 6
living, 219, 236–237
planning, 219, 236
reinforcers, 84
Super, 219
work adjustment theory,
84–86
Rhythm, 71, 74
Risk, 224
Risk taking, 351, 355
Roe's occupational groups, 471
Roe's personality development
theory, 308–321
Maslow's hierarchy of needs,
315–316
occupational classification
system, 308–314
occupational groups of,
309–312, 313
occupations levels, 312,
313–314
parent-child interaction
model, 318–321
propositions of, 316–317
testing and occupational
classification, 314
Role
adolescence, 187
confusion, 187
enactment, 300
home and family, 221
knowledge about, 220, 222
leisure, 221–222
models, 168, 343, 344–345
playing, 345, 465
salience, 220–225, 468
student, 220
worker, 220–221
Role Construct Repertory Test,
284–287
Roles
concept of (Super), 156–157
importance of, 156
indicators of salience of life
roles, 222–225
knowledge of, 220, 222
life, 220–222
Rorschach Test, 35

Safety
needs, 315
work adjustment theory, 69,
70–71
Salience Inventory, 156, 205,
220, 222, 223, 224, 225, 227,
232, 241, 459
Satisfaction, 1, 66, 109
Satisfactoriness, 66
Schemas, 395
Scholastic Assessment Test
(SAT), 28, 29, 30, 86, 341,
458
School adjustment, 382
School-to-work, 179
programs designed for
children, 180–181
transition, 254

Science (Roe), 309, 310, 311, 312, 313
Scoring tests, 13
Screening methods, 463
Search for meaning stage, 262, 456–457
Secondary labor market, 417, 429, 430, 431
Secure pattern, 322
Security, 70, 76
Self-actualization, need for, 315, 316
Self-awareness, 402
Self-concept(s), 154, 155, 156, 163, 170–171, 204
Self-Directed Search (SDS), 14, 32, 94, 101, 102, 104, 105, 106, 107, 108, 109, 110, 111, 112, 116, 457, 458, 463, 464, 469
Self-doubt, 260–261, 456
Self-efficacy theory, 156, 335, 356–364, 366–368, 369, 474
Self-esteem, 156, 206, 265, 270, 315–316, 367
Self-knowledge, 393, 395, 396
Self-observation generalizations, 341–342, 349, 369
Self-talk, 401
Self-understanding, gaining, 27–38
    achievements, 30–31
    aptitudes, 28–30
    example, 36–38
    interests, 32–33
    personality, 35, 36
    values, 34, 35
Semiprofessional and small business occupational level, 314
Semiskilled occupational level, 314
Sensing, 122, 123, 132
    counselors discussing, 143
    and feeling, 124
    and thinking, 124
    work situations effects of, 135
Sensorimotor stage, 166
Separation-attachment concepts, 323
Service (Roe), 309, 310, 311, 312, 313
Service delivery sequence, seven-step, 404–405
Setting in narrative counseling, 291
Sex discrimination, 240
Sexual Experience Questionnaire, 266
Sexual harassment
    career crises and, 265–270
    definition, 266
    effects on career, 268
    example, 269–270
    incidence of, 265–270
    incidence statistics, 267–268

levels of, 266
men versus women's views of, 266–267
responses to, 268
stages, 268–269
work adjustment theory and, 89
Sexual orientation, 2
SIGI PLUS, 16, 54, 464, 465
Simulated job experience, 343, 345–346
Sixteen Personal Factor Questionnaire (16 PF), 35, 36, 53, 458
Skilled occupational level, 314
Skills of counselor, 8–16
    helping, 8–12
    providing occupational information, 15–16
    relating career development theory, 16
    testing, 13–15
Skills work adjustment theory, 67, 82
Sociability, defining, 28
Social
    cognitive career theory, 206, 207, 356–364, 473
    constructivist theory, 156
    economic factor, 154
    factors, 337, 339
    Holland, 99
    interaction, 224
    service, 76
    status, 76
Social cognitive model of career choice, 359–362
Social learning and cognitive theory, 335–373
    applying planned happenstance theory to career counseling, 350–356
    career theory, 356–364
    client cognitive and behavioral skills, 341–343
    cognitive strategies for counseling, 346–349
    combining theories, 452
    counselor behavioral strategies, 343–346
    counselor issues, 369–370
    culturally diverse populations, 368–369, 474
    environmental conditions and events, 337, 339
    genetic endowment, 337
    goals, 349–350, 358–359
    Krumboltz, 336–356
    learning experiences, 339–340
    occupational information, 364–365
    outcome expectations, 358
    self-efficacy, 356, 357–358
    summary, 370
    task-approach skills, 340–341
    testing, 365
    values, 341, 342, 365

women, 365–368, 473
Social relations (Super), 225
Sociological and economic perspectives, 411–447
    approaches, 414, 416–417
    counselor issues, 476–477
Software and work adjustment theory, 80
Spatial ability, 68
Special focus theories, 277–447
Specification
    Ginzberg, 190
    Super, 219
Specifying, 227
Spiritual perspective on decision making, 375, 382–391
    adult career development, 456
    balance, 385
    calling, 386
    career counseling, 387–391
    change, 384–385
    combining theories, 452
    community, 386
    counselor issues, 407–408, 476
    culturally diverse populations, 406–407
    energy, 385–386
    harmony, 386–387
    life purpose and exploring, 461–462
    Lifecareer Theory, 383
    occupational information role, 405
    personal and common realities, 384
    spirituality, 384–387
    testing role, 406
    unity, 387
    women, 406–407
Stabilization, 219, 231
Stages
    adjusting to a choice, 376, 380–381
    adult life stages, 225–239
    advancing, 231
    anticipating a choice, 376–379
    career change, 237
    consolidating, 231
    crystallization, 226
    culturally diverse populations, 242–246
    decelerating, 236
    developmental (Super), 157–159
    developmental (vocation construct systems), 283–284
    establishment, 230–234
    examples, 227–230, 231–234, 235–236
    exploration, 226–230
    holding, 234
    implementing, 227
    innovating, 235
    life, 158
    maintenance, 234–236
    recycling, 158–159, 191, 226, 237–239

retirement living, 236–237
retirement planning, 236
specifying, 227
stabilization, 231
updating, 234
women, 239–242
Standard Occupational Classification Manual, 47, 49–51
Statements and reflections, 10
Statistical discrimination, 432
Status attainment theory, 417, 422–427, 438
Status, work adjustment theory, 69, 70
Stereotypes, 94, 112
 adolescence, 205–209
 African American women, 439
 constructivist career counseling, 303
 counseling example, 176–178
 counselor and recognizing, 437
 education and schools fostering, 174, 176
 gender role, 436
 Gottfredson's theory and, 173–178
 key figures and, 176
 occupational, 340
 societal, 435
 women's behavior, 367
 youth, 418
Storytelling, 292
Strange situations, 322
Strong Interest Inventory (SII), 32, 52, 53, 135, 205, 227, 398, 458, 469
 Basic Interest Scales of, 32, 33
 culturally diverse populations and, 58, 113
 Holland, 102
 Myers-Briggs Type Indicator, 144
Study of Values (SV), 34, 458
Studying, 220
Substantive complexity, 420
Super's and Ginzberg's adolescent life stages comparison, 191–192
Super's conception of career maturity, 194–198
 Career Decision Making, 196
 Career Exploration, 195–196, 197
 Career Orientation, 197–198
 Career Planning, 194, 195, 197
 Knowledge of the Preferred Occupational Group, 196–197
 Realism, 197
 World-of-Work Information, 196, 197
Super's life-span theory, introduction to, 153–161

basic assumptions of, 153–154, 155
career determinants archway figure, 155
counseling example, 208–209
culturally diverse populations, 159–160
developmental stages, 157–159
early adolescence, 453, 455
life stages and substages, 158
occupational information role, 159
roles, 156–157
self-concept, 154, 155
summary, 160
testing role, 159
tests and inventories associated with, 459
theories relating, 454
trait and factor theory versus, 156
vocational development definition, 154
women, 159–160
Super's model of career development of children, 163–173
 curiosity, 163, 164–165
 development of interests, 169–170
 exploration, 165–166
 Gottfredson's theory and, 176
 information, 166–168
 internal versus external control, 169
 key figures, 168
 self-concept and planfulness, 170–171
 time perspective, 170
 usage in counseling, 171–173, 176–178
 women, 173
Supervision-human relations, 70, 76
Supervision-technical, 70, 76
Synchronicity, 384
Synergetic articulation and awareness, 244, 245
Synthesis phase, 397, 399–400

Tardiness on the job, 66
Task-approach skills, 340–341, 343
Taste discrimination, 432
Techniques. *See* Helping skills
Technology (Roe), 309, 310, 311, 312, 313
Tentative stage, 188–193
Tertiary function, 139
Testing, 13–15
 ability, 67–68
 achievements, 205
 adolescence, 204–205
 adult career development, 456
 aptitudes, 28–30, 31

career decision-making approaches, 406
childhood, 181
cognitive information processing theory, 406
constructivist career counseling, 301–302
definition, 13
features of, 15
Holland, 14, 111–112, 181
interpretation, 12
Myers-Briggs, 143–145, 459
norms, 13
reliability, 13–14
Roe, 314
social learning theory, 365
spiritual perspectives on decision making, 406
Super's life-span theory, 159, 204
theories and, 4, 458–459, 469–470
Tiedeman, 406
trait and factor theory, 60
validity, 14–15
work adjustment theory and role of, 86–88
Testing out, 261–262, 265
Tests and disagreement among, 53
Tests and theories, 458–459, 469–470
 career decision-making theories, 469, 470
 life-span theories, 156, 459, 469, 470
 trait and factor theories, 60, 458, 469, 470
Tests in Print V, 27
Thematic Apperception Test (TAT), 35
Theoretical integration, 449–479
Theory. *See also* individual theories
 career development, 3, 4, 5–8, 16, 173–176, 469, 470–472
 chunking and, 7–8
 clarity of, 4, 5
 in combination, 7, 451–479
 constructs, 4, 279–306
 dual-economy, 429–431
 evaluating, 4–5
 human capital, 427–429
 personality, 6–7
 research and, 4, 5
 role of psychology, 4–5
 selection of, 7
 status attainment, 417, 422–427
 testing, 4
 validity of, 4
 women, 472–474
Thinking, 132
 cognitive information processing, 391–405
 counselors discussing, 143
 intuition and, 124, 125

Thinking (*continued*)
  sensing and, 124
  work situation effect of,
    136
Thinking judgment, 123
Tiedeman's perspective on
    process of career decision
    making, 375–382, 452, 456,
    466, 470, 473
Time perspective, 170, 191
Tolerable gender-type
    boundaries, 173–174
Tournament system, 420–421,
    422
Trait(s)
  assessment of, 25–26
  definition, 25
Trait and factor theories, 23,
    25–64
  ability, 28
  achievements, 28, 30–31
  and adolescents, 455
  and adults, 455
  aptitudes, 28–30
  and career decision-making
    theory, 453–457
  classification systems, 39–47,
    48–51, 472
  combined, 452, 457
  computer guidance systems,
    54
  counselor issues, 60–61,
    475–476
  culturally diverse populations,
    58–60, 474
  definitions, 25
  developing, 26
  elaboration, 455
  empowerment, 350
  gaining self-understanding,
    27–38
  and group counseling, 466
  help by counselor, 54–55
  and human capital theory,
    428
  integrating information about
    self and occupations, 53–56
  interests, 32–33
  interviews, 27
  knowledge needed by
    counselor, 52
  and life-span theory, 452–457,
    472
  and Myer-Briggs, 121, 142
  obtaining knowledge about
    world-of-work, 38–53
  occupational information,
    38–39
  personality, 35, 36
  process of counseling by
    using, 54
  requirements, 47, 51–52
  research on, 26
  self-knowledge, 396
  self-understanding, gaining,
    27–38
  summary of, 61

Super's life-span theory
    versus, 156
  testing, 60, 458, 469, 470
  tests and inventories, 458
  validating, 26
  values, 34, 35
  women, 56–58, 472, 473
Trait and type theories, 23–150
Transference, 254
Transitions
  anticipated, 253, 254
  boundaryless career, 254
  categories, 253–256
  chronic hassles, 253
  combining theories, 452
  crises and, 252–276
  definition, 252
  Hopson and Adam's model,
    258–263
  immobilization, 258, 265
  internalization, 262–263
  involuntary, 253, 256, 257, 265
  letting go, 261, 265
  managing, 462
  minimization, 259–260
  models of, 256–257
  nonevents, 253
  nonnormative events, 253,
    254, 255, 256
  normative role, 253
  persistent occupational
    problems, 253–254, 255–256
  search for meaning stage,
    262
  self-doubt, 260–261
  stages model, 259
  testing out, 261–262, 265
  types, 253
  unanticipated, 253, 255, 256,
    265
  voluntary, 253, 254
  women, 264–270
Transition period, 188, 190
Triadic reciprocal interaction
    system, 335, 336
Type combinations for Myers-
    Briggs, 127–131
Type Differentiation Indicator,
    145

Unanticipated transitions, 253,
    255, 256, 265
Unconditional positive regard as
    condition for change, 8
Understanding, need for, 316
Unemployment, 432, 433
United States Employment
    Service, 26, 28, 29, 30
Unity and spirituality, 387
Unskilled occupational level,
    314
Updating, 219, 234

Validity and testing, 14–15
Value(s)
  ability utilization, 223
  achievement, 69, 70, 223

adolescent development, 188,
    190
  adult, 220
  aesthetics, 223
  alternative prioritizing, 397,
    400
  altruism, 35, 69, 70, 223
  autonomy, 69, 71, 223
  clarification, 341
  comfort, 69, 70
  confusion, 256
  constructs, 282–283
  creativity, 223
  development, 188, 190
  economic rewards, 223
  economic security, 225
  expectations, 220, 223–225
  inventories and their scales
    example, 34
  lifestyle, 223–224
  matching reinforcers and
    abilities with, 77–82
  moral, 70
  patterns, 75–77
  physical activity, 224
  prestige, 224
  risk, 224
  safety, 69, 70–71
  Scale (VS). *See* Value Scale
  social interaction, 224
  social learning theory, 341,
    342, 365
  stages, 188, 190
  status, 69, 70
  trait and factor theory, 34,
    35
  types of, 34
  variety, 224
  work, 220
  work adjustment theory, 66,
    68–71, 77–82
  working conditions, 224
Value Scale (VS), 14, 34, 35, 55,
    204, 205, 223, 225, 227, 232,
    458
Variety
  Super, 224
  work adjustment theory, 76
Verbal ability, 68
Vertical mobility, 422
Videotapes, 206, 324, 344, 345,
    366
Vocational Card Sort (VCS),
    289–291, 295, 302
Vocational construct system,
    281, 283–284
Vocational development
    definition (Super), 154
Vocational identity, 109, 200
Vocational Interest Inventory
    (VII), 314
Vocational maturity. *See* Career
    maturity
Vocational Preference Inventory
    (VPI), 14, 94, 102, 104, 108,
    111, 112, 116, 457, 458,
    469

Vocational rehabilitation
counselors, 6
Vocational reptest, 284–287,
301, 302
Voluntary transitions, 253, 254
Volunteer or part-time work, 55

War Manpower Commission, 26
Wisdom of vocational
preference, 193
Women
achievements, 89
activity, 89
adolescence, 205–209
adult development, 473
attitude, 57
career crises, 264–270
career decision-making
theories, 406–407, 473
career development theories,
17–18, 173–176, 472–474
career patterns, 239
commitment to work, 57–58
congruence, 112
constructivist career
development, 303
cultural differences, 56
discrimination, 240, 264,
431–437
earnings, 435
Gottfredson, 173–176
Holland, 112–113, 473
human capitol theory,
428–429
interests, 57
involuntary change, 257
Krumboltz, 366, 473
life-span theory, 472, 473
life stages, 239–242
math self-efficacy, 56, 57, 207,
367, 432, 436, 473
Mexican American, 59
Myers-Briggs, 145–147
nonevent for, 253
parental influence theories,
330
personality factors, 57
Realistic environment, 96–97
reentry into and leave-taking
from labor force, temporary,
264–265
role in work, 434, 435
sciences and, 57
self-confidence, 57
self-efficacy, 366–368, 436
self-esteem, 57, 265, 367
sexual harassment, 265–270
social learning theory,
365–368, 473
spatial ability, 57
stages, 239–242
status attainment theory,
424
stress, 240
Super's life–span theory,
159–160, 207
trait and factor theories,
56–58, 472, 473
unemployment, 432, 433
values, 57, 58
verbal ability, 57
wages, 418, 432, 435
work adjustment theory, 66,
88–90, 473
youth employment, 419
Work activities, general types,
41
Work adjustment definition,
65–66
Work Adjustment Project, 86
Work adjustment theory, 23,
65–93
abilities, 66, 67–68, 77–82
ability patterns, 75, 76–77
achievement, 70, 76
adjustment problems, 67
adult career development,
456
altruism, 70
autonomy, 71
categorizing occupations, 472
counseling example, 72–74
counselor issues, 90, 475–476
culturally diverse populations,
67, 88–90
goal of, 65
group counseling, 466
high school students, 455
instruments used in, 77
interests, 66, 71–72
job adjustment counseling,
82–84
matching abilities, values, and
reinforcers, 77–82
measuring requirements and
conditions of occupations,
74–77
needs, 66, 67, 68, 69, 76
new developments, 86
occupational information role,
88
personality styles, 66, 67, 71
reinforcers, 77–82
retirement, 84–86
safety, 70–71
satisfaction and
satisfactoriness components,
66, 80
skills, 66, 82
status, 70
studies supporting, 81–82
summary, 90–91
testing, 86–88
tests and inventories
associated with, 459
trait and factor theory versus,
66
value patterns, 75–77
values, 66, 68–71, 77–82
women, 67, 88–90, 473
Work contexts, 41, 66, 70, 75, 82
Work environment
Artistic, 98
Conventional, 100
Enterprising, 99–100
Investigative, 97
Realistic, 95
Social, 99
Work environment effect on
individual, 419–422
Work salience, 220
Work settings, changing, 467
Work styles, 41
Work values and interests, 82
Worker characteristics, 41
Worker requirements, 41
Working conditions
Super, 194, 224
work adjustment theory, 76
Working life role, 220–221
Workplace discrimination
culturally diverse populations,
438–441
women, 431–437
World of work. *See*
Occupational information
World-of-Work Information, 194,
196, 197, 204, 207, 210, 222
World-view generalizations, 342

You and Your Career, 464
Youth employment, 417–419